The World Politics of Social Investment (Volume I): Welfare States in the Knowledge Economy

International Policy Exchange Series

Published in collaboration with the
Center for International Policy Exchanges University of Maryland

Series Editors
Douglas J. Besharov
Neil Gilbert

*United in Diversity?
Comparing Social Models in Europe and America*
Edited by Jens Alber and Neil Gilbert

Child Protection Systems: International Trends and Orientations
Edited by Neil Gilbert, Nigel Parton, and Marit Skivenes

The Korean State and Social Policy: How South Korea Lifted Itself from Poverty and Dictatorship to Affluence and Democracy
Stein Ringen, Huck-ju Kwon, Ilcheong Yi, Taekyoon Kim, and Jooha Lee

The Age of Dualization: The Changing Face of Inequality in Deindustrializing Societies
Edited by Patrick Emmenegger, Silja Häusermann, Bruno Palier, and Martin Seeleib-Kaiser

Counting the Poor: New Thinking About European Poverty Measures and Lessons for the United States
Edited by Douglas J. Besharov and Kenneth A. Couch

Social Policy and Citizenship: The Changing Landscape
Edited by Adalbert Evers and Anne-Marie Guillemard

Chinese Social Policy in a Time of Transition
Edited by Douglas J. Besharov and Karen Baehler

Reconciling Work and Poverty Reduction: How Successful Are European Welfare States?
Edited by Bea Cantillon and Frank Vandenbroucke

University Adaptation in Difficult Economic Times
Edited by Paola Mattei

Activation or Workfare? Governance and the Neo-Liberal Convergence
Edited by Ivar Lødemel and Amílcar Moreira

Child Welfare Systems and Migrant Children: A Cross Country Study of Policies and Practice
Edited by Marit Skivenes, Ravinder Barn, Katrin Kriz, and Tarja Pösö

Adjusting to a World in Motion: Trends in Global Migration and Migration Policy

Edited by Douglas J. Besharov and Mark H. Lopez

Caring for a Living: Migrant Women, Aging Citizens, and Italian Families
Francesca Degiuli

Child Welfare Removals by the State: A Cross-Country Analysis of Decision-Making Systems
Edited by Kenneth Burns, Tarja Pösö, and Marit Skivenes

Improving Public Services: International Experiences in Using Evaluation Tools to Measure Program Performance
Edited by Douglas J. Besharov, Karen J. Baehler, and Jacob Alex Klerman

Welfare, Work, and Poverty: Social Assistance in China
Qin Gao

Youth Labor in Transition: Inequalities, Mobility, and Policies in Europe
Edited by Jacqueline O'Reilly, Janine Leschke, Renate Ortlieb, Martin Seeleib-Kaiser, and Paola Villa

Decent Incomes for All: Improving Policies in Europe Edited by Bea Cantillon, Tim Goedemé, and John Hills

Social Exclusion in Cross National Perspective: Actors, Actions, and Impacts from Above and Below
Edited by Robert J. Chaskin, Bong Joo Lee, and Surinder Jaswal

The "Population Problem" in Pacific Asia
Stuart Gietel-Basten

United States Income, Wealth, Consumption, and Inequality
Edited by Diana Furchtgott-Roth

Europe's Income, Wealth, Consumption, and Inequality
Edited by Georg Fischer and Robert Strauss

The World Politics of Social Investment (Volume 1): Welfare States in the Knowledge Economy
Edited by Julian L. Garritzmann, Silja Häusermann, and Bruno Palier

The World Politics of Social Investment (Volume 2): The Politics of Varying Social Investment Strategies
Edited by Julian L. Garritzmann, Silja Häusermann, and Bruno Palier

SCHOOL of
PUBLIC POLICY

THE WORLD POLITICS OF SOCIAL INVESTMENT (VOLUME I)

Welfare States in the Knowledge Economy

Edited by

JULIAN L. GARRITZMANN

SILJA HÄUSERMANN

BRUNO PALIER

OXFORD
UNIVERSITY PRESS

OXFORD
UNIVERSITY PRESS

Oxford University Press is a department of the University of Oxford. It furthers the University's objective of excellence in research, scholarship, and education by publishing worldwide. Oxford is a registered trade mark of Oxford University Press in the UK and certain other countries.

Published in the United States of America by Oxford University Press
198 Madison Avenue, New York, NY 10016, United States of America.

© Oxford University Press 2022

Library of Congress Cataloging-in-Publication Data
Names: Garritzmann, Julian L., editor. | Palier, Bruno, editor. | Häusermann, Silja, editor.
Title: The world politics of social investment / [edited by] Julian L. Garritzmann, Bruno Palier, Silja Häusermann.
Description: New York, NY : Oxford University Press, [2022] | Series: International policy exchange series | Includes bibliographical references and index. | Contents: Volume I. Welfare states in the knowledge economy—Volume II. The Politics of Varying Social Investment Strategies.
Identifiers: LCCN 2021061165 (print) | LCCN 2021061166 (ebook) | ISBN 9780197585245 (hardback ; volume I) | ISBN 9780197601457 (hardback ; volume II) | ISBN 9780197585269 (epub ; volume I) | ISBN 9780197585276 (ebook ; volume I) | ISBN 9780197601471 (epub ; volume II) | ISBN 9780197601488 (ebook ; volume II)
Subjects: LCSH: Welfare economics. | Economic policy--Social aspects. | Social policy—Economic aspects. | Welfare state.
Classification: LCC HB846 .W67 2022 (print) | LCC HB846 (ebook) | DDC 338.9/2—dc23/eng/20220204
LC record available at https://lccn.loc.gov/2021061165
LC ebook record available at https://lccn.loc.gov/2021061166

DOI: 10.1093/oso/9780197585245.001.0001

9 8 7 6 5 4 3 2 1

Printed by Integrated Books International, United States of America

For our children
Alice and Nico
Lena and N.N. (forthcoming)
Lucas, Garance, Mia and Solveig

CONTENTS

CONTENTS OF VOLUME 2

The World Politics of Social Investment (Volume II): The Politics
of Varying Social Investment Strategies

INTRODUCTION

ACKNOWLEDGMENTS

The knowledge economy is centered around the increasing productivity of skills, knowledge, and capabilities, and its determinants and consequences within and across countries around the world. And so is this book and its sister volume. The two books are the result of a large and truly collective endeavor that we could not have done without the immense scholarly work and input of our contributors from around the globe. The 52 contributors to the two WOPSI volumes ("World Politics of Social Investment") have taught us invaluable insights into the fascinating politics of welfare state reform in emerging and developed knowledge economies.

Needless to say, this also has been a challenging journey. From the start (around 2015), our project has been ambitious, aiming to descriptively map and analytically explain how and why policy-makers in such diverse contexts as Argentina, Estonia, Germany, Guatemala, Hungary, Sweden, Spain, Taiwan, or the United States reform their welfare states in different ways to make their countries fit for the knowledge economy. Our vision has been to create a coherent theoretical framework that is broad and general enough to be able to cover social investment reforms and their politics around the globe and over time, while at the same time being substantively meaningful and concrete enough to really grasp the particularities of policy-making in different contexts. We hope that this book as well as its sister volume deliver on these aims.

The two volumes offer two different, but complementary views on the politics of welfare state reform in the century of knowledge—and on social investment policies in particular. While Volume I focuses on the politics of social investment from the perspective of explanatory factors such as structural dynamics, collective political actors, welfare legacies, and institutions ("the independent variables"), Volume II is geographically organized (along the "dependent variables") and offers a systematic and comprehensive analysis of the politics of social investment focused on different world regions, from Nordic Europe, via Continental, Southern, Eastern Europe, North America, Latin America, to North East Asia. All chapters "speak the same analytical language" as they use, apply, and test the same theoretical framework. We are extremely thankful and deeply indebted to all contributors for helping us to develop and to apply this unified framework. Not least, we are thankful that all contributors bore with us during the lengthy process and multiple rounds of revisions that we asked everyone to do for the sake of coherence and uniformity.

We also owe gratitude to a large number of people who commented on first (or later) drafts of our framework and/or individual chapters. Moreover, several people helped us to organize various meetings. In particular, we wish to thank all participants of three larger conferences that we organized in Paris (in 2017 and 2018) and at the EUI (in 2018). At the EUI, Hanspeter Kriesi, Maureen Lechleitner, and Reto Bürgisser generously offered to act as our "local hosts" and made sure we had a wonderful and productive time in the *Badia Fiesolana*. Dorothee Bohle, Giuliano Bonoli, Helen Callaghan, Ellen Immergut, Jane Gingrich, and Anton Hemerijck offered highly valuable feedback on various parts of the project.

We also met and discussed with many of the contributors and discussants at various conferences and workshops and again wish to thank all panelists, discussants, and organizers, for example, at the CES conference in Chicago, the "virtual" CES conference in Iceland, the SASE conference in Kyoto, the ESPAnet conference in Stockholm, the RC19 "hybrid" meeting in Fribourg, and the EU's Social Situation Monitor in Brussels. Moreover, we received excellent questions and feedback at various talks, for example at the University of Oslo, at Oxford, in Milan, and Royal Holloway, and at other occasions. Many participants at these conferenes and workshops have helped us develop, clarify and sharpen our work, and we are grateful to all of them. Special thanks go to Ben Ansell, Pablo Beramendi, Tom Chevalier, Mary Daly, Bernhard Ebbinghaus, Jane Gingrich, Charlotte Haberstroh, Ursula Hackett, Jens Jungblut, Carl Henrik Knutsen, Kati Kuitto, Jim Mosher, John Myles, Agustina Paglayan, David Rueda, and Simone Tonelli.

Andrea Stork and Delia Zollinger provided invaluable help finalizing all material. Both helped enormously in collecting and formatting all materials (countless documents, graphs, tables, CVs, abstracts, appendices, etc.). Thank you! Moreoever, several persons helped us along the way, especially Samira Jebli, Andreana Khristova, Latifa Louaso, and Léonie Trick. Finally, Christine Zollinger worked with us during the beginning of the project and co-authored our first WOPSI publication (a LIEPP working paper). Regina List carefully read and commented on several of our chapters, correcting mistakes and improving our writing. Thank you all!

At Oxford University Press, we particularly wish to thank the series editors, Douglas Besharov and Neil Gilbert, and the editorial board, who were enthusiastic and supportive of the project from the start. In current times, major presses have generally become more critical of edited volumes. At the same time, we are convinced that such integrated collections of studies become increasingly important for advancing the cumulative stock of knowledge, because they connect the dots between ever more specialized empirical research contributions. In this context, our editors at OUP did a wonderful job helping us improve the coherence of the volumes and the integration and synthesis of their findings. Birgit Pfau-Effinger, Espen Dahl, and Martin Potucek provided helpful comments pushing us further. Thanks also to Dana Bliss and Prabha Karunakaran at OUP for working with us efficiently and very supportively during the production process.

Financially, we gratefully acknowledge support from the Goethe University Frankfurt, the University of Zurich, the ANR and the French government under the Investments for the Future program LABEX LIEPP (ANR-11-LABX-0091, ANR-11-IDEX-0005-02) and the Idex University of Paris (ANR-18-IDEX-0001).

Frankfurt, Zurich, Paris
November 2021
Julian L. Garritzmann, Silja Häusermann, and Bruno Palier

CONTRIBUTORS

Melina Altamirano is an Assistant Professor at the Center for International Studies at El Colegio de México (Colmex) in Mexico City. Her research explores the political implications of economic vulnerability and overlapping social inequalities, the political economy of social protection, and the sources of public support for social policy in Latin America. Her work has been published in *Latin American Politics and Society* and *Politics & Society*, among other academic journals.

Armando Barrientos is Professor Emeritus of Poverty and Social Justice at the Global Development Institute at the University of Manchester in the UK. His research interests focus on the linkages existing between welfare programs and labor markets in developing countries, and on policies addressing poverty, vulnerability and population ageing. His most recent books are 'Social Protection for the Poor and Poorest' (2008, edited with D. Hulme, Palgrave); 'Just Give Money to the Poor' (2010, with J. Hanlon and D. Hulme, Kumarian Press) and 'Social Assistance in Developing Countries' (2015, Cambridge University Press).

Juan A. Bogliaccini is Professor of Political Science at the Social Sciences Department, Universidad Católica del Uruguay (UCU); and is Director of the Winter Methods School at UCU. He holds a PhD from the University of North Carolina at Chapel Hill. His research focuses on the political economy of distribution and inequality. He is editor at the Series of Latin American Political Economy at Palgrave.

Björn Bremer is a Senior Researcher in International and Comparative Political Economy at the Max Planck Institute for the Study of Societies in Cologne. He holds a PhD from the European University Institute and his research lies at the intersection of comparative politics, political economy, and political behavior. He is particularly interested in the politics of macroeconomic policies, welfare state politics, and the political consequences of economic crises.

Haohan Chen is an assistant professor of politics and public administration at the University of Hong Kong. He received his Ph.D. in political science and M.S. in statistical science from Duke University. Haohan's research focuses on political economy and quantitative methods. His substantive research interests include redistribution and preference formation in developing democracies and authoritarian regimes. His methodological research focuses on machine learning methods for opinion data on social media.

Claire Dunn is a PhD candidate in Political Science at the University of North Carolina, Chapel Hill. Her research examines questions of social policy and inequality in Latin America with a particular focus on Brazil. Her work has been supported by a Fulbright-Hays Doctoral Dissertation Research Abroad Fellowship and a UNU-WIDER Visiting PhD Fellowship.

Niccolo Durazzi is a Lecturer in Political Economy of Social Policy at the University of Edinburgh. His research focuses on comparative public and social policy with a specific interest on labor markets and skill formation. His work has appeared among others in Journal of European Public Policy, Socio-Economic Review, and Politics & Society.

Margarita Estévez-Abe is an Associate Professor of Political Science at Maxwell School of Citizenship and Public Affairs. She is the author of an award-winning book, *Welfare and Capitalism in Postwar Japan* (Cambridge University Press) and guest-edited special journal issues on Beyond Familialism (*Journal of European Social Policy*) and on Outsourcing Domestic (Care) Work: The Politics, Policies and Political Economy (*Social Politics*). Her field of interest is comparative political economy of advanced industrial countries with focus on welfare states and gender issues.

Julian L. Garritzmann is Professor of Political Science at the Goethe University Frankfurt. He works at the intersection of comparative political economy, public policy, party politics, and public opinion, with a special focus on education and social policies. His previous books include *The Political Economy of Higher Education Finance* (Palgrave), and *A Loud, but Noisy Signal? Public Opinion, Parties, and Interest Groups in the Politics of Education Reform in Western Europe* (Cambridge University Press).

Leonard Geyer is a Researcher in the Work and Welfare Unit at the European Centre for Social Welfare Policy and Research and a PhD candidate at the University of Bamberg. His research focusses on comparative political economy, active labor market policies and vocational education and training systems. His work has been published in *Socio-Economic Review* and the *Journal of European Social Policy*.

Silja Häusermann is Professor of Political Science at the University of Zurich in Switzerland. She studies welfare state politics and party system change in advanced capitalist democracies. She directs the ERC-project "welfarepriorities" (www.welfarepriorities.eu) and is the co-director of the UZH University Research Priority Programme "Equality of Opportunity". She is the co-editor of *The Politics of Advanced Capitalism* (Cambridge University Press 2015). For further information on projects and publications, please see www.siljahaeusermann.org

Evelyne Huber is Morehead Alumni Distinguished Professor of Political Science at the University of North Carolina, Chapel Hill. She studies democratization and redistribution in Latin America and advanced industrial democracies. She is the author and co-author of several books, three of which have won book awards: *Capitalist Development and Dem*ocracy (1992; with Dietrich Rueschemeyer and John D. Stephens), *Development and Crisis of the Welfare State* (2001) and *Democracy and the Left: Social Policy and Inequality in Latin America* (2012; both with John D. Stephens).

Jane Jenson is a professor emerita in the political science department, Université de Montréal and a fellow of the Royal Society of Canada since 1979. Her research focuses on comparative social policy in Europe and the Americas, with particular attention to the narratives surrounding the social investment perspective, and including the consequences for gender relations and women's status. Her most recent book is *Reassembling Motherhood: Procreation and Care in a Globalized World,* Colombia University Press, 2017 (co-edited Y. Ergas & S. Michel).

Herbert Kitschelt is professor of political science at Duke University. He published on the configuration of party systems in advanced democracies (e.g. *The Transformation of European Social Democracy*, 1994; *The Radical Right in Western Europe*, 1995; co-edited *The Politics of Advanced Capitalism*, 2015), post-communism (*Post-Communist Party Systems*, 1999, with co-authors) and Latin America (*Latin American Party Systems*, 2010). One major concern has been the role of clientelism in party systems (co-editor, *Patrons, Clients, and Policies*, 2007), also documented in data and publications within the framework of the Democratic Accountability and Linkage Project (DALP).

Thomas Kurer is a Research Group Leader at the Cluster of Excellence "Politics of Inequality" at the University of Konstanz. Previously, he was a Senior Researcher at the Department of Political Science, University of Zurich, and a Postdoctoral Fellow at Harvard University. He studies the political consequences of technological innovation and occupational change in post-industrial societies.

Margarita León is Professor of Political Science at the Autonomous University of Barcelona (UAB) and a Senior Researcher in the Institute of Government and Public Policies (IGOP) of the same university. Her fields of interest include comparative welfare and social policy research. Her work has been published in *Journal of European Social Policy; Social Politics; South European Society and Politics; and Comparative Politics* among others. In 2018 she was granted with an ICREA ACADEMIA award for a 5 year period for excellence in research (https://www.icrea.cat/es/icrea-academia). She is co-chair of the Spanish Network of Social Policy (Espanet-Spain).

Aldo Madariaga is Assistant Professor at the School of Political Science, Universidad Diego Portales, Chile and Associate Researcher at the Center for Social Conflict and Cohesion Studies (COES). His research focuses on the political economy of development and sustainability, and the relationship between capitalism and democracy. His publications have appeared in Socio-Economic Review, Governance, Policy Studies Journal, Comparative European Politics, among other. His book *Neoliberal Resilience: Lessons in Democracy and Development from Latin America and Eastern Europe* (Princeton University Press, 2020), received two honorary mentions for the best 2021 book (SASE Alice Amsden award, and ISA International Political Economy section).

Rianne Mahon is a distinguished research professor who has published on industrial policy, labour market restructuring, childcare politics, and the redesign of welfare regimes at the local, national and global scales. Mahon has co-edited numerous books including *Achieving the Social Development Goals: Global Governance Challenges* (with S. Horton and S. Dalby), and co-authored *Advanced Introduction to Social Policy* (with Daniel Béland). Her current work focuses on the 'gendering' of global governance, with a focus on migrant domestic workers.

Kimberly J. Morgan is a Professor of Political Science at George Washington University whose work examines the politics shaping public policies in Europe and the United States. She is the author of two books, *Working Mothers and the Welfare State: Religion and the Politics of Work-Family Policy in Western Europe and the United States* (Stanford 2006) and *The Delegated Welfare State: Medicare, Markets, and the Governance of American Social Policy* (Oxford 2011), and co-editor of three volumes, including mostly recently *The Oxford Handbook of the Welfare State, 2d edition* (Oxford 2021).

Bruno Palier is CNRS Research Director at Sciences Po, Centre d'études européennes et de politique comparée. Trained in social science, he has a PHD in Political science. He works on the comparative political economy of welfare state reforms. He was director of LIEPP (Laboratory for Interdisciplinary Evaluation of Public Policies) between 2014 and 2020. He has published numerous articles in international Journals and various books. In 2021, he co-edited with Anke Hassel *Growth and Welfare in Advanced Capitalist Economies*, Oxford University Press. In 2018, he co-edited *Welfare democracies and party politics: Explaining electoral dynamics in times of changing welfare capitalism* (with Philip Manow and Hanna Schwander), Oxford University Press. In 2012, he co-edited *The Age of Dualization: The Changing Face of Inequality in Deindustrializing Societies.* (with Patrick Emmenegger, Silja Häusermann and Martin Seeleib-Kaiser), Oxford University Press, and *Towards a social investment welfare state? Ideas, Policies and Challenges,* (with Nathalie Morel and Joakim Palme) Policy Press.

Emmanuele Pavolini is Full Professor in Economic Sociology and Social Policy at the University of Macerata (Italy). His research interests are: welfare state studies from a comparative perspective, with specific attention to family policies, health care and, more recently, education, inequalities in the access to welfare state provision, occupational welfare, welfare mix and third sector organizations; labor market research and economic development. He is currently co-editor of the Journal of European Social Policy.

Michael Pinggera is a Senior researcher in the Department of Political Science at the University of Zurich, Switzerland. His research focuses on welfare state politics, public opinion, and party competition. Michael Pinggera holds a PhD from the University of Zurich. His work has appeared among others in *Journal of European Public Policy, West European Politics, and European Journal of Political Research*. For further information, please see www.michaelpinggera.com.

Caroline de la Porte is Professor at the Department of International Economics, Government and Business, Copenhagen Business School. She holds a PhD from the European University Institute in Italy. Caroline's research focuses on comparative welfare state reform, the Nordic welfare model, EU governance and the Europeanisation of welfare states. She has published widely on European social policies. Recent publications include "Agents of Institutional Change in EU Policy : The Social Investment Moment," *Journal of European Public Policy*, 25(6) (with David Natali) in 2018, and "The Court of Justice of the European Union and Fixed-term Work : Putting a Brake on Labour Market Dualization?", *Journal of European Social Policy*, 27(3) (with Patrick Emmenegger) in 2017.

Martin Seeleib-Kaiser is Professor of Comparative Public Policy at the Institute of Political Science of the Eberhard Karls Universität Tübingen (Germany). Prior to his appointment at Tübingen in 2017, he held appointments at the University of Oxford (2004–2017), Duke University (North Carolina, USA) (1999–2002) and Bremen University (1993–1999; 2002–2004). His research focuses on the politics of social policy, comparative social policy analysis and the social rights of EU citizens. He has published amongst others in *American Sociological Review, British Journal of Industrial Relations, Journal of Common Market Studies, Journal of European Social Policy, Policy and Politics, Politics and Society, Social Policy and Administration, Social Politics, and West European Politics.*

John D. Stephens is Lenski Distinguished Professor of Political Science and Sociology and Director, Center for European Studies, University of North Carolina, Chapel Hill. He is the author or co-author of five books including the award-winning *Capitalist Development and Democracy* (with Evelyne Huber and Dietrich Rueschemeyer, 1992), *Development and Crisis of the Welfare State* (2001), and *Democracy and the Left* (2012, both with Evelyne Huber).

Bárbara A. Zárate-Tenorio works as a researcher at OsloMet, at the Welfare Research Institute, NOVA. Her research interests include the political economy of social policy, the determinants of political participation and redistributive preferences, and the linkage between welfare policy and violent crime in developing countries, with a special focus on Latin America. She holds a PhD in Social Policy and Intervention from the University of Oxford (2015). Her work has been published in *Comparative Political Studies, The European Journal of Political Research, Governance,* and *The Journal of Development Studies.*

1

TOWARD A WORLDWIDE VIEW ON THE POLITICS OF SOCIAL INVESTMENT

Bruno Palier, Julian L. Garritzmann, and Silja Häusermann

A round the turn of the 21st century, new social policies started to develop all around the world. *Bolsa Familia* in Brazil, *Progresa* in Mexico, *Superémonos* in Costa Rica, *Juntos* in Peru—almost all Latin American countries have developed "conditional cash transfers" (CCTs), a new type of social policy usually conditioning benefits for poor families on their children going to school or attending health checkups. At the same time, some old industrialized countries famously known for being the haven of the male breadwinner model have introduced surprising innovation in their welfare systems: in Germany, massive investment in preschool childcare (*Kita*) since the early 2000s and the introduction of two "daddy months" in a parental leave scheme in 2007; in Japan, a well-paid parental leave in 2014 and universalization of free preschool education for ages 3–5 in 2017; in South Korea, childcare facilities for children below the age of 5 made free of charge in 2013. Policies aimed at investing in children's care and education and in mothers' labor market participation seem to have bloomed almost everywhere. Worldwide there has been a sharp increase in access to secondary and tertiary education. Youth training programs have spread in many Latin American countries, while European countries have introduced youth guarantees, an innovative inclusive policy for their NEETs (young people not in education, employment, or training).

Public spending on social and education policies is less and less a characteristic only of Europe and the rich economies more generally. What is striking is

Bruno Palier, Julian L. Garritzmann, and Silja Häusermann, *Toward a Worldwide View on the Politics of Social Investment*
In: *The World Politics of Social Investment (Volume I)*. Edited by: Julian L. Garritzmann, Silja Häusermann, and Bruno Palier,
Oxford University Press. © Oxford University Press 2022. DOI: 10.1093/oso/9780197585245.003.0001

2 BRUNO PALIER ET AL.

that in many places around the world the focus is progressively shifting toward improving and mobilizing the population's skills and capabilities. This trend in the transformation of social policies and the new emphasis on skill creation, skill mobilization, and skill preservation can be considered to be a general upswing of what has been called in the comparative welfare state literature "social investment" policies (Morel et al., 2012).

Yet the trend is neither universal nor uniform. The reach and requirements of CCTs are quite diverse in Latin America. Some countries are still not really investing in family policies and childcare (in Southern Europe, especially Italy) or female labor market participation (in the Visegrád countries in Central and Eastern Europe). Young adults are still neglected in many welfare states (Chevalier, 2016). Some countries have targeted their social investment benefits to the poorest, while others grant access to social investment services to all. Some others have only increased the availability of these already existing services, allowing the upper middle classes better access but introducing what has been called a "Matthew effect" in the use of social investment (Bonoli et al., 2017). Active labor market policies (ALMPs) aimed at increasing labor market participation can range from very supportive to very coercive ones. Hence, when looking at the details, we see a great variety in the social investment policies that have developed all around the world.

To what degree have countries around the globe developed social investment policies? What kinds of social investments have they implemented? If they did not follow a social investment strategy, what kind of alternative welfare state reforms did they implement? Under what political conditions do social investment reforms develop? What have been the political dynamics behind such diverse social investment and non-social investment welfare state development? These are the many questions that arise about the politics of social investment around the globe. It is to address these issues that we initiated in 2015 a large research project studying the World Politics of Social Investment (the WOPSI project), the results of which are being published as two volumes.

The WOPSI project aims to map and explain the way in which welfare states in a variety of world regions have been adapted by policymakers to take into account the shift toward knowledge economies as constitutive economic and social conditions of the 21st century. Hence, the two main objectives of the WOPSI project are 1) to exhaustively map and describe the various welfare state reforms implemented in different regions of the world, and more particularly the social investment reforms, and 2) to analyze the political processes through which these reforms have been adopted in order to understand the political conditions leading to their adoption and explain the differences in the policies and strategies implemented.

This introduction to the first WOPSI volume presents an overview of the whole project. We start by first proposing a typology of social investment policies and strategies (our dependent variables) on the basis of a review of the various approaches to social investment, the structural changes calling for it, and the diverse policies implementing it. We provide our own definition of social investment and argue that there is not *one* type of social investment but there are *nine*. In the second part of the chapter, we present the constitutive elements of our theoretical approach (explained fully in Chapter 2 in this volume), our main independent variables, our research questions, and the choice of countries. We also present succinctly our main insights on the politics of social investment (discussed fully in Chapter 16 in this volume and Chapter 17 in Volume II [Garritzmann et al., 2022]) and how the two volumes are organized (see the two table of contents presented at the beginning of this volume). Finally, we sketch the content of each chapter of this first volume.

1.1. WHAT IS SOCIAL INVESTMENT? FROM A NEW PARADIGM TO A TYPOLOGY OF POLICIES AND STRATEGIES

"Social investment" has become a buzzword among policymakers and social scientists alike. A simple look at a Google N Gram Viewer on the expression "social investment" shows that the use of the term in published books in Google's collection started to increase in the late 1990s and rose continuously after the 2010s. Social investment is used in many different fields, from personality science and behavioral studies, management and corporate social responsibility, philanthropy and social impact bonds to certain public social and education policies. It is in the latter domains (i.e., public social and education policies) that our project investigates. In the first decade and even more so in the second decade of the 21st century, in the comparative welfare state literature especially, "social investment" has been conceived as the umbrella term for a new set of social policies: policies paying attention to children, to women, to prevention, to human skills and capabilities, and to reconciliation of work and family policies (Jenson & Saint Martin, 2003).

1.1.1. Social investment: A new paradigm for the welfare state

Many ambitious authors, such as Anthony Giddens (1998) or Gøsta Esping-Andersen and colleagues (2002), used the term to name the new orientation they proposed for the welfare state and its new architecture. Many of their ideas have been influenced by Amartya Sen's notion of capabilities (Morel & Palme, 2017), which can be defined as the actual freedom for individuals to choose and achieve the life they value. This freedom relies on a set of institutions, policies, and "capacitating services" that enable people "to foster individual capabilities for self-development and social and economic participation . . . [by] supporting the agency of individuals in achieving a 'flourishing life' " (Morel & Palme, 2017,

p. 153). These ideas have also been influenced by another economist, Nobel Prize winner James Heckman (2006), who emphasized the importance of investing early in children's skills and capacities.

In view of the multiplication of books, reports, debates, and policies referring to the ideas associated with social investment, Morel et al. (2012) have called the social investment perspective the "new paradigm" for the welfare state and its reforms since the late 1990s. This new paradigm follows the era of the Keynesian welfare state (1930s to mid-1970s) and the era of the Schumpeterian or neoliberal welfare state (Jessop, 1993). According to Morel et al. (2012, p. 2),

> The social investment approach rests on policies that both invest in human capital development (early childhood education and care, education and life-long training) and that help to make efficient use of human capital (through policies supporting women's and lone parents' employment, through active labor market policies, but also through specific forms of labor market regulation and social protection institutions that promote flexible security), while fostering greater social inclusion (notably by facilitating access to the labor market for groups that have traditionally been excluded). Crucial to this new approach is the idea that social policies should be seen as a productive factor, essential to economic development and to employment growth.

These proposals for redirecting welfare states toward social investment triggered fierce debate and many criticisms, coming from either a gender equality perspective (Jenson, 2009) or a social citizenship one (Nolan, 2013). The main criticism rests on the economicism associated with the new approach, which is allegedly preoccupied only with the human capital and productivity of the individual. A return to Sen's philosophy as well as the more recent notion of "inclusive growth" seeks to reconcile economic and social objectives associated with social investment (Deeming & Smyth, 2018; see Chapter 3 in this volume). If one cannot deny that the success of the social investment paradigm lies in its promise of economic returns in the context of the emergence of the knowledge-based economy, that success is also linked to its capacity to offer a series of responses to social and demographic developments such as aging and new gender relations. In the next section, we present the socioeconomic context that made the social investment perspective attractive to economists, education and social policy experts, as well as policymakers.

1.1.2. The socioeconomic changes behind the social investment perspective

The social investment perspective (Esping-Andersen et al., 2002; Hemerijck, 2013, 2017; Morel et al., 2012) always emphasizes the necessity to invest in skills, human capital, and human capabilities, to mobilize and to renew them along the entire life course, and to address the new social risks not met by the existing welfare states. The core idea is to "prepare rather than repair only," that is, to equip individuals with skills and education to prepare them ex ante to cope with the life-course risks that prevail in our current economies and societies, rather than to only compensate for such ex post, as do traditional social policies. The socioeconomic changes impelling an increased focus on the social investment perspective are twofold: social and demographic changes leading to new risks of societal welfare loss, on the one hand, and changing capitalism, on the other hand.

Despite their diversity, traditional welfare systems have in common that they emerged and expanded in similar socioeconomic contexts (i.e., within the democratization, national, and industrial revolutions—Rokkan, 1999; Van Kersbergen & Manow, 2009). Initially taking over (or complementing) church-based welfare through assistance policies aimed at providing some minimum support to the poorest in societies, welfare systems have progressively developed into social insurance systems aimed at protecting the market income earned by the "standard" industrial worker when confronted with social risks such as disability, sickness, unemployment, or old age (either through public systems or, if private, publicly regulated and subsidized ones). They were shaped by the male breadwinner model, typical of the late 19th and 20th centuries, assuming that if the income of the man was protected, the whole family would be protected (Lewis, 1992). Most welfare benefits have been conceived as compensating for lack or loss of income and are providing beneficiaries with cash benefits that alleviate their risk of poverty or replace part of their earned income. Traditional policies intervene once a social risk has occurred, ex post, and they deliver the welfare benefits immediately. While assistance policies are typically delivered on a means or income-test basis, social insurance is usually based on the recipient's employment status or situation. Both types mostly take the form of cash transfers and thus can be conceived as compensatory benefits used to support the immediate consumption capacities of their beneficiaries. Beramendi et al. (2015) use the notions of "social compensation," "social consumption," and "consumptive social policies" to refer to these traditional welfare benefits.

In the writings promoting a social investment perspective published in the late 1990s and the first decade of the 2000s, these traditional social policies have been described as ill adapted to the new context and situations of the late 20th century. Indeed, many of the socioeconomic conditions that surrounded the development of traditional welfare systems have progressively been challenged, calling not only for new social policies but also for a new approach to social policies. Several current and ongoing structural dynamics challenge capitalist systems, welfare states, and labor markets. Skill-biased technological change, globalization, automation, changing employment patterns, changing gender relations, and new social risks are but the most visible forms of these. We quickly review these challenges now to better grasp the structural developments that call for a turn to social investment in welfare state policies.

1.1.2.1. Demographic and societal changes

Many countries are experiencing quickly changing sociodemographic dynamics. The aging or "graying" of societies resulting from longer life expectancy and declining fertility has become a major challenge in all developed and emerging economies, challenging labor markets and social security systems in Europe, Asia, and the Americas (Vanhuysse & Goerres, 2013). As people live longer, health and pension expenditures are increasing, while new needs for elderly care emerge. These developments will require the collection of more taxes and contributions to finance these expenditures and, thus, more people participating in the labor market and paying those taxes and social contributions, as well as new care provision services.

While income inequality has increased in many countries, poverty has either stagnated or decreased since the 1980s in all world regions. However, the structure of poverty has changed significantly, shifting the burden from the elderly to the young and children. Child poverty has become an increasing preoccupation as it has increased since the 1980s and remains an important issue (in 2016 half of those living in extreme poverty were children; see UNICEF and the World Bank Group, 2016), especially because of the implementation of neoliberal structural reforms of labor markets and welfare states in emerging and developing countries (see Chapter 3 in this volume). Organisation for Economic Co-operation and Development (OECD) countries are also concerned: in Europe, almost 25% of children and 28% of young people aged 16–24 were at risk of poverty or social exclusion in 2018, compared with "only" 19% of those aged 65 and over (Eurostat, 2018). Though reducing poverty in old age was achieved through pension systems, and thus cash transfers, fighting child and youth poverty and its scars requires much more than cash benefits; it requires additional services such as childcare, education, healthcare, support, and orientation. Tackling child and youth poverty is perceived as the key to avoiding the intergenerational transmission of poverty and the reproduction of inequalities (Esping-Andersen, 2002).

The evolving role of women in society (not least via education and labor market participation) challenges the very fundamentals of many male breadwinner welfare systems (Bonoli, 2007; Esping-Andersen, 1999; Lewis, 1992; Sainsbury, 1996) through changing family structures (fertility, divorce, single parenthood) and changing patterns of labor market attachment (discontinuous employment biographies, school-to-work and family-to-work transitions). In order to avoid women's poverty or dependence and the adversities it brings for their children, welfare states need to support parents' (especially women's) entry into and progression within the labor market and formalize care functions. Such action requires specific gender equality policies in education and the labor market; work–life balance policies, including care services and reorganization of work schedules; as well as changes in parental leave and care responsibilities (Esping-Andersen, 2009; Knijn & Kremer, 1997; Lewis, 2001; Orloff, 2009).

While the post–World War II years in many countries have seen a standardization of work relations around the open-ended formal work contract, the 1980s saw the development of so-called atypical work situations, very often institutionalized by labor market and social protection reforms (Palier & Thelen, 2010). In the OECD countries, between the 1970s and the 2000s, the share of atypical employment in the overall workforce (part-time and fixed-term combined) has grown from around 10% to between 25% and 35%, depending on the specific country. Atypical job situations affect youth, migrants, and women much more than they do men (Emmenegger et al., 2012b). Meanwhile, informal work has increased in emerging economies, particularly in Latin America (Sandberg & Nelson, 2017). Informal and atypical workers are usually very badly (or even not, in the case of informal work) protected by traditional social insurance, which requires full contributions to receive full protection.

By the end of the 20th century, these new social situations were identified as "new social risks" that traditional welfare systems are unable to address (Bonoli, 2007; Esping-Andersen, 1999). The list is long: Informal work, precarious employment, working poverty, long-term unemployment, structural youth unemployment, difficulties of school-to-work transitions, child poverty, changing family patterns, single parenthood, increasing difficulties in reconciling family and work life—all of these generate new welfare demands and require new welfare programs. It is to respond to these situations that many have called for new labor market and social policy responses that, rather than waiting for the risk to occur, would act preventively and structurally to avoid the causes of these risks. Many of the proposals go beyond mere cash transfers to present formal care services and education as the new tools that will be able to cope with new social risks (Hemerijck, 2017; Morel et al., 2012).

Awareness of these new social risks and the social investment perspective proposed to address them owes much to feminist intellectual work. As underlined by Orloff and Palier (2009, pp. 406, 407),

the new concern about women's employment, emphasis on the "care crisis", the promotion of investment in children as well as the reconciliation between work and family life are mostly based on ideas of social policies that have become thinkable thanks to a gendered approach of the welfare state, and promoted by the feminist literature on welfare regimes. . . . Gender is central to the transformations of the contemporary welfare state, in a host of ways. Familial and work arrangements that had underpinned systems of social provision and regulation for many decades have been destabilized by changing gender relations, reflected in increased levels of mothers' employment; women's greater autonomy vis-à-vis partnering, reproduction and sexuality; declining fertility; the terminal decline of housewifery and "male breadwinner" households. Associated political and cultural changes—women's equality movements and the increased presence of women in the formal political sphere, rising support for notions of gender equality, women's political importance as voters, taxpayers, and bearers of the next generation of workers and taxpayers—have shaped contemporary social politics.

Yet, the attractiveness of the social investment perspective also has much to do with its capacity to (ambiguously) reconcile economic and social policies.[1] While neoliberalism relied heavily on the idea of an irreconcilable trade-off between equity (dealt with via "costly" redistributive social policies) and efficiency (dealt with by markets, deregulation, and liberalization of economic policies, leading to cuts in social expenditure), the social investment perspective emphasizes the importance of new social policies for enabling individual and collective economic prosperity in the new context of the knowledge-based economy. Indeed, one of the main economic ideas behind the social investment perspective is to develop education and social policies that collectively invest in and mobilize human capital.

1.1.2.2. Changes in the economy

As a result of the transformation of economies, productivity relies more and more on workers' cognitive skills. The importance of skills is not necessarily built into the traditional welfare states that emerged throughout the 20th century. Already in the 1960s, some economists (Becker, 1964/1993; Bell, 1973; Drucker 1969, 1993) identified skills and knowledge as key capacitating endowments and anticipated the emergence of the "knowledge economy." *Knowledge economies* can be defined as economies placing "a greater reliance on intellectual capabilities than on physical inputs or natural resources" (Powell & Snellman, 2004, p. 199). In the early 21st century, the importance of skills and skill formation systems is widely accepted as part and parcel of countries' politico-economic systems (Barbieri et al., 2018; Estévez-Abe et al., 2001; Hall & Soskice, 2001; Iversen, 2005; Shavit & Müller, 1998), social mobility and inclusion (Becker & Hecken, 2009; Breen & Jonsson, 2005), political participation, and social capital (Marx & Nguyen, 2018; Mettler, 2002; Verba & Nie, 1972).

Three main socioeconomic trends have triggered this increased interest in skill and human capital: deindustrialization, globalization, and technological change. Deindustrialization in the advanced economies and industrialization in the developing and emerging economies are changing labor markets worldwide (Wren, 2013). High-skilled jobs are expanding massively in post-industrial countries

---

1. For a good illustration of this ambiguous relationship between economic and social goals, see Chapter 4 in this volume, which focuses on social investment at the European Union level.

(e.g., Oesch, 2013), while mid-skilled jobs are expanding in emerging economies. Jensen (2011) suggests that deindustrialization amplifies risks for workers who then demand education expansion as a potential protection. The increased demand for skills also means a longer period spent in education, leading to the emergence of a longer early-age span (i.e., "youth") in people's biographies, often insufficiently supported by existing welfare states (Chevalier, 2016).

Globalization of trade and finance as well as migration also contributes to the increased importance of skills. According to the production regime literature on "comparative advantages" (Bohle & Greskovits, 2012; Estévez-Abe, 2009; Hall & Soskice, 2001; Schneider & Paunescu, 2012), firms' incentives to stay in or move away from a certain country depend, among other things, on the skill profile and the education and training system they find in that country. As a consequence of increased competition between countries and pressure on low-skilled jobs, citizens are demanding more education as a new way to be armed and protected in the globalization context (Garritzmann et al., 2018).

Finally, technological change favors skilled workers. Technological change usually is "skill-biased": Technological advancement seems to enhance the productivity of skilled workers, while it replaces or downgrades mid-skilled and low-skilled workers. Goldin and Katz (2008) identified a "race between education and technology," arguing that technological change disproportionately rewards educated workers at the expense of low-skilled workers, resulting in increasing inequalities as governments struggle to catch up with the provision of skills across the entire population. Skills and educational attainment have become an increasingly important determinant of wage inequality and other labor market outcomes (Oesch, 2013). It has been argued that automation, especially of routine work, will have similar effects in the near future since it favors the development of highly skilled and low-skilled jobs and eventually triggers protest and demand for protection from mid-skilled workers and threatened lower middle classes (Kurer, 2020; Kurer & Palier, 2019).

These challenges become visible in somewhat different combinations and to different extents in the different regions of the capitalist world, depending on the region's level and type of economic and societal development. Around the world, skills and human capabilities have become key factors in the distribution of opportunities and hence in the processes of economic distribution and redistribution (see Chapter 8 in this volume). Policies that enhance people's human capital, skills, and capabilities are thus attracting significant interest from economists, governments, and international organizations (as illustrated by Jenson and Mahon in Chapter 3 in this volume). As mentioned, it is also the capacity of social investment policies to deal with new social problems that emerged in post-industrial, post-male-breadwinner societies that attracted attention from social scientists and policymakers.

However, one cannot explain the development of social investment policies only by the fact that these seem to provide an adequate answer to socioeconomic challenges. Such a functionalist and deterministic explanation cannot make sense of the disparity among countries' reactions to these challenges or of the fact that those countries most in need of social investment policies are sometimes those that have the least developed such policies. This is, for instance, the situation in Southern Europe, where the general skill level of the population is relatively low, youth unemployment extremely high, aging developing fast, fertility declining, and women's participation in the labor market still very partial but where social investment policies are scarce to non-existent. Since the 2010s, more and more publications point out the development of social investment ideas and policies in specific countries or some regions of the world (Choi et al., 2020; Deeming & Smyth, 2018; Hemerijck, 2017; Midgley et al., 2017) and evaluate their various economic and social effects, but this variety has been neither conceptualized nor mapped nor systematically explained so far. Doing this is precisely the aim of the WOPSI project. In the next section, we review some of the main developments in social investment policies around the world in order to underline the main commonalities and differences that will form the basis of our conceptualization and categorization of social investment policies.

1.1.3. The variety of social investment strategies and of their effects

Existing research on social investment can be divided into three main strands of literature.[2] The first strand developed the ideas and advocated for the development of social investment policies. The second strand explores the design and emergence of social investment policies in specific policy fields and/or specific countries and regions of the world. The third strand of literature analyzes the effects of social investment policies on socioeconomic and political outcomes, such as social inclusion and poverty reduction. As we discussed the first aspect already in the previous section, we present here selected results from the two other strands of this literature in order to underline the variety of social investment approaches and policies and to determine on what dimensions they vary (goal, coverage, distributive profile, policy domain). It is on the basis of these dimensions that we will build our definition and typology of social investment strategies.

1.1.3.1. The disparate spread of social investment policies

Social investment policies have spread to very different extents and in very different forms across the globe. We sketch these in the following paragraphs.

2. For a review of the publications on social investment, see Wiktorska-Święcka et al. (2016) and Garritzmann et al. (2017). Also, Hemerijck (2017) assembles not all but many of the best experts on social investment and is therefore a kind of state of the art in itself.

1.1.3.1.1. Europe and English-speaking countries

Western European welfare states have implemented social investment reforms to very different degrees (Beramendi et al., 2015; Bonoli, 2013; Hemerijck, 2012, 2013, 2017; Morgan, 2012; Nikolai, 2012). In Europe, the *Nordic European* countries (Denmark, Sweden, Norway, and Finland) are usually mentioned as the most advanced in terms of social investments. These countries have known ample and largely successful programs of this sort for several decades (e.g., Gingrich & Ansell, 2015; Nelson & Stephens, 2012), even though recently there seems to be a certain level of disinvestment in those policies (Van Kersbergen & Kraft, 2017). Social investment can be found in all social policy domains: childcare, elderly care, care for the handicapped, training, as well as work–life balance policies. Services are provided on a universal basis and are publicly financed and accessible to all citizens. All Scandinavian countries invested heavily in all forms of education already during the 1950s, expanding post-secondary education and making universal, high-quality childcare accessible to all children much earlier than most other countries (Busemeyer, 2015; Garritzmann, 2016; Iversen & Stephens, 2008). In addition, compared to other west European welfare states, the Nordic countries spend most on ALMPs and rely on state-provided public services (Bonoli, 2013, pp. 28–46). Privatization of services (in health, care, and education) has contributed to stagnating wages in these sectors and increasing inequalities, less in terms of access since the services remained publicly financed and more through variation in quality (Blomqvist, 2004; Szebehely & Meagher, 2018).

Continental European countries (Bismarckian welfare states such as Germany, Austria, and France), in contrast, have historically been strongly oriented toward compensatory social insurance, with a strong male-breadwinner bias (Esping-Andersen, 1990; Palier, 2010). However, several studies document an expansion of social investment policies, especially in the fields of family policy and, to some extent, activation policy. Germany and Switzerland can be mentioned as examples of continental welfare states, where social investment reforms took the form of care infrastructure, fiscal incentives for childcare, as well as activation programs with regard to the unemployed or persons with disability (Bleses & Seeleib-Kaiser, 2004; Fleckenstein, 2011; Gerlach, 2004; Häusermann & Kübler, 2010; Häusermann & Zollinger, 2014; Hieda, 2013; Morel, 2007; Morgan, 2013; Naumann, 2005, 2012). These reforms have increased the number of services available but not to the point of making them accessible to all so that there is usually a bias toward the educated middle class in their use (Bonoli et al., 2017). Seeleib-Kaiser (2017) speaks of a "truncated" social investment turn for Germany, while Häusermann (2018) underlines the ambiguity of family policies in continental Europe that fluctuate between social transfers and social investment.

Generally, continental European countries have intensified their spending on ALMPs in the 21st century, albeit to a lesser extent than Nordic Europe (Bonoli,

2013, p. 43). Here again, one finds a bias in the implementation of social investment in labor market policies since usually the better-trained get better access to training, while low-skilled persons are activated toward taking any job; these policies thus contribute to the dualization of the labor market (Emmenegger et al., 2012a). Despite the fact that education has become increasingly salient on the political and the public agenda (Ansell, 2010; Busemeyer et al., 2013), in most continental European countries, education systems remain underfunded, especially higher and early childhood education (Busemeyer, 2015; Garritzmann, 2016; Iversen & Stephens, 2008), and stratified (Chevalier, 2016). All in all, the main purpose seems to be to increase the mobilization of existing capacities rather than to create more human capital or improve social or gender equality. One still needs to understand why continental Europe developed this kind of (stratified) social investment and why the evolution varied within this family of welfare systems.

The liberal welfare states of *North America* as well as the United Kingdom, Ireland, Australia, and New Zealand are generally less generous when it comes to social compensation policies (Esping-Andersen, 1990). Regarding some types of social investment, liberal welfare states turned their attention early on to education and skill development. In fact, Heidenheimer (1973) and others (Beramendi et al. 2015; Busemeyer & Nikolai; 2010; Iversen, 2005) argue that while conservative welfare states have focused on compensation and did not develop investment policies, liberal welfare states have focused on investment at the expense of compensatory policies. Thus, despite the fact that social compensation spending is at best average in liberal welfare states, education spending is comparatively high, especially when we include private education spending. Recently, this agenda has been broadened in some liberal welfare states. In the United Kingdom, for example, parents of young children gained the right to ask for a flexible work schedule, paid leave schemes were introduced, and childcare was expanded with support for the poorest families (Morgan, 2013).

The English-speaking countries are low spenders on ALMPs in Europe, even though spending has increased since the late 1990s (Bonoli, 2013, p. 31). English-speaking countries introduced the least expensive ALMPs; in liberal welfare states ALMPs are based on work incentives and pressure on beneficiaries to reintegrate into the labor market rather than on investment in human capital through training (Bonoli, 2013, pp. 33, 43). Social investment mainly takes the form of high levels of public and private spending on education and thus is concerned only with creation of human capital. Some targeted measures have been taken to support poor families in their access to childcare.

Southern European countries (Greece, Italy, Spain, Portugal) were latecomers in introducing social investment reforms. Spending on social investment fields increased only toward the end of the first decade of the 2000s and remains lower than in the other European welfare regimes. However, these countries have made the biggest increase proportionally in spending on ALMPs since then (Bonoli,

2013, p. 31). The structure of their family policies has also changed somewhat. Southern European countries have long been characterized as welfare systems of "unsupported" familialism (Léon & Pavolini, 2014, p. 354). In Spain, however, a social investment turn began in the early 1990s. Most importantly, Spain introduced universal preschool education in 1990, while childcare provision started to expand substantially during the years before the onset of the financial crisis in 2007. In addition, there have been several improvements of maternity and paternity leave and the creation of a national law for long-term care (Léon & Pavolini, 2014, p. 359). Even though there have been many new family and care policies in Spain and even some in Italy, budgetary cuts following the financial crisis have significantly affected these policies. So, one needs to understand why social investment failed to develop much in Southern Europe, except in pre-crisis Spain, though there seems to be a strong need for it.

In Central and Eastern Europe, the *Visegrád* countries (Czech Republic, Hungary, Poland, and Slovakia) spend even less on ALMPs than do countries in Southern Europe (Hemerijck, 2013, pp. 232, 259). However, in the Czech Republic and Poland, spending on ALMPs nearly doubled between 1995 and 2005, while it stagnated in Hungary and even declined in Slovakia. The *Baltic* countries, in contrast to the Visegrád countries, have both favored female employment and invested in higher education (Avlijaš, 2020). In all these formerly socialist countries, women had been encouraged to join the labor force already before the 1990s via special incentives including publicly provided affordable childcare services (Szelewa & Polakowski, 2008). After the collapse of the Soviet Union, the new democratic governments in many of these states closed childcare centers and withdrew financial support. The beginning of the 1990s has been described as the post-communist era of "re-familialization" (Saxonberg & Szelewa, 2007; Szelewa & Polakowski, 2008). The enrollment rates in childcare centers are still comparatively higher in the Czech Republic, Estonia, and Hungary and rather low in Poland and Slovenia (Szelewa & Polakowski, 2008). Regarding higher education, some central and eastern European countries have moved in the direction of "dualized systems," where the best students study free of charge, while students with lower grades are charged considerable tuition amounts (Garritzmann, 2016). One needs here to understand why social investment so differently penetrated the various policy fields and, above all, why there are so many differences between central and eastern European countries.

Taken together, a majority of European countries have reoriented their social policy in the direction of the social investment perspective. The expansion of social investment policies in general seems to be a universal trend and seems to happen across welfare regimes (Hemerijck, 2013). However, we see wide disparities not only between typical families of welfare systems but also within these families. Hence even if welfare regimes still seem to matter, they cannot explain the whole evolution of the systems and the disparate development of social investment. For Europe (and for the North American and other English-speaking countries), we still lack an encompassing overview of social investment agendas and reforms and an exhaustive explanation for existing variations.

1.1.3.1.2. North East Asia

European countries are not the only ones in which we observe an increase in social investment policies (Choi et al., 2020; Hasmath, 2015; Midgley et al., 2017). Since the 1990s, social investment reforms can also be observed in North East Asia as well as in Latin America, which we discuss in the next section. Whereas universal public education is ubiquitous in Japan and South Korea—since this has been a pillar of the growth strategy in those countries since World War II (Peng, 2014)—education in other east Asian countries is almost all private. Regarding higher education, moreover, most Asian countries are still characterized by extremely high private and quite low public spending (Garritzmann, 2016); in this respect, then, social investment has been comparatively underdeveloped. Yet, during the 1990s, governments in Japan and South Korea began to reconfigure their welfare states, mainly by pursuing a new kind of social investment policy. Peng (2014) observes for both countries a shift in the targets of welfare state protection. "Old" social policies (e.g., unemployment and old age insurance) targeted at full-time male industrial workers, public sector employees, military personnel, and teachers have been complemented by "new" social investment policies supporting the labor market participation of outsiders. They incorporate more peripheral, marginalized, and vulnerable population groups such as women, the young, children, and the elderly. This shift has been accompanied by a political rhetoric of social inclusion and was framed in terms of enhancing intergenerational equality. The type and degree of reform, however, also vary across countries and programs.

According to Peng (2014), the social investment strategy in Japan seems mostly focused on reconciliation policies with a primary focus on child- and eldercare. In the 1990s and early 2000s, the government incrementally extended maternity and parental leaves and expanded childcare and family support services. In addition, Japan significantly expanded eldercare services and long-term care insurance. As a consequence of a sharpened insider/outsider problematic, there was also a reform of the employment insurance system. This reform entailed a focus on older workers, women, and youths who were increasingly engaged in precarious working conditions. The reform involved measures to keep workers over the age of 55 in the labor market via a special subsidy paid to employers. The government also institutionalized support programs to address high youth un- and underemployment.

In South Korea a more explicit discourse on social investment garnered much attention during the late 1990s and even more from 2006 onward (Fleckenstein & Lee 2017; Seung-ho & Seung-yoon 2014). In 2006, the Korean government presented the "Vision 2030 for Economic Growth and Welfare," in which the social investment approach was central and social welfare was seen as an investment in the future. In 2006 the government adopted the "Basic Plan for Low Fertility and Aged Society (2006–2010)" (Seung-ho & Seung-yoon, 2014). Addressing child poverty after the 1997 financial crisis and increasing labor market participation were among the main objectives of the turn toward social investment (Fleckenstein & Lee, 2017). In its second implementation period (2011–2016) the "Basic Plan" focused on work–life balance policies. Ambiguously governments have combined cash transfers for families who care for their children at home with the provision of childcare services free of charge as of 2013. According to Fleckenstein and Lee (2017), the main objective is less women's participation in the labor market or investment in human capital than increasing fertility.

Taiwan, as a late industrialized country, needed to deal simultaneously with old and new social risks (Yeh & Lue, 2014). Therefore, traditional income maintenance policies and future-oriented social investment policies came on the political agenda at the same time. However, social investment policies were not supported by a majority in parliament, and social spending increases were concentrated on protective social policies, particularly pension policies, until the early 2010s.

Together, these examples show that North East Asian countries are indeed concerned with social investment agendas. Since the early 2000s, they have introduced social policy reforms particularly in the fields of family and labor market policy—however to very different degrees, more (in South Korea) or less (in Japan and Taiwan) explicitly, with different target groups. Here again, we believe that we still need to understand the political conditions under which these initially very conservative welfare regimes have shifted towards social investment, and to provide comparative analysis of and political explanations for the differences between these countries.

1.1.3.1.3. Latin America

Latin America faces high levels of poverty and income inequality and a sizeable minority being permanently trapped in inferior life trajectories (Fenwick, 2014). For this broad region covering parts of two continents, the literature that relates to a social investment logic of welfare policies seems mostly focused on conditional cash transfers (CCTs) that, as we mentioned at the start of this chapter, have developed in almost all Latin American countries (Stampini & Tornarolli, 2012). CCTs are social assistance programs that provide cash transfers to poor households that are conditional on the families sending their children to school or participating in health plans (Bourguignon et al., 2003; Fenwick, 2014; Huber & Stephens, 2014; Nelson & Sandberg, 2014; Sandberg, 2016; Soares et al., 2009). CCTs have the objective of addressing poverty in the present, while also investing in the future productive capacity of young people, thus reducing the intergenerational transmission of poverty and supporting economic competitiveness. Therefore, social investment in Latin America seems to have predominantly addressed poverty alleviation and investment in enhancing the life chances of the poor.

CCTs have spread in Latin America to compensate for the social cost of structural adjustment programs initiated by the World Bank and the International Monetary Fund at the beginning of the 1990s (Nelson & Sandberg, 2014). Among the first CCT programs were those initiated in the Brazilian municipalities of Campinas and Brasilia in the mid-1990s and nationwide in Mexico. Since then, 18 Latin American countries have introduced CCT programs (Cecchini & Madariaga, 2011). However, comparative analyses of the implementation of CCTs show significant variation, first in the coverage of the benefits, second in the level and capacity of the authority in charge of its administration, and third in the level of conditionality associated with the benefit (Stampini & Tornarolli, 2012). In Brazil, for example, a first program aimed at investing in human capital, initiated at the subnational level in 1995, sought to diminish child vagrancy by providing subsidies to parents who send their children to school. After the program had been extended nationwide and other CCTs using different incentives had emerged, all were brought in 2003 under the umbrella of the *Bolsa Familia*, a national poverty alleviation program that delivers cash benefits to families in situations of extreme poverty (Fenwick, 2014, p. 4ff.). The program's cash benefits are conditional on school attendance, basic health checks, and prenatal care. The strategy was designed to increase both individual capacity and equality of opportunity. The policy focus of Brazil's CCTs was on investing in children and in maternal and early childhood health, whereas gender equality and increasing women's labor market participation were not central pillars of the agenda (Fenwick, 2014, p. 8). As is clear from many reports on CCTs, the objectives and implementation of CCTs have been different in other Latin American countries (see, for instance, Ceccini & Atuesta, 2017). Here again, we need further comparative analysis of and political explanations for the differences between the cases.

In sum, social investment policies have been adopted throughout democratic countries in different world regions. The kind and degree of adapted policies as well as the timing of the introduction and expansion of the respective policies, however, differ starkly across countries. Some have focused on workforce mobilization, while others have improved their human capital creation system. Some have chosen a universal approach, others have targeted public social investment to the poorest, and some others have let the most equipped (in terms of finance and skill) have primary access to social investment services.

1.1.3.2. The varying distributive effects of social investment policies

In addition to the ideational and descriptive strands, a third increasingly established strand in the social investment literature investigates the distributive effects of social investment policies on social, economic, and political outcomes such as social cohesion, poverty reduction, and labor market outcomes. While the WOPSI project does not focus on the consequences of social investment, looking at some of these studies helps us identify the kinds of distributive profiles social investment policies can have and how they are linked to particular institutional designs. It also contributes to figuring out the kind of political support (or rejection) they might receive.

Several studies investigating childcare policies in west European countries have demonstrated the existence of a social bias in access to childcare services: High-quality public childcare services are disproportionately often used by children living in higher-income households (Abrassart & Bonoli, 2015; Ghysels & Van Lancker, 2011; Schlanser, 2011; Van Lancker & Ghysels, 2012). Thus, at least in western European countries, social investment in childcare is likely to benefit those who are better off more than the lower-income quintiles (a finding that we know very well from the other potentially regressive educational sector, namely higher education [cf. Fernandez & Rogerson, 1995; Garritzmann, 2016]). Some analysts maintain that the uneven use of social investment policies causes a strong *Matthew effect* (those who already have will have even more) and therefore increases social inequalities (Bonoli et al., 2017; Cantillon, 2011). However, newer studies show that the effects of preschool care services strongly depend on the design of those policies. A strong positive effect on social inclusion can only be expected if childcare use is universal or targeted to lower strata and if the costs for low-income families are moderate (Abrassart & Bonoli, 2015; Zollinger, 2016). Moreover, if one includes preschool care, elderly care, and primary, secondary, and vocational education as social investment policies, this set of social policies performs better in terms of vertical distribution than more traditional social policies do (Vaalavuo, 2013). In any case, Cantillon (2011) and Taylor-Gooby et al. (2015) have shown that poverty rates in western European countries have stagnated since the 1990s, despite an increase in spending for social investment policies. The implication is that at least in Europe (except in Nordic countries), the main social group benefiting from social investment is the (upper) middle class. This may be one reason why it is precisely this class that seems to be the main supporter of social investment (Beramendi et al., 2015; Busemeyer & Garritzmann, 2017; Gingrich & Häusermann, 2015; Häusermann & Palier, 2017).

Studies on the impact of social investment policies on female employment in South Korea are particularly interesting. Hui and Young (2014) argue that to be effective and to have a social and economic return, social investment policies in South Korea should go beyond family policy and actively address labor market issues. While family policy expenditure in South Korea has risen from 2002 onward, female labor market participation has decreased (Seung-ho & Seung-yoon, 2014). Seung-ho and Seung-yoon (2014) see the decline in female participation as a consequence of the design of family policies, which significantly expanded expenditures on financial transfers for childcare at home but neglected to invest enough in improving the quality of public childcare services. In addition, only few South Korean women are insured for parental leave (insurance is restricted to those employees who are insured by the Korean employment insurance for more than 180 days) since female workers are concentrated in certain occupational segments of the labor market with often precarious working conditions (Seung-ho & Seung-yoon, 2014, p. 5f.). In a case like this, the specific design of social investment reforms can also inform us about which support coalitions we can expect to find, especially regarding the support these policies can gather from different groups of women.

Several evaluation studies have shown positive effects—at least in the short term—of CCT programs (Nelson & Sandberg, 2014, p. 4f.). CCT programs can indeed reduce poverty in the short term, and the conditionality requirements have proven to increase school attendance and the number of health checks. However, the effects of CCTs on the reduction of intergenerational transmission of poverty remain weak (Cecchini & Madariaga, 2011; Nelson & Sandberg, 2014, p. 5ff.). Levy (2008, p. 78) pointed to the fact that without more productive jobs, poor workers will need CCT transfers permanently, which may affect the middle-class support these policies initially benefited from. These studies also underline that the effectiveness of CCTs is contingent on state capacity, as well as on the availability and quality of public services. This interaction effect will also shape the political support coalitions CCT reforms can rely on.

Thanks to a growing number of studies investigating the impacts of social investment policies, we begin to understand the effects of those policies, pointing to the winners (and the losers) and hence to the potential supporters of (and opponents to) social investment programs. These studies emphasize that the redistributive effects of the policies depend hugely on their institutional design, showing thus that social investment policies, depending on the way they are designed, can have different distributive profiles.

Taken together, the three strands of literature reviewed in this and the previous sections have demonstrated a highly diverse turn to social investment across countries in different regions of the world. Indeed, the timing and the extent of the adoption of such policies vary starkly across countries. Moreover, countries in different regions of the world have implemented different types of policy instruments with different functions and different target groups. What the existing literature still lacks, though, is a systematic, encompassing comparison of the varieties of social investment agendas and policies in different regions in the world, as well as an explanation of this variation in terms of the political conditions facilitating or impeding social investment reforms. The WOPSI project aims to both map and explain the diversity of social investment policies adopted around the (democratic) world. In order to fulfill these ambitious objectives, we first need to elaborate a comparative framework able to neatly grasp the diversity of social investment policies and strategies. This is the objective of the next section.

1.1.4. Typologizing the variety of social investment

What is striking from the literature on social investment is that despite an obvious variety of uses of social investment, it has been so far conceived only in the singular form as a paradigm and a family of policies. That is, most literature has assumed that there is "the" social investment approach, "the" social investment paradigm, or "the" social investment strategy. Of course, some authors have underlined the difference between how social investment is implemented in Nordic countries as compared to liberal ones (Morel et al., 2012). Anton Hemerijck proposes a distinction between three welfare functions of social investment: "(1) easing the 'flow' of contemporary labour-market and gendered life-course transitions; (2) raising the quality of the 'stock' of human capital and capabilities; and (3) maintaining strong minimum-income universal safety nets as social protection and economic stabilization 'buffers' in ageing societies" (Hemerijck, 2017, p. 5).[3] But this distinction provides only a potential starting point for identifying and sorting the various types of social investment policies into a systematically elaborated typology.

In order to be able to map the diversity of social investment developments and strategies, we elaborate an approach to social investment that is plural. We find it helpful to think about social investment primarily in terms of goals and functions, and—subsequently—in terms of particular policies. We thereby refrain explicitly from providing a simple, purely policy-based definition because many (if not all) social policies can include elements of social investment that might be overlooked when focusing too quickly and too narrowly on only a few specific policies (Kvist, 2015). We also do not distinguish between transfers and services as both policy instruments can pursue the goals and functions of social investment or not. While services are a core element of every social investment strategy, not all services are per se social investment. Furthermore, some cash transfers do perform social investment functions: For instance, it has been shown that generous and short-term unemployment benefits and sick pay are important for avoiding human capital depletion (Nelson & Stephens, 2012). Also, CCTs are cash transfers (associated with the use of education and healthcare services).

While the overarching social investment paradigm has promoted a similar set of social and economic goals that social investment policies are supposed to share (as described in the next section), our review of actual developments has shown that the programs and policies vary according to their functions and redistributive profiles. Hence, we propose to build our typology of social investment policies on the latter two dimensions. At the close of this section, we

---

3. Anton Hemerijck distinguishes between "stock," "flow," and "buffer" functions; but it is not always clear whether he only refers to social investment policies or in fact refers to all welfare state policies beyond mere social investment, especially for the buffer function which corresponds to income maintenance.

incorporate our social investment framework into an all-encompassing typology of welfare reform strategies more generally.

1.1.4.1. The shared goals of social investment

Social investment aims to prepare, support, and equip individuals in a way that increases their potential to support themselves in the economy (notably through employment) and reduces their future risks of income loss and poverty. Hence, it is about investing welfare resources now in order to generate returns in the future. This strategy involves avoiding social risks and overcoming the intergenerational transfer of disadvantage and poverty (Esping-Andersen, 2002; Jenson, 2010). Social investment aims to prepare individuals to have less to repair later on. The future-oriented social investment logic stands in contrast to purely transfer-oriented compensatory or consumption social policies (Beramendi et al., 2015; Hemerijck, 2012, 2017; Morel et al., 2012). Whereas consumption-oriented policies provide economic security immediately via decommodifying social policies such as income replacement in case of unemployment, old age, or sickness, social investment policies work differently as they focus on future income streams.

Thus, social investment policies are meant to serve both social and economic goals (Kvist, 2016). In terms of social returns, social investment policies are supposed to reduce poverty levels in the longer run, increase social inclusion and social cohesion, narrow inequalities, and contribute to human development. In terms of economic returns to individuals, the social investment perspective expects to enhance labor market opportunities and earnings potential. At the macro-level, a better-educated and better-equipped population is expected to contribute to higher growth rates (since workers can better contribute to the knowledge-based economy). Beyond education and training, social investment is also aimed at helping people to mobilize, preserve, and improve their capabilities and skills.

Against the background of economic structural change, our understanding of social investment relates necessarily to concepts of human capital investments and productivity. However, while employability is an important goal of social investment, it is not enough. The emphasis on both economic and social returns that social investment policies need to pursue to qualify as such brings our concepts beyond human capital in a narrow sense toward the notion of "human capabilities" (i.e., the idea of capacitating individuals to actively shape their own lives) (Sen, 2001; see especially Morel & Palme [2017] on the relationship between social investment and the capabilities approach).

1.1.4.2. The varying functions of social investment

In the cases reviewed earlier in this chapter and throughout both volumes, we see that social investment programs have different functions that we can classify into three main categories: creating, mobilizing, and preserving human capital and capabilities. In a life-course perspective, social investment policies have the function to enable individuals to prevent and/or overcome difficult life events and life transitions without losing their capacity to support themselves economically (Kvist, 2016, p. 6f.). Accordingly, social investment policies help to build, strengthen, maintain, re-establish, and use individuals' capabilities and skills. Social investment policies can first refer to an investment in skill and human capital formation (skill creation). Second, they can comprise an investment in the mobilization of human capital for labor market participation (skill mobilization). Third, they can represent an investment in the preservation and improvement of human skills and capabilities to better handle life events and transitions (skill preservation). Skill creation focuses on the formation of resources (creating capabilities), mobilization on the effective use of existing human resources, and preservation on the maintenance or improvement of these capabilities. Social investment policies aim at fulfilling (one or more of) these functions.

So how can we identify social investment policies concretely? In order to be classified as a social investment policy in our understanding, a policy must aim to achieve (some of) the aforementioned goals and functions. If one looks at the goals and functions of social investment policies, there are sometimes ambiguous domains, such as active labor market policies. The activation of unemployed people to re-enter the labor market via negative incentives such as sanctions and benefit reductions if one refuses any job (even of poor quality and badly paid) is not part of our understanding of the social investment logic (cf. Bonoli, 2013; Taylor-Gooby, 2004). Only positive skill creation, mobilization, and preservation correspond to our understanding of social investment. That is, if spending is retrenched, it can by definition not be "investment," or if individuals are forced to take an unsuitable job that holds them in poverty, it cannot be said to be "social." The goal of social returns can be reached by social inclusion, by fostering capabilities (improving skills and empowering jobless people), and by securing quality jobs (Bonoli, 2013, 23; Morel et al., 2012, p. 9f.). This definition based on goals and function allows us to distinguish between social investment and non-social investment. We, however, need to be able to further distinguish among social investment policies since not only the functions but also the coverage and scope of beneficiaries vary between policies.

1.1.4.3. The varying distributive profiles of social investment

To differentiate social investment policies according to their "distributive profiles," we distinguish three types: "inclusive," "stratified," and "targeted" social investment policies. When we speak of distributive profile, we refer to the question of who is supposed to benefit from the respective social investment proposal or reform, as designated in the corresponding program or bill.

- *Inclusive*: The policy program or bill plans to provide entitlement and provision of services to (almost) everyone. By creating a single pool of beneficiaries, it is intended to reduce inequality and support social cohesion.

- *Stratified*: The policy program or bill plans to provide new social rights and services to only a limited set of potential beneficiaries. It will most likely perpetuate or reinforce inequality, either de jure by directing rights and services to the middle and upper classes explicitly or de facto by not specifying that the rights and services should go to specific vulnerable groups. This is to be associated with the so-called Matthew effect that some authors have attributed to social investment policies (Cantillon, 2011).
- *Targeted*: The policy program or bill explicitly plans to provide entitlement and services to the lower income classes or similar groups such as the outsiders, the NEETs, or those working in the informal sector. It is supposed to fight first and foremost the intergenerational transmission of poverty or precariousness.

When evaluating a specific strategy as "inclusive," "stratified," or "targeted," we look at the respective proposals, programs, reforms, and bills as designed (i.e., the outputs) and not their actual outcomes. In other words, we categorize the policy reform strategy based on the institutional setting and distributive profile of the policy as originally intended and expressed in policy-related documents, not on the policy's outcome.

1.1.4.4. Nine types of social investment policies

What policies serve social investment goals and perform social investment functions? Most immediately and obviously, the social investment perspective translates into strengthening certain education and social policies. Social investment welfare states have a strong leaning toward services. A key focus of the WOPSI project lies on social investment in the field of family, labor market, and education policies (early childhood education and care, school and post-secondary education, as well as lifelong learning and vocational training). However, following our definition of the social investment concept that focuses on goals and functions, other policy fields such as healthcare, housing, and disability policy may also have to do with social investment. As mentioned, Nelson and Stephens (2012) have shown that generous paid sick leaves contribute to preserving human capital. As pointed out by Y.-M. Kim (2007), a precondition for social investment to work is that various factors such as decent home and community environments as well as healthcare are present. Therefore, any strategy to enhance or use human capital in economic terms needs to take into account the influence of the broader social setting. Thus, in addition to the "usual" set of policy domains we have already noted, social investment goals can be pursued via labor market policies that support the move from school to work for young people or by housing policies (Kvist, 2016, p. 7). CCTs take advantage of this complementarity of interventions by making health insurance coverage and/or transfers for poor people conditional on sending children to school and/ or to a physician for regular general checkups.

Since one can distinguish between three functions of social investment and three distributive profiles, there are theoretically nine types of social investment policies (see Table 1.1a).

This comparative analytical grid is mainly aimed at mapping and making sense of the diversity of social investment policies. We provide some basic and abstract examples of different policies in Table 1.1b. These will be explicated in the various case studies presented throughout our two volumes.

Table 1.1a Nine types of social investment policies (typology)

Distributive profile / Function	Inclusive social investment	Stratified social investment	Targeted social investment
Creation of human capital			
Mobilization of human capital			
Preservation of human capital			

Table 1.1b Nine typical social investment policies (examples)

Distributive profile / Function	Inclusive social investment	Stratified social investment	Targeted social investment
Creation of human capital	Universal public childhood education and care of high quality, attended by a vast majority of children aged 1–6	(Semi-)Private education (early childhood or post-secondary/ tertiary), mostly accessible to middle- and upper-middle-class families	Means-tested conditional cash transfers with educational conditions
Mobilization of human capital	Care services accessible to and funded for all households	Childcare prioritized for working parents	Youth guarantee for the NEETs
Preservation of human capital	Public training service available for all unemployed	Contributory (hence proportional and only accessible to those who contributed) sick pay and parental leave schemes	Training targeted to long-term unemployed

Note. NEETs = young people not in education, employment, or training.

1.1.4.5. Six welfare state reform strategies

This grid of the nine types of social investment policies (Table 1.1a) will also help us to figure out which has been the dominant logic of a specific social investment strategy adopted in one particular country at a certain moment in time (see especially cases studied in Volume II, synthesized in Chapter 17 in Volume II [Garritzmann et al., 2022]). When we speak of social investment strategies, we mean the policy objectives and design of a reform of the welfare state that has been inspired by social investment goals and functions. Just like traditional, transfer-based, consumption-oriented welfare policies, social investment policies differ in generosity, scope, and distributive effects.

These various social investment reform strategies are what we ultimately seek to explain in the WOPSI project. Our goal is to understand not only what governments do but also why they do it (hence the notion of welfare reform strategies). This implies that we focus our explanatory effort not on the economic and social outcomes of social investment policies but rather on the actual policy strategies governments pursue.

Of course, policymakers can choose among many welfare state reform strategies. We distinguish six such strategies for reforming the welfare state (see Figure 1.1): three main social investment strategies, "inclusive," "stratified," and "targeted" according to their distributive profile,[4] and three "non-social investment strategies" (i.e., alternative strategies of welfare state development that do not engage with the social investment paradigm). Though social investment remains our focus, these alternative strategies are important to keep in view, not least because they represent "negative" cases that also help us to understand (by default) the political condition for adopting social investment strategies.

Among the "other strategies," three families can be identified: "market liberalism," "social protectionism," and "basic income" strategies. The most

Figure 1.1 Six types of welfare reform strategies.

4. Reintegrating the nine types of social investment policies here would lead to a too complicated framework. Moreover, since we argue below that the explanation of the choice for a specific strategy is political, we believe that the distributive profile (i.e., who will benefit from the reform) is of utmost importance.

straightforward one is pure market liberalism, a strategy of retrenchment, individualization, and privatization of protection against risks (most likely resulting in "forced" commodification). Another welfare strategy that we call social protectionism privileges compensation over investment and decommodification over activation. Finally, some actors favor the development of a (universal) basic income, a strategy that is to date more theoretical than actually empirically observable. Such a reform strategy can be seen in some respects as the antagonist to social investment: A universal (unconditional) basic income breaks the link between expansion of employment and the development of welfare benefits and abandons the provision of specific services (such as childcare, education and training, or elderly care). Though there are certainly many different types of such non-social investment strategies, we do not delve more deeply into possible subcategories since our main focus is on the politics of social investment.

Now equipped with our analytic grid, we can identify and characterize the various types of social investment policies and strategies that have been developed around the world since the late 1990s. We can now also pinpoint the variety of welfare state reforms, both social investment and non-social investment ones, that countries have developed since the 1990s. With these we are able to fulfill the first objective of the WOPSI project, which is to descriptively map which social investment policies countries have pursued and how policies have evolved in these countries. In all chapters in both WOPSI volumes, authors will refer to this typology to characterize the type of policies and strategies they are analyzing. In the conclusion of Volume II (chapter 17), we identify which principal social investment strategy prevailed in which region of the world and how these evolved over time.

The second main aim of the WOPSI project is to explain the situations, trajectories, and differences identified. In order to understand the variety of situations and their evolution, we need a systematic understanding of the political conditions under which social investment agendas and reforms are discussed, elaborated, adopted, or rejected. For this we have forged a theoretical framework that is presented in Chapter 2 in this volume. In the next section, we provide an overview of the main independent variables we think need to be taken into account to explain the politics of social investment, our main research questions, and selected findings. We also present the organization of the two volumes and the content of Volume I's chapters. (See p. xi–xiii the content of volume II).

1.2. THE KEY FEATURES OF THE WOPSI PROJECT AND ITS TWO VOLUMES

In a nutshell, the WOPSI project aims to reveal the political conditions that led to adoption of social investment policies in various political contexts. We break up the process of adopting (or discarding) social investment strategies into two steps. The first is the *politicization* of social investment ideas, debates, and proposals;

in other words, how particular social demands interact with political supply to translate (via collective actors) into political debates and proposals that promote social investment policies. The second consists of the coalitional dynamics and decision-making processes leading to the adoption of specific social investment reform strategies (when interests and parties ally in favor of or against certain types of social investment policies). The various social investment proposals discussed in the public debate and the social investment reform strategies adopted by governments are the two main "dependent variables" of the WOPSI project.

Based on the existing general literature on public policies and specific works focusing on the politics of social investment, we identify four main categories of independent variables: 1) ideas and ideational dynamics, 2) structural socioeconomic changes, 3) institutional legacies, and 4) interests (and their respective interactions). The latter—actors, their positions, and their interactions, leading to different coalitional configurations—are of central interest in both WOPSI volumes.

1.2.1. Our research questions

Our basic and overarching research question is the following: **Which political factors support or inhibit the development of social investment policies across different world regions?** A recent and rapidly growing body of research points to the crucial role of politics to explain the development of social investment policies (Busemeyer et al., 2018; Choi et al., 2020; Häusermann & Palier, 2017). Some of this work highlights the cognitive role of international organizations such as the World Bank, the United Nations, and the OECD in developing a social investment policy paradigm and diffusing it among policymakers (e.g., Jenson, 2010; Morel et al., 2012; see Chapter 3 in this volume). Others see socioeconomic structural change, such as deindustrialization or technological change, as a main explanation for the increasing emphasis on social investments (e.g., Jensen, 2011; see also Chapter 8 in this volume). Still others point to the role of domestic politics and analyze how changing class structures (e.g., Häusermann & Kriesi, 2015; Häusermann & Palier, 2017), public opinion (e.g., Busemeyer et al., 2020), political parties (e.g., Abou-Chadi & Immergut, 2019; Boix, 1998; Gingrich, 2011), or social partners (e.g., Rueda, 2007) affect the adoption of social investment policies.

On the basis of the various potential explanations, we have elaborated a series of seven research questions that allow us and our fellow contributors to detect and analytically grasp the main variations in social investment policies and strategies and to identify and characterize the variables able to explain these variations:

1) *Classifying social investment proposals and reforms*: How can we conceptually distinguish, characterize, systematize, and describe different social investment policies? What are the main political logics followed by the social investment policies?

2) *Social demand*: What are the public/social demands for social investment? Which social groups have a stake in social investment policies? Who are the politically relevant social groups? What do they want? And under what conditions do they get what they want?

3) *Collective actors*: What do collective actors want? Who are the protagonists, antagonists, and consenters of social investment proposals or reforms? And under what conditions are collective actors protagonists, antagonists, or consenters of (different types of) social investment?

4) *Socioeconomic and institutional scope conditions*: What roles do structural dynamics play in the politics of social investment? What are the scope conditions for (successful) social investment reforms? How do political institutions shape the politics of social investment?

5) *Salience*: How politically salient are social investment proposals, programs, and reforms (overall and relative to other welfare reform strategies); and how does this affect the politics of social investment?

6) *Policy legacies*: Are welfare state legacies influential? Do they facilitate, slow, or block reforms?

7) *Coalition formation dynamics*: Which political coalitions are relevant for the adoption of the social investment reforms? Which types of coalitions lead to which types of social investment reforms?

In order to be able to answer these analytical questions as fully as possible and to be able to account for the broadest range of (diverse) situations, we have elaborated a theoretical model regarding how ideational and structural changes, institutional legacies, and actor interests and interactions influence the kind of social investment initiatives that arrive on the public agenda and get discussed, as well as their chances of being adopted. This theoretical framework is elaborated and presented fully in Chapter 2. Next, we only briefly present the main variables we have identified and how they shape the politics of social investment.

1.2.2. The "what" and the "who": The main variables and insights

While existing studies have considerably improved our understanding of the politics of social investment, no single-factor explanation can, of course, explain on its own the large empirical variety (across world regions, countries, time, and policy packages) analyzed in our two volumes. This is why we propose a broad theoretical model that integrates and expands the various variables in order to be able to fully explain variation in social investment policies. Our theoretical framework contextualizes social investment politics in an encompassing macro-level account of ideational paradigmatic and economic structural transformations that shape the politics of social investment: the ideational and structural transition to a knowledge economy and changing valuation and demand of skills. Thereby, the project puts human capabilities and human capital at the very center of welfare state research in the 21st century.

Our framework allows for analysis of the interactions between structural factors and domestic politics in order to arrive at regional accounts of the dynamics of social investment politics. It emphasizes the importance of welfare state legacies and political institutions in shaping the issues raised as well as actors' preferences and their interaction. For each world region studied in this project (Western, Southern, and Central and Eastern Europe; North East Asia; and North and Latin America), the two volumes underline specific aspects of social investment proposals and programs (e.g., the focus on women and demographics in Asia, new instruments to fight poverty in Latin America, a novel human capital perspective in the Baltic region, the focus on activation and family policies in Continental Europe, and de-universalization trends in Scandinavia). In our framework, we adopt a focus on politics and agency and how they filter and moderate structural factors. We also theorize about and analyze empirically how the interaction of public demand (e.g., public opinion, new cleavages, and societal groups) and sociopolitical supply (by parties, social partners, bureaucrats, and specific interest groups) shapes certain social investment proposals and programs and ultimately countries' social investment strategies.

In Chapter 2 of this volume, we elaborate further on how our four sets of factors (ideas, socioeconomic structural factors, policy legacies, and actors' positions and coalitions) interact. Here, we provide a brief glimpse into some of the WOPSI project's main findings.

Changes in economic and social policy paradigms and socioeconomic structural transformations provide the backdrop against which the politicization of social investment happens. As mentioned previously, the politics of social investment have to be understood in the context of several important general developments: deindustrialization, technological change, changing capitalism, the emergence and spread of the knowledge economy, changing demand for skills, and changing demographics and family patterns all exert pressure on welfare states around the globe. These multiple, simultaneously occurring pressures help explain why a focus on skills, education, and lifelong learning has emerged as societies develop from industrial into post-industrial knowledge economies, with accompanying massive middle-class and service sector growth as well as extensive decline of industrial employment. These societal trends articulate the structural changes on the demand side of social investment politics.

Yet, as important as these two types of factors (changes in ideas, on the one hand, and socioeconomic transformations, on the other hand) are in both bringing social investment to the agenda and shaping the demand side of politics, our research shows that neither is the knowledge economy a necessary condition for the politicization of social investment nor do social investments automatically follow from such socioeconomic developments. The social investment paradigm has spread to countries in which social policy objectives are (still) mostly concerned with poverty reduction, and it has remained suppressed in more advanced economies. Hence, an economic-functionalist narrative featuring social investment as the human capital correlate of the knowledge economy cannot fully account for the political reality of social investment development.

Here, a third crucial factor comes in: policy legacies and how they interact with the structural challenges outlined previously. Legacies, particularly pre-existing social policy provisions, matter because, as historical institutionalism teaches us, the interaction of previous policy choices and changing structural conditions affects problem diagnoses, preference configurations, and policy agendas. We show that countries' welfare legacies, particularly the preexisting mix of compensatory social policies and investment policies, in interaction with socioeconomic structural changes, helps explain to what degree and in what form social investments become politicized once these changes become visible in terms of needs and demands (Häusermann & Palier, 2017).

Yet again, legacies alone cannot explain the policy reforms that were ultimately adopted. To illustrate, Spain, Italy, and Portugal share some historical legacies but differ significantly in their social investment reforms, as do Japan and Korea, as well as the Baltics and the Visegrád countries, despite similar legacies. Here, the fourth set of explanations comes in, namely actors' positions and interactions and reform coalitions.

Regarding political, social, and economic actors, we borrow Korpi's (2006) vocabulary from another context and distinguish between reform protagonists (pushing for social investment reforms), antagonists (opposing such reforms), and consenters (taking a neutral position). Who the respective social investment protagonists, antagonists, and consenters are is a key question addressed in many chapters of the two WOPSI volumes. We argue and clearly show that in different contexts different coalitions between protagonists and consenters have formed (and opposition has arisen from different antagonists), resulting in different welfare reform strategies, in general, and different social investment strategies, in particular.

We theoretically and empirically identify several social investment protagonists, antagonists, and consenters in countries around the globe. To start with, we identify the relevant social groups that support or oppose social investments. The main protagonist is the expanded, educated new middle class (see Chapter 12 in this volume; Garritzmann et al., 2018; Häusermann & Kriesi, 2015; Häusermann & Palier, 2017), which favors social investment for both materialistic and ideological reasons. The main antagonists are those groups who benefit least from structural economic and social change toward a knowledge economy, that is, mainly the traditional industrial (male) working class, who favor social compensation to satisfy their needs (Häusermann et al., 2020). Relatedly, the voters of radical populist right parties are crucial antagonists of social investment (Garritzmann et al., 2018), partly for materialistic, partly for ideological reasons.

On the level of collective actors, (new) left parties (especially greens and social liberals) are the main protagonists of social investment policies as they subscribe to the economic and future-oriented social agenda that is associated with social investments. The main antagonists are populist right-wing parties, which—and whose voters—tend to oppose progressive social and economic change and rather defend the status quo (ante) of the industrial era. Christian Democrats and conservatives often have been tacit consenters but in some cases (e.g., the German Christian Democratic Union/Christian Social Union) also have become key protagonists of (stratified) social investment expansion (mainly for electoral reasons related to realignment processes). As the conclusion of this volume underlines (see Chapter 16), the left is usually acting as a protagonist for all types of social investment, playing a major role in developing inclusive social investment policies, while right-wing parties will favor either stratified or targeted social investment.

Moreover, the "social partners" (i.e., unions and employers) play a crucial role in the politics of social investment. The positions on social investment taken by unions (see Chapters 10 and 11 in this volume) and employers (see Chapter 9 in this volume) and their role in the policymaking process are highly context-dependent. Employers might be interested, mostly in human capital mobilization policies. In some contexts, they thus become consenters or even protagonists but remain antagonists in many other situations and regarding other types of social investment. Trade unions' positions vary according to their members' interests (e.g., regarding their skill profiles, risks, and gender balance). For instance, a trade union with traditional blue-collar (male) workers can be expected to have very different preferences than a union comprising high-skilled white-collar (female) employees. Moreover, these preferences also differ according to the degree of union centralization and institutional involvement.

Throughout our volumes, the authors go beyond the mere analysis of the positions of actors in order to understand the political dynamics leading to the adoption of a specific welfare state reform strategy. Many chapters, especially in Volume II, focus on the political coalitions behind the various welfare state reforms. As is summarized in the conclusion of Volume II (Chapter 17 [Garritzmann et al., 2022]), we have identified four main political coalitions behind the various types of social investment reforms: two types of social democratic coalitions based on the alliance between representatives of the (educated) middle class and the working class, with a Nordic version leading to inclusive social investment and a Latin American version leading to targeted social investment; a conservative coalition, where the middle class is allied with employers, leading to stratified social investment favoring human capital mobilization, typical of continental Europe or of some particular period in North East Asia; and a liberal coalition, where the same middle class–employers alliance emerges, but in the context of liberal welfare regimes leads to social compensation retrenchment sometimes substituted by some targeted public social investment (and many private ones publicly supported via fiscal exemption), as in North America and the Baltic countries. We also identified a non-social investment coalition, namely, a situation in which a social compensation coalition emerges when the educated middle class is not large enough to constitute an appealing electoral constituency and social protection legacies are high. In this case, social investment is not likely to emerge as a reform strategy around which a political coalition can be cemented (Southern Europe and partly the Visegrád countries). There still might be social investment protagonists and consenters, but they remain political minorities.

1.2.3. One project, two volumes

Beyond the conceptualization and mapping of reforms, the WOPSI project thus theoretically as well as empirically explains the political conditions for the development or lack of development of social investment policies in democracies around the globe. We aim in particular to understand the content of the social investment proposals, programs, and policies, tracing the political conflicts surrounding social investment and identifying the types of political coalitions that support or prevent a specific social investment strategy.

The two volumes published out of the WOPSI project differ in their orientation. The first volume, subtitled *Welfare States in the Knowledge Economy*, is organized around the explanatory factors (i.e., independent variables) driving social investment reform strategies. We have divided this first volume into four main parts, each corresponding to one set of main independent variables. The first focuses on the ideational dynamics and development of the social investment policy paradigm, looking at and explaining the content and evolution of the social investment ideas of the OECD, the World Bank, and the European Union. The second part comprises chapters on the political and economic scope conditions for social investment reforms to appear. In the third part, the chapters examine the demand for and supply of social investment (i.e., public opinion and social partners' social investment policy preferences). Finally, the last part provides comparative analyses of the politics of various social investment reform strategies, underlining the role played by the variables analyzed in previous parts and adding views on the role played by political parties and political coalitions in different world regions.

The second volume, subtitled *The Politics of Varying Social Investment Strategies*, engages more with the differences between regions and countries and provides systematic comparative analyses of social investment politics for each region of the globe we have covered. Its chapters, organized around the dependent variables, are divided into parts corresponding to four main regions: Western Europe and Northern America, Central and Eastern Europe, North East Asia, and Latin America. For each region, one chapter provides a regional analysis of public opinion regarding social investment topics and policies, and the remaining chapters offer national intraregional comparative studies of the politics of social investment. These chapters situate the policies adopted in our typology of welfare state reform strategies. By comparing different time periods in a single country and different countries within regions, these analyses allow for testing the influence of the various variables identified in our theoretical framework.

In order to maximize our capacity to map and explain the politics of social investment, we have varied as much as possible not only the cases under study but also the methods used. Many chapters use quantitative analysis in order to better characterize and measure the importance of public opinion, actors' positions, and discourses on legislation and policies. Thus, several chapters analyze public opinion survey data, provide large-N overviews covering many countries and years, or quantitatively assess policy agendas or spending patterns. Others, more qualitative in their approach, implement process tracing to understand the political dynamics behind the politicization and adoption of (or failure to adopt) various policies and reforms. But irrespective of their methods, all chapters are integrated thanks to our common typology (see Section 1.1 of this chapter), our common research questions (see the list provided in Section 1.2.1), and the overarching theoretical framework all authors have been working with (see Chapter 2 in this volume).

Taken together, the two volumes provide a systematic and detailed analysis of the politics of social investment and other welfare reform strategies around the globe. Thereby, they provide the empirical knowledge and analytical tools to integrate the analysis of social investment reforms fully in the cumulative body of welfare state research.

1.2.4. Selection of regions and countries

The focus of the WOPSI project is on democratic capitalist countries because we conceive of politics (and mass politics in particular) in a way that presupposes democratic interest representation and competition, as well as programmatic competition between different parties or interest representatives in the context of capitalist knowledge economies. The chapters in Part I of Volume I include also non-democratic countries precisely to make this point. They show that a modicum of institutional-economic development, programmatic voter mobilization, and state capacity is required not only for states to engage in pursuing social investment goals but also for social investment spending to be effective. Put differently, while some social investment policies have also been adopted in non-democracies, the mechanisms of the theoretical model developed in the WOPSI project concentrate on democratic policymaking.

Within the universe of democratic countries, then, we strive to maximize diversity in terms of structural economic change and institutional structures

(welfare legacies and political institutions). The level and type of economic production structure (industrial or post-industrial) influence not only the purpose
and functions of social investment reforms but also whether social investment
reforms are complementary to or substitutive of transfer-oriented welfare reform strategies. This is why we include a wide range of countries from Western
and Southern Europe, Central and Eastern Europe, North East Asia, and Latin
America.

This regional variation allows us to identify the extent to which and the way in
which institutional economic and policy legacies shape the politics of social investment. Hence, only the more developed countries in Latin America can (and
sometimes do) indeed engage in sustained social investment efforts (e.g., backing
up CCTs with the necessary investment in service provision), and these do not
compete against other social programs but are complementary to them, due to
the legacies of truncated welfare states. In North East Asia, by contrast, social
investment is fought over in different terms (i.e., in line with the growth and productivity orientation of the welfare legacy). The contrast between the Visegrád
and the Baltic countries in Europe's eastern countries shows how much the economic growth strategy that is politically pursued (industrial vs. post-industrial)
and the respective actors' coalitions influence the orientation that social investment reforms take. And comparing Northwestern to Southern Europe evidences
how economic development and welfare state legacies shape the political power
and preferences of different societal interests and their representatives.

As far as the time of our analysis is concerned, the main focus is from the
1990s to the late 2010s. In most cases, we focus on the post-neoliberal period
(starting in the 1990s), but some cases take us even further back, when social
investment policies emerged earlier (e.g., in Nordic Europe or when we study the
development of educational policies, as in Chapter 8 in this volume).

1.2.5. Outline of the first volume

In Chapter 2, "The Politics of Social Investment: A Global Theoretical Framework,"
we elaborate the analytical approach the WOPSI project has taken to explain
varying strategies of social investment reforms across regions. The chapter
provides detail on the model's key components (i.e., structural transformations,
changing societal demand, actor configurations, and policy legacies) and their
theorized interactions. From this presentation of the theoretical framework, the
chapter derives a number of general guiding hypotheses regarding favorable and
unfavorable context conditions and coalitional dynamics furthering or impeding
the development of the six welfare state reform strategies we identified, three
oriented toward social investment and three non-social investment alternatives.

This theory chapter makes three contributions: a) it situates the motivation
and ambition of the two-volume project in the existing knowledge and research
on contemporary welfare state development; b) it develops an encompassing

theoretical framework, which systematizes the relative impact of ideational, structural, and institutional factors on the interplay of political supply and demand in structuring social investment reform strategies; and c) it produces a set of concrete hypotheses to explain the politicization of social investment, the prevailing functions and goals social investment is likely to pursue in different institutional contexts, and the distributive profile social investment reforms take, depending on the coalitional dynamics that drive these reforms.

Part I: "The Ideational Context of Social Investment Politics"

The two chapters in this part of Volume I focus on the changing saliency and definition of welfare strategies in the international realm of norm entrepreneurs, namely, international organizations (Chapter 3) and the European Union (Chapter 4). These developments provide the ideational background against which political dynamics unfold.

In Chapter 3, "Multiple Sources of the Social Investment Perspective: The OECD and the World Bank," Jane Jenson and Rianne Mahon trace the development of social investment ideas within the World Bank and the OECD, assuming that these ideas have influenced national policy agendas across the world. In the mid- to late 1990s, the practices of international organizations (IOs) involved in social development began to cohere around new ideas, including social investment, producing since then child-centered strategies and an emphasis on investment in human capital to ensure economic growth, social development, and later inclusive growth. These IOs played key roles in the development and diffusion of the social investment perspective. For the Global South, IOs particularly endorsed the instrument of CCTs to enable very poor families to invest in children's health and education. For IOs working also in the Global North, the social investment perspective added on top of the anti-poverty focus the reliance on children's early education and care and parents' activation in the labor force. All shared the policy objective of breaking the intergenerational cycle of disadvantage.

The diffusion of ideas and practices of social investment followed varied pathways. Unlike social policy, which was diffused after 1945 mainly from the "developed North" toward the "developing world," social investment ideas and practices moved from South to North and even from South to South and North to North. The social investment perspective began to be taken up when IOs were challenged to identify an appropriate strategy for alleviating some of the human costs of the structural adjustments that many of these same IOs had promoted in the 1970s and 1980s. For the World Bank and regional development banks, as well as UNICEF and the OECD, by the mid-1990s the costs of sponsoring structural adjustments had become visible in the form of high poverty rates (even among the employed), child poverty, and—at the societal level—threats to social cohesion.

This chapter thus documents the emergence and deployment of the social investment perspective by the OECD and the World Bank beginning in the mid-1990s and highlights several points of commonality and intersection as well as differences in strategies. Its working hypothesis is that, rather than a single "starting point" and then diffusion to other IOs, each institution began its own work in response to the challenges listed above. Over time, however, some cross-fertilization did occur. The end result was a convergent evolution toward slightly different versions of a social investment perspective focused on children and human capital. Finally, the chapter tracks the fate of the social investment perspective as new approaches come to the fore. These include objectives such as inclusive growth, which is compatible with social investment but broader, and new policy targets such as informal and unpaid work.

In Chapter 4, "The Politics of the European Union Social Investment Initiatives," Caroline de la Porte and Bruno Palier focus on the development of social investment ideas and policy initiatives at the EU level since the early 1990s. The chapter explains why and how the European Union explicitly endorsed the social investment perspective in five "sequences." The authors argue that to explain why the social investment agenda developed at the EU level what matters is national politics (both at the national and at the European Council level) and that to understand the policy process (i.e., how it developed) what matters is the interaction between various EU actors (European Commission bureaucrats but also committees, lobbyists), especially between the "economically oriented" actors and the "socially oriented" actors. The chapter first characterizes the type of social investment promoted in each sequence, after which it analyzes the politics and policy dynamic behind each sequence. It relies on detailed analyses of EU text, proposals, and policy initiatives, as well as a set of interviews with experts and policymakers at the EU level.

In the first sequence identified, ideas about employment and social policies began emerging at the EU level (driven mainly by left-oriented parties at the national level) in the early 1990s as an unintended consequence (a spillover effect) of the furthering of economic integration and of the preparation of the European Monetary Union (EMU). During the second sequence, the idea of a comprehensive social investment policy organized around the notion of a "knowledge-based economy" grew more pronounced in the following years and, as embodied in the Lisbon Strategy (adopted in March 2000), became a cornerstone of the European Union's growth strategy. However, in the middle of the first decade of the 2000s, in a context of changes in the political composition of the new European Commission (reflecting political changes at the national level), as well as policy learning within the Commission, the mid-term evaluation of the Lisbon Strategy called for reducing the whole process to mere human capital mobilization. During this third sequence, center-right parties held the majority in the Council. In the fourth sequence, the Social Investment Package adopted in 2013 was presented as a way to include social concerns and indicators within the European Semester, but it was a merely endogenous initiative, taken by some EU bureaucrats and intellectuals and not really supported by national member states or social forces. Since the Commission changed in 2014, attention turned away from social investment toward a European pillar of social rights, leaving social investment aspects largely unattended and monitoring them only through a "social scoreboard" that is not integrated with the "macroeconomic scoreboard" accompanying EMU governance.

Part II: "The Political and Economic Scope Conditions of Social Investment Reforms"

The chapters in this section discuss the scope conditions of our argument. Chapter 5 starts with the widest perspective, examining the correlation between aggregate indicators of development and the emergence of an investment dimension in social assistance policies in lower- and middle-income countries of the Global South. It probes into the relevance of democratization, among other factors, as a scope condition for social investment policies. Distinguishing between programmatic and clientelistic linkages between voters and parties, Chapter 6 then examines different stages of democratic development as scope conditions for effective social investment politics. Focusing on Latin American cases, Chapter 7 takes up state capacity as an additional scope condition for social investment. Finally, Chapter 8 assesses the interplay of the knowledge economy with changing occupational patterns and societal demands as a context condition for the emergence of social investment politics.

In Chapter 5, "Social Investment and Social Assistance in Low- and Middle-Income Countries," Armando Barrientos takes a very broad perspective on conditions leading to the emergence of social investment. His chapter focuses on lower- and middle-income countries, also described as the "Global South" (in particular many countries in Latin America, Africa, and South East Asia). In these countries, the current challenge to welfare state development differs from that in the "Global North" in one key respect: Poverty is still a significant social problem as a result of both underdeveloped welfare coverage (policy legacies) and low economic productivity. Therefore, where social investment initiatives have developed, they have been closely intertwined with the expansion of poverty reduction policies. Hence, understanding the specific context of policy development in the Global South is essential in order to understand the differences in social investment initiatives both between the North and the South, as well as within the latter.

The chapter makes use of the author's data set of Social Assistance in Low- and Middle-Income Countries, one of the few worldwide social policy data resources that includes the Global South, and analyzes the data from a social investment perspective. The chapter's first section maps the general expansion of social assistance in lower- and middle-income countries, drawing on regional trends in reach and program design. Until the mid-1990s, social assistance in these countries was largely residual, providing ad hoc services to highly vulnerable populations. Since then, social assistance transfers to households in poverty have expanded: Social assistance and CCTs had reached around a third of the population in Latin America by 2015, with similar trends observed in Asia and Africa, although at a slower pace and with a wider diversity in policy instruments. The chapter argues that the expanding social assistance component accommodates a stronger social investment orientation.

After providing a theoretical conceptualization of the social investment orientation social assistance could potentially adopt, the chapter's second section develops a measure of the social investment intensity of different reform types. Some programs are explicitly designed around a social investment strategy, especially CCTs and other forms of conditional family and child transfers such as early childhood interventions. However, even anti-poverty programs without an overt social investment design can have substantive social investment effects. In lower- and middle-income countries, the receipt of social benefits also improves school attendance and retention as well as health status among children.

In the third section, the chapter explores the factors that explain the social investment orientation in social assistance programming (i.e., the scope conditions of the WOPSI project): the degree of democratic development, political objectives of governments and donors, economic openness, employment restructuring, conflict, and economic performance. The analysis shows that a leftward shift in government composition and the level of tertiarization are relevant scope conditions for a social investment orientation of social assistance programs. In addition, since poverty in these countries is closely linked with low economic productivity (i.e., low pay and precarious employment), economic growth rates are also a relevant correlate of the development of social assistance programs with a social investment orientation. Hence, economic development strategies are an important factor accounting for the varieties of social investment strategies in the Global South.

In Chapter 6, "Political Linkage Strategies and Social Investment Policies: Clientelism and Educational Policy in the Developing World," Haohan Chen and Herbert Kitschelt identify programmatic electoral competition as a crucial political precondition for social investment. A distinctive feature of middle-income democracies is that the strategies by which political parties appeal to voters can be clientelistic or programmatic (whereas programmatic competition is the dominant strategy in advanced post-industrial democracies). Clientelistic voter–party linkages imply that political parties adopt policies to provide specific (groups of) voters with concrete benefits. In their chapter, Chen and Kitschelt contribute to our understanding of the political context conditions of social investment by establishing that the prevalence of clientelistic linkages has two detrimental effects on the development of social investment: First, they "crowd out" potentially investive spending in favor of consumptive spending, and second, they degrade the effects of public spending even in typically investment-oriented policy areas. The general insight the overall WOPSI project draws from this chapter is that not all spending in the "typical" fields of social investment (education, active labor market policies, and family care policies) should be considered "investment" as programmatic policymaking is a necessary precondition.

The chapter establishes this contribution by focusing on public spending on primary, secondary, and tertiary education in middle-income countries. Education, particularly secondary education, is critical for the economic advancement of these economies. However, public spending on education can be diverted clientelistically, not only in terms of infrastructure spending but also with regard to teacher demands (with multiplying effects in their families and close communities). The chapter first develops a theoretical argument on the preference configurations of political actors in the field of education policy. It then derives a series of observable implications in terms of spending profiles and educational achievement, depending on the prevailing type of linkages, that is, whether the linkages are programmatic or clientelistic.

These hypotheses are tested empirically with macro- and meso-level data on party competition, linkage types (based on Kitschelt's "Democratic Accountability and Linkages" database), education spending, and education outcomes for a large sample of developing, middle-income countries with multi-party competition. The chapter shows that where clientelistic political linkage mechanisms prevail, consumptive spending prevails, and public education spending has no beneficial effect on educational outcomes, whereas in a context of programmatic competition, public education spending does indeed have an impact. Clientelistic linkages not only reduce (potentially) investive spending but also degrade the nature of the expenditure by diverting resources to the consumption of rent-seeking special interest groups rather than the investments in tangible human skills that can propel the economy. These quantitative findings are supplemented by a case study on rent-seeking and educational investment in Mexico.

In Chapter 7, "State Capacity and Social Investment: Explaining Variation in Skills Creation Reforms in Latin America," Juan Bogliaccini and Aldo Madariaga focus on another crucial scope condition for the development of social investment policies: state capacity. While state capacity features prominently as an explanatory factor in international development research and other subfields, its role has been disregarded in the social investment literature, potentially because the existing literature has focused mainly on countries with comparatively high levels of state capacity (more advanced democracies).

This chapter asks whether a certain degree of state capacity is a necessary condition to establish successful social investment reforms. Using the case of skill formation regimes in Latin American countries as an example, the chapter shows that state capacity does play a role in social investment reforms: It is a necessary, but not in itself sufficient, condition for the implementation of successful social investments. State capacity matters at two crucial moments of the policymaking process: first, as a background variable that affects reform efforts and, second, during the policy implementation period. A second necessary but insufficient condition is the way partisan coalitions interact with policy legacies. The chapter concludes that only the two conditions together allow Latin American countries to advance social investment reforms in a sustainable fashion.

Empirically, the chapter analyzes the political reform processes of vocational education and training in Bolivia, Chile, Guatemala, and Uruguay. While Chile and Uruguay share similarly high levels of state capacity and a legacy of early expansion of skills with an inclusionary strategy, they differ in the success of their reform strategies in coping with the challenges posed by the post-industrial economy. While Chile enacted crucial reforms and universalized coverage, Uruguay is deadlocked in a conflict between timid reforms and a conservative preference for the status quo amidst slow advancement. Bolivia and Guatemala, on the other hand, share comparatively low levels of state capacity and a legacy of exclusionary education policies but still differ in their governments' efforts to generate change since the late 1990s. While Bolivia is a case of successful government-led vocational education reforms, Guatemala's business-backed skills formation schemes lack serious government commitment.

Moreover, the chapter brings vocational education and training, a crucial but often neglected policy area, back to the center of the social investment approach. The authors argue that vocational education and training is, in many circumstances, actually much better able to achieve some of the goals of the social investment state (e.g., the integration of young, low-skilled, vulnerable groups into the labor market) than academic higher education is; yet vocational education still only plays a very minor part in the larger social investment debate (see also Chapter 3 of Volume II [Garritzmann et al., 2022] for a similar argument for Europe). What is more, by offering the first systematic comparison of vocational education and training regimes in Latin America, the chapter adds important knowledge to the literatures on education policy and skill formation regimes, in particular, and to the comparative capitalism literature, more generally.

In Chapter 8, "The Emergence of Knowledge Economies: Educational Expansion, Labor Market Changes, and the Politics of Social Investment," Julian L. Garritzmann, Silja Häusermann, Thomas Kurer, Bruno Palier, and Michael Pinggera trace the development of regional varieties of knowledge economies since the 1870s, focusing on the development of the knowledge economy and its impact on occupational patterns and the politics of social investment.

This chapter reveals a massive educational expansion across all world regions but a specific shift to tertiary education and cognitive skills in the most advanced capitalist democracies (the OECD countries). Then, focusing on the latter countries, the chapter traces the relationship between educational expansion and labor market changes. Using large-scale labor market data, the authors show that the trend toward advanced knowledge economies has coincided with fundamental change in the occupational structure: The data reveals a trend toward a "polarized upgrading," as well as a steady feminization of the workforce. However, occupational transformation varies across contexts, especially according to welfare legacies.

To close, the chapter theorizes on the implications of these two "megatrends" for popular and economic demand for social investment policies and for the politics of social investment more generally. It discusses the various political configurations created by either high or low economic demand for high skill and high or low provision of such a skilled workforce by the education system. It argues that increasing economic and societal demand for high-skilled labor is a precondition for the politicization of social investment and for social investment coalitions and reforms in the advanced capitalist democracies. In case of overeducation or underemployment, *skill mobilization and preservation* are likely to be politicized (likely in a stratified way), while in case of skill-labor scarcity, *skill creation and skill mobilization* are likely to be politicized (also in a stratified way). In case of both high demand and high provision of high skill (i.e., a "knowledge economy" equilibrium), it is the *sustainability* of (inclusive) social investment that is likely to be politicized.

Part III: "Demand for and Supply of Social Investment— Public Opinion and Social Partners' Social Investment Policy Preferences"

The chapters in this third part consider different societal forces that could mobilize political demand for social investment reforms. The first three chapters deal with key actors: Chapter 9 addresses the conditions under which employers might support social investment, while Chapters 10 and 11 address the same question for trade unions in Europe and Latin America, respectively. Chapter 12 then analyzes public opinion in a range of countries across the globe, demonstrating that the educated middle class is the key constituency for social investment reforms in terms of public opinion in all world regions studied in the WOPSI project.

In Chapter 9, "Employers and Social Investment in Three European Countries: The Good, the Bad, and the Ugly," Emmanuele Pavolini and Martin Seeleib-Kaiser focus on one of the potentially most prominent actors in social investment policies: employers. Business has a privileged position in the policymaking process. The power resources approach has claimed that business organizations are antagonists or at most consenters with regard to the introduction and expansion of social policies. Since the late 1980s, a growing body of literature has started to analyze the role of employers and employers' associations in a more nuanced way, but it has so far mainly focused on pension policies and more generally on income maintenance schemes in industrial societies. The role of employers within the politics of social policy in post-industrial society has been less studied. Indeed, both analytical theorization and empirical research are particularly underdeveloped in relation to employers' preferences and strategies concerning the coverage of new social risks and their interests in relation to social investment.

Building on the varieties of capitalism literature, the chapter links the risk perspective and the organizational structure of employer associations in a postindustrial environment. In addition to employer preferences being influenced by structural characteristics of their companies (size, skills, and share of female employment), the chapter hypothesizes that the type of employer representation also matters. Employers' engagement in the politics of social investment policies at the national level can essentially be viewed from three perspectives. First, employers could focus on opposing welfare policies ("antagonists") as costs associated with such policies undermine the profitability of their businesses; in this scenario welfare policies are essentially perceived as policies "against the market." Second, employers could act as "consenters," supporting the expansion of such policies as these policies are relatively cheap compared to other social policy programs. But such support could also have its source in strategic considerations (i.e., employers agree to some consensus reluctantly to prevent even more farreaching policies). Third, employers can develop a first-order preference for the expansion of social investment policies, thus actively pushing such policies ("promoters") or even initiating policies ("protagonists"), as these policies are perceived to support the socioeconomic environment needed for sustainable business activities, especially during times of tight labor markets.

After having elaborated these various possible employer positions, the chapter considers two domains of social investment policies: work–family reconciliation policies and vocational education and training policies. It shows that the level of employers' support for social investment policies depends on the type of policy and the economic sector they represent. The chapter scrutinizes in depth different kinds of social investment policies in Britain, Germany, and Italy. To assess employer preferences and the role of employers' associations in the national policy arena, the authors conduct a qualitative content analysis of core policy documents of employer associations in relation to the two social investment policies since the 1990s. The chapter shows that the support of employers' associations at the national level varies significantly both by country and by policy sector. Despite changed socioeconomic underpinnings and rational arguments to expand social investment policies, national historical patterns and path dependence regarding national policymaking have a significant impact on the approach followed by employers' associations (i.e., whether they are antagonists, consenters, or protagonists of the expansion of social investment policies). Nevertheless, under certain circumstances, significant change can come about, as demonstrated by the preference formation of German employers at the turn of the 21st century.

In Chapter 10, "Social (Investment) Partners? Trade Unions and the Welfare State for the Knowledge Economy," Niccolo Durazzi and Leonard Geyer analyze unions' social investment policy preferences and their role in the politics of social investment. Unlike more traditional welfare state research (in line with power resource theory), the existing literature on social investment has paid surprisingly little attention to trade unions. The chapter provides both theoretical conceptualizations as well as empirical accounts of unions' preferences vis-à-vis social investment as well as their role in the policymaking processes.

This chapter points out that unions' preferences and their influence on social investment agendas and reforms are not as straightforward as they are in terms of compensatory social policies. At first sight, it might seem simple: As social investment policies aim to create, mobilize, or preserve human skills and as unions are committed to full employment and the employability of all, one might assume that unions *grosso modo* are core proponents of social investments. Yet, upon closer inspection several tensions emerge. Some social investment policies such as active labor market policies may be of primary interest to more peripheral members of unions and therefore might find only lukewarm support, if not opposition, from unions. Moreover, social investment policies might undermine unions' power because they often are implemented in a policy arena where unions have little control while weakening policy arenas where unions' control is strong.

Taking a "logic of membership" perspective, the chapter starts at the micro-level of individual union members and develops expectations about unions' preferences by theorizing about their respective individual members' interests. Particularly three factors matter: the skill, age, and gender profile of a union. To give but one example, unions with predominantly low-skilled older male workers are likely to propose very different policies than will unions whose members are mainly high-skilled young women. The argument then moves to the meso-level of union organization and structures and highlights two particularly relevant factors: union density and union centralization. Both higher union density and stronger centralization make unions more inclusive and consequently more prone to support social investment. From a "logic of influence" perspective, which assumes that unions care not only about their members' preferences but also about political power in itself, unions might sometimes be reluctant to support social investments because they could be negotiated in a different political arena than compensatory social policies, stripping unions of influence. In a third step, the argument enters the macro-level and develops expectations about the influence of unions on social investment policymaking. Here, the chapter shows that the same meso-level factors (i.e., union density and centralization) that shaped preferences also affect unions' influence on social investment reforms. All in all, the framework suggests that unions' preferences for and impact on social investment policies depend on a set of micro-level features (i.e., the composition of union membership), meso-level characteristics (i.e., unions' organizational characteristics), and macro-level relationships between unions and governments.

Combining these three analytical levels, the chapter proposes four ideal-typical "contexts" characterized by different expected preferences for and impacts on social investment policy. Case studies of Austria, Germany, Italy, and the United Kingdom are employed to illustrate the framework. Altogether the chapter shows that where unions are centralized and encompassing and enjoy institutionalized involvement in policymaking, they are protagonists in the development of social investment policies. Where, on the other hand, these conditions are partly or entirely missing, unions tend to take a more skeptical or even antagonist position.

In Chapter 11, "Trade Unions, Labor Market Dualization, and Investment in Early Childhood Education and Care in Latin America," Melina Altamirano and Bárbara Zárate-Tenorio focus on the role of organized labor in the context of Latin America. The truncated welfare states of Latin America with strongly dualized labor markets have traditionally provided social protection via insurance only for a selection of employees in regular employment, while leaving informal and low-income workers exposed to significant poverty risks. In such a context, the role of trade unions (as the representatives of the better-organized, formal workforce) in social policy reform becomes particularly interesting since poverty- or inclusion-oriented social investment might not primarily benefit their own workforce or might even come at the cost of their members. Hence, the Latin American context is particularly auspicious for investigating the role of trade unions in the development of social investment policies.

The chapter uses the between-country variance in Latin American labor markets, union organization, and social policy development to identify the factors affecting unions' position on social investment reforms. It focuses on the politics of early childhood education and care (ECEC), which have the dual objective of promoting child development and facilitating female participation in the workforce. The authors argue that the fragmentation of welfare provision and the segmentation of the labor market contribute to explaining union positions regarding ECEC policy expansion. In contexts of low dualization of the labor market, new social policy proposals are more likely to have direct consequences on the formal workers' current system of labor benefits and conditions, which in turn generate incentives for unions to become involved in the policymaking process of social policy expansion. In contrast, in contexts of high labor market dualization, new proposals are less likely to modify current conditions for formal workers due to the political costs this entails; thus, it is unlikely that organized labor will have incentives to speak for (or against) the expansion of policies to outsiders.

To test these arguments, the chapter focuses on two important reforms which expanded ECEC public services to previously excluded segments of the population: *Chile Crece Contigo* ("Chile Grows with You") in Chile (2006) and the *Estancias Infantiles para Madres Trabajadoras* ("Daycare for Working Mothers") program in Mexico (2007). In the two countries, the expansion of ECEC policies has been prominently on the political agenda since the first decade of the 2000s. However, the countries differ in the size of the informal sector and union strength, with Mexico having the largest informal sector and Chile the smallest. The analysis shows that neither in Chile nor in Mexico was organized labor a relevant actor (protagonist) at the agenda-setting stage. Rather, governments were the clear leaders in putting social investment reforms on the agenda. However, unlike the unions in Mexico, which did not attempt to shape the policy at any stage of the process, unions in Chile became highly involved in the post-reform period as consenters to inclusive reforms.

In Chapter 12, "Public Preferences Toward Social Investment: Comparing Patterns of Support Across Three Continents," Björn Bremer studies a key dimension of the demand side of social investment policies: public opinion. Such a focus on public opinion is crucial for at least two reasons: First, the changing occupational configuration of the post-industrial knowledge economy (see Chapter 8 in this volume) has transformed class structures across the advanced capitalist world. Hence, when studying social policy development in this context, a new look at the policy demands of social classes is in order, not least to identify the underlying societal coalitions that drive or impede the development of social investment. Second, previous research has established that individuals' preferences toward social investment are distinct from preferences toward more traditional consumption-oriented social policies: While the working class is the strongest and most consistent supporter of compensatory social policies, parts of the expanded middle class seem to be the champions of social investment. This chapter puts these hypotheses to the test in a larger set of countries across the world and identifies the regional specificities of preference configurations and potential for support for the development of social investment. Its contribution to the volume is twofold: It maps the demand for social investment versus consumption by class and ideology, and it estimates the relative size of the support coalition for social investment across different countries and world regions.

The chapter studies attitudes in more than 40 countries across Europe, Latin America, and Asia on the basis of public opinion data from the Comparative Study of Electoral Systems and the International Social Survey Programme. These cross-national surveys include data on attitudes toward different types of government spending. The analysis compares patterns of support for different forms of social investment against support for traditional transfer-oriented social policies. It uses multivariate regression analysis to explore the determinants of these attitudes. The results indicate that support for social investment and consumption varies by social class: While middle and upper classes are more likely to support social investment policies, lower classes remain the core constituency for social compensation. However, individual-level preference configurations interact with policy legacies, which have feedback effects and influence the size and composition of support coalitions for social investment: Especially in less developed welfare states, support for social investment is more diffuse than in more mature welfare states.

Part IV: "The Comparative Politics of Social Investment Reforms"

The chapters in this section examine the varieties of social investment reform strategies that result from the interplay of societal forces and institutional legacies across regions, specifically focusing on the beneficiaries of social investment reforms, the distributive effects of these reforms, and their underlying political coalitions. In this sense, the chapters combine several of the explanations of Parts I–III to analyze variation in specific regions and policy fields. Chapter 13 develops a systematic comparative analysis of different social investment strategies in Latin America, showing that the concurrence of objectives of poverty relief and activation has contributed to social investment reforms targeted at lower income classes in those countries that managed to simultaneously invest the necessary resources in public services. Comparing familialist countries across Southern Europe and North East Asia, Chapter 14 examines the role of economic and political structures in the variations in the development of social investment policies. Finally, Chapter 15 focuses on differences in the quality of childcare services to detect the distributive targets of social investment reforms across countries in Western Europe, Eastern Europe, and Oceania and the underlying political conditions and coalitions leading to more or less quality in childcare.

In Chapter 13, "Social Investment and Neoliberal Legacies in Latin America: Breaking the Mold?" Evelyne Huber, Claire Dunn, and John D. Stephens examine the extent to which there has been a turn to social investment in Latin America and explain why some countries have seen greater advances than others. It argues that the concept of a "turn" is not useful because it evokes a turn away from transfers, or the passive welfare state, and toward social investment, or the active welfare state. Rather, both transfers and services have been expanded in Latin America since 2000, with transfers growing faster on average than investment in health and education. This is in large part a result of policy legacies, namely the fact that the compensatory welfare state in Latin America had left anywhere from 20% to 80% of the population without coverage and that poverty rates at the turn of the century were high. Thus, in order for social investment to be effective, anti-poverty policies in the form of transfers had to be part of the reform strategy. On the other hand, simple expansion of CCTs, even if tied to school attendance and medical checkups, without accompanying investment in equitable access to health and education services, did not constitute an effective social investment strategy either.

The chapter examines policies in four fields: CCTs, education, ECEC, and healthcare. It assesses progress in these policy areas along three criteria: extent of coverage of the policies, generosity of benefits or quality of services, and equity in access to the benefits and services. The chapter starts by attributing the general wave of social policy expansion in Latin America after 2000 to a backlash against neoliberalism, the rising strength of the left, and the commodity boom. It then explains how the progress of the social investment reform strategies was affected by the partisan orientation of governments, the parliamentary base of governments, and policy legacies.

The research design includes an examination of expenditure patterns over time on transfers, health, and education; a general overview of progress in different social policy areas; and a comparison of different social investment reform experiences. In addition to documenting general trends, the chapter provides a number of brief comparative analyses of different reforms: the spread of CCT programs and the expansion of ECEC programs throughout Latin America; healthcare reforms by right and left governments in Mexico and Uruguay; healthcare reforms by left governments with different policy legacies and partisan control over legislatures in Uruguay, Chile, and Brazil; education reforms by left governments with different policy legacies and relations with civil society in Uruguay and Chile; and ECEC by right and left governments in Mexico and Chile.

To the extent that social investment has been adopted, it has been with the aim to create human capital and reduce vast inequality of opportunity. The emphasis has been on education and healthcare linked to efforts at poverty reduction. The chapter argues that the strength of left parties even when in opposition and the strength of social movements engaged in the struggle for social investment contributed to the advancement of social investment reform strategies. The chapter concludes with a more synthetic assessment of progress of social investment reform strategies in the economically or socially most advanced Latin American countries, Argentina, Brazil, Chile, Costa Rica, Mexico, and Uruguay, and with brief speculation regarding the future of social investment reform strategies after the end of the commodity boom and a potential shift to the right in government.

In Chapter 14, "Different Paths to Social Investment? The Politics of Social Investment in North East Asia and Southern Europe," Margarita Estévez-Abe and Margarita León compare the social investment strategies within familialist countries in Southern Europe and North East Asia (Italy, Spain, Japan, and South Korea) since the 1990s. This chapter aims to better understand the factors that shape the political opportunities for social investment policies and that can potentially explain similarities and differences between these four cases. The choice of this group of familialist states is strategic. The quartet offers good test cases to assess whether social investment policies are applicable to countries beyond a handful of Nordic and northern Continental European countries.

The chapter highlights how specific electoral contexts affect governments' capacity to adopt a social investment turn—particularly in childcare—and how employers' interests intervene in policy decisions that affect their human resources management practices. The chapter explains the variation across the quartet by highlighting the importance of the institutional contexts of party competition, the link between electoral politics and legislative activities, and the economic structure. In the cases of Korea and Spain, governments possess more legislative power than their counterparts in Italy and Japan, and thus electoral promises can more easily enter the policy agenda. Clearer links between national elections and governments mean that political parties compete more on policies. But electoral politics alone are not sufficient to understand the trajectories of the four countries in other social investment policies such as parental leaves. Rather, the economic structure, to the extent that it shapes employers' preferences and labor shortages, is also part of the explanation. In general, employers' preferences matter little in the policy process concerning public subsidization of childcare services—unless the government explicitly forces employers to share the costs. By contrast, the consent of employers is critical for any meaningful paid childcare leave to be legislated. It is not corporatism per se but the predominance of large-scale employers that increases the likelihood that paid parental leave actually gets implemented. Smaller employers are always wary of statutory leaves regardless of the skills of the workers they employ; the cost of managing the temporary loss of an employee is too great. By contrast, large employers have more resources and greater capacity to adjust.

In Chapter 15, "Social Investment or Childcare on the Cheap? Quality, Workforce, and Access Considerations in the Expansion of Early Childhood Education and Care," Kimberly Morgan aims at identifying and explaining differences in childcare quality policies. Since the first decade of the 2000s, governments around the world have employed social investment rationales to help justify increased spending on ECEC services. As ECEC can help parents reconcile paid work and family life, offer enriching education to young children, and provide employment opportunities for those working in this sector, these programs can be an essential component of a social investment strategy. However, simply spending more on ECEC does not ensure that programs will be congruent with social investment objectives. For instance, demand-side subsidies without sufficient regulation can lead to programs that are too expensive to be accessible to low-income families. Services that offer low-paid and inferior jobs for the staff working in them do little to invest in these workers and likely also result in programs of questionable quality. In such instances, the care children receive may even be detrimental to their well-being. The chapter aims at understanding why some countries have expanded ECEC provision with high-quality services for children, good jobs for childminders, and enhanced access for those receiving lower incomes, while others have not.

This chapter analyzes policy developments in six countries that have significantly expanded their spending on ECEC in recent years: France, Germany, Ireland, Slovenia, New Zealand, and Norway. The analysis probes how ECEC expansions have come about in these countries, using indicators that capture the quality of the services provided, their accessibility to low-income families and other marginalized groups, and the quality of the jobs provided by the ECEC sector. On these measures, New Zealand, Norway, and Slovenia rate high on quality, France and Germany fall in a middle category, and Irish policies are least supportive of inclusive high-quality childcare.

At least two factors explain why these countries have pursued varying goals when they have engaged in ECEC expansion. One is the continued weight of historical legacies in influencing the direction countries take as they develop early childhood services. Whether programs are administered by educational or by social welfare administrations shapes the protagonists involved in program expansion. Nonetheless, history is not destiny as countries can change the bureaucratic auspices of ECEC programs. Norway and New Zealand have done just that, bringing all services for children below the mandatory school age under the control of education ministries in an effort to bolster the educational content and quality of these programs.

Left political power is the second factor that influences the nature of ECEC expansions. Governments of both the left and the right have devoted more spending to childcare and early education programs in recent years, in part with an eye on the votes of women and working parents, yet how they pursue these expansions varies markedly. Conservative governments continue to prioritize private market solutions or other ways to limit the level of spending on ECEC services. Thus, even as these parties have increasingly accepted women's employment and sought to woo female voters, their programmatic interventions do less to support social investment objectives. Left parties are more likely to be mindful of both gender equality and class equality concerns. As the chapter shows, these governments are therefore more likely to develop programs that invest in children, their parents, and ECEC workers.

In Chapter 16, "The Politics of Social Investment in the Knowledge Economy: Analytical Insights from a Global Comparison," we provide an encompassing comparative view of the politics of social investment reform strategies across all regions examined in the WOPSI project. The chapter's aim is to summarize and discuss what we have learned about the politics of social investment from the perspective of the independent variables, that is, the factors and actors driving (or impeding) social investment proposals and reforms.

The chapter proceeds in three steps. First, it positions and contextualizes different social investment policies in the typology of reform strategies developed at the outset of the book: the nine types of social investment policies (inclusive, stratified, and targeted social investment combined with their focus on skill creation, mobilization, and/or preservation) and the three non-social investment welfare reform strategies (market liberalism, social protectionism, and basic income). It underpins why this typology is helpful in improving how we think about social investment.

Second, the chapter discusses comparative analytical insights regarding the role of key drivers of social investment politicization and reforms (or non-reforms). More specifically, four elements are discussed: social demands, collective actors, socioeconomic factors, and institutions. The chapter offers strong support for the theoretical model proposed in Chapter 2 of this volume and offers some refinements based on what we have learned. The chapter shows under what conditions parties are social investment protagonists, antagonists, and consenters; it discusses the role of public opinion in this process; and it summarizes to what extent democracy, economic growth, and state capacity are necessary for social investment reforms.

Finally, our concluding chapter in this volume turns toward a more predictive perspective and discusses how we see the prospects for social investment around the globe, based on what we have learned from the global comparison. Moving from the end of the 2010s to the early 2020s, it speculates on which countries are most or least likely to adopt social investment in the near future.

Thus, by the end of this first volume resulting from the WOPSI project, we will have come quite far in our effort to provide a systematic and detailed analysis of the main factors shaping the politics of social investment and other welfare reform strategies around the globe. Having in this volume examined the explanatory factors driving reform strategies, we have also prepared the ground for Volume II, which engages more with differences between regions and countries.

REFERENCES

Abou-Chadi, T., & Immergut, E. (2019). Recalibrating social protection: Electoral competition and the new partisan politics of the welfare state. *European Journal of Political Research, 58*(2), 697–719.

Abrassart, A., & Bonoli, G. (2015). Availability, cost or culture? Obstacles to childcare services for low-income families. *Journal of Social Policy, 44*(4), 787–806.

Ansell, B. W. (2010). *From the ballot to the blackboard: The redistributive political economy of education.* Cambridge University Press.

Avlijaš, S. (2020). Beyond neoliberalism? Revisiting the welfare state in the Baltic states." *Europe-Asia Studies, 72*(4), 614–643.

Barbieri, P., Cutuli, G., & Passaretta, G. (2018). Institutions and the school-to-work transition: Disentangling the role of the macro-institutional context. *Socio-Economic Review, 16*(1), 161–183.

Becker, G. S. (1993). *Human capital. A theoretical and empirical analysis with special reference to education* (3rd ed.). University of Chicago Press. (Original work published 1964)

Becker, R., & Hecken, A. (2009). Higher education or vocational training? An empirical test of the rational action model of educational choices suggested by Breen and Goldthorpe and Esser. *Acta Sociologica, 52*(1), 25–45.

Bell, D. (1973). *The coming of post-industrial society. A venture in social forecasting.* Basic Books.

Beramendi, P., Häusermann, S., Kitschelt, H., & Kriesi, H. (Eds.). (2015). *The politics of advanced capitalism.* Cambridge University Press.

Bleses, P., & Seeleib-Kaiser, M. (2004). *The dual transformation of the German welfare state.* Palgrave Macmillan.

Blomqvist, P. (2004). The choice revolution: Privatization of Swedish welfare services in the 1990s. *Social Policy & Administration, 38*(2), 139–155.

Bohle, D., & Greskovits, B. (2012). *Capitalist diversity on Europe's periphery.* Cornell University Press.

Boix, C. (1998). *Political parties, growth and equality: Conservative and social democratic economic strategies in the world economy.* Cambridge University Press.

Bonoli, G. (2007). Time matters: Postindustrialization, new social risks, and welfare state adaptation in advanced industrial democracies. *Comparative Political Studies, 40*(5), 495–520.

Bonoli, G. (2013). *The origins of active social policy: Labour market and childcare policies in a comparative perspective.* Oxford University Press.

Bonoli, G., Cantillon, B., & Van Lancker, W. (2017). Social investment and the Matthew effect. In A. Hemerijck (Ed.), *The uses of social investment* (pp. 66–76). Oxford University Press.

Bourguignon, F., Ferreira, F. H. G., & Leite, P. G. (2003). Conditional cash transfers, schooling, and child labor: Micro-simulating Brazil's Bolsa Escola program. *The World Bank Economic Review, 17*(2), 229–254.

Breen, R., & Jonsson, J. (2005). Inequality of opportunity in comparative perspective: Recent research on educational attainment and social mobility. *Annual Review of Sociology, 31*, 223–243.

Busemeyer, M. R. (2015). *Skills and inequality. Partisan politics and the political economy of education reforms in Western welfare states.* Cambridge University Press.

Busemeyer, M. R., de la Porte, C., Garritzmann, J. L., & Pavolini, E. (2018). The future of the social investment state: Politics, policies, and outcomes. *Journal of European Public Policy, 25*(6), 801–809.

Busemeyer, M. R., Franzmann, S. T., & Garritzmann, J. L. (2013). Who owns education? Cleavage structures in the partisan competition over educational expansion. *West European Politics, 36*(3), 521–546.

Busemeyer, M. R., & Garritzmann, J. L. (2017). Social investment versus passive transfers: Analyzing public opinion on policy trade-offs in European welfare states with a new comparative survey. *Journal of European Public Policy, 24*(6), 871–889.

Busemeyer, M. R., Garritzmann, J. L., & Neimanns, E. (2020). *A loud, but noisy signal? Public opinion and education reform in western Europe.* Cambridge University Press.

Busemeyer, M. R., & Nikolai, R. (2010). Education. In F. G. Castles, S. Leibried, J. Lewis, H. Obinger, & C. Pierson (Eds.), *The Oxford handbook of the welfare state* (pp. 494–508). Oxford University Press.

Cantillon, B. (2011). The paradox of the social investment state: Growth, employment and poverty in the Lisbon era. *Journal of European Social Policy, 21*(5), 432–449.

Cecchini, S., & Atuesta, B. (2017). *Conditional cash transfer programmes in Latin America and the Caribbean: Coverage and investment trends.* United Nations, Economic Commission for Latin America and the Caribbean.

Cecchini, S., & Madariaga, A. (2011). *Programas de transferencias condicionadas: Balance de la experiencia en América Latina y el Caribe.* United Nations, Economic Commission for Latin America and the Caribbean.

Chevalier, T. (2016). Varieties of youth welfare citizenship. Towards a two-dimensional typology. *Journal of European Social Policy, 26*(1), 3–19.

Choi, Y. J., Huber, E., Kim, W. S., Kwon, H. Y., & Shi, S. J. (2020). Social investment in the knowledge-based economy: New politics and policies. *Policy and Society, 39*(2), 147–170.

Deeming, C., & Smyth, P. (2018). *Reframing global social policy: Social investment for sustainable and inclusive growth.* Policy Press.

Drucker, P. F. (1969). *The age of discontinuity: Guidelines to our changing society.* Harper and Row.

Drucker, P. F. (1993). *Post-capitalist society.* Butterworth-Heinemann.

Emmenegger, P., Häusermann, S., Palier, B., & Seeleib-Kaiser, M. (Eds.). (2012a). *The age of dualization. The changing face of inequality in deindustrializing societies.* Oxford University Press.

Emmenegger, P., Häusermann, S., Palier, B., & Seeleib-Kaiser, M. (2012b). How we grow unequal. In P. Emmenegger, S. Häusermann, B. Palier, & M. Seeleib-Kaiser (Eds.), *The age of dualization. The changing face of inequality in deindustrializing societies* (pp. 3–26). Oxford University Press.

Esping-Andersen, G. (1990). *The three worlds of welfare capitalism.* Princeton University Press.

Esping-Andersen, G. (1999). *Social foundations of postindustrial economies.* Oxford University Press.

Esping-Andersen, G. (2002). A child-centred social investment strategy. In G. Esping-Andersen, G. Duncan, A. Hemerijck, & J. Myles (Eds.), *Why we need a new welfare state* (pp. 26–67). Oxford University Press.

Esping-Andersen, G. (2009). *Incomplete revolution: Adapting welfare states to women's new roles.* Polity Press.

Esping-Andersen, G., Gallie, D., Hemerijck, A., & Myles, J. (Eds.). (2002). *Why we need a new welfare state.* Oxford University Press.

Estévez-Abe, M. (2009). Gender, inequality, and capitalism: The "varieties of capitalism" and women. *Social Politics, 16*(2), 182–191.

Estévez-Abe, M., Iversen, T., & Soskice, D. (2001). Social protection and the formation of skills. A reinterpretation of the welfare state. In P. A. Hall & D. Soskice (Eds.), *Varieties of capitalism. The institutional foundations of comparative advantage* (pp. 145–183). Oxford University Press.

Eurostat. (2018). *Living conditions in Europe, 2018 edition.* European Commission. https://ec.europa.eu/eurostat/documents/3217494/9079352/KS-DZ-18-001-EN-N.pdf/884f6fec-2450-430a-b68d-f12c3012f4d0

Fenwick, T. B. (2014, July 14–19). *From Bolsa Familia to Sem Miséria: Brazil's emerging social investment agenda* [Paper presentation]. International Sociological Association World Congress, Yokohama, Japan.

Fernandez, R., & Rogerson, R. (1995). On the political economy of education subsidies. *Review of Economic Studies, 62*(2), 249–262.

Fleckenstein, T. (2011). The politics of ideas in welfare state transformation: Christian democracy and the reform of family policy in Germany. *Social Politics: International Studies in Gender, State & Society, 18*(4), 543–571.

Fleckenstein, T., & Lee, S. C. (2017). A social investment turn in east Asia? In A. Hemerijck (Ed.), *The uses of social investment* (pp. 266–277). Oxford University Press.

Garritzmann, J. L. (2016). *The political economy of higher education finance. The politics of tuition fees and subsidies in OECD countries, 1945–2015.* Palgrave Macmillan.

Garritzmann, J. L., Busemeyer, M. R., & Neimanns, E. (2018). Public demand for social investment: New supporting coalitions for welfare state reform in western Europe? *Journal of European Public Policy, 25*(6), 844–861.

Garritzmann, J. L., Häusermann, S., & Palier, B. (Eds.). (2022). *The world politics of social investment: Vol. II. The politics of varying social investment strategies.* Oxford University Press.

Garritzmann, J. L., Häusermann, S., Palier, B., & Zollinger, C. (2017). *WoPSI—The World Politics of Social Investment: An international research project to explain variance in social investment agendas and social investment reforms across countries and world regions* [LIEPP Working Paper 64]. Laboratory for Interdisciplinary Evaluation of Public Policy.

Gerlach, I. (2004). *Familienpolitik.* Verlag für Sozialwissenschaften.

Ghysels, J., & Van Lancker, W. (2011). The unequal benefits of activation: An analysis of the social distribution of family policy among families with young children. *Journal of European Social Policy, 21*(5), 472–485.

Giddens, A. (1998). *The third way: The revival of social democracy.* Polity Press.

Gingrich, J. (2011). *Making markets in the welfare state.* Cambridge University Press.

Gingrich, J., & Ansell, B. (2015). The dynamics of social investment: Human capital, activation and care. In P. Beramendi, S. Häusermann, H. Kitschelt, & H. Kriesi (Eds.), *The politics of advanced capitalism* (pp. 282–304). Cambridge University Press.

Gingrich, J., & Häusermann, S. (2015). The decline of the working class vote, the reconfiguration of the welfare support coalition and consequences for the welfare state. *Journal of European Social Policy, 25*, 50–75.

Goldin, C., & Katz, L. F. (2008). *The race between education and technology.* Belknap Press of Harvard University Press.

Hall, P. A., & Soskice, D. (Eds.). (2001). *Varieties of capitalism. The institutional foundations of comparative advantage.* Oxford University Press.

Hasmath, R. (2015). *Inclusive growth, development and welfare policy: A critical assessment.* Routledge.

Häusermann, S. (2018). The multidimensional politics of social investment in conservative welfare regimes: Family policy reform between social transfers and social investment. *Journal of European Public Policy, 25*(6), 862–877.

Häusermann, S., & Kriesi, H. (2015). What do voters want? Dimensions and configurations in individual-level preferences and party choice. In P. Beramendi, S. Häusermann, H. Kitschelt, & H. Kriesi (Eds.), *The politics of advanced capitalism* (pp. 202–230). Cambridge University Press.

Häusermann, S., & Kübler, D. (2010). Policy frames and coalition dynamics in the recent reforms of Swiss family policy. *German Policy Studies, 6*(3), 163–194.

Häusermann, S., & Palier, B. (2017). The politics of social investment: Policy legacies and class coalitions. In A. Hemerijck (Ed.), *The uses of social investment* (pp. 339–348). Oxford University Press.

Häusermann, S., Pinggera, M., Ares, M., & Enggist, M. (2020). *The limits of solidarity. Changing welfare coalitions in a transforming European party system* [Unpublished manuscript]. University of Zurich, https://doi.org/10.5167/uzh-194708

Häusermann, S., & Zollinger, C. (2014, July 14–19). *Political dynamics of social investment reforms in continental welfare states. German and Swiss family policy reforms since 1980* [Paper presentation]. International Sociological Association World Congress, Yokohama, Japan.

Heckman, J. J. (2006). Skill formation and the economics of investing in disadvantaged children. *Science, 312*(5782), 1900–1902.

Heidenheimer, A. J. (1973). The politics of public education, health and welfare in the USA and western Europe: How growth and reform potentials have differed. *British Journal of Political Science, 3*(3), 315–340.

Hemerijck, A. (2012). Two or three waves of welfare state transformation? In N. Morel, B. Palier, & J. Palme (Eds.), *Towards a social investment welfare state? Ideas, policies and challenges* (pp. 1–30). Policy Press.

Hemerijck, A. (2013). *Changing welfare states.* Oxford University Press.

Hemerijck, A. (Ed.). (2017). *The uses of social investment.* Oxford University Press.

Hieda, T. (2013). Politics of childcare policy beyond the left–right scale: Post-industrialisation, transformation of party systems and welfare state restructuring. *European Journal of Political Research, 52*(4), 483–511.

Huber, E., & Stephens, J. D. (2014, July 14–19). *Social investment in Latin America* [Paper presentation]. International Sociological Association World Congress, Yokohama, Japan.

Hui, J. C., & Young, J. C. (2014, April 10–11). *Why women hesitate to work in South Korea: Conditions for effective social investment policies* [Paper presentation]. International Conference on Assessing the Social Investment Strategy, Lausanne, Switzerland.

Iversen, T. (2005). *Capitalism, democracy, and welfare.* Cambridge University Press.

Iversen, T., & Stephens, J. D. (2008). Partisan politics, the welfare state, and three worlds of human capital formation. *Comparative Political Studies, 41*(4–5), 600–637.

Jensen, C. (2011). Capitalist systems, deindustrialization, and the politics of public education. *Comparative Political Studies, 44*(4), 412–435.

Jenson, J. (2009). Lost in translation: The social investment perspective and gender equality. *Social Politics, 16*(4), 446–483.

Jenson, J. (2010). Diffusing ideas for after neoliberalism. The social investment perspective in Europe and Latin America. *Global Social Policy, 10*(1), 59–84.

Jenson, J., & Saint-Martin, D. (2003). New routes to social cohesion? Citizenship and the social investment state. *Canadian Journal of Sociology/Cahiers canadiens de sociologie, 28*(1), 77–99.

Jessop, B. (1993). Towards a Schumpeterian workfare state? Preliminary remarks on post-Fordist political economy. *Studies in Political Economy, 40*(1), 7–39.

Kim, Y.-M. (2007). *Social investment strategy in Korea: Possibilities, issues and prospects* [Paper presentation]. Conference on Social Investment Strategy, Seoul Welfare Foundation.

Knijn, T., & Kremer, M. (1997). Gender and the caring dimension of welfare states: Toward inclusive citizenship. *Social Politics, 4*(3), 328–361.

Korpi, W. (2006). Power resources and employer-centered approaches in explanations of welfare states and varieties of capitalism: Protagonists, consenters, and antagonists. *World Politics, 58*(2), 167–206.

Kurer, T. (2020). The declining middle: Occupational change, social status, and the populist right. *Comparative Political Studies, 35*(10–11), 1798–1835.

Kurer, T., & Palier, B. (2019). Shrinking and shouting: The political revolt of the declining middle in times of employment polarization. *Research and Politics, 6*(1). https://doi.org/10.1177/2053168019831164

Kvist, J. (2015). A framework for social investment strategies: Integrating generational, life course and gender perspectives in the EU social investment strategy. *Comparative European Politics, 13*(1), 131–149.

Kvist, J. (2016). *Social investment reforms: How to achieve more with less* [Unpublished manuscript]. Roskilde University.

León, M., & Pavolini, E. (2014). "Social investment" or back to "familism": The impact of the economic crisis on family and care policies in Italy and Spain. *South European Society and Politics, 19*(3), 353–369.

Levy, S. (2008). *Good intentions. Bad outcomes: Social policy, informality and economic growth in Mexico.* Brookings Institute.

Lewis, J. (1992). Gender and the development of welfare regimes. *Journal of European Social Policy, 2*(3), 159–173.

Lewis, J. (2001). The decline of the male breadwinner model: Implications for work and care, social politics. *International Studies in Gender, State & Society, 8*(2), 152–169.

Marx, P., & Nguyen, C. (2018). Anti-elite parties and political inequality: How challenges to the political mainstream reduce income gaps in internal efficacy. *European Journal of Political Research, 57*(4), 919–940.

Mettler, S. (2002). Bringing the state back in to civic engagement: Policy feedback effects of the G.I. Bill for World War II veterans. *American Political Science Research, 96*(2), 351–365.

Midgley, J., Dahl, E., & Wright, A. C. (2017). *Social investment and social welfare: International and critical perspectives.* Edward Elgar Publishing.

Morel, N. (2007). From subsidiarity to 'free choice': Child-and elder-care policy reforms in France, Belgium, Germany and the Netherlands. *Social Policy & Administration, 41*(6), 618–637.

Morel, N., Palier, B., & Palme, J. (2012). *Towards a social investment state? Ideas, policies and challenges.* Policy Press.

Morel, N., & Palme, J. (2017). A normative foundation for the social investment approach? In A. Hemerijck (Ed.), *The uses of social investment* (pp. 150–160). Oxford University Press.

Morgan, K. J. (2012). Promoting social investment through work–family policies: Which nations do it and why? In N. Morel, B. Palier, & J. Palme (Eds.), *Towards a social investment welfare state? Ideas, policies and challenges* (pp. 153–180). Policy Press.

Morgan, K. J. (2013). Path shifting of the welfare state: Electoral competition and the expansion of work–family policies in western Europe. *World Politics, 65*(1), 73–115.

Naumann, I. K. (2005). Child care and feminism in West Germany and Sweden in the 1960s and 1970s. *Journal of European Social Policy, 15*(1), 47–63.

Naumann, I. K. (2012). Childcare politics in the "new" welfare state. Class, religion, and gender in the shaping of political agendas. In G. Bonoli & D. Natali (Eds.), *The politics of the new welfare state* (pp. 287–307). Oxford University Press.

Nelson, M., & Sandberg, J. (2014, July 14–19). Conditional cash transfers in Latin America: An experiment with social investment? [Paper presentation]. International Sociological Association World Congress, Yokohama, Japan.

Nelson, M., & Stephens, J. D. (2012). Do social investment policies produce more and better jobs? In N. Morel, B. Palier, & J. Palme, *Towards a social investment welfare state? Ideas, policies and challenges* (pp. 205–234). Policy Press.

Nikolai, R. (2012). Towards social investment? Patterns of public policy in the OECD world. In N. Morel, B. Palier, & J. Palme, *Towards a social investment welfare state? Ideas, policies and challenges* (pp. 91–116). Policy Press.

Nolan, B. (2013). What use is "social investment"? *Journal of European Social Policy, 23*(5), 459–468.

Oesch, D. (2013). *Occupational change in Europe: How technology and education transforms the job structure.* Oxford University Press.

Orloff, A. S. (2009). Gendering the comparative analysis of welfare states: An unfinished agenda. *Sociological Theory, 27*(3), 317–343.

Orloff, A., & Palier, B. (2009). The power of gender perspectives: Feminist influence on policy paradigms. *Social Politics, 16*(4), 405–412.

Palier, B. (2010). *A long goodbye to Bismarck? The politics of welfare reform in continental Europe.* Amsterdam University Press.

Palier, B., & Thelen, K. (2010). Institutionalizing dualism: Complementarities and change in France and Germany. *Politics & Society, 38*(1), 119–148.

Peng, I. (2014). The social protection floor and the "new" social investment policies in Japan and South Korea. *Global Social Policy, 14*(3), 389–405.

Powell, W. W., & Snellman, K. (2004). The knowledge economy. *Annual Review of Sociology, 30*, 199–220.

Rokkan, S. (1999). *State formation, nation-building, and mass politics in Europe: The theory of Stein Rokkan, based on his collected works* (P. Flora, Ed., with S. Kuhnle & D. Urwin). Oxford University Press.

Rueda, D. (2007). *Social democracy inside out: Partisanship and labor market policy in industrialized democracies.* Oxford University Press.

Sainsbury, D. (1996). *Gender equality and welfare states.* Cambridge University Press.

Sandberg, J. (2016). Between poor relief and human capital investments— Paradoxes in hybrid social assistance. *Social Policy and Administration, 50*(3), 316–335.

Sandberg, J., & Nelson, M. (2017). Social investment in Latin America. In A. Hemerijck (Ed.), *The uses of social investment* (pp. 278–286). Oxford University Press.

Saxonberg, S., & Szelewa, D. (2007). The continuing legacy of the communist legacy? The development of family policies in Poland and the Czech Republic. *Social Politics: International Studies in Gender, State & Society, 14*(3), 351–379.

Schlanser, R. (2011). *Qui utilise les crèches en Suisse? Logiques sociales du recours aux structures d'accueil collectif pour la petite enfance.* Institut de hautes études en administration publique.

Schneider, M., & Paunescu, M. (2012). Changing varieties of capitalism and revealed comparative advantages from 1990 to 2005: A test of the Hall and Soskice claims. *Socio-Economic Review, 10*(4), 731–753.

Seeleib-Kaiser, M. (2017). The truncated German social investment turn. In A. Hemerijck, *The uses of social investment* (pp. 227–234). Oxford University Press.

Sen, A. (2001). *Development as freedom*. Oxford University Press.

Seung-ho, B., & Seung-yoon, L. S. (2014, April 10–11). *New solution to stagnant female employment rate? Korean female labor market and social investment policies* [Paper presentation]. International Conference on Assessing the Social Investment Strategy, Lausanne, Switzerland.

Shavit, Y., & Müller, W. (1998). *From school to work*. Oxford University Press.

Soares, S., Guerreiro Osorio, R., Soares, F. V., Medeiros, M., & Zepeda, E. (2009). Conditional cash transfers in Brazil, Chile and Mexico: Impacts upon inequality. *Estudios Económicos, 1*, 207–224.

Stampini, M., & Tornarolli, L. (2012). *The growth of conditional cash transfers in Latin America and the Caribbean: Did they go too far?* [IZA Policy Paper 49]. Institute for the Study of Labor.

Szebehely, M., & Meagher, G. (2018). Nordic eldercare–weak universalism becoming weaker? *Journal of European Social Policy, 28*(3), 294–308.

Szelewa, D., & Polakowski, M. P. (2008). Who cares? Changing patterns of childcare in central and eastern Europe. *Journal of European Social Policy, 18*(2), 115–131.

Taylor-Gooby, P. (2004). New risks and social change. In P. Taylor-Gooby (Ed.), *New risks, new welfare?* (pp. 1–28). Oxford University Press.

Taylor-Gooby, P., Gumy, J. M., & Otto, A. (2015). Can "new welfare" address poverty through more and better jobs? *Journal of Social Policy, 44*(1), 83–104.

UNICEF and the World Bank Group. (2016). *Ending extreme poverty: A focus on children*. https://www.unicef.org/reports/ending-extreme-poverty-focus-children

Vaalavuo, M. (2013). The redistributive impact of "old" and "new" social spending. *Journal of Social Policy, 43*(3), 513–539.

Vanhuysse, P., & Goerres, A. (2013). *Ageing populations in post-industrial democracies. Comparative studies of policies and politics*. Routledge.

Van Kersbergen, K., & Kraft, J. (2017). De-universalization and selective social investment in Scandinavia? In A. Hemerijck (Ed.), *The uses of social investment* (pp. 216–226). Oxford University Press.

Van Kersbergen, K., & Manow, P. (2009). *Religion, class coalitions, and welfare states*. Cambridge University Press.

Van Lancker, W., & Ghysels, J. (2012). Who benefits? The social distribution of subsidized childcare in Sweden and Flanders. *Acta Sociologica, 55*(2), 125–142.

Verba, S., & Nie, N. (1972). *Participation in America. Political democracy and social inequality*. University of Chicago Press.

Wiktorska-Święcka, A., Klimowicz, M., Moroń, D., & Michalewska-Pawlak, M. (2016). *Report on scientific literature review on the concept "social investment"*.

A deliverable of the project: "Innovative Social Investment: Strengthening Communities in Europe" (InnoSI). European Commission.

Wren, A. (2013). *The political economy of the service transition.* Oxford University Press.

Yeh, C.-Y., & Lue, J.-D. (2014). *The politics of the social investment turn in Taiwan. Why the social investment turn failed* [Unpublished manuscript].

Zollinger, C. (2016). *Graduell transformativer Politikwandel in postindustriellen Gesellschaften. Die Adaption der Familienpolitik an neue soziale Risiken in der Schweiz* [Dissertationsschrift]. Universität Zürich.

2

THE POLITICS OF SOCIAL INVESTMENT

A GLOBAL THEORETICAL FRAMEWORK

Silja Häusermann, Julian L. Garritzmann, and Bruno Palier

2.1. INTRODUCTION

The overarching ambition of the research project leading up to this book and
its twin volume has been to map and explain the way in which welfare states
in a variety of world regions have been adapted to the continuing—and ever
accelerating—shift toward knowledge economies as constitutive economic and
social conditions of the 21st century. Of course, not all countries rely strongly or
even predominantly on cognitive work, and baselines of occupational patterns
differ massively across countries and regions; but a trend toward economies
placing "a greater reliance on intellectual capabilities than on physical inputs or
natural resources" (Powell & Snellman, 2004, p. 199) is indeed ubiquitous, as we
demonstrate in Chapter 8 in this volume. This greater reliance on intellectual
capabilities implies a certain shift toward a production regime in which cognitive
work becomes the key source of productivity and value creation, while a major
purpose of manual and non-cognitive service work is then to sustain the production capacity of the knowledge economy. This shift, although at different levels
and speeds, is very much real and material (cf. the sharp divide that emerged in
the 2020 COVID-19 crisis between those able to work from a distance and those
whose work was tied to manual labor, i.e., physical presence; see Hatayama et al.,
2020). But the change is also ideational and thereby translates into an emerging
economic and intellectual framework that informs policymakers' and citizens'
analyses, diagnoses, and policy preferences across the world regions.

Silja Häusermann, Julian L. Garritzmann, and Bruno Palier, *The Politics of Social Investment* In: *The World Politics of Social Investment (Volume I)*. Edited by: Julian L. Garritzmann, Silja Häusermann, and Bruno Palier, Oxford University Press.
© Oxford University Press 2022. DOI: 10.1093/oso/9780197585245.003.0002

Social investment policies are *one* way in which many governments have addressed the challenges and opportunities of the transformation of capitalisms since the end of the 1990s. Social investment policies aim to prepare, mobilize, and equip individuals in a way that increases their chances of supporting themselves in the knowledge economy (notably through employment) and reduces their future risks of income loss and poverty. The two volumes at hand define social investment policies as policies that aim to create, mobilize, and/or preserve human skills and capabilities. The social investment perspective (Bonoli, 2005; Esping-Andersen, 1999, 2002; Hemerijck, 2013; Morel et al., 2012) has always emphasized the necessity to invest in, mobilize, and renew human capital and human capabilities along the entire life course in order to address social risks. The core idea is to "prepare rather than repair," that is, to equip individuals ex ante with the skills and education needed to cope with risks over the life course, rather than to merely compensate for the incidence of such risks ex post. Social investment as a policy strategy hence involves proactively avoiding social risks and overcoming the intergenerational transfer of disadvantage and poverty (Esping-Andersen, 2002; Jenson, 2010). Today, the social investment "paradigm" (Morel et al., 2012) is providing orientation in welfare reform discussions in a vast array of countries and across highly different contexts.

Adapting to the changing economic and societal conditions via social investment policies is, however, by no means the *only* policy option. We see three main alternative strategies that have gained some degree of prominence in the early 21st century: market liberalism, social protectionism, and basic income strategies. *Market liberalism* denotes a strategy of retrenchment, individualization, and privatization of protection against risks, based on the assumption that the economy will not yield the mass employment and productivity growth (also in lower- and medium-skilled work) that would be necessary to sustain wage compression and universal, equalizing social transfer schemes. Rather, according to this policy strategy, welfare states need to adapt to the conditions of changing capitalism by forcing or pushing commodification, on the one hand, and by allowing for more choice, flexibility, and stratification, on the other hand. For large parts of the society, such a strategy de facto implies stronger incentives for or constraints on commodification under market conditions, without effective support in achieving stable and well-qualified employment. Even though social investment and market liberalism share a focus on employment, it would be wrong to equate the two approaches as they are distinguished by, among other things, the active or passive role the state takes in supporting people's opportunities in the labor market and the valorization of their human capital and capabilities.

Aside from market liberalism, two additional strategies seem possible. First, a welfare strategy of *social protectionism* privileges compensation over investment and decommodification over activation. This is indeed the portfolio of welfare state policies that has been predominantly used traditionally and that comes to most minds intuitively when thinking about "social policy." The key goal of these policies is to shield people from the changing labor markets through ex post material compensation, in case they do not manage to support themselves and their families through employment. The main idea is to focus on "repairing" rather than "preparing" them for (future) labor market or other socioeconomic losses.

Finally, some voices favor *basic income strategies*, such as the universal and/or unconditional basic income (UBI). Such a strategy, more theoretical to date than actually empirically observable, can be seen in some respects as the actual antagonistic paradigm to social investment as UBI entirely cuts the reciprocal link between employment and welfare benefits and implies no concept at all of the state providing specific services, such as childcare, education and training, or care for the elderly.[1]

While not the only strategy available, social investment policies have certainly become *the* key toolbox for policymakers facing the challenges of rapidly changing markets and social inequalities. As our two volumes document, the social investment paradigm has entered the discourse of international organizations, national political arenas, scholarly debates, and the general public both at an astounding pace and with an impressive global reach, despite the different world regions exhibiting strongly divergent levels of capitalist development, welfare states, and reform challenges. This is why we devote these two volumes to the study of the politics of social investment across world regions.

The goal of the World Politics of Social Investment project is twofold. First, we seek to *map* the development (or absence) of social investment reforms in different countries and world regions comparatively, from conditional cash transfers in Latin America to expanded educational opportunities in the Baltic states to early childcare and education reforms across the OECD (Organisation for Economic Co-operation and Development) countries and support for female employment in North East Asia and Western Europe. To grasp the range and variance of these policies, we introduce a *novel typology of social investment reforms* based on their functions (creating, mobilizing, or preserving human skills and capabilities) and distributive effects (inclusive, stratified, or targeted). The new typology should allow us to move beyond a lumped—and often maximalist—definition of social investment in order to understand these policies as having different welfare effects, just like social compensation policies have been understood since the early milestone contributions of the 1980s and early 1990s (Korpi & Palme, 1998; Esping-Andersen, 1985, 1990, 1992). It should facilitate integration of the study of social investment into the regular scholarly canon of comparative welfare state and public policy research.

The project's second goal is to introduce an encompassing theoretical framework to *explain* the dynamics of *the politicization of social investment* (i.e., the

---

1. In this sense, Gough's (2019) concept of a "universal basic service" welfare state is closer to the idea of universally providing inclusive social investment than to the idea of a UBI.

extent to which and the terms in which social investment becomes salient on reform agendas) and *social investment reforms* (i.e., which concrete policies and which distributive profiles social investment reform strategies pursue). Politicization and reforms are the two main phenomena we explain (i.e., the "dependent variables" of our project), whose findings are presented in the two volumes at hand. Distinguishing them is important as they combine in different ways and are driven by distinctive factors. Politicization (i.e., the contentiousness of social investment reforms in political debates, demands, and proposals) depends largely on structural factors such as the maturity of welfare states and democratic institutions, socioeconomic development and context, and the societal implications of these developments on political demand for and supply of public policy responses. Whether and how social investment demands and proposals then materialize in actual reforms, though, are matters of politics (i.e., of coalitional dynamics), which in turn are structured by policy legacies. Politicization can occur without being followed by actual reforms, if initiatives are aborted, hindered, or vetoed or simply do not find the relevant majorities (as, e.g., in several Southern European cases of failed reform attempts). And reforms can happen without widespread politicization if they are driven by international or national technocrats (as, e.g., in the case of cash transfer programs in certain Central and Latin American countries).

Against the background of changing structural dynamics, the probabilistic framework we propose points to the interaction of societal demand and political supply in the politicization of social investment and theorizes about the role of domestic politics in the dynamics of coalition formation and decision-making. Our approach departs from and complements the rich body of research on aspects of social investment welfare reforms that tends to be narrower in geographical scope, the policy fields addressed, or the explanatory factors studied. We strive to show that the study of social investment across world regions opens our eyes to the systematic variation of the functions and distributive effects of social investment policies. Despite this variation, the large-scale comparison also shows that social investment is indeed a meaningful concept of welfare reform as all these reforms adapt social policy by implementing a consistent set of mechanisms according to which welfare policies are and should be aimed at the active development, use, and care of human capital and capabilities.

The purpose of this particular chapter is to introduce and explain our theoretical framework (in Section 2.2) and to develop concrete hypotheses that could explain social investment politicization and reforms (in Section 2.3). Hence, we begin the next section by establishing which factors and developments we need to take into account when theorizing about welfare state change in the 21st century in general: structural societal, demographic, and economic change; the actual development and level of maturity of the welfare state itself; ideational changes; changing preferences and concerns among the general public; and political transformations such as electoral de- and realignment of party systems. Based on this, we present and explain our integrated theoretical framework. We thereby also discuss how our approach deviates from other theoretical perspectives on welfare state development in the knowledge economy, such as structural determinism or a universalistic conception of median voter politics. Contrary to these approaches, we emphasize and theorize about the role of agency and coalitions at the level of both citizens and political elites.

We then proceed to develop specific hypotheses regarding the determinants of social investment politicization and regarding the substance and likelihood of political coalitions forming in favor of or against particular types of social investment policies (i.e., "protagonists," "antagonists," or "consenters," borrowing Korpi's [2006] terminology). In a nutshell, we argue that while a modicum of programmatic-democratic politics and state capacity are scope conditions for the politicization of social investment, the development of the knowledge economy and the maturity of the welfare state contribute to shaping political demand and supply in such a way as to bring social investment to the political agenda as a contested issue. The specific ways in which social investment is thus politicized depend on the interaction between institutional legacies of the existing welfare state and structural-economic developments. By "ways" we mean the functions and goals associated with social investment and the main social policies at stake. Finally, we theorize about the distributive profile of social investment reforms (inclusive, stratified, or targeted) as being conditional on political power configurations and coalitional dynamics among interest groups, political parties, and, in some contexts, experts and bureaucrats. Hence, ultimately, our key argument is that *politics*, both mass politics and producer group politics (themselves endogenously rooted in structural and institutional developments), are key to explaining both the politicization of social investment and the choice of social investment reform strategies. The chapters in this volume then focus on particular factors or sets of factors of our theoretical framework (i.e., our "independent variables") to assess the validity of our hypotheses and to evaluate the relative importance of the factors shaping the salience and occurrence of social investment reforms and their distributive profile.

2.2. A THEORETICAL FRAMEWORK FOR UNDERSTANDING WELFARE POLITICS IN THE 21ST CENTURY

Comparative welfare state research is a long-established field at the intersection of political science, sociology, and economics that has achieved a cumulative stock of knowledge on the factors that explain differences in the types, generosity, design, and effects of social policies being adopted and implemented in various contexts. When theorizing about the development of social investment reforms, we can draw on this knowledge while also considering the inherent and contingent specificities of social investment policies. At the most general level, we know that any explanation of social policy development in democratic settings needs to pay attention to both citizens and organized collective political actors, their action repertoires and resources, and their interactions in the context of ideas (such as perspectives on social justice), institutions, and structural constraints (such as budgetary limits). Hence, at least within democratic contexts, the building blocks for theorizing about and explaining social policy development are largely universal across time and regions. Yet, one still needs to integrate, adapt, and reconceptualize these elements to account for the particular ideational, structural, and institutional conditions of welfare politics in the 21st century.[2]

2.2.1. Explaining welfare politics in the 21st century

The existing scholarly knowledge on welfare state development tells us that the historical context—and "time" more generally (Pierson, 2004)—is key for understanding the incentive structures, belief systems, preferences, and strategies of political actors and how they are likely to use their room to maneuver (Bonoli, 2007). When theorizing about welfare politics in the 21st century—generally, not specific to social investment—two aspects thus need to be considered: the specific structural social and demographic changes that mark this particular era and the existing institutional policy legacies that differ across countries and contexts.

First, most societies, not only in the Western world but also in North East Asia and parts of Latin America, have experienced transformative changes since the 1980s when it comes to demographics, gender roles, and family structures. On the one hand, the aging or "graying" of societies as a result of medical advances, wealth, lower fertility, and particular social policies has become a major cause for concern, especially in advanced democracies, challenging labor markets and social security systems in particular in Europe and in the countries of North East Asia (Vanhuysse & Goerres, 2013). Also, the massive educational expansion across all world regions (traced empirically in Chapter 8 of this volume) has contributed to the emergence of a longer early age span (i.e., "youth") in people's biographies, but youth-specific social risks often remain only weakly addressed by existing welfare states (Chevalier, 2016). On the other hand, the changing role of women in society (not least via more education and labor market participation) challenges the very fundamentals these capitalist labor markets and familialist welfare states were built upon (Lewis, 1992; Orloff, 2009; Sainsbury, 1996). Family structures (think of fertility, divorce, single parenthood, and dual-earner families) and patterns of labor market attachment (e.g., discontinuous

2. The reference to the century is not used here as a precise temporal indication but rather indicates the "contemporary" era of welfare state restructuring that started in most world regions in the last decade of the 20th century, when demographic, economic, and political changes created a new context of welfare politics (Hall, 2020).

employment biographies and family-to-work transitions) are no longer the same. In the advanced capitalist democracies, "new social risks" (Bonoli, 2007; Esping-Andersen, 1999) such as working poverty, precarious employment, long-term unemployment, structural youth unemployment, difficulties of school-to-work transitions, and increasing difficulties in reconciling family and work life have given rise to new (or renewed) welfare demands. In less developed countries, these forms of precariousness have, of course, always been present, especially in labor markets; but changing demographic patterns and gender dynamics give them renewed importance. These sociodemographic transformations and their implications for the type and prevalence of social risks are challenges that *all* welfare reforms in the 21st century need to come to terms with, irrespective of the specific reform orientation (social investment, market liberalism, social protectionism, or basic income strategies).

Second, *any* theorization of welfare politics in the 21st century needs to pay close attention to the ways in which existing welfare institutions influence these politics. Indeed, a key theoretical insight (based on Lowi, 1972; see also Longstreth et al., 1992) in comparative welfare state research after the 1980s was that institutional policy legacies shape politics. The politics of reforming existing social policies (i.e., the "new politics of the welfare state") are by no means the same as the "old politics" of creating and introducing new policies (Pierson, 1996, 2001). For one, policy legacies fundamentally and structurally affect the actual problems at hand which welfare reform is supposed to resolve. The extent and distribution of risks, poverty, inequalities, and employment opportunities are largely endogenous to institutional legacies (Scharpf & Schmidt, 2000). Hence, when addressing the issue of single-parent poverty, for example, the existing supply of either public, private, or interfamilial care services makes a massive difference regarding the problem at hand and regarding the functionality and availability of different policy responses.

Moreover, the "new politics" differ from the old because existing institutional legacies shape the actual or perceived fiscal leeway for welfare state expansion (Bonoli, 2012; Stephens et al., 1999). For mature welfare states, such as the conservative social insurance regime in continental Europe or the productivist welfare state in North East Asia (Kim, 2016), reforms that imply an investive policy logic that deviates from the established protectionist or productivist models represent more of a disruption, or budgetary trade-off, than they do for welfare states whose degree of development is widely perceived as "still incomplete" or "fragmented." Depending on the legitimacy an existing regime or equilibrium enjoys, such a disruption or reinvention may even be perceived as a budgetary or political zero-sum choice in a reform process.

Legacies are a key factor of any theory of welfare state politics in the 21st century also because they shape both actors and their power resources through positive or negative institutional feedback effects (Pierson, 1992; Skocpol, 1992). This holds for both societal "actors" such as classes or risk groups as well as collective, organized political actors such as political parties, employer associations, or trade unions. With respect to societal groups, welfare policies not only endogenously affect risk structures; they also "produce" welfare constituencies that may either support or challenge the welfare state. For the mature welfare states of Western Europe, Esping-Andersen (1993) theorized how the distinctive welfare regimes shape class structures, and Oesch (2015) has followed up on this by demonstrating how closely intertwined the type of welfare institutions and the expansion of the new middle classes are. Similarly, potential welfare constituencies such as labor market "insiders and outsiders" are themselves endogenously forged by the welfare state (Esping-Andersen, 1999; Häusermann, 2010; Rueda et al., 2015), for example, by the crucial and defining difference between formal and informal labor market status in Latin America (Barrientos, 2009; Pribble, 2013). Skocpol (1992) and Pierson (1992, 1994, 1996) pioneered this reasoning while applying it to the emergence of veterans and particularly the elderly and pensioners as a relevant social and political constituency in welfare politics.

But institutional legacies also more immediately shape the role and preferences of collective political actors. In the corporatist, insurance-based welfare regimes of the coordinated market economies of continental Europe, for instance, employer organizations and trade unions are essential actors that control not only positions of power but also concrete organizational resources of the welfare state (Palier, 2010; Palier & Martin, 2009). They thereby become stakeholders of existing social policy, and their preferences regarding further reform are shaped by existing institutional arrangements and incentives. In particular, the distributive and stratifying effects of institutional legacies shape the payoffs of particular policy reforms. This is why actor preferences are conditional on the institutional framework (Ansell, 2010). Thus, for example, trade unions in dualized and stratified welfare states might be more resistant to inclusive and equality-oriented reforms (Clegg, 2007; Gingrich & Ansell, 2015), as is analyzed systematically in Chapter 10 of this volume. Similarly, teachers' unions or private sector providers in Latin America might oppose equality-oriented reforms of the educational system (Bogliaccini & Madariaga, 2020; Chambers-Ju & Finger, 2016).

2.2.2. Explaining social investment politics in the 21st century

As we have seen, both societal demographic transformations and existing institutional arrangements are key variables of *any* theory of welfare state change in our times. However, existing frameworks (such as the power resources or "new politics" approaches) are by no means sufficient to understand social investment as a *particular* strategy of welfare state development. We are indeed in need of a specific theoretical framework to address the politics of social investment because *transnational ideational dynamics*, the development of the *knowledge economy*, and the *transformation of party competition in advanced democracies* all bear massive and distinctive significance for the politics of social investment in ways that do not apply to other welfare reform strategies. We address each of them sequentially.

First, regarding ideational dynamics, as retraced by Jenson and Mahon in Chapter 3 as well as by de la Porte and Palier in Chapter 4 of this volume, the practices of various international governmental organizations involved in social development began to cohere around new ideas, including social investment, in the mid- to late 1990s, producing since then early-life intervention and child-centered strategies and emphasizing investment in human capital to promote economic growth, well-being, and social development (Jenson, 2010). More recently, these organizations have gathered around the concept of "inclusive growth," promoting a more encompassing understanding of human capacities and a preoccupation with reducing inequalities, while maintaining a focus on skills and social investment. In the Global South, international organizations (in particular UNICEF, the World Bank, and regional development banks) have played key roles in the development and diffusion of the social investment perspective. In their discourse in relation to social investment policies, they recommended policies that had the potential to break the intergenerational cycle of disadvantage and poverty. Similarly, in the Global North, the OECD and the European Union (from the Lisbon Strategy launched in 2000 to the Social Investment Package adopted in 2013 and the European Pillar of Social Rights proclaimed in 2017; see Chapter 4 in this volume) have engaged in similar capacity-building-oriented visions of welfare state discourse, with the OECD in particular turning ever more strongly toward a focus on reducing inequality and expanding opportunities in the context of economic structural change from the early 2000s onward (Chapter 3 in this volume). The approaches behind these capacity-building-oriented policies were developed—in different variants—by intellectuals such as Anthony Giddens and Gøsta Esping-Andersen and have framed what has been called a new social policy paradigm (Hemerijck, 2017; Jenson & Saint Martin, 2003; Morel et al., 2012). These ideational influences have deeply marked the perspectives and ideas for addressing economic and social transformations in all the regions our project covers.

The second—and possibly most important—factor that affects the politics and development of social investment is the emergence of the knowledge economy as both a political reality and a cognitive framework. *Knowledge economies* can be defined as economies placing "a greater reliance on intellectual capabilities than on physical inputs or natural resources" (Powell & Snellman, 2004, p. 199). The social investment perspective (Bonoli, 2007; Esping-Andersen, 2002; Hemerijck, 2013; Morel et al., 2012) always emphasizes the necessity to invest in human capital and human capabilities to address social risks not met by the existing welfare state. Hence, our understanding of social investment against the background of economic-structural change relates it necessarily to concepts of human capital investment and productivity. However, while employability is an important goal of social investment, it is not enough. The emphasis on both economic and social returns that social investment policies need to pursue in order to qualify as such brings our concepts closer to the notion of "human capabilities" than strictly that of human capital because "human capabilities" brings with it the idea of capacitating individuals to actively shape their own lives (Sen, 2001; see also Morel & Palme [2017] on the relationship between social investment and the capabilities approach). Nevertheless, there is indeed a close nexus between changing incentives and payoff structures in the economy and the politics of social investment. To some extent, social investment has often been seen as the "natural correlate" of the knowledge economy because this economy places heightened value on cognitive and interpersonal skills for both individual well-being and welfare, as well as for macroeconomic performance. Today, the importance of skills and skill formation systems is widely accepted as integral to countries' politico-economic systems (Estévez-Abe, 2008; Hall & Soskice, 2001; Iversen, 2005; Müller & Shavit, 1998; Schneider, 2013; Thelen, 2004), as well as social mobility and inclusion (Becker & Hecken, 2009; Breen & Jonsson, 2005).

Hence, the structural and institutional underpinnings of the politics of social investment need to be understood with reference to processes of educational expansion, occupational upgrading, and the conditions of an "era of knowledge-based growth" (Hall, 2020). This increasing focus on human skills and capabilities is not necessarily built into the traditional welfare states that have emerged throughout the 20th century, nor is it essential to the politics of welfare reform when it comes to alternative strategies such as social protectionism or market liberalism. However, for understanding the politics of social investment, the changing demand for skills in the labor market and the transformed social structure that results from educational expansion and occupational change need to be placed front and center.

Finally, there is a third development whose significance is distinctive for theorizing about social investment as a welfare reform strategy: the transformation of party competition in advanced democracies. In the early 21st century, the mass political context of welfare state politics could hardly be more different from what it was in the mid-20th century (Häusermann et al., 2013). During the heyday of Western welfare state expansion in the second half of the 20th century, parties of the mainstream left and right had dominated the landscape, and in all the advanced democracies they had counted on joint vote shares of 70%–80% or even more; the early decades of the 21st century, however, have seen massive and transformative changes in the system of collective interest representation. This transformation regards not only the substance of the most important programmatic dimensions of party competition but also the size of political parties and, associated with this, the role and opportunity structures for their allies among trade unions and employer organizations. In terms of substantive transformation, the emergence in the 1980s of a new dimension of deeply divisive sociocultural policy choices regarding minority rights, gender equality and diversity, environmentalism, immigration, as well as internationalism and supranational integration has led to an increased heterogeneity within both the left and the right, with some parties taking universalistic and culturally liberal positions and others opting for more traditionalist and communitarian stances (Bornschier, 2010; Häusermann & Kriesi, 2015; Kitschelt, 1994; Kitschelt & McGann, 1997; Kriesi et al., 2006, 2008; Marks & Steenbergen, 2004).

From then onward, the economic-distributive dimension of party competition pitting state interventionist left-leaning parties against market liberal right-leaning parties was not only complemented by a salient "second dimension" of sociocultural politics debating individual and societal organization and liberties; in most countries, this second dimension has clearly surpassed the economic one in terms of both salience and polarization (Hutter & Kriesi, 2019; Kitschelt & Rehm, 2015; Kriesi et al., 2008, 2012). However, not only have existing mainstream parties been enlarging their programmatic profile to accommodate either universalistic or particularistic positions, but new challenger parties on both the left-libertarian and the right-authoritarian sides have increased their vote shares at the expense of the mainstream parties, to the extent that center-left and center-right parties in many countries no longer hold dominant positions even within their own ideological camp. This diversification of what it means to be "left-wing" or "right-wing" has also complicated the relationship between mainstream left parties and trade unions, as well as between mainstream right parties and business, as complex trade-offs have emerged, for example, between insider protection and universalism on the left (Pribble, 2013; Rueda, 2005) and between economic liberalism, integration, and migration control on the right (Dancygier & Walter, 2015). This reconfigured landscape of mass politics in advanced democracies is impacting all politics of welfare reform, of course, through the altered relative salience of economic-distributive versus sociocultural topics, as well as through the altered coalitional options that result from a multidimensional political space and an increasingly fragmented party system (Bonoli & Natali, 2012; Häusermann, 2010; Manow et al., 2018).

The emergence of a polarizing and salient second dimension of political competition is *particularly* relevant for the politics of social investment for at least three reasons. First, there is a substantive affinity between cultural liberalism and inclusive social investment which relies on the universalistic-egalitarian foundations of both policy goals. The extended time horizon and the less predictable distributive gains of inclusive social investment—as opposed to social protectionism—resonate with the universalistic goals of equal rights and opportunities that underlie many of the left-libertarian claims (Beramendi et al., 2015). Second, there is a substantive overlap between the electoral constituencies of left-libertarian and right-authoritarian parties and the constituencies supportive of social investment and social consumption or social compensation, respectively. The educated middle class, especially in the post-industrial, public, and semi-public sectors, tends to be both the key electorate of the New Left and the key advocate of social investment policies (Beramendi et al., 2015; Garritzmann et al., 2018; Häusermann & Palier, 2017; see Chapter 12 in this volume). Evidence points to a range of explanations for this: from its universalistic values to economic opportunities to political trust and to a self-interest in the expansion of (semi-)public services (Busemeyer & Garritzmann, 2017; Häusermann et al., 2021; Kitschelt & Rehm, 2013). On the other hand, both the petty bourgeoisie and voters of the skilled working class and lower middle class are champions of social protectionism, as well as the key constituencies of the far right (Häusermann et al., 2020; Oesch & Rennwald, 2018; Zhen et al., 2019). While the reasons for this overlap are still being debated, its empirical occurrence has been shown consistently. Irrespective of its causes, these overlaps imply at least two consequences that are relevant for understanding the politics of social investment. First, social investment is most likely to be politicized at least partially in sociocultural terms, with strong references to, for example, gender equality and "new" risk groups and minorities. Furthermore, programmatic choices between social protectionism and social investment may entail significant trade-offs in advanced welfare states (Busemeyer & Garritzmann, 2017; Häusermann et al., 2020), much like the dilemmas between focusing on their traditional and new core electorates that the second dimension has created for the left on sociocultural policy choices since the 1980s (Oesch & Rennwald, 2018).

Hence, a theoretical framework for understanding the politics of social investment needs to pay specific attention to 1) actors and processes fueling ideational diffusion and learning worldwide; 2) the economic consequences and implications of the emergence of the knowledge economy, especially in the form of changing demand for particular skills; and 3) the emergence of new political preference divides at the level of public demand and political supply (i.e., organized action).

2.2.3. The theoretical framework: Explaining social investment politicization and reforms

Figure 2.1 depicts the theoretical framework that will guide our analyses of both the politicization of social investment and coalition formation and decision-making in concrete social investment reform strategies across different world regions in both this volume and its sister volume. It highlights ideational, structural, and institutional context conditions that affect the interaction of political supply and demand, as well as the dynamics of coalition formation among antagonists, protagonists, and consenters of social investment. Figure 2.1 also emphasizes that our analytical focus is on the politics of social investment, rather than on the implementation and effects of social investment reforms.

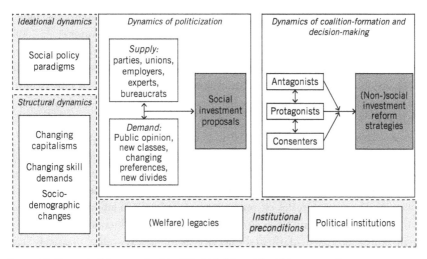

Figure 2.1 Theoretical framework of the "World Politics of Social Investment" project.

2.2.3.1. Context conditions

Figure 2.1 shows how much we emphasize the structural, ideational, and institutional context conditions that affect politics. Somewhat paradoxically, acknowledging the fundamental and transformative effects of these context conditions is indeed key for understanding the relevance of and leeway for political choice, voluntarism, and agency that we highlight in the explanation of both the politicization of social investment proposals and the decision-making process in social investment reform strategies. Not carefully theorizing about these context conditions would not only preclude a comparative analysis across world regions but also entail a risk of neglecting the ways in which context shapes actors, their preferences, and power relations. In the following, we explain how in different institutional contexts, ideational and structural change affects political demand and supply both at the societal level and at the level of organized actors.

As mentioned, capitalist systems around the world are changing. At the core of these ongoing transformations is an increasing focus on human skills and capabilities, which is also reflected in the discourses and perceptions of international and national epistemic communities that increasingly define skills and capabilities as key to individuals', families', and countries' prosperity and welfare. Depending on both the level of development and the preexisting institutional framework, this shift occurs at different speeds and levels in different countries, but the underlying structural dynamic is virtually universal across capitalist democracies. Technological change, deindustrialization, and globalization/financialization are structural economic and political dynamics that (can) contribute to and accelerate this shift toward skill-centered economies. Technological change triggers changes in occupational patterns across economic sectors, strongly impacting the distribution of opportunities and constraints across social classes (Oesch, 2013) as it increases returns particularly for higher-skilled groups in both services and industry (Acemoglu, 2002; Autor et al., 2008). Technological change is also leading to ever-increasing premiums on education and a "race between education and technology" (Goldin & Katz, 2008). It has been argued that automation (of routine work) will have similar effects in the near future as its consequences are likely to be skill- and task-biased too (Frey & Osborne, 2017; Thewissen & Rueda, 2016).

Closely related but not identical to processes of technological change, de-industrialization in the advanced economies (Iversen & Cusack, 2000; Oesch, 2013) and the transformation of industrial production in the developing and emerging economies result in ever more complex global value chains that are changing the opportunities citizens are presented with in labor markets world-wide (Iversen & Wren, 1998; Wren, 2013). In all deindustrializing countries, high-skilled jobs particularly in the service sector are expanding massively (e.g., Oesch, 2013) at the expense of medium-skilled, lower middle-class jobs especially in the manufacturing sector (Autor et al., 2003; Peugny, 2019). In less developed economies, occupational upgrading may take place at a lower echelon, with the main focus being on the expansion of post-secondary education and vocational skills (e.g., see Chapters 7 and 8 in this volume). Even there, however, structural economic change over time prizes educational expansion.

The globalization of goods (trade), money (finance), and people (migration), implying a strengthening of (transnational) financial institutions, also feeds into this increased attention to skills and human capital. Along the lines of the compensation thesis that globalization ultimately leads to welfare state expansion because risk-averse workers demand stronger welfare protection (Cameron, 1978; Katzenstein, 1985), Busemeyer and Garritzmann (2018) show the positive effect of globalization on demand for public education spending, an effect that—at least in the most advanced economies—is even stronger than the effect on demand for traditional compensatory social policies. Furthermore, (transnational) financialization and the interdependence of labor markets and production chains fuel the complexity of production processes and the transformation of occupational structures.

In such a context of rapidly changing capitalism and changing demand for skills across economic sectors, two developments are of political significance. First, governments more or less explicitly have to determine a specific strategy of economic growth (Hassel & Palier, 2020a). And second, the structural change itself affects the preferences of firms, different sectors of employers, and producer interests, as well as the composition and preferences of social classes and the democratic public. This is precisely why taking structural developments into account is so crucial to understanding the politics of social investment.

Let us first look at government choices. The recent and burgeoning literature on political-economic models, growth strategies, growth models, and growth regimes (Beramendi et al., 2015; Baccaro & Pontusson, 2016; Hall,

2020; Iversen & Soskice, 2019; Hassel & Palier, 2021a; Thelen, 2014) illustrates that the rapid transformation of economic production structures requires attention to agency and political steering. The term "strategies" should not suggest an overly rationalistic assumption but simply the shared idea in these political economy approaches that governments have "some intention" (Hassel & Palier, 2020b) when it comes to how they intend to support (employment) growth and that there is some coherence in policy decisions. To understand the choices governments make, all the above-mentioned approaches consider ideational influences, as well as preexisting institutional legacies as important, even though they tend to emphasize somewhat different factors: While growth regime theories such as those of Thelen (2014) and Hassel and Palier (2021b) emphasize the effects of the institutions organizing the economy (market regulation, industrial relations, modes of financing the economy, skill formation, and welfare institutions), more structuralist approaches, such as those of Beramendi et al. (2015) and Baccaro and Pontusson (2016), focus mainly on the composition of aggregate supply and demand. Equally important are the political institutions such as the electoral system, the development of democratic linkages, and the representative institutions since they condition the leeway governments have in orienting policies and government accountability. Thereby, these institutions are relevant scope conditions for our argument as well (see, e.g., Chapter 6 in this volume).

2.2.3.2. Political demand and supply

However, these institutional context factors do not determine policies as governments indeed make choices, which may depart from previous arrangements depending on, for example, the performance and legitimacy of the previous institutional arrangements. In this sense, all of these recent approaches to different degrees go beyond the more static regime typologies they respond to, such as the welfare capitalism regimes (Esping-Andersen, 1990) or the varieties of capitalism (Estévez-Abe, 2008; Hall & Soskice, 2001; Nölke & Vliegenhart, 2009; Schneider, 2013). Good examples of this renewed attention to agency and choice within our project are the divergent strategies pursued by governments in the Baltic countries and the Visegrád states (see Chapter 9 in Volume II [Garritzmann et al., 2022]) or the different post-industrial growth strategies in the North East Asian welfare states, which integrate the legacies of the productivist welfare model in different ways (see Chapters 10–13 in Volume II [Garritzmann et al., 2022]).

But not only do governments need to make choices; they also need to make these choices in the context of—and sometimes under the pressure of—new political claims by the public, voters, producer groups, trade unions, and political parties. Our theoretical framework focuses on both political demand (structural societal and economic demands) and political supply (aggregated, politically organized interests), which are interdependent in complex ways.

Regarding political demand, we focus on the societal and economic changes that economic tertiarization, the emergence of the knowledge economy, and educational expansion have brought about. In particular, we build on these trends to identify the relevant socioeconomic groups we need to look at, their preferences, and the political divides that are likely to shape the politics of social investment in the contexts of changing capitalism (see Figure 2.1). To start with labor markets, one consequence of technological change, tertiarization, and societal changes (across both more advanced and developing economies, see Chapter 5 in this volume) is the massive increase of employment in skilled occupations. This trend has been fueling the emergence of a strongly expanded middle class, especially in the more advanced capitalist democracies (Manning, 2003; Oesch, 2013). This expanded middle class needs, in turn, to be subdivided into "new" and more "traditional" parts. The new middle class is characterized by employment in the (cognitive-creative and/or interpersonal) skilled and high-skilled service sector, a high degree of feminization, and more frequent atypical and non-standard work contracts (Emmenegger et al., 2012), whereas the more traditional or "old" middle class refers to the petty bourgeoisie, as well as skilled and high-skilled employees predominantly in the manufacturing industry. It is important to acknowledge that the expansion of high-skilled middle-class jobs is not purely a result of tertiarization as skill-upgrading has also taken place in (diversified) industrial production.

On the opposite end of the new middle class lies a relative decline in labor demand for medium-skilled and routine manufacturing production workers and for mid-skill routine-based services (Autor et al., 2003; Kurer, 2020; Oesch, 2013). This decline is more specific to the most advanced political economies of Western Europe, the Baltics, North America, and North East Asia (which have become service economies to an overwhelming extent; see Wren [2013]), while demand for skilled routine work remains relatively more important in Latin America and parts of Central and Eastern Europe. Even in the more manufacturing- and export-oriented countries of Western Europe (such as Germany), mid-skilled industrial jobs have declined massively, with employees in services outnumbering employees in industrial production by a ratio of 2:1 as of the late 2010s (see Chapter 8 in this volume). However, this is not to say that low-skilled work is generally in lower demand as a considerable—and in some places growing—share of workers remains employed in low-paid (service) jobs, resulting in an increasing gap between high-skilled and low-skilled workers. The overall pattern might thus be best described as "polarized upgrading" (see Goos et al., 2014; Spitz-Oener, 2006; Oesch & Rodriguez-Menes, 2010; see also Chapter 8 in this volume).

Scholars have attempted to capture these broader societal transformations and changing occupational structures with new class schemes. The class schemes that capture the occupational structure of post-industrial economies best help us make sense of the politically relevant dynamics in these countries. Oesch (2006,

2013) as well as Kitschelt and Rehm (2013), in particular, introduce not only the divide within the higher-skilled middle-class occupations but also a potential divide within the working class between the production workers, on the one hand, and a newly growing service sector working class, on the other hand (Beramendi et al., 2015). The latter shares with the new middle class both the higher degree of feminization as well as weaker labor market protection and social rights.

These occupational transformations are closely intertwined with the massive educational expansion that all capitalist economies have experienced since the 1980s (see Chapter 8 in this volume). In the more advanced capitalist democracies, we see near-universal enrollment in secondary education by the early 21st century, with large shares of young cohorts attending tertiary education as well, especially in the Anglo-Saxon countries, Nordic Europe, and North East Asia but increasingly so also in Continental, Southern, Central and Eastern Europe. In the less developed and developing economies, the bulk of educational expansion has taken place at the secondary and post-secondary levels (see Chapter 6 in this volume).

These socio-structural transformations in the relative size, significance, and dynamic of the different labor market sectors and occupational categories bear direct political relevance for theorizing about the politics of social investment and welfare state reforms more generally. The new middle class is both the product and the main beneficiary of the massive expansion of education and human capital formation and is therefore—contrary to the traditional conceptualization of labor as the key pro-welfare state force—likely to be a (new) pivotal actor in welfare politics (Beramendi et al., 2015; Busemeyer & Garritzmann, 2017; Häusermann & Palier, 2017). The declining medium-skilled lower middle class (formerly working class) belonged and still belongs to the main beneficiaries of social protectionism or "compensatory social policies" (Beramendi et al., 2015), such as unemployment benefits, pensions, health insurance, and accident coverage, which historically were built targeted to their needs (Esping-Andersen, 1990; Huber & Stephens, 2001). Hence, while one could imagine their demand for upskilling to rise (to update their skills for the new economy), an equally plausible scenario is to see this class hold on most tightly to established compensation-oriented policies, particularly when challenged by the rise of the knowledge economy. Similarly, in developing economies, middle-class voters and their children are the main beneficiaries of expansion of (post-)secondary and partly tertiary education, whereas the poor continue to be more reliant on poverty-relieving compensatory policies, on social investment that relates to basic social services (healthcare, primary education), or on clientelistic benefits (Chapter 6 in this volume).

However, beyond the implications these socio-structural and economic changes have for the policy preferences and priorities of these social classes, one key insight here is that the relative size of these (old and new) social classes and their political representation—via political parties and interest groups—will vary greatly across regions and countries as a function of the structural changes undergone. Hence, the relative weight of their different demands is also likely to vary, which is a crucial factor in our theoretical framework (see Chapter 12 in this volume).

At the same time, these rapidly and deeply transforming context conditions are equally likely to shape preferences among supply-side actors (i.e., organized collective political actors such as interest groups and political parties) not only through aggregation effects but also more directly. This is most visible when it comes to the interests of employers and trade unions because they represent distinctive economic interests. The emergence of the knowledge economy and occupational polarization tend to change the demand for skills in the workforce in terms of both level and type. In most advanced democratic economies, there are shortages of highly skilled labor, both generally and specifically skilled. At the same time, the demand for lower- and medium-skilled labor is generally declining, most clearly so regarding manual and specific skills. This should affect the preferences of businesses in these contexts, reinforcing their interest in the creation and mobilization of cognitive skills through public policies (see Chapter 2 in Volume II [Garritzmann et al., 2022] and Chapters 9 and 14 in this volume). This is not to say that we should expect business associations to wholeheartedly support an encompassing social investment agenda as they may contest both the inclusiveness and the quality of service provision (see Chapter 15 in this volume). But it does imply that where the most productive sectors are knowledge-intensive, business may more strongly support social investment— at least much more strongly than more traditional theories of welfare politics would assume. These effects of structural change on the preferences of capital again depend very much on the speed and level of the economic-structural transformations, as well as on the growth strategies pursued by governments (see Chapter 8 in this volume). Also, as shown in volume II, there is considerable regional variation in these growth strategies, with, for example, some Visegrád countries explicitly countering the emergence of knowledge economy structures by reinforcing manufacturing production.

On the side of labor (i.e., trade unions), the changing demands for skills and occupational polarization also raise interesting questions regarding the likely preferences and heterogeneity of unions' demands (Becher & Pontusson, 2011). In particular, trade unions should have an incentive to push for public educational investments in order to support and represent their rising middle class and medium/high-skilled membership (and in order to appeal more systematically to women), while at the same time claiming stronger social compensatory policies to mitigate the consequences of declining demand for mid-skill level and routine labor (see Chapter 10 in this volume).

Like trade unions, political parties experience both pressure to adapt to the changing representational patterns and the need to position themselves strategically in the transformed space of party competition outlined in Section 2.2.2.

Again, like trade unions, most centrist parties across developed democracies represent increasing shares of middle-class and high-skilled voters, which affects their incentives to support social policies that support these classes and their interests (Gingrich & Häusermann, 2015). At the same time, parties try to hold on to traditional segments of the (working class) electorate for both ideological and strategic reasons since most countries by now have left and right challenger parties competing for their votes (Manow et al., 2018).

Finally, experts and bureaucrats are important actors on the political supply side. They are less interdependent with socio-structural demand-side changes than interest groups and parties are. However, they have an important role in structuring in particular agenda-setting dynamics and the politicization of social investment reforms because they tend to be more tightly connected to national and international epistemic communities, particularly when it comes to international organizations. Hence, understanding and including experts and bureaucrats is crucial for taking ideational dynamics into account. Furthermore, in terms of scope conditions, bureaucrats can be decisive political actors especially in the context of countries with lower levels of democratic development (see Chapter 15 in Volume II [Garritzmann et al., 2022]) and in highly centralized and statist countries.

2.2.4. Specificities and distinctiveness of our approach

Is our theoretical framework too generic and encompassing as it integrates ideational, structural, institutional, and political factors? No, we contend, it is not. Our framework needs to be encompassing in order to suit very different political and regional contexts. Yet, it has a clear, testable, and distinctive argument: *politics, both mass politics and producer group politics—themselves endogenously rooted in structural and institutional developments, as well as ultimately political choice—are key in explaining the politicization of social investment or lack thereof, as well as social investment reform strategies.*

This argument is non-deterministic, implying a range of potential outcomes that can be systematically accounted for. In this sense, our framework differs clearly from structurally deterministic, functionalist, culturalist, as well as politically monocausal rival explanations (for a discussion of different perspectives on social investment, see Hemerijck [2017]).

First, we clearly diverge from structurally deterministic models of capitalism, capitalist development, and economic institutions. We do not assume that there is a universal and uniform trend of capitalist development toward liberalization (Streeck, 2009) or toward the knowledge economy, let alone toward an inherent expansion of complementary social policy (i.e., an "updated" Wagner's law). More importantly even, we depart from functionalist hypotheses or claims according to which deindustrialization and the (exogenous) emergence of the knowledge economy would inevitably lead to expanded educational systems (Jensen, 2011).

In our model, both political institutions supporting and sustaining the development of a knowledge economy and the expansion of social policies that would sustain the creation, mobilization, and preservation of human capabilities and skills are matters of political choice, which is neither straightforward nor necessarily coherent.

Our framework also differs explicitly from culturalist and predominantly ideational models of policy development. While we acknowledge the role of framing, discourse, and ideational influences, we consider them a conditioning factor and part of the political process, seen as conflictive and coalitional dynamics between actors whose preferences diverge. Social investment policies are neither the direct result of a diffusion of best practices among policymakers and technocrats nor an inherent correlate of the progressive expansion of a knowledge-based world society (Meyer et al., 1997). They are also by no means the result of political-cultural "narratives" of sustainable political responses to economic development (Piketty, 2019). Rather, our framework emphasizes the role of economic structures, material preferences, as well as political conflict over these preferences and over the distributive effects of social investment policies. As any other policy, social investment reform strategies entail winners and losers, and the distribution of gains and losses is first and foremost a matter of power and coalitional politics.

Finally, we take a multidimensional approach to the explanation of social policy. Just as welfare states can be reformed via a variety of strategies, policy debates involve several dimensions, for example, social investment versus compensation or inclusiveness versus stratification and targeting. Voters, interest groups, and political parties take different positions along these multiple dimensions. Hence, we depart both from a straightforward median voter story of policy development (Iversen & Soskice, 2019) and from predominantly structural-elitist neo-Marxist models of institutional choice and development (Amable, 2017; Baccaro & Pontusson, 2019). Iversen and Soskice (2019) argue that the preferences of the median voter for capitalist development, economic modernization, and educational expansion will eventually prevail in the political process over elite preferences for pure liberalization, on the one hand, and preferences for exclusive social protectionism, on the other hand. By contrast, Baccaro and Pontusson (2019) claim that policy choices are ultimately made by a narrow, hegemonic "social bloc" of elite capitalist interests of the dominant economic production sectors, with any deviation or complement to their main interests being mere concessions and side payments to minor allies of this "bloc."

Since our model is multidimensional, it is inherently probabilistic. We argue that social investment policies, just like any social policy, differ on several dimensions, including eligibility, generosity, provision, and financing—in short, regarding their functions and distributive profiles, as discussed in Chapter 1 of this volume. Furthermore, various strategies of social policy development are debated simultaneously (e.g., social investment and social protectionism). Hence, variable coalitions can form both in the arena of electoral politics and in the arena of producer group politics (as well as, of course, across these arenas).

Therefore, our model is radically non-deterministic. It allows for agency and choice, as well as for potentially inconsistent or incoherent policy strategies. From this more open and probabilistic perspective, which results from placing politics and coalitional dynamics front and center, our approach is closest to two related theoretical contributions on mass politics and producer group politics in contemporary political economy: "constrained partisanship" and "growth strategies." The constrained partisanship framework (Beramendi et al., 2015) theorizes about institutional reform options of political parties and governments—called "feasibility sets"—in different contexts of institutional legacies and structural demands. In this model, social investment is a feasible, but never necessary, option in most contexts, but not in all, depending on the preexisting ratio of consumption to investment spending and on the relative size and power of new versus old middle-class voters (Beramendi et al., 2015, p. 29). The framework acknowledges the multidimensionality of the political space and thus the indeterminacy of coalition formation and outcomes.

The growth strategies framework similarly theorizes the leeway and choice sets of political decision-makers in different varieties of export- or demand-led production regimes (Hassel & Palier, 2021a). It focuses on producer groups—employers and trade unions—as key actors in political decision-making but also places political choice front and center. Again, social investment is one political strategy but only one among others; and its prevalence is highly conditional on the production regime, actor preferences, and other policy choices regarding the institutions organizing the economy.

While these two approaches confer very different theoretical and empirical weight on electoral and producer group politics, they are similar in their focus on agency and coalition-building and in the acknowledgment that social investment reforms are the result of political conflict and power asymmetries, that they are only one among several possible strategies, and that their actual design will reflect the coalitional politics that brought them about.

All chapters in the two volumes that present the output of our project situate their analysis and their findings in this theoretical framework. They usually focus on a subset of factors and specific dependent variables, but they adhere to the joint frame of reference in order to produce an integrated understanding of the political factors that are conducive to or prohibitive of particular social investment reform strategies. The following section develops more concrete, testable hypotheses to explain the politicization of social investment, the type of policy field and function that is likely to prevail in a particular context, and the coalitional politics that are likely to lead to a particular distributive profile of social investment reforms.

In order to address and test such a wide range of research questions, our project relies on a mixed-methods strategy, of course. Depending on the particular aspect of the theoretical framework chapters seek to explain, they make use of administrative, media, or public opinion data for large-N statistical analyses, they content-code reforms for more mid-range quantitative analyses, or they rely on case studies to causally trace the prevailing coalitional dynamics.

2.3. DETERMINANTS OF SOCIAL INVESTMENT POLITICIZATION AND SOCIAL INVESTMENT REFORM STRATEGIES

This section develops a range of hypotheses at a relatively abstract level, both with regard to the factors driving social investment politicization as well as with regard to the social investment policy fields and their functions (skill creation, preservation, and mobilization) that are likely to prevail in different contexts. The hypotheses also involve the actors and actor coalitions that we would expect to drive particular distributive profiles (inclusive, stratified, or targeted) of social investment reform strategies.

2.3.1. Social investment politicization

The first question we are interested in is under what conditions social investment is likely to become a politicized issue on the welfare reform agenda. In other words, how does social investment—among the many different options on the menu of welfare reform strategies in the 21st century—become a visible and explicit option on a country's reform agenda, if at all? We refer to this as the "politicization" of social investment. Broadly defined, *politicization* refers to the rising importance of issue competition around a topic (Green-Pedersen, 2007), that is, whether political actors address the issue, formulate particular positions on it, and devote attention to defending these positions (against opponents) in the political arena. Politicization goes beyond mere agenda-setting as it implies the development of political debate and some level of political conflict. It also goes beyond mere salience as it also refers to competing stances of political actors, which are specific to the policy field in question. At this point of the development of our theoretical framework, however, we focus on salience because the specific policy fields and actor configurations will depend on more proximate factors that we will theorize about in Section 2.3.2. of this chapter.

2.3.1.1. Necessary scope conditions

When theorizing about the politicization of social investment, it makes sense to think about scope conditions, that is, whether there are necessary conditions that are required for social investment to be meaningfully politicized (i.e., contested between different political actors as a genuine policy option). We argue—and test in Chapters 5–7 of this volume—that a certain level of state capacity and democratic politics are indeed such scope conditions.

Regarding *state capacity*, the key element to consider is that social investment requires effective services to be provided to the target populations. Conditional cash transfers, for instance, cannot be considered social investment policies unless they are accompanied by the services that allow for the implementation of the—usually health- and education-related—conditionality (see Chapters 7 and 13 in this volume). As long as states cannot provide these services or cannot even reach the target populations to implement policies, social investment cannot become a real policy reform option; that is, it cannot be effectively politicized in the policymaking arena (e.g., see Chapter 15 in Volume II, [Garritzmann et al., 2022]).

The potential to effectively enact social investment through services is also the mechanism that explains why *programmatic democratic competition* is a scope condition for the politicization of social investment. Clientelistic linkages between patrons and voters not only crowd out resources that would be needed for the development of social investment but also undermine the actual enhancement of human capital and capabilities that is at the very heart of any social investment policy (e.g., see Chapter 6 of this volume). To be clear, full-grown democracy is not a precondition for human capital-developing policies. Even autocratic regimes in lower- and middle-income countries can and have expanded investment-oriented social assistance schemes (see Chapter 5 in this volume). However, we argue that while democracy in itself is not relevant for the politicization of social investment (and countries' reform effort), *within* democracies the quality of democracy, understood as the political linkages between voters and parties, does matter. Consequently, the focus of our project on democratic countries is not because autocrats by definition could or would not pursue human capital expansion. Rather, we chose this focus because we conceive of *politics* (and mass politics in particular) in a way that presupposes democratic interest representation and competition, as well as programmatic competition between different parties or interest representatives. Hence, if social investment proposals are brought forward in the absence of state capacity and programmatic competition, they fulfill alternative political functions (e.g., clientelistic ones) and cannot be seen as the actual, valid politicization of social investment.

2.3.1.2. Probabilistic scope conditions

Beyond state capacity and a certain level of programmatic democratic linkages, we identify no other necessary scope conditions for social investment to become a real political option. Rather, institutional legacies (notably the level of welfare state "maturation") and structural change (notably the state of capitalist development) appear to be *probabilistic* factors, which may enhance or reduce the likelihood that social investment would become politicized, but should not be considered necessary.

Let us first discuss the role of *institutional legacies*. While in the more advanced, mature welfare states of Western democracies, social investment is oftentimes conceptualized in terms of a "further development" or "next stage" relative to the preceding compensation-oriented welfare state (Hemerijck, 2017; Morel et al., 2012)—a stage ridden with hard choices and trade-offs (Garritzmann et al., 2018; Häusermann et al., 2021)—a mature welfare state is not a precondition for the politicization of social investment. There is no reason to assume that welfare states would necessarily have to go through a phase of "compensation maturation" for social investment to be politicized or that such a compensation-oriented phase would necessarily lead to the politicization of social investment. In the "truncated welfare states" of many Latin American countries (Holland, 2018), for instance, the focus of the social policy agenda in the first two decades of the 21st century has focused strongly on social security and poverty relief for the lower classes, in particular for people in the informal sector. This may lead to a "residual"—or, better, targeted—expansion of social policy, but these policy goals can be pursued by either social compensation or social investment or both at the same time (see Chapter 14 in Volume II [Garritzmann et al., 2022]). Hence, there is no (logical or temporal) precedence of a fully developed compensatory welfare state on social investment. Furthermore, several countries in Central and Eastern Europe, especially in the Visegrád region, indeed have developed, "mature" social insurance welfare states (Cerami & Vanhuysse, 2009; Inglot, 2008) and yet largely avoid the politicization of social investment (see Chapter 8 in Volume II [Garritzmann et al., 2022]). Hence, a certain type or level of preexisting welfare state is not a scope condition for the politicization of social investment.

The development of the *knowledge economy* and more so the adoption of a "knowledge economy strategy" by governments are somewhat stronger (but still probabilistic) factors affecting the politicization of social investment. The link is more political than functionalist, even though the demand for skilled labor might explain why economic tertiarization correlates positively with social investment even outside of democracies (see Chapter 5 in this volume). Politically, however, the stage of tertiarization, as well as educational and occupational upgrading, affects both the size of different constituencies that might claim or oppose social investment and the stakes of these policy choices. Hence, it is in the most advanced capitalist democracies that preferences toward traditional consumptive social policies differ most strongly from preferences toward social investment (e.g., Busemeyer & Garritzmann, 2017; Fossati & Häusermann, 2014; Garritzmann et al., 2018). In particular, it is mostly knowledge economies that display the sizeable and politically mobilized new middle-class constituencies that articulate societal demands for social investment explicitly and distinctively (Häusermann & Palier, 2017; see Chapter 12 in this volume for an empirical overview of the differences in the relative size of different occupational groups and their preference profiles). Where the knowledge economy is less developed, other actors such as experts and bureaucrats are likely to become the key actors in the politics of social investment (if social investment appears on the public agenda at all). In such conditions, the link between socio-structural transformations and political demand regarding social investment is likely to be less tight, and policymaking is supposedly driven more strongly by other factors (e.g., ideational influences, international organizations, and the like[3]) than by the bottom-up political and societal demands that are to some extent endogenous in the knowledge economy.

Beyond shaping the demand side of policymaking, however, the knowledge economy, of course, also affects the politicization of social investment through its effects on supply-side preferences and the priorities of bureaucrats, employers, and producer groups more generally. On the technocratic side, international and supranational organizations are increasingly likely to promote social investment policies as an integral part of a coherent political strategy furthering the development of knowledge economies (see Chapter 3 in this volume). On the side of producer groups, the demands from business organizations in particular are likely to be conditional on the interplay between their demand for enhanced human capital and skills and the existing supply thereof. Where the labor market demand for highly skilled labor is large and sustained (in extremis, a scarcity of skilled labor), we expect business to become a protagonist of the politicization of social investment (see Chapters 8, 9, and 14 in this volume), potentially stirring political conflict between market liberal and conservative forces within the right-wing political spectrum (see Chapter 6 in Volume II [Garritzmann et al., 2022]).

A final important remark here is, of course, that the development of a knowledge economy is itself not an exogenous influence on welfare politics. It can be part and parcel of a political growth strategy (Hassel & Palier, 2020a). Where this is the case, social investment is certainly likely to become a politicized reform option. However, it can also become politicized despite governments or economic elites, if the latter should actively choose to divest. In this case, whether social investment becomes politicized or is absent from the agenda of reform options depends on the level of friction between structural or external constraints and government strategies and on the presence of competing political entrepreneurs.

To conclude, a mature welfare state and the emergence of the knowledge economy are expected to be conducive, but not necessary, factors to the politicization of social investment as one option of welfare reform.

---

3. Ideational dynamics by themselves are likely to be neither necessary nor sufficient for the politicization of social investment at the level of countries. Certain countries implemented social investment long before international and supranational organizations put it on the agenda. Rather, ideational dynamics can acquire particular significance in certain domestic political contexts (e.g., if bureaucrats or strong political leaders are leading actors of social investment politicization) (see Chapter 15 in Volume II [Garritzmann et al., 2022]).

2.3.2. Social investment reform strategies

Once social investment has become politicized in a particular context, the second step in theorizing about the politics of social investment consists of explaining the variety of resulting substantive policy reform strategies.[4] We analytically divide this question into two: on the one hand, explaining the main *goals and functions* social investment reforms pursue and, on the other hand, the *distributive profile* of these reforms. We suggest that the prevailing goals and functions depend primarily on the interaction between institutional legacies and structural-economic and demographic developments and that the distributive profile inherent in policy reforms depends primarily on the political actors and coalitions driving these reforms and reform proposals.

2.3.2.1. Explaining goals and functions: Human capital creation, mobilization, or preservation

Social investment policies can pursue one or several of three goals and functions (see also Chapter 1 in this volume): investment in the development of human capabilities and skills (*human capital creation*), investment in the mobilization of human capital for labor market participation and individual as well as aggregate employment performance (*human capital mobilization*), and investment in the preservation and improvement of human skills and capabilities to better handle life events and transitions (*human capital preservation*). In order to be classified as a social investment policy in our understanding, a policy must aim to achieve at least one of the aforementioned goals and functions.[5]

Certain policy fields obviously coincide more closely or more loosely with these different goals and functions. Education policies, vocational education and training, early childhood education and care policies, cash transfers conditional on school attendance and health checkups, and investments in the quality of teaching staff are typical examples of human capital–creating policies. Active labor market policies, work–life balance policies, and policies of active aging belong to the realm of human capital–mobilizing reform strategies. Finally, short and well-paid parental leave schemes, social insurance for atypical work contracts, and certain types of retraining policies are part of the package of human capital–preserving policy instruments. However, we do not assign specific policy fields to functions or goals as the same instrument, for example, early childhood education and care policies, can pursue different or several goals at the same time (in this case human capital creation for young children and human capital mobilization for parents). Hence, when theorizing about the determinants of policy

---

4. Similar to Hassel and Palier (2021a), we do not use the term "strategy" in a purely procedural or instrumental way here, but as—with reference to Mintzberg (1978)—"a pattern in the stream of decisions." Hence, our focus here is on substantive policy decisions.

5. Negative employment incentives only such as sanctions and benefit reductions are precisely not part of our understanding of the social investment logic (cf. Bonoli, 2013; Taylor-Gooby, 2005).

strategies, the intentions and goals associated with a reform are more important than the policy field as such.

While several goals and functions can obviously appear on the reform agendas of countries and regions, the prevailing objectives and fields are likely to be context-specific. A country's policy legacies reflect the economic production strategy and related welfare state policies it has pursued in the past. They entail mechanisms of path dependency, but through interaction with structural developments, they also shape the type and prevalence of social risks and economic needs in a particular context.

We operationalize these legacies in terms of the ratio of welfare resources that are bound in policies entailing immediate (consumptive) versus future (investment) distributive effects (Beramendi et al., 2015). This legacy in terms of an investment/consumption ratio structures the relative salience of particular problem diagnoses and thus policy functions pursued in a country or geographic region (Beramendi et al., 2015; Hassel & Palier, 2020a). To stay in line with the terminology developed in this chapter, we label the dimension of consumptive policies "compensation" as they refer to income- and welfare-compensating policies. This allows us to deduce specific challenges that the welfare state is confronted with, and based on this, we can theorize what a "social investment" approach to these challenges would look like. Of course, this by no means implies that a country will follow such an approach. Functional problem pressure does not directly explain the type of problems policymakers perceive as relevant, the diagnosis they make, or the solutions they adopt. But the specific institutional context interacts with structural developments and leads to different ways of conceiving of the "problem" at hand for different types of welfare and production regimes (Iversen & Wren, 1998; Scharpf & Schmidt, 2000). Whether, to what extent, and with which distributive implications these problems are then addressed via social investment reforms in different countries will depend on political factors further theorized in the next section of this chapter. Figure 2.2 stylizes the profiles of such legacies in a two-dimensional space (loosely based on Häusermann & Palier, 2017), in which the quadrants—not by accident—tend to relate to established theories of institutional regimes.

In countries that build on a legacy of both consumptive and investive welfare policies (upper left quadrant of Figure 2.2), all three goals and functions are likely to be present on the agenda and in the political debate. The main challenge, however, refers to the *sustainability* of simultaneously maintaining these policies universally, in fiscal terms (e.g., tax levels) as well as in social and political terms (in light of political polarization, migration, and international integration). In these countries (think of the Nordic welfare states, for example), the politics of social investment are likely to center around the question *for whom* such an encompassing social investment strategy can and should be pursued (Lindvall & Rueda, 2014). Indeed, even though broad support for social investment goals in this context is the result of strong positive feedback mechanisms of existing (and

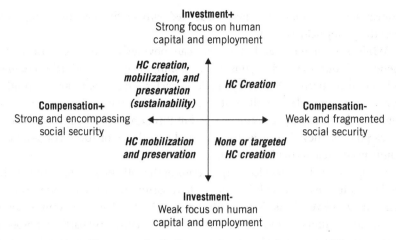

Figure 2.2 Institutional legacies and prevailing social investment functions in the political debate. Note: HC stands for "human capital, skills and capabilities".

long-established) policies, there is always a risk that a (growing, upwardly mobile) middle class would consider opting out of universal coverage by embracing policies that would allow for more choice or lower tax burdens (see Chapter 2 in Volume II [Garritzmann et al., 2022]).

The situation is very different where the policy legacy is weaker on compensation and relatively stronger on investment (upper right quadrant of Figure 2.2), a context exemplified by liberal Anglo-Saxon countries, partly by countries of North East Asia, and by the Baltics. As these countries tend to exhibit relatively good employment performance and flexible labor markets, mobilizing human capital is not the key challenge when considering the interaction of institutional legacies with economic structural change.[6] Rather, their relative emphasis on investment in the past and particularly the scarce provision of compensation policies[7] tend to bring skill development and education (how, by whom, and to whom it should be provided in what quality) to the center when debating social investment policies, possibly with a focus on the low-skilled who are likely to struggle particularly in this context.

---

6. At least as long as they experience a relatively sustainable demographic development. When the demographic development is very unfavorable, as in North East Asian countries, and this problem is reinforced by weak female labor market participation, human capital mobilization becomes, of course, a challenge as well.

7. Comparatively analyzing education and social policies in the United States and Europe, Heidenheimer (1981) theorized already in 1973 that education policies and social policies were functional equivalents so that some countries tilt more toward educational investments (the Anglo-Saxon world), whereas others focus on compensation (Continental Europe). In still other countries (e.g., Scandinavia), however, education and social policies are treated as complementary.

Countries that have relied more heavily on compensation policies in the past (lower left quadrant of Figure 2.2) generally have rather effective income protection schemes, but they face the challenges of rather weak employment rates as well as segmented or dualized labor markets (mostly continental European countries as well as North East Asian countries, specifically with re-gard to female employment rates, and several economically more advanced Latin American countries). These institutional legacies (and rigidities) create friction with the increasing demand for (and scarcity of) high-skilled labor, with the increasing demand for personal services, and with changing family and gender patterns. Given the prevalence of new social risks and dualization, the politicization of social investment in such a context will likely center on easing transitions into the labor market, increasing labor market participation (especially of women and outsiders), and preserving skills through periods of non- or atypical employment. Consequently, we would expect human capital mobilization and preservation to take a key place in discussions of social in-vestment reform strategies.

Finally, Southern European countries and most Latin American countries gen-erally have had a tradition of highly fragmented labor markets *and* welfare states (lower right quadrant of Figure 2.2). They tend to be only weakly productivity-oriented (i.e., they have hardly any social investment legacy to build on), and ac-tual poverty and poverty risks remain a key challenge when it comes to welfare. Just like the North East Asian and continental European economies, they are relatively ill prepared to meet the structural challenges of changing capitalism to-ward knowledge- and service-based growth. However, not least because of their fragmented and dualized welfare institutions, economic-structural change tends to occur more slowly. Massive emphasis on human capital creation would not be met with adequate labor demand on behalf of employers (see Chapter 8 of this volume). Hence, social investment policies in these contexts are likely to re-main comparatively narrow, focused on residual forms of outsider support and activation, and often of lower quality (empirically see Chapters 5 and 13 in this volume). In the case of the Latin American countries still plagued by high levels of poverty, the poverty-alleviating aspect of social investment programs is very important. The conditional cash transfer programs in Latin American countries (increasingly also in Africa and South East Asia) are among the most visible examples of such a debate centered on investment in breaking the intergenera-tional cycle of poverty.

We do not adopt a functionalist perspective. The goals and functions that empirically prevail in a particular context do not directly follow and cannot be derived straightforwardly from either structural-economic developments or the preexisting institutional framework. Rather, it is the interaction between the two that allows us to theorize how (i.e., under what conditions) social invest-ment reforms are likely to be politicized in terms of concrete reform proposals. Again, our argument is probabilistic: There can, of course, and most likely will be domestic or international actors pushing for other, contextually more deviant welfare reforms and strategies. Furthermore, political actors can actively promote economic growth strategies that defy endogenous tendencies. However, we would expect such claims to resonate less strongly in the respective domestic political arenas.

2.3.2.2. Explaining distributive policy designs: Inclusive, stratifying, and targeting social investment

As a final step in the theorization of social investment reform strategies, we address their *distributive policy design*. Reforms in very different policy fields and with very different policy goals in terms of creation, mobilization, and preservation of human skills can also vary significantly with regard to the distribution of benefits and costs they entail for different social strata. This distributive profile of reforms is, of course, a key dimension of any analysis of social policy—in some sense it is the very core of such analyses. We theorize that the choice of distributive profile depends primarily on the political actors and coalitions who propose, defend, or oppose these reforms and their alliances and coalitions. To be clear, this crystallization of our theoretical focus on distinctive sets of variables at the different stages of the theoretical framework is, of course, an analytical simplification. As developed throughout this chapter, the very actors themselves, their power relations, their preferences, and their alliances are structured and influenced by institutional legacies, by the structural and ideational imprints these institutions hold and perpetuate, and by exogenous structural and ideational dynamics. However, we focus more narrowly and immediately on political actors and their interaction here because we want to identify the coalitional dynamics that can be expected to underlie the distributive design of particular social investment policies.

Hence, this step of the theoretical framework mainly focuses on the meso-level of organized political actors (especially parties, employers, unions, interest groups, and experts) who participate directly in political decision-making processes. This actor-centered perspective is key also because political actors actively influence the framing of policy proposals, which is as crucial in the area of social investment as in any social policy reform. Policies, and certainly social investment policies, can embody different rationales, from activation to redistribution, education, human capital mobilization, gender equality, or social inclusion. Therefore, the processes of framing are key for coalition formation as they make actor alliances malleable and prone to political exchange and ambiguous agreements (Palier, 2005; Häusermann, 2010; Häusermann & Kübler, 2011). In this sense, the ambiguities of social investment instruments are an integral part of the politics of social investment (Busemeyer et al., 2018; Häusermann, 2018); therefore, a close empirical focus on actors and policymaking processes is required for their analysis.

The comparative welfare state literature distinguishes between three main distributive profiles social policies can take: they can be 1) *inclusive*, that is, encompassing and egalitarian, including all or large parts of society in a joint policy scheme, with benefits being widely and relatively equally distributed, thereby creating a large societal coalition of stakeholders; 2) *stratified*, distributing different benefits to different (vertical) segments of the society, thereby also creating a large coalition of stakeholders but a more fragmented one, stabilizing the existing stratification of society; or 3) *targeted* and needs-based, channeling benefits to lower social classes and precarious social groups only, which may target particularly pressing needs but at the same time lacks the political effect of broadening the societal support base for the policy as such.

These three distributive principles have been at the heart of welfare state analysis for many decades (with Esping-Andersen [1990] as well as Korpi & Palme [1998] providing probably the most relevant and renowned theorizations). However, their variety has so far been studied mostly with regard to social compensation policies (i.e., income stabilization and transfers). It is one of the central arguments of this volume that social investment policies should and can be conceptualized using the very same categories of distributive effects. As they simultaneously pursue the twin goals of social inclusion and economic prosperity, there is a risk—also rampant in the scholarly literature—of portraying social investment policies as a "magic bullet," devoid of distributive costs and flaws. Given the cumulative knowledge of comparative welfare state research, however, holding social investment policies to such a standard would be highly inadequate theoretically and implausible empirically. Just as pension systems or unemployment insurance can be more or less inclusive and more or less redistributive, so can social investment policies. But because of their distinctive functions regarding the creation, mobilization, or preservation of human capital and capabilities, the preferences of different political actors relative to the distributive profiles of social investment policies may differ from their preferences when it comes to consumptive policies.

When proposals are debated and decisions are made, organized actors may act either as *protagonists* (i.e., actively pushing in favor of some social investment policies), as *consenters* (agreeing to support such proposals if they believe that their constituencies would not lose or if they obtain some concession in other domains), or as *antagonists* (opposing such orientation of social policies) (see Figure 2.1).[8] In the following, we develop a few rather general hypotheses on who the relevant actors are in social investment reform politics and what positions they are likely to defend in terms of social investment reform strategies. The goal here is not—and cannot be—to theorize about the specific alliances

---

8. Following the contribution of Emmanuele Pavolini and Martin Seeleib-Kaiser to our project (Chapter 9 in this volume), we adopt the vocabulary suggested by Walter Korpi (2006) to define employers' position regarding the development of welfare states across history; however, we apply the vocabulary to all kinds of organized actors involved in the politics of social investment.

in every policy function and context. It is only the concluding chapters of this volume (Chapter 16) and its sister volume (Chapter 17 [Garritzmann et al., 2022]) that can take stock of all empirical findings regarding the specific actor configurations that are likely to lead to a particular social investment reform strategy. Rather, our goal here is to pave the way for empirically linking distinctive actor configurations to social investment reform strategies. When theorizing about the preferences of political actors, we focus mostly on the societal groups and constituencies whose interests these actors defend or represent. Here again we distinguish our approach from more culturalist approaches, which tend to consider ideational dynamics and hegemonic discourses to predominate in structuring actor preferences (e.g., Baccaro & Pontusson, 2019).

The set of actors who are politically relevant in social policy reform processes is not the same in every circumstance. When social investment is a salient, "loud" topic on the domestic reform agenda, the electoral arena of mass politics is the most important arena to consider. If mass politics is a decisive arena, then it is important to consider not only governments and political parties but also public opinion and attitudes in the respective electoral constituencies, to which parties in particular are sensitive (see Chapter 3 of Volume II [Garritzmann et al., 2022]). By contrast, when social investment is not a salient issue, interest groups and/or national and international bureaucrats and experts are likely to be the most important "quiet" actors, depending on the development of the intermediary representative system (Culpepper, 2010).

We start by discussing the roles of non-partisan actors, that is, those not associated with a particular political party (i.e., experts, bureaucrats, and interest organizations). Experts are relevant actors for political decision-making, especially when either the political-representative democratic system is relatively weak (such as in Latin American countries; see Chapter 15 of Volume II [Garritzmann et al., 2022]) or when there is a strong (financial) dependency of domestic politics on international organizations, which has been the case not only in Latin America but also in the development of social policy reforms in Central and Eastern Europe and, more recently, in several countries across Southern Europe. Under conditions of strong constraint and/or weak contestation and politicization, experts and bureaucrats can have more direct impact on policy proposals. There is no specific distributive profile of reforms that we assume to be associated with such a direct impact, however.

The role, importance, and position of interest organizations representing labor and capital are similarly context-dependent but somewhat more closely associated with distinctive distributive preferences. Labor organizations (i.e., trade unions) should at first glance be expected to be protagonists of inclusive social investment (see Chapter 10 of this volume) as these policies are conducive to higher employment rates (Kenworthy, 2017; Nelson & Stephens, 2012), particularly in permanent and high-quality jobs. However, our hypotheses in this regard need to be more differentiated. Ample research has shown that trade union preferences are sensitive to the type and composition of their (current and targeted) membership (e.g., Mosimann & Pontusson, 2018). Hence, the role and preferences of unions are likely to be conditional on their membership structure (i.e., representational concerns) as well as on institutional factors.[9] Where unions have weak legitimacy and highly selective membership, not only is their role supposedly more marginal to begin with but their position regarding social investment reforms is highly uncertain. Selective industrial sector unions or fragmented unions that organize specific and more privileged sectors of the labor market may well oppose inclusive social investment reforms as they would threaten the (insider) advantages of their members. Teachers' unions in Latin America (see Chapters 6 and 7 in this volume; Chambers-Ju & Finger, 2016) or industrial sector unions in the Visegrád countries (see Chapter 8 of Volume II [Garritzmann et al., 2022]) can be regarded as examples of such a dynamic. Moreover, social investment policies oftentimes target social risk groups that are not the core constituencies of trade unions and whose policy concerns are not a priority on the trade unions' agendas, such as early childhood education and care or education policies more generally (Bonoli, 2005; Häusermann, 2010, p. 5; Thelen, 2014). Hence, there is a risk that trade unions approach these policy fields with a more selective focus on the situation of the professionals in the respective services (schools, childcare centers), rather than with a (simultaneous) focus on the societal benefits for users.

Consequently, we would expect trade unions to be protagonists of inclusive social investment reforms when they represent encompassing membership, particularly in processes in which policies are closely related to labor market protection. However, when reforms are outside their key policy concerns, we would expect trade unions (even trade unions with encompassing membership) to act more in the role of consenters. We would then anticipate that more selective, fragmented trade unions would be protagonists or consenters of stratified social investment, in order to protect more narrowly the interests of their members. However, when confronted with a shrinking insiders' constituency, trade unions may endorse (inclusive) social investment in order to conquer new socioeconomic groups in a logic of influence (see Chapter 10 in this volume).

Business and employer organizations also hold a specific place in the theorization of actor configurations relative to social investment reform strategies. Quite distinctively from social compensation policies, the literature has theorized and found business groups to even be among protagonists of social investment reforms in some contexts, especially when such policies are intended to expand labor supply in times of scarcity (Fleckenstein & Seeleib-Kaiser, 2011; Korpi, 2006; see Chapters 9 and 14 in this volume). If social investment policies are

---

9. Therefore, Durazzi and Geyer (Chapter 10 in this volume) as well as Altamirano and Zarate-Tenorio (Chapter 11 in this volume) analyze how micro-, meso-, and macro-factors condition unions' preferences.

perceived as a (cheaper) alternative to income compensation policies, employer groups may also act as consenters of reform even when there is no immediate labor shortage. However, their primarily economic rationale for supporting these policies selectively implies three correlates. First, they will likely be more involved in social investment policies that are closely linked with labor market issues (such as parental leave or vocational training). The second correlate projects heterogeneity across employer associations, depending on their specific labor demand and occupational structure. Third, employer organizations are likely to support stratified (or perhaps targeted) social investment policies since reducing inequality is less important than creating specific and selective incentives for particular groups of beneficiaries. These hypotheses regarding employer preferences should be rather universal across institutional contexts, even though the actual prevalence of problems and incentives is likely to vary across regions.

When it comes to the electoral arena, governments appear to be highly important actors both because they convey a political demand via parties and because they respond to the ideational and structural demands of interest organizations and international actors. Hence, governments are likely to be policy protagonists if the electoral institutions allow them some leeway to initiate, frame, and manage reform processes, allowing them to shape social investments in line with their policy, vote, and office motivations. To understand the actual material and distributive social investment reform strategies governments promote, however, partisanship, on the one hand,[10] and growth strategies, on the other,[11] are key. Where governments start from a compensation-based welfare system and engage in a knowledge economy strategy, they are likely to act as protagonists and push (possibly among other proposals) for stratified policies of human capital creation and mobilization, not unlike employer organizations.

In most contexts, however, we expect that the distributive profile of social investment policies is related primarily to partisanship. At the level of political parties, we suggest that left-wing parties advocate more inclusive social investment policies than right-wing parties, for both ideological and electoral reasons. "More inclusive" may mean egalitarian, but it may also mean to privilege stratified over purely targeted measures, in order to expand eligibility beyond the lower social strata and to build a broader support coalition. As explained in Section 2.2.2, the electorate of mainstream left-wing parties has changed significantly across developed democracies since the 1980s, with mostly middle-class voters prevailing among the core constituencies today (Gingrich & Häusermann, 2015). Given their stronger focus on the needs of new risk groups, women, and the

10. See, for example, Ansell (2010), Busemeyer (2015), Iversen and Stephens (2008), and Manow et al. (2018); see also various chapters from this project, for example, Chapters 13 and 15 in this volume and Chapters 12 and 13 in Volume II (Garritzmann et al., 2022).
11. See, for example, Hassel and Palier (2021b) and Kazepov and Ranci (2017); see also various chapters from this project, such as Chapters 5 and 7–9 in Volume II (Garritzmann et al., 2022).

high-skilled more generally, we would expect socioculturally progressive new left parties to place stronger emphasis on inclusive social investment, whereas more industrial worker–oriented left parties might prioritize social compensation and act merely as consenters to inclusive social investment reforms (Beramendi et al., 2015; Häusermann et al., 2021).

Electoral realignment is also relevant to consider when theorizing about the positions of right-wing political parties. Hypotheses regarding moderate right parties can follow lines similar to those of employer organizations. Overall they are rather unlikely to be protagonists of inclusive social investment, but they may consent to social investment (as an alternative to social compensation) and may even push actively for stratified provision of social investment services, not least to capture potential support from centrist (female) voters (e.g., Morgan, 2013; Schwander, 2018). In countries where targeted social policies have traditionally prevailed, right-wing parties are a priori unlikely to support any social investment. The case is somewhat different when it comes to the radical (populist) right or right-wing nationalist parties. In line with their strong electoral affinity to the industrial working class (and self-employed small business), as well as their opposition to economic and societal modernization and its correlates, these parties are expected to be the most vocal antagonists of social investment in general (Enggist & Pinggera, 2021; Häusermann et al., 2020; Michel & Lefkofridi, 2017; Pinggera, 2020; Rathgeb, 2021).

In terms of class coalitions, we hence argue that, in many countries, members of the educated middle class are most likely the key supporters of social investment. In the developed world, the educated middle class is predominantly represented by the left parties (social democrats, green, or social liberal parties, depending on the country). Even though the educated middle class is the main supporter of social investment, this class by itself is generally not big or strong enough to carry a policy re-orientation to success, not even in the most likely case of Nordic Europe (see Chapter 2 of Volume II [Garritzmann et al., 2022]). It is certainly true that the size of the educated middle class varies greatly across countries (depending itself strongly on the welfare state legacy; see Oesch [2015]): in the Nordic countries, for instance, educated people in interpersonal service occupations represent about a fourth of the workforce, whereas the same group remains way below 10% in the Southern European countries (Beramendi et al., 2015; see also Chapter 12 in this volume). Hence, there is a need for cross-class coalitions to press for actual policy change (Häusermann & Palier, 2017). We see potential for two main class coalitions: a middle class–business alliance, on the one hand, and a middle class–working class alliance, on the other hand. The policy packages likely supported and adopted by these two alliances obviously differ, especially in terms of the emphasis they are likely to place on different distributive profiles of the social investment reform strategy.

Based on these basic considerations regarding class and actor preferences, we would expect coalitions led by left-wing parties or governments to advocate inclusive social investment policies, especially if they ally with working-class constituencies. In such cases, business and possibly parts of the right may act at best as consenters. By contrast, when business or moderate right parties act as protagonists of coalition formation (even if with the left), we would expect more stratified reforms to prevail. Trade unions could be consenters in both scenarios, while (populist) radical right parties are expected to be the most important antagonists across institutional and economic contexts. It is more difficult to identify leading protagonists for targeted social investment reforms, especially in the more developed capitalist democracies. In less developed welfare states, where there is a stronger focus (domestically and by international organizations) on poverty and poverty relief and where existing (compensatory) policies fail to cover lower social strata (mainly because of informal labor markets, lacking resources, or state capacity problems), we would expect left-wing partisan actors and governments to be (the only) protagonists of targeted expansion of human capital creation among the poor.

2.4. CONCLUDING REMARKS

In this chapter, we have discussed the key concepts of this volume's approach to the politics of social investment. We examine social investment policies as one potential answer to the social, economic, and political challenges that welfare states are facing in the 21st century. Social investment is not the only possible response: Market liberalism, social protectionism, and basic income strategies are alternatives that governments, parties, and interest organizations can pursue. However, social investment policies are the most direct and explicit answer to the joint social and economic challenges that come with the emergence of the knowledge economy in 21st-century capitalism.

The politicization of social investment (i.e., the development of a conflictive, salient debate about the type and design of social investment reforms) is neither universal nor straightforward. To become a viable political and politicized option, social investment needs to rely on a modicum of state capacity, and—under conditions of democratic politics—it requires programmatic linkages between parties and voters. Beyond these two basic conditions, welfare state maturity, the emergence of a knowledge economy, and electoral realignment are probabilistic, but not necessary, conditions that are likely to contribute to the politicization of social investment on the menu of welfare reform strategies.

We have refrained explicitly from defining social investment policies via policy fields. Rather, the goals and functions of social investment are key, and they can be pursued by means of highly different social policies, for example, education policies, labor market policies, and even pension policies. As developed in this chapter, these functions are the creation, mobilization, and/or preservation of human capital and human capabilities. We expect social investment to be politicized in terms of one or several of these functions, depending mostly on institutional policy legacies that, in interaction with structural socioeconomic changes, shape both the challenges that emerge as well as the ways in which political actors perceive these challenges and potential solutions. Therefore, we mainly expect regional variation in the emphasis that different countries place on human capital creation, mobilization, or preservation.

Lastly, the distributive design of social investment policies can be as heterogeneous as the distributive design of social compensation policies, irrespective of the policy field and function concerned: Benefits can be targeted toward the poor, they can be stratified toward specific social strata, and they can be inclusive and thereby contribute to alliances between lower- and middle-class beneficiaries. As determinants of these distributive profiles, we point primarily to the likely coalitional alignments between political actors driving reforms, these actor configurations being themselves influenced by institutional legacies and structural developments.

By theorizing about the politicization, functions and goals, and distributive profiles of social investment policies sequentially in a combined framework (see Figure 2.1) as the outcome of a complex interplay of ideational and structural dynamics, institutional legacies, societal changes, the interaction of political supply and demand, and, ultimately, coalition-building, we have developed an explanatory framework that is encompassing enough to account for the politics of social investment across highly different world regions. At the same time, the framework is testable and distinctive in its emphasis on political agency and choice, against functionalist, structural-deterministic, and culturalist approaches that have a strong voice in the current scholarly literature.

On the basis of the above framework, we expect parties of the "New Left" (i.e., left-wing parties which emphasize cultural liberalism, universalism, and socially progressive values) to be the most ardent and most explicit protagonists of social investment policies. We foresee the radical (populist) right as the most likely and vocal antagonist. With these poles of a politicized debate, it becomes also clear why we would expect social investment to be most politicized where electoral realignment has progressed the furthest: The occupational and socio-structural effects of the emerging knowledge economy in terms of job polarization and new social needs and demands contribute to both electoral realignment and the politicization of social investment in terms of new electoral divides. Where social investment is less salient in the electoral arena, the same political divide can unfold in terms of antagonistic growth strategies between governments privileging the strengthening of dynamic, high-skilled services and those prioritizing economic growth through manufacturing or lower-wage production of goods and services. In less developed capitalist contexts, we expect left-wing partisan actors to promote inclusive or targeted social investment with a strong focus on poverty relief, against the interests of actors who defend stratification of old or new social policy schemes.

The roles and positions of trade unions and employer organizations are not straightforward as they depend on membership structure, the type of labor demand in a particular context, and macro-institutional factors. Overall, however, we would expect these actors—as well as moderate right parties—to be more likely to advocate stratified social investment policies that either preserve existing distinctions or mobilize or benefit specific social groups in a less inclusive and egalitarian way.

To what extent do the implications of our theoretical framework ultimately resonate with the alignments and predictions concerning traditional social compensation schemes? And to what extent do we expect the distributive profile of social investment policies to match the regime characteristics that have been conceptualized for decades on the basis of social compensation policies? To some extent, a match between existing welfare regimes and the politics of social investment indeed exists, as can be expected given the endogenous and interrelated nature of institutional and structural developments and their link to actors. We indeed expect political agency in favor of inclusive social investment to be strongest in the universal welfare states and to some extent in the most advanced capitalist economies. Similarly, we expect stratification to prevail more strongly where institutions and structures have reinforced stratified policies over decades, such as in Continental or Southern Europe, North East Asia, and the economically more advanced welfare states of Latin America. And we, of course, predict that stratification will be highly politicized and present (vs. inclusiveness or targeting) in those contexts where preexisting welfare states are truncated and fragmented such as in Latin America and to some extent Southern Europe.

However, we also anticipate important and notable deviations with regard to the determinants of social investment, three of which we point out here. For one, while trade unions have been conceptualized as key protagonists of inclusive policies of social compensation, they cannot be seen as the "natural" ally of left-wing protagonists of inclusive social investment since a) they may have reservations regarding the "commodifying" aspect of social investment policies and b) many trade unions do not represent the core constituencies of social investment. Rather they may be merely consenters of social investment or, depending on the context, protagonists of stratified social investment. Second, while employer organizations may be consenters to particular, insurance-based social compensation policies (Mares, 2003), at least some members of business groups are likely to become protagonists of human capital-creating or -mobilizing policies under conditions of labor scarcity. Such a more active role for capital is, of course, likely to remain selective and context-dependent, but—especially in combination with the transformed role of trade unions as key stakeholders of social compensation policies—such a more active role has the potential to alter coalitional patterns and alignments when there is a choice between social investment and social compensation.

Finally, inclusive, stratified, and targeted social compensation policies have been theorized as key policy strategies in social democratic, corporatist, and liberal welfare regimes, respectively. When it comes to social investment, however, there is little reason to expect targeted policies to become a key and prioritized strategy for any political actor. Targeted compensation policies represent the "basic security" that even liberal states provide for people who do not manage to provide for themselves in the labor market. In a social investment logic, targeted social investment policies are likely to be no actor's first choice. Rather, they are likely to be an explicit policy option only where social investment is more fundamentally oriented toward fighting poverty and its transmission in a sustainable and capacitating way. In the more advanced capitalist democracies, the main rival of inclusive or stratifying social investment as a political strategy is thus not targeted social investment but rather social protectionism, as a potential first choice for parts of the left, or market liberalism and commodification, as a potential first choice for the political right. In this way, the alternative options of welfare reform strategies in the 21st century may indirectly also affect the coalitions that drive social investment reform strategies.

REFERENCES

Acemoglu, D. (2002). Technical change, inequality, and the labor market. *Journal of Economic Literature, 40*(1), 7–72.

Amable, B. (2017). *Structural crisis and institutional change in modern capitalism: French capitalism in transition.* Oxford University Press.

Ansell, B. (2010). *From the ballot to the blackboard. The redistributive political economy of education.* Cambridge University Press.

Autor, D. H., Katz, L. F., & Kearney, M. S. (2008). Trends in U.S. wage inequality: Revising the revisionists. *Review of Economics and Statistics, 90*(2), 300–323.

Autor, D. H., Levy, F., & Murnane, R. J. (2003). The skill content of recent technological change: An empirical exploration. *The Quarterly Journal of Economics, 118*(4), 1279–1333.

Baccaro, L., & Pontusson, J. (2016). Rethinking comparative political economy: The growth model perspective. *Politics & Society, 44*(2), 175–207.

Baccaro, L., & Pontusson, J. (2019). *Social blocs and growth models: An analytical framework with Germany and Sweden as illustrative cases* [UNEQUAL DEMOCRACIES Working paper 7]. Université de Genève.

Barrientos, A. (2009). Labour markets and the (hyphenated) welfare regime in Latin America. *Economy and Society, 38*(1), 87–108.

Becher, M., & Pontsson, H. J. (2011). Whose interests do unions represent? Unionization by income in western Europe. In D. Brady (Ed.), *Research in the sociology of work: Vol. 22B. Comparing European workers* (pp. 181–211). Emerald.

Becker, R., & Hecken, A. E. (2009). Why are working-class children diverted from universities? An empirical assessment of the diversion thesis. *European Sociological Review, 25*(2), 233–250.

Beramendi, P., Häusermann, S., Kitschelt, H., & Kriesi, H. (2015). *The politics of advanced capitalism*. Cambridge University Press.

Bogliaccini, J., & Madariaga, A. (2020). Varieties of skills profiles in Latin America: A reassessment of the hierarchical model of capitalism. *Journal of Latin American Studies, 52*(3), 601–631.

Bonoli, G. (2005). The politics of the new social policies. Providing coverage against new social risks in mature welfare states. *Policy and Politics, 33*(3), 431–449.

Bonoli, G. (2007). Time matters: Postindustrialization, new social risks, and welfare state adaptation in advanced industrial democracies. *Comparative Political Studies, 40*(5), 495–520.

Bonoli, G. (2012). Blame avoidance and credit claiming revisited. In G. Bonoli & D. Natali (Eds.), *The politics of the new welfare state* (pp. 93–110). Oxford University Press.

Bonoli, G. (2013). *The origins of active social policy: Labour market and childcare policies in a comparative perspective*. Oxford University Press.

Bonoli, G., & Natali, D. (2012). *The politics of the new welfare state*. Oxford University Press.

Bornschier, S. (2010). *Cleavage politics and the populist right: The new cultural conflict in western Europe*. Temple University Press.

Breen, R., & Jonsson, J. (2005). Inequality of opportunity in comparative perspective: Recent research on educational attainment and social mobility. *Annual Review of Sociology, 31*, 223–243.

Busemeyer, M. R. (2015). *Skills and inequality. Partisan politics and the political economy of education reforms in Western welfare states*. Cambridge University Press.

Busemeyer, M. R., De La Porte, C., Garritzmann, J. L., & Pavolini, E. (2018). The future of the social investment state: Policies, outcomes, and politics. *Journal of European Public Policy, 25*(6), 801–809.

Busemeyer, M. R., & Garritzmann, J. L. (2017). Public opinion on policy and budgetary trade-offs in European welfare states: Evidence from a new comparative survey. *Journal of European Public Policy, 24*(6), 871–889.

Busemeyer, M. R., & Garritzmann, J. L. (2018). Compensation or social investment? Revisiting the link between globalisation and popular demand for the welfare state. *Journal of Social Policy, 48*(3), 427–448.

Cameron, D. R. (1978). The expansion of the public economy: A comparative analysis. *American Political Science Review, 72*(4), 1243–1261.

Cerami, A., & Vanhuysse, P. (2009). *Post-communist welfare pathways. Theorizing social policy transformations in central and eastern Europe.* Palgrave Macmillan.

Chambers-Ju, C., & Finger, L. (2016). Teachers' unions in Mexico: The politics of patronage. In T. Moe & S. Wiborg (Eds.), *The comparative politics of education: Teachers unions and education systems around the world* (pp. 215–238). Cambridge University Press.

Chevalier, T. (2016). Varieties of youth welfare citizenship. Towards a two-dimensional typology. *Journal of European Social Policy, 26*(1), 3–19.

Clegg, D. (2007). Continental drift: On unemployment policy change in Bismarckian welfare states. *Social Policy & Administration, 41*(6), 597–617.

Culpepper, P. (2010). *Quiet politics and business power. Corporate control in Europe and Japan.* Cambridge University Press.

Dancygier, R., & Walter, S. (2015). Globalization, labor market risks and class cleavages. In P. Beramendi, S. Häusermann, H. Kitschelt, & H. Kriesi (Eds.), *The politics of advanced capitalism* (pp. 133–156). Cambridge University Press.

Emmenegger, P., Häusermann, S., Palier, B., & Seeleib-Kaiser, M. (2012). *The age of dualization. The changing face of inequality in deindustrializing societies.* Oxford University Press.

Enggist, M., & Pinggera, M. (2021). Radical right parties and their welfare state stances—Not so blurry after all? *West European Politics.* Advance online publication. https://doi.org/10.1080/01402382.2021.1902115

Esping-Andersen, G. (1985). *Politics against markets: The social democratic road to power.* Princeton University Press.

Esping-Andersen, G. (1990). *The three worlds of welfare capitalism.* Princeton University Press.

Esping-Andersen, G. (1992). The making of a social democratic welfare state. In K. Misgeld (Ed.), *Creating social democracy* (pp. 35–66). Penn State Press.

Esping-Andersen, G. (1993). *Changing classes: Stratification and mobility in post-industrial societies.* Sage.

Esping-Andersen, G. (1999). *Social foundations of postindustrial economies.* Oxford University Press.

Esping-Andersen, G. (2002). A child-centred social investment strategy. In G. Esping-Andersen, G. Duncan, A. Hemerijck, & J. Myles (Eds.), *Why we need a new welfare state* (pp. 26–67). Oxford University Press.

Estévez-Abe, M. (2008). *Welfare and capitalism in postwar Japan.* Cambridge University Press.

Fleckenstein, T., & Seeleib-Kaiser, M. (2011). Cross-national perspectives on firm-level family policies: Britain, Germany, and the US compared. In J. Clasen (Ed.), *Converging worlds of welfare?* (pp. 129–154). Oxford University Press.

Fossati, F., & Häusermann, S. (2014). Social policy preferences and party choice in the 2011 Swiss elections. *Swiss Political Science Review, 20*(4), 590–611.

Frey, C. B., & Osborne, M. A. (2017). The future of employment: How susceptible are jobs to computerisation? *Technological Forecasting and Social Change, 114,* 254–280.

Garritzmann, J. L., Busemeyer, M. R., & Neimanns, E. (2018). Public demand for social investment: New supporting coalitions for welfare state reform in western Europe? *Journal of European Public Policy, 25*(6), 844–861.

Garritzmann, J. L., Häusermann, S., & Palier, B. (Eds.). (2022). *The world politics of social investment: Vol. II. The politics of varying social investment strategies.* Oxford University Press.

Gingrich, J., & Ansell, B. (2015). The dynamics of social investment: Human capital, activation and care. In P. Beramendi, S. Häusermann, H. Kitschelt, & H. Kriesi (Eds.), *The politics of advanced capitalism* (pp. 282–304). Cambridge University Press.

Gingrich, J., & Häusermann, S. (2015). The decline of the working class vote, the reconfiguration of the welfare support coalition and consequences for the welfare state. *Journal of European Social Policy, 25,* 50–75.

Goldin, C., & Katz, L. F. (2008). *The race between education and technology.* Belknap Press of Harvard University Press.

Gough, I. (2019). Universal basic services: A theoretical and moral framework. *The Political Quarterly, 90*(3), 534–542.

Goos, M. Manning, A, & Salomons, A. (2014). Explaining Job Polarization: Routine-Biased Technological Change and Offshoring. *American Economic Review, 104*(8), 2509-2526.

Green-Pedersen, C. (2007). *The reshaping of west European party politics. Agenda-setting and party competition in comparative perspective.* Oxford University Press.

Hall, P. A. (2020). The electoral politics of growth regimes. *Perspectives on Politics, 18*(1), 185–199.

Hall, P. A., & Soskice, D. (2001). *Varieties of capitalism. The institutional foundations of comparative advantage.* Oxford University Press.

Hassel, A., & Palier, B. (2021a). *Growth and welfare in advanced capitalist economies. How have growth regimes evolved?* Oxford University Press.

Hassel, A., & Palier, B. (2021b). Tracking the transformation of growth regimes in advanced capitalist economies. In A. Hassel & B. Palier (Eds.), *Growth and welfare in advanced capitalist economies. How have growth regimes evolved?* (pp. 3–56). Oxford University Press.

Hatayama, M., Viollaz, M., & Winkler, H. (2020). *Jobs' amenability to working from home: Evidence from skills surveys for 53 countries.* [Policy Research Working Paper 9241]. World Bank.

Häusermann, S. (2010). *The politics of welfare state reform in continental Europe. Modernization in Hard Times.* Cambridge University Press.

Häusermann, S. (2018). The multidimensional politics of social investment in conservative welfare regimes: Family policy reform between social transfers and social investment. *Journal of European Public Policy, 25*(6), 862–877.

Häusermann, S., & Kriesi, H. (2015). What do voters want? Dimensions and configurations in individual-level preferences and party choice. In P. Beramendi, S. Häusermann, H. Kitschelt, & H. Kriesi (Eds.), *The politics of advanced capitalism* (pp. 202–230). Cambridge University Press.

Häusermann, S., & Kübler, D. (2011). Policy frames and coalition dynamics in the recent reforms of Swiss family policy. *German Policy Studies, 6*(3), 163–194.

Häusermann, S., & Palier, B. (2017). The politics of social investment: Policy legacies and class coalitions. In A. Hemerijck (Ed.), *The uses of social investment* (pp. 339–348). Oxford University Press.

Häusermann, S., Picot, G., & Geering, D. (2013). Rethinking party politics and the welfare state. Recent advances in the literature. *British Journal of Political Science, 43*(1), 221–240.

Häusermann, S., Pinggera, M., Ares, M., & Enggist, M. (2020). *The limits of solidarity. Changing welfare coalitions in a transforming European party system* [Unpublished manuscript, Department of Political Science, University of Zurich].

Häusermann, S., Pinggera, M., Enggist, M., & Ares, M. (2021). Class and social policy in the knowledge economy. *European Journal of Political Research.* Advance online publication. https://doi.org/10.1111/1475-6765.12463

Heidenheimer, A. J. (1981). Education and social security entitlements in Europe and America. In P. Flora & A. J. Heidenheimer (Eds.), *The development of welfare states in Europe and America* (pp. 269–304). Routledge.

Hemerijck, A. (2013). *Changing welfare states.* Oxford University Press.

Hemerijck, A. (2017). *The uses of social investment.* Oxford University Press.

Holland, A. (2018). Diminished expectations: Redistributive preferences in truncated welfare states. *World Politics, 70*(4), 555–594.

Huber, E., & Stephens, J. D. (2001). *Development and crisis of the welfare state. Parties and policies in global markets.* University of Chicago Press.

Hutter, S., & Kriesi, H. (2019). *European party politics in times of crisis.* Cambridge University Press.

Inglot, T. (2008). *Welfare states in east central Europe, 1919–2004.* Cambridge University Press.

Iversen, T. (2005). *Capitalism, inequality, and welfare.* Cambridge University Press.

Iversen, T., & Cusack, T. R. (2000). The causes of welfare state expansion: Deindustrialization or globalization? *World Politics, 52*(3), 313–349.

Iversen, T., & Soskice, D. (2019). *Democracy and prosperity. Reinventing capitalism through a turbulent century.* Princeton University Press.

Iversen, T., & Stephens, J. (2008). Partisan politics, the welfare state and the three worlds of human capital formation. *Comparative Political Studies, 41*(4–5), 600–637.

Iversen, T., & Wren, A. (1998). Equality, employment, and budgetary restraint: The trilemma of the service economy. *World Politics, 50*, 507–546.

Jensen, C. (2011). Capitalist systems, deindustrialization, and the politics of public education. *Comparative Political Studies, 44*(4), 412–435.

Jenson, J. (2010). Diffusing ideas for after neoliberalism: The social investment perspective in Europe and Latin America. *Global Social Policy, 10*, 59–84.

Jenson, J., & Saint-Martin, D. (2003). New routes to social cohesion? Citizenship and the social investment state. *Canadian Journal of Sociology/Cahiers canadiens de sociologie, 28*(1), 77–99.

Katzenstein, P. J. (1985). *Small states in world markets: Industrial policy in Europe.* Cornell University Press.

Kazepov, Y., & Ranci, C. (2017). Why no social investment in Italy? Timing, austerity, and macro-level Matthew effects. In A. Hemerijck (Ed.), *The uses of social investment* (pp. 287–300). Oxford University Press.

Kenworthy, L. (2017). Enabling social policy. In A. Hemerijck (Ed.), *The uses of social investment* (pp. 89–96). Oxford University Press.

Kim, M. M. S. (2016). *Comparative welfare capitalism in East Asia. Productivist models of social policy.* Palgrave Macmillan.

Kitschelt, H. (1994). *The transformation of European social democracy.* Cambridge University Press.

Kitschelt, H., & McGann, A. (1997). *The radical right in western Europe. A comparative analysis.* Michigan University Press.

Kitschelt, H., & Rehm, P. (2013). Occupations as a Site of Political Preference Formation. *Comparative Political Studies, 47*(12), 1670–1706.

Kitschelt, H., & Rehm, P. (2015). Party alignments. Change and continuity. In P. Beramendi, S. Häusermann, H. Kitschelt, & H. Kriesi (Eds.), *The politics of advanced capitalism* (pp. 202–230). Cambridge University Press.

Korpi, W. (2006). Power resources and employer-centered approaches in explanations of welfare states and varieties of capitalism: Protagonists, consenters, and antagonists. *World Politics, 58*(2), 167–206.

Korpi, W., & Palme, J. (1998). The paradox of redistribution and strategies of equality: Welfare state institutions, inequality, and poverty in the Western countries. *American Sociological Review, 63*(5), 661–687.

Kriesi, H., Grande, E., Dolezal, M., Helbling, M., Höglinger, D., Hutter, S., & Wüest, B. (2012). *Political conflict in western Europe.* Cambridge University Press.

Kriesi, H., Grande, E., Lachat, R., Dolezal, M., Bornschier, S., & Frey, T. (2006). Globalization and the transformation of the national political space: Six European countries compared. *European Journal of Political Research, 45*(6), 1–36.

Kriesi, H., Grande, E., Lachat, R., Dolezal, M., Bornschier, S., & Frey, T. (2008). *West European politics in the age of globalization.* Cambridge University Press.

Kurer, T. (2020). The declining middle: Occupational change, social status, and the populist right. *Comparative Political Studies, 53*(10), 1798–1835.

Lewis, J. (1992). Gender and the development of welfare regimes. *Journal of European Social Policy, 2*(3), 159–173.

Lindvall, J., & Rueda, D. (2014). The insider–outsider dilemma. *British Journal of Political Science, 44*(2), 460–475.

Longstreth, F., Steinmo, S., & Thelen, K. A. (1992). *Structuring politics: Historical institutionalism in comparative analysis*. Cambridge University Press.

Lowi, T. (1972). Four systems of policy, politics and choice. *Public Administration Review, 32*(4), 298–310.

Manning, A. (2003). Comment on: "The patterns of job expansions in the USA: A comparison of the 1960s and 1990s", by Erik Olin Wright and Rachel E. Dwyer. *Socio-Economic Review, 1*(3), 327–333.

Manow, P., Palier, B., & Schwander, H. (2018). *Welfare democracies and party politics. Explaining electoral dynamics in times of changing welfare capitalism.* Oxford University Press.

Mares, I. (2003). *The politics of social risk: Business and welfare state development.* Cambridge University Press.

Marks, G., & Steenbergen, M. R. (2004). *European integration and political conflict.* Cambridge University Press.

Meyer, J., Boli, J., Thomas, G. M., & Ramirez, F. O. (1997). World society and the nation-state. *American Journal of Sociology, 103*(1), 144–181.

Michel, E., & Lefkofridi, Z. (2017). The electoral politics of solidarity. In K. Banting & W. Kymlicka (Eds.), *The strains of commitment: The political sources of solidarity in diverse societies.* Oxford University Press.

Mintzberg, H. (1978). Patterns in strategy formation. *Management Science, 24*(9), 934–948.

Morel, N., Palier, B., & Palme, J. (2012). *Towards a social investment welfare state? Ideas, policies and challenges* (pp. 233–266). Policy Press.

Morel, N., & Palme, J. (2017). A normative foundation for the social investment approach? In A. Hemerijck (Ed.), *The uses of social investment* (pp. 150–160). Oxford University Press.

Morgan, K. J. (2013). Path shifting of the welfare state: Electoral competition and the expansion of work–family policies in western Europe. *World Politics, 65*(1), 73–115.

Mosimann, N., & Pontusson, J. (2018). Solidaristic unionism and support for redistribution in contemporary Europe. *World Politics, 69*(3), 448–492.

Müller, W., & Shavit, Y. (1998). Bildung und Beruf im institutionellen Kontext: Eine vergleichende Studie in 13 Ländern. *Zeitschrift für Erziehungswissenschaft, 1*(4), 501–533.

Nelson, M., & Stephens, J. D. (2012). Do social investment policies produce more and better jobs? In N. Morel, B. Palier, & J. Palme (Eds.), *Towards a social investment welfare state?* (pp. 205–234). Policy Press.

Nölke, A., & Vliegenthart, A. (2009). Enlarging the varieties of capitalism: The emergence of dependent market economies in east central Europe. *World Politics, 61*(4), 670–702.

Oesch, D. (2006). *Redrawing the class map: Stratification and institutions in Germany, Britain, Sweden and Switzerland.* Palgrave Macmillan.

Oesch, D. (2013). *Occupational change in Europe: How technology and education transforms the job structure.* Oxford University Press.

Oesch, D. (2015). Welfare regimes and change in the employment structure: Britain, Denmark and Germany since 1990. *Journal of European Social Policy, 25*(1), 94–110.

Oesch, D., & Rennwald, L. (2018). Electoral competition in Europe's new tripolar political space: Class voting for the left, centre-right and radical right. *European Journal of Political Research, 57*(4), 783–807.

Oesch, D., & Rodriguez-Menes, J. (2010). Upgrading or polarization? Occupational change in Britain, Germany, Spain and Switzerland, 1990–2008. *Socio-Economic Review, 9*(3), 503–531.

Orloff, A. S. (2009). Gendering the comparative analysis of welfare states: An unfinished agenda. *Sociological Theory, 27*(3), 317–343.

Palier, B. (2005). Ambiguous agreement, cumulative change: French social policy in the 1990s. In K. Thelen & W. Streeck (Eds.), *Beyond continuity: Institutional change in advanced political economies* (pp. 127–144). Oxford University Press.

Palier, B. (2010). *A long goodbye to Bismarck? The politics of welfare reforms in continental Europe.* Amsterdam University Press.

Palier, B., & Martin, C. (2009). *Reforming the Bismarckian welfare systems.* John Wiley & Sons.

Peugny, C. (2019). The decline in middle-skilled employment in 12 European countries: New evidence for job polarization. *Research and Politics, 6*(1), 1–7.

Pierson, P. (1992). "Policy feedbacks" and political change: Contrasting Reagan and Thatcher's pension-reform initiatives. *Studies in American Political Development, 6*(2), 359–390.

Pierson, P. (1994). *Dismantling the welfare state? Reagan, Thatcher and the politics of retrenchment.* Cambridge University Press.

Pierson, P. (1996). The new politics of the welfare state. *World Politics, 48*(2), 143–179.

Pierson, P. (2001). Coping with permanent austerity: Welfare state restructuring in affluent democracies. In P. Pierson (Ed.), *The new politics of the welfare state* (pp. 410–465). Oxford University Press.

Pierson, P. (2004). *Politics in time: History, institutions, and social analysis.* Princeton University Press.

Piketty, T. (2019). *Capital and ideology.* Harvard University Press.

Pinggera, M. (2020). Congruent with whom? Parties' issue emphases and voter preferences in welfare politics. *Journal of European Public Policy.* Advance online publication. https://doi.org/10.1080/13501763.2020.1815825

Powell, W. W., & Snellman, K. (2004). The knowledge economy. *Annual Review of Sociology, 30*, 199–220.

Pribble, J. (2013). *Welfare and party politics in Latin America.* Cambridge University Press.

Rathgeb, P. (2021). Makers against takers: The socio-economic ideology and policy of the Austrian Freedom Party. *West European Politics, 44*(3), 635–660.

Rueda, D. (2005). Insider–outsider politics in industrialized democracies: The challenge to social democratic parties. *American Political Science Review,* 99(1), 61–74.

Rueda, D., Wibbels, E., & Altamirano, M. (2015). The origins of dualism. In P. Beramendi, S. Häusermann, H. Kitschelt, & H. Kriesi (Eds.), *The politics of advanced capitalism* (pp. 89–111). Cambridge University Press.

Sainsbury, D. (1996). *Gender, equality and welfare states.* Cambridge University Press.

Scharpf, F. W., & Schmidt, V. A. (2000). *Welfare and work in the open economy: Vol. 1. From vulnerability to competitiveness in comparative perspective.* Oxford University Press.

Schneider, B. R. (2013). *Hierarchical capitalism in Latin America: Business, labor, and the challenges of equitable development.* Cambridge University Press.

Schwander, H. (2018). Electoral demand, party competition, and family policy: The politics of a new policy field. In P. Manow, B. Palier, & H. Schwander (Eds.), *Welfare democracies and party politics: Explaining electoral dynamics in times of changing welfare capitalism* (pp. 197–224). Oxford University Press.

Sen, A. (2001). *Development as freedom.* Oxford University Press.

Skocpol, T. (1992). *Protecting soldiers and mothers. The political origins of social policy in the United States.* Belknap Press of Harvard University Press.

Spitz-Oener, A. (2006). Technical change, job tasks, and rising educational demands: Looking outside the wage structure. *Journal of Labor Economics,* 24(2), 235–270.

Stephens, J. D., Huber, E., & Ray, L. (1999). The welfare state in hard times. In H. Kitschelt, P. Lange, G. Marks, & J. D. Stephens (Eds.), *Continuity and change in contemporary capitalism* (pp. 164–192). Cambridge University Press.

Streeck, W. (2009). *Re-forming capitalism. Institutional change in the German political economy.* Oxford University Press.

Taylor-Gooby, P. (2005). *Ideas and welfare state reform in western Europe.* Palgrave Macmillan.

Thelen, K. (2004). *How institutions evolve: The political economy of skills in Germany, Britain, the United States and Japan.* Cambridge University Press.

Thelen, K. (2014). *Varieties of liberalization and the new politics of social solidarity.* Cambridge University Press.

Thewissen, S., & Rueda, D. (2016). *Automation and the welfare state: Technological change as a determinant of redistribution preferences* [Oxford INET Working Paper Series 2016-02]. Institute for New Economic Thinking.

Vanhuysse, P., & Goerres, A. (2013). *Ageing populations in post-industrial democracies. Comparative studies of policies and politics.* Routledge.

Wren, A. (2013). *The political economy of the service transition.* Oxford University Press.

Zehn, Z. J., Mayer, N., Palier, B., & Rovny, J. (2019). The "losers of automation": A reservoir of votes for the radical right? *Research & Politics,* 6(1), 1–7.

PART I

THE IDEATIONAL CONTEXT OF SOCIAL INVESTMENT POLITICS

3

MULTIPLE SOURCES OF THE SOCIAL INVESTMENT PERSPECTIVE

THE OECD AND THE WORLD BANK

Jane Jenson and Rianne Mahon

3.1. INTRODUCTION

The Organisation for Economic Co-operation and Development (OECD) and the World Bank merit attention in this volume because they have played key roles in the development, diffusion, and evolution of social investment perspectives at the scale of the international system, both North and South. The practices of these two international organizations (IOs) began to cohere around the ideas and policies of social investment in the mid-1990s as evidence accumulated that their previous economistic paradigms for promoting growth and social development were failing to achieve their announced goals. Indeed, they were challenged to identify a strategy for alleviating some of the human costs of the structural adjustments that they, along with other IOs, had promoted in the 1980s. While hewing to a common core, their interpretations of social investment differed in several respects, especially in initial formulations, distinctions reflecting in part their organizational mandates and different starting points of problem definition.

Both organizations seek to use the cognitive authority of their policy expertise to influence state actions (Mahon, 2018, p. 564). Both are "knowledge organizations," undertaking policy-oriented research in which economists predominate.

Jane Jenson and Rianne Mahon, *Multiple Sources of the Social Investment Perspective* In: *The World Politics of Social Investment (Volume I)*. Edited by: Julian L. Garritzmann, Silja Häusermann, and Bruno Palier, Oxford University Press.

As knowledge organizations, they contribute to the development and diffusion of new perspectives on policy. Each has historically focused on particular regions of the world: the Paris-based OECD on its member countries primarily situated in the North; the Washington-based World Bank on the South. Documenting and comparing the development of social investment ideas, objectives, and instruments within the OECD and the Bank helps to identify elements common to diverse perspectives on social investment as they appeared around the globe beginning in the 1990s.

This chapter argues that each IO started from its own assessment of challenges and its knowledge network. Nonetheless, they shared "the overarching social investment aim of breaking the intergenerational transmission of social disadvantage" (Hemerijck, 2018, p. 815). In the first major section we document that in the 1990s the OECD intensified its search for social policy ideas and instruments to address the new social risks associated with changing family forms and practices as well as post-industrial labor markets marked by growing precarity, dualization, and feminization, including their poverty-generating effects. By 1997 it could claim its "social investment approach . . . stresses interventions that take place early in the life-cycle" as well as activation (OECD, 1997a, pp. 5–6). The World Bank's social investment perspective took hold at the same moment, when the costs of the Washington Consensus' structural adjustments became too high to ignore (Jenson, 2010, p. 60). It followed policy ideas about mitigating risk and reducing poverty, relying on policy instruments focused on families with children and the "early years" (ages 0–6). The objective was both to alleviate poverty and to break its intergenerational cycle.

In the second major section, we argue that in the middle of the first decade of the 21st century and especially after the 2008 financial crisis, there was convergence toward a revised perspective as both IOs embraced "inclusive growth" as a macroeconomic paradigm, one which aims to reduce inequalities in society because they hinder growth (Hasmath, 2015). The social investment instruments of each were folded into a much larger agenda of reducing inequalities across the population. Both IOs still hewed to some of the policy instruments of the social investment perspective but with the larger policy objective of reducing social inequality in general, a goal not part of the social investment perspective.[1] This meant that policies covered more of the population than the families and young children who initially captured the attention of the initiators of the social investment perspective. Knowledge networks advocated new forms of "universality" across income and age groups.

---

1. On the distinction we make here between instruments and objectives, see, among others, Hall (1993).

3.2. DIVERSE ROOTS AND ROUTES OF DISCOVERY

Each organization "discovered" social investment ideas in the 1990s. Yet neither IO simply seized on this agenda; seeds had been planted in the 1980s. In both organizations too the emphasis on social investment, with its notions of breaking intergenerational cycles of disadvantage and poverty and creating and maintaining human capital, was a social policy strategy that had to be embedded in macro-frames about the pursuit, promotion, and achievement of economic growth and societal well-being—the OECD's growth paradigm and the Bank's development paradigm. For the OECD this imperative meant devoting attention to the employability, including human capital, of working-age adults, while the World Bank's poverty-reduction objective generated forms of targeting in its social investment initiatives.

3.2.1. The OECD: Investments in the work–family life course

Once considered a club of rich capitalist countries, since the 1990s OECD membership has grown from the traditional core to include several Eastern European countries, Korea, Mexico, Chile, and Israel; and it undertakes various "enhanced engagement" activities with others. Expansion has helped stretch its gaze in ways that have begun to dissolve the North–South binary that long shaped its actions. The available levers for advancing its positions are, however, limited. With the mission "to promote policies," its major tool is networking its expertise. It combines broad policy advice with detailed comparative peer review and the development of indicators to facilitate the benchmarking of country performance on growth. The OECD's mandate is to promote economic growth. Nonetheless, its "growth paradigm was not a monolithic or unified set of discourses. Rather it was continuously renegotiated and remade in an open and contingent process," making it "remarkably flexible in adapting to changing circumstances, integrating newly emerging problems and perspectives without changing its basic tenets" (Schmelzer, 2016, p. 14). Many emerging problems are handled by particular directorates, such that although the Economics Department remains the guardian of the core mandate, other units have been able to challenge its truth claims. Two that played roles in our story are the Directorate for Employment, Labour and Social Affairs (DELSA) and the Education Directorate. While the former advocated policies to facilitate women's employment, the latter looked primarily to creation of human capital.

The OECD's social investment approach has relied upon the "lynch-pin" of the perspective, the "work–family life course" (Hemerijck, 2018, p. 816). The organization began to reflect on challenges to, and the future of, the welfare state in the 1980s. Hints of a new approach appeared at the 1988 meeting of social policy ministers, who agreed that the goal was an "active society in which all members have a constructive role (Mahon, 2014, p. 91)." The position was informed by the work of DELSA's predecessor, which developed a conception of the mobilization of the labor force in an active society where social policies would "maximise both the number of people who have *opportunities* for active social roles, and the duration of their lives over which they can experience such activity" (Mahon, 2014, p. 89). By 1992 the Employment, Labour and Social Affairs Committee asserted that "many types of social expenditure are an investment in society which enhance its growth potential."[2] DELSA developed its thinking more fully in *New Orientations for Social Policy*, which promoted the ability to participate in a globalized knowledge-based economy (OECD, 1994, p. 12). In terms of public expenditures, the report advocated shifting from income maintenance to measures for facilitating labor market participation, while recognizing the need to support the most vulnerable.

A major focus of the analysis, reflecting the general social policy discussions of the time, was pension reform, although in 1992 the organization was also in the midst of drafting its jobs strategy. Eschewing the latter's neoliberal willingness to sacrifice equity concerns in the name of labor market flexibility, DELSA's publication drew attention to new social risks. Ministerial approval of *New Orientations* allowed DELSA to proceed with its agenda, including through events such as the November 1996 high-level conference Beyond 2000: The New Social Policy Agenda that brought ministers together with invited experts. The latter included Gøsta Esping-Andersen, who called "for a radical rethinking of family policy . . . that helps reduce dependence on a single income earner, and . . . that makes it possible to combine high fertility rates with female careers" (OECD, 1997b, p. 65). Reporting on the conference, Pearson and Scherrer (1997) of DELSA stressed new social risks (including divorce and lone-parenthood), called for interventions early in life, and advocated spending to underwrite adults' establishment and re-establishment in the labor market. In the conceptualization used in this volume, this analysis might be seen as, among other things, one combining creation, mobilization, and maintenance of human capital, although the OECD authors were not using that term.

The next milestone was the report *A Caring World: The New Social Policy Agenda*, which advanced the life-course perspective, highlighting four new social risks: the rise of lone-parent families, the increase in dual-earner households, the threat of falling fertility, and the low-skill, low-wage nexus (OECD, 1999, p. 13). Thus, while women's labor force participation might reduce family risks, it also raised demographic concerns for society about deferred fertility (OECD, 1999, pp. 14–15). The conclusion was clearly emerging that public policy needed to help young families reconcile work and family life via public investment in childcare and appropriate leave policies. Beyond the immediate labor market

2.

advantages were the long-term positive effects of investing in the creation of human capital via early childhood interventions to combat the deleterious effects of disadvantage and childhood poverty. While a variety of programs—such as teaching parenting skills—might help, the analysis reported the greatest payoffs from early education. Thus, the notion of the mutually reinforcing benefits of childcare for the whole life course was developing (OECD, 1999, pp. 84–85). It was seen this way: Childcare increased parental employment, thus combatting the poverty of young families, and allowed women to maintain the benefits of their own human capital investments, while investments in children's human capital would hopefully also contribute to breaking the intergenerational cycle of disadvantage.

The analysis took a leap forward with an initiative launched in 2001. The thematic review *Babies and Bosses* planted the OECD's flag for expertise in the domain of work and family. Being an area of innovation for the OECD and therefore in need of appropriate indicators for benchmarking, a series of analyses proceeded via four in-depth peer reviews involving 13 countries. The goal was to give sufficient attention to diverse institutional arrangements, thereby also fostering the internal debates that could provoke policy learning. The *Babies and Bosses* studies scrutinized tax and benefit policies, seeking to identify barriers to displacing the male breadwinner model and increasing mothers' employment. It endorsed the adult-worker family, focusing policy proposals on family–work reconciliation in general via public support for childcare, flexible work schedules, and shared parental leave. Critical of policies that allowed, even encouraged, lone parents to remain out of the labor force, the final report called for elimination of disincentives to participation, even retaining the idea of "moderate benefit sanctions" for not seeking work, an idea that had been part of the OECD's toolbox in the 1990s (OECD, 2007, p. 20; Pearson & Scherer, 1997, p. 8). Thus, DELSA's work on a social investment strategy led it to focus on mobilization of more of the labor force, by including incentives and support for full-time work for women and policies responding to the needs of the adult-worker family, whether with one or two parents.

A second initiative that contributed to the OECD's life-course perspective on social investment came from the Education Directorate. Its premise was that education interventions should minimize risks associated with life-course transitions and, among things, avoid the long-term consequences of childhood poverty. A major document prepared for the 1996 ministerial meeting on life-long learning for all shared key social investment premises: We now live in a "learning economy" characterized by rapid change, social cohesion is at risk if learning opportunities are unfairly distributed, and social policy should move from passive transfer payments toward "active policies that contribute directly to the formation of human capital" (OECD, 1996, pp. 90–91). The Directorate's analytic framework drew on the concept of human capital, leading it to focus on its creation, notably via wider access to high-quality early childhood education (OECD, 1996, p. 95).

The view that the risks of disadvantage started young but could be overturned by early intervention engendered a mandate for another thematic review of early childhood education and care (ECEC) beginning in 2001, particularly targeting disadvantaged children (Mahon, 2006, p. 188). It was labeled "Starting Strong," after the publication titles. The choice of John Bennett, who had been deeply involved in the United Nations (UN) Committee on the Rights of the Child, to head the review and a team of experts in early education generated an immediate tension within the approach over the view of children as active learners and rights-bearers and a more instrumental view (Mahon, 2010, p. 184). Debate aside, the third report, for example, reported that "research findings have led education and social policy makers to re-think their investment patterns in children and families and to take a 'life-cycle' view on child development and family support" (OECD, 2012a, p. 17). The report described positive state actions as resting on a social investment perspective's view of ECEC as a policy instrument useful for fighting child poverty and educational disadvantage, for reaping the societal benefits of education in a "learning economy," and for boosting female employment (OECD, 2012a, p. 18).

Studies intensified along the same lines, pushing measurement and data development, including new databases on family policies and outcomes. In *Doing Better for Children*, DELSA's Social Policy Division called for careful and planned investments across the "child life cycle," with concern still focused on social risks, via chapters on lone parenthood and intergenerational lack of mobility (OECD, 2009).[3] The document deployed a "well-being" lens and reviewed the evaluation data for a wide range of policy interventions—from universal cash transfers and childcare to conditional cash transfers (CCTs) and a "service cascade" approach combining some universal programs with supplementary measures targeting the disadvantaged. It recommended concentrating spending early in the child life cycle, even in utero, and concentrating on at-risk children in order to change the intergenerational transmission of disadvantage (OECD, 2009, pp. 178–183). This report's conclusions were then added to insights from *Babies and Bosses* to produce *Doing Better for Families* (OECD, 2011a), which returned to demographic concerns and child poverty. Recommendations for interventions continued to focus on employment strategies for making work pay and with supports for work–family balance as well as on early interventions, especially for young children at risk of developmental delays and socio-emotional difficulties.

---

3. The investment language was quite fully developed: "It is common to liken spending on children to an investment, reflecting the strong future focus in child policy. . . . The investment metaphor is a useful one, reflecting the fact that much of the child's well-being is experienced in the future. This metaphor can be usefully extended into thinking about investment in children in terms of a portfolio of investments of different types" (OECD, 2009, pp. 183–184).

We see that the OECD responded to the new social risks, which challenged long-standing analytic premises about social policy, by inserting into the core of its growth paradigm commitments to human capital investments and to increasing labor force participation so as to reduce the drivers of disadvantage. The consolidation of this life-course approach to social investment emerged from separate organizational venues over the course of two broad policy exercises. The first, led by DELSA beginning in the 1990s, analyzed and promoted social policy practices in support of employment of the adult-earner family—childcare, shared parental leave, and more flexible work arrangements, including a more equal gender division of labor in two-parent, heterosexual families. The second, beginning at the start of the new millennium, was led by the Education Directorate. It positioned early education's human capital creation effects as complements to broader social protection measures needed to overcome life-course transition risks associated with child poverty and disadvantage. Both policy exercises utilized all the propositional repertoire of the OECD to disseminate knowledge, data, and policy advice that would advance their shared goal of investing in prevention as well as promoting labor market success.

3.2.2. The World Bank: Ending poverty by investing in children

An international development paradigm has been at the core of the World Bank's actions since its foundation, with the mission being "working for a world free of poverty." Its conception of development has changed over time, however, from an emphasis on physical infrastructure in its first decades to poverty alleviation, schooling, and health in the 1970s; the neoliberal structural adjustment lending of the Washington Consensus in the 1980s; and then a return to a poverty-reduction focus via social investments in the 1990s and into the new millennium. Like the OECD, the Bank sees itself as a knowledge organization with strong internal research capacity, but it can also deploy its tools of conditional and negotiated loans to lever its policy expertise into action. It "aims to be the authoritative international voice defining what economic development is and what the development agenda should be" (Hammer, 2013, p. 12). Despite the integration of social science disciplines into the research apparatus and their own efforts to shift understandings of the "poverty problem," the hurdle has been high because of the embedded "econocentric response to social problems," that is, the need to frame social interventions in economistic ways, promising to measure their contributions to economic growth and enhanced project effectiveness (Vetterlein, 2012).

A social investment approach fit well with such econocentrism (Jenson & Saint-Martin, 2006). It could deploy economists' language that transformed "spending" into "investments." It could rest on a popular economic theory about the role of human capital in wealth creation. Indicators could be developed, and returns could be quantified. It nonetheless took some time to move the Bank toward a social investment perspective. This happened in the mid-1990s. While concerns about poverty, schooling, and health had shaped Robert McNamara's presidency (1968–1980), for a decade and a half afterward the Bank sidelined social development, embraced neoliberalism's Washington Consensus, and focused lending on structural adjustment programs, with their conditionality of trade liberalization, privatizations, cuts to government spending, and so on. By the early 1990s, however, it was clear that structural adjustment programs "were an unmitigated public relations disaster, triggering a global backlash against the Bank and throwing it into a state of internal crisis and drift" (Hammer, 2013, p. 1). Major rethinking accompanied preparations for the Bank's 50th anniversary and the World Summit on Social Development in Copenhagen, both in 1995 (Vetterlein, 2012, p. 48). There was an opening for survivors of the McNamara era within the Bank to argue again that social welfare spending and growth were complementary, not contradictory: that "investment in human resources through health, education and population was good for growth" (Hall, 2007, p. 155), while retaining its preference for the basics of neoliberalism—"investments in people, by themselves, will not be fully effective unless the overall economic policy framework for these investments is conducive and supportive. This implies macroeconomic stability, an open economy, access to world markets, the right structure of incentives, and the proper functioning of capital and labor markets" (World Bank, 1995, p. vi). *Investing in People. The World Bank in Action* was published with the explicit purpose of laying out the Bank's support for new directions for human development (Jenson, 2017, p. 209). Overseen by the directors of the Education and Social Policy Department and the Population, Health and Nutrition Department, the document proclaimed, "Investing in people means helping people invest in themselves and their children. It means empowering households, especially poor households, to increase the quantity and quality of investments in children" (World Bank, 1995, p. 3).

The document's origins in these units of the Bank bureaucracy meant that education and hence human capital creation were designated as drivers of growth and development. In contrast to earlier decades, however, the process would begin well before primary schooling. The Bank's concern with poverty reduction led it to a targeted approach in which early childhood development (ECD) became a central policy idea via the focus on enabling poor children to develop their human capital and thus to break the intergenerational cycle of poverty. Like the OECD, the consolidation of the perspective drew on earlier work. The Human Development Network (HDN) in the late 1980s had turned its attention to the "early years," with the work of ECD experts such as Robert Myers and Mary Eming Young. Then, as ideas about social investment circulated more widely, between 1998 and 2006 Young commissioned numerous studies and several conferences. The approach drew heavily on Anglo-American studies such as the numerous evaluations of US welfare programs and the work of economist

James Heckman on the high rate of return on multiple forms of investment in the early years (Mahon, 2010, pp. 176–177). Later analyses retained the emphasis on a range of interventions for preschool children but included more evidence from across the Global South as that evidence accumulated, in part because of research by the international banks and other actors.

With evidence about the effects of early intervention on overcoming the effects of poverty, new policy instruments were added to the arsenal. While traditional interventions such as center-based programs for school readiness; programs to improve health, nutrition, and parenting; and even communication campaigns were highlighted, a new policy instrument for the ECD domain gained significant attention: the CCT (Naudeau et al., 2011, pp. 139–150).[4] As policy attention turned to the effects of insecurity and "shocks"—whether because of conflict, weather, or economic reform—CCTs were highlighted as a tool for promoting the health of the youngest children and ensuring the education of older children (Alderman, 2011; Fiszbein & Schady, 2009).

The incorporation into the policy instrument toolbox of a monetary transfer conditioned by use of health and education programs also followed from a shift in the Bank's understanding of poverty that was laid out in the controversial 2000/2001 *World Development Report* (WDR), *Attacking Poverty* (Vetterlein, 2012, p. 40). As the research on ECD had already been doing, that WDR used a definition of poverty that "encompassed not only low income and consumption but also low achievement in education, health, nutrition, and other areas of human development" (World Bank, 2001, p. v). This analysis altered the lens. It built on *Voices of the Poor*, a Bank background study that had uncovered through attitudinal surveys that poverty was experienced as insecurity and as lack of income (Vetterlein, 2012, p. 40). The WDR turned to a consideration of security and its flipside, risk. Many risks were identified and interventions sought that would enable individuals to mitigate and cope with risk by providing assets. Moreover, "supporting the institutions that help poor people manage risk can enable them to pursue the higher-risk, higher-return activities that can lift them out of poverty," such as keeping their children in school (World Bank, 2001, p. 40). Among the policy instruments identified were familiar insurance and assistance programs as well as the workfare, microfinance, and social funds of the neoliberal years; but CCTs were also singled out, particularly as conditional subsidies for school attendance (World Bank, 2001, pp. 151–158). This turn to moderating

---

4. Enthusiasm for CCTs spread rapidly from the initial mid-1990s experiments in Brazil and Mexico (see Chapter 15 in Volume II [Garritzmann et al., 2022]; Jenson & Nagels, 2018). The major overview commissioned by the World Bank in 2009 assessed an immense body of evaluation data available from programs already underway in virtually every country in Latin America as well as large-scale ones in Bangladesh, Indonesia, and Turkey and pilot projects in Cambodia, Malawi, Morocco, Pakistan, and South Africa. The report maps the expansion over the preceding decade (Fiszbein & Schady, 2009, pp. 1, 40). Its Appendix A lists in detail all the programs covering most regions of the globe in place at the time of writing.

the potential effects of risks was a strategy of prevention that underpinned the Bank's understanding of social investment, just as prevention was the goal of the social investment perspective in other settings (Morel et al., 2012, p. 9).

Thus, alongside its work on ECD with a child development paradigm, the HDN generated significant work on CCTs as a tool for advancing a social investment agenda focused on children's nutrition and health as important contributors to the creation of human capital. One key report provided a global overview of the effects of CCTs paid to mothers of young and school-age children and their consequences for risk mitigation. It claimed that CCTs, available when a shock hit, could be preventive because "sharp deteriorations in income can have potentially irreversible effects on education and child nutritional status—and that, in turn, may be one of the mechanisms whereby poverty is transmitted across generations" (Fiszbein & Schady, 2009, p. 161). Overall, the report rehearsed all of the arguments about CCTs as social investments in children. The authors were the chief economist of the HDN, Ariel Fiszbein, who teamed with Norbert Schady, who had produced a summary report on the long-term consequences of nutritional and other deficits and considered in detail the effects of CCTs, among other instruments (Schady, 2006). The CCTs often highlighted were Latin American, from Brazil and Mexico especially. Not surprisingly, with the HDN containing many experts as well as nationals of Latin American countries—like Fiszbein, for example—these experiments attracted attention and were quickly scaled up to become standard models for intervention, propagated by the Bank's—and other key IOs'—experts (Ancelovici & Jenson, 2013; Foli et al., 2018).

We see then that by the 2010s the HDN of the Bank had incorporated into its rethought and revised social development agenda and broader development paradigm policy tools for investments in the form of services as well as transfers that it argued could reduce the intergenerational transmission of poverty and that would support human capital acquisition in "the early years." Its loans as well as technical expertise went to countries willing to institute such programs, thereby ensuring the instruments' diffusion as well as the worldwide dissemination of knowledge about them. The targeting strategy was, however, a residual one that retained from neoliberalism the notion that universal and quality services were likely primarily to benefit the "elite"—not only the wealthy but also the middle class and workers in the formal sector. Convinced of the possibility of such Matthew effects, the Bank discouraged, by refusing to support, more widely available public services and promoted "choice" in private services (Deacon, 2005, p. 21; World Bank, 1995, p. 8).[5]

---

5. On this fear of a "Matthew effect" in social investment policies, see, among others, Cantillon (2011, pp. 441, 446).

3.3. THE SOCIAL INVESTMENT PERSPECTIVE FACES NEW CHALLENGES

The social investment perspective that emerged in the North in the mid-1990s consolidated around strategies to support labor force participation, particularly of women, by making work pay and providing support for work–family reconciliation. Investments in early childhood served a dual purpose of creating human capital and raising employment rates, especially of adult women. The social investment perspective in the South concentrated much more on human capital creation, with policy instruments to support ECD, health, nutrition, and schooling in order to mitigate risk and reduce poverty.

After more than two decades of innovations and adjustments to social policy, the challenges were no longer exactly the same. New research was beginning to turn attention to a range of inequalities that were leaving middle-income earners struggling. Although Gini coefficients fell in a few southern countries, patterns of income distribution caused Gini coefficients to rise in the North. In addition, the appearance of pro-equality movements like Occupy and *Podemos* served to underline the need to address concerns about inequality. Indeed, social movements around the world rejected the familiar nostrums about the positive benefits of economic globalization in the wake of the 2007 food crisis and the 2008 financial crisis.

There was also an important geopolitical dimension to the challenges. Robert Zoellick, president of the World Bank, symbolically declared "the end of the Third World," claiming "it is time we put old concepts of First and Third Worlds, leader and led, donor and supplicant, behind us. We must support the rise of multiple poles of growth that can benefit us all" (Hammer, 2013, p. 140–141). The breakthrough of the "emerging" economies and the dissolution of the East–West divide seemed to herald a world with multiple poles of growth, symbolized for many at mid-decade by the popular identification of the BRIC countries— Brazil, Russia, India, China, now usually written as BRICS since the addition of South Africa. In similar category-breaking actions, the OECD opened accession discussions in 2007, eventually broadening its membership to include several Eastern European and Latin American countries and instituting "enhanced engagement" with four BRICS (China, India, Brazil, South Africa) and Indonesia.

In this context, international idea-sets were shifting by the middle of the first decade of the 2000s. Virtually simultaneously and perceptively in advance of the global economic crisis, policy research in the two organizations was turning to identification and analysis of growing inequality in both North and South. Under the guidance of the Bank's chief economist, François Bourguignon (2003–2006), the 2006 WDR focused on equity and development. Building on earlier work by Michael Förster (2000), in early fall 2008 the OECD launched the publication, *Growing Unequal? Distribution and Poverty in OECD Countries*, quickly followed by two other reports (OECD, 2008, 2011b, 2015a). Support was already building for approaches that "shift emphasis from measuring economic production to measuring people's well-being" (Stiglitz et al., 2009), for the UN Social Protection Floor (SPF) initiative launched in 2009 and led by the International Labour Organization and the World Health Organization (ILO-WHO), and for strategies of inclusive growth. The lead-up to the 2015 adoption of the Sustainable Development Goals (SDGs) also opened new horizons consistent with the increasingly multipolar, non-binary world; the SDGs, unlike their predecessor Millennium Development Goals, applied across the globe, signaling that the whole world needed to improve.

3.3.1. The OECD's agenda realignment— Inclusive growth

The 2008 crisis shook the very analytic premises of the OECD's growth paradigm: Collapse of deregulated financial institutions, impoverishment of middle-class workers, and record levels of youth unemployment were not supposed to happen. Several countries as well as the secretary-general called for a major reflection process to provide the organization with adjusted theory and new tools to enable building "a more solid path for economic growth and well-being" (OECD, 2012b, p. 2). Launched in 2012, this reflection process covered significantly more of the organization than had the exercises that consolidated a social investment perspective in the 1990s and early 2000s. The Ministerial Council Meeting endorsed an organization-wide process (led by Gabriela Ramos, OECD chief of staff, and out of the secretary-general's office) to identify "new approaches to economic challenges" (NAEC). The exercise was supposed to identify lessons from the crisis, use these to develop a renewed and adjusted framework to address complex macroeconomic challenges, and understand their structuring of interconnections and trade-offs between different policy objectives such as growth/inequality/employment, growth/environment, and environment/inequality (OECD, 2012b, pp. 4–5). This was, in other words, a major enterprise, potentially shifting ideas and practices across the whole organization.

An embedded element of the NAEC was the Inclusive Growth Initiative (IGI), also begun in 2012 under the same ministerial mandate. Its framework report, ready 2 years later, provided a structure for thinking about social policy and growth. The report first asserted that inequality of income and opportunity "undermines growth prospects in the long term" (OECD, 2014, p. 8) and then spent a major part of its analytic effort on mapping inequalities. Inclusive growth was defined as "economic growth that creates opportunity for all segments of the population and distributes the dividends of increased prosperity, both in monetary and non-monetary terms, fairly across society" (OECD, 2014, p. 80). Charting a route to inclusive growth required a new analytic framework with three pillars: multidimensionality, emphasis on distribution, and policy relevance.

The IGI brought a new analytic lens to the OECD, and like *Beyond 2000* (OECD, 1997a), this framing incorporated work already underway in the organization (OECD, 2014, pp. 1, 79). *Multidimensionality* built on the Better Life Initiative begun in 2011 to develop a database of objective and subjective indicators of well-being (OECD, 2013b). From the Better Life indicators, the IGI selected income, health, and jobs (OECD, 2014, pp. 80–82). The analysis of *distribution* was well anchored by existing reports on inequalities across the OECD, such as *Growing Unequal* (2008, 2011b) and for specific categories such as women (OECD, 2013a). Group-based—sex, citizenship status, age, and so on—inequalities were a particular focus. Moving well beyond attention to those disadvantaged by new social risks, the condition of middle classes around the world was central to the analytic frame. Indeed, the median household became an analytic focus. To *achieve policy relevance*, the lens needed to shift: "conventional economic growth theory focuses essentially on average material living standards, whereas Inclusive Growth looks at the distributional effects of policies along the entire distribution of outcomes. The task ahead is therefore more complex and requires a better understanding of the causal links between policies and outcomes in various areas" (OECD, 2014, pp. 84–85). Analysis should look at how living standards were driven by policy (and non-policy) choices. It should identify how choices were hindering growth by generating inequalities or failing to mitigate their effects.

NAEC's synthesis report (OECD, 2015b) again stressed the need to change objectives and perspectives. It covered a full array of macroeconomic, fiscal, and environmental domains and devoted significant attention to finding useful modeling and measurement tools as well adding attention to the way institutions are "shaped by history, social norms and political choices." The overall framing reflected an agenda shared with the IGI: "a greater focus on well-being and its distribution to ensure that growth delivers progress for all" and attention to the "multidimensionality and distributional effects of policy" which "requires a comprehensive approach to inclusive growth" because "large income inequality undermines growth and well-being, by reducing investment in skills by low-income households" (OECD, 2015b, pp. 3–4). This synthesis, emerging from a very ambitious and whole-organization project, had to cover a wide range of themes, from insufficiently flexible employment to tax evasion and environmental degradation. But not everything had to be invented. When it turned to social policy recommendations "to mitigate trade-offs between growth and other dimensions of well-being, in particular equity," it reached back to the earlier work described here, calling for high-quality education beginning in early childhood (with a particular focus on disadvantaged and at-risk groups), attention to job quality (building on the multidimensional conceptualization and measures of earnings, working conditions, and employment security already developed by the Better Life Initiative), and gender equality in education, employment, and entrepreneurship (OECD, 2015b, pp. 4, 15, 41–42).

Given the ambition of the recalibration involved in the NAEC exercise, it represented a challenge to long-standing ideas, particularly of the powerful Economics Department. Its propositions may have been strengthened by the exercise's location in the Office of the Secretary General and having the chief of staff as its champion. Advocates claim an impact on the Going for Growth project (the Economics Department's main project for the last decade), as well as the latter's Economic Outlooks and Economic Surveys (OECD, 2015b, p. 12). However, they also accept that more is needed to fully realize their ambition. This same ambition meant that follow-up went in many directions over varied policy domains. In particular, for social policy the 2017 IGI update report *Bridging the Gap* returned to well-worked themes. Thus, the life-course and intergenerational perspectives headed the policy chapter: "a central pillar of this new policy setting concerns the role that national governments should play to enable individuals to flourish throughout their lives. If the government is to rise to the challenge of addressing unequal outcomes and to prevent disadvantage cascading down generations, whilst acting as a catalyst for stronger productivity growth, it needs to be reconfigured to serve its citizens as a launch pad" (OECD, 2017, p. 41). While recognizing that successful labor force participation requires learning opportunities over all of working life, more familiar child-centered nostrums held center stage. The assertion that "early childhood is a key phase for later life development and success" generated detailed attention to child development as the foundation for human capital and for socio-emotional skills, generating a call for ECEC but also for the kinds of parenting interventions and support for high-risk groups considered in *Doing Better for Children* (OECD, 2009, 2017, pp. 42–44). A later study highlighted the need for policies to grapple with the greater incidence of informal cohabitation and parental separation among poor and working-class parents (Miho & Thévenon, 2020).

Overall, we see that the instruments associated with the social investment perspective, meant to reform post-1945 welfare states, now have visibility in a policy context of promoting inclusive growth. Initially primarily confined to DELSA and the Education Directorate where the policy ideas as well as measurement work were institutionalized, these instruments have been integrated into the organization-wide Inclusive Growth agenda and the NAEC approach. Moreover, in recognition of the multiple poles of economic growth, the OECD's research has been broadened to include emerging economies, including some policy instruments previously confined to them (Jenson, 2017, p. 214). Taken together, these changes have brought attention to multidimensionality, incorporating numerous aspects of well-being, including a focus on gender-based inequalities and on job quality (OECD, 2018). The NAEC initiative has sought a new growth narrative that would include "a new conception of economic progress based on a deeper understanding of the relationship between growth, human wellbeing, a reduction in inequality, and environmental sustainability to inform economic policy making and politics" (OECD, 2019, p. 5). Reaching even further, the

NAEC initiative has turned its attention to systemic resilience, including in the aftermath of the COVID-19 pandemic and other systemic threats (OECD, 2020).

3.3.2. The World Bank: Investing in shared prosperity

Just as the 1997 Asian crisis had sounded the death knell of the Washington Consensus, the later crises prompted significant change in World Bank discourse and practice by significantly broadening its targets for social inclusion. In moving to an inclusive growth frame, as did the OECD, the Bank turned to ongoing staff work to identify appropriate instruments. The WDR 2006, *Equity and Development*, had postulated that "good economic institutions are equitable in a fundamental way: to prosper a society must create incentives for the vast majority of the population to invest and innovate" (World Bank, 2005, p. 9). The route to achieving such prosperity was to "level the playing field," creating equality of opportunity (but not outcomes) because inequities are "wasteful and inimical to sustainable development and poverty reduction." Moreover, policy must focus on long-run complementarities not simply short-run trade-offs of equity and efficiency: "greater equity implies more efficient economic functioning, reduced conflict, greater trust, and better institutions, with dynamic benefits for investment and growth" (World Bank, 2005, p. 3). The Bank's Poverty Reduction and Economic Management Network (PREM) was also working on better understanding of issues of inclusive growth. An early analysis co-authored by the director of the Diagnostic Facility for Shared Growth within the PREM provided a definition of inclusive growth and noted how it differed from the OECD Development Assistance Committee's view of pro-poor growth: "the pro-poor approach is mainly interested in the welfare of the poor while inclusive growth is concerned with opportunities for the majority of the labor force, poor and middle-class alike" (Ianchovichina & Lundstrom, 2009, p. 1, fn 2).[6]

This distinction signaled a key shift the Bank was undergoing, away from an exclusive focus on poverty toward another view of growth. In these years, however, change was slow-moving and had still not integrated all the implications of the 2006 WDR. Nor did it reflect fully the work around the Bank's 2005 Social Development Strategy. After the appointment of Jim Yong Kim as president, however, in 2013 the Board of Executive Directors took a further step, making "shared prosperity" the second of two official goals, the other being ending extreme poverty by 2030. This addition turned attention to distributional patterns and policies and put into question the previous strategy of targeting the poorest. The second and "complementary" goal allowed the Bank to include detailed analytic attention to the bottom 40% of the population. There was a call for more nuanced policy analysis because "policy interventions that reduce extreme

---

6. Bank staff was engaged in discussions of the concept with their OECD counterparts, for example, at the joint workshop held in Paris in 2011 (De Mello & Dutz, 2012).

poverty may or may not be effective in boosting shared prosperity if the two groups—the poor and the bottom 40—are composed of distinct populations" (World Bank, 2016, pp. 1, 53).

With the addition of a second goal of shared prosperity, a first task for in-house researchers was to demonstrate continuity with past work, that the addition was innovative but not a fundamental break from long-standing thinking. Thus, major measurement work was accompanied by a short history recalling earlier Bank discussions. One tack was to evoke the 1970s and Robert McNamara's emphasis on the bottom 40% (World Bank, 2015, p. 75, Box 2.1). A second was to review debates about definitions of relative and absolute poverty. A third reminder was of earlier suggestions of the need for measures of well-being beyond income and including education and more equitable distribution of goods and services (as the OECD was also doing with its Better Life Initiative). The latter was the position taken by, inter alia, Kaushik Basu, who became chief economist under Jim Yong Kim. The overview could thus conclude that "shared prosperity" belonged in Bank discourse, that it was complicated but measurable, and that it did not threaten the Bank's core business: "adoption of the goal of achieving shared prosperity inherently implies that ensuring the well-being of the most vulnerable in a society is a key goal of development" (World Bank, 2015, pp. 74–77).

But how? In 2016 the first Poverty and Shared Prosperity report, *Taking on Inequality*, appeared. It was in many ways a parallel to the OECD's *All on Board* (2014). It provided a comprehensive overview of data on many kinds of inequalities, considered policies to raise incomes, and identified best practices. As President Kim summarized the idea-set, "More equal countries tend to have healthier people and be more economically efficient than highly unequal countries. And countries that invest smartly in reducing inequality today are likely to see more prolonged economic growth than those that don't. Less inequality can benefit the vast majority of the world's population." The echo of the OECD's (2015a) title was loud.

The policy conclusions were both clear and complex. Certain general conditions characterized countries with successful experiments: "The building blocks of success have been prudent macroeconomic policies, strong growth, functioning labor markets, and coherent domestic policies focusing on safety nets, human capital, and infrastructure" (World Bank, 2016, p. 15, also Chapter 5). Among the six domestic policies highlighted, three were policy instruments familiar from the social investment perspective: ECD, CCTs, and universal access to good-quality education. Going much further, the analysis stressed universal healthcare, improved rural roads and electrification, and taxation.

In the analysis, ECD was saved from the equity-efficiency trade-off because of the long-term benefits throughout the life cycle: it "promotes physical, socio-emotional, language and cognitive development during a child's early years. . . . Investing in such interventions shapes an individual's educational attainment, health, social behavior, and earnings in adulthood" (World Bank,

2016, p. 131). The policies reviewed and approved included teaching parenting, preschool learning, breastfeeding, and improved nutrition, all drawing extensively on traditional Bank work on schooling and health. Similar considerations led to positive assessments of CCTs as protection from shocks and for improving health and educational outcomes in addition to reducing Gini coefficients in some cases (World Bank, 2016, p. 140ff.). With the overall emphasis on reducing inequalities in access to health and education, from the early years and through the life cycle, the familiar policy instruments of a social investment perspective had been harnessed to the much larger inclusive growth and shared prosperity agendas focused on reducing societal inequalities.

The 2019 WDR, *The Changing Nature of Work*, reiterates the themes. In its chapter on lifelong learning it singles out "learning before 7" as one of the key domains for investment, alongside tertiary education and adult learning (World Bank, 2019, Chapter 3). It also, however, takes something of a new tack. It provides a subsection on social assistance.[7] In the same section, it assesses social minima. It adds "progressive universalism," which emerged in the health field: "At its centre lies a determination to ensure that people who are poor gain at least as much as those who are better off at every step of the way toward universal coverage, rather than having to wait and catch up as that goal is eventually approached" (Gwatkin, 2011, p. 2161). Alongside this notion of progressive universalism the WDR has suggested even a universal basic income is not inconceivable (World Bank, 2019, p. 89). Thus, in a chapter on "ideas for a new social contract," the WDR notes that, in addition to investment in education and skills training, working-age adults may need a social contract that "could provide a minimum income, combined with basic universal social insurance, decoupled from how or where people work. A guaranteed social minimum could take many forms, achieved through a series of programs or by expanding individual interventions" (World Bank, 2019, p. 129). In other words, in line with the proposals for a worldwide SPF developed by the ILO-WHO report, the Bank was willing to (and as already taken up in the 2013 WDR) consider basic social assistance programs, especially those covering the "hardest to reach," publicly financed and mandatory social insurance programs, and extension of labor rights to the informal sector (World Bank, 2019, p. 2012).

Thus, the World Bank's shared prosperity agenda extends concerns about distribution and access to benefits and services beyond a concern with the very poor, reaching into the middle class in many emerging and developing economies. Even as it maintains commitments to instruments familiar from earlier strategies, it is transforming CCTs into "social assistance"; and ECD and lifelong learning become contributions to social and emotional as well as human

---

7. See Chapter 5 in this volume for a discussion of social assistance as part of a social investment approach.

capital. More significantly, concepts such as progressive universalism and a universal basic income as well as universal basic services shift the principles and objectives of the strategy. Is it still a social investment perspective?

3.4. CONCLUDING REMARKS

The social investment perspective first emerged in response to worries about growth paradigms. In the North, there were fears that growth was inhibited by a malfunctioning welfare state designed in the post-1945 years for an era of male-breadwinner families, of stable and reasonably paid employment, and of unmet needs for pensions, healthcare, and education. Initially new social risks associated with gaps in coverage as well as changing families, economies, and labor markets sparked calls for policies that could ensure successful labor market integration of women, lone parents, and youth; reduce child poverty; and break the intergenerational transmission of disadvantage as well as divert a looming demographic crisis. New policy instruments but, more importantly, policy objectives turning on the work–family life course as part of a strategy for mobilizing human capital emerged but without consistent attention to improving equality (among others, Cantillon, 2011; Nolan, 2013; Saraceno, 2015). In the Global South, the challenges were somewhat different. The Washington Consensus approach to economic growth and development blazed out with the Asian crisis of 1997. Years before, however, there was already ample evidence that poverty was being exacerbated by structural adjustment experiments. Strategies to mitigate risk and ensure the physical and intellectual well-being of the children of the poor led to instruments to encourage ECD, adequate nutrition, and family investment in schooling, especially for girls. ECD programs and CCTs as policy instruments were promoted in the name of health, education, and breaking the intergenerational transmission of poverty, with concern focused on ending extreme poverty rather than on achieving equality.

However, also beneath this thinking about the welfare state—whether liberal, social democratic or Bismarckian—larger changes were occurring. By the 2000s, it was clear that the Matthew effect was no longer being successfully countered in many countries, and inequalities in the OECD world were on the rise, including in unexpected places such as Sweden (OECD, 2015c). In the South, some emerging economies, such as Brazil, were improving their equality measures; but others were stuck or deteriorating. Then crisis hit in 2007 and 2008. The certainties of growth paradigms were shaken, and some of the principles of post-neoliberalism, particularly a lack of attention to inequalities within society, came up of reconsideration. Along with comparative analysis of inequality came new measures of inclusive growth, incorporating well-being. In social policy communities, discussions of the need for universal or at least more inclusive rather than targeted social services and transfers had already begun to percolate through the thinking of several IOs (Deacon, 2005). Such ideas gained traction, particularly in the proposals for the SPF and SDG, where both North and South were described as suffering from similar problems and in need of shared solutions.

In the OECD, DELSA and the Education Department found new allies in those framing the NAEC, which challenged the neoliberal economic model housed in the Economics Department. Introducing an analysis of the costs of deepening inequality—not simply disadvantage or childhood poverty—forced a reconsideration of that dominant department's approaches to growth and its macroeconomic ideas. Multidimensional measures of well-being for adults and children took hold while the commitment to universality was found in several policy proposals. Novel measures and new data were more easily generated than new policy directions, however. Existing policy instruments were turned to new uses. For example, inequalities in human capital acquisition became a hindrance to growth more than a sign of impending intergenerational transmission of disadvantage. Activation was reconfigured from "any job" to avoid child poverty to quality work with job protection and good working conditions in order to maximize growth. Inserted in an updated growth paradigm, such policies could provide the pillars on which new macroeconomic objectives could rest.

Elsewhere other IOs were also moving toward new paradigmatic objectives. The ILO-WHO proposals for a SPF rehabilitated social assistance measures as well as basic social insurance. Novel ways of talking about "universality" of coverage circulated, and the World Bank was listening. CCTs, for example, lost one of their letters: conditions often dropped away for want of enforcement (Ancelovici & Jenson, 2013, p. 307). They became a cash transfer (CT), a policy instrument that could be directed toward any population group—including the elderly and disabled—in need (Foli et al., 2018). CTs to families with children began to resemble a "family allowance" and in some cases a "citizenship right" (Fenwick, 2016, p. 8). Transfers or basic pensions also covered a wider range of categories. There has been an ideational shift away from targeting the poor and the young to an approach covering the whole population no matter what age or family status. For several years, some countries and regional organizations, in Latin America and elsewhere, have been moving toward commitments to "basic universalism" that would scale up from the poor to the better-off, much like progressive universalism would (Huber, 2009; Molina, 2006). They were linking with discussions of a citizen's income that have circulated on the margins in Europe and North America for several years. Thus, while the policy instruments may still be those that institutionalized the social investment perspective, the principles and objectives that are their rationales are in flux as population-wide inequalities take center stage, and universality enters from stage left.

REFERENCES

Alderman, H. (2011). *No small matter: The impact of poverty, shocks and the human capital investment in early child development*. World Bank.

Ancelovici, M., & Jenson, J. (2013). Standardization for transnational diffusion: The case of truth commissions and conditional cash transfers. *International Political Sociology, 7*(1), 294–312.

Cantillon, B. (2011). The paradox of the social investment state. Growth, employment and poverty in the Lisbon era. *Journal of European Social Policy, 21*(5), 432–449.

Deacon, B. (2005). From "safety nets" back to "universal social provision." *Global Social Policy, 5*(1), 19–28.

De Mello, L., & Dutz, M. (2012). *Promoting inclusive growth: Challenges and policies*. Organisation for Economic Co-operation and Development.

Fenwick, T. B. (2016). From CCTs to a social investment welfare state? Brazil's "new" pro-poor strategy. *Development Policy Review, 35*(5), 659–674.

Fiszbein, A., & Schady, N. (2009). *Conditional cash transfers. Reducing present and future poverty*. World Bank.

Foli, R., Béland, D., & Fenwick, T. B. (2018). How instrument constituencies shape policy transfer: A case study from Ghana. *Policy and Society, 37*(1), 108–124.

Förster, M. (2000). *Trends and driving factors in income distribution and poverty in the OECD area* [OECD Labour Market and Social Policy Occasional Paper 42]. Organisation for Economic Co-operation and Development.

Garritzmann, J. L., Häusermann, S., & Palier, B. (Eds.). (2022). *The world politics of social investment: Vol. II. The politics of varying social investment strategies*. Oxford University Press.

Gwatkin, D. (2011). Universal health coverage: Friend or foe of health equity? *The Lancet, 377*(9784), 2160–2161.

Hall, A. (2007). Social policies and the World Bank: Paradigms and challenges. *Global Social Policy, 7*(2), 151–175.

Hall, P. A. (1993). Policy paradigms, social learning and the state. *Comparative Politics, 4*(1), 275–296.

Hammer, P. J. (2013). *Change and continuity at the World Bank: Reforming paradoxes of economic development*. Edward Elgar.

Hasmath, R. (2015). *Inclusive growth, development and welfare policy*. Routledge.

Hemerijck, A. (2018). Social investment as policy paradigm. *Journal of European Public Policy, 25*(6), 810–827.

Huber, E. (2009). Including the middle classes? Latin American social polities after the Washington Consensus. In M. Kremer, P. Van Lieshout, & R. Went (Eds.), *Doing good or doing better: Development policies in a globalizing world* (pp. 137–155). Amsterdam University Press.

Ianchovichina, E., & Lundstrom, S. (2009). *Inclusive growth analytics. Framework and application* [Policy Research Working Paper WPS4851]. World Bank Economic Policy and Debt Department Economic Policy Division. Retrieved April 22, 2020, from https://pdfs.semanticscholar.org/ab02/6bd02ef6ed4c71d f844d28d94ab7e4853788.pdf

Jenson, J. (2010). Diffusing ideas for after neoliberalism: The social investment perspective in Europe and Latin America. *Global Social Policy, 10*(1), 59–84.

Jenson, J. (2017). Developing and spreading a social investment perspective: The World Bank and OECD compared. In A. Hemerijck (Ed.), *The uses of social investment* (pp. 207–215). Oxford University Press.

Jenson, J., & Nagels, N. (2018). Social policy instruments in motion. Conditional cash transfers from Mexico to Peru. *Social Policy & Administration, 52*(1), 323–342.

Jenson, J., & Saint-Martin, D. (2006). Building blocks for a new social architecture: The LEGO™ paradigm of an active society. *Policy & Politics, 34*(3), 429–451.

Mahon, R. (2006). The OECD and the work/family reconciliation agenda. In J. Lewis (Ed.), *Children, changing families and the welfare state* (pp. 173–200). Edward Elgar.

Mahon, R. (2010). After neoliberalism? The OECD, the World Bank and the child. *Global Social Policy, 10*(2), 172–192.

Mahon, R. (2014). The OECD's search for a new social policy language: From welfare state to active society. In D. Béland & K. Petersen (Eds.), *Analysing social policy concepts and language: Comparative and transnational perspectives* (pp. 81–100). Policy Press.

Mahon, R. (2018). Through a fractured gaze: The OECD, the World Bank and transnational care chains. *Current Sociology Monograph, 66*(4), 562–576.

Miho, A., & Thévenon, O. (2020). *Treating all children equally? Why policies should adapt to evolving family arrangements* (DELSA/ELSA/WE/SEM(2020)5). OECD.

Molina, C. G. (2006). *Universalismo básico: Una nueva política social para América Latina.* Inter-American Development Bank.

Morel, N., Palier, B., & Palme, J. (2012). *Towards a social investment welfare state? Ideas, policies and challenges.* Policy Press.

Naudeau, S., Kataoka, N., Valerio, A., Neuman, M. J., & Elder, L. K. (2011). *Investing in young children: An early child development guide for policy dialogue and project preparation.* World Bank.

Nolan, B. (2013). What use is "social investment?" *Journal of European Social Policy, 23*(5), 459–468.

Organisation for Economic Co-operation and Development. (1994). *New orientations for social policy* (Social Policy Studies 1).

Organisation for Economic Co-operation and Development. (1996, January 16–17). *Lifelong learning for all* [Paper presentation]. Meeting of the Education Committee at Ministerial Level, Paris, France.

Organisation for Economic Co-operation and Development. (1997a). *Beyond 2000: The new social policy agenda. Summary of the high-level conference held at the Chateau de la Muette, Paris, 12th–13th November 1996* (OCDE/GD(97)66).

Organisation for Economic Co-operation and Development. (1997b). *Family, market and community: Equity and efficiency in social policy* (Social Policy Studies 21).

Organisation for Economic Co-operation and Development. (1999). *A caring world: The new social policy agenda.*

Organisation for Economic Co-operation and Development. (2007). *Babies and Bosses: Reconciling work and family life: A synthesis of findings for OECD Countries.*

Organisation for Economic Co-operation and Development. (2008). *Growing unequal: Income distribution and poverty in OECD countries.*

Organisation for Economic Co-operation and Development. (2009). *Doing better for children.*

Organisation for Economic Co-operation and Development. (2011a). *Doing better for families.*

Organisation for Economic Co-operation and Development. (2011b). *Divided we stand: Why inequality keeps rising.*

Organisation for Economic Co-operation and Development. (2012a). *Starting Strong III: A quality tool-box for early childhood education and care.*

Organisation for Economic Co-operation and Development. (2012b, May 23–24). *New approaches to economic challenges—A framework paper* [Paper presentation]. Meeting of the OECD Council at Ministerial Level, Paris, France. Retrieved on April 22, 2020, from https://www.oecd.org/general/50452415.pdf

Organisation for Economic Co-operation and Development. (2013a). *Closing the gender gap: Act Now.*

Organisation for Economic Co-operation and Development. (2013b). *How's Life? 2013: Measuring Well-Being OECD publishing.* Retrieved October 27, 2021, from http:/dx/doi.org/10.1787/9789264201392-en

Organisation for Economic Co-operation and Development. (2014). *All on board: Making inclusive growth happen.*

Organisation for Economic Co-operation and Development. (2015a). *In it together: Why less inequality benefits us all.*

Organisation for Economic Co-operation and Development. (2015b, June 3–4). *Final synthesis: New approaches to economic challenges* [Paper presentation]. Meeting of the OECD Council at Ministerial Level, Paris,

France. Retrieved April 22, 2020, from http://www.oecd.org/naec/Final-NAEC-Synthesis-Report-CMIN2015-2.pdf

Organisation for Economic Co-operation and Development. (2015c). *Sweden Policy Brief: Achieving greater opportunities and outcomes for all.* Retrieved April 22, 2020, from https://www.oecd.org/sweden/sweden-achieving-greater-equality-of-opportunities-and-outcomes.pdf

Organisation for Economic Co-operation and Development. (2017). *Bridging the gap: Inclusive growth 2017 update report.*

Organisation for Economic Co-operation and Development. (2018). *Good jobs for all in a changing world: The OECD jobs strategy.*

Organisation for Economic Co-operation and Development. (2019). *Beyond growth: Towards a new economic approach: Report of the Secretary General's Advisory Group on New Growth Narrative.* Retrieved April 9, 2020, from https://www.oecd.org/naec/averting-systemic-collapse/SG-NAEC(2019)3_Beyond%20Growth.pdf

Organisation for Economic Co-operation and Development. (2020). *A systemic resilience approach to dealing with Covid-19 and future shocks.* Retrieved April 22, 2021, from https://www.oecd.org/coronavirus/policy-responses/a-systemic-resilience-approach-to-dealing-with-covid-19-and-future-shocks-36a5bdfb/

Pearson, M., & Scherer, P. (1997, April–May). Balancing security and sustainability in social policy. *The OECD Observer, 205,* 6–9.

Saraceno, C. (2015). A critical look to the social investment approach from a gender perspective. *Social Politics, 22*(2), 257–269.

Schady, N. (2006). *Early childhood development in Latin America and the Caribbean* [Policy Research Working Paper WPS3869]. Washington: World Bank. Retrieved April 22, 2020, from https://openknowledge.worldbank.org/handle/10986/9

Schmelzer, M. (2016). *The hegemony of growth: The OECD and the making of the economic growth paradigm.* Cambridge University Press.

Stiglitz, J., Sen, A., & Fitoussi, J.-P. (2009). *Report by the Commission on the Measurement of Economic Performance and Social Progress.* Paris: The Commission. Retrieved April 22, 2020, from http://hdl.voced.edu.au/10707/47743

Vetterlein, A. (2012). Seeing like the World Bank on poverty. *New Political Economy, 17*(1), 35–58.

World Bank. (1995). *Investing in people: The World Bank in action.*

World Bank. (2001). *World development report 2000/2001. Attacking poverty.*

World Bank. (2005). *World development report 2006: Equity and development.*

World Bank. (2015). *A measured approach to ending poverty and boosting shared prosperity: Concepts, data, and the twin goals* (Policy Research Report).

World Bank. (2016). *Poverty and shared prosperity 2016: Taking on inequality.*

World Bank. (2019). *World development report 2019: The changing nature of work.*

4

THE POLITICS OF EUROPEAN UNION'S SOCIAL INVESTMENT INITIATIVES

Caroline de la Porte and Bruno Palier

4.1. INTRODUCTION

Like the Organisation for Economic Co-operation and Development (OECD) and the World Bank at the global level (see Chapter 3 in this volume), the European Union institutions have been important protagonists for social investment initiatives at the EU level since the mid-1990s. In 2013, the European Union adopted the ambitious Social Investment Package, which proposed policies to invest in human capital throughout the life course. The package focuses on and identifies policies with a high social investment orientation, including developing early childhood education and care policies, active labor market policies, education and lifelong learning, as well as housing support, rehabilitation, healthcare, and long-term care services. The Social Investment Package is the apex of a series of initiatives taken at the EU level since the mid-1990s aimed at providing EU member states with a common vision for the modernization and reform of their welfare states and labor markets that is compatible with the EU growth strategy. The Social Investment Package builds on these earlier EU initiatives that developed from the mid-1990s onward in a series of politically significant sequences.

With its initiatives, the European Union contributed to elaborating and legitimizing the social investment perspective in Europe. As shown in previous work, the European Union has ideational influence on member states (Moreno & Palier, 2005). Moreover, in contrast to the OECD, which works exclusively

Caroline de la Porte and Bruno Palier, *The Politics of European Union's Social Investment Initiatives* In: *The World Politics of Social Investment (Volume I)*. Edited by: Julian L. Garritzmann, Silja Häusermann, and Bruno Palier, Oxford University Press.
© Oxford University Press 2022. DOI: 10.1093/oso/9780197585245.003.0004

through soft power (see Chapter 3 in this volume), the EU level is a higher tier of governance for the EU member states, exercising political influence, especially in socioeconomic policy. The European Union has various means of regulation, ranging from legislation in areas where it has exclusive or shared authority with member states to soft regulation, especially policy coordination, in areas of member state competency (such as labor market and social policies). At the EU level, social investment issues are mainly addressed through policy coordination, which consists of political agreement among the EU member states on common policy aims, key benchmarks, member state reporting, and country-specific recommendations (de la Porte & Pochet, 2012). Through various channels documented in the Europeanization literature, EU policy coordination has been instrumental in leading to changes in members states in the domain of social investment policies, especially when EU orientation and the political priorities of governments converged (Barcevicius et al., 2014; de la Porte & Pochet, 2012; Erhel et al., 2005; Graziano et al., 2011; Jessoula & Madama, 2018). Here, we focus not on member states' policies but on the EU's social investment initiatives.

This chapter maps and then explains the metamorphoses in the European Union's social investment welfare state reform strategy, following the general theoretical framework of the World Politics of Social Investment (WOPSI) project (see Chapter 2 in this volume). To start, we show that there have been five main sequences in the development of the European Union's social investment initiatives. Each sequence is identified inductively by a significant political reorientation of the strategy, promoting a particular type of social investment. The social investment perspective proposed by the EU institutions started with a focus on labor market participation (hence focusing on the skill mobilization function of social investment) before being broadened in 2000 to a perspective that included skill creation as much as skill mobilization and preservation. It then changed again toward a return to workforce mobilization and experienced a specific "social investment moment" with the Social Investment Package (de la Porte & Natali, 2018), before being embedded within a broader European pillar of social rights (EPSR) in 2019.

In order to explain the adoption of and subsequent changes in the social investment strategy proposed by the European Union, we then examine the politics of EU social investment. To understand the content and variation of the EU social investment framework, we focus on why and how key protagonists among relevant actors (EU commissioners and directors-general, EU political parties, heads of state and ministers of EU member states, as well as European intellectuals) have influenced EU social investment ideas and initiatives.

We argue that two main dynamics explain the metamorphoses of the European Union's approach to social investment. First, there is an "internal" dynamic, consisting of internal battles within the European institutions between what we call (following de la Porte & Pochet, 2002) "economically oriented" actors[1] and "socially oriented" actors.[2] The general dynamic is that through various spillover effects, and at different moments, the economically oriented actors try to capture the labor market and social policy fields and impose their market-liberalizing view on them, pushing for labor market deregulation, cost containment and privatization in social policies, while the socially oriented actors react and negotiate compromises that allow for a more social solution in order to maintain equitable welfare states and fair labor markets (de la Porte & Pochet, 2002). Since social investment combines both an economic perspective (investing for the knowledge-based economy) and a social preoccupation (to avoid the reproduction of inherited inequalities and to promote gender equality as well as autonomy and social progress for all), it became essential to elaborate "ambiguous agreements" (Palier, 2005) that allow each of these antagonistic actors to claim achievement of its objectives.

However, we also need to look at a second dynamic to fully understand the politics of social investment at the EU level; that is, we need to look at the support or opposition on the part of member states to the Commission's initiatives. Coalitions of member states and/or political parties on particular issues do indeed explain the content of EU initiatives, as has been demonstrated by Tallberg (2008) and Tallberg and Johansson (2008) regarding the adoption of the Lisbon Strategy in 2000. As Tallberg (2008) has shown, for socioeconomic issues the left–right divide does matter; and depending on the political center of gravity of the European Council, different perspectives will be taken on labor market and social policies. In these political dynamics, the reference to national socioeconomic models that are perceived to be successful at a particular moment in time will be key to achieving compromises between various EU actors and member states.

This chapter is organized as follows. In the first part, we present EU social investment initiatives in five distinct sequences, underlining each one's primary orientation in terms of social investment functions and distributive profiles, following the WOPSI typology. In the second part, for each sequence, we analyze, first, the politics behind the EU social investment initiatives and, second, the substantive content of EU social investment policy and the national socioeconomic model(s) associated with it.

1. The Directorate-General in charge of economic affairs at the Commission, the Economic Policy Committee (providing analyses for the Economic and Financial Affairs Council), the European Central Bank, and employer organizations.
2. The Directorate-General in charge of social affairs, the Employment Committee, and the Social Protection Committee (the latter two providing analyses for the Employment and Social Affairs Council), plus some left-leaning members of the European Parliament. The two terms "economically oriented" and "socially oriented" correspond to the vocabulary used by the actors themselves (at least in interviews) and have been used in different studies (see de la Porte & Pochet, 2002; Mandin, 2001).

4.2. FIVE SEQUENCES IN THE DEVELOPMENT OF SOCIAL INVESTMENT INITIATIVES AT THE EU LEVEL

Prior to the launch of the European Monetary Union (EMU), social policy at the EU level mainly concerned equal treatment, which related primarily to labor market policies, or highly technical areas, such as health and safety at work, that were not part of the core domains of welfare states. In these areas, the Court of Justice of the European Union played a very active role in interpreting EU law (Leibfried & Pierson, 1995; Martinsen, 2015).

By the 1990s, however, labor market and social policy had entered the EU agenda. Welfare state reforms, previously considered to be in the realm of member states' sovereignty, began to be addressed at the EU level, due to a spill-over from the preparation and then implementation of the EMU. In 1993, by adopting the Maastricht Treaty, member states agreed to have sound macro-economic policy, including low inflation, yearly balanced budgets (low budget deficits), and relatively stable (and low) public debt. Yet, the Maastricht Treaty should not be seen as imposing only technical criteria for the single currency (limiting the level of inflation, public deficit, and debt). It also meant that all the European countries accepted a profound shift in the economic policy paradigm, with implications for welfare states and labor markets: Welfare state expenditures were supposed to be kept at bay and markets to be more competitive, favored by low inflation. For labor markets, this meant wage moderation, ensuring labor costs were not too high, which implied reducing non-wage labor costs (de la Porte & Pochet, 2002; Palier, 2010). In the context of the Maastricht Treaty, welfare transfers and services were more often seen as comprising an element of rigidity and as a burden for companies (labor cost) and states (budget deficits). Those supporting Maastricht criteria–based monetarism increasingly denounced passive and costly welfare programs as impediments to the competitiveness of firms and countries in this new context. New policies aimed at retrenching social expenditure and liberalizing labor markets were promoted as necessary to meet the Maastricht criteria.

Increasingly, the focus of welfare reforms was on adapting and realigning the social policy paradigm to the new economic paradigm that had gained prominence at the EU level. With increased economic integration, the European Union started to take more and more initiatives to try to harmonize welfare state reforms among member states (at least ideationally; see Moreno & Palier, 2005; Palier & Pochet, 2005). As Morel et al. (2012) show, the social investment perspective is explicitly aimed at combining economic objectives (increasing labor market participation and preparing the workforce of the knowledge-based economy) with social policy concerns (addressing new social risks that the old welfare states were neglecting) and instruments (childcare, active labor market policies, reconciliation policies, and the like). The social investment perspective thus appeared to be a fitting starting point for building a new European vision that could realign the region's welfare states with the new European economic context and policies.

Before analyzing the political processes that led to such EU social investment initiatives, we present the (cognitive) social policy framework(s) developed to reconcile welfare states and labor markets with the new economic context. We identify five institutionally significant sequences of social investment and relate them to the human capital mobilization, creation, and preservation functions of social investment, as well as the redistributive profiles that were adopted.

1) *The European Employment Strategy* (1993–1997). The first sequence in development of the EU series of initiatives began in the early 1990s and ultimately led to the adoption of Title VIa on Employment in the Amsterdam Treaty in 1997. The title specifies an overall EU objective of mobilization of human capital ("high level of employment") and preservation of human capital ("trained and adaptable workforce"). These policies were to be implemented in member states via policy coordination (an iterative policy cycle of common objectives, national reports, evaluation, and peer review), later called the Open Method of Coordination (OMC). Within the framework of the European Employment Strategy (EES), the first set of specific employment policy guidelines were adopted at the end of 1997, organized around "employability," "entrepreneurship," "adaptability," and "equal opportunities." The "employability" policies of the employment guidelines encourage a lifelong learning approach and comprehensive training but also policies to enable rapid labor market integration. The EES also included "equal opportunities" objectives aiming to increase the employment rate of women by promotion of measures for reconciling work and family life, mainly by ensuring access to affordable and high-quality day care but also ensuring equal wages for men and women. The promoted policies were centered on labor market policies, and childcare was included to support labor market participation. Thus, the main approach taken by the EU social investment initiatives during this first phase was skill mobilization, and the distributive profile was a combination of targeted policies (for those out of the labor market) and inclusive ones (lifelong learning for all).

2) *The Lisbon Strategy* (1998–2004). The second sequence pertains to the adoption and first implementation of the Lisbon Strategy, a growth strategy that implied specific labor market but also welfare state reforms. With preparation already begun in 1998, the Lisbon Strategy was adopted in March 2000 by the European Council. It aimed to make the European Union "the most competitive and dynamic

knowledge-based economy in the world capable of sustainable economic growth with more and better jobs and greater social cohesion" by 2010. It was first implemented under the Prodi Commission (1999–2004). With this strategy, the perspectives on mobilization of human capital were reinforced, with quantitative employment rate targets for the European Union to be reached by 2010: a 70% overall employment rate and 60% female employment rate (European Council, 2000). There was also a strong focus on quality in work, highlighting in particular the importance of decent wages. Moving beyond employment and labor market policy, it expanded the social investment perspective to human capital creation. The focus on childcare, previously a subelement of the EES, was strengthened, and childcare targets (at least 30% of children aged 0–3 attending childcare) were agreed in 2002 (European Council, 2002). Higher education was also high on the agenda, with specific targets set for completion of tertiary education. A social inclusion strategy was also developed which included integration through work and a rights-based approach to fighting poverty. An annual (spring) summit, exclusively concentrating on social and economic issues, was institutionalized to discuss progress in social investment–type policies.

3) *Constricting the Lisbon Agenda* (2005–2010). The third sequence comprises a reformulation of the Lisbon Strategy under the first Barroso Commission (2004–2009) in a more liberal direction. It led to a stronger focus on mobilizing human capital, while creation and preservation became less significant. The notion of flexicurity became flagged by the European Union as a means for European countries to ensure competitiveness on labor markets but also protection and skills. It was partly inspired by the Danish and Dutch labor market models (i.e., a combination of flexible labor markets, training, and decent unemployment benefits). Quality in employment and quality of social protection were no longer on the agenda. Reconciliation of work and family life and childcare became side issues. When adopting the new "Europe 2020" growth strategy in 2010, only three (limited) social investment objectives survived: further increasing labor market participation (in any jobs), increasing the level of tertiary education, and reducing the number of people at risk of poverty or social exclusion. The Europe 2020 growth strategy was integrated with the "European Semester," the governance procedure around the EMU, which is driven by economic and financial affairs ministers and European Commission directorates-general. EU commitment to inclusive social investment was weakened and refocused on targeted workforce mobilization.

4) *The Social Investment Package* (2011–2013). The fourth sequence leads to the adoption of the Social Investment Package. It was an attempt

by experts to counteract increasing economic pressures on social policies coming from the new EU economic governance. Social investment protagonists, who had been active in previous sequences, were keen on developing a more inclusive and comprehensive social investment policy. The resultant Social Investment Package, adopted in 2013, encouraged member states to develop and strengthen policies such as early childhood education and care, education, active labor market policies, training, and lifelong education. It also mentioned the social protection aspects of the comprehensive social investment policies that had been key between 2000 and 2004. These included housing support, rehabilitation, healthcare, and long-term care services. The life-course perspective, entailing lifelong learning but also possibilities to have temporary periods away from the labor market for childcare, was emphasized more than in the previous periods (de la Porte & Natali, 2018). The focus of social investment was thus on creation and mobilization of human capital and capabilities and, to some extent, preservation. However, as will be shown, despite much activity by social investment protagonists and the actual adoption of the Social Investment Package, there were no strong political commitments among member states or within the second Barroso Commission (2009–2014) to develop and strengthen instruments for social investment.

5) *Toward European Social Rights?* (2014–2019). The fifth sequence represents a reorientation of EU social policy toward a focus on rights and principles, with little emphasis on social investment. It begins with the Juncker Commission, which took office in 2014. Juncker aimed to boost the social dimension of Europe following austerity, high unemployment (especially among young people), and sluggish growth. Part of this response was to tackle the youth unemployment that resulted from the Eurocrisis through a "youth guarantee," a co-funded EU activation scheme for young people not in education, employment, or training, so-called NEETs (Tosun, 2017). The Juncker Commission also launched the European Pillar of Social Rights (EPSR), adopted as a solemn declaration by all EU institutions in November 2017 in Gothenburg. According to its Article 14, the EPSR "expresses principles and rights essential for fair and well-functioning labor markets and welfare systems in 21st century Europe. It re-affirms some of the rights already present in the Union acquis and includes new principles which address the challenges arising from societal, technological and economic developments." It identifies 20 principles in three areas: access to the labor market, fair working conditions on the labor market, and social protection and inclusion. Some of the social investment orientations which had been developed during the fourth sequence

were included in the pillar (namely education, training and lifelong learning, active support to employment, work–life balance, childcare, and support to children). Announced as a series of rights that should become accessible to all citizens, hence potentially promoting inclusive social investment, these principles remain vague since, as Article 14 states, "For them to be legally enforceable, the principles and rights first require dedicated measures or legislation to be adopted at the appropriate level". The social investment aspects of the pillar were not the central focus of the Juncker Commission.

4.3. THE POLITICAL PROCESSES EXPLAINING THE METAMORPHOSES OF SOCIAL INVESTMENT AT THE EU LEVEL

EU social investment initiatives thus started with labor market concerns; then comprised a comprehensive approach to skills, equality, and social cohesion during the late 1990s and early 2000s; and then shifted to a narrower perspective, mostly focused on labor force mobilization within an agenda concerned with austerity. It ended up being absorbed (and diluted) within the broader European Pillar of Social Rights. We now analyze the politics of social investment metamorphoses in the five sequences we identified. Before presenting our analysis, we present the various types of actors that have played prominent roles in these politics and the mechanisms through which their influence operates.

The European Union's social investment ideas have been influenced by various European intellectuals and experts and by what appeared to be the "successful" models provided by different EU countries. Perspectives depended on the economic context: relative economic growth during the late 1990s and the early 2000s, deep economic crisis in 2008 and 2009 followed by the EU debt crisis starting in 2010, and the subsequent dualization of Europe (Palier et al., 2018). In these various contexts, countries fared differently, providing a succession of "models" that were perceived as having been successful. The European Union's social investment initiatives were initially strongly influenced by the (Anglo-) Nordic successes of the 1990s. From 2005, the German model gained traction, a trend that was strengthened following the financial crisis beginning in 2008 and the EU austerity policies after 2010. Various waves of EU enlargement and the changes of political leadership in the European Commission (and in the directorates-general) have also contributed to shaping EU social investment.

In order to understand how these influences have translated into concrete EU initiatives, we look at the political activity of specific and relevant actors. European intellectuals have been central in framing social investment at the EU level. However, the extent of their influence has been highly dependent on whether they found political support within EU institutions and among member states. We thus also analyze the role of EU actors within EU institutions (such as EU commissioners, functionaries, or members of the European Parliament) and especially the political activity of the Commission leadership and the Commission directorates-general,[3] as well as various technical issue-specific committees, the European Parliament, and experts. As mentioned in the introduction, de la Porte and Pochet (2002) have shown that these actors can be separated into two distinct groups: the "economically oriented" actors (directorates-general and issue-specific committees focusing on financial and economic matters, favoring a liberal approach involving welfare state retrenchment and labor market deregulation) and "socially oriented" actors (directorates-general and issue-specific committees focusing on employment and social protection, favoring a strong social dimension of Europe). The content of the EU social investment perspective partly varies according to the power of one of these groups over the other one. But these European Union actors are not autonomous as far as EU concrete actions are concerned; they rely on the decisions taken by the member states. These decisions depend on the political orientation of the EU institutions that reflect the composition and varying coalitions among member states. Hence, the EU social investment framework has been substantively influenced by the political orientation of the EU decision-making institutions, in particular the European Council (gathering the heads of states and of governments, who give the general orientation to EU policies), the Council of the European Union (which passes legislation and is composed of ministers from the member states[4]), and the European Commission (which is the executive branch of the European Union, has the monopoly on policy initiatives, and has become more and more politicized since the early 2000s). We thus look at the left–right orientation of the political leaders within the European Council (see our tables), and we also checked that the political composition of the Councils of Ministers corresponded to the main political orientation of the European Council of heads and governments (for this we use the Armingeon et al. [2019] database; see appendix).[5]

3. The Commission is organized into policy departments, known as "directorates-general," which are responsible for different policy areas. They develop, implement, and manage EU policy, law, and funding programs.
4. Its composition varies according to the policies at stake. The Ecofin Council gathers national ministers of economy and finance (and sometimes budget) and deals with economic and financial issues and policies; the Council of Social and Employment Affairs gathers national ministers in charge of social and employment affairs and deals with the corresponding issues. It can sometimes convene both, such as during the Spring Summit institutionalized in 2000.
5. Other scholars have conducted a more advanced analysis of preference heterogeneity in the Council and other European institutions, but we focus mainly on the social investment protagonists here, where the left–right composition of the European Council and member states is the most important dimension to be considered (Tallberg & Johansson, 2008).

In sum, the two main political dynamics that shape the European Union's social investment initiatives are the internal struggle between economically and socially oriented actors and the variation in the political center of gravity of the European Council. The general dynamic of the EU politics of social investment is the following: the more left-leaning[6] the EU member states, the more inclusive are the social investment initiatives introduced by the European Union (strongly influenced by socially oriented actors), and the more right-leaning, the more focused on activation and mere human capital mobilization (strongly influenced by economically oriented actors). We now turn to our analyses of the politics of each sequence.

4.3.1. Sequence 1: The European Employment Strategy (EES)—An Anglo-Nordic model (1993–1997)

4.3.1.1. Politics: A spillover effect from EU economic integration supported by left-leaning European actors

The discussions on core redistributive policy among EU member states, that is, on how to maintain national welfare states in the context of the EMU, began following the 1992 signing of the Maastricht Treaty, which institutionalized the EMU. During national debates regarding whether to adopt the Maastricht Treaty, many European governments discovered that European integration was not always perceived as a good thing by their citizens, who saw only economic constraints, not social advantages. This is reflected in the referendums on the EMU, including in France, where the Maastricht Treaty was barely approved, and in Denmark, where it was rejected. In these circumstances, some European actors tried to promote a more social Europe, aimed at full employment in a period of economic recession (1992–1993), in order to increase the Union's legitimacy.

Within the European Commission, the Directorate-General for Employment and Social Affairs (called DG V at the time, but was renamed DG EMPL in the mid 1990s) had prepared two recommendations on social protection that were adopted by the European Council in 1992. The first concerned ensuring sufficient resources and social assistance in social protection systems (European Council, 1992a). The second proposed a convergence of social protection objectives and policies, aimed at "improving and modernizing national social protection systems." This recommendation advocated the reduction of "social burdens" (i.e., social contributions) on firms in order to make social protection more employment-friendly. It proposed to move from a passive to an active social policy framework and promoted the notion of "productive" social policy (European Council, 1992b). As for employment policies, the idea of using the

---

6. "Left-leaning government," as coded by Armingeon et al. (2019), denotes when a party from the socialist or social democratic party family dominates the governmental coalition.

classic European method of integration was given up in favor of a softer approach, elaborating common objectives for different national policies.

In December 1993, after several months of consultation and despite a political
context unfavorable for a European social turn (right-wing parties were dominant in 1993 and 1994; see Table 4.1), Commission President Jacques Delors
published a white paper on growth, competitiveness, and employment that
called for greater concern about unemployment at the EU level and for linking
European macroeconomic policy with welfare reforms aimed at raising employment levels (European Commission, 1993).

Table 4.1 Left-leaning heads of state and government in the European Council,
1993–1997

	1993	1994	1995	1996	1997
Left-leaning heads of state and government	3	4	8	8	9
Number of member states	12	12	15	15	15

Source. Armingeon et al. (2019).

In parallel, as part of the first program of the newly founded Party of European
Socialists, the European Employment Initiative was launched. Influenced by its
Nordic members, the European Socialists attempted to better connect issues of
welfare and employment (Wincott, 2003). With an active employment policy
becoming a focal point of the party, attention turned to activation, productivity,
and high employment rates. This turn reflected a shift to the "new left" perspective that was emerging among Democrats in the United States under Bill
Clinton (elected president in 1992) and the United Kingdom's "New Labour"
under Tony Blair (who took over leadership of the Labour Party in 1994 and
was elected prime minister in 1997) and that was also visible in the evolution
of Nordic social democrats in the mid-1990s. The debate was informed by the
Delors white paper but also by a 1993 report written by Allan Larsson for the
Party of European Socialists, entitled "Put Europe to Work," also known as the
"Larsson Report" (de la Porte, 2011; Lightfoot, 2003). The issue of how to develop labor market policy to support the aims of the EMU was central. The orientation proposed in the white paper and reiterated in the Larsson Report were
eventually adopted in 1994 at the Essen European Council, which was the last
attended by Delors as Commission president (European Council, 1994).

At that meeting, the European Council approved five axes around which to
organize the convergence of national employment policies: improving employment opportunities, increasing the employment intensity of growth, developing
active labor market policies, targeting measures to reactivate the long-term unemployed, and reducing non-wage labor costs to encourage employers to hire
low-skilled workers (de la Porte & Pochet, 2002). However, because of political

blockages from conservative governments, there was no real political push toward concrete implementation of policies along these axes.

There was a wind change with the 1995 enlargement. As shown in Table 4.1, the political composition of the European Council changed dramatically in 1995. When Sweden and Finland became EU members along with Austria, a strong momentum eventually emerged for developing a common European employment policy. Allan Larsson, former finance minister of Sweden, member of the Party of European Socialists, author of the party's Larsson Report, and designated director general of the European Commission's DG EMPL in 1995, worked with Swedish Prime Minister Ingvar Carlsson (1994–1996) to develop EU employment policy. An influential protagonist at the time, Larsson presented a paper, "A Vision for the IGC [Intergovernmental Conference]: A European Employment Union—To Make EMU Possible," as part of the preparations for treaty revisions that were planned for 1997. In the paper, he introduced the idea of developing an employment union alongside the EMU, emphasizing that "the creation of an Employment Union would be the expression of a common European commitment to give a central role to the battle against unemployment" (Larsson, 1995, pp. 5–6). In the paper, active labor market policy was identified as a necessary means to enhance skills and to increase labor market participation.

However, until 1997, no commitment was made at the EU level to follow through on these new proposals, especially because of continuing blockages from conservative governments in member states such as Germany and Spain. It is the deepening of the competition over welfare issues between "economically oriented" and "socially oriented" European actors and a change in majority within the European Council that permitted increasing involvement of European institutions in social policies.

After the 1994 Essen summit, the Directorate-General for Economic and Financial Affairs (DG ECFIN, previously called DGII) seized on the European Council's new interest in employment policy to promote its own views on these policies, shaped by monetarism: In various communications, it repeatedly proposed to liberalize the labor market and make it more flexible in order to reduce unemployment (following here the perspectives adopted in the OECD job studies of the early 1990s; see Mahon, 2011). Meanwhile, in some reports, the Economic Policy Committee (EPC) was calling for a more flexible labor market and more liberal employment policies. In response, the Directorate-General for Employment and Social Affairs (DG EMPL) tried to counteract these trends by using the term "security" next to "flexibility" in Commission texts. Meanwhile, it lobbied national governments to make employment an explicit, positive goal of the Union. The DG EMPL claimed that otherwise national ministers of employment would be stripped of their role by the Council of Economic and Finance Ministers (Ecofin Council) (Mandin, 2001).

The battle for shaping employment policy was strongly influenced by the newcomers to the European Union. Austria, Finland, and Sweden who joined the European Union in 1995 had pro–social policy traditions. Sweden, with strong support from Finland, supported a common EU employment and social policy. Employment policy coordination, including active labor market policy, at the EU level was presented to the national electorates of Sweden and Finland as a means of safeguarding national social standards (de la Porte, 2011). Meanwhile, left/social democratic governments were increasingly numerous across Europe. In June 1997, the recently elected French Socialist prime minister, Lionel Jospin, pressed European countries to take action in this field even before the treaty was adopted.

In this context, a new chapter section on employment (Title VIa) was included in the Amsterdam Treaty signed in October 1997 so that Europe explicitly recognized the goal of full employment. The "Employment Title" contained the main ideas proposed by Larsson. An exceptional European Council summit on employment was organized in Luxembourg in November 1997 to launch the EES, even before the Amsterdam Treaty was ratified by all EU countries. It is the shift toward left-wing governments and prime ministers among the powerful EU countries, in particular the United Kingdom (Blair, Labour Party) and France (Jospin, Parti Socialiste), that enabled agreement on the Employment Title. This left-leaning political coalition in the Council also then promoted the development of an EU employment policy (Tallberg & Johansson, 2008). Helmut Kohl (Christian Democratic Union, Germany), who had been opposed to the Employment Title since the 1994 Essen summit, and Jose Maria Aznar, representing the conservative coalition in Spain, agreed to include the title in the treaty because of its soft law character. Wim Kok, then prime minister of the Netherlands and later to be a key protagonist in reorienting the EES and the Lisbon Strategy, signed the Treaty of Amsterdam for his country. The title represents a legal commitment to the political objective of a high level of employment through an iterative policy cycle based on soft governance (de la Porte, 2011).

The Nordic economic and employment models were at the time perceived to be the most successful in the European Union and would thus serve as a blueprint for the EES, which represents the foundation of the European Union's social investment policy. Allan Larsson, who was director of the DG EMPL from 1995 to 2000, argued, based on his idea of an employment union, that an active labor market policy was essential for employment growth. The focus at the time was on the mobilization of human capital (enhancing employment rates) but also on the creation and preservation of human capital through training and active labor market policy, particularly based on the Swedish model. Although inspired by the Nordic model, this policy proposal was also congruent with the "new left" approach to the "investment welfare state" (Giddens, 1998) promoted especially by UK Prime Minister Blair, who supported the supply-side type of employment policies which were central in the EES. The compromise was to increase employment rates by deregulating labor markets but also by ensuring that the labor force was equipped with the necessary skills. This entailed a shift from a passive to an active labor market policy, rather than an increase in expenditure, in order to remain on target with the budget deficit limits of the EMU. It was the countries with low employment rates, especially among women and older workers (i.e., corporatist-type welfare states) that were targeted implicitly.

Once the Employment Title had been integrated into the Amsterdam Treaty and the EES launched, the DG EMPL under Larsson's leadership focused on identifying goals that would form the basis of a Commission communication (European Commission, 1997). In the communication, 20 employment policy aims were proposed under four headings: entrepreneurship, adaptability, employability, and equal opportunities. In addition, the Commission communication proposed a quantitative employment rate target—70%—for the European Union. The Commission's strategy, defined by the DG EMPL but also supported by the DG General Secretariat and the DG ECFIN, was to place more pressure on member states to increase their employment rates. The employment rate across the European Union at the time was 60%, due to a large extent to low rates of employment among women, youth, and older workers, especially in the corporatist-type welfare states where a labor shedding strategy was implemented all along the 1980s and early 1990s (Palier, 2010).

On the basis of the Commission's proposals, the Commission worked together with member states to agree on employment policy aims. All 20 guidelines proposed by the Commission were accepted, with employability—embodying mobilization of human capital—prioritized most by member states. The objectives for the EES and its European employment guidelines were endorsed at the extraordinary Jobs Summit, held in Luxembourg in November 1997 (European Council, 1997). However, the proposal to have a 70% employment rate benchmark was not accepted by the Council at that time.

4.3.1.2. Social investment output: An Anglo-Nordic policy model

With Larsson as the first EU social investment protagonist, the Swedish model, with its focus on mobilization and creation of human capital, was a strong source of inspiration for the EES. But the first sequence of EU social investment also reflects the UK approach to labor market participation, especially under Prime Minister Blair. Thus, the initial EU social investment, with a legal basis for policy coordination in the Employment Title and specific employment policy aims in the EES, reflected the Anglo-Nordic approach to labor market policy. Employment and labor market policy focused on encouraging employment participation among all categories of citizens through an active approach to labor force participation, including upskilling policies, such as vocational training and lifelong learning. At the same time, workers and labor markets were encouraged to be flexible (adaptability) and entrepreneurial. Furthermore, there was a strong focus on gender-equalizing policies to support women, including enhancing the supply of childcare. Through the EES, an Anglo-Nordic approach to social investment started to emerge and was institutionalized at the EU level through policy coordination. This implied that the continental and Southern European countries had to reform their welfare systems. The European Union encouraged and, where politically viable, would partially shape, or at least inspire, national reforms (de la Porte & Jacobsson, 2012; Palier, 2010).

Thus, initially, EU social investment combined an inclusive social investment distributive profile focused on mobilization of human capital for all with a targeted distributive profile, aiming to mobilize groups that were not active on the labor market (women and older workers), especially in conservative corporatist-type welfare states. There was also a focus on preservation and upskilling human capital since the proposed policies entailed high-quality training and lifelong learning so that workers would be able to respond to shifts in the labor market. This approach was based on the Nordic model where traditionally training was central to active labor market policies but also integrated other active labor market policies aimed at facilitating rapid (re-)entry into the labor market, more in line with the liberal type of active labor market policies. The ideas were thus influenced by the Nordic model as well as by the "third way" thinking—emphasizing social rights and responsibility for all to contribute to the labor market.

4.3.2. Sequence 2: The Lisbon Strategy—The (Anglo-) Nordic model (1998–2004)

4.3.2.1. Politics: The consolidation and broadening of the EU social investment perspective

In the late 1990s, the European Union accelerated preparations for the single currency which would be launched in January 1999. To ensure that all the countries participating in the EMU would follow a similar economic policy that would guarantee the strength and stability of the Euro, the Stability and Growth Pact (SGP) was adopted in 1997. The SGP defined a process of policy coordination with EU benchmarks and policies, national reports, and EU surveillance, as well as corrective mechanisms in case of deviation from the agreed-upon aims. Most important in this initial institutional architecture are the limits for public debt (maximum 60% of gross domestic product [GDP]) and budget deficits (maximum 3% of GDP) and the pursuit of low inflation. The SGP thus asserted that a stable single currency needed sound public finance. The economically oriented European actors (especially DG ECFIN and the EPC, under the Ecofin Council) understood that they had a responsibility to guarantee that member states balance their budgets. They promoted an extensive version of the pact, imposing the view that public expenditure had to be controlled or even diminished for the sake of a stable euro. Multiple reports and studies from the EPC and the DG ECFIN showed that for many European countries public spending increased most for health and that demographic aging would soon cause a sharp increase in public pension expenditure. They started to suggest cost containment and structural reforms of health and pension systems. These reforms often meant a partial privatization of health and pension systems (Crespy & Vanheuverzwijn, 2019; de la Porte & Heins, 2015; Palier, 2009). The challenges were present in all EU countries but were more acute in the conservative-type welfare regimes, where public debt was higher than the 60% limit and where social protection expenditure, especially on pensions, was high (Palier, 2010).

However, the economically oriented actors could not totally win this battle. The Santer Commission (1995–1999) and the Prodi Commission (1999–2004) supported a more left-wing agenda. Under these two Commission leaderships, the DG EMPL had significant resources and was very strong. In reaction to the fiscal consolidation and structural reform agenda put forward by the DG ECFIN, the DG EMPL argued that, left to unfold, these dynamics would lead to the dismantling of national welfare systems and the demise of the European social model. Socially oriented actors thus argued that, instead of keeping social protection formally outside EU competence but in reality under the control of purely budgetary constraints and economic actors, it was time for Europe to endorse some common action in order to preserve and modernize European welfare systems. This argument was received in a politically favorable context: Between 1998 and 2002, left-leaning governments were in the majority in the European Union (see Table 4.2). These circumstances paved the way for the Lisbon Strategy that incorporated guidelines for welfare state reforms very much inspired by a social investment approach (Mandin, 2001; Palier, 2009).

Table 4.2 Left-leaning heads of state and government in the European Council, 1998–2004

	1998	1999	2000	2001	2002	2003	2004
Left-leaning heads of state and government	11	11	11	9	8	5	5
Number of member states	15	15	15	15	15	15	15

Source. Armingeon et al. (2019).

In July 1999, just before it resigned, the Santer Commission published a communication proposing "A concerted strategy for modernizing social protection" aimed at combining economic efficiency with social justice. The communication put forward "social protection as a productive factor" and "employment policy as a bridge between economic and social policy." The focus was on adapting social protection to aging populations, making social protection systems more employment-friendly, and adapting social protection to greater individualization of rights (European Commission, 1999). Key protagonists within the

Commission from Nordic countries, in particular Allan Larsson but also Juhani Lönnroth, a Finn and director of employment within the DG EMPL at the time, were active in developing the European Union's social dimension on the basis of social investment policies that are inherent in the Nordic model (de la Porte, 2011). These ideas resonated with the "new left" initiatives concerning social protection, as presented by Tony Blair and Gerhard Schröder in their paper published on the eve of European elections in June 1999, "Europe: The Third Way/Die Neue Mitte," in which they call for the transformation of the "social safety net of entitlements into a springboard to personal responsibility" (Blair & Schröder, 1999, p. 10). The DG EMPL was, at the time, the authoritative actor that shaped EU social policy to accompany economic and monetary policy in the EMU.

While the broader debate on social protection was being framed mainly in the DG EMPL, other actors also played a significant role. In particular, the European Anti-Poverty Network (EAPN), a non-governmental platform for networks of organizations battling poverty and social exclusion, also provided input to the debate on what was termed "social inclusion" policy (i.e., fighting social exclusion through labor market participation) in dialogue with the Commission and EU member states. The EAPN underlined the risk of poverty and social exclusion that would arise with public policy reforms designed to comply with the convergence criteria of the SGP if the focus would exclusively be on the financial sustainability of social protection. Thus, the EAPN emphasized social exclusion as a multifaceted problem and proposed a rights-based approach to inclusion that also focused on (re-)entry into the labor market. Partly due to the active role of the EAPN, one of the main objectives of the 1999 Commission communication on social protection was to develop a social inclusion policy, where work was identified as the best way to combat social exclusion (European Commission, 1999).

The Finnish, Portuguese, and French governments were also quite active in the debate on social inclusion in the 1999–2000 period. The Finnish government, with a prominent role of the minister of social affairs, Marja Perho, pushed for having social exclusion as one of the issues on the agenda of its presidency in the second half of 1999. The Finns advocated developing an EU social protection strategy, comparable to the one in employment policy. In view of Portugal's forthcoming presidency in early 2000, the country's minister of social affairs, Eduardo Ferro Rodrigues, supported an EU social inclusion strategy, while Prime Minister António Guterres (1995–2000), who was also president of the Portuguese Socialist Party, presented to the Party of European Socialists already in January 1999 a plan for a European growth strategy and, with it, a social inclusion strategy. This was met with strong support among the left-leaning governments in the European Union, which were in strong majority at the time (see Table 4.2).

As Portugal prepared its presidency, it sought to convince European governments that national welfare reforms should be coordinated through a balanced compromise between economic requirements and social objectives, in particular tackling poverty and promoting social inclusion. Prime Minister Guterres' aim was to develop a more comprehensive socially oriented growth strategy that would prepare Europe to better compete with the United States in the knowledge-based economy and that would include strong social protection. At the same time, he wanted to institutionalize a means to develop a common policy approach regarding national reforms of research and development, education, and social policy. To reach that aim, he appointed Maria Rodrigues, who had been minister of employment from 1995 to 1997, as his special advisor. To elaborate a new compromise between economic and social policy, several major studies were commissioned from European experts. As a result of one of these, Maurizio Ferrera, Anton Hemerijck, and Martin Rhodes prepared a publication on the future of welfare states ("recasting the welfare state"), calling for recalibration, rather than retrenchment, of social and employment policies (Ferrera et al., 2000). They proposed modernization of social protection but at the same time argued for an active shift of welfare states to include a stronger component of social investment, especially creation and mobilization of human capital. Thus, the Lisbon Summit of March 2000 was prepared with a focus on the knowledge-based economy and reforming social policy (de la Porte, 2011).

At the Lisbon Summit,[7] member state leaders met to agree on a socioeconomic strategy for the European Union for the coming decade. The resulting Lisbon Strategy set out the European Union's goal of becoming the world's most competitive knowledge-based economy, with more and better jobs. In this new approach, social policies were supposed to focus more on prevention and social investment than on compensating for immediate difficulties. Social policy is constructed as a necessary feature of a well-functioning modern economy, particularly one that hopes to position itself in the high stakes of the knowledge economy. In its declaration, the European Union promotes the notion of "quality" as a way to reconcile economic and social policies. For the European Union, promoting quality in employment and social policy is a key element in reaching the goals of building more and better jobs, creating a competitive and cohesive knowledge-based economy, and ensuring a positive mutual interaction between economic, employment, and social policies (Jenson & Pochet, 2002).

This signified that the skill creation and mobilization goals of social investment were center stage at the EU level. Importantly, member states committed to achieving an average employment rate of 70% by 2010, a target they had not agreed to at the launch of the EES. Member states also agreed to strive for

---

7. This was the first so-called Spring Summit. Since then, the European Council has held a meeting every spring devoted to economic and social questions.

an average female employment rate of 60% and an employment rate for older workers (aged 55–65) of 50%. Also during the Lisbon Summit, the principles of the OMC were adopted, in order to address common challenges through benchmarking, policy coordination, and monitoring of member state policies. Following the Lisbon Summit, the OMC was applied in various areas of social protection (social exclusion/inclusion, making work pay, pensions, and healthcare) and in other areas related to the knowledge economy (research and development, education).

In institutional terms, the Ecofin Council formally (legally) carried the most weight in the Council of the European Union,[8] but politically—supported by a strong representation of left-leaning governments (see Table 4.2)—the Employment and Social Affairs Council (EPSCO) had considerable influence at the time as well. As for employment policies, in the field of social protection, the Nordic model and the "new left" approach were the strongest sources of inspiration for EU policies. Recently arrived in power, left-leaning political leaders from corporatist-type welfare states (including Germany and France) also supported social investment since they wanted EU policy commitments to be able to drive changes domestically (Palier, 2010). Parallel to the framing of social protection on the EU agenda, the Commission, politically supported by Employment and Social affairs Council (EPSCO), initiated a process to institutionalize the intergovernmental Social Protection Committee, which was formally included in the Nice Treaty (adopted in 2001). Even the skeptical member states—Denmark and Germany—agreed to set up the working group to advise EPSCO, as long as it would not intervene in national welfare systems.

France, which held the EU presidency in the second half of 2000, was very keen on an EU social inclusion policy. On this basis, and with still a solid majority of left-leaning governments and prime ministers in the European Union, the social inclusion OMC strategy was adopted in December 2000. Its aims were to promote participation and integration through employment, reduce social risks, target actions toward vulnerable groups, and mobilize relevant actors to formulate and implement social inclusion goals. This OMC was of particular importance for the United Kingdom in light of its focus on children in poverty and for Portugal due to its relatively high rate of poverty.

The momentum to develop social policy initiatives successfully continued for the remainder of this period. In the first half of 2001, during the Swedish presidency, the OMC was launched in the area of pensions, whereby the economically and socially oriented actors worked together to propose reforms that would be fiscally responsible but also socially fair ("sustainable and adequate pension"). Under the Belgian presidency in the second half of 2001, a framework for investing in quality in employment and social policies was adopted (European Commission, 2001). Furthermore, Frank Vandenbroucke, Belgian minister of social affairs, commissioned Gøsta Esping-Andersen and colleagues to write a

---

8. See note 4.

report about a new welfare architecture for Europe. It was later published as a book, *Why We Need a New Welfare State*, advocating for social investment, especially focusing on investing in children from a young age and in female labor market participation (Esping-Andersen et al., 2002). The academic work by Esping-Andersen and colleagues reinforced Larsson's idea of "social protection as a productive factor" and offered policy recommendations on how to reform social protection toward social investment.

Childcare had been on the EU agenda since the launch of the EES, but there were initially no headline targets on this. In 2002, during the Spanish presidency, the European Union specified two benchmarks: 90% of children from age 3 until mandatory school age and 33% of children 0–2 years old should be in childcare by 2010 (European Council, 2002). The policy proposal supported the dual-earner model that became central to the EU social investment approach, with a strong focus on mobilizing (female) human capital to participate in the labor market. At the same time, the strategy also underlined the importance of childcare for human capital creation (investing in children's cognitive skills).

4.3.2.2. Social investment output: A "new left"–oriented (Anglo-)Nordic model

This second sequence in EU social investment focused on dual earners, with employment rate targets for the European Union (70% overall employment rate to be reached by 2010), in particular a female employment rate target (60% female employment rate to be reached by 2010). This focus is accompanied by an emphasis on creation of human capital for children (early childhood education and care) as well as for those who can participate in the labor market (lifelong learning). The Nordic model is the main source of inspiration, especially pertaining to the creation and mobilization of human capital. At the same time, however, the focus on children and child poverty entailed policies targeted at families with poor children based on the UK model. Social protection was seen as a productive factor but should be made more effective, among other ways, by enabling labor market participation of many groups of citizens. This type of goal is central in the Nordic countries, which focus on a strong relationship between universal social investment rights and responsibility to contribute to the labor market (see Chapter 2 in Volume II [Garritzmann et al., 2022]). The overall policy orientation of social investment at this time was inclusive.

4.3.3. Sequence 3: Constricting the Lisbon agenda—Toward an (Anglo-)German model (2005–2010)

4.3.3.1. Politics against inclusive and broad social investment

The political context among member states changed in 2004 in conjunction with the eastward enlargement of the European Union. With the arrival of the

Table 4.3 Left-leaning heads of state and government in the European Council, 2005–2010

	2005	2006	2007	2008	2009	2010
Left-leaning heads of state and government	10	9	10	11	10	9
Number of member states	25	25	27	27	27	27

Source. Armingeon et al. (2019).

new member states, the liberal political agenda weighed heavily in the Council, and right-wing parties and coalitions dominated the EU institutions (see Table 4.3). The social dimension of Europe was no longer central, partly because the left-leaning political parties in the European Council had lost ground (see Table 4.3). Already during the first term (2005–2009) of Jose Manuel Barroso, a former center-right Portuguese prime minister, the Commission itself became more center-right in its orientation.

André Sapir, an academic, contributed to shifting the political debate at that time. The Sapir Report, gathering the views of a high-level expert group, emphasized the need to strengthen competitiveness (Sapir et al., 2003). This resonated well with member states' political priorities in the enlarged configuration and their center-right political orientation. The focus on competitiveness in the Sapir Report strongly influenced the assessment of the Lisbon Strategy conducted in 2004–2005, under the leadership of Wim Kok, a former prime minister of the Netherlands who had strongly supported the EES in the 1990s. The *Jobs, Jobs, Jobs* report produced by the Employment Taskforce led by Kok shifted the debate from growth, employment, and social cohesion (including high-quality jobs and high-quality training) toward competitiveness, growth, and jobs. It recommended that the link between economic and employment policies (EMU and employment policy coordination) be strengthened, while the social inclusion OMC and other social policy initiatives were to continue but without the same political weight. In the mid-term revision of the Lisbon Strategy adopted in 2005, this orientation was supported by the center-right political majority among member states in the European Council and in the European Parliament (see Table 4.3). This meant that mobilization of human capital, especially focused on increasing employment rates, was central. Policies focused on initial and inclusive creation of human capital were sidelined, as were gender equality concerns (Jacquot, 2015).

Following the financial crisis late in the first decade of the 21st century, this workfare-based policy agenda became even more pronounced. The economies of the peripheral countries suffered dramatically, leading to sovereign debt crises whereby these countries were at risk of not being able to pay back their public debt without financial aid. When the second Barroso Commission began its tenure in 2009, the main issue on the EU agenda was regaining stability in the

Eurozone area. The emphasis at the EU level was on fiscal consolidation to contain the effects of the crisis in the Eurozone.

When preparing the successor of the Lisbon Strategy, the aim of the new Commission was to narrow the focus of the EES and OMCs to better support competitiveness and jobs. The OMCs were not central on the EU agenda, and social protection reform was seen mainly from the perspective of financial sustainability. Economic and employment policy were tied closely together in national reform programs that each country had to write and send to the Commission every year. They embodied the leaner version of social investment, which was a prelude to what would feature in "Europe 2020," the new growth strategy that would be adopted in 2010, where the general goals are organized around key priorities (fiscal consolidation, employment, climate, training, anti-poverty) but weakly institutionalized.

By the time the Europe 2020 strategy was agreed upon in 2010, it had an extremely low status. Since the global financial crisis hit Europe, the European Union's agenda was mostly occupied with reacting to the crisis and strengthening EMU governance. The European Union had moved toward requiring much tougher fiscal consolidation, embodying the thinking in Germany, developed among others by Wolfgang Schäuble, who became German minister of finance in 2009. Europe 2020 was integrated with the more centralized European Semester that was to govern economic and public policy. With the European Semester, the DG ECFIN's role as promoter of stable finances and consolidation was strengthened, while the DG EMPL was weakened considerably (de la Porte & Heins, 2015).

In the Europe 2020 strategy, the European Union adopted new headline targets in the areas covered by the Lisbon Strategy. The aim to increase labor market participation is stronger than ever: The previous target of an average overall employment rate of 70% was raised to 75% (to be reached by 2020). It also emphasizes ensuring that workers are skilled and can adapt to changes in the labor market. Human capital mobilization and creation are both present during this sequence. In terms of creation, there are two headline targets: to decrease the rate of school dropouts to 10% and to increase the proportion of young people with a tertiary education to 40% by 2020. However, attention to the quality of jobs was dismissed in favor of a high rate of (any) jobs, including low-wage service jobs.

In the years of the Great Recession, there was virtually no room for social policy initiatives. Significant dossiers, such as labor markets, were temporarily shifted from the DG EMPL to the DG ECFIN. This signified that the targets for employment rates and flexibilization, linked closely to the EMU, were prioritized, whereas quality in work, high-quality childcare, and lifelong learning were de-emphasized (de la Porte & Natali, 2018). During the financial crisis, employment subsidies and targeted reductions of non-wage labor costs as well as the promotion of self-employment—arguably of precarious character in the context of a major economic crisis—were among the measures proposed in the Europe 2020 strategy to stimulate job creation (de la Porte & Heins, 2015; Morel, 2015).

4.3.3.2. Social investment output: Toward an Anglo-German model

During this sequence, social investment at the EU level shifted from the (Anglo-)Nordic model to an Anglo-German model. This development mirrors developments in member states, where policy focused on enabling the creation of low-wage service jobs. This shift is embodied in the landmark Hartz reforms in Germany of the early 2000s, which dualized the labor market and whereby stratified and targeted social investment policies were reinforced (Emmenegger et al., 2012; Palier & Thelen, 2010). The focus was on the mobilization of human capital readily available in the labor market, and the principal aim was to increase employment rates. The focus on more jobs crowded out any effort to produce better jobs. Flexicurity—with some reference to the Danish model but also to the Dutch one (more focused on workfare than the Danish case)—was again flagged at the EU level as a means to combine flexible labor markets, investments in human capital through training, and relatively generous unemployment benefits (preservation of human capital). However, it was flexibility that was actually central, with little attention to skills and training or protection. Labor markets have been flexibilized in the eastern European countries and partially flexibilized in corporatist-type welfare states, but mostly for the low-skilled and in the service sector, while the middle class and skilled workers maintained secure positions in the labor market. Overall, activation has mainly been pursued through incentive reinforcement and employment assistance, which is strongly focused on mobilization of workers to enter the labor market, while upskilling, focused on the creation of human capital, has been under-prioritized (Bengtsson et al., 2017).

Thus, the social investment strategy at the EU level has, during this sequence, shifted more toward the mobilization of human capital. Furthermore, in corporatist-type welfare states, social investment is taken on board; but it is mainly stratified and targeted, and in liberal countries (among which we would include central and eastern European countries) it is targeted and meager (de la Porte & Jacobsson, 2012; see Chapter 8 in Volume II).

4.3.4. Sequence 4: A social investment package with no national political anchor (2011–2013)

4.3.4.1. Politics: The desperate attempt to revive social investment

In the period after 2010, center-right parties continued to dominate among EU countries (see Tables 4.4 and 4.5). This facilitated, in 2011–2013, rapid decisions to strengthen the governance of the EMU, which enhanced the surveillance

Table 4.4 Left-leaning heads of state and government in the European Council, 2011–2013

	2011	2012	2013
Left-leaning heads of state and government	8	9	12
Number of member states	27	27	27

Source. Armingeon et al. (2019).

capability of the DG ECFIN vis-à-vis member state budgets (de la Porte & Heins, 2015). The general approach mirrored the German growth strategy focused on exporting capacities and the moderation of labor costs (Scharpf, 2021). There was no questioning of the fiscal restraint underlying this model. Its pursuit led to austerity in most EU countries, especially in the countries at the Union's periphery that were most severely hit by the financial crisis (Dukelow, 2015; Pavolini et al., 2015; Theodoropoulou, 2015).

The political response to austerity policy in the south has been the strengthening of far-left parties, while the north has seen a strong shift to populist-nationalist movements (Palier et al., 2018). In this context, several actors in and around the Commission sought to develop alternative policy responses to austerity, such as social investment, but also social rights, to respond to increasing political dissatisfaction in countries strongly affected by the financial crisis.

Academics were first-movers in proposing a more inclusive and pro-active approach to social investment. In 2011, Frank Vandenbroucke, Bruno Palier, and Anton Hemerijck wrote an opinion paper, "The EU Needs a Social Investment Pact," intended to influence policymakers (Vandenbroucke et al., 2011). These three academics were also very active in advocating social investment as a policy frame in the European Commission and in the European Parliament. Hemerijck presented the opinion paper to the European Parliament, which debated the issue and later adopted a resolution on this topic (European Parliament, 2013).

Laszlo Andor, who became commissioner for employment and social affairs under the second Barroso Commission in 2009, wanted to move beyond the fiscal consolidation agenda being pursued by the economically oriented actors. When he entered office, most of Europe 2020 had already been planned, and its salience was low as attention was placed on the tightening of governance of the EMU (de la Porte & Heins, 2015). To facilitate progress with his social policy ambitions, Andor appointed high-level staff in the DG EMPL, including in 2011 Lieve Fransen as director for social policy and Europe 2020. Andor and Fransen decided, following interaction with key intellectuals on social investment, to explore the possibility of developing an EU social investment policy and to establish an expert group for this purpose. Fransen became leader of the ad hoc social investment expert group, to which she recruited various academics, including Joakim Palme, Frank Vandenbroucke, Maurizio Ferrera, and later on Bruno

Palier (European Commission, 2017). The expert group had a clear objective to reach consensus on a strong narrative about social investment and to elaborate a series of indicators aimed at tracking the social and economic return of social investment policies. The social investment protagonists hoped that social investment would contribute to adding a social dimension to the European Semester, like the EES and social OMC had added a strong social dimension to the Lisbon Strategy (de la Porte & Natali, 2018). The slight increase in left-leaning leaders in the European Council in 2012 and 2013 (see Table 4.4) signified that there might be more interest in EU social policy initiatives.

On the basis of the expert group's work and influenced by the legacy of earlier social investment experience in the European Union, the Commission developed a new social investment narrative. The EU Social Investment Package (SIP) issued by the Commission in February 2013 was shaped by the policies discussed in the expert group (de la Porte & Natali, 2018). The centerpiece of the SIP was a communication stressing "the need to invest in human capital throughout life and ensure adequate livelihoods" (European Commission, 2013). It included policies focused on creating (lifelong learning, education, training, and childcare), mobilizing (facilitating entry to the labor market, active labour market policy), and to a lesser extent preserving human capital (healthcare). While the aims were not new, presenting social investment as a unifying framework was novel as the SIP proposed to merge the EES and the social policies of the Lisbon Strategy in one overarching policy framework. Similar to the Commission's thinking in 1999, social investment was framed as a complement to social protection. Compared to the EES and the Lisbon Strategy, there is more emphasis on the life-course perspective on social investment and on starting investment in human capital very early.

However, within the Commission, and especially since the introduction of the new economic procedures agreed upon between 2009 and 2011, the balance of power had shifted even more in favor of the DG ECFIN. The DG EMPL was simply not able to convey its social investment vision to the rest of the Commission. While the SIP included a range of initiatives, no agreement could be reached on the (new) social investment indicators that were to be integrated into the European Semester. Only the targets for employment rate, childcare, training, and higher education from previous sequences were still present in the European Semester (de la Porte & Natali, 2018).

The DG ECFIN's strength is reflected by the indicators centered around fiscal consolidation and budgetary restraint. It is especially the 0.5% structural budget deficit indicator that has become the new focus of the DG ECFIN, leaving little room for expansive fiscal spending, including for social investment. In 2011, the DG ECFIN designed a macroeconomic imbalance procedure (MIP), which comprises 14 key indicators—although this number has changed over time—as well as an elaborate system of DG ECFIN-driven analyses and instruments enabling the European Union to require that member states take corrective action when not meeting MIP targets. The MIP includes key labor market indicators such as activity rates, long-term unemployment rates, and youth unemployment rates, which are framed from an economic rather than social perspective (de la Porte & Heins, 2015).

After the "social investment moment" that culminated in the SIP communication and other documents, it became "lost in translation" when trying to shift from ideational consensus to indicators and to renewed political commitment (de la Porte & Natali, 2018). The other social policy issue that Andor had mobilized for as political entrepreneur, a European Unemployment Insurance System, was stopped in its tracks before rising to decision-making levels due to its redistributive implications for member states. After Andor's term in the Commission ended in 2014, no strong social investment protagonists remained there. The social investment working group was dissolved, Fransen left the Commission, and the main intellectual entrepreneurs of social investment were no longer active in the EU arena.

Despite the formal adoption of the SIP, there was virtually no national backing or engagement with social investments among member states. The Nordics had become more euro-skeptic, and Eastern Europe had never bought into the idea of social investment. Most member states, especially the southern countries, which had frequently been under excessive deficit procedure since 2010, were cutting budgets for social protection and social investment (Palier et al. 2018; Pavolini et al., 2015). Thus, there were no national promoters of social investment (Ferrera, 2017) as there were in the period at the end of the 1990s and the early 2000s. By contrast, the political priorities in the early 2010s were centered around strengthening and improving existing EMU governance procedures, cost containment, and increasing growth. With the main implicit national models being either liberal (Anglo and Eastern Europe) or corporatist-dualized (especially Germany), social investment was de facto restricted to a lean targeted version. In view of the policies implemented, the second Barroso Commission (2009–2014) was even more liberal than the first one.

4.3.4.2. Social investment output: The domination of the German-liberal model

At the EU level, the 2011–2013 years were mostly characterized by a reinforcement of the German model, reflected in the strengthened governance of the EMU. As of 2010, Germany was no longer considered to be the "sick man" of Europe, but had become a symbol of stability and economic success, with a pragmatic conservative approach to social policy reforms, although it institutionalized dualism (Palier & Thelen, 2010). The EU response to countries experiencing a sovereign debt crisis represents the underlying German paradigm. The European Union supports "growth-friendly fiscal consolidation," which entails cutting public expenditure (especially social expenditure, including social investment) and limiting tax increases, which should in turn create market confidence and enhance private sector investment and economic growth.

The growth strategy for countries under Memorandums of Understanding since 2010 or 2011 (among them Ireland, Greece, Portugal, and partly Spain) was inspired by the German export-led growth strategy, that is, budgetary discipline, market credibility, and competitiveness (Scharpf, 2021). Ireland was the country that most clearly followed this strategy and was subsequently commended by the European Commission as a blueprint for other debt-ridden countries (Dukelow, 2015).

In contrast to the first two sequences, the EU social investment reform strategy that was put forward with the SIP did not resonate politically with priorities and reforms undertaken in member states. In corporatist-type welfare states, labor markets were dualized, particularly due to the Hartz reforms in Germany and its replicas in other countries. Across the countries of the European Union, especially those badly hit by the Great Recession, all areas of social protection, including social investment, were affected by austerity policy (de la Porte & Heins, 2016; Pavolini et al., 2015).

The adoption of the SIP (2013) had little political impact in member states, but it did encourage some protagonists in the Commission to make further efforts to develop a strong social dimension for EU social policy in the subsequent sequence and look for more political backing for their social policy initiatives. The work to prepare the SIP led to a new initiative in the following years.

4.3.5. Sequence 5: Toward social rights? (2014–2019)

4.3.5.1. The politics of the renewal of a social Europe
The year 2014 marks the beginning of the presidency of Jean-Claude Juncker in the European Commission. His agenda was focused, on the one hand, on rendering the EMU more solid (he chaired the Eurogroup from 2005 to 2013) and, on the other hand, on strengthening social rights. In light of his assessment that all the previous initiatives regarding a social Europe lacked a legal base, he sought to provide more comprehensive social rights for EU citizens. He proposed a European Pillar of Social Rights (EPSR) in 2016, arguing that fair, inclusive, and empowering welfare systems and labor markets are crucial for boosting productivity, strengthening social cohesion, and increasing standards of living. Thus, he integrated the thinking of social protection as a productive factor into the motivation to launch the EPSR (European Commission, 2016). The social (and social investment) ambition of the EPSR was not new as it has been omnipresent since the Lisbon Strategy, but the dominance of the rights-based language in the EPSR, which could imply more regulation prompted by the EU level, was novel.

Social investment policies that had been present in the early 2000s and revived with the SIP were partly included in the pillar. The European Parliament report on the EPSR concluded that it "will not deliver without social investment, especially in available and affordable high-quality infrastructure for caring for children and other dependent persons and also measures to combat discrimination between women and men" (European Parliament, 2016, para. 37). Social investment is mentioned throughout the European Parliament report and is framed there as a productive factor, following the initial framing by Allan Larsson in the 1990s but covering a broader range of areas. The presence of social investment in the EPSR can be partially explained by the fact that some of the central individuals involved in developing it were key protagonists in the previous sequences of EU social investment. For example, Maria Rodrigues, a key protagonist behind the Lisbon Strategy, mobilized on behalf of social investment from her position as rapporteur in the European Parliament on the EPSR (European Parliament, 2016). Allan Larsson, one of the main actors in developing the EES, advised the European Commission on the EPSR (de la Porte & Natali, 2018).

This EPSR initiative was taken in a context of political polarization and ideological cleavages between member states and regions. On the one hand, left-wing populist parties emerged in countries most strongly affected by the financial and sovereign debt crises. In these economies that experienced stringent international and EU conditionality requiring reforms in areas of social protection (Pavolini et al., 2015; Sacchi, 2015; Theodoropoulou, 2015), a persistent demand for more EU solidarity surfaced. Even if the left was not in the majority in the European Council, its presence was somewhat more significant in 2014 and 2015 than before the crises (see Table 4.5). On the other hand, countries calling for fiscal conservatism, led by Germany, wanted to maintain stringent EU rules and policies, with strict macroeconomic policy and without further EU integration in social policy.

Table 4.5 Left-leaning heads of state and government in the European Council, 2014–2017

	2014	2015	2016	2017
Left-leaning heads of state and government	14	13	11	12
Number of member states	27	27	27	27

Source. Armingeon et al. (2019) (note that only data until 2017 is available).

The EPSR was eventually adopted in November 2017 in Gothenburg, in a solemn declaration, by the European Parliament, the Council of the European Union, and the European Commission (2017). It is notable that while the EPSR initially aimed to develop extensive (new) social rights, through hard regulatory instruments, at the end, the regulatory instruments used were mainly soft. For example, after formal consultation with the main stakeholders, it became clear that legislating a European minimum wage did not seem politically or institutionally feasible, considering the variety of wage-setting and welfare systems in member states. Yet, in 2020 the Commission proposed a directive on minimum wages. In addition, there are three other directives: on work–life balance, on basic labor rights (information and consultation) targeted at the most vulnerable workers, and on health and safety. All three are updates of previous directives, which were at the origins of EU social policy. The remainder of the principles, including those on social investment, are to be implemented via soft law and integrated into the European Semester, where the economically oriented actors continue to dominate.

4.3.5.2. Social investment output: Integration in a broader framework, with low political salience for social investment

In 2016, when the Commission launched the consultation on the EPSR (European Commission, 2016), it echoed the Nordic-inspired discourse from the late 1990s: Social policy is a "productive factor" within well-functioning and fair labor markets and welfare systems, which in turn boosts productivity, strengthens social cohesion, and increases standards of living (European Commission, 2016). The European Parliament, the European Commission, and the Council of the European Union (2017) officially proclaimed their support for the 20 principles enumerated in the EPSR in a solemn declaration at the Gothenburg social summit in November 2017. The principles are organized under three headings: equal opportunities and access to the labor market, fair working conditions, and social protection and inclusion. Despite advertising the EPSR as a framework for "rights," most principles, in particular those pertaining to social investment, are to be implemented via soft law (policy coordination or the new "social scoreboard"). Some of the social investment policies proposed already in the 1990s and early 2000s and reiterated in the SIP developed in sequence 4 are picked up again in the EPSR: education, training and lifelong learning, active support to employment, work–life balance, childcare, and support to children.

The policies and outcomes associated with these policy orientations are monitored via the "Social Scoreboard," which comprises EU headline indicators, descriptions, and targets and tracks trends and performance. The process, although aiming to feed into the European Semester, is a secondary concern as the Semester focuses primarily on fiscal restraint and long-term reduction of public debt in the EMU. There are no linkages between the Social Scoreboard and the MIP, even if some of the indicators cover the same trends. Although the Commission can issue country-specific recommendations to member states in these areas, they are weak, due to a weaker legal basis. By contrast, until 2020 and the new COVID crisis context, the country-specific recommendations pertaining more directly to the EMU had a stronger legal base and are directly linked to the deficit and debt targets of the EMU.

4.4. CONCLUSION

In this chapter, we have traced five main sequences in the development of the European Union's social investment reform strategy. Each of these sequences promotes different types of social investment, but changes overall are cumulative and respond to different economic, societal, and political challenges. In a first sequence, during the late 1990s, social investment ideas emerge in relation to the mobilization of human capital, including labor market activation but also lifelong learning, quality training, and quality jobs. In the second sequence, in the early 2000s, the prominence of social investment at EU level is reinforced, goes beyond employment policies, and focuses on the creation and mobilization of human capital. During the third sequence, from the middle of the first decade of the 2000s, social investment is less salient on the EU and national political agendas, while the focus is on labor market participation and growth, as reflected in the European Semester, which strengthens EMU governance and distracts interest from Europe 2020. In the fourth sequence, which covers the years following the Great Recession, this trend continues, with a pronounced emphasis on austerity and labor market participation and less on quality lifelong learning. During this sequence, EU social investment policy is developed by intellectuals and Commission actors as a counterdiscourse to austerity and fiscal restraint. However, this did not reflect political priorities in member states, and the policy framework was not effective. During the fifth sequence, the new EPSR includes social investment aims from previous sequences but no great effort to pursue them in EU member states.

In 2020, the impetus for EU social policy instigated by the EPSR was reaffirmed in the Ursula von der Leyen Commission (2019–2024) (European Commission, 2019). In the economic crisis European Union set off by the COVID-19 pandemic, social policy initiatives in the EPSR and beyond seem to have taken center stage at the EU level. However, the north and the south continue to disagree regarding how much the European Union should be involved in social policy, especially concerning fiscal matters (Vandenbroucke et al., 2020).

When tracing the development of social investment ideas and initiatives at the EU level, we found two political dynamics to be of importance. First, the political orientation of the European Union's socioeconomic strategy has been a battlefield between the European Union's socially and economically oriented actors, the former favoring a focus on fiscally sustainable yet fair welfare systems and labor markets and the latter favoring an exclusive focus on balanced budgets and supply-side policies. Social investment appeared to be a good candidate for enabling compromises, entailing ambiguous agreements (Palier, 2005) since it combines the aim of supporting an economic goal (i.e., favoring economic growth and the development of the knowledge-based economy through human capital formation and mobilization) and a social goal (i.e., fostering social inclusion and preventing the reproduction of inherited poverty). Second, the changes in emphasis on social investment in the European Union over time reflects political priorities in member states. The higher the number of left-leaning governments within the European Union, as indicated by the heads of government in the European Council, the more inclusive and broad are the proposed social investment perspectives. Conversely, the higher the number of right-leaning governments, the more concentration there is on stratified and targeted social investment, focused merely on workforce mobilization.

ACKNOWLEDGMENTS

We would like to thank Hanna Kviske for coding the left–right composition of the European Council and Francesco Fioretti for research assistance. This work is supported by a public grant overseen by the French National Research Agency as part of the "Investissements d'Avenir" program LIEPP (ANR-11-LABX-0091, ANR-11-IDEX-0005-02).

REFERENCES

Armingeon, K., Wenger, V., Wiedemeier, F., Isler, C., Knöpfel, L., Weisstanner, D., & Engler, S. (2019). *Comparative political data set 1960–2017*. Institute of Political Science, University of Zurich.

Barcevicius, E., Weishaupt, T., & Zeitlin, J. (2014). *Assessing the open method of coordination: Institutional design and national influence of EU social policy coordination*. Palgrave Macmillan.

Bengtsson, M., de la Porte, C., & Jacobsson, K. (2017). Labour market policy under conditions of permanent austerity: Any sign of social investment? *Social Policy and Administration, 51*(2), 367–388.

Blair, T., & Schröder, G. (1999). *Europe: The third way/Die neue mitte*. Labour Party.

Crespy, A., & Vanheuverzwijn, P. (2019). What "Brussels" means by structural reforms: Empty signifier or constructive ambiguity? *Comparative European Politics, 17*, 92–111.

de la Porte, C. (2011). Principal-agent theory and the open method of co-ordination: The case of the European employment strategy. *Journal of European Public Policy, 18*(4), 485–503.

de la Porte, C., & Heins, E. (2015). A new era of European integration? Governance of labour market and social policy since the sovereign debt crisis. *Comparative European Politics, 13*(1), 8–28.

de la Porte, C., & Heins, E. (2016). *The sovereign debt crisis: The EU and welfare state reform*. Palgrave Macmillan.

de la Porte, C., & Jacobsson, K. (2012). Social investment or re-commodification? Assessing the employment policies of the EU member states. In N. Morel, B. Palier, & J. Palme (Eds.), *Towards a social investment welfare state? Ideas, policies and challenges* (pp. 117–152). Policy Press.

de la Porte, C., & Natali, D. (2018). Agents of institutional change in EU policy: The social investment moment. *Journal of European Public Policy, 25*(6), 828–843.

de la Porte, C., & Pochet, P. (2002). *Building social Europe through the open method of coordination*. Peter Lang.

de la Porte, C., & Pochet, P. (2012). Why and how (still) study the open method of co-ordination (OMC)? *Journal of European Social Policy, 22*(3), 336–349.

Dukelow, F. (2015). "Pushing against an open door": Reinforcing the neo-liberal policy paradigm in Ireland and the impact of EU intrusion. *Comparative European Politics, 13*(1), 93–111.

Emmenegger, P., Häusermann, S., Palier, B., & Seeleib-Kaiser, M. (2012). *The age of dualization: The changing face of inequality in deindustrializing societies*. Oxford University Press.

Erhel, C., Mandin, L., & Palier, B. (2005). The leverage effect. The open method of coordination in France. In J. Zeitlin & P. Pochet (Eds.), *The open method of co-ordination in action* (pp. 217–247). Peter Lang.

Esping-Andersen, G., Gallie, D., Hemerijck, A., & Myles, J. (2002). *Why we need a new welfare state*. Oxford University Press.

European Commission. (1993). *Growth, competitiveness, employment: The challenges and ways forward into the 21st century* [White paper COM (93) 700].

European Commission. (1997). Proposal for guidelines for member states employment policies 1998 [Commission Communication COM (97) 497].

European Commission. (1999). A concerted strategy for modernising social protection [Commission Communication COM (99) 347].

European Commission. (2001). Employment and social policies: A framework for investing in quality [Commission Communication COM (2001) 313].

European Commission. (2013). Social investment package: Towards social investment for growth and cohesion [Commission Communication COM (2013) 83].

European Commission. (2016). Launching a consultation on the European Pillar of Social Rights [Commission Communication COM (2016) 127]. https://eur-lex.europa.eu/legal-content/EN/TXT/?uri=COM%3A2016%3A127%3AFIN

European Commission. (2017). Expert group on social investment for growth and cohesion. http://ec.europa.eu/transparency/regexpert/index.cfm?do=groupDetail.groupDetail&groupID=2819

European Commission. (2019, November 27). Speech by president-elect von der Leyen in the European Parliament Plenary on the occasion of the presentation of her College of Commissioners and their programme. https://ec.europa.eu/commission/presscorner/detail/en/SPEECH_19_6408

European Council. (1992a). 92/441/EEC: Council recommendation of 24 June 1992 on common criteria concerning sufficient resources and social assistance in social protection systems. *Official Journal of the European Union*, *L245*, 46–48.

European Council. (1992b). 92/442/EEC: Council recommendation of 27 July 1992 on the convergence of social protection objectives and policies. *Official Journal of the European Union*, *L245*, 49.

European Council. (1994). *Essen European Council, presidency conclusions.*

European Council. (1997). *Extraordinary European Council meeting on employment, presidency conclusions.*

European Council. (2000). *Lisbon European Council, presidency conclusions.*

European Council. (2002). *Barcelona European Council, presidency conclusions.*

European Parliament. (2013). Resolution of 12 June 2013 on the Commission communication "Towards social investment for growth and cohesion—including implementing the European social fund 2014–2020" (2013/2607(RSP)). *Official Journal of the European Union*, *C65*, 68–78.

European Parliament. (2016). *Report on a European Pillar of Social Rights* (2016/2095) Employment and Social Affairs Committee.

European Parliament, Council of the European Union, & European Commission. (2017). *Solemn declaration on the European Pillar of Social Rights*. https://ec.europa.eu/commission/publications/european-pillar-social-rights-booklet_en

Ferrera, M. (2017). Impatient politics and social investment: The EU as "policy facilitator." *Journal of European Public Policy*, *24*(8), 1233–1251.

Ferrera, M., Hemerijck, A., & Rhodes, M. (2000). *The future of social Europe: Recasting work and welfare in the new economy*. Celta Editora.

Garritzmann, J. L., Häusermann, S., & Palier, B. (Eds.). (2022). *The world politics of social investment: Vol. II. The politics of varying social investment strategies*. Oxford University Press.

Giddens, A. (1998). *The third way: The renewal of social democracy*. Polity Press.

Graziano, P., Jacquot, S., & Palier, B. (2011). *Europa, Europae: The EU and the domestic politics of welfare state reforms*. Palgrave Macmillan.

Jacquot, S. (2015). *Transformations in EU gender equality policy: From emergence to dismantling*. Palgrave.

Jenson, J., & Pochet, P. (2002, December 5–8). Employment and social policy since Maastricht: Standing up to the European Monetary Union [Paper presentation]. The Year of the Euro, Nanovic Institute for European Studies, University of Notre Dame, Notre Dame, IN, USA.

Jessoula, M., & Madama, I. (2018). *Fighting poverty and social exclusion in the EU: A chance in Europe 2020*. Routledge.

Larsson, A. (1995). *A vision for IGC 1996: A European employment union to make EMU possible.*

Leibfried, S., & Pierson, P. (1995). *European social policy: Between fragmentation and integration*. Brookings Institution.

Lightfoot, S. (2003). The party of European socialists and the treaty of Amsterdam: Really a policy-seeking party? *Perspectives on European Politics and Society, 4*(2), 217–242.

Mahon, R. (2011). The jobs strategy: From neo-to inclusive liberalism? *Review of International Political Economy, 18*(5), 570–591.

Mandin, C. (2001). *L'Union Européenne et la réforme des retraites: Mémoire de DEA*. Sciences po.

Martinsen, D. (2015). *An ever more powerful court? The political constraints of legal integration in the European Union*. Oxford University Press.

Morel, N. (2015). Servants for the knowledge-based economy? The political economy of domestic services in Europe. *Social Politics: International Studies in Gender, State & Society, 22*(2), 170–192.

Morel, N., Palier, B., & Palme, J. (2012). *Towards a social investment welfare state? Ideas, policies and challenges*. Policy Press.

Moreno, L., & Palier, B. (2005). The Europeanisation of welfare: Paradigm shifts and social policy reforms. In P. Taylor-Gooby (Ed.), *Ideas and welfare state reform in western Europe* (pp. 145–175). Palgrave Macmillan.

Palier, B. (2005). Ambiguous agreement, cumulative change: French social policy in the 1990s. In K. Thelen & W. Streeck (Eds.), *Beyond continuity: Institutional change in advanced political economies* (pp. 127–144). Oxford University Press.

Palier, B. (2009). L'Europe et les états-providence. *Sociologie du travail, 51*(4), 518–535.

Palier, B. (2010). *A long goodbye to Bismarck? The politics of welfare reform in continental Europe*. Amsterdam University Press.

Palier, B., & Pochet, P. (2005). Toward a European social policy—At last? In N. Jabko & C. Parsons (Eds.), *The state of the European Union: Vol. 7. With US or against US? European trends in American perspective* (pp. 253–273). Oxford University Press.

Palier, B., Rovny, A. E., & Rovny, J. (2018). European disunion? Social and economic divergence in Europe, and their political consequences. In P. Manow, B. Palier, & H. Schwander (Eds.), *Welfare democracies and party politics: Explaining electoral dynamics in times of changing welfare capitalism* (pp. 281–297). Oxford University Press.

Palier, B., & Thelen, K. (2010). Institutionalizing dualism: Complementarities and change in France and Germany. *Politics & Society, 38*(1), 119–148.

Pavolini, E., León, M., Guillén, A. M., & Ascoli, U. (2015). From austerity to permanent strain? The EU and welfare state reform in Italy and Spain. *Comparative European Politics, 13*(1), 56–76.

Sacchi, S. (2015). Conditionality by other means: EU involvement in Italy's structural reforms in the sovereign debt crisis. *Comparative European Politics*, *13*(1), 77–92.

Sapir, A., Aghion, P., Bertola, G., Hellwig, M., Pisani-Ferry, J., Rosati, D., Viñals, J., & Wallace, H. (2003). *An agenda for a growing Europe: Making the EU system deliver*. European Commission.

Scharpf, F. (2021). Forced structural convergence in the Eurozone. In A. Hassel & B. Palier (Eds.), *Growth & welfare in advanced capitalist economies: How have growth regimes evolved?* (pp. 161–201). Oxford University Press.

Tallberg, J. (2008). Bargaining power in the European Council. *Journal of Common Market Studies*, *46*, 685–708.

Tallberg, J., & Johansson, M. (2008). Party politics in the European Council. *Journal of European Public Policy*, *15*(8), 1222–1242.

Theodoropoulou, S. (2015). National social and labour market policy reforms in the shadow of EU bail-out conditionality: The cases of Greece and Portugal. *Comparative European Politics*, *13*(1), 29–55.

Tosun, J. (2017). Promoting youth employment through multi-organizational governance. *Public Money & Management*, *37*, 39–46.

Vandenbroucke, F., Andor, L., Beetsma, R., Burgoon, B., Fischer, G., Kuhn, T., Luigjes, C., & Nicoli, F. (2020, April 6). *The European Commission's SURE initiative and euro area unemployment re-insurance*. VOX, CEPR Policy Portal. https://voxeu.org/article/european-commission-s-sure-initiative-and-euro-area-unemployment-re-insurance

Vandenbroucke, F., Hemerijck, A., & Palier, B. (2011). *The EU needs a social investment pact* [OSE Opinion paper no. 5]. Observatoire Social Européen.

Wincott, D. (2003). The idea of the European social model: Limits and paradoxes of Europeanization. In K. Featherstone & C. Radaelli (Eds.), *The politics of Europeanization* (pp. 279–302). Oxford University Press.

APPENDIX 1

Table A-4.1a Heads of state and government in EU member states, organized according to country (1993–2017)

Country	1993	1994	1995	1996	1997	1998	1999	2000	2001	2002	2003	2004	2005	2006	2007	2008	2009	2010	2011	2012	2013	2014	2015	2016	2017
Austria (AT)	C	C	L	L	L	L	L	L/C	C	C	C	C	C	C	C/L	L	L	L	L	L	L	L	L	L	L/C
Belgium (BE)	C	C	C	C	C	C	C/R	R	R	R	R	R	R	R	R	R/C	R	R	R	R	L	L/R	R	R	R
Bulgaria (BG)															L	L	L/R	R	R	R	R/L	L/R	R	R	L/R
Croatia (HR)																						L	L	L/C	C
Cyprus (CY)													R	R	R	R/L	L	L	L	L	L/R	R	R	R	R
Czech Republic (CZ)													L	L/R	R	R	R/Ind.	Ind.	R	R	R/Ind.	Ind./L	L	L	L/R
Denmark (DK)	L	L	L	L	L	L	L	L	L/R	R	R	R	R	R	R	R	R	R	R/L	L	L	L	L/R	R	R
Estonia (EE)			L	L	L	L	L	R	R	R	R	R	R	R	R	R	R	R	R	R	R	R	R/C	C	C
Finland (FI)			L	R	R/L	L	L	L	L	L/R	L/C	C	C	C	C	C	C	C	C/R	R	R	R/C	R/C	C	C
France (FR)	R	R	R	R	R/L	L	L	L	L	L/R	R	R	R	R	R	R	R	R	R	R/L	L	L	L	L	L/R
Germany (DE)	C	C	C	C	C	C/L	L	L	L	L	L	L	L/C	C	C	C	C	C	C	C	C	C	C	C	C
Greece (EL)	L	L	L	L	L	L	L	L	L	L	L	L/R	R	R	R	R	R/L	L	L/Ind.	Ind./R	R	R/L	R/L	L	L
Hungary (HU)															L	L	L	L/R	R	R	R	R	R	R	L
Ireland (IE)	R	R/C	C	C	C/R	R	R	R	R	R	R	R	R	R	R	R	R	R	R/C	R/C	R/C	R/C	R/C	R/C	R/C
Italy (IT)	L	R	Ind.	Ind./C	C	C/L	L	L/Ind.	Ind.	R	R	R	R	R/L	L	L/R	R	R	R/Ind.	Ind.	Ind./L	L	L	L	L
Latvia (LV)	R	R	Ind.	C	R	C/L	L	R	R	R	R	R	R	R	R/C	C	C/R	R	R	R	R	R	R	R/C	C

(continued)

Table A-4.1a Continued

Country	1993	1994	1995	1996	1997	1998	1999	2000	2001	2002	2003	2004	2005	2006	2007	2008	2009	2010	2011	2012	2013	2014	2015	2016	2017
Lithuania (LT)													L	L	L	L/R	R	R	R	R/L	L	L	L	L	L
Luxembourg (LU)	C	C	C	C	C	C	C	C	C	C	C	C	C	C	C	C	C	C	C	C	C/R	R	R	R	R
Malta (MT)				L	L	L	L	L	L	L/C	C	C	C	C	C	C	C	C	C	C	C/L	L	L	L	L
Netherlands (NL)	C	L	L	L	L	L	L	L	L	L/C	C	C	C	C	C	C	C	C/R	R	R	R	R	R	R	R
Poland (PL)													L/R	R	R	R	R	R	R	R	R	R	R	R	R
Portugal (PO)	R	R	L	L	L	L	L	L	L	L/R	R	R	R/L	L	L	L	L	L	L/R	R	R	R	R/L	L	L
Romania (RO)														R	R	R	R	R	R	R/L	L	L	L/Ind.	Ind.	Ind./L
Slovakia (SK)													C	C	C/L	L	L	L/C	C	C/L	L	L	L	L	L
Slovenia (SL)													L	L	L	L	L	L	L	L	L	L/R	R	R	R
Spain (ES)	L	L	L	L/C	C	C	C	C	C	C	C	C/L	L	L	L	L	L	L	L/C	C	C	C	C	C	C
Sweden (SE)	R	L	L	L	L	L	L	L	L	L	L	L	L	L/R	R	R	R	R	R	R	R	R/L	L	L	L
United Kingdom (UK)	R	R	R	R	R/L	L	L	L	L	L	L	L	L	L	L	L	L	L/R	R	R	R	R	R	R	R

Methodological notes.

1. A data set was retrieved from "Comparative political data set" (https://www.cpds-data.org) where government composition and heads of state are categorized according to left (L), center (C), and right (R). Technocratic or non-partisan caretakers are also considered.

2. Data for the period 1995–2017 was then coded according to the political spectrum. For the leaders of the European Council, the code options are L, R, C, or independent (Ind.), which refers to all extraordinary forms of government leadership, for example, non-partisan caretaker, technocratic government. Those were only considered if they exceeded a period of 6 months.

In the instance that elections led to a political shift, the change is indicated by a /. For example, if a left head of state was replaced by a conservative head of state the code for that year will read "L/C." The government composition of member states was coded in descending order; this means that if the government is made up of more than one party, the first letter indicates the largest share of the coalition. For example, if the code reads "LRC," this means that the largest share of the government belongs to the left spectrum.

If there is a change in government, the code for year x reflects the newly elected government. For example, if a left government is replaced by a right government, the code for year x will read "R."

Table A-4.1b Heads of state of EU member states, organized according to various combinations of the L–R spectrum (1993–2017)

Political spectrum	1993	1994	1995	1996	1997	1998	1999	2000	2001	2002	2003	2004	2005	2006	2007	2008	2009	2010	2011	2012	2013	2014	2015	2016
L	4	4	8	7	7	9	11	9	8	5	4	3	7	6	8	8	8	6	3	5	8	9	9	10
L/R	0	0	0	0	0	0	0	0	1	2	1	1	1	2	0	2	1	2	1	0	1	3	1	0
L/C	0	0	0	1	0	0	0	1	0	1	0	0	1	0	0	0	0	1	1	0	0	0	0	1
L/Ind.	0	0	0	0	0	0	0	1	0	0	0	0	0	0	0	0	0	0	0	0	0	0	1	0
R	4	4	2	2	0	1	1	2	2	4	6	9	9	9	11	9	9	11	12	11	10	11	11	10
R/L	0	0	0	0	2	0	0	0	0	0	0	0	1	1	0	1	1	0	1	3	1	1	2	0
R/C	0	1	0	0	0	0	0	0	0	0	0	0	0	0	1	1	0	0	1	1	1	1	2	3
R/Ind.	0	0	0	0	0	0	0	0	0	0	0	0	0	0	0	0	1	0	0	0	1	0	0	0
C	4	3	4	4	5	3	2	2	3	3	4	4	6	7	5	6	6	5	4	4	2	2	2	3
C/L	0	0	0	0	0	2	0	0	0	0	0	1	0	0	2	0	0	0	1	1	1	0	0	0
C/R	0	0	0	1	0	0	1	0	0	0	0	0	0	0	0	0	1	1	1	0	1	0	0	0
C/Ind.	0	0	0	0	0	0	0	0	0	0	0	0	0	0	0	0	0	0	0	0	0	0	0	0
Ind.	0	0	1	0	0	0	0	0	1	0	0	0	0	0	0	0	0	0	0	1	0	0	0	1
Ind./L	0	0	0	0	0	0	0	0	0	0	0	0	0	0	0	0	0	0	0	0	0	1	0	0
Ind./R	0	0	0	0	0	0	0	0	0	0	0	0	0	0	0	0	0	1	0	1	0	0	0	0
Ind./C	0	0	0	1	0	0	0	0	0	0	0	0	0	0	0	0	0	0	0	0	0	0	0	0
All variations including L	4	4	8	8	9	11	11	11	9	8	5	5	10	9	10	11	10	9	8	9	12	14	13	11
All other variations (C, R, Ind.)	8	8	7	7	6	4	4	4	6	7	10	10	15	16	17	16	17	18	19	18	15	14	15	17
Overall sum	12	12	15	15	15	15	15	15	15	15	15	15	25	25	27	27	27	27	27	26	27	28	28	28

Methodological note: After the governments were coded in Table A-4.1a, all variations were counted for each year, and all combinations including the code "L" were summarized, indicating changes in the political center of gravity in the European Council, 1993–2017. This was the data that we used in Table 1.5 in the analysis of the politics of the sequences of social investment.
Source. Comparative political data set (https://www.cpds-data.org).

PART II

THE POLITICAL AND ECONOMIC SCOPE CONDITIONS OF SOCIAL INVESTMENT REFORMS

5

SOCIAL INVESTMENT AND SOCIAL ASSISTANCE IN LOW- AND MIDDLE-INCOME COUNTRIES

Armando Barrientos

5.1. INTRODUCTION

In contrast to welfare states in Europe and North America, welfare institutions in low- and middle-income countries (LMICs) remain limited in their reach of the population and in their coverage of social risks. According to the International Labour Organization's (ILO's) World Social Protection Report 2017–19, the share of the population covered by social protection (including social insurance and social assistance) was 12.9% for sub-Saharan Africa, 38.9% for Asia and the Pacific, 39.2% for North Africa, and 61.4% for Latin America and the Caribbean (ILO, 2017). Social protection institutions reach a minority of the population in developing regions.

These shortcomings are structural. Where economic development has taken place, it has not been associated with a transformation in welfare institutions yielding comprehensive and inclusive provision. All Latin American countries have now secured middle-income country status, with Chile and Uruguay graduating into high-income country status. Yet their welfare institutions remain segmented, truncated in some cases (see also Chapter 13 in this volume). As a first approximation, we might study welfare institutions in LMICs as dual, with a social insurance component covering workers in formal employment and their families and with a focus on employment-related and life-course risks and a social assistance component targeting low-income groups and workers in informal employment and their families and addressing consumption risks and low productivity.

Armando Barrientos, *Social Investment and Social Assistance in Low- and Middle-Income Countries* In: *The World Politics of Social Investment (Volume I)*. Edited by: Julian L. Garritzmann, Silja Häusermann, and Bruno Palier, Oxford University Press. © Oxford University Press 2022. DOI: 10.1093/oso/9780197585245.003.0005

Since 2000 LMICs have embarked on a significant upgrading of social protection provision. The focus of the recent expansion has been on budget-financed, citizenship-based, rules-based programs providing targeted transfers to disadvantaged groups, with selection based on socioeconomic status and vulnerability (Barrientos, 2013a). The growth in social assistance provision has been remarkable. By 2015, close to a billion people lived in households in receipt of a social assistance transfer (Barrientos, 2018b).[1]

Social investment figures prominently in the recent expansion of social assistance in LMICs. This is in line with an understanding that poverty is a consequence of low productive capacity and that, to be effective, social assistance must be designed to support human development and economic inclusion.[2] The main objective of this chapter is to assess the social investment orientation of social assistance, construct measures of social investment, and identify relevant correlates. The analysis relies on a new data set, Social Assistance in Low and Middle Income Countries (SALMIC) (Barrientos, 2018b), which will be described in more detail. In the context of the volumes, this chapter focuses on targeted social investment strategies aimed at creating human capital. It addresses research questions associated with the identification and measurement of social investment reforms, their political salience, societal demand, and legacies and institutions.

The design of social assistance programs provides an indication of their social investment orientation. There is wide diversity in practice among LMICs, but it will be useful to focus on four "ideal types": 1) *pure income transfers*, old age or family and child transfers, for example, aimed at subsidizing consumption; 2) *employment guarantees*, focused on community asset accumulation; 3) *conditional income transfers*, providing transfers with conditions on human capital accumulation; and finally 4) *integrated anti-poverty transfers*, providing multidimensional support and intermediation (Barrientos, 2013a). Conditional income transfers and integrated anti-poverty transfers have an explicit focus on social investment. Pure income transfers lack explicit social investment objectives by design but might in practice support social investment depending on context, for example, where pensioners co-reside with children of school age and use their

---

1. The World Bank's *State of Social Safety Nets 2015* report estimated the reach of social assistance transfers in LMICs at 2 billion (World Bank, 2015). This is based on figures from the ASPIRE database, calculated from household survey data (World Bank, 2016). In fact, the World Bank measures the reach of safety nets, which include social assistance and emergency assistance. The latter is important in lower-income countries, and it remains a front-line instrument in the World Bank's lending and technical support operations. This chapter focuses on social assistance alone.
2. In LMICs, social policy is approached as a component of broader economic, social, and political development policies, with the implication that productivism is the default position. This approach is described as international development and promoted by United Nations agencies, donors, and international nongovernmental organizations. It will now apply to high-income countries under the Sustainable Development Goals (see Chapter 3 in this volume).

transfer to facilitate schooling. Employment guarantees lack social investment features and might actually undermine it, for example, where mothers' employment adversely affects children's schooling. Program design will provide an entry point to assessing the social investment orientation of social assistance in LMICs.

The emphasis on social investment in LMICs' social assistance expansion raises interesting questions in the context of political economy models explaining social investment in high-income countries. In the latter, social investment is associated with reforms to social insurance institutions—family, labor market, and education policies—addressing the interests of the middle and upper classes affected by the knowledge economy (see Chapter 12 in this volume). The trends studied in this chapter highlight critical issues for the application of this model globally. As the chapter will demonstrate, LMICs' social investment has emerged as a focus of social assistance expansion, directed at low-income groups. Social assistance is grounded on vertical redistribution, from the better off to the worse off, in contrast to the horizontal redistribution at the core of social insurance. This raises important questions about the political economy conditions likely to facilitate such policies.

The chapter divides into four main sections. Section 5.2 describes the expansion of social assistance in LMICs, sketching regional trends. Section 5.3 develops measures of social investment orientation based on program design. Section 5.4 identifies trends in social investment in the recent expansion of social assistance in LMICs. Section 5.5 estimates regression models to identify key factors associated with social investment orientation. A final section concludes.

5.2. SOCIAL ASSISTANCE EXPANSION

Beginning from the mid-1990s, most LMICs have introduced or expanded programs providing rules-based, budget-financed regular and reliable transfers to disadvantaged households. There is considerable variation across countries and regions as regards the design, scope, and reach of emerging social assistance. Flagship programs have led the expansion. This section provides a broad description of developments.

In Latin American countries, the return to democracy following structural adjustment was accompanied by strong demand for social policies. Brazil is a paradigmatic case (Barrientos, 2013b). The restoration of democracy in 1985 following 20 years of dictatorship led to a new constitution in 1988, enshrining social rights. Early policy reforms focused on extending coverage of existing social insurance to informal workers in agriculture, while also establishing a nationwide social assistance pension scheme. Municipal innovation beginning in 1995 focused instead on conditional income transfers, providing income transfers to families in extreme poverty conditional on children attending school. They eventually became a federal program in 2001 as *Bolsa Escola*—itself the main component of *Bolsa Família* in 2003. In Brazil, as in the rest of Latin America, social protection policy evolved from—largely unsuccessful—efforts to extend social insurance to informal and low-income groups to the establishment of separate social assistance institutions. The expansion of budget-financed transfers to older people has taken a variety of forms: subsidized entry into social insurance schemes (Brazil, Argentina); categorical schemes (Bolivia, Trinidad and Tobago); and selective social assistance old age transfers (most countries in the region) (Rofman et al., 2015). Conditional income transfers are in place in all countries in the region and reach around a quarter of the population (Cecchini & Madariaga, 2011). In lower income countries in Central America they are smaller and less institutionalized.

In former Soviet Union (FSU) countries in Europe and Central Asia, social protection systems relied on comprehensive social insurance sustained by a commitment to full employment and low wage dispersion. Family and child transfers provided additional support. Structural transformation and liberalized labor markets have exerted considerable pressure on social insurance funds (Falkingham & Vlachantoni, 2010). Reforms have focused on categorical transfers and especially on family and child transfers with a view to strengthening their protective and productivist orientation (Gassmann, 2018). In Central Asia, countries have experimented with conditional income transfers with mixed success.

In Asia, the expansion of social assistance is apparent from developments in the most populous countries. In China, the liberalization of state-owned enterprises in urban areas at the turn of the century undermined work-based social protection and generated rising unemployment. A relatively small social assistance program first piloted in Shanghai in 1993, the Minimum Living Standards Scheme commonly referred to as *DiBao*, provided support to mainly elderly people and people with disabilities in urban areas (Gao et al., 2009; Wang, 2007). It expanded from 2.5 million beneficiaries in 1999 to 22.4 million by 2003. It is managed by city authorities, who control eligibility and transfer levels. In 2006 the government decided to extend *DiBao* to rural areas, reaching a further 46 million beneficiaries (Golan et al., 2015). *DiBao* is an integrated anti-poverty transfer program, including a range of transfers supporting consumption, health, and schooling. The 1997 financial crisis led to large-scale reforms and expansion of South Korea's Minimum Living Standard Scheme.

India's flagship program is the Mahatma Ghandi National Rural Employment Guarantee Scheme established in 2004–2005. It provides 100 days of work on demand to households in rural areas, reaching over 45 million households. It is a hybrid program, as much a guaranteed employment program as a transfer program with work conditions. In addition, India's National Social Assistance Scheme provides old age, disability, and schooling transfers to over 20 million households. Lacking a productivist orientation, India's anti-poverty transfers have very limited human development objectives (Mehrotra, 2011). By contrast, Pakistan and Bangladesh have implemented large-scale conditional income transfer programs and scholarship schemes.

South East Asian countries have rapidly expanded social assistance provision (Weber, 2010). The 1997 financial crisis was the catalyst. Indonesia and the Philippines have introduced large-scale conditional income transfers (Fernandez & Olfindo, 2011; Sumarto et al., 2008). Old age transfers have also expanded across the region. The Philippines has also recently introduced a budget-financed old age transfer scheme.

The global expansion of social assistance has been slower and more uncertain in Africa (Monchuk, 2014). In Southern Africa, South Africa's long-standing social assistance and disability grants have been the core of its welfare institutions. The fall of apartheid led to an expansion of social assistance. In 1998 a Child Support Grant was introduced to address child malnutrition (Lund, 2008). The means-tested grant was subsequently extended to children under 18 years of age. Today, social assistance reaches around half the population in South Africa (Leibbrandt et al., 2011). East African countries have introduced a range of income transfers, including conditional income transfers, to address poverty and conflict; but with few exceptions, they remain limited in reach and dependent on donor support (Davis et al., 2016). In Western and Central Africa, progress has been slow due to low implementation capacity and policy legacies, but several countries have piloted conditional income transfers with varying degrees of success (Garcia & Moore, 2012).

To summarize, LMICs have rapidly expanded social assistance provision, even in regions with long-standing social insurance institutions like Latin America and the Caribbean. Social assistance dominates social protection institutions in LMICs in terms of reach.[3] The expansion of social assistance in LMICs has a protective and a social investment orientation. The next sections explore the relative weight of social investment in the expansion of social assistance in LMICs.

5.3. ASSESSING SOCIAL INVESTMENT IN PROGRAMMING

The expansion of social assistance described in the previous section is an important pointer for emerging welfare institutions as it prefigures the institutional setting that will consolidate in LMICs.[4] In this section we propose how to assess social investment orientation.

---

3. Focusing on budgets or expenditure would reverse this assessment.
4. Here, the focus is on institutional development, but outcomes are important too. The expansion of social assistance is making an important contribution to the reduction of global poverty.

5.3.1. Social investment in programming

The balance of protection and promotion objectives is central to emerging welfare institutions. In LMICs, social assistance programs are seldom designed in the income maintenance tradition dominant in Europe in the Golden Age (Atkinson, 1995). Only in South Korea and China transfers were designed to fill in beneficiaries' poverty gaps. Even there, practice diverges from the European model. In China, transfers are meant to secure income levels at the poverty line set by local authorities, but in practice these are set to meet budgetary restrictions (Gao et al., 2009). Outside these two countries, social assistance transfers are usually a fixed contribution to household budgets, often below the average poverty gap.[5] As a consequence, the protective properties of social assistance transfers are widely perceived to be limited.

A program's direct transfer recipient may also provide clues about the balance of protection and promotion. Old age and disability transfers suggest that compensation is the primary objective for policy designers. On the other hand, transfers to mothers and children underline a social investment objective. Social assistance in LMICs taken as a whole has a pro-old bias, in the sense that old age transfers are common with transfers directed at mothers and children less in evidence. Old age transfers are significantly more generous than family transfers.

Conditions are common to social assistance programs, but some types of conditions suggest a social investment orientation (on different types of conditionality, see also Chapter 16 in Volume II [Garritzmann et al., 2022]). Human capital–related conditions invariably signal social investment. Work conditions are more likely to reflect a program's reliance on self-selection than a concern with activation.[6] This suggests that protective objectives are dominant. Active labor market policies are scarce in LMICs (Alderman & Yemstov, 2013). Increasingly, conditional income transfers include activation components to support program exit, consistent with the social investment objectives of these programs (Economic Commission for Latin America and the Caribbean & ILO, 2014). Anti-poverty policies focusing on physical or financial asset accumulation might be inimical to social investment. Most child laborers in LMICs are employed in micro-enterprises. And mothers working in small enterprises or self-employed have very limited access to creches and childcare facilities.

In sum, program design features indicating an explicit social investment orientation include those with a focus on families and children, links to human development interventions or conditions, mothers as the direct recipient, and human development conditions.[7]

---

5. As a rough average, transfer levels are around 20% of household consumption.
6. In the context of LMICs, it is important to distinguish between short-term public works and employment guarantees. The former are common in emergency assistance. Employment guarantees are social assistance instruments because they generate rules-based entitlements.
7. Social assistance programs lacking these design features might nevertheless generate social investment depending on context. This point will be taken up in the next section.

5.3.2. "Ideal types" and social investment

The four "ideal types" of social assistance programs provide an entry point to assessing the social investment orientation of social assistance programs in LMICs.

Pure income transfers have no explicit human capital accumulation objective. Old age and disability transfers are prime examples. They provide a consumption subsidy with no reference to human capital accumulation. Protection objectives are dominant.

Employment guarantees create regular entitlements with a work condition. India's National Rural Employment Guarantee is a paradigmatic example. On paper, participants are offered 100 days of employment annually on demand at a wage below the market rate. In practice, implementation and process deficits restrict access to guaranteed employment (Dutta et al., 2012). The associated work by participants generates community productive assets, irrigations, and roads, for example. Employment guarantees might possibly generate household investment in human capital through the income effects of the transfers, but employment of mothers (and children) could in fact produce adverse effects of human development (Mani et al., 2014; Shah & Steinberg, 2015).

Conditional income transfers combine consumption subsidies with subsidies supporting human capital accumulation (Fiszbein & Schady, 2009). Transfers are ruled-based, regular, and reliable for prespecified periods of time. Selection is based on socioeconomic status and household demographics. At their core is an insight into the role of low productive capacity as a key factor explaining poverty. Conditional income transfers are explicitly designed around a social investment strategy. The objective is to improve current consumption deficits while ensuring a minimum investment in the human capital of children. Typically, conditional income transfers have two parts: 1) a fixed household transfer, sometimes described as a nutrition transfer, and 2) schooling-related variable transfers often associated with the age/grade/gender of children. The variable part of the transfer conveys signals about the human capital accumulation objective to participant households. Conditions attaching to children's schooling, healthcare, and nutrition ensure actual investment. The structure of the transfers and the design and monitoring of the conditions describe the design intensity of the social investment orientation of conditional income transfers.[8]

Integrated anti-poverty programs combine transfers and intermediation. They include interventions on a wider range of dimensions than under conditional income transfers. Chile's *Chile Solidario*, a program introduced in 2002 with the aim of eradicating extreme poverty, combined interventions on income,

---

8. A growing literature measures outcomes from conditional income transfer program (Baird et al., 2014; Glassman et al., 2013), but the focus here is the design implications for social investment (Barrientos, 2018a).

employment, health, education, housing, intrahousehold relations, and registration (Barrientos, 2010). The key issue addressed by program designers was the absence of coordination among the many public agencies and programs addressing poverty, resulting in the limited inclusion of groups in extreme poverty. In addition to addressing consumption deficits and deficits in human capital, integrated anti-poverty transfer programs pay attention to social inclusion with a broader perspective on capacitation. Social investment objectives are met by the relevant interventions packaged into the programs and by the structuring of conditions and intermediation. In Latin America and elsewhere, most conditional income transfers have incorporated a wider set of interventions and intermediation for participant households who find it hard to comply with conditions or require additional support (e.g., Brazil, whereas others emphasize the sanctioning aspect of conditionality, e.g., Mexico; see Chapter 16 in Volume II [Garritzmann et al., 2022]).

Program design features and objectives provide clues as to the social investment orientation of social assistance programs. Taking account of the considerable diversity in program design in LMICs, a focus on "ideal types" and their distribution will support an accurate assessment of social investment orientation. Conditional income transfers and integrated anti-poverty programs have a strong social investment orientation. They share a core objective in improving the productive capacity of groups in poverty, and their design features favor children's schooling, healthcare, and, in some cases, adult skills accumulation. By contrast, pure income transfers lack explicit social investment objectives and features and show a compensatory orientation. Employment guarantees have labor supply conditions, but these are in place to facilitate beneficiary self-selection. They lack capacitating objectives and are therefore primarily a compensatory instrument. There are concerns, supported by evaluation studies, that they are inimical to social investment through the impact of mothers' participation in children's schooling. The next section will rely on "ideal types" of social assistance to measure social investment orientation.

Relying on program types to measure social investment orientation will provide a lower-bound, conservative measure. In the context of LMICs, pure income transfers without an explicit social investment design can have measurable social investment effects. The latter are contingent on contextual conditions. Studies on the second-order effects of old age transfers in LMICs find that transfers are shared within households. In countries with extensive co-residence of pensioners and their grandchildren, pension transfers are best described as household transfers that come through older members. Where old age transfers are generous, as in South Africa, they have a measurable impact on the health status of household members (Case & Wilson, 2000), schooling of children (de Carvalho, 2008; Duflo, 2000; Yañes-Pagans, 2008) and labor migration (Ardington et al., 2009). Where old age transfer levels are ungenerous, effects on the human capital of household members are hard to find. Unintended social investment

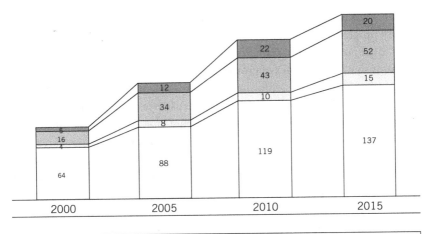

Figure 5.1 Social assistance programs in LMICs by type.
Source. SALMIC data set.

outcomes of pure income transfers largely depend on household demographics, intrahousehold allocation, and the generosity of transfers. Pure income transfers can be capacitating, but in the analysis that follows we focus on programs with explicit social investment objectives and instruments. As noted, this will provide a conservative measure of social investment.[9]

5.4. SOCIAL INVESTMENT TRENDS

Using program data from the SALMIC data set (Barrientos, 2018b), this section provides measures of social investment. The SALMIC database collected data on social assistance programs in all LMICs annually from 2000 to 2015. It focused on flagship programs, defined as programs with an institutional basis, scaled up or in the processes of scaling up, and leading poverty reduction in their respective countries. The justification for this focus is the fact that many LMICs have large numbers of highly fragmented small-scale interventions. Program data was harmonized to facilitate aggregation at the country and region levels.

Figure 5.1 provides a breakdown of social assistance programs by type. As can be seen from the figure, all four types of social assistance programs show growth in the 2000–2015 period. By 2015, pure income transfer programs more than doubled to 137, and they remain the dominant type of provision. Conditional

---

9. Measuring unintended social investment outcomes in pure income transfers requires analysis of impact evaluation studies. This is available for a handful of programs in particular years (Bastagli et al., 2016), but this data is too patchy to provide a global picture at this point in time.

income transfers were the second most common type at 55. Integrated anti-poverty programs number 20. Finally, employment guarantees number 15. In terms of the number of programs, compensatory and social investment groups of programs show similar rates of growth, roughly a threefold expansion.

Counting programs is informative when considering trends in program design, but tracking the reach of social assistance, that is, the number of beneficiaries from the programs, better accounts for the global significance of social assistance expansion in LMICs. Figure 5.2 provides a measure of reach by program type. It shows that a large expansion of social assistance can be traced to the first decade of the 21st century. This trend reflects a significant number of new large-scale programs coming on stream, such as India's National Rural Employment Guarantee Scheme, the expansion of China's *DiBao*, and Brazil's *Bolsa Família*. The numbers in the figure refer to direct and indirect beneficiaries. Where program agencies report only the number of direct recipients, as in pension programs, the numbers are multiplied by the relevant country's average household size to capture both direct and indirect beneficiaries. This facilitates a like-for-like comparison with programs that are household-based, conditional income transfers, for example. The figure shows a stronger equivalence between compensatory and social investment–oriented social assistance than in program incidence. Focusing on reach, as opposed to the number of programs, provides an accurate picture of the expansion of social investment in LMICs.

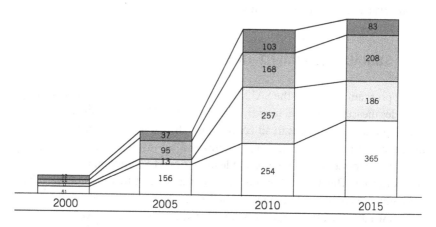

Figure 5.2 Social assistance reach in LMICs by program type (millions of direct and indirect beneficiaries).
Source. SALMIC data set.
Note. "Reach" describes the number of direct and indirect beneficiaries of social assistance programs. Where programs report only the number of direct beneficiaries, pensions, for example, this figure is multiplied by the average household size in that particular country to arrive at a figure for direct and indirect beneficiaries. Figures might be an underestimate due to missing data for some programs in some years.

Figure 5.3 shows the relative weight of protection and social investment in terms of reach across regions. Diversity is as expected. Some regions are protection-oriented, South, East, and Central Asia in particular. Conditional income transfers are important in Latin America and the Caribbean and in East Asia. In part, diversity reflects institutional legacies. For example, the preeminence of protective objectives in FSU countries in Central Asia reflects the focus on family and categorical transfers that dominated social assistance under Soviet rule. In part, it reflects transition in welfare institutions. It will be some time before the emerging institutions are consolidated. Within regions, the influence of large countries is important. China, the Philippines, and Indonesia have surged ahead with social investment–oriented social assistance; but this is not a generalized trend in other countries in their respective regions.

To sum up, the discussion in this section tracked the expansion of social assistance and the trends in social investment. Employing ideal program types, it measured social investment orientation by comparing program incidence and reach. Conditional income transfer and integrated anti-poverty programs have an explicit social investment orientation. Protection objectives dominate in pure income transfers. Employment guarantees are inimical to social investment. Pure income transfers are the largest type of program as regards program numbers or incidence. Program numbers increase more or less proportionally over time across protection and social investment types. When the focus is on reach, the numbers of direct and indirect beneficiaries, the expansion of social assistance looks closely balanced between protection and social investment objectives. Close to one-half of global social assistance beneficiaries participate in programs

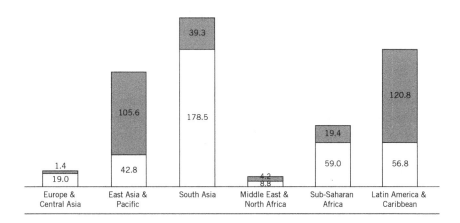

□ Pure transfers ■ Conditional Income transfers plus Integrated Anti-poverty transfers

Figure 5.3 Reach of compensatory and social investment transfers by region (millions of direct and indirect beneficiaries)
Source. SALMIC data set.
Note. Figures exclude employment guarantees.

with an explicit social investment orientation. There is diversity across regions, highlighting the role of institutional legacies and the transitional nature of current welfare institutions.

5.5. CORRELATES OF SOCIAL INVESTMENT

To date, few studies have attempted to explain the main factors behind the global expansion of social assistance (Barrientos, 2019), despite many references in the policy literature to facilitating or contextual factors. Globalization and de-industrialization have undermined social insurance institutions, where these had developed. The re-establishment of democratic processes and the retrenchment of authoritarianism created political conditions in which the social policy demands, accumulated during the spread of economic liberalization and structural adjustment in the 1980s and 1990s, can force policy reforms. Financial and economic crises are important drivers of social protection expansion as they add urgency to social policy demands.[10] These are "demand" factors, but "supply" factors are important too. Sustained economic growth and the commodity boom in the first decade of the new century unexpectedly enlarged fiscal space and enabled governments to respond to pressures for stronger social policy.

Favorable conditions for the expansion of social protection in general may not necessarily help explain why LMICs have focused on expanding social assistance and why the expansion of social assistance has a social investment orientation.[11]

Linear explanations presuming that the expansion of social assistance is an antecedent to their future evolution into social insurance run counter to the fact that social assistance and social investment expansion has been stronger in Latin American countries with long-standing social insurance institutions (illustrating that—contrary to the most economically advanced welfare states—social investment and social consumption do not operate as alternatives in LMICs; see also Chapters 7 and 13 in this volume).

Studies on social investment expansion in high-income countries in the Organisation for Economic Co-operation and Development emphasize the crucial role of societal demand by middle- and upper-income classes (see Chapter 12 in this volume). "Demand" for social investment is hypothesized to be stronger where a "new" middle class dependent on employment in open and technology-intensive occupations is influential and weaker where an "old" middle class

10. The 1997 financial crisis in Asia led to a rapid expansion of social assistance in countries like Indonesia and South Korea (Kwon, 2002; Sumarto et al., 2008).
11. Carnes and Mares (2014, 2015) argue that the growth of social assistance in Latin America is grounded on changes in employment brought about by economic liberalization that has extended employment vulnerability to the middle classes. Their hypothesis applies to demand for compensatory transfers, especially pensions.

linked to manufacturing employment is capable of resisting reforms of compensatory welfare institutions. But in LMICs the expansion of social assistance benefits mainly low-income groups. In the Latin American context, Pribble and co-workers emphasize the role of left coalitions, in power in the first decade of the new century, in driving a redistributive agenda (Pribble et al., 2009).[12] This is relevant because social assistance implies vertical redistribution, in contrast to horizontal distribution which defines social insurance. Political economy explanations for the social investment orientation of emerging social assistance institutions in LMICs need to explain *jointly vertical redistribution and social investment*.

In the context of aid-dependent low-income countries in sub-Saharan Africa and Asia, it has been suggested that the focus on social investment is associated with the influence of multilateral organizations. In particular, the spread of conditional income transfers has been associated with the influence of the World Bank and other multilaterals (Jenson, 2010; Peck & Theodore, 2015; Yeates, 2018). This hypothesis requires substantive critical scrutiny. Analysis of the distribution of the World Bank's financial support across social assistance instruments fails to support this hypothesis (Andrews et al., 2014). The data in Figure 5.3 confirms this point: The World Bank has advocated conditional cash transfers but alongside a multiplicity of instruments. And the role of multilaterals is often exaggerated in discussions of social protection policies in LMICs, especially by the multilaterals themselves. It is worth recalling that conditional income transfers were not an invention of Bretton Woods institutions but emerged from domestic policy innovations in Brazil and Mexico in the mid-1990s.

Figure 5.3 suggests that institutional and policy legacies are important, particularly in retarding reform. The pattern of social assistance programs in FSU countries reflects a transition from social protection systems based on guaranteed full employment and family transfers to welfare institutions addressing liberalized labor market conditions. This institutional legacy makes it hard for countries to move away from compensatory transfers, often attached to groups perceived to be deserving and/or vulnerable. In sub-Saharan Africa policy legacies privileged humanitarian and emergency assistance—food transfers, food/cash for work, and school feeding—supported by international aid. The shift to social investment–oriented social assistance has encountered resistance from both donors and local elites. Sustained economic growth, including natural resource revenues, and democratization are rapidly opening reform options in some countries, an additional explanation for the social investment orientation in low-income countries. Institutional and policy legacies in South Asia favored welfare policies linked to rural development, but rapid urbanization and participation

---

12. Experimental research on preferences for human capital conditions in social assistance, especially conditional income transfers, suggests that support is greatest among low- and high-income groups (Zucco et al., 2020).

in global production chains, in garments, for example, are likely to strengthen a social investment orientation.

The explanatory power of alternative hypotheses was tested in a multivariate context. Table 5.1 reports on the results of two regression estimations.

Model 1 reports the results of estimating a panel probit in which the dependent variable is whether countries have social investment–oriented programs, conditional on having social assistance. This model seeks to identify potential factors distinguishing countries' institutional approach to social investment, conditional on having social assistance.

Model 2 reports the results of a linear random intercept model in which the independent variable is the reach of social assistance, the total number of direct and indirect beneficiaries of programs with a social investment orientation, conditional on countries having social assistance. The advantage of the linear random intercept model is that it enables explicit estimation of the effects of changes within countries and the effects of differences between countries.[13] Distinguishing between and within effects throws light on the factors explaining the expansion of social investment–oriented social assistance, conditional on countries having social assistance.

The analysis employs social assistance data from the SALMIC data set introduced in the last section, supplemented by panel country data from the Quality of Government data collection (Teorell et al., 2018). The independent variables aim to capture the factors identified in this section. The *fh_ipolity2* variable captures the level of democracy on a 10-point scale. A series with imputed values for missing observations will be used to maximize country/year coverage. The *left* variable, from the Database of Political Institutions, is a dummy variable with 1 where the largest party in the governing coalition is left-oriented. The variable *ictd_taxnresexsc* captures tax revenues excluding resource taxes and social security contributions as a proportion of gross domestic product (GDP). This variable captures fiscal capacity. The variable *serv* represents the share of the labor force in services. The variable *lngdpcap* is the log of GDP per capita in 2011 purchasing power parity terms. It measures countries' economic growth. Finally, both models include region dummies to capture institutional legacies.

Focusing on Model 1, changes in the level of democracy within a country are positively correlated with the presence of social investment programs, but the level of significance attached to this parameter is marginal at 10%. Differences in the levels of democracy across countries are not significantly different from zero. Within-country changes to the left in governing coalition have large and significant positive effects on the presence of social investment assistance programs. However, differences in left orientation across countries are associated with a negative parameter, although with marginal significance at 10%.

---

13. Bell and Jones (2015) and Bartels (2008) discuss the linear random intercept model in detail; see an application of the model to social investment in Nöel (2020).

Table 5.1 Estimation results

Variables	Model 1 Incidence (SI is [1,0])	Model 2 Reach (SI as fraction of population)	Descriptives Mean	SD
fh_ipolity2 (within)	0.6008*	0.0023	6.46	2.55
	(0.343)	(0.003)		
fh_ipolity2 (between)	−0.4995	−0.0008	6.45	2.5
	(0.500)	(0.004)		
left (within)	1.6849***	0.0305**	0.35	0.47
	(0.611)	(0.012)		
left (between)	−3.2304*	−0.0458**	0.45	0.38
	(1.811)	(0.020)		
ictd_taxnresexsc (within)	0.1211	0.0018	16.14	5.98
	(0.092)	(0.001)		
ictd_taxnresexsc (between)	−0.4507**	−0.0028*	16.13	5.61
	(0.209)	(0.002)		
serv (within)	0.2081***	0.0011	46.33	15.42
	(0.080)	(0.001)		
serv (between)	−0.2775***	−0.0022**	46.52	15.42
	(0.099)	(0.001)		
lngdpcap	3.1596**	0.0319***	8.72	0.84
	(1.445)	(0.012)		
East Asia and Pacific	3.1097	0.0293*	0.12	0.32
	(3.386)	(0.016)		
South Asia	3.2999	0.1056	0.06	0.24
	(3.544)	(0.067)		
Middle East and North Africa	−1.9949	0.0015	0.08	0.27
	(3.517)	(0.010)		
Sub-Saharan Africa	1.5807	0.0226*	0.22	0.41
	(2.386)	(0.013)		
Latin America and the Caribbean	6.3091**	0.0969***	0.26	0.44
	(2.451)	(0.020)		
lnsig2u	3.6898***			
	(0.125)			
Snidjers-Bosker R2 level 1		0.2594		
Snidjers-Bosker R2 level 2		0.3264		
Incidence			0.45	0.49
Reach			0.03	0.08
Observations	1018	1018	1018	
Number of countries	96	96	96	

Note. Robust standard errors in parentheses. Reference region is Europe and Central Asia. SI = social investment; SD = standard deviation.
*p < 0.1, **p < 0.05, ***p < 0.01.

The within-country service employment share variable has a positive and significant parameter. The between-country parameter is also significant but negative. These results suggest that tertiarization within country is consistent with social investment.

The variables capturing "supply"-side variables provide conflicting signals. Changes in the level of GDP per capita, as captured by its log transformation, are associated with a strong and positive effect on the incidence of social investment. This is in line with expectations that economic growth, and perhaps associated implementation capacity, would facilitate a social investment orientation. The within-country tax revenue parameter is not significant, but the between-country parameter is negative and significant. This suggests that countries with large revenue to GDP ratios are less likely to support a social investment orientation.

Finally, the regional dummies have the expected signs, recalling Figure 5.3. The reference region is Europe and Central Asia. As expected, the Latin America and Caribbean region has a large positive parameter.

Turning to Model 2 results, the focus is on identifying factors associated with the expansion of reach of social investment programs. Reassuringly, the Model 2 results largely confirm the main gist of the findings from Model 1. Democracy levels and changes do not appear to have significant effects on the expansion of social investment reach. Left-leaning coalitions have a positive and significant correlation with the reach of social investment–oriented social assistance but a negative correlation across countries. Tax revenues have a marginal association with social investment. Economic growth retains a positive effect on social investment reach. The within-country parameter associated with tertiarization is not significant with respect to changes within country but retains a negative and significant correlation across countries. With respect to the regional dummies, the East Asia and Pacific and the sub-Saharan Africa dummies now show marginal significance at the 10% level, compared to the Europe and Central Asia reference region. This again reflects the data presented in Figure 5.3.

These results suggest that democratization, while having a positive effect of social investment, might not be a hugely important factor, conditional on countries having social assistance. Democratization might be a highly important factor in the expansion of social assistance (Barrientos, 2019) but not decisive as regards its social investment orientation.[14] On the other hand, within-country shifts to left-leaning governing coalitions have large explanatory power on social investment orientation. In sum, these results suggest that social investment–oriented vertical redistribution is explained by shifts to left-leaning governing coalitions and tertiarization, especially in countries traditionally with non-left-leaning

14. The data covers the period 2000–2015, following the retrenchment of authoritarianism in the 1990s.

coalitions and lower levels of tertiarization. Economic growth is important in explaining the social investment orientation of social assistance provision. Institutional legacies are likely to have played an important role in constraining social investment expansion.

5.6. CONCLUSIONS

The chapter tracked the recent expansion of social assistance programs in LMICs and examined their social investment orientation. This represents a large global expansion of targeted policies directed at creating human capital among low-income groups. Emergent welfare institutions have considerable political salience domestically and internationally.

Distinguishing "ideal types" of social assistance programs in LMICs helped identify social investment orientation. Whereas pure income transfers are primarily protective and compensatory, conditional income transfer and integrated anti-poverty programs share an explicit social investment orientation. Pure income transfers might also have social investment outcomes depending on context. A fourth type, the employment guarantee, lacks social investment features. Measures of social investment relying on "ideal types" provide lower-bound, conservative estimates as pure income transfers might also be capacitating depending on context.

Analysis of a new data set of social assistance programs, SALMIC, shows that the expansion of social assistance programs in LMICs is fairly well balanced between protection and social investment objectives. In terms of reach, programs with an explicit social investment orientation account for close to one-half of direct and indirect beneficiaries globally. Differences in social investment orientation across subregions point to the influence of institutional and policy legacies, constraining the pace and extent of reforms.

The social investment orientation associated with emergent social assistance institutions in LMICs raises important questions regarding political economy scope conditions and supporting coalitions. Social assistance represents vertical redistribution, and the associated social investment engages general skills. What possible political and economic factors could explain support for these institutions? Multivariate analysis of social investment correlates throws some light on this important question. The results of this analysis suggest that social investment–oriented vertical redistribution is partially explained by shifts to left-leaning governing coalitions and tertiarization, especially in countries characterized by non-left-leaning coalitions and lower levels of tertiarization. Economic growth is also important in explaining the social investment orientation of social assistance provision. The analysis also suggests that institutional legacies might play a role in constraining social investment expansion.

REFERENCES

Alderman, H., & Yemstov, R. (2013). *How can safety nets contribute to economic growth?* [Policy Research Working Paper 6437]. World Bank.

Andrews, C., Kryeziú, A., & Seo, D. (2014). *World Bank support for social safety nets 2007–2013. A review of financing, knowledge services and results* [Discussion Paper 1422]. World Bank.

Ardington, C., Case, A., & Hosegood, V. (2009). Labour supply responses to large social transfers: Longitudinal evidence from South Africa. *American Economic Journal: Applied Economics, 1*(1), 22–48.

Atkinson, A. B. (1995). On targeting social security: Theory and Western experience with family benefits. In D. van de Walle & K. Nead (Eds.), *Public spending and the poor* (pp. 25–65). John Hopkins University Press.

Baird, S., Ferreira, F., Ozler, B., & Woolcock, M. (2014). Conditional, unconditional and everything in between: A systematic review of cash transfer programs on schooling outcomes. *Journal of Development Effectiveness, 6*(1), 1–43.

Barrientos, A. (2010). Protecting capabilities, eradicating extreme poverty: Chile Solidario and the future of social protection. *Journal of Human Development and Capabilities, 11*(4), 579–597.

Barrientos, A. (2013a). *Social assistance in developing countries.* Cambridge University Press.

Barrientos, A. (2013b). The rise of social assistance in Brazil. *Development and Change, 44*(4), 887–910.

Barrientos, A. (2018a). Conditional income transfers, social policy and development. In J. Midgley, R. Surender, & L. Alfers (Eds.), *Handbook of social policy and development* (pp. 373–392). Edward Elgar.

Barrientos, A. (2018b). *Social assistance in low and middle income countries dataset (SALMIC).* Global Development Institute, University of Manchester. www.social-assistance.manchester.ac.uk

Barrientos, A. (2019). *Does a general theory of welfare institutions explain the expansion of social assistance in low and middle income countries?* [Working Paper 1; SOCIUM SFB 1342]. University of Bremen.

Bartels, B. L. (2008). *Beyond "fixed versus random effects": A framework for improving substantive and statistical analysis of panel, time-series cross-sectional, and multilevel data* [Mimeo]. Stony Brook University.

Bastagli, F., Hagen-Zanker, J., Harman, L., Barca, V., Sturge, G., & Schmidt, T. (2016). *Cash transfers: What does the evidence say? Annex 1 Overview of existing cash transfer reviews.* Overseas Development Institute.

Bell, A., & Jones, K. (2015). Explaining fixed effects: Random effects modelling of times series cross-sectional and panel data. *Political Science Research and Methods, 3*(1), 133–153.

Carnes, M., & Mares, I. (2014). Coalitional realignment and the adoption of non-contributory social insurance programmes in Latin America. *Socio-Economic Review, 12*, 695–722.

Carnes, M., & Mares, I. (2015). Explaining the "return of the state" in middle-income countries: Employment vulnerability, incomes, and preferences for social protection in Latin America. *Politics and Society, 43*(4), 525–550.

Case, A., & Wilson, F. (2000). *Health and wellbeing in South Africa: Evidence from the Langeberg Survey* [Mimeo]. Princeton University.

Cecchini, S., & Madariaga, A. (2011). *Conditional cash transfer programmes. The recent experience in Latin America and the Caribbean* (Report LC/G.2497-P). Economic Commission for Latin America and the Caribbean.

Davis, B., Handa, S., Hypher, N., Winder, N., Winters, P. C., & Yablonski, J. (2016). *From evidence to action: The story of cash transfers and impact evaluation in sub-Saharan Africa*. Oxford University Press.

de Carvalho, I. E. (2008). *Household income as a determinant of child labour and school enrollment in Brazil: Evidence from a social security reform* [IMF Working Paper WP/08/241]. International Monetary Fund.

Duflo, E. (2000). *Grandmothers and granddaughters: Old age pension and intra-household allocation in South Africa* [Working Paper 8061]. National Bureau of Economic Research.

Dutta, P., Murgai, R., Ravallion, M., & van de Walle, D. (2012). *Does India's Employment Guarantee Scheme guarantee employment?* [Policy Research Working Paper 6003]. World Bank.

Economic Commission for Latin America and the Caribbean & International Labour Organization. (2014). *The employment situation in Latin America and the Caribbean. Conditional cash transfer programmes and the labour market* (No. 10). United Nations.

Falkingham, J., & Vlachantoni, A. (2010). *Pensions and social protection in central Asia and south Caucasus: Development in the post-Soviet era* [CRA Discussion Paper 1002]. Centre for Research on Ageing, School of Social Sciences, University of Southampton.

Fernandez, L., & Olfindo, R. (2011). *Overview of the Philippines' conditional cash transfer program: The Pantawid Pamilyang Pilipino Program (Pantawid Pamilya)* [Social Protection Discussion Paper 62879]. World Bank.

Fiszbein, A., & Schady, N. (2009). *Conditional cash transfers: Reducing present and future poverty*. World Bank.

Gao, Q., Garfinkel, I., & Zhai, F. (2009). Anti-poverty effectiveness of the minimum living standards assistance policy in urban China. *Review of Income and Wealth, 55*(1), 630–655.

Garcia, M., & Moore, C. M. T. (2012). *The cash dividend: The rise of cash transfer programs in sub-Saharan Africa*. World Bank.

Garritzmann, J. L., Häusermann, S., & Palier, B. (Eds.). (2022). *The world politics of social investment: Vol. II. The politics of varying social investment strategies.* Oxford University Press.

Gassmann, F. (2018). Social assistance. In S. W. Handayani (Ed.), *Asia's fiscal challenge: Financing the social protection agenda of the Sustainable Development Goals* (pp. 132–167). Asian Development Bank.

Glassman, A., Duran, D., Fleisher, L., Singer, D., Sturke, R., Angeles, G., Charles, J., Emrey, B., Gleason, J., Mwebsa, W., Saldana, K., Yarrow, K., & Koblinsky, M. (2013). Impact of conditional cash transfers on maternal and newborn health. *Journal of Health Population and Nutrition, 4*(Suppl 2), 548–566.

Golan, J., Sicular, T., & Umapathi, N. (2015). *Unconditional cash transfers in China: An analysis of the rural minimum living standard guarantee scheme* [Policy Research Working Paper 7374]. World Bank.

International Labour Organization. (2017). *World social protection report 2017–19.*

Jenson, J. (2010). Diffusing ideas for after neoliberalism: The social investment perspective in Europe and Latin America. *Global Social Policy, 10*(1), 59–84.

Kwon, H.-J. (2002). Advocacy coalitions and the politics of welfare in Korea after the economic crisis. *Policy and Politics, 31*(1), 68–93.

Leibbrandt, M., Wegner, E., & Finn, A. (2011). *The policies for reducing income inequality and poverty in South Africa* [Working Paper 64]. Southern Africa Labour and Development Research Unit, University of Cape Town.

Lund, F. (2008). *Changing social policy. The Child Support Grant in South Africa.* HSRC Press.

Behrman, J. R., Galab, S., & Reddy, P. (2014). *Impact of the NREGS on schooling and intellectual human capital* [GCC Working Paper GCC14-01]. University of Pennsylvania.

Mehrotra, S. (2011). *Introducing conditional cash transfers (CCTs) in India: A proposal for five CCTs* [IAMR Occasional Paper 2]. Institute of Applied Manpower Research.

Monchuk, V. (2014). *Reducing poverty and investing in people.* World Bank.

Noël, A. (2018). Is social investment inimical to the poor? *Socio-Economic Review, 18*(3), 857–880.

Peck, J., & Theodore, N. (2015). *Fast policy: Experimental statecraft at the thresholds of neoliberalism.* University of Minnesota Press.

Pribble, J., Huber, E., & Stephens, J. D. (2009). Politics, policies, and poverty in Latin America. *Comparative Politics, 41*(4), 387–407.

Rofman, R., Apella, I., & Vezza, E. (2015). *Beyond contributory pensions: Fourteen experiences with coverage expansion in Latin America.* World Bank.

Shah, M., & Steinberg, B. M. (2015). *Workfare and human capital investment: Evidence from India* [Working Paper 21543]. National Bureau of Economic Research.

Sumarto, S., Suryahadi, A., & Bazzi, S. (2008). Indonesia's social protection during and after the crisis. In A. Barrientos & D. Hulme (Eds.), *Social protection for the poor and poorest: Concepts, policies and politics* (pp. 121–145). Palgrave.

Teorell, J., Dahlberg, S., Holmberg, S., Charron, N., Rothstein, B., Alvarado Pachon, N., & Svensson, R. (2018). *The quality of government dataset, version January 2018* [Dataset]. Quality of Government Institute, University of Gothenburg. https://www.gu.se/en/quality-government/qog-data

Wang, M. (2007). Emerging urban poverty and effects of the Dibao program on alleviating poverty in China. *China and World Economy, 15*(2), 74–88.

Weber, A. (2010). Social assistance in Asia and the Pacific: An overview. In S. W. Handayani & C. Burkleys (Eds.), *Social assistance and conditional cash transfers* (pp. 47–59). Asian Development Bank.

World Bank. (2015). *The state of social safety nets 2015.* World Bank.

World Bank. (2016). *Atlas of social protection indicators of resilience and equity* [Database]. http://datatopics.worldbank.org/aspire/home

Yañes-Pagans, M. (2008). *Culture and human capital investments: Evidence of an unconditional cash transfer programme in Bolivia* [Discussion Paper 3678]. Institute of Labor Economics.

Yeates, N. (2018). *Global approaches to social policy* (2018–2). United Nations Research Institute for Social Development.

Zucco, C., Luna, J. P., & Baykal, O. G. (2020). Do conditionalities increase support for government transfers? *Journal of Development Studies, 56*(3), 527–544.

6

POLITICAL LINKAGE STRATEGIES AND SOCIAL INVESTMENT POLICIES

CLIENTELISM AND EDUCATIONAL POLICY IN THE DEVELOPING WORLD

Haohan Chen and Herbert Kitschelt

6.1. INTRODUCTION

People can protect themselves from the loss of market income (wages, profits) through communal networks (family, religion, neighborhood, etc.), insurance contracts (financial markets), or government-provided support (welfare state social benefits). The latter may substitute lost income with government transfers ("social compensation") or enable people to acquire skills and capabilities that increase their chances of supporting themselves through employment and reduce their future risks of income loss and poverty ("social investment"). An important ingredient of such social investment policies—serving specifically the function of human capital *creation*—is public education and training. This chapter will show that for public education and training spending to actually serve this purpose, it is critical whether it is delivered in terms of "policy," with eligibility to obtain the benefit for anyone who meets certain universalistic criteria (like residence status, age, previous qualification, insurance contribution, or labor market status), or in terms of "clientelism," as a favor delivered by politicians and their brokers to those who support them to get elected and hold public office. In other words, this chapter establishes the absence or weakness of clientelistic partisan practices as a

Haohan Chen and Herbert Kitschelt, *Political Linkage Strategies and Social Investment Policies* In: *The World Politics of Social Investment (Volume I)*. Edited by: Julian L. Garritzmann, Silja Häusermann, and Bruno Palier, Oxford University Press. © Oxford University Press 2022. DOI: 10.1093/oso/9780197585245.003.0006 condition for social investment and thereby underlines the key argument of the book that social investment needs to be defined through its goals and functions, rather than via policy fields. The chapter also builds on the findings of the previous chapter by Barrientos (Chapter 5 in this volume) that formal democracy itself is not an important determinant of social investment expansion. Rather, the actual functioning of democracy is crucial.

An earlier study comparing 66 developing countries with at least a modicum of multi-party competition showed that clientelistic benefits tend to operate as a *substitute* for social policies of compensation (Kitschelt, 2015). Where weak state capacities prevent the implementation of encompassing effective pension and unemployment insurance schemes, people may resort to clientelism as a "second best" strategy of income risk-hedging. Both clientelistic hedging and social insurance, however, address the same problem with different arrangements of social compensation.

In contrast to social compensation, however, we show in this chapter that clientelism is no substitute when it comes to social investment in capacities to earn a market income. We develop a theory on how clientelistic politics in developing countries negatively affects public education and its outcomes for skill formation by both "crowding out" educational inputs and "degrading" educational outputs and outcomes. First, clientelism "crowds out" resource inputs that could have been devoted to education. Second, clientelism "degrades" the investment effect of resources allocated to public education because they are often diverted to the personal consumption of rent-seeking clients, frequently the titular providers of such education services. In other words, clientelistic politics reduce both the magnitude of financial effort and the efficiency of public education in developing countries.

The chapter is organized in five parts. In Section 6.2, we explain why government input in education should not always be considered social investment at face value. Educational effort can be deployed as an investment in educational recipients, but it can also be a strategy of social compensation and/or consumption mostly benefiting its producers, managers, contractors, and teachers in the education system. In Section 6.3 we introduce our theoretical arguments on how clientelism "crowds out" (Stage I) and "degrades" (Stage II) social investment efforts. In Section 6.4, we present an illustrative case study of Mexico's educational politics detailing the mechanisms postulated in our theoretical argument. Section 6.5 introduces a large-N cross-national study. We first describe the data we use in Section 6.5.1. Then, in Section 6.5.2, we provide evidence indicating that clientelism "crowds out" (Stage I) input in public education. In Section 6.5.3, we show that resources devoted to education under clientelistic politics often result in very poor educational skills, thus "degrading" (Stage II) the investment momentum of public educational resource commitments. Section 6.6 concludes.

Table 6.1 Attributes of the educational process

Level	Inputs	Throughputs	Outputs	Outcomes
Primary	• Government spending on education (percentage of GDP)	• Teacher–pupil ratio (levels) • Children out of school (ratios) • Teacher training at different levels • Educational staff expenditure as percentage of total school expenditure	• School level completion and certification (graduation) rates (primary, secondary, tertiary educational attainment)	• Literacy rates (youths, adults) • Percentage of labor force with primary, secondary, upper secondary, tertiary school completion • Math, science, reading performance at different school levels
Secondary	• Per student capita educational spending on different tiers of the sector (as percentage of GDP per capita)			
Tertiary	• Capital investments in education (buildings, software, machines) • Teachers' salaries • Non-teaching staff salaries			

6.2. WHEN DO EFFORTS IN EDUCATION SIGNAL A SOCIAL INVESTMENT?

Education is a Janus-faced good in at least two ways: First, it can be *consumption*, but also *investment*. Second, it can be a *private* good, but also has *public* goods qualities.[1] Consumption uses up a resource and creates benefits in a single time period. Investments deploy resources to yield benefits to the owner over a multitude of time periods. Education as a consumption good is privately appropriated. However, as an investment good, it has both *private* benefits and *public* spillovers, while it is never just a collective good with non-excludable provision and non-rival consumption (Kosack, 2012, p. 24). When a government makes efforts in the field of education, the type of goods provided—private or public, investment or consumption—cannot be directly observed or measured by any simple indicator. It is essential to distinguish four operational and observable aspects of education and consider their goods characters, as summarized in Table 6.1.

1) *Educational Inputs*: These are financial resources allocated to education, converted into buildings, teaching materials, salaries, and other operating budgets. This fiscal flow is easily measurable in budget ratios

1. This property of education is similar to water supply and electricity (Min, 2015).

and gross domestic product (GDP) shares, disaggregated by public and private sources. Such inputs have consumption qualities for their providers (builders, teachers, administrators, service personnel) but may be investments from the perspective of students.

2) *Educational Throughputs*: This denotes the organizational *process* of education, or how recipients of treatment (student populations) are interfaced with inputs (teachers, facilities, etc.). Indirect measures of the throughput process are the ratios of age cohorts included in the educational process and student–faculty ratios. Also, teacher–non-teaching support staff ratios are relevant. The quality of the throughput process determines to a considerable extent whether and how inputs are actually converted into educational investment outputs and outcomes or mostly consumption for the participants of the process, education providers (incomes) or recipients: Presence in educational institutions could consume students' time without adding marketable skills (see Chapter 15 in this volume for a similar argument regarding early childhood education and care policies).

3) *Educational Outputs*: These are the formal certifications graduates earn as a result of an educational process, in as much as employers recognize degrees, student grades associated with degrees, and degree-issuing institutions as signals of skill and ability and reward recipients by salary levels for their effort. From the recipient's vantage point, a degree is thus a private investment good. From an aggregate societal perspective, the density of degree holders may create a collective investment goods as high-quality employers locate in areas with more degree holders and promote economic expansion.

4) *Educational Outcomes*: These are the measured operational skills of the labor force that may or may not be associated with the distribution of educational outputs (e.g., percentage of degree holders in a population). There are general verbal, mathematical, and scientific skills and specific skills applicable only in narrowly defined professions. Measures of general educational outcomes, especially verbal and mathematical skills, have become available only recently and will be employed in our analysis. They are the ultimate and most desirable measure of educational investment, both private at the individual level and public.

These four aspects of education show interesting features upon examining World Bank data and our data on clientelistic linkages. Figure 6.1 is a correlation matrix. The first four variables are (from left to right) measures of input, throughput, output, and outcome in secondary education. The final variable (bottom right) is an indicator of political linkage strategy—the effort of political

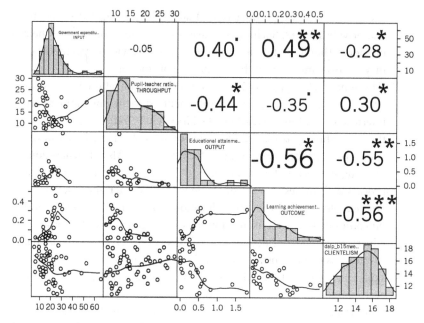

Figure 6.1 Correlation matrix of educational input, throughput, output, outcome, and clientelism.

Note. The variables, from left to right, are 1) government expenditure per student, secondary education (percentage of GDP per capita); 2) pupil–teacher ratio, upper secondary; 3) educational attainment, at least completed upper secondary, population 25+, total (percentage; cumulative); (4) learning achievement in mathematics (level 4) for upper secondary school; 5) parties' effort in clientelism (DALP b15nwe). Variables 1–4 are averages of data points from 2008 to 2014. Variable 5 is based on the DALP expert survey from 2008–2009; see description in the text.

parties in mobilizing voters using clientelistic benefits. The data points include a set of 66 developing democratic countries. The first observation derived from the matrix is that inputs, throughputs, outputs, and outcomes of education are at best moderately correlated. For example, student spending does nothing to explain teacher–pupil ratios and is a rather feeble predictor of educational degree outputs or measured citizen educational competences. Much of the variation among the variables remains unexplained. This suggests that the rates of "conversion" from educational inputs into outputs and outcomes vary among developing countries. Second, the level of clientelistic effort in a developing democracy is negatively associated with educational input, throughput,[2] and especially output and outcome.

Based on the four aspects of education we have defined and motivated by patterns found in the data, we propose a theory of clientelism and social

---

2. A higher pupil–teacher ratio means worse educational throughput. Thus, a positive correlation indicates a negative correlation.

investment in education in developing countries. We argue that the degree to which a government provides education as private and public *investment* depends on two factors: 1) the abundance of public resources allocated to educational *inputs* and 2) the efficiency of conversions from inputs and throughputs to outputs and outcomes. Both factors are shaped by the dynamics of distributive politics. Specifically, choices of governments in the generosity and quality of educational inputs are a function of interest alignment of voters on the demand side and linkage strategies of politicians and parties on the supply side. In the context of developing democracies, the degree to which political parties mobilize voters with clientelistic benefits is the key mechanism on which our chapter is focused. We argue that clientelism both *crowds out* educational input ("Stage I effect") and *degrades* ("Stage II effect") the efficiency of converting educational input and throughput to output and outcome.

6.3. THEORY: INTERESTS, CHOICE, AND IMPLEMENTATION IN EDUCATIONAL INVESTMENT STRATEGIES

Econometric models leave little doubt that beyond the individual economic and social benefits they generate in terms of human capital, skills, and capabilities, educational investments, albeit measured only with input or throughput indicators, are one critical ingredient of countries' economic performance, even when controlling for a host of other variables (cf. Barro, 1998; Bleaney & Nishiyama, 2002; Glaeser et al., 2004; Halter et al., 2014; Jones, 2015). But not all education is equally important at every level of development. Moreover, different tiers of education yield different political conflict alignments, predicated on diverging distributive interests of groups and classes.

Disparities in delivering primary schooling and achieving basic literacy to account for economic performance matter most for the poorest countries. But in our comparison of more than 60 countries with multi-party elections, basic literacy rates among 15-year-olds and older vary rather little. Moreover, no social group—defined in terms of class, ethnicity, or even gender—challenges the access of any other group to basic education.[3] The political conflict about primary education has become a valence issue where politicians compete on competence.[4]

At the other extreme, tertiary education, often intertwined with technological innovation, becomes a critical contributor to economic growth primarily among countries situated near the global innovation frontier (see Chapter 8 in

3. In an earlier age, in Western countries, the struggle about primary education also was mostly not a distributive-economic conflict but one about ideological control between emerging states and religious regimes (e.g., Ansell & Lindvall, 2013).
4. Of course, there are quality issues, but they may require a fine-grained sociological and economic analysis of educational governance and delivery mechanisms (Banerjee & Duflo, 2011).

this volume). Affluent countries exhibit big variance in post-secondary and university educational sectors (Ansell, 2010; Busemeyer, 2014; Garritzmann et al., 2017). In middle-income countries outside the post-communist region, however, tertiary education captures only a small fraction of each student age cohort.[5]

The greatest economic educational challenge for middle-income countries is to raise large portions of their low-skilled but literate workforce to higher skill levels to enable companies to move up the global production chain to production processes with higher value-added. Chances for employment are mostly expanding for (higher) secondary education graduates. Especially in countries in the $ 5,000–$20,000 GDP (2010) per capita income at purchasing power parity (PPP) range, the critical political action is in the realm of improving secondary education systems, including a lower tier (8th–10th grade) and an upper tier (11th–12th grade), often supplemented by vocational education (see Chapter 7 in this volume, on social investment via technical and vocational education and training policies in the economically less advanced countries of Latin America).

Secondary education commands the largest share of total education spending (40%–60%) almost everywhere. Inputs as percentage of GDP vary substantially across countries and even more so quality of outputs and outcomes. This variance, we submit, has to do with conflict of interest among social groups and political organizations that impinge upon education politics in two stages. In the first, group conflict of interest leads to a lesser or greater funding allocation to secondary education inputs. In the second stage, the conflict results in a greater or lesser productivity of educational effort in terms of outputs and outcomes. Where clientelism becomes a dominant pattern of politics, it *crowds out* education spending in the first stage and *degrades* educational effort in the second stage by turning inputs into consumer goods for the providers of educational services rather than investments (i.e., improvements of the professional capabilities of the recipients of educational services).[6]

In this chapter, we show the empirical effect of lesser or greater clientelism in politics on crowding out and degrading educational effort. Due to length and data limitations, we will only sketch in the barest fashion preference schedules and conflict alignments that affect the role of clientelism in educational efforts. We will then *specify the hypotheses linking clientelism to educational investments at different stages of the educational process with more emphasis on the second stage* (converting inputs into outputs) as the literature has paid less attention to that issue.

---

5. World Development Indicators show hardly any of the countries outside the post-communist region with BA or higher tertiary-level certification degrees of 15% or more in any age cohort.

6. Economists, of course, have noticed the problem that educational inputs are uncorrelated to outputs and outcomes but have solely looked for causes in the governance and organization of educational systems (degree of centralization, teacher job security, private/public schools), without endogenizing any of these features to politics and considering clientelism (see Pritchett, 2001, 2013).

6.3.1. Societal preferences over educational effort

In middle-income countries, introducing early and simple reforms—such as elementary education to achieve universal literacy—may be widely supported, while more advanced reforms—such as secondary school expansion—crystallize conflict among contrasting distributive coalitions (Doner & Schneider, 2016). The literature on educational policy quite appropriately considers secondary school reform as an economic distributive choice over different groups' opportunities for social mobility (cf. Ansell, 2008, 2010; Boix, 1998; Busemeyer, 2014; Heidenheimer, 1981; Iversen & Stephens, 2008). Like Ansell (2010), let us distinguish three stylized groups—the poor, the middle, and the rich. Their political representatives make choices over the allocation and use of scarce resources: 1) whether or not to put them at all into educational investments or clientelistic consumption, with education as just one possible channel; 2) if educational investments, how much effort to dedicate to secondary education; 3) if educational investment, how much effort to dedicate to tertiary education.

The middle-income tier's upward mobility aspirations will be satisfied most if investment in secondary education becomes the policy prerogative. As a secondary objective, this group may acquiesce to an emphasis on tertiary educational investments as it funds a more distant step on the ladder of upward social mobility this group ventures to reach. Middle-income earners will abhor the waste of educational resources for clientelistic consumption and give it lowest priority.

High-income recipients with resources to enroll their offspring in private primary and secondary education will want to preserve closure of middle-class paths to higher education through public secondary school investments. They favor strong investment in an exclusive public higher education system, as long as it serves only their own children, but oppose expansion of secondary education to the children of the middle class. Rather than producing more competitors for their own offspring with higher secondary and tertiary educational certificates, they would rather waste educational resources on clientelistic provisions. The poor, finally, in a struggle to survive have a short time horizon and discount their children's future access to secondary and higher education. They begrudgingly opt for clientelistic politics as the least bad and most expedient option[7] if it delivers a modicum of immediate satisfaction of needs, for example, by a high ratio of unskilled non-teaching to teaching staff in the educational system.[8] But clientelistic policies outside the area of education may deliver more direct

---

7. Strong clientelism is therefore associated with higher turnout of the poor (Kasara & Suryanarayan, 2015).
8. Students of clientelism have often used public employment as a tracer of clientelistic political effort. See, for example, Weitz-Shapiro (2014). In countries without effective welfare states, expansion of public employment is a form of "embedded liberalism" to protect the poor from destitution (Nooruddin & Rudra, 2014).

Table 6.2 Group preferences over educational policies

Priority	Low-income poor group (P)	Intermediate-income group (M)	High-income rich group (R)
1	1. Clientelistic delivery of educational inputs	1. Secondary school investments	1. Tertiary school investments
2	2. Secondary school investments	2. Tertiary school investment	2. Clientelistic benefits of educational inputs
3	3. Tertiary school investments	3. Clientelistic delivery of educational inputs	3. Secondary school investments

access to public resources. As runner-up preference, the poor would rather see investments in secondary than tertiary education as they reckon that the probability of their own offspring going to secondary school is higher than attending university.

The three groups thus have different preference schedules (Table 6.2), which opens up the feasibility of different coalitions if none of them unilaterally controls the political system. The role clientelism may play in each configuration has consequences both for the allocation of public resources to education (Stage I) as well as for the conversion of educational inputs into outputs/outcomes (Stage II).

6.3.2. Stage 1: Interest alignments and political coalitions over secondary education policy

A strong emphasis on clientelism as a distractor from educational investments may result especially from a rich–poor coalition. At the stage of financial allocation to education, poor voters may rather see resources diverted to other programs than education as they offer a higher yield of clientelistic side-payments. Aside from outright direct vote buying and gifts during electoral campaigns, such alternatives include direct social transfers (disability pensions, housing subsidies, nutrition aid, and medical services) or public works and general administrative jobs that often exist only on paper and do not involve any operational tasks.

If a coalition of politicians and parties dominates that assembles rich and poor voters, it is most inimical to public educational spending. A coalition of poor and middle-income voters may strike a compromise in which the poor concede some secondary educational spending. Most favorable for public sector educational budgets, and particularly for secondary education, should be a rich–middle income coalition. Empirically, this framework implies at the micro-level that those who are receptive to clientelism put less emphasis on educational investments. At the meso-level of political parties, the more clientelistic parties should lend less support to educational investments. And we should find that this applies to both clientelistic parties attracting the rich and the poor.

At Stage I, we should observe that where the average proclivity of political parties toward clientelism is more pronounced, governments spend less on education, especially secondary education. In line with the focus of this book on the democratic politics of social investment, our country sample is confined to polities with a modicum of multi-party competition and in most, but not all, instances a sufficiently level playing field that incumbents face a realistic risk of electoral defeat and expulsion from government. With our country sample we are able to explore whether greater clientelistic effort is associated with less educational budget allocation, even once regime properties have been largely controlled for.

6.3.3. Stage II: Conversion of educational effort into educational outcomes

In the second stage, dominant coalitions catering to the rich and the poor may subvert middle-class preferred secondary education investment by converting public educational expenditures into consumption expenses. This conversion may take many forms: Politicians may retain contractors to build schools and supply textbooks because they make their employees support their political benefactor in elections. Elected politicians may hire a high ratio of non-teaching to teaching staff and/or hire teachers with more concern for their political loyalty than their pedagogical competence. Also awarding scholarships to the offspring of political loyalists without regard for their educational merits will diminish the quality of educational outputs and outcomes (Hicken & Simmons, 2008, p. 112). Much of the clientelism at stake here is not single-shot vote buying but enduring "relational" exchange throughout legislative terms. This intertemporal resilience of relational clientelism alleviates problems of opportunism, monitoring, and sanctioning involved in clientelism (Kitschelt & Wilkinson, 2007; Nichter, 2010, 2014; Yıldırım & Kitschelt, 2020).

Clientelism thus tends to misallocate people and resources in the education process for the sake of powerful partisan actors' short-term political and material consumption purposes. Because clientelistic producers and consumers of educational services obtain more resources than would correspond to an open competitive allocation in educational exam contests and in occupational markets, the educational outputs (degrees) and outcomes (skills, competences) are degraded. The hypothesis we can test, then, is that—net of expenditure input—polities with parties exerting strong clientelistic effort exhibit weaker academic outputs and outcomes. Where (input) expenditures are high yet outputs and outcomes are weak, clientelism is expected to be at its most intense.

6.3.4. Potential mediating mechanisms: "Friendly extensions" of the theoretical argument

There are at least five intervening mechanisms between clientelism and degradation of educational investment effort. They are correlated with clientelism and may make the latter statistically insignificant as predictors of educational inputs/outputs/outcomes, although they are closely intertwined with the intervening variables in ways that may be impossible to disentangle in terms of causal direction. There may be a "coevolution" or "complementarity" of clientelism with these mechanisms.[9]

1) *State Capacity*: Where the government machinery is staffed by professionals hired because of their operational skills and independently of considerations of political loyalty, state capacity is higher and clientelism tends to be lower. Investment efficiency of educational policy will also be higher.

2) *Between-Group Ethnic Income Inequality*: Ethnic divides, but only if they involve ethnic division of labor and systematic group-based income differentials, foster clientelism (Wang & Kolev, 2019, building on Baldwin & Huber, 2010). Polities with high between-group inequality may produce fewer club and collective goods (Alesina et al., 1999) and consequently invest less (Stage I)—and less efficiently as investments (Stage II)—in education.

3) *Left Redistributive Programmatic Parties*: Where developing countries do incorporate "left" parties with a programmatic redistributive agenda, clientelistic effort will be lower, with more educational inputs (Stage I) and more efficient investments (Stage II).

4) *Post-Communist Polity Context*: Communist systems emphasized educational investments, and this legacy may color the appeals and policies of both post-communist successor parties and liberal-democratic or nationalist competitors. This effect may come to the fore more in the efficiency of converting inputs into outputs than the generosity of educational funding in a time of economic liberalization.

5) *Generic Strength of Programmatic Parties*: The presence of more programmatic parties, regardless of ideological bent or legacies, may undercut clientelism and improve efficiency, if not effort, in educational policy investments. Some diversified linkage parties combine clientelistic and programmatic strategies (Kitschelt & Singer, 2016), but most programmatic parties do not. Programmatism involves 1) internal cohesion of parties around public policy objectives, interacting with 2) differentiation of the parties' objectives in the party system and 3) salience of those issues on which parties show internal programmatic cohesiveness and external, systemic difference (Kitschelt & Freeze, 2010).

---

9. Besley and Persson (2011), among others, have invoked the idea of "coevolution" where causal relations may be impossible to identify.

6.3.5. Rival accounts of educational investment efforts and outcomes

There is, however, also a set of mechanisms that may influence the effort and efficiency of educational investment independent of partisan clientelism and related political processes. When entered as controls, they may prove our argument to be wrong or serve as complementary explanations.

1) *Particularist Electoral Institutions*: Personalistic electoral systems (open list proportional representation, single-member districts) have been alleged to promote clientelism, but there is little evidence in a broad cross-national comparison (Kitschelt, 2011). Nevertheless, particularistic electoral institutions could work through some other mechanism of rent-seeking politics to diminish educational expenditures and degrade educational outputs and outcomes.

2) *Open Economies*: Open economies cannot afford an underfunded, inefficient educational system. They offer more opportunities for high-skill jobs and make the elites less inclined to seek system closure (Ansell, 2010). Openness may enhance educational expenditure and efficiency.

3) *Economic Inequality*: Inequality may make it hard for individuals to invest at a socially optimal rate in education, and it thereby reduces economic growth (Berg et al., 2018; Halter et al., 2014). Inequality may also reduce educational investment and efficiency as it weakens the middle-income strata most keen on such outcomes. Inequality may work on policymaking through clientelism (You, 2015), but empirically this relationship may be tenuous.[10] The channel between inequality and education policy may be distinct.

6.4. A CASE STUDY OF DEGRADING EDUCATIONAL INVESTMENT: MEXICO

There is little systematic work available on the passage of policy and the implementation of educational strategies beyond the study of educational expenditures (critically: Gift & Wibbels, 2014). But Mexico is an exception, primarily because the high-profile politics of its teachers' union appear to have degraded the quality of educational results (see Chambers-Ju & Finger, 2016; Fernandez, 2012).

---

10. You's findings rely on a questionable inequality data set and cannot be replicated with better indicators (contact Kitschelt for data upon request).

Teachers' unions may not invariably bring about such outcomes.[11] But the combination of a corporatist, authoritarian party instrumentalizing unions—with receptive and profiteering union bosses enmeshed in clientelistic networks—certainly does.

In the 1940s the ruling Mexican Revolutionary Institutionalized Party (PRI) merged fragmented teachers' associations into a single teachers' representation. Once centralized and with loyalists displacing intermittent leftist challengers, the teachers' union became the party's "political brigade" to mobilize the broader electorate (Chambers-Ju & Finger, 2016, p. 219; see Chapters 11 and 13 in this volume). Electoral manipulation was part of the deal as ballot stations were typically sited in schools.

An oligarchy of union leaders and power brokers benefited from this design as teachers' functionaries, controlling teachers' hiring and firing decisions; governing teachers' training, wages, and performance evaluation; and shaping the governance structure of schools (choice of principals and district managers). Over the course of decades, this system delivered weak educational results and failed to keep up with the demands of labor markets for better-trained workers. The clientelistic ruling party crafted an extremely politicized and centralized teaching system that simply could not deliver quality.

Decentralizing reforms came with Mexico's political liberalization and democratization in the 1990s and early 2000s under the first non-PRI president. With the waning power of the old PRI, the union's imperious boss, Elba Esther Gordillo, founded her own party and in 2006 was said to have unofficially sold off the union's electoral support to the winning Partido Acción Nacional (PAN) presidential contender.[12] Most likely this was a defensive act to protect the union's clientelistic network and the existing educational infrastructure from reform, thus exacerbating the performance crisis of the education system (Hecock, 2014).

Ester Gordillo swung the teachers' union back into the PRI camp for the 2012 presidential election, even though the PRI's presidential candidate, Enrique Peña Nieto, ran against the power of the teachers' union and the inefficiency of Mexico's education system. The union paid a price for the opportunism of auctioning off its clientelistic capabilities to competing parties: Once in office, Nieto had Gordillo arrested for embezzlement of $156 million to finance her lavish lifestyle (including a private jet), and public opinion swung

---

11. By raising wages, unionization may attract more talented, high-quality teaching staff. By weakening performance oversight and competition among teachers, unions may lower teachers' efforts in the classroom.

12. Nevertheless, it is unclear whether the union's operatives—as brokers—were actually materially useful for the PAN as the unofficially endorsed party. Larreguy et al. (2017), at least, find that teacher-brokers effectively raised the allied party's tally only where the brokers were ideologically sympathetic to the party the union was committed to support. This was definitely not the case for the PAN.

against the union. Lately, however, after almost 5 years in jail without trial and conviction, Gordillo was released from prison as the PRI appeared to need the teachers' union again in its losing struggle to defend the presidency in the 2018 election.[13]

By being tied into and taking advantage of a clientelistic partisan struggle, the Mexican teachers' union could amass unparalleled power and resources, much of which was extracted from budgetary expenditure lines to promote education as an investment. The union's clientelistic capacities even survived the regime and then oscillated between benefiting different parties.

Clientelistic political connections of teachers' unions play a role in degrading the conversion of educational inputs into outputs elsewhere, such as Colombia (Eaton & Chambers-Ju, 2014). In India, the intimate political connections of the public school teachers to political parties may be one element to account for the inefficiency of the Indian school system (e.g., Pritchett, 2013). Overall, however, much work needs to be done to uncover and document the significance of clientelism in school systems and in the teachers' unions more specifically.

6.5. A LARGE-N CROSS-NATIONAL STUDY

6.5.1. The data

We engage in a simple national cross-sectional analysis of correlational patterns. In contrast to Hicken and Simmons (2008), we have direct measures of clientelism as well as of educational performance for that exercise. The universe of cases is limited by our data sources. We exclude here from consideration the Western advanced post-industrial democracies and cover a maximum total of 66 countries in Central and Eastern Europe, Latin America, Asia and the Middle East, and sub-Saharan Africa. These are all countries with at least a modicum of multi-party competition, although in some instances hampered by hegemonic dominant parties. We therefore cannot adequately test the familiar regime hypothesis but engage in a more fine-grained analysis of the mechanisms prevailing in educational effort and outcomes in countries with multi-party competition.

If the statistical analysis included the old (post)industrialized world with very affluent countries as well, one dominant variable would have drowned all other contenders in accounting for educational expenditure and efficiency: economic development. If development is the only critical correlate of high quality of education, it should come to the fore even in a slightly truncated set of countries that includes those with per capita GDP under $25,000 in 2008 (at PPP).

---

13. See the report in *The Guardian* on December 21, 2017: https://www.theguardian.com/world/2017/dec/21/release-of-mexican-union-boss-a-sign-of-the-times-for-pena-nieto (accessed May 4, 2018).

6.5.1.1. Dependent variables

We rely on the World Bank's (World Bank n.d.) education indicators for financial input, organizational throughput, and degree earnings (lower and upper secondary degrees among 25+-year-olds) as our dependent variables.[14] We can rely on a direct outcome variable for secondary school degree earners, and it is the World Inequality Database on Education (WIDE), sponsored by UNESCO (UNESCO Institute for Statistics, n.d.). It measures the percentage of school students situated in different tiers of educational systems (primary, secondary, tertiary) who pass different thresholds of competence in math, science, and reading tests. Clear and equivalent patterns emerge for students' math and science achievements in a cross-national perspective. To save space, we report only results for national percentages of students mastering the highest math test level (4). Performance results of reading tests, however, follow no pattern that is theoretically discernable to us, and we set them aside for future study.

6.5.1.2. Independent variables of interest

We are ultimately interested in the consequences of *parties' and entire party systems' efforts in clientelistic partisan linkage formation.* We take the parties' clientelistic effort variable(s) from the Democratic Accountability and Linkage Project (DALP, n.d.), with expert judgments of parties' linkage strategies collected in 88 countries in 2008–2009 (see Appendices 1–3).

We report findings for the summary index of five different clientelistic exchange relations that parties may establish with voters and that was scored by DALP experts (gift giving, social benefits, office patronage, regulatory favors, procurement contracts). We also employ a composite index of *parties' programmatic appeals.* Construction of the programmatism variables is sketched in Appendix 2. Another variable "hand-constructed" from the DALP is *left party strength,* the construction of which is also described in the Appendix (originally from Kitschelt, 2015). On a 4-point scale it measures a party's commitment to progressive income redistribution.

We also add in a specification of the educational inputs, measured as per capita spending on secondary school pupils as a percentage of the per capita GDP of a country. We know from Figure 6.1 that educational inputs have some, albeit not an overwhelming, relationship to outputs and outcomes.

6.5.1.3. Control variables

The *between-group inequality index for multicultural polities* comes from Baldwin and Huber (2010) but is employed here in the expanded version constructed for Wang and Kolev (2019). All other independent variables are drawn from

---

14. Because statistical estimations yield similar results, we confine ourselves to reporting upper-division secondary degree earnings only.

established data providers. State capacity is measured in terms of the World Bank's Governance Indicator for "government effectiveness." The more or less democratic character of the multi-party regimes included in our study is measured by *Polity IV's political democracy index*, running over a 21-point scale (from –10 to + 10). Johnson and Wallack (2008) offer the variables tapping *institutional electoral particularism called "ballot" and "pool."* Export (as a percentage of a country's GDP) and per capita GDP at PPP calculations originate in the usual World Bank economic statistics files. And the market income-based Gini coefficients are from Frederick Solt's (2009) Standardized World Income Inequality Database, with the best and most reliable income inequality data currently available.

Some variables reflecting features of the education system are not available for all 66 countries in the DALP study, thus reducing the available comparison cases to anywhere between 34 and 66. Most of our estimations therefore include only between 45 and 52 cases, or about 69%–79% of the maximal number of DALP country observation points. This small number of degrees of freedom in the data severely limits the complexity of statistical analysis. We avoid operating with multivariate models of more than five independent variables and try to confine ourselves to reduced-form models that delete irrelevant controls in order to preserve degrees of freedom and prevent statistical patterns to be influenced by irrelevant alternatives.

6.5.2. The crowd-out effect

Let us begin here with an overview of primitive results that relate measures of inputs, throughputs, outputs, and outcomes at the three levels of educational services to the summary measure of clientelism, with a singular control for economic development added. Displayed in Table 6.3 are only relations that are statistically significant at the 0.05 level.

On the educational input and throughput side, there is an array of indicators (see Table 6.1) that shows no correlation with clientelism at all. Consistent with the crowding out hypothesis, secondary education public expenditure is negatively correlated with clientelism. But, consistent with Harding and Stasavage (2013), gross secondary school enrollment may go up without adding any new resources, thus deteriorating student–expenditure ratios, something that may then degrade educational output/outcomes (Stage II hypothesis). The same effect of clientelism is also suggested by the fact that clientelism is associated with greater expenditure for school staff, especially in tertiary education.

The table communicates rough evidence directly about the second stage degradation hypothesis we take up in more detail in the next section: After controlling for development levels, lower and higher secondary school completion rates as well as secondary school students' math and science competence are negatively correlated with clientelistic partisan effort. In more partisan clientelistic polities, there is a smaller pool of the labor force with secondary education but a large pool with only primary schooling, and the female labor force participation is negatively correlated with clientelism. But let us first focus on the crowding out hypothesis.

Table 6.4 explores the evidence for the crowding out hypothesis and conveys the message of Table 6.3 in more precise numerical terms. Partisan clientelism does reduce secondary educational effort, measured by student expenditure as a percentage of GDP per capita. None of the "friendly" potential mediators

Table 6.3 Where does clientelistic partisan effort "subvert" or "distract from" the educational effort? A preliminary exploration (coefficients of the relationship of overall clientelistic partisan effort [as measured DALP B15.nwe] to educational measures [input, throughput, output, and outcome] after controlling for economic development only [GDP per capita @ PPP 2008])

Level	Inputs	Throughputs	Outputs	Outcomes
Primary				• Percentage of labor force with only primary education (and male) is greater where B15 is higher
Secondary	• Government expenditure per secondary student (percentage of GDP) declines with higher clientelistic effort/B15	• Gross secondary school enrollment goes up with clientelistic effort/B15	• Educational attainment/ school completion in lower secondary and higher secondary schools is lower, where clientelistic effort/B15 is higher (all ≥25 years old)	• Percentage of secondary school students who receive top-level math and science results declines with rise in clientelistic effort/B15
Tertiary	• Tertiary school staff compensation goes up with clientelistic effort/B15			
All levels	• Educational staff expenditure rises with clientelistic effort/B15			• Percentage of women in the labor force declines with more clientelistic effort/B15

Table 6.4 Clientelism crowding out educational inputs

	Dependent variable		
	Government expenditure per student, secondary (percentage of GDP per capita)		
	(1)	(2)	(3)
Partisan clientelistic effort	−1.479**	−2.610***	−2.345***
(dalp_b15nwe)	(0.681)	(0.690)	(0.739)
Development: per capita GDP		−5.299***	−5.952***
(dalp_lg_GDPpcPPP)		(1.467)	(1.593)
Post-communism			3.544
(X3.9.postcomm)			(3.329)
Constant	41.344***	104.148***	104.760***
	(10.088)	(19.633)	(19.928)
Observations	56	56	54
R^2	0.080	0.262	0.284
Adjusted R^2	0.063	0.234	0.241
Residual standard error	10.552 (df = 54)	9.541 (df = 53)	9.649 (df = 50)
F statistic	4.721** (df = 1; 54)	9.412*** (df = 2; 53)	6.600*** (df = 3; 50)

Note. df = degrees of freedom.
*$p < 0.1$, **$p < 0.05$, ***$p < 0.01$.

between clientelism and educational inputs—state capacity, ethnic divisions, left party strength, post-communist region, or programmatic partisan crystallization—make a difference in this direct relationship. As an example, we show here the resilience of the partisan clientelistic effort to the inclusion of the post-communist region variable. Likewise, none of the "unfriendly" rival hypotheses advanced by alternative theories pans out, regardless of whether we introduce democratic institutions (ballot format, district size), export share of the economy, degree of civil and political liberties (various indicators), or market income inequality.

6.5.3. The degradation effect

To investigate the Stage II degradation hypothesis, we turn to the relationship between clientelism and secondary school educational output—measured by completion of lower or upper secondary school degrees among the population aged 25 and older—and/or educational outcomes—measured by the percentage of secondary school students performing at the highest mathematical (or science) achievement level (4) in the WIDE study. The relationships between economic development levels and educational outputs ($r = 0.71$, $n = 51$) and outcomes ($r = 0.76$, $n = 34$) are strong, in contrast to those with educational inputs. In the restricted sample we can include in the multivariate analysis, there is a strong relationship between outputs and outcomes ($r = 0.66$, $n = 34$).

Table 6.5 first numerically replicates what was already announced in Table 6.3: Holding constant for economic development, clientelism indeed covaries with a degradation of the educational outputs. This result vanishes, however, when we add the presence of programmatically redistributive parties in a party system or the prevalence of a post-communist partisan context—imbued with more programmatic parties and/or the strength of parties with economic programs—into the equation. These are "friendly" amendments to the main theoretical proposition: All three factors militate against clientelism and appear to be the proximate correlates of the negative relationship between clientelism and educational deterioration.

A similar pattern appears when we examine educational outcomes, measured by the percentage of secondary school students reaching the highest math scores. The direct effect of clientelism on educational quality disappears when programmatic parties are added as predictors, in conjunction with either post-communist legacies or Gini market income inequality (Table 6.6).

Table 6.7 ignores the complexity of multivariate relations and mechanisms. Instead, it presents an illustration with a simpler, and hence likely to be noisier, exploration of the degradation hypothesis: Do countries with relatively generous educational inputs but weak outcomes exhibit particularly strong clientelistic partisan efforts? Indeed, the shaded quadrant of Table 6.7 shows rather high clientelism in that combination of educational inputs and outcomes. Mexico certainly fits that bill (Fernandez, 2012). Brazil and Venezuela also exemplify the pattern well. Less fitting is the placement of Costa Rica and Malaysia in this cell: Both are rather high-income countries and thereby spend absolutely greater amounts of funds on education. The distribution of cell averages across the table, however, also suggests that the association between clientelism and educational outcomes is stronger than that between clientelism and educational inputs.

Once again, other theoretically "friendly" mediators between clientelism and educational outcomes do not matter. Likewise, rival hypotheses about institutions and political-economic arrangements do not contribute to an account of the observable educational efficiency patterns.

Let us finally turn to an argument that overarches the input/crowding out and output/degradation hypotheses: Can we detect anywhere indications of different social coalition politics in educational policymaking and especially of an alliance of poor and rich voters, on the face of it the most unlikely union? Just to recall, the former demand a well-endowed but exclusive tertiary educational system that keeps middle-income contenders at bay by limiting public higher secondary education. But the rich may concede to the poor the generous (non-teaching, low-skill) staffing of educational services in clientelistic fashion, and thus accept low efficiency in the conversion of educational inputs into outputs.

Table 6.5 Clientelism degrades educational output

	Dependent variable					
	Educational attainment, at least completed upper secondary, population 25+, total (%) (cumulative)					
	(1)	(2)	(3)	(4)	(5)	(6)
Partisan clientelistic effort	−6.591***	−7.423***	−2.400	−0.997	−1.021	−0.061
(dalp_b15nwe)	(1.369)	(1.494)	(1.637)	(1.677)	(1.103)	(1.585)
Educational input		−0.465	0.219	0.156	0.007	0.146
Government expenditure per student, secondary (percentage of GDP per capita)		(0.324)	(0.304)	(0.297)	(0.206)	(0.272)
Development: per capita GDP			17.427***	15.573***	11.932***	14.589***
(dalp_lg_GDPpcPPP)			(3.764)	(3.833)	(2.688)	(3.430)
Redistributive programmatic parties				6.719**		
(X3.6.left.party.strength)				(2.714)		
Postcommunist legacy an party context					30.983***	
(X3.9.postcomm)					(4.165)	
Parties with economic programmatics						7.230***
(dalp_new_CoSalPo_Econ_kf_c)						(2.001)
Constant	144.946***	166.544***	−74.114	−85.026	−52.558	−99.669*
	(20.057)	(24.477)	(55.723)	(54.681)	(37.619)	(49.914)
Observations	51	45	45	43	43	44
R^2	0.321	0.370	0.586	0.620	0.820	0.689
Adjusted R^2	0.307	0.340	0.556	0.580	0.801	0.657
Residual standard error	21.233 (df = 49)	20.889 (df = 42)	17.133 (df = 41)	16.506 (df = 38)	11.350 (df = 38)	15.163 (df = 39)
F statistic	23.193*** (df = 1; 49)	12.340*** (df = 2; 42)	19.373*** (df = 3; 41)	15.476*** (df = 4; 38)	43.322*** (df = 4; 38)	21.633*** (df = 4; 39)

Note. df = degrees of freedom.
*$p < 0.1$, **$p < 0.05$, ***$p < 0.01$.

Table 6.6 Clientelism degrades educational outcome

	Dependent variable					
	Learning achievement in mathematics (level 4) (upper secondary by country total all, average)					
	(1)	(2)	(3)	(4)	(5)	(6)
Partisan clientelistic effect	-0.038***	-0.038***	-0.021**	-0.018*	-0.010	-0.011
(dalp_b15nwe)	(0.010)	(0.011)	(0.009)	(0.009)	(0.010)	(0.010)
Educational input		0.006*	0.005**	0.004	0.003	0.003
Government expenditure per student, secondary (percentage of GDP per capita)		(0.003)	(0.002)	(0.002)	(0.003)	(0.002)
Development per capita GDP			0.144***	0.139***	0.134***	0.142***
(dalp_lg_GDPpcPPP)			(0.029)	(0.030)	(0.030)	(0.027)
Postcommunist legacy and party context				0.050	0.019	
(X3.9.postcomm)				(0.034)	(0.040)	
Parties with economic programmatics					0.024	0.022*
(dalp_new_CoSalPo_Econ_kf_c)					(0.015)	(0.012)
Income inequality						-0.005*
(gini_market_m_00s)						(0.002)
Constant	0.673***	0.544***	-1.014***	-1.011***	-1.105***	-0.953***
	(0.139)	(0.192)	(0.342)	(0.347)	(0.349)	(0.327)
Observations	34	30	30	28	27	27
R^2	0.315	0.463	0.726	0.729	0.757	0.797
Adjusted R^2	0.293	0.423	0.694	0.682	0.700	0.748
Residual standard error	0.118 (df = 32)	0.113 (df = 27)	0.082 (df = 26)	0.079 (df = 23)	0.078 (df = 21)	0.072 (df = 21)
F statistic	14.694*** (df = 1; 32)	11.621*** (df = 2; 27)	22.962*** (df = 3; 26)	15.496*** (df = 4; 23)	13.115*** (df = 5; 21)	16.446*** (df = 5; 21)

Note. df = degrees of freedom.
*$p < 0.1$, **$p < 0.05$, ***$p < 0.01$.

Table 6.7 Educational inputs, outcomes, and clientelism

		Outcomes: Percentage math scores (4)		
		<–¼ SD below global mean	Within ±¼ SD around the global mean	>¼ SD above global mean
Inputs: Education expenditure as percentage of GDP	>¼ SD above global mean	BRA (15.3) CRI (12.66) MDA (13.93) MEX (15.78) MYS (12.3) VEN (16.99) Average clientelism: 14.49		EST (11.49) ISR (12.19) LTU (14.44) LVA (10.52) SVN (10.89) Average clientelism: 11.91
	Within ±¼ SD around the global mean	ARG (16.98) COL (15.7) URY (11.64) Average clientelism: 14.77	SRB (13.5) Average clientelism: 13.5	HUN (14.85) KOR (12.13) POL (11.78) Average clientelism: 12.92
	<–¼ SD below global mean	ALB (13.97) CHL (12.22) GEO (13.98) IDN (14.81) MUS (16.63) PAN (17.28) PER (13.51) ROU (14.64) THA (13.29) Average clientelism: 14.48	BGR (15.81) HRV (13.56) Average clientelism: 14.68	CZE (10.63) JPN (12.21) RUS (12.86) SVK (11.22) Average clientelism: 11.73

Note. Shading indicates high clientelism in that combination of educational inputs and outcomes. SD = standard deviation.

Indirectly a very big gap in tertiary (university) educational access between the social elites, on one side, and everyone else but particularly the middle strata, on the other, would indicate a possible poor–rich coalition. The WIDE survey happens to break down educational performance by income quintiles, measuring the mean percentage of those 25–29 years old in the income quintiles with university degrees. The standard deviation between these means is a good measure of the exclusiveness of higher education: Most likely, the greater that standard deviation is, the more successful completion of tertiary education is skewed toward a thin layer of the rich. This is the dependent variable in Table 6.8. Equations show independent variables that ultimately mattered, plus a control for overall educational expenditures (as a percentage of GDP).

The table discloses that clientelistic partisan effort systematically and robustly contributes toward making the access gradient to tertiary university degrees more uneven, by contributing to the standard deviation in the percentage of different income quintiles achieving tertiary university degrees. This applies once development levels are controlled for, as well as the supply of upper secondary school graduates who potentially could enter the university. Upper classes manage to

Table 6.8 Tertiary education completion variance and clientelism: Are there indications of a poor–rich coalition? Does clientelism exacerbate the disparity of educational investment strategies?

	Dependent variable		
	Tertiary completion rate (25–29 years old) (all by country wealth index quintiles, standard deviation)		
	(1)	(2)	(3)
Partisan clientelistic effort	0.008	0.017***	0.010**
(dalp_b15nwe)	(0.005)	(0.005)	(0.004)
Development: per capita GDP		0.035***	0.037***
(dalp_lg_GDPpcPPP)		(0.010)	(0.008)
Education expenditure as percentage of GDP		0.001	0.0001
("dalp_pegdpeducexp")		(0.007)	(0.005)
Selection into the pool of tertiary school entrants			0.513***
(Upper secondary completion rate, 3–5 years above upper secondary school graduating year)			(0.086)
Constant	0.046	−0.397***	−0.389***
	(0.072)	(0.144)	(0.108)
Observations	54	48	48
R^2	0.045	0.256	0.593
Adjusted R^2	0.027	0.205	0.556
Residual standard error	0.072 (df = 52)	0.064 (df = 44)	0.048 (df = 43)
F statistic	2.445 (df = 1; 52)	5.049*** (df = 3; 44)	15.688*** (df = 4; 43)

Note. df = degrees of freedom.
$^*p < 0.1$, $^{**}p < 0.05$, $^{***}p < 0.01$.

restrict access to higher education better, where there is more clientelistic partisan effort. Of course, further research would have to probe into this interesting correlation to reconstruct the causal process that might yield this outcome. Elements along the way could be 1) less secondary education funding where clientelistic staffing policies prevail throughout the educational system and tertiary university certification is highly restricted and/or 2) worse conversion of inputs into outputs, where clientelistic exchange pervades educational policy implementation.

6.6. CONCLUSION

Our chapter shows that clientelism is a critical form of political mediation impacting social investment strategies in terms of both fiscal effort as well as substantive political-economic effectiveness and efficiency. It goes beyond the familiar regime hypothesis that democracies spend more on education and Hicken and Simmons' (2008) exploration of educational effectiveness with rather indirect independent and dependent variables and a smaller number of observations.

Clientelism "crowds out" educational investment in favor of more direct clientelistic fiscal exchanges. Clientelism also "degrades" educational effort by undercutting professional quality control of educational service delivery in favor of diverting funds to rent-seeking educational service providers (builders, managers, teachers, maintenance staff) and political favorites among the recipients (politically connected but intellectually unfit students). While clientelism may address liabilities that call for social compensation (old age, unemployment, invalidity) where universal insurance systems are weak (Kitschelt, 2015), it does nothing to address social investment policies: It is clearly a net value subtractor. The critical area of secondary education in middle-income countries demonstrates this sharply. Behind the clientelistic penetration of educational services stands a logic of social power that this chapter could barely touch: The ruling elites of all times have known that nothing is more dangerous to their continued predominance than to equip the downtrodden and exploited, or even potential middle-income challengers, with knowledge and skills. This may shine through in the deliberate deployment of clientelism as a technique of domination.

Finally, let us situate our investigation within the framework of the overall volume on social investment strategies. We are contributing to the advancement of our understanding of the politics of creating social capital in low- to middle-income countries. The question is whether this capital is generated as an inclusive or a targeted social investment. Strong clientelism points the way not only to a targeted design of investment but in many ways to a subversion of the goals and functions of social investment as resources are drained away from the purpose of empowering citizens with better labor market opportunities.

Our chapter does not lay out and test an explicit model of the micro-level preferences of groups of social actors and their aggregate collective action (parties, interest groups), but it develops implications of a socioeconomic interest-based configuration of conflict that can be tested at an aggregate level. It suggests that economic group interests are behind the different educational social investment strategies. If an urban middle stratum (we do not dare say "class") gets its way, it advances educational investment efforts and efficiency while containing clientelism. The rule of economic and political oligarchies, as well as their co-optation of poor constituencies, however, undermines educational investments through proliferating clientelism.

Our chapter suggests that it is likely that educational investments are highly salient issues in many polities, particularly investments in secondary education. The sketch of a Mexico case study suggests as much, and so do Chapters 7 and 13 in this volume.

Political legacies may play an important role in shaping the extent to which thriving clientelism undermines educational investment policies. A history of communist rule as well as the presence of programmatic parties outside of a post-communist context contain clientelism and favor more educational effort and investment.

REFERENCES

Alesina, A., Reza, B., & Easterly, W. (1999). Public goods and ethnic divisions. *The Quarterly Journal of Economics, 114*(4), 1243–1284.

Ansell, B. W. (2008). University challenges: Explaining institutional change in higher education. *World Politics, 60*(2), 189–230.

Ansell, B. W. (2010). *From the ballot to the blackboard: The redistributive political economy of education.* Cambridge University Press.

Ansell, B., & Lindvall, J. (2013). The political origins of primary education systems: Ideology, institutions, and interdenominational conflict in an era of nation-building. *American Political Science Review, 107*(3), 505–522.

Baldwin, K., & Huber, J. D. (2010). Economic versus cultural differences: Forms of ethnic diversity and public goods provision. *American Political Science Review, 104*(4), 644–662.

Banerjee, A., & Duflo, E. (2011). *Poor economics: A radical rethinking of the way to fight global poverty.* PublicAffairs.

Barro, R. J. (1998). *Determinants of economic growth: A cross-country empirical study.* MIT Press.

Berg, A., Ostry, J. D., Tsangarides, C. G., & Yakshilikov, Y. (2018). Redistribution, inequality and growth. new evidence. *Journal of Economic Growth, 23*(2), 259–305.

Besley, T., & Persson, T. (2011). *Pillars of prosperity: The political economics of development clusters.* Princeton University Press.

Bleaney, M., & Nishiyama, A. (2002). Explaining growth: A contest between models. *Journal of Economic Growth, 7*(1), 43–56.

Boix, C. (1998). *Political parties, growth and equality: Conservative and social democratic economic strategies in the world economy.* Cambridge University Press.

Busemeyer, M. R. (2014). *Skills and inequality: Partisan politics and the political economy of education reforms in Western welfare states.* Cambridge University Press.

Chambers-Ju, C., & Finger, L. (2016). Teachers' unions in Mexico. The politics of patronage. In T. M. Moe & S. Wiborg (Eds.), *The comparative politics of education: Teachers unions and education systems around the world* (pp. 215–238). Cambridge University Press.

Democratic Accountability and Linkages Project (DALP). N.d. Database on Citizen-Politician Linkages. Duke University. https://sites.duke.edu/democracylinkage/

Doner, R., & Schneider, B. R. (2016). The middle-income trap: More politics than economics. *World Politics, 68*(4), 608–644.

Downs, A. (1957). An economic theory of political action in a democracy. *Journal of Political Economy, 65*(2), 135–150.

Eaton, K., & Chambers-Ju, C. (2014). Teachers, mayors, and the transformation of clientelism in Colombia. In D. Alberto Brun & L. Diamond (Eds.), *Clientelism, social policy, and the quality of democracy* (pp. 88–113). Johns Hopkins University Press.

Fernandez, M. (2012). *The political economy of education* [Unpublished doctoral dissertation]. Duke University.

Garritzmann, J. L., Häusermann, S., Palier, B., & Zollinger, C. (2017). *WOPSI: The World Politics of Social Investment* [LIEPP Working Paper 64]. Sciences Po.

Gift, T., & Wibbels, E. (2014). Reading, writing, and the regrettable status of education research in comparative politics. *Annual Review of Political Science, 17*, 291–312.

Glaeser, E. L., La Porta, R., Lopez-de Silanes, F., & Shleifer, A. (2004). Do institutions cause growth? *Journal of Economic Growth, 9*(3), 271–303.

Halter, D., Oechslin, M., & Zweimüller, J. (2014). Inequality and growth: The neglected time dimension. *Journal of Economic Growth, 19*(1), 81–104.

Harding, R., & Stasavage, D. (2013). What democracy does (and doesn't do) for basic services: School fees, school inputs, and African elections. *The Journal of Politics, 76*(1), 229–245.

Hecock, R. D. (2014). Democratization, education reform, and the Mexican teachers' union. *Latin American Research Review, 49*(1), 62–82.

Heidenheimer, A. (1981). Education and social security entitlements in Europe and America. In P. Flora & A. Heidenheimer (Eds.), *The development of welfare states in Europe and America* (pp. 269–306). Routledge.

Hicken, A., & Simmons, J. W. (2008). The personal vote and the efficacy of education spending. *American Journal of Political Science, 52*(1), 109–124.

Iversen, T., & Stephens, J. D. (2008). Partisan politics, the welfare state, and three worlds of human capital formation. *Comparative Political Studies, 41*(4–5), 600–637.

Johnson, J. W., & Wallack, J. S. (2008). Electoral systems and the personal vote [Database]. https://dataverse.harvard.edu/dataset.xhtml?persistentId=hdl:1902.1/17901

Jones, C. I. (2015). *The facts of economic growth*, version 2.0. http://web.stanford.edu/~chadj/facts.pdf

Kasara, K., & Suryanarayan, P. (2015). When do the rich vote less than the poor and why? Explaining voter turnout across the world. *American Journal of Political Science, 59*(3), 613–627.

Keefer, P. (2007). Clientelism, credibility, and the policy choices of young democracies. *American Journal of Political Science, 51*(4), 804–821.

Kitschelt, H. (2011, September 1–4). Do institutions matter for parties' electoral linkage strategies? [Paper presentation]. Annual Meeting of the American Political Science Association, Seattle, WA, USA.

Kitschelt, H. (2015, November 7). Social policy, democratic linkages, and political governance [Paper presentation]. Workshop on Social Policy and Clientelism, University of Cologne, Cologne, Germany.

Kitschelt, H., & Freeze, K. (2010, September 1–5). Programmatic party system structuration: Developing and comparing cross-national and cross-party measures with a new global data set [Paper presentation]. Annual Meeting of the American Political Science Association, Washington, DC, USA.

Kitschelt, H., & Kselman, D. (2013). Economic development, democratic experience, and political parties' linkage strategies. *Comparative Political Studies, 46*(11), 1453–1484.

Kitschelt, H., Mansfeldova, Z., Markowski, R., & Toka, G. (1999). *Post–Communist Party systems: Competition, representation, and inter-party cooperation.* Cambridge University Press.

Kitschelt, H., & Singer, M. (2016, April 14–16). Diversified partisan linkage strategies [Paper presentation]. 23rd Council of Europeanists Conference, Philadelphia, PA, USA.

Kitschelt, H., & Wilkinson, S. I. (2007). *Patrons, clients and policies: Patterns of democratic accountability and political competition.* Cambridge University Press.

Kosack, S. (2012). *The education of nations: How the political organization of the poor, not democracy, let governments to invest in mass education.* Oxford University Press.

Larreguy, H., Montiel Olea, C. E., & Querubin, P. (2017). Political brokers: Partisans or agents? Evidence from the Mexican teachers' union. *American Journal of Political Science, 61*(4), 877–891.

Min, B. (2015). *Power and the vote: Elections and electricity in the developing world.* Cambridge University Press.

Nichter, S. C. (2010). *Politics and poverty: Electoral clientelism in Latin America* [Unpublished doctoral dissertation]. University of California Berkeley.

Nichter, S. (2014). Political clientelism and social policy in Brazil. In D. A. Brun & L. Diamond (Eds.), *Clientelism, social policy, and the quality of democracy* (pp. 130–151). Johns Hopkins University Press.

Nooruddin, I., & Rudra, N. (2014). Are developing countries really defying the embedded liberalism compact? *World Politics, 66*(4), 603–640.

Pritchett, L. (2001). Where has all the education gone? *The World Bank Economic Review, 15*(3), 367–391.

Pritchett, L. (2013). *The rebirth of education: Schooling ain't learning.* Brookings Institution Press.

Frederick Solt. (2009). The Standardized World Income Inequality Database v1-v7. https://doi.org/10.7910/DVN/WKOKHF. Harvard Dataverse, V20.

Stokes, S. C., Dunning, T., Nazareno, M., & Brusco, V. (2013). *Brokers, voters, and clientelism: The puzzle of distributive politics.* Cambridge: Cambridge University Press.

UNESCO. Institute of Statistics. (n.d.). *World Inequality Database on Education.* https://www.education-inequalities.org/about

Wang, Y.-T., & Kolev, K. (2019). Ethnic group inequality, partisan networks, and political clientelism. *Political Research Quarterly, 72*(2), 329–341.

Weitz-Shapiro, R. (2014). *Curbing clientelism in Argentina: Politics, poverty and social policy.* Cambridge University Press.

World Bank. No date. Online database education. https://data.worldbank.org/topic/education

Yıldırım, K., & Kitschelt, H. (2020). Analytical perspectives on varieties of clientelism. *Democratization, 27*(1), 20–43.

You, J.-s. (2015). *Democracy, inequality and corruption.* Cambridge University Press.

APPENDIX

A.1. MEASURES AND INDEX OF PARTIES' CLIENTELISTIC EFFORT

For a more detailed analysis of the notion of clientelism and the individual questionnaire items, as well as the construction of the summary index of clientelism, see Kitschelt (2011), downloadable from the DALP website at http://sites.duke.edu/democracylinkage/. Experts rated parties on 5-point scales on five different types of clientelistic exchange, displayed in Table 6.1. Here, we display a correlation matrix for the five variables. These correlations are extremely high, but this feature is driven by the presence of a substantial number of parties in Western advanced post-industrial democracies that have virtually no clientelism. As shown in Kitschelt (2011), the correlation is substantially lower between some of the five indicators, when affluent countries are excluded. Especially the correlation between providing gifts/vote buying (b1) as a spot-market, individually targeted clientelistic technique and the relational clientelistic techniques (whether targeted at individuals as patronage [b3] or procurement [b4] at business firms and nonprofit associations) as well as the spot-market "wholesale" technology of regulatory favors account for only 40%–45% of the variance. Nevertheless, in spite of the diversity of clientelistic linkage profiles across parties and countries, even then a principal components analysis generates just one very strong underlying latent variable that captures the variance of most of the scores on all five clientelism indicators (Chronbach's alpha = .955). Let us here display only the very high correlations among the five variables, when all 506 parties in 88 countries are included:

```
pwcorr b1 b2 b3 b4 b5
        |    b1      b2      b3      b4      b5
--------------+-----------------------------------------------
     b1 |  1.0000
     b2 |  0.8192  1.0000
     b3 |  0.7722  0.8267  1.0000
     b4 |  0.7965  0.8137  0.9023  1.0000
     b5 |  0.7537  0.7926  0.8037  0.8924  1.0000
```

A.2. PROGRAMMATIC STRUCTURING ("CRYSTALLIZATION") OF PARTY COMPETITION: COSALPO_4 (FROM DALP)

The DALP survey's fourth module[15] asked experts to identify parties' precise policy positions on a series of issue dimensions.[16] In addition to standardized policy questions asked in each country, the latter included nationally idiosyncratic issues and issue dimensions that could not be scored across the entire data set of 88 countries.[17] Experts were also given the options *Don't Know* and *Party Has no Clear Position*. We will make use of this policy placement data to identify whether or not a party meets three criteria that Downs (1957) outlined to enable voters to choose among parties based on their programmatic commitments: The party must issue appeals that are (1) distinct from the appeals of other parties, (2) internally shared (coherent) by the relevant party operatives, and (3) salient for the party's activities. A more detailed development of the operationalization of these attributes and of the overall measure of programmatic appeals can be found in Kitschelt and Freeze (2010), available on the DALP website (http://sites.duke.edu/democracylinkage).

First, to measure the distinctiveness of a party's position on any issue dimension, we compute the average distance between a party j's mean position (across experts) on issue k and the mean positions of all other parties (across experts) on the same issue k. The resulting indicator represents the average differentiation of party j's position on issue k from that of all other parties in the system.

Second, we operationalize the parties' internal programmatic coherence by the consistency of the experts' policy placements. Parties characterized by

15. Data can be downloaded from http://sites.duke.edu/democracylinkage
16. Each was measured on a 10-point scale.
17. The five core policy issues cover (1) the defense of national identity, (2) moral–cultural governance (tradition versus individual choice), and (3) various aspects of economic governance and distribution (redistributive spending on the poor, state role in the economy, universalistic social insurance). Precise question wordings can be found on the DALP website.

internal dissension and temporal inconsistency are more likely to generate inconsistent expert policy placements. We adopt the conventional approach and operationalize party j's cohesion on any single issue k as the standard deviation of expert judgments for j on issue k.[18]

Third, as a second measure of programmatic variance but also of the salience of the issue dimension for the political pursuits of a party, we use the share of experts who do not attribute a position to j on dimension k (i.e., the share of experts who chose *Don't Know* or Party *Has no clear Position* or left the question blank). To the extent that experts fail to score parties on a particular issue dimension, this is also a sign that said parties do not meet the minimal level of cohesion and consistency required for responsible and reliable programmatic choice.

For each party j on issue dimension k, this leaves us with three distinct indicators: differentiation, cohesion, and non-attribution. As a first step toward an integrated measure, we normalize each of these three measures to [0,1] such that each is increasing in the extent to which it satisfies the relevant programmatic criterion (i.e., higher scores indicate more distinctiveness, greater cohesion, and lower levels of expert non-attribution). The absence of any one of these properties is sufficient to undermine a party's programmatic capacity: Parties which do not differentiate from their competitors will generate a "rationality crisis," regardless of whether or not their platform is unified and consistent (thus satisfying the responsibility/reliability criterion); parties which generate extremely low response rates are unlikely to satisfy the responsibility/reliability criterion, even if the small number of experts who judge place them consistently and distinctly from other parties; and so on. To create a single, integrated index operationalizing party j's programmatic capacity on issue dimension k, we thus calculate the product (distinctiveness × cohesion × non-attribution), which yields a programmatism score in the range [0,1] for j on k.

One approach to measuring a party's aggregate programmatic capacity would be to average its programmatism scores across all of a country's issue dimensions. However, different parties may give different emphases to different issues in campaigns and governance, and we may not want to classify a party as *non-programmatic* for failing to generate high programmatism on all conceivable issues. For the aggregate index of programmatic partisan effort, we therefore select the four issue dimensions on which party j has the highest programmatism scores and take the average of j's scores on these four dimensions. Label this indicator *PROGRAM*. A range of different indices employing fewer or more items were constructed and compared (Kitschelt & Freeze, 2010). The PROGRAM index turns out to provide scores that are highly correlated with the range of alternative

---

18. To take out an individual expert's idiosyncratic anchor, however, we have transformed expert i's party positions jk into differences from the mean position k-bar they assign to all parties j on issue k, by subtracting party j's position from that mean k-bar.

indices with different numbers of issues aggregated into a single party-based programmatism score.

To arrive at an overall national score of programmatism across all parties, then, first for each party the average CoSalPo scores are being calculated across the selected policy dimensions to construct the index. Then, the party scores of CoSalPo_x, where x stands for the issues from which parties' programmatism was constructed, are weighted by the electoral size of each party in the preceding two legislative elections.

The index can numerically vary from 0 to 1; among the 506 parties in our data set it empirically varies from .059 to .513, with a mean (standard deviation) of .226 (.119). Another index was constructed in similar fashion including for each party the three economic issues (CoSalPo_3.econ) on which experts rated the parties. More details can be found in Kitschelt and Freeze (2010).

Operationalizing the Downsian criteria for rational programmatic choice is, as can be seen, no simple task. The PROGRAM indicator is a composite of three distinct measures, each of which is likely subject to measurement error arising from the methodological pitfalls of expert surveys. Before proceeding, it is thus essential to establish a minimum of construct validity. The Kitschelt and Freeze (2010) exploratory paper reports the bivariate relationship between the PROGRAM indicator and four distinct variables with which, a priori, one would expect it to be associated. Past research suggests that policy-based accountability should be associated with both higher levels of economic development and higher levels of democratization (Keefer, 2007; Kitschelt & Kselman, 2013; Stokes et al., 2013). In both cases the association is strong and in the expected direction (correlations of $r = .62$ and $r = .33$). The other two construct validity tests draw on information provided in the DALP data set. Parties' programmatic effort should not be perfectly correlated with the parties' clientelistic effort, measured in ways described in Appendix A.1. But there should be—on average—a negative relationship between the two, even though some parties may simultaneously engage in intense clientelistic and programmatic efforts. Indeed, the overall relationship between programmatism and clientelism across 506 parties in 88 countries is $r = -.52$. Finally, the DALP also asks experts to provide a "round-about" assessment of the extent to which parties pursue votes based on their programmatic policy promises. Although this item is noisy and measures programmatic "effort" rather than programmatic coherence and distinctiveness, the positive correlation ($r = .40$) again suggests that our more detailed measure of programmatism varies in ways which satisfy at some basic level the criteria for construct validity.

A.3. STRENGTH OF LEFT-REDISTRIBUTIVE PARTIES PRESENT IN PARTY SYSTEMS (FROM DALP)

Constructing the index of left-redistributive party strength requires two operations. First, identify the parties that count, and measure the crystallization and extremism of their distributive programmatic propensities. Second, score the competitive strength of these parties for the entire party system as a function of the electoral weight of these parties in the two legislative elections preceding 2008 and the radicalism and cohesion of their positions. The DALP survey again is the empirical reference for the construction of a simple 0–3 scale. Score computation can be requested from the author. To provide a flavor of the scoring, here are the criteria to be met to reach the highest score (3) for the strength of the left-redistributive parties in a party system:

- The parties counting as redistributive must have scoring averages on the three core economic issues in the expert survey of <4.0 on a 1–10 scale, with lower values indicating more redistributive positions.
- The cohesion score on these issues, averaged over those parties in a polity that meet the first criterion, must exceed an average of .25, substantially above the average of all parties/issues scored in DALP.
- The experts' left–right placement of the parties must be 4.0 or lower on a 1–10 scale, with 1 indicating the most leftist position.
- The combined share of leftist-redistributive parties must be >20% of the vote in the two most recent legislative elections preceding the 2008–2009 DALP survey.
- The age of the left-redistributive parties must exceed a weighted average of 10 years.

By way of illustration, using the scoring scheme, Hungary achieves a score of 1.0 in 2008, although its major left party was in government with 42.6% of the average vote in the preceding two legislative elections. This is so because the party embraced centrist economic policy positions barely on the left side of the scoring scale's midpoint (4.92) with a high level of internal incohesion, indicated by the low level of agreement among experts about the appropriate score of the party (average cohesion score 0.092). By contrast, many other post-communist countries in 2008 displayed smaller, albeit more cohesive and more programmatically redistributive, parties than Hungary and therefore earned higher scores of 2 or 3.

A.4. POST-COMMUNIST LEGACIES: NATIONAL-ACCOMMODATIVE AND BUREAUCRATIC-AUTHORITARIAN COMMUNISM (DUMMY VARIABLE)

For the construction of the legacy of communist rule types, see Kitschelt et al. (1999, pp. 35–42). Bureaucratic-authoritarian and national-accommodative communisms are here collapsed into score 1 of the dummy variable. Both types reflect pre-communist conditions under which, compared to patrimonial communism (dummy variable = 0), higher state capacities, more cumulative experience with bottom-up political action under conditions of a modicum of civil liberties, and the mobilization of socialist-redistributive parties interacted with each other to shape communist regimes after the end of Stalinism, which eventually permitted a direct transition toward liberal democracy, relative strong structuration with programmatic parties (albeit not necessarily stable party labels and organizations), and a transformation of risk-hedging regimes toward an emphasis on social insurance systems with rather little clientelism in the mix. National-accommodative and bureaucratic-authoritarian communisms include the Central European and East Central European formerly communist countries. Most fission products of the former Soviet Union, except the Baltic countries but including Russia's Central Asian colonial periphery, South Eastern Europe (Albania, Bulgaria, Macedonia, Romania, and Serbia), as well as Mongolia, belong to the patrimonial type of communism.

A.5. STATE CAPACITY: GOVERNMENT EFFECTIVENESS 2008 IN THE WORLD BANK'S WORLDWIDE GOVERNMENT INDICATORS

Government effectiveness captures perceptions of the quality of public services, the quality of the civil service and the degree of its independence from political pressures, the quality of policy formulation and implementation, and the credibility of the government's commitment to such policies. Access this table to see a list of the individual variables from each data source used to construct this measure in the Worldwide Governance Indicators at http://info.worldbank.org/governance/wgi/index.aspx#doc

A.6. POLITY IV SCHEME OF POLITICAL REGIME FORM (AUTHORITARIANISM–DEMOCRACY)

The Polity IV scheme intends to measure political competition more so than civil liberties. Its complex scoring procedures cover several subjects—political competition, constraints on executive authority, elite political recruitment, and mass political participation. The combined index of autocracy and democracy has a 21-point scale running from (closed) dictatorship (−10) to (open) democracy (+10), with scores exceeding 5 typically labeled *democracy*. Data sources can be located at http://www.systemicpeace.org/polity/polity4.htm. The variable constructed here averages a country's index scores in the 5 years leading up to the DALP expert judgments of partisan linkage strategies.

7

STATE CAPACITY AND SOCIAL INVESTMENT

EXPLAINING VARIATION IN SKILLS CREATION REFORMS IN LATIN AMERICA

Juan A. Bogliaccini and Aldo Madariaga

7.1. INTRODUCTION

In the final decades of the 20th century, the collapse of the model of import substitution industrialization (ISI) and the accompanying socioeconomic transformations, as well as a new international policy agenda, compelled Latin American governments to move from compensation-based social policy to a new policy paradigm centered on activation and skills creation.[1] The rationale was that higher skills and training should attract investments in capital and technology, leading to higher growth and productivity (Inter-American Development Bank, 2003, p. 108). The outcome was rather, as usually, a combination of compensation-based social policy with well-designed instruments to expand social investment (SI) policy to the informal sector and other previously uncovered sectors.

This chapter intends to make sense of the unequal advancement of the SI agenda in Latin America, by analyzing the politics of skills creation reforms in four countries: Bolivia, Chile, Guatemala, and Uruguay. Arguing in favor of

1. In our previous work, we have used the term "skills formation" following a well-established notion in the literature that takes technical and vocational education and training as the center of analysis (Bogliaccini & Madariaga, 2020). In order to differentiate this broader approach to skills from that presented in this chapter, which focuses on the relationship between skills and social investment, we follow Chapter 1 in this volume and refer instead to "skills creation."

Juan A. Bogliaccini and Aldo Madariaga, *State Capacity and Social Investment* In: *The World Politics of Social Investment (Volume I)*. Edited by: Julian L. Garritzmann, Silja Häusermann, and Bruno Palier, Oxford University Press. © Oxford University Press 2022. DOI: 10.1093/oso/9780197585245.003.0007

including skills creation within the core of research on SI, we show that success in expanding SI in skills creation reflects the wide variance in state capacity
among countries in the region. By "skills," we refer to the abilities acquired
through formal and informal education that provide concrete know-how and
allow the performance—and potential improvement—of specific tasks at the
workplace (Bogliaccini & Madariaga, 2020).[2] These abilities are acquired in, for
the most part, standardized educational and training contexts and comprise both
specific and broad knowledge. The analysis of skills creation in Latin America,
we argue, needs to consider the narrower definition as technical and vocational
upper secondary and tertiary education and training and as a broader intake including upper secondary general education in the equation because the average
worker in the region will not attain such a level. This means that the policy goals
regarding skills creation in Latin America are related to schooling and attainment at the secondary level as much as improving cognitive scores.

Since the emergence of the SI agenda, Chile, the country ranking with the
highest state capacity and among social policy frontrunners in the region,
excelled the others in universalizing educational coverage, attainment, and cognitive scores and increasing the share of technical and vocational education and
training (TVET). On the contrary, countries with historical problems in terms
of state capacity, institutional-building, and construction of welfare institutions,
like Guatemala, have remained the absolute regional laggards. We thus point at
the crucial—but hitherto neglected—role of state capacity in the politics of SI.

However, we argue and show that state capacity is a necessary, but not a
sufficient, condition for advancing skills creation in Latin America (Goertz &
Mahoney, 2012). Uruguay, a country with among the highest state capacity and
most advanced welfare state in the region, has remained deadlocked in a conflict
between timid reforms and low advancement. Bolivia, on the contrary, managed
to build reform coalitions to expand SI and overcome its laggard situation, albeit
encountering problems at the moment of implementing SI reforms, mostly because of low levels of state capacity.

We argue, therefore, that successful SI reform strategies depend on two
conditions that are necessary but individually not sufficient: 1) state capacity and
2) SI-enhancing reform coalitions interacting with the respective policy legacies
(see Doner & Schneider, 2020). We find that only Chile has had a decided advancement of SI reforms in the education realm, while Bolivia and Uruguay have
fallen short because of problems associated with either state capacity or the interaction between reform coalitions and policy legacies.

---

2. The concept of "skills" is a contested one between disciplinary boundaries, but also, it acquires
   different meanings in time and space. For a discussion, see Payne (2017). It is important to note
   that focusing on the formal dimensions of skills acquisition—like we do here—should not ob-
   scure the fact that much of this acquisition occurs through prolonged experience and routinized
   problem-solving on the job.

This chapter offers several contributions to research on the politics of SI. First, it highlights skills creation as a key component of the SI agenda, focusing on a region where skills creation has been largely neglected (see Chapter 3 in Volume II [Garritzmann et al., 2022] for an analysis of skills creation in Western Europe). Second, it extends research on the scope conditions for SI, studying state capacity as a key prerequisite for SI in less advanced countries, although one that is not sufficient, as the Uruguay case shows. Third, we propose that the interaction between reform coalitions and policy legacies is also a necessary condition for SI reforms, although also in itself insufficient, as the Bolivian case will make clear.

The chapter is structured as follows: First, we develop our understanding of skills creation as SI and show the shift in the international social policy agenda that affected skills creation during 1980–1990. Second, we develop our analytical argument about the importance of state capacity for SI reforms alongside the interaction between policy legacies and reform coalitions. Third, we analyze our four cases under these premises. We conclude by summarizing the contributions to the SI research agenda.

7.2. SKILLS CREATION AS SI IN LATIN AMERICA

Skills creation (i.e., our broader definition comprising general and TVET upper secondary and post-secondary education) has hitherto not elicited the interest it deserves in the SI discussions, both in Latin America and in other countries around the globe. This is surprising given the fact that SI is all about strengthening people's skills and capacities to participate fully in employment and social life (Morel et al., 2012). These volumes define SIs as policies aiming to create, preserve, or mobilize human skills and capabilities (see Chapter 1 in this volume). We argue that skills creation should lie prominently in the SI agenda.

Current research on skills creation has focused on TVET, highlighting its capacity to foster adaptability, employability, productivity, and the flexibility of the economy to respond to changing demands and technological requirements, generating virtuous complementarities. However, in the case of non-advanced countries, the discussion on effective skills creation is usually part of greater efforts to think of strategies to universalize and increase the quality of education as part of the shift from compensatory-only to compensatory plus activation policies. In other words, the transformation of the social policy agenda toward an SI one in Latin America needs to deal with closing basic educational gaps.

In this section we show how the quest for moving away from a pure compensatory social policy approach put skills creation at the center of social policy reforms in Latin America. We also show that governments's ability to carry this agenda further varied greatly in the region.

7.2.1. Skills creation metamorphosis: From ISI to the open market economy

In Latin America, the focus on skills creation and training for the job market arrived with the change from ISI to the open market model. During ISI, social policy followed a direction similar to that in Southern Europe (Barrientos, 2009; Filgueira, 2005): a bias toward the urban and male workforce and a heavy weight of social security benefits, particularly pension schemes, on labor market insiders in social expenditure. In the case of education, the focus was on universalizing primary education, but significant resources ended up being put into tertiary academic education (see Chapter 8 in this volume). TVET developed only in a few countries and only as a subsidiary policy under the wing of education ministries. Countries like Brazil, Chile, Colombia, and Mexico also built vocational training institutions similar to those existent in Continental Europe; but with the exception of Brazil, these were established rather late and did not figure prominently in these countries' development strategy (see Economic Commission for Latin America and the Caribbean & International Labour Organization, 2013). At the end of the 1980s, it became clear that the social policy regimes associated with ISI had configured a situation of strong focus on compensatory measures and segmentation between insiders and outsiders.

This neglect of education contrasted starkly with the success of the East Asian economic miracles and their human capital–oriented social policy and industrialization processes (see Haggard & Kaufman, 2008, pp. 35–38). This was a key antecedent for the shift in the international social policy agenda in the 1990s. The new development mainstream dictated that education should be a priority in the reform of the social policy sector. International organizations forcefully put education on the policy agenda, increasing their loan portfolios for education programs and strongly advocating the new approach (Grindle, 2004, pp. 40, 47; Hunter, 2000; see also Chapter 3 in this volume). This agenda highlighted the focus on the quality of education, skills creation, lifelong learning and training, education to work transitions, and active labor market policy (Inter-American Development Bank, 2003; Saavedra, 2003; Wolff & Moura de Castro, 2003). TVET programs born from this agenda grew mostly detached from mid-century TVET programs. Rather than generating and promoting new skills, old and new institutions were placed under the radar of labor ministries and their mission directed to activating outsiders in the context of structural change and massive unemployment.

7.2.2. Latin America after two decades of SI reforms

Latin American countries have advanced at diverse speeds in reforming their skills creation systems. When we analyze the outcome of SI reforms since the 2000s in terms of coverage and attainment of general and vocational education (see our definition of "skills creation" in the introduction), we see two results worth highlighting (see Bogliaccini & Madariaga, 2020). First, countries tend to cluster around groups that coincide roughly with the advanced, intermediate, and laggard groups of welfare development found in the literature (Figure 7.1) (Bogliaccini & Madariaga, 2020; Filgueira, 2005; Segura-Ubiergo, 2007; see also Chapter 13 in this volume). This shows that the capacity of states to expand welfare institutions in general during the 20th century is a key antecedent when analyzing their ability to pursue an SI agenda in the new millennium. Second, our data also shows inconsistencies between groups that reflect the uneven success of SI reforms. Our assessment of SI in the 21st century is based on the typology of skills supply profiles elaborated in Bogliaccini and Madariaga (2020), based on a cluster analysis using the variables presented below.

Within the advanced group, Chile is the only country that closed coverage gaps with the Organisation for Economic Co-operation and Development

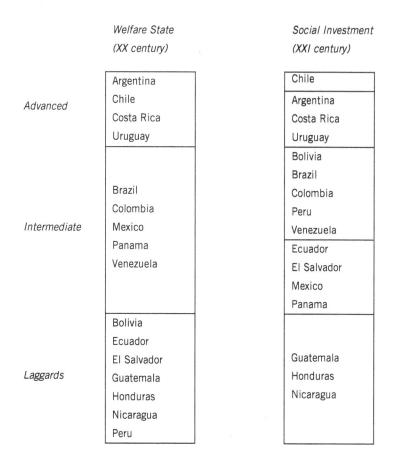

Figure 7.1 Welfare state development and social investment reforms.
Source. Author's elaboration based on Filgueira (2005), Segura-Ubiergo (2007), and Bogliaccini and Madariaga (2020).

(OECD) countries—although quality and equality remain major concerns. The other advanced welfare states (Argentina, Costa Rica, and Uruguay), on the contrary, have been unable to further reduce gaps, particularly with respect to the attainment of secondary education among young adults. This implies a cautionary note when analyzing the high cognitive test scores of these countries, particularly Costa Rica and Uruguay: Higher quality of education here comes at the expense of leaving a substantive share of students behind. Despite the differences, there is a striking commonality with Chile: Except for Costa Rica, Program for International Student Assessment (PISA) scores show that quality tends to be lower for TVET than for general education programs (see Table 7.1). In this regard, some studies suggest that TVET is used as an alternative to incorporate poorer populations excluded from the general education system (see Sevilla, 2017).

Intermediate welfare states show important advances in their SI agendas but can be further divided into two subgroups. One subgroup, composed of Bolivia, Brazil, Colombia, Peru, and Venezuela, has made an important universalization effort, significantly reducing the share of the population with only primary education and increasing the completion of secondary education (see Table 7.2). It has also significantly improved the share of students who attend TVET programs, particularly at the post-secondary level. While still lagging in the reduction of population with only primary schooling, they have reached the regional frontrunners in terms of secondary completion among youngsters. Worthy of recognition are the cases of Peru and Bolivia, previously laggard welfare states and now in the group of higher SI advancement. With the partial exception of Brazil, they have done so at the peril of educational quality, having the lowest cognitive test scores in the region.

The second subgroup, composed of El Salvador, Ecuador, Mexico, and Panama, has improved skills portfolios, albeit in a more uneven and heterogeneous way.

Table 7.1 Average PISA scores for general and TVET programs (2015)

	Math			Reading			Science		
	General	TVET	Diff	General	TVET	Diff	General	TVET	Diff
Chile	423	416		459	446		447	443	
Argentina	409	408		427	415		432	433	
Costa Rica	397	422	*	424	451	*	417	441	*
Uruguay	418	410	*	437	409	*	436	429	
Brazil	374	443	*	404	482	*	397	471	*
Colombia	386	405	*	418	449	*	411	433	*
Mexico	402	426	*	417	442	*	410	433	*

Source. Authors' elaboration based on data from the OECD.
*Differences are significant at the 0.05 level.

Table 7.2 Advancement in skills creation indicators 1995–2015

	Highest educational degree = primary education (%) [a]			Highest educational degree = secondary education (%) [b]			Cognitive test scores [c]			Population in TVET alternatives [d]	
	ca. 1995	ca. 2015	% change	ca. 1995	ca. 2015	% change	2006	2013	% change	Secondary	Post-secondary
Chile	14.9	6.7	-8.2	58	84.2	26.2	539.7	575.9	36.2	23.2	45.0
Average	14.9	6.7	-8.2	58	84.2	26.2	539.7	575.9	36.2	23.2	45.0
Argentina	9.7	3.1	-6.6	49.9	65.6	15.7	511.5	521.4	9.8	14.9	13.0
Costa Rica	22.5	10.4	-12.1	30	58.2	28.2	556.0	539.0	-17.0	15.7	9.0
Uruguay	21.1	8.7	-12.4	31.9	42.1	10.2	550.5	545.4	-5.2	15.3	8.0
Average	17.8	7.4	-10.4	37.3	55.3	18.0	539.3	535.2	-4.1	15.3	10.0
Bolivia	50.1	29.9	-20.2	44.1	79.1	35	—	—	—	4.7	15.0
Brazil	55.6	25.5	-30.1	23	62.2	39.2	501.5	519.5	18.0	8.0	14.0
Colombia	47.8	29.8	-18	38.1	70.1	32	501.6	516.9	15.3	19.0	37.0
Peru	40.7	23.4	-17.3	29.7	82.6	52.9	482.0	524.3	42.3	1.1	32.0
Venezuela	22.2	11	-11.2	37	72.8	35.8	—	—	—	15.0	24.0
Average	43.3	23.9	-19.4	34.4	73.4	39.0	495.0	520.2	25.2	9.6	24.4
Ecuador	—	13.5	—	—	63.3	—	456.0	510.8	54.8	21.5	12.0
El Salvador	49.7	31	-18.7	27.2	45.9	18.7	N/A	N/A	N/A	17.4	13.0
Mexico	33.3	15.5	-17.8	21.3	51.1	29.8	536.0	542.9	6.8	16.2	23.0
Panama	—	10.3	—	—	58.6	—	459.4	475.7	16.3	15.3	5.9
Average	41.5	23.3	-18.3	24.3	48.5	24.3	483.8	509.8	26	17.6	13.5

Table 7.2 Continued

	Highest educational degree = primary education (%)[a]			Highest educational degree = secondary education (%)[b]			Cognitive test scores[c]			Population in TVET alternatives[d]	
	ca. 1995	ca. 2015	% change	ca. 1995	ca. 2015	% change	2006	2013	% change	Secondary	Post-secondary
Guatemala	61.8	52.4	−9.4	21.2	33	11.8	451.4	491.4	40.0	28.0	4.6
Honduras	48.2	34.7	−13.5	18	42.7	24.7	—	488.3	—	46.0	4.4
Nicaragua	53.4	39.2	−14.2	14.4	35.8	21.4	463.9	470.2	6.3	5.0	9.0
Average	54.5	42.1	−12.4	17.9	37.2	19.3	457.7	483.3	25.6	26.3	6.0

Note. N/A = not available.

[a] Economically active population with 0–5 years of education (percentage). From Economic Commission for Latin America and the Caribbean (2017).

[b] Population aged 20–24 who completed secondary education. From Economic Commission for Latin America and the Caribbean (2017).

[c] SERCE and TERCE regional standardized tests, averages for math and reading in each year (UNESCO, 2014).

[d] From Sevilla (2017) and the UNESCO-UIS Database (for Bolivia and Guatemala).

Source. Authors' elaboration using different sources (see notes).

Thus, while showing a similar effort as the former group in terms of reducing the population with only primary education, they have not been able to emulate this success at the secondary level. With the partial exception of Mexico, these countries show very low cognitive test scores, even failing to improve quality for the insiders.

While these two groups have followed different strategies for increasing TVET provision, they share the fact that cognitive test scores for TVET are higher than for general education (see Table 7.1). This suggests that secondary TVET might be having a special role in skills creation. Our hypothesis for this pattern is that innovation in curricula and practices has been more likely to occur in novel TVET-oriented curricula than in entrenched academic programs where the clash between government and unions tends to produce costly stalemates.

Finally, the group composed of Guatemala, Honduras, and Nicaragua has made negligible advances with the SI agenda. This group combines a low capacity to provide a minimum of education (as shown in the primary and secondary education attainment scores) and low quality (as shown in cognitive test scores) with among the highest enrollment rates in secondary TVET of the region (except for Nicaragua). The magnitude of enrollment in secondary TVET vis-à-vis academic programs leads us to hypothesize that secondary TVET is being used as a substitute for traditional education to get around the problem of low enrollment, low completion, and large dropout and not as a source of skills creation per se.

We interpret these data in the following way: In the advanced countries with broader coverage of secondary education and more equal—for regional standards—access to tertiary education, the quality between general and TVET alternatives in secondary education tends to be similar (and, if anything, biased toward general education). This reflects the fact that as middle classes increased their opportunities to go to tertiary education, secondary TVET became most important for increasing educational opportunities for poorer populations. Data for countries in the advanced group shows that the majority of students enrolled in secondary TVET comes from the lower socioeconomic strata, in contrast with the post-secondary level where this trend is equilibrated with a similar attendance by higher and lower socioeconomic strata in TVET courses (Sevilla, 2017). Contrariwise, in countries of the intermediate group with narrower overall coverage of secondary education—and in particular of secondary TVET—higher-quality TVET appears to be an important alternative, at least until recently, for middle- and lower-middle-class families in Brazil, Colombia, and Mexico, while tertiary education (either general or TVET) for the most part continues to be a privilege for the higher classes (Bruns et al., 2012, p. 87; Jacinto & García de Fanelli, 2014). As TVET alternatives in these countries expand, especially at the secondary level, this becomes more and more an alternative for poorer populations, potentially putting a limit on the capacity of these countries to significantly increase TVET coverage while maintaining the high quality of their secondary TVET systems and expanding at the same time coverage of tertiary education for middle-class families (Jacinto & García de Fanelli, 2014). Conversely, in the laggard group, TVET is mostly conceived as a way to provide a labor market exit in the context of very low attendance rates in secondary education and high rates of dropout from the general education system.

In the next section we analyze the role of state capacity and the interaction between policy legacies and reform coalitions for reforming education and TVET policies in four countries representing four different trajectories: Bolivia, Chile, Guatemala, and Uruguay.

7.3. STATE CAPACITY: A NECESSARY BUT INSUFFICIENT CONDITION FOR SI REFORM SUCCESS

State capacity is a multidimensional concept related to the ability of state institutions to reach into society and affect individual behavior (Kurtz, 2013, p. 3). Extractive, steering, legitimation, and coercive capacities have been usually recognized as key dimensions of this concept (Centeno, 2002; Giraudy, 2012; Kurtz, 2013; Soifer, 2015). In the case of public policy, state capacity reflects the overall ability of countries to establish, accomplish, implement, and, perhaps most notably, enforce and sustain over time policy objectives across their entire national territory. In this sense, state capacity is as much about administrative structures capable of delivering as it is about authoritative power to get individuals or groups to obey commands and to pursue policy objectives with autonomy from pressure groups (Evans & Heller, 2013; Kurtz, 2013).

Low state capacity imposes severe obstacles for pursuing a (successful and sustainable) SI agenda and affects the choice of policy instruments of reform coalitions. The differential capacities Latin American states have in providing public goods, in this case related to skills creation, act in two moments in our analytical framework: first, as a background variable that affects current reform efforts (for example, the capacity to raise revenue to properly fund new policies and to use competent civil servants to design reforms). Second, even if SI-proposing coalitions manage to advance reforms and overcome existing constraints in the short term, a lack of adequate state capacity may impair the results of those reforms, for example, through the (in)ability to execute mandated budgets or implement reforms evenly across the territory following the law and without discretion. In this latter sense, state capacity affects the implementation and sustainability of SI reforms. That is why we argue that having SI-enhancing reform coalitions is not sufficient for successful reform outputs and outcomes— whether these are successful and sustainable depends (at least to some degree) on the level of state capacity.

Another important aspect is that over time high levels of state capacity can also strengthen policy legacies. Policy legacies (i.e., the design and functioning of past policies) have "long-lasting effects on the ability of reformers to alter the [current] design and scope [of those policies]" (Pribble, 2013, p. 27). Policy legacies, therefore, also set opportunities and constraints in the formation of reform coalitions and the pursuing of policy alternatives (see Chapters 1 and 2 of this volume). These legacies inform political strategies and coalitional alternatives to foster SI reforms (Busemeyer, 2015; Pribble, 2013; see also Pierson, 1994). Such legacies structure the sort of problems that reform coalitions need to address for reform. Existing policies empower certain societal groups over others. This influences how organized actors define their political goals and how they pursue their policy preferences. We can expect policy legacies to bear especial influence in the context of gradual processes of policy and institutional development (Mahoney & Thelen, 2010). Occasionally, however, disruptive processes or critical junctures may allow a disregard for these legacies and permit substantive overhauls of the existing systems, as we will argue was the case in Chile during the military period (see Levitsky & Murillo, 2013).

Skills creation is intimately related to state capacity (Evans & Heller, 2013; Kurtz, 2013). In Latin America, the construction of educational institutions closely followed that of welfare systems and the relative levels and evolution of state capacity. By analyzing gross enrollment rates in primary education for our selected cases, we observe differences in state capacity to carry educational reforms in history, in particular with respect to the movement from elite education to mass education (see Table 7.3; see also the discussion in Chapter 8 of this volume). Data shows how Chile and Uruguay were among the top 5 countries in the region in crossing the enrollment rate benchmarks of 60% and 90% for primary education, while Bolivia and Guatemala are placed among the laggards (for a global analysis of enrollment levels, see Chapter 8 in this volume).

The fact that Bolivia and Guatemala universalized a minimum level of education only recently is telling with regard to the capacity of states to pursue more complex SI strategies. Now, state capacity not only reflects historical efforts at

Table 7.3 Evolution in gross enrollment rate at primary level

	Decade in which gross enrollment rates reached 60%+	Decade in which gross enrollment rates reached 90%+
Chile	1910 (1)	1950 (3)
Uruguay	1940 (4)	1960 (4)
Bolivia	1960 (15)	1990 (15)
Guatemala	1980 (17)	2000 (17)

Note. The numbers in brackets are the countries' position among 17 Latin American countries in passing the selected benchmarks.

Source. Authors' elaboration based on Frankema (2009).

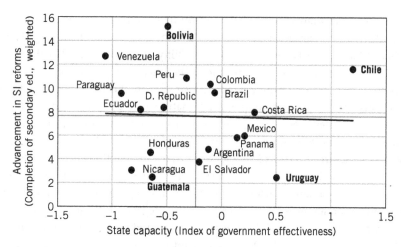

Figure 7.2 State capacity and advancement of SI reforms.
Source. Authors' elaboration based on World Development Indicators, World Bank, and CEPALSTAT. Division lines are drawn at the respective mean.

skills creation but also affects current reform strategies. Figure 7.2 aligns Latin American countries according to the index of government effectiveness (a broad measure of state capacity that is available for all countries in the region and an indicator of success in the expansion of SI and the success in secondary education completion). While the first takes the average government effectiveness score between 1995 and 2015, the second takes the change in secondary education attainment among young adults (20–24 years old) in 1995–2015. We weighted this indicator by the initial level in each country in order to control for the decreasing returns of public investment and social incorporation: It may be relatively easy to expand supply and attainment at early stages of coverage through drastic increases in the education budget and public effort; however, once a threshold is reached, countries face increasing problems in tackling the remaining bottlenecks and continuing to expand supply and attainment in specific populations not yet incorporated. Thus, a country with a high advancement but starting at a relatively low level will see its score decreased, while a country having a lower advancement but starting at a relatively higher level will have its score increased. Given the challenges of skills creation in the region—not least the lack of quality data available for all countries—we believe this is a rough but accurate measure of countries' skills creation efforts since the 2000s.

Figure 7.2 does not show a clear-cut picture. We divided the figure into four quadrants for a clearer visualization. While some countries with low state capacity indeed have low SI effort (e.g., Guatemala) and while some with high state capacity show high SI (e.g., Chile), we also observe several "off-diagonal" cases: Uruguay, for example, stands out in the quadrant of countries with low SI effort despite high state capacity; Bolivia, in contrast, reaches high scores on SI reforms despite comparatively low levels of state capacity.

In the remainder of this chapter, we analyze one country from each quadrant to better understand the role that state capacity and its interaction with political coalitions and policy legacies have played. To foreshadow the results, we will argue that Bolivia shows success despite low state capacity and Uruguay shows failure despite high state capacity because of the importance of the interaction between policy legacies and reform coalitions. We propose that weak legacies and strong coalitions in the case of Bolivia allowed a short-term improvement in SI reforms, albeit confronting long-term challenges of sustainability because of the underlying state capacity problems. In Uruguay, high and valued legacies by strong advocacy groups such as teachers' unions in combination with reform coalitions unwilling to take the costs associated with reform conflicts blocked the advancement of SI reforms in spite of high levels of state capacity.

7.3.1. Guatemala: SI gridlocked by chronic low state capacities

Guatemala is a country where feeble state capacity is reinforced by a legacy of poor social policy and weak political coalitions. Although democracy returned in 1986 and the signing of peace accords in 1996 that followed a decades-long Civil War, marked the initiation of a new era after a decades-long civil war, institutionalization of the political system has been deceptive. Low state capacity has translated into state capture, corruption, and criminality. Due to the gravity of the situation, in 2006 the United Nations set an unprecedented organism in order to promote accountability and strengthen the rule of law, the International Commission Against Impunity in Guatemala (CICIG). Working as an international prosecutor under Guatemalan law, the CICIG investigation was a deciding factor for President Otto Pérez (2012–2015), who was forced to resign before the termination of his term and prosecuted for corruption and fraud. Earlier, in 2010, another president, Alfonso Portillo (1998–2002), had also been convicted for corruption and fraud. After Otto Perez was jailed, another case involved his successor: in a publicized affair with diplomatic repercussions, President Jimmy Morales expelled in 2017 the head of CICIG from the country after finding it was investigating dirty campaign donations affecting him (Malkin, 2017).

Guatemala ranks today among the countries with the greatest education and health coverage problems and among the highest rates of poverty, extreme poverty, and inequality in the region. Highlighting the urgency of tackling these problems, the peace accords committed to increase educational and health expenditures by 50%, for which a tax reform was needed, increasing state revenues by another 50%. However, the tax reform failed miserably, and so did efforts at increasing expenditure up until 2020 (Schneider, 2012). As a result, as of 2020 Guatemala was among the countries with the lowest tax revenues and is the country with the lowest public expenditure overall and the lowest expenditure in education in Latin America.[3]

In this context, Guatemala remains unable to build a long-term reform coalition and advance SI reforms. For example, following the wave of conditional cash transfer (CCT) programs in Latin America (see the various chapters on Latin America in Volume II [Garritzmann et al., 2022]), the Colom government established in 2008 *Mi Familia Progresa* (MFP), a cash transfer conditioned on, among other things, school attendance. However, MFP was poorly designed and funded since the beginning. Although the program was formally means-tested, the inexistence of procedures for targeting beneficiaries or accountability for the use of resources made transfers de facto discretionary, therefore increasing the danger of clientelistic practices (see Cecchini et al., 2009, pp. 44–45). In terms of resources, at the time of launching, the program involved a meager 0.06% of gross domestic product (GDP) (Economic Commission for Latin America and the Caribbean, 2017); and no permanent resources were earmarked to maintain it alive. Already 1 year after being implemented, the government had to settle a loan from the Inter-American Development Bank (IADB) to maintain the program running. A new IADB loan had to be secured in 2012. Moreover, it suffered from severe political weakness. MFP was hosted by the Presidency's Executive Coordination Secretariat and depended directly on the Office of the First Lady, its future being strongly dependent on the incumbent government (Cecchini et al., 2009, p. 41). In fact, after the government turnover in 2012, the new Pérez government canceled the program and launched a new—albeit strikingly similar—one, *Mi Bono Seguro*.

Guatemala has bet on secondary-level TVET to offer an educational alternative to those who stay in formal education. There is also the Instituto Técnico de Capacitación (INTECAP), a public TVET institute offering formal secondary education titles and—mostly—post-secondary short-cycle courses to an elite of cherry-picked candidates. This institute is funded through payroll taxes and, albeit a public institution, is led by business; and governments have little to no capacity to influence its management and/or strategies (see Bogliaccini & Madariaga, 2019). Very low levels of state capacity have impeded the government from effectively incorporating this institution: on the one hand, due to the fact that since its creation governments have failed to provision budget resources to complement payroll taxes as established in the institute's governing law and, on the other, because of the effective refusal on the part of the employers to relinquish control of the institute to the state. In this context, the state has had to use resources from external cooperation projects (e.g., USAID, Millennium Challenge Corporation, German Agency for International Cooperation) to further expand the coverage of TVET, while employers maintain their capacity to manage a small but high-quality

---

3. Data from Economic Commission for Latin America and the Caribbean (2017).

public institution to their own interests, producing an important gap between employers' skills creation capacities and the lower-quality and poorly funded public education system. The result is a complete stalemate in terms of historically low enrollment and quality.

In short, the case of Guatemala shows how low levels of state capacity prevented the expansion of skills creation SI policies as lacking state capacity hindered proper funding, organization, and design of these policies.

7.3.2. Bolivia: SI breakthrough endangered by low state capacity

Bolivia's political and institutional history is not unlike that of Guatemala: revolutionary challenges, military dictatorships, secession attempts, and a polarized ethnic society. It departs from Guatemala, however, in that a long-term government coalition led by a political outsider managed to temporarily overcome state capacity problems and enact significant SI reforms. Yet, these reforms were much more impressive on paper than they were in practice as considerable state capacity problems undermined the policies' effectiveness (see also Chapter 15 in Volume II [Garritzmann et al., 2022]).

Evo Morales—who governed between 2006 and 2019—was the leader of a union of small indigenous farmers, which led mass mobilizations with anti-neoliberal and ethnic demands against the establishment in the late 1990s and early 2000s (Garay-Molina, 2010; Silva, 2009). Building on the support of a strong and experienced union movement, mobilized impoverished rural workers, and sectors of urban middle classes and capitalizing on the neoliberalization of traditional left-wing parties, Morales led the leftist *Movimiento al Socialismo* (MAS) to the presidency, with a strong popular backing and the resistance of business and regional elites (see Anria, 2016; Garay-Molina, 2010).

Morales devised two strategies for expanding SI: First, in the context of low expenditure on education and low tax revenues, Morales decided to reinforce support from poorer populations by subsidizing the demand for education to quickly increase enrollment and attainment rates. To this end, he devised a cash transfer for children in public schools conditioned on school attendance: the *Bono Juancito Pinto*. Spending only about 0.3% of GDP, Bolivia's CCT reached around 10% of the Bolivian population and over one-third of the targeted population in 2007, its first year of operation (Economic Commission for Latin America and the Caribbean, 2017). The transfer was expanded with government funds in the subsequent years, reaching 50% of the targeted population in 2010 (Economic Commission for Latin America and the Caribbean, 2017). The second strategy was increasing supply. To this end, and in order to circumvent the strong opposition of domestic businesses to increasing taxation, he implemented a tax on hydrocarbons and a policy of nationalization, which hurt the mostly foreign natural gas companies operating in the country (Fairfield, 2015). This allowed a significant increase in revenues and expenditure (Garay-Molina, 2010, pp. 66–67). In fact, compared to the early 1990s, Bolivia has doubled its educational expenditure.[4] Following this, Morales engaged in important institutional reforms. In 2010 the MAS government passed the *Avelino Siñani-Elizardo Pérez* bill, with a marked emphasis on strengthening the link between education and the productive sector, in both its general and TVET components. Catering to its support base, the bill has a strong emphasis on communitarian economies and integrating indigenous culture to productive activities (Sevilla, 2017, pp. 26–27; Yapu, 2015). The law also created new public post-secondary TVET institutions, the *Escuelas Superiores Tecnológicas Fiscales*. This emphasis on state-provided TVET was instituted in the Bolivian constitution of 2009 and paralleled with the creation of a national system of competences (*Sistema Plurinacional de Certificación de Competencias*).

Nonetheless, despite these reform advances, low state capacity significantly impaired the implementation of reforms and their sustainability. The TVET component of the Morales reform was difficult to implement due to limited infrastructure in public schools, lack of trained teachers, and difficulty in adapting curricula to the new normative (Sevilla, 2017, p. 27). In other words, despite the presence of an SI-enhancing reform coalition, the result of the reform in terms of implementation was not unlike that of previous reform attempts in the country (e.g., Lizárraga, 2015, p. 15). Low state capacity also decreased the ability to execute the larger budgets brought about by higher tax revenues. For example, the tax on hydrocarbons allocated a fixed 8% of revenue to public universities. However, for several reasons, including their low focus on research and development, public universities were unable to spend the extra resources: In 2012, budget execution was only 60% (Lizárraga, 2015, p. 16).

In sum, the Bolivian case shows that lacking state capacity hindered the implementation and sustainability of skills creation policies, despite the fact that an SI-friendly government pushed for them. This shows, on the one hand, that state capacity is a necessary condition for successful and sustainable SI reforms; on the other hand, the Bolivian case also shows that an SI-friendly reform coalition alone is not sufficient to achieve sustainable reforms. We thus argue that both state capacity and an SI-friendly reform coalition are necessary (but in themselves insufficient) conditions for successful SI reforms.

7.3.3. Uruguay: SI gridlocked in the political arena despite high state capacity

The case studies so far have shown why state capacity is a necessary condition for successful SI reforms. Uruguay will illustrate why state capacity is a necessary, but in itself not a sufficient, condition for such successful reforms. Despite high

4. Data from Economic Commission for Latin America and the Caribbean (2017).

levels of state capacity, Uruguay has only managed to enact and implement some meager skills creation reforms and lags behind other countries in terms of enrollment levels—because Uruguay lacked the political reform coalitions pushing for SI reforms.

Contrary to Chile and confronted with the need to reform educational institutions under democracy, Uruguayan reformers have been heavily constrained by past legacies, despite having strong state capacities. Strong unions and the inherited narrow-corporatist institutions have been pervasive to the necessary reform of the once model public educational system by regional standards. Divided elites have been unable to agree on the need to provide political shielding to reformers. Massive middle-class allegiance to public education has made it more difficult to propose privatization, while a historically state-led TVET system has made it difficult for a dispersed business community to participate in training efforts. Therefore, a legacy of state-led education with a pervasive focus on academic programs over TVET but one of the lowest attainment rates in the region has proven resistant to several reform attempts since the 1990s.

Carrying on the most comprehensive educational reform in 1995 by the center-right Colorado Party government, Uruguay secured almost universal pre-primary access and strengthened primary education quality and equality. However, reformers failed completely to advance necessary reforms in secondary-level education aimed to increase enrollment and attainment rates. By 2016, only Guatemala and Nicaragua lagged behind Uruguay in terms of secondary education attainment rates (Table 7.2).

By 2005, the labor-backed *Frente Amplio* government began an aggressive policy of budgetary increases for education, from an initial 2% in terms of GDP to 4.5% by 2015. However, in spite of massive investment in education, there is a political stalemate regarding institutional reform. The *Frente Amplio* governments have confronted strong opposition from teachers' unions with respect to education reform agendas, similarly to center-right Colorado governments a decade before. Under such circumstances, the *Frente Amplio* administrations (2005-2020) targeted educational expenditure for academic programs on the demand side, doubling it as a share of GDP in just 10 years. The inability to pair an increase in resources with a necessary institutional reform resulted in a sluggish advance in enrollment at all levels.

Two policies were successful during the *Frente Amplio* administrations in terms of education, alongside the massive increase in investment. First, the continuation of the successful inherited pre-primary programs. Second, the "one laptop per child" program. These two policies are worth mentioning because, having been inaugurated by two different governments in two different decades, they share a key common factor: Institutional responsibility was allocated outside the education administration in order to circumvent opposition from teachers' unions. In other words, a strong policy legacy of corporatism and union control of education administration—particularly at the secondary level—played against reforms aimed at expanding education access at this level, and advancement in other levels was achieved only when institutional reforms placed the new policies outside the realm of the education authority controlled by teachers' unions.

In spite of this gridlock, secondary-level TVET programs have been partially enhanced by the inclusion of an upper secondary-level TVET path toward tertiary education, which contributes to easing internal formal barriers between academic and TVET programs. Tertiary education programs, even at the university level, have slowly begun to open enrollment for students coming from the TVET path. This was achieved, again, thanks to the lower barriers to change in TVET programs given teachers' lower organization in this level and in the context of an educational system strongly oriented toward academic programs (see Bogliaccini & Madariaga, 2020). However, the extremely poor figures in terms of secondary education attainment signal a de facto barrier to the improvement of the skills portfolios among youngsters.

In terms of tertiary-level TVET, Uruguay lagged behind other Latin American countries until a specific training institution was founded in 2008. This new institution, under the wing of the Labor Ministry, generously funded by a tax levied from every formal employee, and with active participation of both organized labor and business, was mostly oriented toward the labor supply until 2014, concentrating both on the unemployed and on small niches of high-skilled service exports. Since 2015, a second impulse from the third *Frente Amplio* government (2015–2020) slowly began to focus on firm demands and to seek a more active relationship between firms and experts. However, this government initiative, while fully supported by organized labor, encountered some difficulties in getting business decisively involved in it, partially because of internal divisions in the business community, partially because of an excessive focus on historical concerns associated with TVET in the country, namely, unemployment alleviation and supply-side demands.

In sum, the case of Uruguay shows that although state capacity is a necessary condition for successful SI reforms, it is not a sufficient condition in itself. Whether SI reforms are launched as well as how they are designed and implemented also crucially depend on the respective political reform coalitions, as also argued in this volume's theoretical framework (Chapters 1 and 2 in this volume).

7.3.4. Chile: SI enhances policy legacies in a context of high state capacity

In a scenario of high state capacity, Chile represents a positive case in the success of SI reforms.[5] Chile's policy legacies are tightly connected with the unique conditions under which educational institutions were reshaped: a harsh

---

5. Chile is a case of success in SI reforms by regional standards but not so when compared to the OECD. See Bogliaccini and Madariaga (2020).

dictatorship that displaced educational institutions and actors in order to rebuild the system on two main pillars, to subsidize and to privatize the supply of education. These extraordinary conditions allowed the Pinochet dictatorship to disregard a previous legacy of strong state involvement and the power of teachers' unions. Results after three decades are mixed: While coverage and attainment increased in a sustained way to put Chile at the top of the region, access and quality became stratified, producing important within-system inequality and opportunity segmentation.

The *Concertación* coalition governed between 1990 and 2010 as a center-left political alliance between the Christian Democrats, the Socialists, and other minor parties. In the post-authoritarian period, these parties successfully reorganized themselves in a professionalized and technocratic manner and therefore severed their previously strong linkages to organized civil society (Flores-Macías, 2010; Levitsky & Roberts, 2011; Luna, 2014; Pribble, 2013). This allowed the *Concertación* governments to contain the strong social pressure accumulated during the years of dictatorship, particularly among middle classes left behind from neoliberal modernization. Thus, while a tax reform negotiated across the political spectrum allowed important increases in social expenditure, the *Concertación* governments strengthened the legacies of the Pinochet dictatorship by reinforcing freedom of choice and subsidizing private education through expanding voucher schemes paid directly to schools and post-secondary institutions. These governments also enhanced private provision of TVET at the tertiary level.

Chile's CCT program (*Chile Solidario*), established in 2003, is among the smallest in the region. The logic behind this was explicitly that Chile counted on an extensive supply of services and near universal coverage, and the program was highly targeted to those few families still remaining outside the public–private network. In this context, unlike other CCTs, the key was not the transfer nor the conditionality but the associated program of social work with excluded families.

Demand-side educational subsidies served to increase per student expenditure in the private supply of education and not as a direct transfer to students and their parents. Over time, these subsidies substantially increased matriculation in the private sector. In fact, today, private education comprises over 50% of enrollment in secondary and tertiary education. In the case of post-secondary TVET, private provision is virtually full (Sevilla, 2017, p. 36). Post-secondary TVET is also noteworthy for legally accepting for-profit institutions—unlike private universities, which exploit regulatory loopholes to extract profits that are legally prohibited. Therefore, the sharp increase in public expenditure during the democratic governments compared to the previous period masks the fact that an important part of these extra resources went to subsidize private education.

Although Chile did not build specific institutions to incorporate business into the management of TVET, during the dictatorship it privatized state-owned educational institutions, delegated the management of key secondary TVET schools to the private sector, and set up new training schemes—including a tax break program and several targeted programs to incorporate outsiders—with training provision subcontracted to private providers. In this context, private actors have been able to set up their own educational and training institutions and manage the training-related tax break program with little involvement of state actors and even less from the country's weak unions.

The necessary cautionary note on Chile's strategy comes from the inability of the privatized system to increase quality or induce coordination among labor market actors to improve the existing skills mismatch, in addition to a significant stratification of education access (see Torche & Mizala, 2012). This has induced a change of orientation but with uncertain outcomes. After strong student demonstrations since the 2006 demanding higher state involvement to secure educational quality and counting on a strong political mandate and congressional support, the second government of Michelle Bachelet (2014–2018) pushed important educational reforms in order to restrict the expansion of the private for-profit sector, reduce subsidies to private institutions, and strengthen state provision of education. Particularly important in the last case is the founding of 15 state-run TVET post-secondary institutions, which will change the privatized character of the sector, and the elimination of tuition fees in post-secondary institutions (TVET and academic) receiving funds from the state. To this end, Bachelet implemented a new tax reform to meet the new expenditure needs. The advancement of these initiatives illustrates the importance of partisan coalitions to either reinforce or attempt to break the existing pattern of skills creation in Chile. In fact, Bachelet's governing coalition included the Communist Party for the first time since re-democratization, a party with strong ties to the student unions behind the protests. The following Piñera government sought to reverse some of these reforms, catering to the interests of the segment of reluctant middle classes, educational entrepreneurs, and business in general, albeit without success.

In sum, Chile shows how high state capacity and a good fit between reform coalitions and policy legacies produced successful—for the region—SI reforms and outcomes. State capacity allowed Chile to raise revenues through tax reforms each time governments had substantive educational reform commitments. At the same time, reform coalitions attuned to previous policy legacies allowed for a high continuity of reform efforts during the two decades following democratization, while changes to this trajectory followed political negotiation in Congress and majoritarian will.

7.4. CONCLUSION

In this chapter, we have highlighted the importance of skills creation as an SI strategy and studied the politics of SI reforms in a region historically characterized by a legacy of compensatory social policies, state capacity problems, and unstable political coalitions impairing political and policy sustainability. Moreover, we have pointed at the complex but crucial relationship between state capacity and SI reforms, showing that state capacity is a necessary, but in itself not a sufficient, condition for successful SI reforms.

Latin America entered the new millennium with a low-skilled workforce and significant educational coverage and quality gaps. In this context, international organizations diffused an SI agenda with emphasis on covering basic gaps and serving labor market and economic flexibility and adaptation to new economic requirements. Latin American countries have responded variably to this agenda, reforming their educational and training systems through strategies with diverse degrees of success. In this chapter, we have put emphasis on state capacity. We have argued that state capacity is a necessary but insufficient factor affecting the expansion of SI. This not only in terms of policy design and political support but, most notably, in terms of implementation and the sustainability of SI reforms. Latin American countries find challenges in investing in state capacity precisely due to the urgency of coverage gaps. As we showed, Chile and Uruguay present consistently higher levels of state capacity than Bolivia and Guatemala, which have allowed these countries to pass from elite to mass education and to provide a minimum of welfare and education to the population.

However, state capacity does not ensure the sustainability of SI reforms. Drawing on the context of specific policy legacies, reform coalitions can advance an SI agenda even at low levels of state capacity by gathering support from new constituencies, increasing resources, and expanding access. Yet, lacking state capacity hinders the implementation and sustainability of these reforms in practice, making state capacity a necessary condition for successful SI reforms. The case studies also showed that existing policy legacies and organized actors could act as veto players for further institutional reforms, even in the context of high state capacity and institutional strength. State capacity can therefore be regarded as a necessary, but not in itself sufficient, factor for successful SI reforms.

Overall, the differential advancement of SI reforms in the region is consistent with state capacity levels, as expected, but also responds, mostly in the short run, to the interplay of policy legacies and reform coalitions. That is, our analysis argues in favor of the importance of state capacity for the sustainability of SI reforms, although the sole presence of high levels of state capacity is not a sufficient factor to observe such an advancement. Policy legacies and reform coalitions have to be brought into the analysis to portray a complete picture of the politics of the advancement of SI reforms.

ACKNOWLEDGMENTS

We thank Julian Garritzman, Silja Häusermann, Bruno Palier, and the participants at the WOPSI conferences in Paris and Florence for their comments and suggestions. We also thank Cecilia Giambruno and Martin Opertti for valuable research assistance. The research for this chapter was partly funded by the Center for Social Conflict and Cohesion Studies (ANID/FONDAP/15130009), the Clemente Estable Fund (FCE-1-2017-1-135444) awarded by the Uruguayan Agency for Research and Innovation, and the Fondecyt de Iniciacion (11190487) and REDES (ANID/PCI/REDES190097) projects awarded by the Chilean Agency for Research and Development.

REFERENCES

Anria, S. (2016). Democratizing democracy? Civil society and party organization in Bolivia. *Comparative Politics, 48*(4), 459–478.

Barrientos, A. (2009). Labour markets and the (hyphenated) welfare regime in Latin America. *Economy & Society, 38*(1), 87–108.

Bogliaccini, J., & Madariaga, A. (2019, May 13–14). The discreet charm of the oligarchy: Business power and democratic instability in Guatemala [Paper presentation]. REPAL Annual Meeting, New Orleans, LA, USA.

Bogliaccini, J., & Madariaga, A. (2020). Varieties of skills supply profiles in Latin America. *Journal of Latin American Studies, 52*(3), 601–631.

Bruns, B., Evans, D., & Luque, J. (2012). *Achieving world-class education in Brazil: The next agenda.* World Bank.

Busemeyer, M. (2015). *Skills and inequality: Partisan politics and the political economy of education reforms in western welfare states.* Cambridge University Press.

Cecchini, S., Leiva, A., Madariaga, A., & Trucco, D. (2009). *Desafíos de los programas de transferencias con corresponsabilidad: Los casos de Guatemala, Honduras y Nicaragua.* Economic Commission for Latin America and the Caribbean.

Centeno, M. (2002). *Blood and debt: War and the nation-state in Latin America.* Penn State University Press.

Doner, R., & Schneider, B. R. (2020). Technical education in the middle income trap: Building coalitions for skill formation. *The Journal of Development Studies, 56*(4), 680–697.

Economic Commission for Latin America and the Caribbean. (2017). *Noncontributory social protection programmes database: Latin America and the Caribbean.* https://dds.cepal.org/bpsnc/index-en.php

Economic Commission for Latin America and the Caribbean & International Labour Organization. (2013). *The employment situation in Latin America and the Caribbean: Challenges and innovations in labour training.*

Evans, P., & Heller, P. (2013). Human development, state transformation and the politics of the developmental state. In S. Leibfried, E. Huber, M. Lange, J. D.

Levy, & J. D. Stephens (Eds.), *The Oxford handbook of transformations of the state* (pp. 691–713). Oxford University Press.

Fairfield, T. (2015). *Private wealth and public revenue in Latin America: Business power and tax politics.* Cambridge University Press.

Filgueira, F. (2005). *Welfare and democracy in Latin America: The development, crises, and aftermath of universal, dual, and exclusionary social states.* UNRISD Project on Social Policy and Democratization.

Flores-Macías, G. A. (2010). Statist vs. pro-market: Explaining leftist governments' economic policies in Latin America. *Comparative Politics, 42*(4), 413–433.

Frankema, E. (2009). The expansion of mass education in twentieth century Latin America: A global comparative perspective. *Revista de Historia Economica-Journal of Iberian and Latin American Economic History, 27*(3), 359–396.

Garay-Molina, G. (2010). The challenge of progressive change under Evo Morales. In K. Weyland, R. Madrid, & W. Hunter (Eds.), *Leftist governments in Latin America: Successes and shortcomings* (pp. 57–76). Cambridge University Press.

Garritzmann, J. L., Häusermann, S., & Palier, B. (Eds.). (2022). *The world politics of social investment: Vol. II. The politics of varying social investment strategies.* Oxford University Press.

Giraudy, A. (2012). Conceptualizing state strength: Moving beyond strong and weak states. *Revista de Ciencia Política, 32*(3), 599–611.

Goertz, G., & Mahoney, J. (2012). *A tale of two cultures: Qualitative and quantitative research in the social sciences.* Princeton University Press.

Grindle, M. S. (2004). *Despite the odds: The contentious politics of education reform.* Princeton University Press.

Haggard, S., & Kaufman, R. (2008). *Development, democracy and welfare states.* Princeton University Press.

Hunter, W. (2000). World Bank directives, domestic interests, and the politics of human capital investment in Latin America. *Comparative Political Studies, 33*(1), 113–143.

Inter-American Development Bank. (2003). *Good jobs wanted: Labor markets in Latin America.*

Jacinto, C., & García de Fanelli, A. (2014). Tertiary technical education and youth integration in Brazil, Colombia and Mexico. *International Development Policy/Revue internationale de politique de développement, 5.* https://doi.org/10.4000/poldev.1776

Kurtz, M. J. (2013). *Latin American state building in comparative perspective: Social foundations of institutional order.* Cambridge University Press.

Levitsky, S., & Murillo, M. (2013). Lessons from Latin America: Building institutions on weak foundations. *Journal of Democracy, 24*(2), 93–107.

Levitsky, S., & Roberts, K. M. (2011). *Latin America's left turn.* Johns Hopkins University Press.

Lizárraga, K. (2015). *Formación para el trabajo en Bolivia: La paradoja de un país extractivo* [Development Research Working Paper 03/2015]. Institute for Advanced Development Studies.

Luna, J. P. (2014). *Segmented representation: Political party strategies in unequal democracies.* Oxford University Press.

Mahoney, J., & Thelen, K. (2010). *Explaining institutional change.* Cambridge University Press.

Malkin, E. (2017, August 17). Guatemala president who championed honesty orders anticorruption panel chief out. *New York Times.* https://www.nytimes.com/2017/08/27/world/americas/jimmy-morales-guatemala-corruption.html?mcubz=3

Morel, N., Palier, B., & Palme, J. (2012). *Towards a social investment welfare state? Ideas, policies and challenges.* Policy Press.

Payne, J. (2017). The changing meaning of skill: Still contested, still important. In C. Warhust, K. Mayhew, D. Finegold, & K. Buchanan (Eds.), *The Oxford handbook of skills and training* (pp. 54–71). Oxford University Press.

Pierson, P. (1994). *Dismantling the welfare state? Reagan, Thatcher and the politics of retrenchment.* Cambridge University Press.

Pribble, J. (2013). *Welfare and party politics in Latin America.* Cambridge University Press.

Saavedra, J. (2003). Labor markets during the 1990s. In P. Kuczynski & J. Williamson (Eds.), *After the Washington Consensus: Restarting growth and reform in Latin America* (pp. 213–263). Institute for International Economics.

Schneider, A. (2012). *State-building and tax regimes in Central America.* Cambridge University Press.

Segura-Ubiergo, A. (2007). *The political economy of the welfare state in Latin America: Globalization, democracy, and development.* Cambridge University Press.

Sevilla, M. P. (2017). *Panorama de la educación técnica profesional en América Latina y el Caribe* (Serie Políticas Sociales 222). Comisión Económica para América Latina y el Caribe.

Silva, E. (2009). *Challenging neoliberalism in Latin America.* Cambridge University Press.

Soifer, H. D. (2015). *State building in Latin America.* Cambridge University Press.

Torche, F., & Mizala, A. (2012). Bringing the schools back in: The stratification of educational achievement in the Chilean voucher system. *International Journal of Educational Development, 32*(1), 132–144.

Wolff, L., & de Moura Castro, C. (2003). Education and training. The task ahead. In P. Kuczynski & J. Williamson (Eds.), *After the Washington Consensus: Restarting growth and reform in Latin America* (pp. 181–211). Institute for International Economics.

Yapu, M. (2015). Desafíos de la educación técnica y profesional y política educativa en Bolivia. *EDETANIA, 48,* 81–100.

8

THE EMERGENCE OF KNOWLEDGE ECONOMIES

EDUCATIONAL EXPANSION, LABOR MARKET CHANGES, AND THE POLITICS OF SOCIAL INVESTMENT

Julian L. Garritzmann, Silja Häusermann, Thomas Kurer, Bruno Palier, and Michael Pinggera

8.1. INTRODUCTION

Social investment policies pursue the joint goal of enhancing economic well-being as well as social inclusion both at the individual level and for society as a whole. Hence, while social investment is by no means merely an instrumental approach to enhance productivity, it indeed focuses on skills, capabilities, and human capital because these are key for citizens with regard to their social and economic well-being and mobility. Skills and capabilities have become ever more important in a context of changing capitalism toward the knowledge economy. At the core of these ongoing transformations is an increasing focus on human skills. Early visionaries (Becker, 1964/1993; Bell, 1973; Drucker, 1969, 1993) identified skills and knowledge as the key endowments of today's societies already in the 1960s and famously predicted the emergence of the "knowledge economy."

Knowledge economies can be defined as economies placing "a greater reliance on intellectual capabilities than on physical inputs or natural resources" (Powell & Snellman, 2004, p. 199). In this sense, Hall (2021) characterizes the post-1995 period as an "era of knowledge-based growth." Today, the importance of skills and skill formation systems is widely accepted to be part and parcel for countries'

Julian L. Garritzmann, Silja Häusermann, Thomas Kurer, Bruno Palier, and Michael Pinggera, *The Emergence of Knowledge Economies* In: *The World Politics of Social Investment (Volume I)*. Edited by: Julian L. Garritzmann, Silja Häusermann, and Bruno Palier, Oxford University Press. © Oxford University Press 2022. DOI: 10.1093/oso/9780197585245.003.0008 politico-economic systems (Hall & Soskice, 2001; Iversen, 2005; Iversen & Soskice, 2019; Thelen, 2004), economic growth (Glaeser et al., 2004; Hanushek & Woessmann, 2015; Organisation for Economic Co-operation and Development [OECD], 2008), as well as modernization and democratization more generally (Inglehart & Welzel, 2005; Lipset, 1959). On the micro-level, we witness rising educational returns (Lemieux, 2007), pointing at the ever-increasing labor market relevance of skills; and we know that education is also positively associated with social engagement and political participation (Mettler, 2002).

This chapter traces the emergence of features of the knowledge economy across different world regions and studies their implications for labor markets as well as for the politics of social investment. Up until the 19th century, education was a "luxury good," reserved for the offspring of the socioeconomic elites and the clergy. Since the (late) 19th century, however, we have witnessed a massive expansion of educational attainment, increasingly covering also lower societal strata. Expansion has spread from primary education (in the 19th century) via secondary education (in the 1950s–1990s) to tertiary education (since the 1980s) (Barro & Lee, 2013; Lee & Lee, 2016; Windolf, 1997), as we detail in Section 8.2. These developments are tightly intertwined with countries' structural-economic development as they have developed from agrarian societies to industrialized economies and—more recently—to post-industrial knowledge economies. Although the pace, degree, and content of these developments have differed starkly across regions, the trend toward more knowledge- and skill-based economies can be observed in all world regions.

The goal of this chapter is threefold. First, we descriptively map the massive educational expansion and increasing importance of education and skills in more than 100 countries around the globe (covering almost all countries that are analyzed in our two volumes), using time-series data going back to the 1870s. We also show that while countries on all continents exhibit this pattern, educational expansion has occurred at different points in time, to different degrees, and with different kinds of education so that important differences between world regions and between countries within world regions remain.

In the second part of the chapter we concentrate on those countries where the trend toward the knowledge economy has gone the furthest (i.e., the advanced capitalist democracies). For these countries we analyze the relationship between educational expansion—"supply" of skills—and changing labor markets (i.e., sectoral and occupational change)—"demand" for skills. In line with the massive educational expansion and the rise of the knowledge economy, we document a steady shift from jobs in sectors more reliant on physical input toward the service sector; moreover, we uncover a strong trend of occupational "upskilling": Cognitively demanding jobs, often requiring higher education, have grown in all countries. However, while economic modernization has created many high-skilled jobs, a similarly consistent trend is the decline in "medium-skilled" jobs and an increase in low-paid jobs. A considerable—and in some places growing—share of workers are employed in low-paid jobs, resulting in a widening spread between two kinds of service workers: the high-skilled, high-paid ones and the low-paid ones, employed in non-routine interpersonal services. The overall pattern might thus be best characterized as "polarized upgrading" (see Oesch & Rodriguez-Menes, 2010; Spitz-Oener, 2006).

In the final part of the chapter, we theorize and reflect on the likely implications of educational expansion and labor market change for societal and economic demand for social investment and how this demand affects the politics of social investment more generally. We argue that—and show how—the politics of social investment have to be understood against the background of these two interacting trends of educational expansion and labor market polarized upgrading. We identify four different trajectories of how "demand for" and "supply of" skills interact and theorize how these in turn affect the politics of social investment. We argue that these trajectories help explain why social investment is politicized *to different degrees* and *in different forms* in different contexts.

This chapter does not offer causal analyses of the relationship between education, labor markets, and the politics of social investment. Its purpose instead is to descriptively map the relationship between educational expansions and labor market changes and to reflect on the implications of these trends for the politics of social investment. Several subsequent chapters of our two volumes extend these arguments in different directions, by empirically investigating patterns of social investment support among particular occupational classes (e.g., Chapter 12 in this volume), employers (Chapter 9 in this volume), and trade unions (Chapters 10 and 11 in this volume) and by analyzing the interplay of structural changes and actual political processes in specific contexts (e.g., Chapter 4 for Southern Europe in Volume II [Garritzmann et al., 2022] or Chapter 15 for childcare policies in this volume). These chapters (as well as all chapters in Volume II [Garritzmann et al., 2022]) also show that while the macro-level trends identified here provide the crucial background against which the politics of social investment have to be understood, the relationship between structural change and policy reform is far from deterministic. As the theoretical framework of these volumes (see Chapter 2 in this volume) lays out, structural change matters, but there always remains space for political agency.

8.2. TRANSITION TOWARD KNOWLEDGE ECONOMIES: THE GLOBAL EDUCATIONAL REVOLUTION

8.2.1. Educational expansion worldwide

This section traces the massive educational expansion that has happened around the globe, using enrollment data for more than 100 countries over 140 years, enriched with qualitative evidence. We analyze this trend and demonstrate how the expansion of education has spread from primary education in the 19th century to secondary education in the mid-20th century and has more recently been continued in tertiary education. We use data on educational enrollment by Lee and Lee (2016). Figure 8.1 shows the evolution of enrollment in primary, secondary, and tertiary education. The enrollment ratios were calculated as the number of students enrolled in a certain education level divided by the size of the population at that age that could be enrolled at that level in a given country.

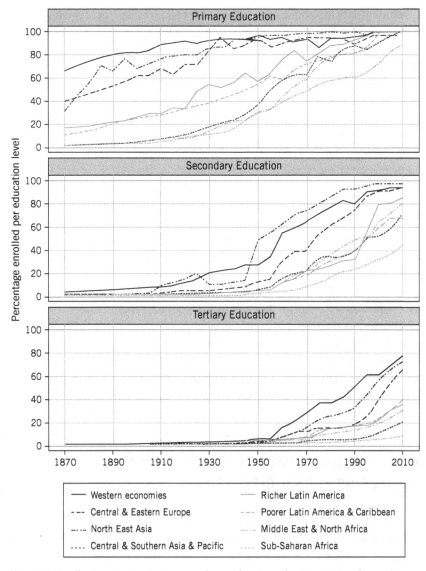

Figure 8.1 Enrollment rates in primary, secondary, and tertiary education (regional averages are weighted by country population size).

For a detailed discussion of the primary sources, the data quality, and meticulous process of dealing with comparability problems (such as different definitions of primary, secondary, and tertiary education), see Lee and Lee (2016).

We show developments for eight world regions from 1870 until 2010[1] (i.e., in all regions—and almost all countries—covered in our two volumes): 1) the "Western economies" (i.e., Western Europe and the English-speaking countries),[2] 2) Central and Eastern Europe,[3] 3) North East Asia,[4] 4) Central and Southern Asia and the Pacific,[5] 5) the comparatively richer Latin American countries (see Chapter 13 in this volume for a differentiation of the Latin American countries),[6] 6) the comparatively poorer Latin American and Caribbean countries,[7] 7) the Middle East and North Africa,[8] and 8) sub-Saharan Africa.[9] Figures 8.1 and 8.2 show average values of the countries in these groups, weighted by the countries' population size in order to acknowledge different country sizes.

Before we start interpreting the findings, we hasten to add a note of caution: While the grouping of countries in these eight groups is helpful for the purpose of this chapter, trying to group these 110 countries over 140 years is difficult and has to remain arbitrary to some degree. This is so because if we zoom in more closely, the development in each country is unique, and grouping them into larger categories will necessarily brush over variation within regions as well as within countries. First, while the countries in each of our eight groups share many similarities, they all have unique developments so that some countries at some points in time could even fit better into other categories as they are over- or underperforming their regional neighbors. Second, while we use countries as the unit of analysis here, we acknowledge that there is also (considerable) variation within countries. To mention an extreme example, in Spain nowadays the most common highest educational level is tertiary education in the northern and eastern regions but primary education in the southwest. Similar variation can be

1. The data by Lee and Lee (2016) goes even further back in time, to the 1820s. Yet, we lack data on population size before 1870, which we need as we weight the regional averages by population size. This chapter thus focuses on the post-1870 period, which is sufficient for our purpose.
2. Australia, Austria, Belgium, Canada, Denmark, Finland, France, Germany, Greece, Iceland, Ireland, Italy, Luxembourg, the Netherlands, New Zealand, Norway, Portugal, Spain, Sweden, Switzerland, the United Kingdom, the United States.
3. Albania, Bulgaria, Czech Republic, Hungary, Poland, Romania.
4. Hong Kong, Japan, Korea, Taiwan.
5. Afghanistan, Bangladesh, Cambodia, China, Fiji, India, Indonesia, Malaysia, Myanmar, Nepal, Pakistan, Philippines, Sri Lanka, Thailand.
6. Argentina, Brazil, Chile, Costa Rica, Mexico, Uruguay.
7. Barbados, Belize, Bolivia, Colombia, Cuba, Dominican Republic, Ecuador, El Salvador, Guatemala, Guyana, Haiti, Honduras, Jamaica, Nicaragua, Panama, Paraguay, Peru, Trinidad and Tobago.
8. Algeria, Cyprus, Egypt, Iran, Iraq, Jordan, Kuwait, Libya, Malta, Morocco, Syria, Tunisia, Yemen.
9. Benin, Cameroon, Congo D.R., Cote d'Ivoire, Gambia, Ghana, Kenya, Lesotho, Liberia, Malawi, Mali, Mauritius, Mozambique, Niger, Reunion, Senegal, Sierra Leone, South Africa, Sudan, Swaziland, Togo, Uganda, Zambia, Zimbabwe.

found in other contexts, for example, in the United States or in India. In sum, we acknowledge that no country grouping will be perfect. Yet, we want to get at some broader patterns rather than describing each specific context. Thus, some simplification is necessary, at the danger of oversimplifying. Here, we therefore identify eight groups that—while not being perfect—in our view tell us a lot about the different developments in different world regions. In later parts of this chapter as well as in subsequent chapters we acknowledge in more detail that considerable within-region differences exist, by zooming in on specific contexts. With this note of caution, we now turn to our results.

Figure 8.1 reveals three remarkable trends. First, enrollment rates have increased over time for all educational levels and in all world regions. We do not see a decline in educational attainments in any world region. Put differently, all countries develop in the direction of more knowledge-intensive societies. Second, the expansion of the three levels of schooling has happened (and for secondary and tertiary education is still happening) at different periods of time. While the expansion of primary education is mainly a story of the 19th and early 20th centuries in all countries, the expansion of secondary education started much later (the pace changed quickly around 1950). Tertiary education was expanded still 20 years later, beginning in the 1970s in most countries. Third, despite these common trends, we also observe ample differences between world regions: The "Western democracies" (Western Europe plus English-speaking countries) are the forerunners of educational expansion (especially in primary and tertiary education), but countries in North East Asia as well as in Central and Eastern Europe also moved comparatively early (especially for secondary education).

Focusing more specifically on *primary* education in the top panel of Figure 8.1, we see that the Western economies showed considerably high enrollment rates above 60% already in the mid-19th century, whereas in the other regions the share of each generation attending primary school was (much) lower: In Central and Eastern Europe and in North East Asia it was around 40% and in all other world regions below 20% at this time. Thereafter, primary education enrollment ratios started to converge as countries with lower enrollment rates also started expanding education massively. While the Western economies reached (quasi)universal enrollment already around 1910, Central and Eastern Europe as well as North East Asia also had high levels at this time and achieved quasi-universal enrollment around 1930. Expansion occurred more gradually in the other five regions: They all achieved quasi-universal enrollment in primary education around 1990, except for sub-Saharan Africa, where primary education enrollment rates only currently cover the entire population.

The second panel in the middle of Figure 8.1 shows enrollment ratios for *secondary* education,[10] which is particularly crucial for economic advancement and

---

10. Lee and Lee (2016, p. 149) state, "The classification of vocational and teacher training schools is often complicated . . . for the most part, they are classified as secondary schools, but some

social mobility in a context of industrialization (see Chapter 6 in this volume, which focuses on secondary education as a key political-distributive issue in low- and middle-income countries). Although the expansion of secondary education started some 100 years after the expansion of primary education, the trends and regional differences are comparable to those of primary education. The "Western economies" were again forerunners but were closely followed and then overpassed by North East Asia; they started expanding secondary education already before the outbreak of the First World War, while North East Asian countries surpassed them after World War II. In Central and Eastern Europe, the expansion of secondary education began in the 1930s and quickly picked up pace in the 1960s. The other Asian, Latin American, and North African countries showed similar trends but some 40 years later, as enrollment levels rose much quicker in the 1980s and 1990s. From a global perspective, change is slowest in sub-Saharan Africa, where—despite a clearly expansive trend—enrollment levels remained much lower until the present day (around 45% in 2010).

Panel three in Figure 8.1 shows the development of *tertiary* education. The data again reveals a similar pattern but with a lag of several decades. The Western economies heavily expanded tertiary education from around 10% in 1960 to slightly above 70% on average in 2010. The trend was a bit slower in North East Asia and Central and Eastern Europe but shows similarly high levels today. While we do not observe a (strong) upward trend for sub-Saharan Africa and Central and Southern Asia (yet?), tertiary education has also been expanded in Latin America and in the Middle East and North Africa, especially in the first decade of the 21st century. This data nicely illustrates the expansion of higher education, which is in turn the foundation for the rise of the knowledge economy in the Western economies, in North East Asia, and in Central and Eastern Europe.

In sum, Figure 8.1 demonstrates a massive global expansion of educational enrollment, which has spread subsequently from primary education to secondary education and—more recently—to tertiary education. Yet, important differences in educational enrollment remain across countries in different world regions. This can be seen even more clearly when rearranging the data to show the respective shares of the population with the highest educational degrees obtained: Figure 8.2 shows the development of educational *attainment* in the same eight world regions over 140 years. Educational attainment captures the highest level of education attained and is reported as a percentage of the working-age population (15–64). Looking at educational attainment offers a different perspective than in the previous sets of presented data since it illustrates the predominant types of skills available in a country at a certain period in time, which is important to

technical schools and teacher training colleges (which require the completion of secondary-level education) are classified as tertiary institutions." See Lee and Lee (2016) for details and our detailed discussion in this chapter based on qualitative literature.

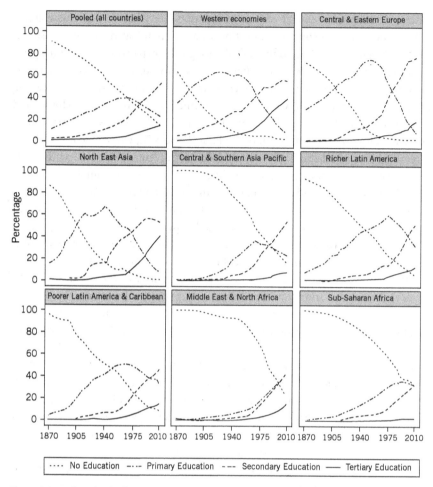

Figure 8.2 Highest level of educational attainment of the working-age population.

understand countries' stock of skills and thereby their human capital potential in the economy.

Figure 8.2 shows several interesting trends. First, the percentage of the working-age population that did *not* experience any schooling has monotonously declined in all regions. In the Western economies, in Central and Eastern Europe, and in North East Asia, basically everyone had experienced some schooling already in the mid-20th century. Latin America achieved similar levels several decades later. But in Central and Southern Asia and the Pacific as well as in the Middle East and North Africa and especially in sub-Saharan Africa, considerable parts of the working-age population still have not attained any educational degrees. Second, due to the expansion of secondary and tertiary education, the percentage of people whose highest degree is primary education is decreasing everywhere, which further underlines the trend toward knowledge economies.

Third, it is also interesting to see that in all regions people with secondary education still are the majority of the working-age population. That is, even in the most advanced capitalist economies, the majority of the working-age population holds a secondary education degree, which points to both the crucial importance of this educational stage for social mobility and the needs of the economy as well as to the potential for further educational upgrading. Finally, the trend toward knowledge economies becomes most explicit by analyzing the development of tertiary education. Especially in North East Asia and in the Western economies, we observe impressive numbers showing that by now on average around 40% of the population have attained tertiary education.

In sum, the figures in this section show that when we conceive of the interplay between schooling and skill creation systems, labor markets, and social policy, the dynamic "action" and interesting variation nowadays are in the areas of secondary and tertiary education, rather than in primary education. The figures also show that educational upskilling does not equal tertiarization: secondary and vocational education are still massively important for large numbers of citizens and countries' economies, and they are thus key in the matching between skills and labor markets.

8.2.2. Educational expansions in the advanced capitalist democracies

In the remainder of this chapter, we focus on those countries that have gone the furthest in transforming into knowledge economies, namely the advanced capitalist democracies in the Western economies, in North East Asia, and in Central and Eastern Europe, because these are the contexts in which educational expansion has gone the furthest and where the economies (can) rely the most on human capital rather than on physical capital or natural resources (see the definition in the introduction of this chapter). We start with a more differentiated look at the enrollment data, in order to offer a more fine-grained classification of countries into the country groups that we identify in our two volumes, focusing on seven "groups" of advanced economies: 1) Nordic Europe,[11] 2) Continental Europe,[12] 3) Southern Europe,[13] 4) the Visegrád countries,[14] 5) North America,[15] 6) English-speaking non-America,[16] and 7) North East Asia[17] (unfortunately, comparable data are not available for the Baltics, which would otherwise be the eighth group).

11. Denmark, Finland, Iceland, Norway, Sweden.
12. Austria, Belgium, France, Germany, Luxembourg, the Netherlands, Switzerland.
13. Italy, Greece, Spain, Portugal.
14. Czech Republic, Hungary, Poland.
15. United States and Canada.
16. Australia, Ireland, New Zealand, United Kingdom.
17. Hong Kong, Japan, Korea, Taiwan.

Figure 8.3 clearly shows that the countries in these seven groups today should be characterized as having developed a high level of education of their population, hence having the highest potential to be knowledge economies: Enrollment in primary education has been quasi-universal for more than 50 years now, and enrollment in secondary education reached high levels shortly after the Second World War. Today, large shares of the population also attend tertiary education, especially in North America and Nordic Europe but increasingly also in the

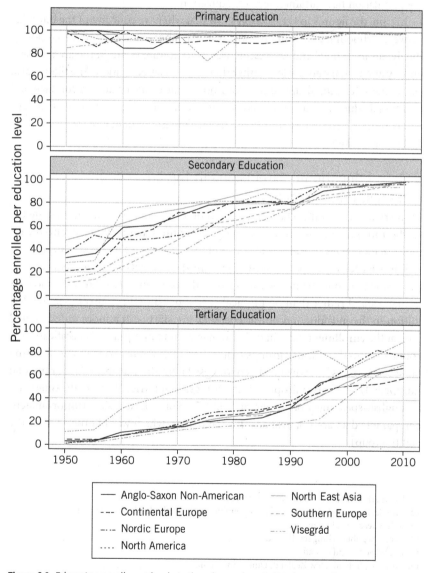

Figure 8.3 Education enrollment levels in the advanced capitalist democracies.

other regions. The pace here is somewhat slower though in Continental Europe (which traditionally has focused on vocational rather than academic training).

Despite these smaller differences in timing, we might conclude from Figure 8.3 that these countries' education systems have become similar by now. What the enrollment data cannot show, however, are important differences within the educational sectors (i.e., in the *kinds of education* that students attend). For reasons of space, we focus here on important differences in *tertiary* education as post-secondary education is increasingly becoming relevant in an age of post-industrialization and increasing focus on "high skills" in the knowledge economy (see Durazzi, 2018). A crucial distinction here is whether students attend *academic* or *vocational* tertiary education (Hall & Soskice, 2001). Moreover, it matters what kind of vocational education and training (VET) countries offer (i.e., whether it is more school- or more firm-based or a mixture of both) (Busemeyer & Trampusch, 2012; Thelen, 2004).

This distinction is important for two reasons. On the one hand, the type of tertiary education has massive socioeconomic consequences: While educational inequality is lower in more academically oriented systems, wage inequality is higher (Busemeyer, 2015). Moreover, youth unemployment is much lower in countries with strong dual apprenticeship systems (i.e., where VET takes place both in schools and in firms) than in countries with purely school-based vocational education (Blossfeld & Shavit, 1993; Breen, 2005). Also, the type of tertiary education is tightly connected to the types of capitalism as vocational systems are the crucial backbone of coordinated market economies, whereas liberal market economies (Hall & Soskice, 2001; Thelen, 2004) and hierarchical/dependent market economies (Bohle & Greskovits, 2012; Schneider, 2009) focus more on general academic (and low) skills. Besides these socioeconomic consequences, the vocational and academic orientations, on the other hand, also have important political implications as their match or mismatch with labor market demand affects the politics of social investment (as we discuss in the final section of this chapter).

Important here is that four groups exist: Some regions have focused almost entirely on academic higher education (the English-speaking rich countries and Southern Europe), whereas others rely on a mix of academic higher and school-based vocational education (France, Nordic Europe except Denmark). A third group combines academic higher education and strong VET systems ("dual apprenticeship systems" in the German-speaking Continental Europe, Denmark, the Netherlands) while in a fourth we find a mix of academic higher education and employer-dominated vocational training (North East Asia) (Busemeyer & Trampusch, 2012; Hall & Soskice, 2001; Thelen, 2004).

North America, particularly the United States, took the lead in the expansion of academic higher education. In the United States, this expansion can be traced back to the crucial impact of the G.I. Bill in the 1940s, which offered generous financial student aid to returning war veterans to attend higher education

(Skocpol, 1992). Such student aid was further expanded under all Democrat-led administrations, particularly under Lyndon B. Johnson (Strach, 2009). Due to these policies, the United States preceded the developments in other countries by almost 20 years and moved quickly toward academization, while putting little weight on vocational skills.

In most other countries, access to academic higher education was only widened in the 1960s and 1970s, often as a result of left-leaning governments, student protests, and increasing employer demands for educational expansion (Garritzmann, 2016). Outside the North American context, the *Nordic European countries* have expanded academic higher education the most and the quickest as governing coalitions led by social democrats have aimed at achieving equality of opportunities and socioeconomic equality, while stimulating economic growth (Garritzmann, 2016; and see Chapter 2 in Volume II [Garritzmann et al., 2022]). Vocational education in these countries is much less developed and takes the form of school-based training (with the exception of Denmark).

The *Continental European* and the *North East Asian countries*, in contrast, have been much slower at widening access to higher education. One main reason for this is that their more conservative governments held more conservative and critical views on education expansion (Garritzmann, 2016). But another important reason for the different pattern is the prevalence of strong VET programs in these countries, at both the secondary and the post-secondary levels (Nikolai & Ebner, 2012). Having well-functioning VET systems that are highly interwoven with their coordinated type of market economies (Hall & Soskice, 2001; Thelen, 2004), the Continental European countries were much more hesitant toward "academization" as their comparative advantage relied on strong vocational skills and there was lower economic demand for more academic skills. The same is largely true for North East Asia, although the enrollment levels in vocational education were somewhat lower and training took a more segmentalist form there (i.e., being dominated by strong employers and weak public and union engagement) (Estévez-Abe, 2008).

Like the English-speaking countries, the *Southern European countries* also placed much emphasis on academic education, while their vocational education and training systems have remained underdeveloped to this date. In contrast to their English-speaking counterparts, however, access to tertiary education in Southern Europe has been more constrained and less open. Moreover, graduates struggle to enter the well-protected labor market, leading to very high levels of youth unemployment and over-education, and/under-employment (Ansell & Gingrich, 2017).

In sum, while all of these more advanced economies have transformed massively toward knowledge economies in terms of enrollment, important country differences remain, particularly regarding the type of tertiary education. The implications of these differences for the societal and economic demand for particular skills and skill-creating policies can only be understood with reference to their production regime and type of capitalism (Hall & Soskice, 2001), their growth strategies (Hassel & Palier, 2020), and the interaction of the education and training system with the development of labor markets, which is what we focus on next.

8.3. "DEMAND FOR EDUCATION": LABOR MARKET CHANGES IN THE ADVANCED CAPITALIST DEMOCRACIES

The chapter so far has demonstrated that educational expansion is a global phenomenon but has gone the furthest in the advanced capitalist democracies in the Western economies, in Central and Eastern Europe, and in North East Asia.[18] Next, we zoom in on occupational labor market changes in these countries. The aim is to point out the crucial parallel developments of education and labor market changes because the distributive effects and hence the consequences for politics depend on the interplay of the production of skills (education) and the demand for skills (labor). Hence, we aim at exploring how the "supply of education" and "demand for education" interplay in the most advanced economies. We show the extent to which occupational profiles in the advanced capitalist democracies have changed with regard to sectoral composition, task structures, and gender.

8.3.1. Sectoral change: The rise of the service economy

The available sectoral OECD data does not allow us to go back in time as far as and for as many countries as the time series on educational enrollment presented in the previous Section 8.2. Figure 8.4 provides information on the changing composition of the economy since the 1960s in different parts of the world by offering an in-depth look at seven economies representative of the respective regions: Denmark (Nordic Europe), Germany (Continental Europe), Japan (North East Asia), Spain (Southern Europe), Estonia (Baltics), the Slovak Republic (Visegrád), the United Kingdom (Anglo-Saxon non-North American), and the United States (North America). The figure displays striking similarities regarding the broad pattern but also some noteworthy differences in the level and timing of change.

The first sector, agriculture, has reduced to a few percent of the labor force in all Western capitalist democracies: In Germany and the United States, this

18. Interesting related work has argued that, and analyzed why, the advanced capitalist democracies, including Japan and Korea, are special and other countries struggle to catch up with this group, pointing at what has been termed the "middle-income trap" (Eichengreen et al., 2012; Iversen & Soskice, 2019; Kharas & Kohli, 2011).

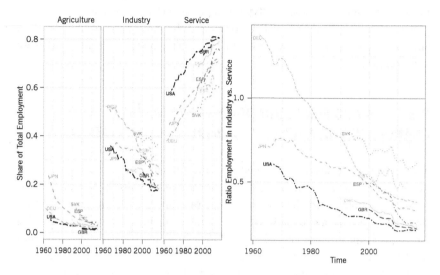

Figure 8.4 Employment in agriculture, industry, and services over time.
Source. OECD Employment Outlook—employment by economic activity.

development took place before the 1960s, when agricultural workers were drawn
to the industrial companies in urban areas. In Japan, the share of the agricultural
sector was still above 20% in the beginning of our period of observation but has
decreased to numbers comparable to those of the two other countries displayed
since then. In Southern and Eastern Europe, this trend was somewhat slower but
has converged to similar levels nowadays.

Moreover, as is well known, contemporary advanced capitalist democracies
have become to an overwhelming extent service economies (Wren, 2013). The
share of the labor force in the service sector nowadays exceeds 50% in all the
selected countries and even exceeds 70% in several countries. Today's service
sector dominance reflects both a massive and rapid expansion of service jobs
since the middle of the 20th century and a consistent shrinking of the industrial sector, which nowadays represents in most countries less than a third of all
workers.

This trend started earlier and has gone the furthest (more than 80% of
employees work in services) in North America and the other English-speaking
"liberal market economies" (in the Varieties of Capitalism typology). But even
in industry-reliant "coordinated market economies" such as Germany, industrial jobs have undergone massive decline—even if on a somewhat lower level.
While in Germany industrial workers clearly outnumbered service workers in
the 1960s, we nowadays find more than two service workers for each industrial
worker in the German labor force. The same is true for Japan, which shows a
similar trend to Germany but started deindustrializing even earlier. The rise of
service jobs is somewhat less pronounced in the Visegrád countries (represented

in Figure 8.4 by the Slovak Republic), where we observe a more resilient industry sector, whereas it is quicker in the Baltics (represented by Estonia in Figure 8.4). This corresponds to the Visegrád countries' focus on "complex industrial manufacturing" and the Baltics' turn toward information and communication technologies (ICTs) and services (Bohle & Greskovits, 2012; see Chapters 8 and 9 in Volume II [Garritzmann et al., 2022]).[19] Spain showed an equally quick shift toward the service economy, at least since the 1990s—but might be less representative for the group of Southern European countries overall in this respect (cf. the composition of occupational tasks in Figure 8.5 as well as Chapter 4 in Volume II [Garritzmann et al., 2022]).

In sum, Figure 8.4 impressively demonstrates the turn away from work relying on physical inputs or natural resources toward service occupations, a large share of which require more intellectual and communication capabilities than industrial production (i.e., the emergence of the knowledge economy). At the same time, we witness differences in the extent and timing of these changes, even within the group of the advanced capitalist democracies.

8.3.2. The cognitive turn: Task-biased occupational change

Besides looking at the size of economic sectors, labor market changes can also be assessed through an occupational lens. Studying occupational change in addition to sectoral composition allows one to evaluate the demand for more or less cognitively skilled human capital. The most important force behind the profound transformation of the employment structure in past decades has been technological change (Autor et al., 2003; Goos et al., 2014; Manning, 2003; Oesch, 2013). The fact that new technology is a core driver of this gradual, long-term development has important implications on how we study occupational change. In their seminal contribution, Autor et al. (2003) emphasize the very particular way in which the increasing presence of robots, computers, and smart software at the workplace altered skill demand. Rather than replacing workers in a "linear" fashion (i.e., "lowest skills first and highest skills last"), technology is particularly powerful in replacing so-called routine tasks. Examples can be found in blue-collar jobs (e.g., machine operators and assemblers) but also in white-collar jobs—think of mid-skilled office clerks or accountants. Such routine tasks might be complex and demanding, perhaps even requiring considerable formal education or training; but they are essentially repetitive and follow clearly defined rules. This latter aspect makes routine jobs susceptible to automation since such tasks, however complex, are codifiable. Autor et al.'s (2003) important contribution has

19. In contrast to the Visegrád group, the Baltics have moved much more in the direction of high skill- and ICT-focused service economies, showing quicker deindustrialization (Bohle & Greskovits, 2012; data not shown here).

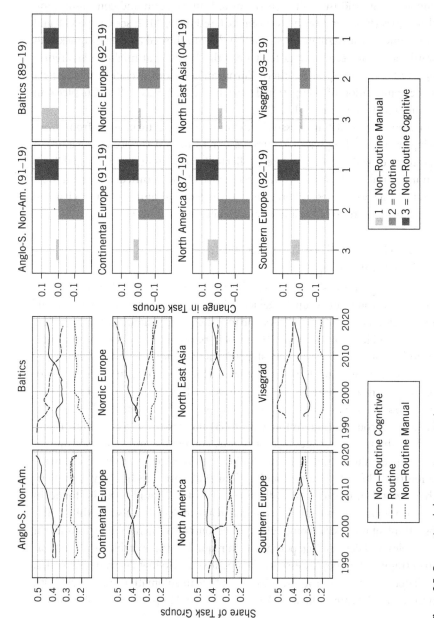

Figure 8.5 Occupational change across countries.

Source. ILO modeled estimates, November 2019 (Employment by sex and occupation, ILO modelled estimates, November 2019 [thousands], annual).

thus led to a shift from a pure focus on a jobs' *skill* content toward an increasing focus on jobs' *task* content. The fact that *routineness* matters in addition to the skill requirements of a job is consequential with respect to which changes in the aggregate employment pattern we would expect.

The most important implication of these developments for our study is the following: Since non-routine jobs can be found in both non-routine manual and interpersonal service work as well as in high-skilled (e.g., managers) occupations, while routine jobs are mainly performed by mid-skilled employees, labor markets might polarize rather than upgrade. That is, while we see an increasing and continuous rise in the level of skills in a country (i.e., the "supply" of skills, as demonstrated in the first part of this chapter), we might not find the same parallel trend of continuous upgrading also in the labor market (i.e., the "demand" for skills). Rather, we might see a pattern of employment polarization.

To investigate this empirically, we show the development of the relative share of routine jobs compared to both high-skilled and manual and interpersonal non-routine jobs in the left panel of Figure 8.5. We use data from the International Labour Organization (ILO) for 27 advanced capitalist democracies, which we aggregate into the same world regions as in the previous section.[20] Regional averages are weighted by the size of the countries' respective labor force. The time period for which data is available varies slightly from country to country, but we can cover most of them since at least the early 1990s.

A first remarkable trend is the consistent growth in non-routine cognitive jobs (solid line on the left side of Figure 8.5) in every region displayed. First, in line with all the evidence provided so far in this chapter, advanced capitalist democracies are characterized by a massive shift toward high-skilled jobs during the past decades. In this sense, we see the emergence of the knowledge economy. Second, there is another similarly consistent trend: the decline in mid-skilled routine jobs. When looking at relative changes from the first to the last observations plotted in the right panel of Figure 8.5 (due to data availability, the time period to calculate this change varies slightly), we see that the magnitude of the decline in routine jobs is on average even larger than the increase in non-routine cognitive jobs. Third, with respect to the development on the lower end of the skill spectrum, the evidence is more mixed. While we observe some growth in manual and interpersonal non-routine jobs in a majority of the countries, changes in non-routine manual work are smaller and less consistent. Taken together, the term that might best describe the predominant pattern of occupational change is

20. The country grouping remains the same, but data was missing for a few countries. The following are included: Nordic Europe = Denmark, Finland, Norway, Sweden; Continental Europe = Austria, Belgium, Switzerland, Germany, France, the Netherlands; Southern Europe = Greece, Italy, Spain; Baltics = Estonia, Latvia, Lithuania; Visegrád = Czech Republic, Hungary, Poland, Slovakia, Slovenia; North America = United States, Canada; Anglo-Saxon non-American = Australia, Great Britain, New Zealand; North East Asia = Korea (occupation-specific data from Japan is not available in the same quality, but Japan is added to this region for Figure 8.6 on female employment).

"polarized upgrading" (Oesch & Rodriguez-Menes, 2010; Spitz-Oener, 2006; but see Oesch & Piccitto, 2019): strong job growth at the top of the skill distribution, a consistent decline in the middle, and more or less limited growth in manual and interpersonal non-routine jobs.

Figure 8.5 also shows that the historical evolution of the employment structure differs between regions, at least partly because domestic institutions, legacies, and policies moderate the impact of structural developments and produce variance in the exact shape of the pattern and the magnitude of changes (Fernandez-Macias, 2012; Peugny, 2019). Figure 8.5's left panel reveals quite pronounced differences in the *levels* of employment shares: While labor markets in Central, Eastern, Southern, and, to a lesser degree, Continental Europe were still dominated by routine work in the 1990s, the Nordic European and English-speaking countries had already largely transformed to knowledge economies with large shares of high-skilled non-routine cognitive work.

Looking at *changes* in employment shares (right panel of Figure 8.5), it appears that Nordic European, North East Asian, and the Visegrád countries underwent more clear-cut upgrading with very limited or even absent growth in non-routine manual and interpersonal service sector jobs. In line with existing work (e.g., Goos et al., 2014), polarization is more pronounced in the liberal Anglo-Saxon labor markets—but a similar trend of a growing non-routine manual and interpersonal service sector can be witnessed in Continental and Southern Europe (Emmenegger et al., 2012; Palier & Thelen, 2010). Despite their focus on knowledge-extensive ICT sectors (Bohle & Greskovits, 2012; see Chapters 8 and 9 in Volume II [Garritzmann et al., 2022]), the Baltics have seen a particularly strong increase in non-routine manual and interpersonal work, which, however, started from very low levels, as is visible in the panel on the left-hand side.

In sum, the occupational perspective adds important shades to the narrative of general up-skilling and educational expansion. The main trend certainly is a strong push to an ever-larger number of highly educated workers in cognitively demanding jobs. That is, the "demand" for highly skilled and educated workers in the labor market increases. At the same time, job prospects for workers without college degrees are increasingly bleak: Mid-skilled routine jobs are slowly going extinct, which only leaves the option of non-routine manual and interpersonal, low-paid service sector jobs. Educational expansion and occupational up-skilling are thus not equivalent to linear upward mobility and the experience of "collective ascent" many western European countries had in the decades after World War II (Mau, 2015). Yet, the data reveals systematic country differences in these developments.

8.3.3. Gender: Feminization of the workforce

The final aspect of large-scale labor market changes we want to illustrate here relates to female employment rates. These are—of course—to a large extent endogenous to educational expansion, occupational change, as well as social transformations. However, the extraordinary and rapid increase in female labor market participation (Figure 8.6), in particular in Continental European and English-speaking countries over only a few decades (while it had been higher in the Nordic countries much earlier and has until this day remained at lower levels in Southern Europe and the Visegrád countries), is important to understand the link between the structural trends emphasized in this chapter and the politics of social investment.

When both men and women are active in the workforce, this naturally changes the entire purpose and focus of social policy, not only regarding social investment and new social risks (Armingeon & Bonoli, 2006; Bonoli, 2007) but also the role of the family in the provision of welfare overall (Leitner, 2003) and the importance of education for both girls and boys. Female employment rates reflect the massive and broad implications of economic, social, and cultural change for social policy overall. It follows that many social investment policies (from childcare provision to continuous training to active aging and the provision of good, well-insured, typical employment) are heavily gendered in their target population and distributive effects. It thus emphasizes the importance of the "mobilization of human capital" function within social investment strategies to guarantee women's access to the labor market. Figure 8.6 plots the share of female employment in the eight groups of advanced capitalist democracies. While we do witness a common trend toward high female labor force participation, there are important differences between countries: Nordic Europe clearly leads

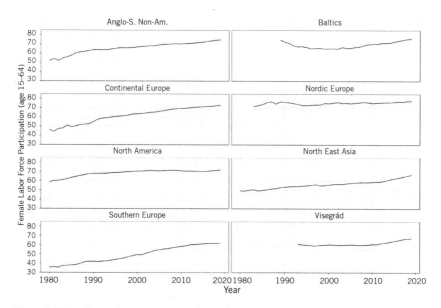

Figure 8.6 Female employment rates in advanced capitalist democracies.
Source. ILO.

the field, showing female employment rates around 70% already since the 1980s. Yet, we witness similarly high levels in the Baltics (see Chapters 8 and 9 in Volume II [Garritzmann et al., 2022]). Between 1980 and 2010, the English-speaking and the Continental European countries have continuously caught up in this development, also showing high female employment rates by now. North East Asia also witnesses a steady increase, especially during the most recent period (see Chapters 12 and 13 in Volume II [Garritzmann et al., 2022]). The Visegrád countries, and especially Southern Europe, show considerably lower levels (potential reasons are discussed in Chapters 4 and 8 in Volume II [Garritzmann et al., 2022]).

8.4. HOW EDUCATIONAL EXPANSION ("SUPPLY OF SKILLS") AND LABOR MARKET CHANGE ("DEMAND FOR SKILLS") AFFECT DEMAND FOR SOCIAL INVESTMENT

In this final section we reflect on and discuss the implications of the educational expansion and the identified labor market changes for the kind of political demand for social investment we would expect. More specifically, we hypothesize how changing educational attainment as well as changes in the size of economic sectors and occupational patterns shape the politics of social investment by providing a particular "functional" context within which business and voters may or may not request skill formation policies.

Hence, let us start by briefly sketching out how we think the demand for social investment by business and voters relates to this context. The most obvious link between a change toward the knowledge economy, occupational change, and the demand side of social investment policies runs through the incentives for *employers* in the economically growing sectors to support the creation, preservation, and mobilization of human capital. Employers in the knowledge economies require a higher skilled workforce. This implies not only specific support for particular educational profiles but also a demand for measures increasing female employment rates (in particular through childcare provisions), especially for high-skilled women. This is not to say that we should expect business to wholeheartedly support an encompassing social investment agenda as it may contest both the universal design and the quality of service provision (see Chapter 15 in this volume). But it does imply that where the most productive sectors are knowledge-intensive and where there is a scarcity of skilled labor supply, business can sustain the political demand for social investment to achieve such a workforce (which is shown comparatively in Chapter 9 in this volume).

At the level of *popular demand* (i.e., social groups demanding social investment reforms), the structural trends we have sketched obviously create a functional need for social investment since the prospects for employment, social inclusion, and mobility increasingly depend on human capital formation. However, there is, of course, no direct link between a functionalist need and a political and politicized demand for social investment, in particular if we consider that structural change also creates losers. In political terms, the expanded (and strongly feminized) new middle class of middle- and high-skilled employees in non-routine, cognitive and interpersonal service occupations entails the strongest demand for social investment policies (see Chapter 12 in this volume; Garritzmann et al., 2018; Häusermann & Palier, 2017). The high-skilled middle class' labor market prospects depend on education and on the possibility to work (in terms of both available good jobs and childcare and elderly care provision). In addition, they might support good-quality public education of their children (if private provision is not affordable or available to all). Therefore, there is a point in suggesting that—in a self-reinforcing way—the expansion of higher education and of the service economy creates its own support base for social investment policies (just as power resource theorists argued for the expansion of compensatory social policies [e.g., Huber & Stephens, 2001]).

However, the link between educational expansion and occupational polarized upgrading is not as trivial as it may seem as these two developments are not necessarily aligned.[21] Rather, it is only when the economic production structure (i.e., the labor market) matches the education regime that human capital formation actually results in wage premiums, labor productivity, and in—overall—good life prospects for large segments of society. Hence, we need to theorize the interaction between labor market change and the educational expansion in a way that allows for both equilibria and mismatches.

8.4.1. Combining demand and supply of skills

Theorizing the interaction of the education profile in a country (i.e., the "supply of skills") and the skill orientation of its labor market (i.e., "demand for skills") is likely to be fruitful in order to understand not only the strength and scope of the support coalition but also the functions of social investment that are likely to be supported (skill creation, skill mobilization, and skill preservation). Table 8.1 presents a stylized, theoretical 2×2 table of how structural change might relate to the politics of social investment. We combine the educational expansion (i.e., the "supply of skills") with the labor market's "economic demand for skills" to theorize on how different combinations might affect the politics of social investment.

In Figure 8.7 we provide some cross-sectional empirical evidence for the empirical distribution of advanced capitalist democracies across the two dimensions.

---

21. For a different, but interesting, related perspective, see Durazzi (2018). Durazzi analyzes why higher education systems differ across contexts and why higher education institutions have been active in different ways in higher education reforms, arguing that their makeup and role depend on the type of knowledge economy (whether based on advanced manufacturing or ICT and services) as well as on the degree of competition within the higher education sector.

Table 8.1 Theorizing on how different combinations of demand for and supply of high-skill labor might lead to different kinds of politicization of social investment.

		Demand for high-skilled labor	
		Weak	Strong
Supply of high-skilled labor	Strong	II Over-education/ Under-employment → *Skill mobilization and preservation are politicized, probably in a stratified way*	I Knowledge economy → *Sustainability of (inclusive) social investment of all functions (skill creation, mobilization, preservation) is politicized*
	Weak	IV Non-knowledge economy → *Social investment not politicized (if not for elite top-down action, then probably in a targeted way)*	III Skilled-labor scarcity → *Skill creation and skill mobilization are politicized, probably in a stratified way*

As one measure of supply of high skills, we plot the tertiary enrollment ratio on the y-axis; the x-axis shows the share of non-routine cognitive jobs as a measure of demand for skills. The data is the same as discussed so far in this chapter.[22] As in the previous section, we focus on the most advanced countries in terms of their educational enrollment. Were we to include more (diverse) countries, we would expect the variation to be even broader. In the following, we discuss our theoretical expectations for and the empirical cases in each of the four scenarios.

To be sure, once again, we do not claim that a functionalist perspective on the demand for and supply of skills alone can explain the respective policies that countries adopt. As theorized in Chapter 2 of this volume, we expect political actors to play an important role in this process. Nonetheless, focusing on demand for and supply of skills is interesting and revealing because it teaches us about the different contexts and the different socioeconomic conditions that political actors face and how these (might) affect the politicization of social investment. We theorize in the following how these socioeconomic factors can affect the politics of social investment. The subsequent chapters in this volume focusing on political actors (as well as all chapters in Volume II [Garritzmann et al., 2022]) then analyze the positions and strategies that political actors choose in these different contexts.

First, if a country produces a high-skilled workforce as well as the respective demand for it (i.e., "Scenario I" in the top right corner of Table 8.1), we can characterize the context as one of a "knowledge economy" in the purest sense. We could expect that the Nordic European countries may come closest to this pattern, which indeed is supported by Figure 8.7 as we find Finland, Denmark, Sweden, and Norway in this quadrant (we also find the United States and Australia here).

---

22. As enrollment data was missing for some of the Baltic countries, we added information using data provided by the World Bank.

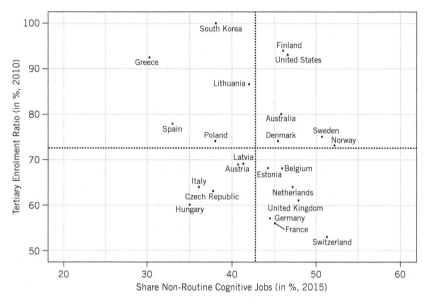

Figure 8.7 Scatterplot of demand and supply of high-skill labor. (Note: The dotted lines show average values for both dimensions.)
Source. ILO, World Bank.

In such a context, both the social partners (employers and unions) as well as the general public should be in favor of expansive social investment policies, to maintain the high-supply—high-demand equilibrium. Employers and unions should favor social investment to be equipped with a skilled workforce to maintain the skill-focused economy. Likewise, a large share of the general public (i.e., the large, educated middle class) should support strong social investment for both themselves and their children. Such a context should stabilize the demand and support for social investment. Regarding the type of social investment policy, we could expect that there is demand for (maintenance and further improvement of) social investment policies of all functions (skill creation, skill preservation, skill mobilization) and that inclusive social investment policies are demanded. Discussion in these countries could center around the question of how encompassing the social investment policies should be (i.e., whether they should be inclusive or rather stratified; see this book's typology in Chapter 1 in this volume and Chapter 2 in Volume II [Garritzmann et al., 2022] for an analysis of Scandinavia along these lines). Moreover, the economic and political sustainability of the model could be a topic of political discourse as maintaining an inclusive social investment state in many policy areas also comes at a price (e.g., high taxation or high public debt).

Empirically, as Figure 8.7 shows, besides Nordic Europe, also the United States and Australia fall into this box as they are characterized by high-skilled workforces and skill-intensive labor markets. Interestingly, as shown in Chapter 6 in Volume II (Garritzmann et al., 2022), unlike in Scandinavia, this

274 JULIAN L. GARRITZMANN ET AL.

nonetheless does not translate into high demand for public social investments in these English-speaking countries, arguably because of preexisting private human capital investments, which stabilize the private-heavy policy path via self-reinforcing feedback effects (Garritzmann, 2016). This underlines, once again, that a functionalistic perspective alone cannot explain the variation. Also, job polarization is most developed in these countries, which sets some limits on the extent to which people can expect to obtain a good job out of (some) education, thus refraining from any demand for inclusive social investment. Finally, the Baltics also have recently moved in the direction of the high-supply, high-demand scenario. While none of them fall into the top right quadrant in Figure 8.7 (yet), Lithuania scores at the edge of the quadrant and Latvia and Estonia locate in the middle of the figure (see Chapters 7 and 9 in Volume II [Garritzmann et al., 2022] for details). What this shows then, is that the combination of high-supply and high-demand of high skills leads to demand for further skill investments—yet, whether this functional pressure transforms into policy and what form these social investments take (public or private and inclusive, stratified, or targeted) cannot be explained by a functionalistic perspective alone as it depends on the interaction of the legacies and reform coalitions, as argued in Chapter 2 in this volume.

Second, in countries where higher education has been expanded but the labor market does not produce enough demand for the skilled workforce ("Scenario II" in the top left corner of Table 8.1), we find a pattern of over-education and under-employment, especially among young people. Ansell and Gingrich (2017) demonstrate this configuration most tellingly for Southern Europe (see also Kazepov & Ranci, 2016): While the effect of holding a tertiary degree on wages and job quality (the "education premium") has increased in almost all Western economies over the past 20 years, it has stagnated or even declined in Southern Europe (see also Weisstanner & Armingeon, 2020). The results are not only high rates of youth unemployment and emigration ("brain drain") but also declining political trust and increasing dissatisfaction. Besides Southern Europe, we could expect that a similar situation applies—if at lower levels—for the Visegrád countries, which have witnessed some educational expansion but not similar expansions in the labor market as they remained highly dependent on routine jobs in complex industrial manufacturing.

Figure 8.7 shows that the pattern is the clearest for Southern Europe: Greece and Spain clearly fit our expectation, but Italy shows lower skill-supply levels. Moreover, we find Korea in this box, with high tertiary enrollment levels but below-average (in this group) labor market usage of these skills.[23] This fits interpretations of Korea increasingly facing problems of over-education (Fleckenstein & Lee,

---

23. The primary data shows values of 100% enrollment for Korea. Given other reports (e.g., Fleckenstein & Lee, 2018; OECD, 2009), this seems over-estimated, but not by much, as Korea by now has one of the highest—if not the highest—tertiary enrollment rates.

2018). The Visegrád countries do not cluster clearly in one box as Poland shows high supply but low demand, while Hungary and the Czech Republic show lower skill-supply levels. This underlines once again that a pure functionalistic story is not enough to understand the complex empirical reality and points at the relevance of domestic politics in shaping demand and supply (see the respective country chapters for detailed analyses). The high-supply, low-demand scenario thus teaches us that in these contexts there might be less demand for additional social investments (especially skill creation policies) but rather pressure on easing school-to-work transitions (e.g., with skill mobilization and skill preservation policies) and on matching the labor market to the available skills.

Theorizing on the implications of this situation, we should expect lower economic and popular demand for additional social investment in general. Both economic actors (employers and unions) as well as the general public could, however, perceive the main socioeconomic problem not as one of skill-supply (i.e., that there is "too much" education) but as relating to the labor market and employment policy (i.e. that there are too few "good jobs"). Social investment might thus be less politicized and discussion more focused on (the quality of) jobs and macroeconomic performance (e.g., [un-]employment and inequality). Moreover, the educated middle class—a core support group of social investment—is simply much smaller in Southern Europe (see Chapter 12 in this volume) and is not ready to expand access to higher education when it sees its children's difficulties with finding a job fitting their expectation and adequate to their level of education. If social investment policies are politicized, focus should be particularly on skill mobilization and skill preservation policies, rather than on skill creation policies as the main (perceived) challenge is less about the skill supply than about putting skills to use. Moreover, it is likely that the demand does not ask for inclusive social investment policies but rather stratified (or maybe targeted) ones because it applies to a certain stratum of society.

Third, the mirror image to this configuration is a context where the economy demands a high-skilled workforce, but the educational system under-produces the supply of tertiary education ("Scenario III" in the bottom right corner of Table 8.1), either through shortages in education or because the country has been long focusing on specific skills for manufacturing industry or because women are de facto forced to (partially) retreat from the labor market when they have children.

Empirically, this is confirmed in Figure 8.7 as we especially find Continental European conservative welfare states in this quadrant, Switzerland being the most extreme example. Moreover, we also find the United Kingdom here. In these contexts, both educational expansion and (full-time) female labor force participation remain lower, whereas the demand for cognitive non-routine work is very high. To solve this mismatch, policymakers can turn to (skilled) migration, the integration of (skilled) women, or—at least in the long-term—technology (e.g., robotics). They may be confronted with a relatively small, reluctant educated middle class that may prefer to maintain high wages (because of scarce supply) and oppose the universalization of social investment that would mean more competition for their jobs and risk of lower wages and higher un-employment (hence stratified social investment to restrain the policies for the educated middle class). Given that technological solutions seem rather futur-istic and given a rather strong conservative attitude toward migration in many of these countries, the most likely reaction might be a reluctant and gradual opening toward the labor market integration of women (and some immigration but potentially on a limited temporal basis). In terms of social investment, eco-nomic and popular demand might thus politicize and push for (skill mobilizing) social investment policies that facilitate women's labor market (re-)entry (e.g., through training and family policies), as well as for skill creation social invest-ment policies. The societal demand for social investment can be potentially high but may be hindered by social conservatism and protectionism of the established positions. Social investment policies are thus unlikely to take an inclusive form and will rather be stratified.

Finally, many countries fall into Scenario IV (i.e., low economic demand for skills and low supply of skills). As we focus on the more advanced economies here, Figure 8.7 largely underestimates the number of countries in this box—in fact, we would expect most less advanced economies to show in this scenario. The less advanced Latin American countries (see the classification in Chapter 13 in this volume), many sub-Saharan African countries, and many Central and Southern Asian countries can be characterized as showing this combination most clearly. In this scenario, we would expect skill creation policies to have a rather different function (i.e., less directly labor market–related but more closely linked to pov-erty alleviation and social inclusion; see Chapter 5 in this volume). The condi-tional cash transfer policies that have been implemented in most Latin American countries can be understood in this direction (for details, see Chapter 14 in this volume as well as Chapters 14–16 in Volume II [Garritzmann et al., 2022]). A medium- to long-term strategy of policymakers might, moreover, be to aim to attract businesses (or foreign direct investment) by increasing the country's stock of human capital by investing in skill creation policies. Whether this road is chosen, however, is a political question and depends on political coalitions, as well as the country's economic situation ("factor endowments") and state ca-pacity (see Chapter 7 in this volume).

8.4.2. Demand "against"? Who opposes social investment?

So far, we have focused on *demand* for and the potential coalitions *supporting* social investment. Yet, it is equally important to think about potential *opposition* to such expansion. While this chapter has focused on identifying the drivers of economic and societal demand for social investment, it is important to under-stand the flipside of structural change, which also feeds back into the politics of social investment: While educational and occupational upgrading have sustained the demand for social investment, they have also created two other important groups. On the one hand, there are losers of structural change (especially the routine, often medium-skilled manual workers, especially in industrial manufacturing). The increasingly redundant "old" working class obviously belongs to the main beneficiaries of compensatory social policies, which historically were built around their needs (Esping-Andersen, 1990; Huber & Stephens, 2001). The most likely scenario for this group is to stick to the status quo and defend existing compensation policies, particularly when challenged by the rise of the knowledge economy, and even to oppose social investments (Garritzmann et al., 2018) (i.e., to become social investment antagonists). Considering the respective size of this potentially powerful electoral group will help to explain the social investment–social compensation mix that countries' policymakers choose. Hence, social investment should be much less controversial in contexts where deindustrialization has started earlier (e.g., in Nordic Europe and the Baltics) or where its aim at supporting an increase in labor force participation is crucial in the context of aging (as in North East Asia), while it should be more controversial where it occurred late and rapidly (e.g., in Continental Europe) or only slowly sets in (e.g., the Visegrád countries). On the other hand, the structural transformation has also led to an expansion of employment among non-routine interpersonal (service sector) workers. Their political stance (toward social investment) is not evident: They are least likely to participate politically overall (Marx & Nguyen, 2018). But even if they do, they have an equally strong interest in compensating social policy as in (targeted or universal) social investment and thus might demand both—or focus on compensation first as they might prioritize a "safety net" over social investments.

8.5. CONCLUSION

This chapter discussed the relationship of two "mega-trends" (educational expansion and labor market changes) and their implications for the politics of social investment. We first identified a massive educational expansion in (almost) all countries across the globe but also pointed at considerable regional and temporal variation across world regions. In the second part, we analyzed labor market changes regarding their skill orientation and identified a pattern of "polarized upgrading" as more people find work in both high-skilled and manual and interpersonal non-routine jobs but as medium-skilled jobs have vanished. In the final part we theorized on the implications of these two crucial developments for the politics of social investment. We argued that different patterns of skill demand and skill supply lead to four different contexts or trajectories of politicization of social investment. These contexts are crucial for understanding the politics of social investment in the respective countries.

We do not claim that welfare state *reforms* can be explained by these functional pressures alone since domestic political and socioeconomic actors and their interaction with welfare legacies play a major role in shaping the respective welfare state reforms (see Chapters 1 and 2 in this volume). But the four trajectories that we identified help explain why social investment is politicized *to different degrees* and *in different forms* in different contexts. Several of the subsequent chapters in this volume, as well as the geographically structured chapters in Volume II (Garritzmann et al., 2022), will build upon these insights to explain the politicization and specific welfare state reforms in these contexts. The finding that, despite witnessing similar broad socioeconomic transformations ("the emergence of the knowledge economy"), there are important differences in the country-specific trajectories highlights why it is important to study the interaction of legacies and reform coalitions. Domestic factors can and do influence how structural socioeconomic factors affect politics (as argued in Chapter 2 in this volume)—and how this in turn affects outcomes such as inequality (see also Hope & Martelli, 2019), growth, and social inclusion.

REFERENCES

Ansell, B. W., & Gingrich, J. (2017). Mismatch: University education and labor market institutions. *PS: Political Science and Politics, 50*(2), 423–425.

Armingeon, K., & Bonoli, G. (2006). *The politics of post-industrial welfare states: Adapting post-war social policies to new social risks.* Routledge.

Autor, D., Levy, F., & Murnane, R. J. (2003). The skill content of recent technological change: An empirical exploration. *The Quarterly Journal of Economics, 118*(4), 1279–1333.

Barro, R. J., & Lee, J. W. (2013). A new data set of educational attainment in the world, 1950–2010. *Journal of Development Economics, 104*, 184–198.

Becker, G. S. (1993). *Human capital: A theoretical and empirical analysis with special reference to education* (3rd ed.). University of Chicago Press. (Original work published 1964)

Bell, D. (1973). *The coming of post-industrial society: A venture in social forecasting.* Basic Books.

Blossfeld, H. P., & Shavit, Y. (1993). *Persistent inequality: Changing educational attainment in thirteen countries.* Westview Press.

Bohle, D., & Greskovits, B. (2012). *Capitalist diversity on Europe's periphery.* Cornell University Press.

Bonoli, G. (2007). Time matters: Postindustrialization, new social risks, and welfare state adaption in advanced industrial democracies. *Comparative Political Studies, 40*(5), 495–520.

Breen, R. (2005). Explaining cross-national variation in youth unemployment: Market and institutional factors. *European Sociological Review, 21*(2), 125–134.

Busemeyer, M. R. (2015). *Skills and inequality: Partisan politics and the political economy of education reforms in western welfare states*. Cambridge University Press.

Busemeyer, M. R., & Trampusch, C. (2012). *The political economy of collective skill formation*. Oxford University Press.

Drucker, P. F. (1969). *The age of discontinuity: Guidelines to our changing society*. Harper and Row.

Drucker, P. F. (1993). *Post-capitalist society*. Butterworth-Heinemann.

Durazzi, N. (2018). The political economy of high skills: Higher education in knowledge-based labour markets. *Journal of European Public Policy, 26*(12), 1799–1817.

Eichengreen, B., Park, D., & Shin, K. (2012). When fast-growing economies slow down: International evidence and implications for China. *Asian Economic Papers, 11*(1), 42–87.

Emmenegger, P., Häusermann, S., Palier, B., & Seeleib-Kaiser, M. (2012). *The age of dualization: The changing face of inequality in deindustrializing societies*. Oxford University Press.

Esping-Andersen, G. (1990). *The three worlds of welfare capitalism*. Polity Press.

Estévez-Abe, M. (2008). *Welfare and capitalism in postwar Japan*. Cambridge University Press.

Fernandez-Macias, E. (2012). Job polarization in Europe? Changes in the employment structure and job quality, 1995–2007. *Work and Occupations, 39*(2), 157–182.

Fleckenstein, T., & Lee, S. C. (2018). The political economy of education and skills in South Korea: Democratisation, liberalisation and education reform in comparative perspective. *Pacific Review, 32*(2), 168–187.

Garritzmann, J. L. (2016). *The political economy of higher education finance: The politics of tuition fees and subsidies in OECD countries, 1945–2015*. Palgrave Macmillan.

Garritzmann, J. L., Busemeyer, M. R., & Neimanns, E. (2018). Public demand for social investment: New supporting coalitions for welfare state reform in western Europe? *Journal of European Public Policy, 25*(6), 844–861.

Garritzmann, J. L., Häusermann, S., & Palier, B. (Eds.). (2022). *The world politics of social investment: Vol. II. The politics of varying social investment strategies*. Oxford University Press.

Glaeser, E. L., La Porta, R., Lopez-de-Silanes, F., & Shleifer, A. (2004). Do institutions cause growth? *Journal of Economic Growth, 9*, 271–303.

Goos, M., Manning, A., & Salomons, A. (2014). Explaining job polarization: Routine-biased technological change and offshoring. *The American Economic Review, 104*(8), 2509–2526.

Hall, P. A. (2021). How political economies change: The evolution of growth regimes in the developed democracies. In A. Hassel & B. Palier (Eds.), *Growth and welfare in advanced capitalist economies: How growth regimes evolve* (pp. 57–97). Oxford University Press.

Hall, P. A., & Soskice, D. (2001). *Varieties of capitalism: The institutional foundations of comparative advantage.* Oxford University Press.

Hanushek, E., & Woessmann, L. (2015). *The knowledge capital of nations: Education and the economics of growth.* MIT Press.

Hassel, A., & Palier, B. (2020). *Growth and welfare in advanced capitalist economies: How growth regimes evolve.* Oxford University Press.

Häusermann, S., & Palier, B. (2017). The politics of social investment: Policy legacies and class coalitions. In A. Hemerijck (Ed.), *The uses of social investment* (pp. 339–348). Oxford University Press.

Hope, D., & Martelli, A. (2019). The transition to the knowledge economy, labor market institutions, and income inequality in advanced democracies. *World Politics, 71*(2), 236–288.

Huber, E., & Stephens, J. D. (2001). *Development and crisis of the welfare state: Parties and policies in global markets.* University of Chicago Press.

Inglehart, R., & Welzel, C. (2005). *Modernization, cultural change, and democracy: The human development sequence.* Cambridge University Press.

Iversen, T. (2005). *Capitalism, inequality, and welfare.* Cambridge University Press.

Iversen, T., & Soskice, D. (2019). *Democracy and prosperity: Reinventing capitalism through a turbulent century.* Princeton University Press.

Kharas, H., & Kohli, H. (2011). What is the middle income trap, why do countries fall into it, and how can it be avoided? *Global Journal of Emerging Market Economies, 3*(3), 281–289.

Lee, J.-W., & Lee, H. (2016). Human capital in the long-run. *Journal of Developmental Economics, 122,* 147–169.

Leitner, S. (2003). Varieties of familialism: The caring function of the family in comparative perspective. *European Societies, 5*(4), 353–375.

Lemieux, T. (2007). The "Mincer equation" thirty years after schooling, experience, and earnings. In S. Grossbard (Ed.), *Jacob Mincer: A pioneer of modern labor market economics* (pp. 127–148). Springer.

Lipset, S. M. (1959). Some social requisites of democracy: Economic development and political legitimacy. *American Political Science Review, 53*(1), 69–105.

Manning, A. (2003). Comment on: "The patterns of job expansions in the USA: A comparison of the 1960s and 1990s", by Erik Olin Wright and Rachel E. Dwyer. *Socio-Economic Review, 1*(3), 327–333.

Marx, P., & Nguyen, C. (2018). Political participation in European welfare states: Does social investment matter? *Journal of European Public Policy, 25*(6), 912–943.

Mau, S. (2015). *Inequality, marketization and the majority class: Why did the European middle classes accept neo-liberalism?* Palgrave Macmillan.

Mettler, S. (2002). Bringing the state back in to civic engagement: Policy feedback effects of the G.I. Bill for World War II veterans. *American Political Science Review, 96*(2), 351–365.

Nikolai, R., & Ebner, C. (2012). The link between vocational training and higher education in Switzerland, Austria, and Germany. In M. R. Busemeyer & C.

E. Trampusch (Eds)., *The political economy of collective skill formation* (pp. 234–258). Oxford University Press.

Oesch, D. (2013). *Occupational change in Europe: How technology and education transform the job structure*. Oxford University Press.

Oesch, D., & Piccitto, G. (2019). The polarization myth: Occupational upgrading in Germany, Spain, Sweden, and the UK, 1992–2015. *Work and Occupations, 46*(4), 441–469.

Oesch, D., & Rodriguez-Menes, J. (2010). Upgrading or polarization? Occupational change in Britain, Germany, Spain and Switzerland, 1990–2008. *Socio-Economic Review, 9*(3), 503–531.

Organisation for Economic Co-operation and Development. (2008). *Tertiary education for the knowledge society* (2 vols).

Organisation for Economic Co-operation and Development. (2009). *OECD review of tertiary education: Korea.*

Palier, B., & Thelen, K. (2010). Institutionalizing dualism: Complementarities and change in France and Germany. *Politics & Society, 38*(1), 119–148.

Peugny, C. (2019). The decline in middle-skilled employment in 12 European countries: New evidence for job polarisation. *Research & Politics, 6*(1). https://doi.org/10.1177/2053168018823131

Powell, W. W., & Snellman, K. (2004). The knowledge economy. *Annual Review of Sociology, 30*, 199–220.

Schneider, B. R. (2009). *Hierarchical capitalism in Latin America: Business, labor, and the challenges of equitable development*. Cambridge University Press.

Skocpol, T. (1992). *Protecting soldiers and mothers: The political origins of social policy in the United States*. The Belknap Press of Harvard University Press.

Spitz-Oener, A. (2006). Technical change, job tasks, and rising educational demands: Looking outside the wage structure. *Journal of Labor Economics, 24*(2), 235–270.

Strach, P. (2009). Making higher education affordable: Policy design in postwar America. *Journal of Policy History, 21*(1), 61–88.

Thelen, K. (2004). *How institutions evolve: The political economy of skills in Germany, Britain, the United States, and Japan*. Cambridge University Press.

Weisstanner, D., & Armingeon, K. (2020). How redistributive policies reduce market inequality: Education premiums in 22 OECD countries. *Socio-Economic Review, 18*(3), 838–856.

Windolf, P. (1997). *Expansion and structural change: Higher education in Germany, the United States, and Japan, 1870–1990*. Westview Press.

Wren, A. (2013). *The political economy of the service transition*. Oxford University Press.

PART III

DEMAND FOR AND SUPPLY OF SOCIAL INVESTMENT

PUBLIC OPINION AND SOCIAL PARTNERS' SOCIAL INVESTMENT POLICY PREFERENCES

PART II

9

EMPLOYERS AND SOCIAL INVESTMENT IN THREE EUROPEAN COUNTRIES

THE GOOD, THE BAD, AND THE UGLY

Emmanuele Pavolini and Martin Seeleib-Kaiser

9.1. INTRODUCTION

Business has a privileged position in the policymaking process (Lindblom, 1977). The power resources approach has claimed that social policy can be understood as politics against markets (Esping-Andersen, 1985); business organizations are antagonists or at most consenters with regard to the introduction and expansion of social policies (see Korpi, 2006). Since the 1990s, a growing body of literature has started to analyze the role of employers from a different perspective. These approaches have in common the idea that employers and their associations do not under all circumstances oppose social policies but might even provide support. Building on this literature, the chapter aims at offering an analytical contribution on the role of employers as important actors in explaining the development of social investment (SI) policies. SI can be understood as policies that promote both economic efficiency and equal opportunity (especially for socioeconomically disadvantaged people) (Widmaier, 1970; cf. Morel et al., 2012); such approaches to SI may be inclusive, stratified, or targeted (as outlined in Chapter 1 of this volume). Within the domain of SI policies, we will focus on employment-oriented family policies as well as vocational education and training (VET). Employment-oriented family policy is often perceived to be an

Emmanuele Pavolini and Martin Seeleib-Kaiser, *Employers and Social Investment in Three European Countries* In: *The World Politics of Social Investment (Volume I)*. Edited by: Julian L. Garritzmann, Silja Häusermann, and Bruno Palier, Oxford University Press. © Oxford University Press 2022. DOI: 10.1093/oso/9780197585245.003.0009 element of human capital mobilization. Within the literature, VET policy has been rarely included in the analysis of SI policies, despite the fact that its quality can be of fundamental importance for the transition from school to work of the majority of young people not attending university.[1] In this context we want to highlight the low levels of youth unemployment; the proportion of young people not in education, employment, or training; and the relatively smooth transition from school to work in a number of countries with comprehensive VET systems (see O'Reilly et al. 2019). The European Commission (2010, p. 2) states, "VET must play a dual role: as a tool to help meet Europe's immediate and future skills needs; and, in parallel, to reduce the social impact of and facilitate recovery from the crisis."

Employers' engagement in the politics of SI policies at the national level can essentially be viewed from three perspectives. First, employers could focus on opposing welfare policies ("antagonists") as costs associated with such policies undermine the profitability of their businesses; in this scenario, welfare policies are essentially perceived as policies "against the market" (Esping-Andersen, 1985). Second, employers could act as "consenters," supporting the expansion of such policies as these policies are relatively cheap compared to other social policy programs. But such support could also have its source in strategic considerations (i.e., employers agree to some consensus reluctantly to prevent even more far-reaching policies). Third, employers can develop a first-order preference for the expansion of SI policies, thus actively pushing such policies ("protagonists"), as these policies are perceived to support the socioeconomic environment needed for sustainable business activities, especially during times of tight labor markets (Fleckenstein & Seeleib-Kaiser, 2011; Korpi, 2006).

We analyze empirically SI policies in Britain, Germany, and Italy. Britain is usually characterized as a liberal welfare state within a liberal market economy (LME) with a "pluralist" model of interests' representation. Germany has been described as a conservative or Christian democratic welfare state within a coordinated market economy (CME), with a model of "sectoral coordination" in terms of interests' representation. Italy belongs to the Mediterranean welfare state regime and has a mixed-market economy (Esping-Andersen, 1990; Ferrera, 1996; Hall & Soskice, 2001; Molina & Rhodes, 2008) with fragmented "sectoral coordination." To assess employer preferences and the role of employers' associations in the national policy arena, we analyzed secondary literature and core policy documents of employers' associations in relation to SI policies since the 2000s. We thus focus on the dimension of politicization and coalition-building in the decision-making process.

---

1. For exceptions, see Chapter 7 in this volume and Chapter 3 in Volume II (Garritzmann et al., 2022).

9.2. STATE OF THE ART

In order to investigate the role of employers in SI policies, there is a need to bridge two different recent research streams: the welfare state literature focusing on the politics of new social risks (Bonoli & Natali, 2012) and the varieties of capitalism (VoC) literature focusing on skill formation and risks (Mares, 2003; Swenson, 2002) as well as the organizational structure of employer associations (Martin & Swank, 2012). Both streams of research share the view whereby employers' associations might support SI policies. Within the welfare state literature, Bonoli (2005) can be considered as the scholar who introduced a new way of looking at employers within the analysis of the politics of new social risks. In his view, there might be a convergence of interests between employers and welfare state reformers willing to expand coverage in typical SI policies. The reasons are twofold. First, these policies are generally not as costly as the more traditional forms of social intervention, and therefore they may be supported in a political exchange between cuts to old social risks protection programs (e.g., pensions and passive labor market policies) and expansion in SI policies; in this respect, employers might be considered "consenters." Second, SI policies have a favorable impact on labor supply because their goal is not decommodification, but, on the contrary, they are oriented toward a commodification of the workforce, helping individuals to participate and to remain in the labor market; policies aimed at making it easier for families to reconcile work and family life can be expected to significantly increase the labor supply of women; active labor market policies encourage the transition from non-employment to employment of individuals, such as youth and long-term unemployed people; VET policies can contribute to match labor supply and demand. In this respect, they might even be "promoters" of SI policies. Bonoli's approach has fostered a growing literature which discusses welfare state transformations adopting a similar view and in particular argues that employers' associations might join reform coalitions willing to expand SI policies (see, for example, Bonoli & Natali, 2012; Häusermann, 2012, 2018).

However, the differences among employers and their associations in different countries have received only scant attention. In order to build an analytical toolkit for studying employers' preferences and strategies toward SI policies, we build on the work of Mares (2003) and Martin and Swank (2012). Mares' (2003) starting questions were, under what conditions do employers favor private, firm-level welfare programs, and how do employers regard proposals that attempt to socialize risks? Mares creates a typology with three types of social policies (pp. 18–19): a) "firm-level social policies," with the lowest value along the risk redistribution axis (the risk pool is restricted to the members of the single firm) and the highest value on "control" (the policies are directly administered by the single company), often directly paid by employers; b) "contributory insurance," in which employers retain a limited role in terms of "control" (administration) and the level of risk redistribution of these policies can vary (from medium-high to medium-low); c) "universalistic social policies" that take high values on the risk redistribution among social groups and enterprises and low values on the control dimension (business plays no role in the administration of universalistic social policies) and are usually funded through taxation. Mares considers also the factors that influence the social policy model preferred by different firms (Table 9.1). The main factors are the firm size and the type of workers' skills needed by the enterprise, as well as the incidence of social risks among their employees. Mares argues that firms with a) a high incidence of risk, a small size, and low skills should prefer "universalistic" social policies; b) a low incidence of risk, a small size, and low skills should opt for no policy at all; c) a high incidence of risk, a large size, and high skills should prefer "contributory" social policies; and d) a low incidence of risk, a large size, and high skills should prefer "private" social policies.

Martin and Swank (2012) shift their attention to another dimension of companies' characteristics: the forms of collective action. In particular, they differentiate among three types of labor market coordination by firms (p. 7):

- The "macro-corporatist" model, where employers are organized into hierarchically ordered groups, and the peak association negotiates broad political agreements with labor and the state through collective bargaining and tripartite policymaking committees.
- The "sectoral coordination" model, where employers wield power largely at the industry level—employers' associations within specific industries engage in significant coordination with corresponding labor unions; but the encompassing multisector peak associations are much weaker, and the state is largely absent from negotiations.
- The "pluralist" model, where employers are represented by a panoply of conflicting groups, with many purporting to aggregate business interests and none having much policymaking authority.

They argue that these three models not only represent employers' interests to different degrees and with different outcomes but are also able to partially shape single employers' preferences: "employers are social animals and, as such, develop their policy interests in packs; consequently, their business organizations

Table 9.1 Prediction on social policy outcomes preferred by different firms

Incidence of risk		Size and Skill Intensity	
		Small/Low	Large/High
	High	Universalistic	Contributory
	Low	None	Private

Source. Mares (2003, p. 37).

are deeply determinative of how they think about the world in general and welfare state programs in particular" (Martin & Swank, 2012, pp. 1–2). The pivotal role of employer associations to foster and shape social policy preferences by their members produces its maximum strength in macro-corporatist and lowest strength in pluralist models. The way employer associations work in macro-corporatist environments (centralized, functionally specific, hierarchically ordered, encompassing, and unitary peak associations) helps companies not only to represent their interest but to form political identities and policy preferences.

> Fragmented, *pluralist* interest groups do not have these effects on employers, as the groups do not foster collective wage setting and compete with one another for members. These structures encourage concessions to the particularistic self-interests of members and work against agreements to solve collective action problems. In countries with *sector coordination*, one is likely to find deals between business and labor at the sectoral level, which offer core workers high levels of social protections but which neglect the interests of labor-market outsiders . . . industrial sector–based organizations simply have few if any incentives to significantly contribute to the costs of programs that address the needs of marginalized workers. (Martin & Swank, 2012, pp. 23–24)

Most of the literature on the role of employer associations and employers' preferences in social policy (partially with the exception of Martin & Swank, 2012) focuses on the role of these associations during the industrial/Fordist era. But do the VoC findings also apply in deindustrialized economies? Deindustrialization and technological change reduce firms' need for medium-skilled workers (usually defined as workers with "specific skills"), while the labor market is increasingly polarized/dualized between workers in high (often export-oriented) and low (often offering services for the internal market) productivity industries, reducing employers' incentives to cooperate (see Chapter 8 in this volume). Thus, merging the "politics of new social risks" research stream with the VoC approach can be quite fruitful in developing a more comprehensive analytical framework for analyzing the role of employers in the politics of SI policies.

9.3. THE LABOR MARKET AND THE ECONOMIC STRUCTURE: CHANGED FUNCTIONAL UNDERPINNINGS

9.3.1. The structural changes in the skills required in the labor market

In order to assess employers' preferences toward SI policies, we first need to understand if the findings identified in the VoC literature still hold for

Table 9.2 Composition of the workforce by industry (excluding the primary sector) as shares of total employees: 1995–2017

	Germany		Italy		United Kingdom	
	1995	**2017**	**1995**	**2017**	**1995**	**2017**
Manufacturing	27.0%	20.6%	29.7%	21.5%	21.0%	10.0%
Construction and public utilities	11.5%	8.0%	8.8%	7.1%	6.1%	6.9%
Consumption services [a]	28.5%	32.8%	23.3%	37.0%	34.0%	35.5%
Europe2020 "Smart growth" sectors [b]	8.5%	10.8%	7.9%	9.1%	12.2%	14.7%
Welfare and public administration	24.5%	27.8%	30.3%	25.3%	26.7%	32.8%
Total	100.0%	100.0%	100.0%	100.0%	100.0%	100.0%

[a] Sectors included wholesale and retail trade; transportation and storage; accommodation and food service activities; real estate activities; administrative and support service activities; arts, entertainment, and recreation; other service activities.
[b] Sectors included information and communication; financial and insurance activities; professional, scientific, and technical activities.
Source. Eurostat EU-LFS online database.

deindustrialized economies (Table 9.2). Between 1995 and 2017, the share of employment in manufacturing declined to approximately 21% in Italy and Germany, a reduction by almost 40%. In the United Kingdom, the share of employment in manufacturing declined to 10% of the workforce. Conversely, an expansion took place in the tertiary sector, especially in the retail and hospitality (consumption) and welfare sectors (but not in Italy) and, partially, in the so-called smart growth sectors (information and communication; financial and insurance activities; professional, scientific, and technical activities).

According to the VoC literature, specific skills predominate in CME models, and employers are generally keen to support educational and social policies fostering support and training for workers with specific skills, whereas LMEs rely on general skills complemented by company-level education and training (Hall & Soskice, 2001). Have employer preferences changed as a result of deindustrialization and changing skills compositions? Building on the work of Fleckenstein et al. (2011), we differentiate employment by three skill categories: workers with high general skills (managers, professionals, technicians), workers with specific skills (craft and related trades workers, plant and machine operators and assemblers), and workers with low general skills (clerical support workers, service and sales workers, employment in elementary occupations) (cf. Wiss, 2017).[2] Over time we have witnessed a polarization in all three countries (see Table 9.3). While the proportion of workers with specific skills has declined, the share of workers with high general skills (the largest group in Germany and the United

---

2. We have used the International Standard Classification of Occupations first-digit classification of occupations.

Table 9.3 Skill composition of employees (as shares of total employees) in 1995 and 2017

	Germany		Italy		United Kingdom	
	1995	**2017**	**1995**	**2017**	**1995**	**2017**
High–general skills workers	35.0%	42.9%	27.8%	33.0%	37.2%	49.1%
Specific-skills workers	30.0%	20.1%	31.8%	21.0%	19.7%	11.4%
Low–general skills workers	34.9%	37.0%	40.4%	46.0%	43.1%	39.5%
Total	100.0%	100.0%	100.0%	100.0%	100.0%	100.0%

Source. Authors' elaboration on Eurostat EU-LFS online database (indicator: lfsa_egais).

Kingdom) as well as with low general skills has increased. Although polarization took place in all three countries, they have followed different paths. The United Kingdom represents a case of an increasingly strong polarization between jobs requiring high general skills (49.1%) and jobs only requiring low general skills (39.5%), with a marginal role played by workers with specific skills (11.4%). In Germany we witness a different kind of polarization; on the one hand, we see workers with specific skills have been partially replaced by workers requiring high general skills, while at the same time the proportion of workers with low general skills has only marginally increased—a development which we might characterize as upgrading of the production system in a post-industrial environment. The Italian labor market is characterized by a limited growth of employees with high general skills and a replacement of workers requiring specific skills by workers in low–general skill occupations—a development which can be described as downgrading.

This trend is not only related to deindustrialization but is also occurring within manufacturing, which historically has been the economic sector primarily relying on workers with specific skills (Table 9.4).

Given such structural changes, we can expect preferences of employers to have evolved. First, we hypothesize that the pressure to train and to safeguard workers with specific skills has become less important even in CMEs such as Germany (with Italy being a hybrid). Second, companies relying on workers requiring low general skills have no preference for a more universal provision of training and education. Third, the increasing importance of workers requiring high general skills has led to a further diversification between CMEs (Germany) and LMEs (the United Kingdom) in relation to VET at the secondary and tertiary education levels.

9.3.2. Labor shortages and unemployment

In this section we use the economic sector and workers' profiles as a way to understand the risk associated with labor shortages. Table 9.5 shows job vacancies[3]

---

3. A *job vacancy* is defined as a paid post that is newly created, unoccupied, or about to become vacant for which the employer is taking active steps and is prepared to take further steps to find a

Table 9.4 Changed skill composition in the manufacturing sector (as shares of total employees—excluding the primary sector)

	Germany		Italy		United Kingdom	
	1998	**2017**	**1998**	**2017**	**1998**	**2017**
High–general skills workers	24.8%	33.3%	21.1%	29.2%	34.4%	42.8%
Specific-skills workers	52.9%	41.9%	62.9%	53.5%	46.1%	39.5%
Low–general skills workers	22.3%	24.8%	16.0%	17.3%	19.5%	17.7%
Total	100.0%	100.0%	100.0%	100.0%	100.0%	100.0%

Source. Authors' elaboration on Eurostat EU-LFS online database (indicator: lfsa_egais).

in the three countries over time and by economic sector. Although data are not fully comparable, job vacancies are particularly a problem, more prominently since 2007, in both the United Kingdom and Germany, whereas this is less of a problem in Italy. The data provided by Eurostat does not allow a decomposition of results by occupation (and worker's skills) but only by economic sector. However, the data on the economic sector can be used as a proxy of the skills required. There are no particular labor shortages in manufacturing in Italy and Germany, whereas this is partially the case in the United Kingdom. Construction is instead a sector where labor shortages are more severe, especially in Germany and, partially, the United Kingdom. If we shift to sectors typical requiring low general skills, we witness that in both Germany and the United Kingdom companies have (often very severe) shortages. The same applies to sectors usually requiring high general skills, defined in the table 9.5 "'Smart growth' sectors" (e.g., from transportation and communication to financial intermediation and business activities).

In sum, the data provide a general idea on the importance of skill shortages for companies: Labor shortages for workers requiring high general skills, and to a lesser degree for workers requiring low general skills, appear to be a problem in Germany and the United Kingdom, whereas the opposite seems to be the case in Italy.

9.3.3. The feminization of the labor market and its impact on skills

Since the 1990s all EU countries have witnessed an increase in female labor market participation. In addition to the increase in the overall activity rates of

suitable candidate from outside the enterprise concerned and which the employer intends to fill either immediately or within a specific period of time. The job vacancy rate compares the proportion of total vacant posts to the sum of the total number of occupied posts and those vacant.

Table 9.5 Job vacancies in Germany, Italy, and the United Kingdom by economic sector (2001–2017)

		Total				10 employees or more		
		2001	2004	2007	2017	2004	2007	2017
Total	Germany	3.1	2.1	3.5	2.7	1.8	3.1	2.6
	Italy	—	—	—	—	1.0	1.1	0.9
	United Kingdom	2.4	2.3	2.4	2.6	—	—	—
Manufacturing	Germany	—	1.0	1.7	1.7	0.8	1.5	1.6
	Italy	—	—	—	—	0.8	1.0	0.8
	United Kingdom	1.7	1.8	1.9	2.1	—	—	—
Construction and public utilities	Germany	—	1.1	2.2	4.2	0.7	1.7	3.9
	Italy	—	—	—	—	1.2	1.3	1.0
	United Kingdom	2.1	1.8	1.7	2.0	—	—	—
Other services	Germany	—	2.8	3.0	3.2	2.2	2.6	2.9
	Italy	—	—	—	—	1.4	1.2	1.3
	United Kingdom	2.8	2.8	2.8	3.2	—	—	—
"Smart growth" sectors	Germany	—	3.5	5.6	4.0	3.7	5.4	2.7
	Italy	—	—	—	—	1.0	1.1	1.0
	United Kingdom	2.5	2.7	3.1	2.8	—	—	—

Source. Eurostat EU-LFS online database (indicator lfsa_eegan).

women, we witness significant shifts in the skill composition of the workforce. The increased female labor force participation and the changed skill composition can provide the functional underpinning for policy change (Fleckenstein et al., 2011). We could speculate that the stronger female labor market participation has become, the more employers will tend to support employment-oriented family policies. However, the willingness of enterprises is mediated by the type of female labor market participation of a country and the size of companies (see Chapter 14 in this volume).

Table 9.6 shows the changed female labor market participation by occupational profile since the 1990s. This overall increase in female labor market participation took different directions depending on the type of occupational profile. In 2017 more than half of employees with jobs requiring high general skills were female (51.6%) in Germany; the share was only slightly lower in the United Kingdom (48%) and in Italy (49.4%). At the same time the majority of workers with jobs requiring low general skills jobs are female in all three countries; while their relative share decreased in Germany and the United Kingdom, it increased in Italy.

Table 9.7 presents female employees as a proportion of total employees by industry. Public administration and welfare services are the sectors mostly characterized by women's employment (69%–71% in Germany and the United

Table 9.6 Female employees as a share of total employees by skills (1995–2017)

	Germany		Italy		United Kingdom	
	1995	2017	1995	2017	1995	2017
Female workers with jobs requiring high general skills	48.1	51.6	45.7	49.4	42.1	48.0
Female workers with jobs requiring specific skills	12.7	12.3	19.5	13.9	14.7	9.4
Female workers with jobs requiring low general skills	65.7	63.4	47.5	58.1	68.1	63.0
Total	43.3	46.9	37.6	45.4	47.7	49.4

Source. Authors' elaboration on Eurostat EU-LFS online database (indicator: lfsa_egais).

Table 9.7 Female employees as a share of total employment by industry (1995–2017)

	Germany		Italy		UK	
	1995	2017	1995	2017	1995	2017
Manufacturing	28.5	27.1	30.5	25.6	28.0	24.6
Construction and public utilities	12.2	15.3	5.5	8.3	14.7	18.7
Public administration and welfare provision	60.8	68.7	52.3	63.0	68.6	70.8
Consumption services	52.8	49.9	38.4	46.7	49.1	46.2
"Smart growth" sectors	44.4	49.1	30.9	48.9	41.0	40.8
Total	43.3	46.9	37.6	45.4	47.7	49.4

Source. Eurostat EU-LFS online database.

Kingdom, 63% in Italy). The service sector in general has high female participation, especially in Germany and Italy. In particular, half of employees in these two countries are women in the so-called Europe 2020 smart growth industrial sectors (information and communication; financial and insurance activities; professional, scientific, and technical activities). Manufacturing and, even more so, construction have a low share of female employment.

9.4. POLICY PREFERENCES OF EMPLOYERS' ASSOCIATIONS IN GERMANY, BRITAIN, AND ITALY

Employers could be "antagonists," "consenters," or "protagonists" with regard to the politics of SI policies (Korpi, 2006; cf. Fleckenstein & Seeleib-Kaiser, 2011), as suggested in the introduction. To assess their preferences in the national policy arena, we analyzed secondary literature and core policy documents of employers' organizations with regard to VET and employment-oriented family policy.

9.4.1. The good: German employers increasingly "promoting" SI

Germany's vocational training system is considered "the crown jewel of the country's political economy" (Thelen, 2014, p. 85)—supported by employers and their interest in the formation of specific skills (Wood, 2001). The need for significant reforms of the system was voiced on and off by employer representatives, especially during years of economic crisis in the 1990s and early 2000s; however, over the years, political actors established a consensus, whereby the system needed to be updated and reformed (Hassel, 2007; see Chapter 3 in Volume II [Garritzmann et al., 2022]). The German Employers' Association, the Bundesvereinigung der Deutschen Arbeitgeberverbände (BDA; 2005), identified a number of points to be addressed in a reform of the VET system. The main points included the need to increase the appeal of vocational training to young people and to allow more flexibility and deregulation within the vocational training system. Schools should play a central role in promoting vocational education. Concrete suggestions included increasing the number and length of internships available to secondary school students to increase the appeal of vocational training and decrease the number of dropouts, increasing the occupational and geographic mobility of vocational training applicants, focusing on competencies of apprentices rather than learning contents, developing simple and transparent quality assurance criteria (e.g., analogous to the European Qualifications Framework), and opening up higher education access to those with advanced vocational qualifications (e.g., Meister, Fachwirt, Fachkaufmann, or equivalent), which is severely restricted and varies by the respective German state (*Länder*). Eventually, the 2005 Vocational Training Act (*Berufsbildungsgesetz*) was passed with general support by the BDA, which was able to significantly influence the final law (see Busemeyer, 2009)—overall, the law can be considered a continued commitment to vocational training and a rejection of an overall path to downgrading. The association representing hotels and restaurants (Deutscher Hotel- und Gaststättenverband [DEHOGA]) was pushing for some downgrading with regard to the flexibilization of remuneration and working time; however, the two demands did not make it into the final law (DEHOGA, 2005).[4]

At the beginning of the 21st century, German businesses developed an overall positive position toward comprehensive employment-oriented family policies proposed by the grand coalition government, after having opposed family policy expansion in the mid-1980s (BDA, 1985). In its 2006 position paper, the BDA argued that the economy required more women in employment and more children to ensure sufficient labor supply in the future, particularly

---

4. For an extensive analysis of the politics of the VET reform in Germany, see Chapter 3 in Volume II (Garritzmann et al., 2022).

skilled labor. Without promoting an increase in human capital mobilization, the country would not be able to maintain its capacity for innovation and competitiveness, as well as the system of social security. Consequently, the BDA called for family policies that placed parents in a better position to make the choice of having children and to continue working, instead of policies that "compensate" parents for the costs of children. The latter was considered to be inefficient, while the former was supposed to boost economic development. In 2005, the president of the BDA stated, "Based on the increased scarcity of skilled employees, we can no longer forgo the potential of highly qualified women and mothers" (FAZ, 2005, authors' translation). Insufficient childcare provision was identified as the greatest barrier to increasing female employment, which was viewed as imperative in light of the need for highly qualified employees (BDA, 2006, pp. 3–9). The family policy strategy of the BDA called for an expansion of childcare provision, in particular emphasizing the need to expand facilities for the under-3s and subsequently supported childcare legislation, including the introduction of a legal entitlement to childcare for children older than 1 year in 2013 (BDA, 2008).

The BDA also fully supported the 2007 reform of leave policies as the earnings-related leave benefit was in principle thought to facilitate the fast return of parents to their workplaces. In fact, organized business was pushing for a more comprehensive reform guided by the adult worker model. Driven by labor supply arguments, German business was calling for greater generosity for full-time working parents, proposing a flat-rate monthly benefit of 300 euros for parents who wanted to engage in more than 30 hours of employment. The employers' association also suggested incrementally reducing the maximum duration of the job guarantee for parents from 3 years to 1 year, following the expansion of childcare provision (BDA, 2006, pp. 17–21; 2008).[5] Especially noteworthy is the position of the German Chambers of Industry and Commerce (Deutscher Industrie- und Handelskammertag [DIHK]), primarily representing small- and medium-sized companies, which not only supported the new overall policy trajectory but also specifically considered the two "daddy months" in principle fairly unproblematic in light of experiences in Sweden (DIHK, 2006). Overall, the role of employers' organizations becoming promoters and even protagonists of an employment-oriented family policy focusing on an inclusive SI approach in order to mobilize the female workforce has been crucial for the coalition-formation and decision-making dynamics (Seeleib-Kaiser, 2010).

5. The other main employers' associations also promoted the drive for employment-oriented family policies, although they did differ on minor issues (cf. Deutscher Industrie- und Handelskammertag, 2006; Zentralverband des Deutschen Handwerks, 2007; Bundesverband der Deutschen Industrie, 2008).

9.4.2. The bad: British employers as antagonists and limited consenters of SI

In Britain, employers can by and large be considered as antagonists of a comprehensive approach toward public SI beyond universal education as voluntarism has characterized many aspects of British social policy and industrial relations (see Marchington et al., 2004). This approach has had significant economic and social consequences: Britain's "low-skill equilibrium" (Finegold & Soskice, 1988) not only has had negative consequences for the economic development of the country but has had a detrimental social impact on the lives of many young people not attending university, by locking them into low-skilled and low-wage jobs (Mayhew, 1985). In almost regular intervals, government and employers have identified the situation as in need of improvement. In 1989, the main employer association, the Confederation of British Industry (CBI), characterized the British labor force as "under-educated, under-trained and under-qualified" (CBI, 1989, p. 16); and three decades later political actors still struggle to improve the skills of young workers. Despite an increase of apprenticeships in the aftermath of the Great Recession and the desire to rebalance the economy, many of the new apprenticeships focus on rather short courses and on the unemployed. Many of the apprenticeships are deemed to be insufficient to acquire higher-level skills (cf. King, 1997; Fleckenstein & Lee, 2018). To address the unsatisfactory situation, the Conservative government somewhat surprisingly announced the introduction of an apprenticeship levy in 2015, to increase companies' investments in VET. While the CBI supported the notion of improving the availability of apprenticeships, it opposed the introduction of a mandatory levy and highlighted the need for flexibility of companies (CBI, 2015). The Engineering Employers' Federation (2017) consented to the government's policy, which is also not surprising as 92% of the large manufacturing companies offer apprenticeship programs. Eventually, an apprenticeship levy of 0.5% of an employer's wage bill was introduced in 2017 to create an additional 3 million apprenticeship starts in England by 2020 (Fleckenstein & Lee, 2018). Nevertheless, first assessments are quite critical with regard to the kind and quality of apprenticeships that were introduced—according to a report "nearly 40 per cent of the money raised by the apprenticeship levy is being spent on MBA-style executive programs or low-skills training that fail to meet the standard of teaching young people a trade" (Moules, 2018). To conclude, although employers were not able to stop the introduction of the apprenticeship levy, they have at least partially structured the apprenticeships within their companies in such a way that they meet their short-term needs, instead of contributing to a more inclusive SI and addressing the long-term economic and social needs of the country.

The CBI was also very critical of the various employment-oriented family measures, highlighting the costs for small- and medium-sized enterprises. Nevertheless, the CBI consented to the minimum requirements set out in the

1999 legislation regarding maternity leave and the introduction of parental leave (CBI, 1999, p. 3). In the subsequent years, employers unsurprisingly provided only lukewarm support for the increase in statutory maternity pay and the introduction of paid paternity leave. Moreover, they strongly opposed the extension of the duration and the splitting of the leave between mothers and fathers as well as the entitlement to flexible working hours proposed by the government (CBI, 2001, p. 11ff.; 2006). Apparently, the CBI's first-order preference is a voluntaristic approach based on occupational provision. Employers that consider a business case for family policies as given are assumed to directly provide occupational policies. Thus, instead of supporting a comprehensive public approach, employers consented to a minimalistic public approach vis-à-vis parental leave, while their first-order preference is rooted in a selective occupational approach to support skilled workers based on a cost argument (Fleckenstein & Seeleib-Kaiser, 2011).

With regard to childcare, however, the business community has been a promoter in advocating an expansion of affordable childcare. In 2001 the CBI stated,

> [I]t is the role of the state to provide childcare facilities that meet the diverse needs of working parents. Improving the quality, quantity, affordability and flexibility of childcare is key and will give parents—particularly lone parents—more opportunity to fully participate in the labour market and better balance the needs of work and family. The CBI supports the government's National Childcare Strategy and believes it has led to positive developments in state-funded childcare provision. . . . But the level of state-funded childcare in the UK remains low in comparison with other EU countries and the CBI believes that more can be achieved in this area. The government should place more support behind childcare provision to raise it to a level in line with other member states. (CBI, 2001, p. 23)

In fact, business support for childcare expansion dates back to the late 1980s, when the CBI urged the Conservative government to invest in public childcare facilities in order to facilitate female employment participation. Employer calls for childcare were explicitly linked with anticipated labor shortages associated with demographic change, which was considered to undermine the competitiveness of British businesses (CBI, 1989; see also Lister, 1996; Randall, 2000).[6]

---

6. More recent changes to family policy, such as the possibility of shared parental leave introduced in 2015, have been driven by considerations of improving gender equality and should not be considered as elements of a larger social investment strategy; by and large employers have consented to the sharing option (Groom, 2011).

9.4.3. The ugly: The Italian selective "consenters" approach to SI based on fiscal welfare

When looking at the Italian employers' associations and SI policies, it is important to distinguish between VET policies and employment-oriented family policies: The former have received quite more attention compared to the latter. However, for business two important underlying principles are at the core of the overall approach to SI: selectivity and fiscal welfare. The employers' associations agree with an expansion of SI policies, as long as a) they support a stratified SI (they are not universal and allow enterprises to decide if they want to use them) and b) the expansion of coverage is not primarily achieved through "social welfare" (using Titmuss' terminology) but by "occupational welfare" and, even more importantly, by "fiscal welfare." The core preference of employers is for the state to foster SI through fiscal incentives to companies interested in exploiting the advantages of these policies. The selectivity lies exactly in the idea that these policies have to expand just on the base of the demand from (single) enterprises and economic sectors (Pavolini & Jessoula, 2020).

In the Italian education debate, there has been an ongoing discussion for decades on whether the system should move toward a more generalist system, like the Anglo-Saxon one, or a "dual model," like the German one (Ballarino, 2016; Ventura, 1998). Several attempts to shift toward a dual model received limited support until the turn of the century. However, since the beginning of the international economic crisis especially, all employers' associations have started to advocate a shift toward the German "dual model" of education and VET (Ballarino, 2016). In this respect they have been the main promoters and supporters of the 2015 school system reform (the so-called good school reform), which introduced the so-called *Alternanza Scuola-lavoro* ("alternation between school and work") (Argentin & Barone, 2016). The new reform prescribes that all upper secondary school students have to spend 400 hours[7] (out of a total amount of around 3000) in practical activities within companies during the last 3 years of school. Employers' associations present this experience in their documents as the first real attempt to move forward toward the "dual" model (Confartigianato, 2016; Confindustria, 2015b, 2018), and they have given quite a positive evaluation of the reform. Hence, the employers' associations were among the main supporters of the reform introduced by the Renzi government in 2015. However, employers' associations have been asking for more fiscal incentives in order to host and to integrate students in the case of VET policies and the "good school reform."

Employment-oriented family policies are not high on the agenda of the most representative employer associations. An analysis of the main documents produced by Confindustria (the most representative employer associations for

---

7. Or 200 hours in the case of lyceum students.

medium and large companies) since the turn of the century shows that these types of policies have received relatively little attention. In order to exemplify Confindustria's position, it is useful to analyze the main documents it has produced since 2014 in parliamentary hearings in relation to two bills, one on reconciliation needs and policies (*Schema di decreto legislativo recante misure di conciliazione delle esigenze di cura, di vita e di lavoro*), the other on labor market policies (the so-called Jobs Act) (Confindustria, 2014, 2015a).

There are very few suggestions with regard to employment-oriented family policies. At a very general level, Confindustria supports more public effort, but

> a wider and more generous coverage should be carefully considered. . . . If financed either through social contributions or through general taxation, it is necessary to avoid that these programmes will cause an increase in labour costs, which are already high. . . . It is important that the Bill contemplates fiscal incentives to employment-oriented family policies and provides fiscal incentives for collective agreements between social partners in relation to flexible working times and reconciliation practices. . . . Fiscal incentives should be offered also to companies that invest in work life balance also directly and autonomously. (Confindustria, 2015a, p. 12, authors' translation)

These documents do not make specific reference to either the strengthening of formal childcare provision or the proposal to use parental leave in a more flexible way. The only increases of public expenditure considered acceptable are fiscal incentives directly given to companies or provided in order to support industrial sector–level or company-level agreements in relation to employment-oriented family policies (e.g., the introduction of reconciliation services in exchange for wage increase moderation) (Ascoli et al., 2018).

Associations of small and medium-sized employers (SMEs), primarily employing workers requiring specific skills (*Confartigianato* in the industrial and manufacturing economic branch) or companies employing mainly low-skilled workers (e.g., *Confcommercio* in the retail industry) emphasized even more their strong opposition to any new regulation which would increase costs (also the worry of Confindustria) and make more complicated the organization of working times in SMEs through new or more generous forms of parental leave and flexible working time rules (Confartigianato, 2015; Rete Imprese Italia, 2016).

In sum, although the employer associations' world is fragmented and divided based on size and skill requirements, they all agree in limiting employment-oriented family policies which would increase costs, with the associations representing SMEs or sectors employing low-skilled workers even more fundamentally opposed; and they all agree on introducing or strengthening the use of fiscal incentives (Confcommercio, 2016; Rete Imprese Italia, 2016).

The positions expressed in recent years have not changed over time. The analysis of the debate around the legislation on reconciliation from 2014 on, introducing more rights for parents, shows that practically the associations' positions have remained skeptical and opposed to more rights in this policy field, even if since the 2000s all main employers' associations have introduced specific internal bodies which should represent women's interests and needs inside the companies. The employer associations in Italy have not linked SI policies and an increase of women's employment as an important asset in order to improve the competitiveness of the Italian economy and the Italian companies, especially in the high-skilled and highly productive sectors, as has been the case in Germany.

Overall, the position that the employers' associations in Italy have adopted in relation to SI has followed a similar line in relation to employment-oriented family and VET policies. The presence of a weak version of the "sectoral coordination" model, getting closer and closer to a "pluralist" model, helps explain the strongly stratified approach to SI.

9.5. CONCLUSIONS

The support of employers' associations at the national level has varied significantly, and path dependence regarding national policymaking seemed to have had a significant impact on whether they were antagonists, consenters, or protagonists. Whereas German social policymaking was historically characterized by its consensus orientation and the role of social partnership within the overall framework of a social market economy, decision-making in the United Kingdom was much more driven by conflictual processes and employer organizations opposing an active role of the state. The Italian case has historically followed a middle path between the other two countries: Social partnership was not institutionalized as in Germany, but at the same time employer associations were not very vocal against an active role of the state. The changed functional underpinnings with regard to labor market developments seemed to have had less of an impact than hypothesized as we would have expected a much more active role of British employers and, partially, Italian ones in supporting SI policies.

Although the term "social investment" is rarely used in German political discourse, the salience of the concept has significantly increased. There seems to be a common understanding about investing in the future of the workforce in light of current and future skill and labor shortages, which are significantly driven by demographic change. German employer organizations (seemingly independent of the size of the companies they are representing) continued to support a reformed VET system and became promoters of universalist employment-oriented family policies at the turn of the 21st century. The continued support for SI in the VET sector can be explained by path dependence as well as the high levels of skill shortages, especially in the smart growth sectors. The aim of this policy is to adapt and update a VET system, historically very much catering to the formation of specific skills, to the requirement of facilitating the formation of high general skills. It could be argued that by adding this element the system becomes more stratified, while at the same time it could also be understood as inclusive as it aims to improve the future job opportunities of those who do not attend university and to contribute to a smooth school-to-work transition. Regarding employment-oriented family policies, German employer associations have made a complete U-turn, which is very much the result of the current and anticipated labor and skill shortages. The design of the employment-oriented family policy at the federal level can be characterized as inclusive SI—the support of employers' organizations has been crucial for the successful enactment of this policy (Seeleib-Kaiser, 2010).

British employers continued to favor voluntarism and acted as consenters in relation to some employment-oriented family policies. Their overall approach to SI in family policies was much more targeted as they seem to be primarily interested in mobilizing low-skilled female workers. Employers' associations were able to limit and influence the overall design of SI policies in the domain of employment-oriented family policies. The skill shortage does not seem to have had a significant impact on changing the preferences of the British employers' associations regarding vocational education and training policy. Here it seems that the Conservative government acted as an ideal capitalist in the long-term interest of British employers.

Italian employers only paid lip service to the expansion of SI policies, with the exception of some support for reforms in the education system. Their core idea has been support for a stratified SI with expansion based mostly on selective incentives (via fiscal welfare) to those companies that could benefit the most from it. In a situation characterized, on the one hand, by a weak "sectoral coordination" model among companies and, on the other, by much diversified needs in terms of skills and skill shortages within the private sector, the employer associations have chosen a line of minimum support for SI. It is also very likely that the high unemployment rate has significantly impacted on the preference formation of Italian employers.

To conclude, despite changed socioeconomic underpinnings and rational arguments to expand SI policies in the three countries under scrutiny, it seems to be the case that national historical patterns and path dependence significantly shape policies in the domain of SI. However, under certain circumstances, significant change can come about, as demonstrated by the preference formation of German employers at the turn of the 21st century.

REFERENCES

Argentin, G., & Barone, C. (2016). La riforma della scuola: Innovazione e retorica del cambiamento. In M. Carbone & S. Piattoni (Eds.), *Politica in Italia: I fatti dell'anno e le interpretazioni Edizione 2016* (pp. 172–194). Il Mulino.

Ascoli, U., Natali, D., & Pavolini, E. (2018). Still a weak occupational welfare in southern Europe? Evidence from the Italian case. *Social Policy & Administration, 52*(2), 534–548.

Ballarino, G. (2016). Higher education policies. In U. Ascoli & E. Pavolini (Eds.), *The Italian welfare state in a European perspective* (pp. 143–164). Policy Press.

Bonoli, G. (2005). The politics of the new social policies. Providing coverage against new social risks in mature welfare states. *Policy and Politics, 33*(3), 431–449.

Bonoli, G., & Natali, D. (2012). *The politics of the new welfare state*. Oxford University Press.

Bundesverband der Deutschen Industrie (2008). *BDI Manifest für Wachstum und Beschäftigung*. Berlin, BDI.

Bundesvereinigung der Deutschen Arbeitgeberverbände. (1985). Stellungnahme zum Regierungsentwurf eines Gesetzes über die Gewährung von Erziehungsgeld und Erziehungsurlaub. Deutscher Bundestag, Ausschuß für Jugend, Familie und Gesundheit, Ausschußdrucksache 10/151.

Bundesvereinigung der Deutschen Arbeitgeberverbände. (2005). *BILDUNG schafft ZUKUNFT—Das Bildungsprogramm der Arbeitgeber*.

Bundesvereinigung der Deutschen Arbeitgeberverbände. (2006). *Familie schafft Zukunft*.

Bundesvereinigung der Deutschen Arbeitgeberverbände. (2008). *Ausbau der Kinderbetreuung richtig und überfällig*.

Busemeyer, M. R. (2009). Die Sozialpartner und der Wandel in der Politik der beruflichen Bildung seit 1970. *Industrielle Beziehungen, 3*, 273–294.

Confartigianato. (2015). *Audizione Commissioni Congiunte Bilancio Senato della Repubblica e Camera dei Deputati. Disegno di legge di stabilità 2016*. Parlamento Italiano.

Confartigianato. (2016). *Audizione Commissioni Congiunte Bilancio Senato della Repubblica e Camera dei Deputati. Disegno di legge di stabilità 2017*. Parlamento Italiano.

Confcommercio. (2016). *Donne motore della ripresa. Relazione del Presidente Patrizia Di Dio*.

Confederation of British Industry. (1989). *Towards a skills revolution: Report of the Education and Training Taskforce*.

Confederation of British Industry. (1999). *CBI's response to the consultation on parental and maternity leave*.

Confederation of British Industry. (2001). *CBI response to "Work & parents: Competitiveness and choice" green paper*.

Confederation of British Industry. (2006). *Work and families bill.*

Confederation of British Industry. (2015). *CBI response to the government's consultation on the introduction of an apprenticeship levy.*

Confindustria. (2014). *Proposte per il mercato del lavoro e per la contrattazione.*

Confindustria. (2015a). *Camera dei Deputati. Audizione decreti attuativi Jobs Act. Schema di decreto legislativo recante misure di conciliazione delle esigenze di cura, di vita e di lavoro.* Camera dei Deputati.

Confindustria. (2015b). *Audizione Commissioni Congiunte Bilancio Senato della Repubblica e Camera dei Deputati. Disegno di legge di stabilità 2016.* Parlamento Italiano.

Confindustria. (2018). *Assise Confindustria 2018. La visione e la proposta.*

Deutscher Hotel- und Gaststättenverband. (2005). Berufsbildungsgesetz (BBiG). Retrieved April 27, 2020, from http://osthoga.de/wp-content/uploads/2015/03/berufsbildungsgesetz.pdf

Deutscher Industrie- und Handelskammertag. (2006). *Stellungnahme: Referentenentwurf eines Gesetzes zur Einführung des Elterngeldes.*

Engineering Employers' Federation. (2017). *Lifting the lid on the levy: Making the apprenticeship levy work for industry.*

Esping-Andersen, G. (1985). *Politics against markets.* Princeton University Press.

Esping-Andersen, G. (1990). *The three worlds of welfare capitalism.* Princeton University Press.

European Commission. (2010). *A new impetus for European cooperation in vocational education and training to support the Europe 2020 strategy* (COM(2010) 296 final).

FAZ (2015). Das "familienfreundlichste Land in Europa." *Frankfurter Allgemeine Zeitung*, April 13, 2015.

Ferrera, M. (1996). The "southern model" of welfare in social Europe. *Journal of European Social Policy*, 6(1), 17–37.

Finegold, D., & Soskice, D. (1988). The failure of training in Britain. *Oxford Review of Economic Policy*, 4(3), 21–53.

Fleckenstein, T., & Lee, S. (2018). Caught up in the past? Social inclusion, skills, and vocational education and training policy in England. *Journal of Education and Work*, 31(2), 109–124.

Fleckenstein, T., Saunders, A. M., & Seeleib-Kaiser, M. (2011). The dual transformation of social protection and human capital: Comparing Britain and Germany. *Comparative Political Studies*, 44(12), 1622–1650.

Fleckenstein, T., & Seeleib-Kaiser, M. (2011). Business, skills and the welfare state: The political economy of employment-oriented family policy in Britain and Germany. *Journal of European Social Policy*, 21(2), 136–149.

Garritzmann, J. L., Häusermann, S., & Palier, B. (Eds.). (2022). *The world politics of social investment: Vol. II. The politics of varying social investment strategies.* Oxford University Press.

Hall, P. A., & Soskice, D. (2001). *Varieties of capitalism*. Oxford University Press.

Hassel, A. (2007). What does business want? Labour market reforms in CMEs and its problems. In B. Hancké, M. Rhodes, & M. Thatcher (Eds.), *Beyond varieties of capitalism* (pp. 253–277). Oxford University Press.

Häusermann, S. (2012). The politics of new and old social risks. In G. Bonoli & D. Natali (Eds.), *The politics of the new welfare state* (pp. 127–152). Oxford University Press.

Häusermann, S. (2018). The multidimensional politics of social investment in conservative welfare regimes: Family policy reform between social transfers and social investment. *Journal of European Public Policy*, 25(6), 862–877.

King, D. (1997). Employers, training policy, and the tenacity of voluntarism in Britain. *Twentieth Century British History*, 8(3), 383–411.

Korpi, W. (2006). Power resources and employer-centered approaches in explanations of welfare states and varieties of capitalism. *World Politics*, 58(2), 167–206.

Lindblom, C. E. (1977). *Politics and markets*. Basic Books.

Lister, R. (1996). Back to the family. In H. Jones & J. Millar (Eds.), *The politics of the family* (pp. 11–31). Avebury.

Marchington, M., Goodman, J., & Berridge, J. (2004). Employment relations in Britain. In G. J. Bamber, R. D. Lansbury, & N. Wailes (Eds.), *International and comparative employment relations* (pp. 36–66). Sage.

Mares, I. (2003). *The politics of social risk: Business and welfare state development*. Cambridge University Press.

Martin, C. J., & Swank, D. (2012). *The political construction of business interests: Coordination, growth, and equality*. Cambridge University Press.

Mayhew, K. (1985). Reforming the labour market. *Oxford Review of Economic Policy*, 1(2), 60–79.

Molina, Ó., & Rhodes, M. (2008). The political economy of adjustment in mixed market economies: A study of Spain and Italy. In B. Hancké, M. Rhodes, & M. Thatcher (Eds.), *Beyond varieties of capitalism: Conflict, contradictions and complementarities in the European economy* (pp. 223–252). Oxford University Press.

Morel, N., Palier, B., & Palme, J. (Eds.). (2012). *Towards a social investment welfare state? Ideas, policies and challenges*. University of Chicago Press.

Moules, J. (2018). Poor quality apprenticeships set to waste £600m, says think-tank. *Financial Times*, April 13, 2015.

O'Reilly, J., Leschke, J., Ortlieb, R., Seeleib-Kaiser, M., & Villa, P. (2019). *Youth labor in transition: Inequalities, mobility, and policies in Europe*. Oxford University Press.

Pavolini, E., & Jessoula, M. (2020). *Il welfare invisibile. Il ruolo del welfare fiscale nel sistema di protezione italiano fra politica, politiche e diseguaglianze*. Il Mulino.

Rete Imprese Italia. (2016). *Audizione 16 marzo 2016. Senato della Repubblica. 11a Commissione Lavoro, previdenza sociale*. Senato della Repubblica.

Randall, V. (2000). *The politics of day childcare in Britain*. Oxford University Press.

Seeleib-Kaiser, M. (2010). Socio-economic change, party competition and intra-party conflict: The family policy of the grand coalition. *German Politics, 19*(3–4), 416–428.

Swenson, P. (2002). *Capitalists against markets: The making of labor markets and welfare states in the United States and Sweden*. Oxford University Press.

Thelen, K. (2014). *Varieties of liberalization and the new politics of social solidarity*. Cambridge University Press.

Ventura, S. (1998). *La politica scolastica*. Il Mulino.

Widmaier, H. P. (1970). Aspekte einer aktiven Sozialpolitik. Zur politischen Ökonomie der Sozialinvestitionen. In H. Sanmann (Ed.), *Zur Problematik der Sozialinvestitionen* (pp. 9–44). Duncker & Humblot.

Wiss, T. (2017). Paths towards family-friendly working time arrangements: Comparing workplaces in different countries and industries. *Social Policy & Administration, 51*(7), 1406–1430.

Wood, S. (2001). Business, government, and patterns of labor market policy in Britain and the Federal republic of Germany. In P. Hall & D. Soskice, *Varieties of capitalism* (pp. 247–274). Oxford University Press.

Zentralverband des Deutschen Handwerks (2007). *Positionspapier für eine Integrierte Familien- und Bildungspolitik*. Berlin: ZDH.

10

SOCIAL (INVESTMENT) PARTNERS?

TRADE UNIONS AND THE WELFARE STATE FOR THE KNOWLEDGE ECONOMY

Niccolo Durazzi and Leonard Geyer

10.1. INTRODUCTION

Social investment (SI) is to be understood as a set of policies aimed at the creation, mobilization, and preservation of human capital (Garritzmann et al., 2022), and it is increasingly seen as a key ingredient to foster simultaneously economic competitiveness and social inclusion (Hemerijck, 2015, 2017; Morel et al., 2012). At first sight, therefore, trade unions should wholeheartedly support these policies to the extent that such policies have the capacity to ease the transition to a high-skill/high-wage knowledge-based economy (Durazzi, 2019; Esping-Andersen et al., 2001). For example, evidence suggests that SI policies are conducive to higher employment rates (Kenworthy, 2017; Nelson & Stephens, 2012), thus making SI an attractive option for trade unions, especially if employment gains are achieved in permanent and high-quality jobs (Nelson & Stephens, 2012), where unionization capacity tends to be higher (Esping-Andersen, 1990). In addition, it has been noted that SI—as a future-oriented and service-heavy set of policies—needs a significant policy infrastructure to work well (Sabel et al., 2017), and unions can theoretically play a part in these policy frameworks as informational logics have often been important reasons for governments to seek cooperation with unions and empower them (Culpepper, 2002; Simoni, 2013).

Yet, despite these potential "ladders," SI also confronts trade unions with a number of "snakes" (Crouch, 2000). Two issues stand out. Firstly, unions are

Niccolo Durazzi and Leonard Geyer, *Social (Investment) Partners?* In: *The World Politics of Social Investment (Volume I).* Edited by: Julian L. Garritzmann, Silja Häusermann, and Bruno Palier, Oxford University Press. © Oxford University Press 2022. DOI: 10.1093/oso/9780197585245.003.0010 faced with a *representational* problem. Most SI policies—especially those of a "targeted" type (see this volume's typology), for instance, think of active labor market policies (ALMPs) or family policies—primarily target weakly organized segments of society that have not been traditionally incorporated within unions' domain of action. These groups, broadly speaking, correspond to those identified by Bonoli (2005) as most exposed to new social risks: young people, non-permanent workers, and women. Hence, the extent to which unions would firmly stand behind the development of these policies is uncertain. The "insider–outsider literature" pushes the argument further and provides a decisively negative answer to the question of whether unions would support SI policies. Taking one of the chief SI policies—ALMPs—insider-outsider models predict that unions will systematically oppose ALMPs because they are not of direct benefit to their core members. As SI policies are of primary benefit to poorly unionized labor market outsiders, while "old" social policies (e.g., insurance-based unemployment benefits) are of primary benefit to insiders, the argument goes, unions are expected to support the latter and oppose the former (Rueda, 2005, 2006).

Secondly, there is a potential *institutional* dilemma that unions are faced with. The perspective of taking part in the administration and management of SI policies might in fact be seen by unions not so much as an opportunity but rather as a threat to the extent that SI policies entail a loss of institutional control over other policy areas. In other words, some SI policies might be implemented in policy arenas where unions have little control while weakening a (competing) policy arena where union control is strong; and, as such, again, unions might oppose a shift toward SI (Clegg & Van Wijnbergen, 2011; Davidsson & Emmenegger, 2013; Durazzi & Geyer, 2020).

In line with theoretical arguments that posit unions both potentially supporting and opposing SI policies, the literature provides us with empirical evidence along both lines. To mention but a few, unions were at the heart of a broad coalitional realignment that favored SI in Denmark, leading to a path of "embedded flexibilization" which kept together economic competitiveness and social solidarity (Ibsen & Thelen, 2017; Thelen, 2014); German unions were part of a broad coalition supporting the development of family policy in the first decade of the 2000s (Häusermann, 2018), and unions were the crucial actors behind the establishment of a system of high-quality training for low-skilled young people in Austria. On the other hand, instances of opposition to SI are also well documented: German unions strongly opposed the expansion of school-based training to support young people who could not find an apprenticeship place (Busemeyer, 2012; Thelen, 2014; Thelen & Busemeyer, 2012); Italian unions have been depicted as largely focused on insider-oriented social policies at times of economic adjustment, focusing most of their efforts in the social policy domain on protecting the pension rights of existing members (Madama et al., 2013); and French unions have traditionally looked with suspicion at training measures as they feared that they would increase government power in the overarching framework of unemployment protection while weakening the role of the unions (Bonoli, 2012).

As examples of both unions' support for and opposition to SI manifest empirically, and given that there are plausible theoretical reasons to hypothesize both unions' support and opposition, the question that arises is the following: Under what conditions should we expect unions to support SI policies? Moreover, against the background of the larger picture of the politics of SI analyzed in this book, a second question ensues: When does union support "matter" in the SI policymaking process? The chapter formulates theoretical insights to tackle these questions by focusing on 1) the preference formation of trade unions with respect to SI policy and 2) the potential role of trade unions in the policy process leading to the adoption—or lack thereof—of SI policies. Short case studies on four diverse cases are then employed to illustrate the main theoretical insights.

10.2. MICRO-, MESO-, AND MACRO-DIMENSIONS OF UNIONS' PREFERENCE FORMATION AND POLICY IMPACT

10.2.1. Micro-level preference formation: Age, gender, and skills across sectors

We start off by assuming a simple "logic of membership" (Schmitter & Streeck, 1999) at the level of individual trade unions along industry lines whereby unions position themselves according to the economic self-interest of their members.[1] Self-interest influences individuals' preferences toward childcare, education, and ALMPs (see Garritzmann et al. 2018) as well as SI policies as a whole, in particular when respondents are faced with trade-offs between spending on different policy areas (Neimanns et al., 2018; see also Chapter 12 in this volume). We therefore hypothesize in particular that *age, gender, skill-level,* and *the respective employment sector (agriculture, industry, services)* play roles in shaping individual preferences toward SI policies and that therefore the concentration of union members along these four variables determines which SI policies will be high on unions' agendas and which, conversely, will not be met with significant interest.

---

1. Mosimann and Pontusson (2017) show not only that union members influence the position of their organization but that being a member of a union also increases an individual's support for redistributive policies. This means that unions not only aggregate but also shape preferences, an argument which is supported by Bremer's finding (see Chapter 12 in this volume) that union members are significantly more likely to support spending on education. From our perspective, it is less important, however, if unions aggregate or form their members' preferences. Rather, it is important that either way they position themselves according to the economic self-interest of their dominant members.

To exemplify the point, we can think of one policy for each of the skill creation, mobilization, and preservation components of SI. The most obvious skill creation policy is education and training: Receiving good-quality education and training is expected to be crucial to land a job in a high-skilled sector and to maintain it in today's knowledge economies. In line with this argument, more educated people are more supportive of further spending on education (Busemeyer & Garritzmann, 2017; Garritzmann et al., 2018; Neimanns et al., 2018; see Chapter 12 in this volume), and trade unions in high-skill sectors (e.g., high-end manufacturing, dynamic services) will be certainly supportive of (various forms of) education and training policies.

If we turn to an example of skill mobilization, such as employment- and child-oriented family policies, the primary beneficiaries are different, namely young parents and particularly female employees. Indeed, these policies have gained prominence as more women have entered the labor market in recent decades (Fleckenstein et al., 2011), and several studies have found women and families with young children to be more supportive of childcare policies (Garritzmann et al., 2018; Neimanns et al., 2018; see Chapter 12 in this volume). Yet, female employment is not evenly distributed across sectors. The public sector, in which an average 58.3% of employees across Organisation for Economic Co-operation and Development (OECD) countries is female, is the obvious example of a sector with above-average female employment (OECD, 2017). We might therefore expect unions in sectors with a high share of female employment to be strong supporters of family policies, such as childcare or gender-neutral parental leave policies.

If we move on to skill preservation and updating, of which skill-oriented ALMPs are a crucial component, we would expect yet another picture: Here, the main beneficiaries are labor market outsiders, especially those in sectors where atypical forms of employment are prevalent, such as low-end services, where we therefore expect to find the strongest support for ALMPs as improving workers' skills by updating them might operate as a bridge toward better employment conditions. Clearly, other forms of skill updating, such as lifelong learning, might find support at the opposite end of the labor market spectrum as those employed in high-end dynamic services—often faced with radical forms of innovation and technological change (Hall & Soskice, 2001)—might also favor forms of skill updating. But certainly this would apply to a much lesser extent to sectors where neither atypical employment nor radical innovation features prominently (e.g., manufacturing, public sector).

Lastly, and independent of the other factors, the expansion of SI policies can benefit employees in the public sector by securing existing and providing additional employment. In this sense, the SI state as an employer can create and secure jobs. For example, teachers can expect to benefit from additional funds allocated toward education policies, or employees of the public employment service (PES) might benefit from increased emphasis on ALMPs. Therefore, public sector workers and their unions are expected to be more supportive of SI policies than their private sector peers. Again, this mechanism has distributive implications as we know that the expansion of public sector employment has particularly benefited (high-skilled) women, as workers.

Table 10.1 provides examples of the expected SI preferences for unions in different sectors, based on the stylized composition of the sectoral membership along the three key variables of age, gender, and skill level.

However, the power resources of different union federations at the sectoral level vary widely, and we therefore anticipate that different priorities also have different political weight within the union movement. To take a simple example, the profile of workers in core sectors (e.g., manufacturing) is such that it makes them significantly more likely to join a union compared to, say, workers in low-end services, giving unions in core sectors a much stronger power—and voice—than unions in weakly organized sectors. This consideration is crucial because SI policies—although widely supported by the middle class (Garritzmann et al., 2018)—are often of primary benefit to traditionally weaker or less represented segments of the workforce who tend to be those more exposed to "new social risks" (Bonoli, 2005, 2006; Martin & Swank, 2012). To understand under which circumstances the interests of weaker workers might be represented, we need to move "up" from the micro-level and introduce a set of meso-level features.

Table 10.1 Hypothesized SI preferences based on stylized membership composition

Sector	Age composition	Gender composition	Skill composition	Unions' SI preferences
Manufacturing industry	Above-average old employees	Above-average male employees	Medium/high	Skill creation
Public sector	Balanced	Above-average female employees	Medium/high	Skill mobilization, skill creation (+ general support to increase public sector employment)
High-end services	Balanced	Balanced	High	Skill creation, skill mobilization, skill preservation and updating (lifelong learning)
Low-end services	Above-average young employees	Balanced	Low	Skill preservation and updating (ALMPs), skill mobilization

Source. Authors' own elaboration.

10.2.2. Moving to the meso-level: Density, centralization, and institutional involvement

While individual workers' profiles are useful to establish the micro-foundations of unions' preferences, the literature shows that there are several mechanisms by which unions' preferences might move away from narrow sectoral interest representation. Firstly, *density* and *centralization* have been shown to matter when it comes to considering how narrow or wide unions' perimeter of interest representation is. Where union density is high, it is more likely that the membership base is more representative of the entire workforce, and therefore the demands of otherwise weakly unionized members are more likely to be heard (Benassi & Vlandas, 2016). The same holds true for the level of centralization: Where peak confederations have strong power vis-à-vis sectoral federations, weaker parts of the union movement are more likely to be empowered even in the absence of particularly high density (Benassi & Vlandas, 2016; Durazzi et al., 2018; Durazzi & Geyer, 2020; Gordon, 2014; Oliver, 2010). More specifically, the literature presents us with three variants when it comes to different degrees of centralization: The Nordic and Mediterranean countries are characterized by high or medium-high levels of centralization, while the Continental European and Anglo-Saxon countries tend to have low levels of confederal authority over their affiliate unions (see, e.g., Benassi & Vlandas, 2016). Yet, within the latter group, a further distinction should be made. In Continental European countries (e.g., Germany), the various sectoral unions are involved in national-level policymaking, hence a logic of interest—and of potential conflict between confederation and affiliated unions—is likely to play out. In Anglo-Saxon countries, instead, sectoral (or, rather, occupational) unions tend not to participate in national-level policymaking but to focus primarily on furthering their members' interest at the workplace, in line with the business unionism ideal type (Hyman, 2001), while the confederation is more likely to have a voice in national policymaking, though often unheard by the government and not necessarily representative of its affiliate unions. Hence, in the latter case, lack of confederal authority is unlikely to culminate in conflict, but it would rather lead to a "division of labor" between confederation and sectoral/occupational unions.

To illustrate how different levels of centralization play out in the preference formation process, let us consider a simple example of the formulation of a policy preference for labor market policy, and in particular let us consider the support for either unemployment benefit (UB) or ALMPs (i.e., a typical "old" consumption-oriented social policy vis-à-vis one of the chief "new" investment-oriented social policies). Firstly, where density and centralization are low, unions in core sectors (such as the metal-working industry) are likely to be the most powerful players within the union movement, and their policy preference is expected to lean toward UB, making it difficult for the union movement to adopt a strong position in favor of ALMPs, which would be most demanded by sectoral unions in weakly unionized sectors (e.g., the low-end services). If, however, this sector is either well unionized (i.e., high density) or empowered through a strong peak organization (i.e., high centralization), it is more likely that a policy preference in favor of ALMPs will emerge. In other words, both density and centralization broaden the perimeter of interest representation by making it more inclusive toward weaker segments of the workforce. High density and/or high centralization are therefore hypothesized to increase inclusionary preferences and support for SI policies. Moreover, thinking about the type of SI policy preferred by the unions, we can expect that in contexts of high union density and/or a high degree of centralization unions support "inclusive" SI policies (covering as many citizens as possible). Less centralized or encompassing unions may support inclusive policies as well, if these are not in conflict with the interests of core members. However, if conflicts emerged, they would be more likely to support "stratified" SI (focusing on their respective members).

Secondly, unions not only act according to a logic of (narrow or broad) interest representation but might also follow a *logic of influence* (Schmitter & Streeck, 1999). In this case, unions' policy preferences will be driven primarily by the aim of *maintaining* or *increasing* their degree of influence over the policy process (Davidsson & Emmenegger, 2013; Emmenegger, 2014). This logic is particularly relevant for SI policies because these are more likely to be implemented in institutional arenas where unions' power is traditionally low compared to "old" social policies. Let us go back to the example of the preference formation process over UB and ALMPs. The institutional arenas within which these two policies are implemented differ starkly: While unions have a significant degree of influence over UB administration across most Western European countries (either directly or indirectly), their influence over ALMPs might be much more limited because their role in PES is not as strong compared to the administration of UB. In these circumstances, an "activation turn" weakening UB and strengthening ALMPs might be perceived as lowering their general political influence, and it might be therefore opposed. To the extent that SI policies involve a direct reduction of union influence or a shift of resources from areas of high union influence to others of low influence (Clegg & Van Wijnbergen, 2011; Durazzi & Geyer, 2020), unions face an institutional trade-off which puts them in opposition to SI policies.

The exposure to institutional trade-offs, however, is likely to vary across countries, according to three scenarios: Firstly, if unions are systematically involved across policy areas, they are unlikely to face significant institutional trade-offs; secondly, and for opposite reasons, if unions are marginal actors—and therefore not involved in policymaking altogether—they will not be faced with an institutional trade-off either; thirdly, the middle-ground situation, where unions enjoy strength in some areas but not all and where they are involved in policymaking but not systematically, is where unions are more likely to be faced with an

314 NICCOLO DURAZZI AND LEONARD GEYER

institutional trade-off. In addition, trade-offs are more likely to occur in policy areas which are traditional strongholds of union power—notably labor market or vocational training policy—and less so in the field of childcare or general education. Both of the latter are areas where unions enjoyed little institutionalized powers or, in other words, areas where unions have less to lose in terms of influence.

10.2.3. SI policymaking: (When) Do unions matter at the macro-level?

Having reviewed how micro-level foundations and meso-level features might influence unions' preference formation, the last step is to theorize whether and how unions' preferences make it into the policymaking process. Here, we build again on the same meso-level factors just introduced. We suggest that these factors not only shape the linkage between micro- and meso-levels in terms of preference formation but also shape the linkage between the preference formation process and macro-level policymaking. In line with the power resource literature (Korpi, 1978, 1983), we assume that unions matter most when their density and/or institutional involvement are medium or high: in these circumstances, unions' voice is strong (i.e., they can act as protagonists) and their veto power credible (i.e., they can perform the antagonist role).

However, in the field of SI it is also worthwhile to ask when the influence of trade unions is pivotal (i.e., when the intervention of unions is more likely to alter the political outcome). This question is relevant because, at least since the "activation turn" in the late 1990s, SI policies have been embraced by various political actors, and they tend to be supported by large cross sections of the population (Garritzmann et al., 2018). Therefore, unions' pro-SI positions may not necessarily be pivotal for pushing through SI policies (i.e., they would appear as enthusiastic or reluctant consenters). Against this background, we contend that the role of unions is most consequential when a given SI policy entails a degree of class conflict or when it entails a trade-off with their established interests. For example, the position of the Austrian trade unions was consequential when they managed to push through an SI-oriented training reform against the opposition of organized employers (Durazzi & Geyer, 2020): They were, in other words, protagonists in the development of an SI policy. Similarly, the example of French unions opposing training measures to prevent state intervention in the union-administered unemployment funds was consequential and limited the development of more SI-oriented policies (Bonoli, 2012): They were, in other words, credible antagonists.

In contrast, unions may matter less in policy areas where such conflicts or trade-offs are unlikely to occur, such as family policy or general education. Here, unions would be best characterized as (enthusiastic or reluctant) consenters. The expansion of childcare illustrates this logic. In line with the general turn toward SI policies, measures that allow mothers to reconcile family and paid employment tend to be supported by encompassing coalitions. A case in point is Germany, where several policies in this field introduced in the early 2000s were supported by all major parties, the social partners as well as welfare organizations (Häusermann, 2018). Under these conditions, the support of the unions for this reform certainly did not hurt. However, if all other relevant actors support this policy as well, the position of the unions is unlikely to have significantly altered the outcome. From this perspective, the impact of unions might have been higher or more visible if they opposed childcare policies. However, this is unlikely because, as argued, unions do not face stark institutional trade-offs in this field. Hence, with respect to policy impact, we assume that unions are less relevant with regard to SI policies that do not present them with significant institutional trade-offs (e.g., childcare or general education) compared to SI policies that might directly affect unions' power in traditional social policy areas (e.g., ALMPs vs. UB).

10.3. DENSITY, CENTRALIZATION, AND INSTITUTIONAL INVOLVEMENT: WHERE AND HOW DO THEY MANIFEST THEMSELVES EMPIRICALLY?

We have argued in Section 10.2 that preferences at the level of the *individual* union are a function of their members' interests but that (varying degrees of) density, centralization, and institutional involvement mediate unions' logic of membership and that they are therefore key features to hypothesize unions' preferences for SI policies and their impact on SI policymaking at the macro-level. In this section we sketch out how these three meso-level features manifest themselves empirically across a set of advanced industrialized countries. To capture our three features of interest, we use the following indicators from the Database on Institutional Characteristics of Trade Unions, Wage Setting, State Intervention and Social Pacts (ICTWSS) (Visser, 2019)[2]:

- *Union density* is measured as the share of union members among all wage earners in employment (ranges from 0 to 1).
- *Union centralization* is measured by the authority of confederations over their affiliate federations (which also ranges from 0 to 1, indicating none to full authority of the confederation).
- *Institutionalized involvement of unions* in the policymaking process is captured by two indicators measuring 1) whether there is routine

2. We use the indicators "ud," "cfauthority," and "ri" and "tc" from the ICTWSS data set to measure density, authority, and institutional involvement, respectively. For more information on the indicators, see the ICTWSS Codebook (Visser, 2019).

involvement of unions and employers in government decisions on social and economic policy and 2) whether there is a standard (institutionalized) tripartite council concerning social and economic policy. The unweighted average of both measures is used to construct a single indicator on union involvement, which ranges from 0 (no involvement) to 1 (high level of involvement).

In Table 10.2, we provide average data for advanced capitalist countries over the years 1990–2000 (when SI emerged as a paradigm) and 2001–2014 (when SI became gradually institutionalized). We only include in the sample those countries for which at least one data-year is available across each indicator of interest in each of the two periods of interest. The countries are ranked according to the unweighted average of their value across the three dimensions in each period ("mean").

The ranking along the unweighted average reveals a picture that will be broadly familiar to scholars in comparative political economy and that is also fully consistent with recent contributions in the field of comparative employment relations (see Benassi & Vlandas, 2016): We find four macro-combinations of union movements (identified through different shadings in Table 10.2), which will be used in the next section to formulate expectations around unions' preferences for and impact on SI policies:

1) Unions in Scandinavian countries, Austria, Belgium, and the Netherlands combine high or medium-high density, high or medium-high centralization, and high institutional involvement.
2) Unions in Southern European countries display medium density, medium-high centralization, and medium institutionalized involvement.
3) Unions in Continental European countries display medium density, medium-low centralization, and medium institutionalized involvement.
4) Unions in Anglo-Saxon countries (with the exception of Ireland) plus Japan feature medium-low density, low centralization, and low institutional involvement.

10.4. BRINGING TOGETHER MICRO, MESO, AND MACRO: HYPOTHESIZING UNIONS' PREFERENCES AND THEIR IMPACT ON POLICY

Having discussed theoretically why we expect density, centralization, and institutional involvement to matter when it comes to unions' preference formation for and impact on SI policies (Section 10.2) and having reviewed how density,

Table 10.2 Institutional involvement, centralization, density, and expected SI of trade unions

Country	1990–2000				2001–2014			
	Involvement	Centralization	Density	Mean	Involvement	Centralization	Density	Mean
Belgium	1.00	0.65	0.53	**0.73**	1.00	0.65	0.55	**0.73**
Norway	0.75	0.76	0.57	**0.69**	0.75	0.70	0.54	**0.66**
Denmark	0.75	0.60	0.75	**0.70**	0.75	0.52	0.69	**0.65**
Austria	0.98	0.78	0.41	**0.72**	0.90	0.67	0.31	**0.63**
Finland	0.75	0.48	0.78	**0.67**	0.75	0.46	0.71	**0.64**
Sweden	0.43	0.54	0.84	**0.60**	0.37	0.60	0.73	**0.57**
Netherlands	1.00	0.53	0.24	**0.59**	1.00	0.50	0.20	**0.57**
Ireland	0.59	0.35	0.46	**0.46**	0.67	0.36	0.34	**0.46**
Italy	0.43	0.45	0.37	**0.42**	0.48	0.50	0.35	**0.44**
Spain	0.43	0.38	0.17	**0.33**	0.63	0.48	0.16	**0.42**
Portugal	0.52	0.39	0.25	**0.39**	0.44	0.40	0.20	**0.35**
Switzerland	0.50	0.11	0.22	**0.28**	0.50	0.10	0.18	**0.26**
France	0.32	0.30	0.09	**0.24**	0.29	0.30	0.08	**0.22**
Germany	0.32	0.13	0.29	**0.25**	0.27	0.11	0.20	**0.19**
Canada	0.00	0.20	0.34	**0.18**	0.00	0.20	0.30	**0.17**
New Zealand	0.05	0.04	0.30	**0.13**	0.25	0.10	0.21	**0.19**
Japan	0.00	0.15	0.24	**0.13**	0.00	0.20	0.19	**0.13**
United Kingdom	0.05	0.00	0.35	**0.13**	0.00	0.00	0.27	**0.09**

Source. Authors' elaboration based on Visser (2019).

centralization, and institutional involvement manifest empirically across countries (Section 10.3), we now move on to the formulation of hypotheses for both unions' preferences and their impact on policymaking. Table 10.3 brings together the insights developed so far.

10.5. AN ILLUSTRATION OF THE THEORETICAL FRAMEWORK

Having set out our theoretical expectations regarding unions' preference formation and impact on policymaking, we illustrate the theoretical framework by making use of a set of diverse case studies (Seawright & Gerring, 2008) covering the four macro-groups of unions, based on their institutional features and identified through the comparative data in Section 10.3 (see also Table 10.2). While limited space does not permit a systematic empirical test here, the following concise case studies aim at illustrating the key features of the proposed theoretical framework, touching upon both unions' preferences toward SI policies and their impact in terms of SI policymaking. We use the same country cases as the chapter on employers (Chapter 9 in this volume) so that readers can easily link between both sides of the social partners.

10.5.1. Contexts I and III: High union density, high centralization, strong involvement (Austria) versus medium density, medium-low centralization, and medium-low involvement (Germany)

A comparison of training policies for the low-skilled in Austria and Germany clearly illustrates the difference between the first and the third scenarios. Austria is a prime example of a country that is located at the top end of the presented indices: union movements that are unlikely to be faced with an institutional trade-off and that build on encompassing organizations with strong preeminence of the confederation over the sectoral federations. The Austrian case is contrasted with that of Germany, which illustrates how the presence of institutional trade-offs might turn unions from "SI protagonists" to "SI antagonists," thus touching upon one case in the "middle" of the index and revealing broader insights on the workings of unions fragmented along sectoral lines.

When confronted with a crisis of the apprenticeship market in the late 1990s, both the Austrian and German governments opened a debate with the social partners on potential solutions to be adopted for those low-skilled young people who were unable to secure an apprenticeship in the dual system of vocational training (Busemeyer, 2012). Yet, despite the fact that the negotiations took place in two "most similar" countries (regarding other political-economic factors), the outcome was significantly different: In the Austrian case, a highly inclusive

Table 10.3 Hypothesized preferences and impact on policymaking of trade unions across countries

Unions' institutional features			SI policy preference	SI policy impact	Country examples
Density	**Centralization**	**Involvement**			
High	High	High	• Broad logic of membership leading to inclusive, pro-SI preferences as weaker segments of unions are empowered via high centralization and/or density • Unlikely veto position because institutional trade-offs are unlikely to occur through extensive institutional involvement	• Likely protagonists as unions are powerful and their involvement is strongly institutionalized across "old" and "new" policy areas	Scandinavian countries, Benelux (+ Austria)
Medium	Medium-high	Medium	• Broad logic of membership leading to targeted, pro-SI preferences as weaker segments of unions are empowered via high centralization • Possible veto position because of potential institutional trade-offs	• Likely protagonists but targeted at weaker members • Likely antagonists if SI policy undermines institutional involvement	Southern European countries
Medium-low	Medium-low	Medium	• Narrow logic of membership and potential for insider–outsider conflicts. Support if SI policies is directly or indirectly beneficial to core members and their unions, lip service for policies neither benefiting nor conflicting with core members' interest, opposition against policies harmful to core members. • Possible veto position because of potential institutional trade-offs	• Likely protagonists/consenters if SI policies are of direct/indirect benefit to core members • Likely antagonists if SI policy goes against interest of core members or reduces involvement	Continental European countries
Medium-low	Low	Low	• Narrow logic of membership of occupational union unlikely to formulate preferences for social policymaking • Inclusive but not representative position of the confederation • Unlikely veto position because of lack of institutional involvement	• Likely (reluctant or enthusiastic) consenters and SI agenda to be left to government due to lack of involvement in policymaking	Anglo-Saxon countries

training system—which developed into a training guarantee—was set up in parallel to the apprenticeship system (Bundeskanzleramt, 2008; Bundesministerium für Wirtschaft und Arbeit, 1998). This means that young people unable to land an apprenticeship place were offered a place in a state-funded training system, leading to the same certification as the dual apprenticeship system. The unions were key in setting up this system, which they managed to push through against employers' will.[3]

The German case shows a starkly different picture: There, too, the government proposed to (temporarily) upgrade training outside of the dual system to award equal certifications, but the unions fiercely opposed this proposal (Busemeyer, 2012; Busemeyer & Trampusch, 2013). The lack of institutional trade-offs for trade unions in Austria—and a significant institutional trade-off in Germany—goes a long way in explaining the divergent outcome. In Austria, unions' involvement in policymaking is institutionalized across policy areas (Durazzi & Geyer, 2020). This allowed the unions a wide range of potentially feasible policy choices to solve the apprenticeship crisis. Setting up a training guarantee delivered primarily through workshops in the PES was the option that they pushed for as they considered it to be the most politically likely to succeed. The absence of an institutional trade-off was crucial in shaping unions' preferences: Moving (part of) training from the apprenticeship system to the PES did not lower their influence and control over this policy area. The Austrian case provides an example of both a *targeted* and an *inclusive* SI policy: It is de facto targeted because it caters for unsuccessful apprenticeship seekers who often come from disadvantaged backgrounds, but it is de jure inclusive as its institutionalization through the training guarantee means that all young people have a right to a fully qualifying training place and that this right is underwritten by the state.

In Germany, in contrast, unions were pushed into a politically constrained territory as the only available option on the table was to move (part of) training into the school system (i.e., education policy)—an area in which unions' control is very weak (especially when compared to their power over the dual apprenticeship system). In this context, unions—jointly with employers—fiercely opposed this government proposal, which therefore never materialized. This left young people who do not land an apprenticeship to enter the so-called transition system"—a patchwork of measures not leading to recognized certification and carrying little value in the labor market (Thelen, 2014; Thelen & Busemeyer, 2012). The opposition of the unions to a shift from the dual training to school-based training was in large part motivated by an institutional trade-off: Had it happened, unions would have lost control and power over a key policy area such as training. The outcome was therefore one of *stratified* SI, whereby successful apprenticeship seekers continued enjoying high-quality training but unsuccessful ones ended up in a significantly lower-quality system, thus perpetuating inequalities.

---

3. Interview with a representative of the Austrian Arbeiterkammer conducted in May 2016.

Furthermore, the German case speaks to two additional theoretical predictions. Firstly, the only union that supported the upgrade of the school-based system to bridge the lack of apprenticeship places was the (left-leaning) teachers' union (Busemeyer, 2012), testifying to the rather peculiar role of public sector unions in the context of SI policy (recall Section 10.2) insofar as expansion of public sector employment may be a reason for public sector unions to support SI policies. Secondly, in the context of the discussions around the lack of apprenticeship places, the option of introducing shorter and less demanding 2-year apprenticeships was also part of the debate, next to the upgrading of the school system. Here, unions' preferences and their role in the policy process again mapped onto the theoretical expectations: The confederal union (Deutscher Gewerkschaftsbund—DGB) took a more conciliatory stance on this proposal and stated its availability to explore this option. The blue-collar metal-working union (IG Metall), on the other hand, played the predicted antagonist role. The introduction of 2-year apprenticeships was not in the interests of its members as it would have led to a segmentation of the labor market in its sector, and, as such, it strongly opposed considering this option. Indeed, in a clear sign of escalating inter-union conflict, senior IG Metall officials openly reminded the DGB in an article in the union's newspaper that "[t]he DGB is not appointed to formulate the IG Metall's training policy" (Ehrke et al., 2004, p. 28).

10.5.2. Context II: Medium-strong union density, medium-high centralization, and medium involvement (Italy)

This case study focuses on Italy to touch upon a union movement with a high degree of centralization in its (social) policy preference formation process (similarly to the countries at the top of our index) but also with a varying degree of involvement in policymaking (similarly to the countries at the middle of our index), which, if anything, has been decreasing in the most recent years (Durazzi et al., 2018). We focus on the case of ALMPs for labor market outsiders to understand unions' behavior in Italy toward SI, and we illustrate how ALMPs for labor market outsiders were convincingly embraced by unions, which played the protagonist role in the establishment of a noteworthy framework of training measures of temporary agency workers (TAWs).

A landmark event in this respect was the establishment of a bilateral fund, Forma.Temp, jointly managed by unions and employers to fund training. The establishment of Forma.Temp followed the 1997 labor market reforms, which liberalized the Italian labor market and allowed widespread use of agency work, which was previously banned in Italy. Just 1 year after the labor market reform passed, the unions provided a crucial contribution in filling the implementation vacuum left by the 1997 reform, which did not detail how training for temporary workers should be organized (Johnston et al., 2011, p. 357). Through the creation of the bilateral fund, four types of training have been offered to agency workers since 2001: 1) basic training, which focuses on general skills such as foreign languages or information technology literacy; 2) professional training, to which most of the resources are devoted, aiming to equip workers with specific and technical skills that can be of immediate use at the workplace; 3) on-the-job training, aiming to (re-)align workers' skills to those needed for their jobs; and 4) continuous training, which consists of a training voucher that allows TAWs to attend a specific training program of their choice (Durazzi, 2017). These training opportunities have been enjoyed by Italian agency workers to comparatively high levels. In contrast to an overall expenditure on ALMPs still significantly lower than many Western European countries (Jessoula et al., 2010, p. 577), significant resources are invested in training for TAWs, and a comparatively very high share of agency workers have access to training (Durazzi, 2017, pp. 274–275), to the point that commentators referred to it as "a good practice" (Leonardi, 2008, p. 216). The decisive role of the unions in this policy area was precisely explained on the grounds that a strong confederal union has as a core objective the representation of all workers, including labor market outsiders.[4] In this respect, training was seen as crucial in helping labor market outsiders to secure a permanent, better-paid job (Durazzi, 2017).

Yet, in the context of progressive liberalization of the labor market and of their progressive marginalization from the policy process since the late 1990s (Durazzi et al., 2018), the unions coupled *targeted* pro-outsider SI strategies with a general defensive position, aimed at preserving the security of labor market insiders (e.g., in the realm of pension policy or dismissal rules). Thus, unions never fully realigned their preferences toward a comprehensive transformation of the welfare state in an SI direction (see also Chapter 5 in Volume II [Garritzmann et al., 2022]), and reforms since the 1990s do not suggest that such a reorientation has been convincingly pursued by governments (see also Chapter 5 in Volume II [Garritzmann et al., 2022]) or has found support from other relevant collective actors (e.g., employers did not lend particular support to SI policies, see Chapter 9 in this volume). In this context, the unions used targeted SI policies as a bridge for labor market outsiders to secure a better position in the labor market.[5] Unions' inclusive stance toward labor market outsiders was shaped primarily by their confederal nature (Durazzi, 2017) that, as hypothesized, facilitated the inclusion of weaker segments of the labor market within unions' representation and agency. Yet, the behavior of Italian unions stands in contrast with a broader realignment of union preferences that are found in countries where unions are firmly involved in social policymaking (i.e., those at the top of our index; see, for instance, Thelen [2014] on Denmark and the Netherlands).

---

4. Interview with a representative of the General Confederation of Labour conducted in May 2013.
5. Interview with a representative of the Italian Confederation of Workers' Trade Unions conducted in May 2013.

This might be understood—in the light of the proposed framework—as the outcome of different degrees of institutional involvement in policymaking of Italian unions compared to their Scandinavian counterparts, fueling the suspicion that a broader realignment of the welfare state might have ultimately led to unions' (further) marginalization from the policy process and to a labor market–welfare state nexus characterized by "flexibility-without-security."

10.5.3. Context IV: Low union density, low centralization, low involvement (Britain)

Our final case study illustrates the role of labor unions at the bottom of our index by assessing the role of British unions in the context of the development of ALMPs for young people (for additional cases, see also the analysis of North America in Chapter 6 of Volume II [Garritzmann et al., 2022]). In these cases, we expect that union involvement in policymaking is strictly optional for policymakers as unions do not benefit from any institutionalized structure of involvement. At the same time, the absence of institutional involvement and hence institutional trade-offs means that unions are free to take inclusive positions. Three subsequent policy packages neatly illustrate this point. The first is the New Deal for Young People (NDYP) introduced in 1998 by Tony Blair's New Labour government. The unions were involved in the implementation of the NDYP through local partnerships (House of Commons, 2001), and while the Trade Union Congress (TUC) generally regarded the policy as a success, it supported additional SI efforts by paying attention to the quality of measures. Specifically, the unions called for a focus on "real" work experience in combination with intensive and accredited training as the most effective measure (House of Commons, 2001). In 2009, against the background of the world financial crisis, Labour replaced the NDYP with the Young Persons' Guarantee and its principal component, a direct-job creation scheme called the Future Jobs Fund (FJF). Again, the government consulted with the unions and invited them to participate in the implementation of the program, in particular to monitor that the employment opportunities offered under the program provided youth with quality work experience.[6] Thus, the TUC, unbound by the institutional constraints that unions in the "middle" of Table 10.1 face (recall the German example), contributed to increasing the SI content of policies targeted primarily at outsiders by providing skill formation opportunities to disadvantaged young people. Yet, as the coalition government came to power in 2010, it scrapped the FJF against the strong opposition of the TUC and replaced New Labour's framework of ALMPs for young people with the so-called Youth Contract. In this context, the involvement of the TUC—by its own admission—was significantly curtailed.[7] Furthermore,

---

6. Interview with a representative of the TUC conducted in September 2016.
7. Interview with a representative of the TUC conducted in September 2016.

the unions criticized the widespread use of "bad" work experience—which in their view too often resulted in the exploitation of youth and the replacement of regular employment—and the reduction of standards in the new program (House of Commons, 2012; Wintour & Mulholland, 2011). However, their voice was just not heard by the government—and indeed there was no institutional structure guaranteeing that it should have been. Unions, in other words, were forced into a "reluctant" consenter role.

The British case provides three insights regarding the preferences and impact of fragmented unions in a weakly institutionalized policy environment, such as that of the Anglo-Saxon countries. Firstly, in this context of low union density, centralization, and involvement, unions' involvement is a choice that policymakers may or may not take; and it is therefore by no means guaranteed. Secondly, the TUC engaged with the government when it was given the opportunity to do so, but all the sectoral/occupational unions by and large refrained from even taking part in the consultations with government. And thirdly, in the absence of trade-offs, the TUC preferences were genuinely along the lines of an SI approach, emphasizing the importance of (inclusive) skill formation for young people, and—as they were left out of the consultations by the coalition government—a workfarist *non-SI strategy*, inspired by market liberalism principles, became predominant.

10.6. CONCLUSION

How, then, should we characterize the role of trade unions with respect to SI policymaking? Our chapter suggests that the answer is, *it depends*. Overall, our theoretical expectations and empirical evidence do not identify strong reasons to believe that unions would in general oppose the objectives commonly associated with SI policies. However, we have shown how SI policies might at times conflict with other policy areas that are also important to unions and on which unions have a historically established authority and a strategic interest (see Bledow, 2019). In these cases, we suggest that a strong and credible institutional involvement of unions across policy areas is key for policymakers to have their support when it comes to the realignment of the welfare state toward SI. With strong and credible involvement in the reform process—including in the "new" SI-oriented policy areas—it is conceivable that unions might play a protagonist role. Conversely, where such involvement is patchy and/or government's commitment to include unions in the policy process is not credible, their position might be expected to come closer to that of antagonists. On top of the institutional trade-offs, the chapter also suggests that—as hypothesized—encompassing unions tend to be at the outset more favorable to SI policies. In short, we argued that the degree of union density, centralization, and involvement is key to understanding unions' preferences and respective role in the politics of SI.

To what extent do we expect the arguments developed in this chapter to travel to other regions? Due to the limited availability of data and space, the evidence has been drawn only from advanced capitalist countries. However, Chapter 11 in this volume on the Latin American context shows that unions with strong collective representation in countries with a smaller informal sector are more likely to effectively push for the broadening of early education and childcare policies compared to unions with weaker collective representation in countries with a large informal sector. In the former, unions act in the interests of the wider population and effectively expand the benefits of SI policies to them, while in the latter, unions' primary concern is the well-being of protected insiders in the formal sector. These findings are in line with the basic micro-, meso-, and macro-logic of our theoretical framework, suggesting therefore that it may be applicable to other parts of the world as well. We also acknowledge that, given limited space availability, we have illustrated our theoretical framework only with short cases and have not provided a full and exhaustive test to the theory (e.g., more policy areas/countries could be included), although findings from research that included other policy areas as well seem to resonate with the main hypotheses generated by our theoretical framework (see, e.g., Bledow, 2019). The aim of this chapter was rather to develop a theoretical framework that provides a useful heuristic to conceptualize unions' role in the politics of SI.

REFERENCES

Amsterdam Institute for Advanced Labour Studies. (2016). *Database on institutional characteristics of trade unions, wage setting, state intervention and social pacts* (Version 5.1).

Bundeskanzleramt. 2008. *Second Austrian reform programme for growth and jobs 2008–2010.* http://ec.europa.eu/archives/growthandjobs/pdf/member-states-2008-2010-reports/Übersetzung_2_%20NRP_2008-2010_final_EN.pdf

Benassi, C., & Vlandas, T. (2016). Union inclusiveness and temporary agency workers: The role of power resources and union ideology. *European Journal of Industrial Relations, 22*(1), 5–22.

Bledow, N. (2019, September 5–7). Compensatory policy for the elderly? Investigating reform skepticism and seniority biases of labor unions in the welfare state [Paper presentation]. ESPAnet, Stockholm, Sweden.

Bundesministerium für Arbeit, Gesundheit und Soziales, Bundesministerium für wirtschaftliche Angelegenheiten & Bundesministerium für Unterricht und kulturelle Angelegenheiten. (1998). Nationaler Aktionsplan für Beschäftigung Österreich. ec.europa.eu/social/ajax/BlobServlet?docId=5771&langId=de

Bonoli, G. (2005). The politics of the new social policies: Providing coverage against new social risks in mature welfare states. *Policy & Politics, 33*(3), 431–449.

Bonoli, G. (2006). New social risks and the politics of post-industrial social policies. In K. Armingeon & G. Bonoli (Eds.), *The politics of post-industrial welfare states: Adapting post-war social policies to new social risks* (pp. 3–26). Routledge.

Bonoli, G. (2012). Active labour market policy and social investment: A changing relationship. In N. Morel, B. Palier, & J. Palme (Eds.), *Towards a social investment welfare state? Ideas, policies and challenges* (pp. 181–204). Policy Press.

Busemeyer, M. R. (2012). Business as a pivotal actor in the politics of training reform: Insights from the case of Germany. *British Journal of Industrial Relations, 50*(4), 690–713.

Busemeyer, M. R., & Garritzmann, J. L. (2017). Academic, vocational or general? An analysis of public opinion towards education policies with evidence from a new comparative survey. *Journal of European Social Policy, 27*(4), 373–386.

Busemeyer, M. R., & Trampusch, C. (2013). Liberalization by exhaustion: Transformative change in the German welfare state and vocational training system. *Zeitschrift für Sozialreform, 59*(3), 291–312.

Clegg, D., & Van Wijnbergen, C. (2011). Welfare institutions and the mobilization of consent: Union responses to labour market activation policies in France and the Netherlands. *European Journal of Industrial Relations, 17*(4), 333–348.

Crouch, C. (2000). The snakes and ladders of 21st-century trade unionism. *Oxford Review of Economic Policy, 16*(1), 70–83.

Culpepper, P. D. (2002). Powering, puzzling, and "pacting": The informational logic of negotiated reforms. *Journal of European Public Policy, 9*(5), 774–790.

Davidsson, J. B., & Emmenegger, P. (2013). Defending the organisation, not the members: Unions and the reform of job security legislation in western Europe. *European Journal of Political Research, 52*(3), 339–363.

Durazzi, N. (2017). Inclusive unions in a dualized labour market? *Social Policy & Administration, 51*(2), 265–285.

Durazzi, N. (2019). The political economy of high skills: Higher education in knowledge-based labour markets. *Journal of European Public Policy, 26*(12), 1799–1817.

Durazzi, N., Fleckenstein, T., & Lee, S. C. (2018). Social solidarity for all? Trade union strategies, labor market dualization, and the welfare state in Italy and South Korea. *Politics & Society, 46*(2), 205–233.

Durazzi, N., & Geyer, L. (2020). Social inclusion in the knowledge economy: Unions' strategies and institutional change in the Austrian and German training systems. *Socio-Economic Review, 18*(1), 103–124.

Ehrke, M., Heimann, K., & Vitt, E. (2004). Anschluss statt Ausschluss—Zweijährige Berufe helfen benachteiligten Jugendlichen nicht. *Gewerkschaftliche Bildungspolitik,* 1/2004, 25–29.

Emmenegger, P. (2014). *The power to dismiss: Trade unions and the regulation of job security in Western Europe.* Oxford University Press.

Esping-Andersen, G. (1990). *The three worlds of welfare capitalism*. Princeton University Press.

Esping-Andersen, G., Gallie, D., Hemerijck, A., & Myles, J. (2001). *A new welfare architecture for Europe* [Report submitted to the Belgian presidency of the European Union].

Fleckenstein, T., Saunders, A. M., & Seeleib-Kaiser, M. (2011). The dual transformation of social protection and human capital comparing Britain and Germany. *Comparative Political Studies, 44*(12), 1622–1650.

Garritzmann, J. L., Busemeyer, M. R., & Neimanns, E. (2018). Public demand for social investment: New supporting coalitions for welfare state reform in Western Europe? *Journal of European Public Policy, 25*(6), 844–861.

Garritzmann, J. L., Häusermann, S., & Palier, B. (Eds.). (2022). *The world politics of social investment: Vol. II. The politics of varying social investment strategies*. Oxford University Press.

Gordon, J. C. (2014). Protecting the unemployed: Varieties of unionism and the evolution of unemployment benefits and active labor market policy in the rich democracies. *Socio-Economic Review, 13*(1), 79–99.

Hall, P. A., & Soskice, D. (2001). An introduction to varieties of capitalism. In P. A. Hall & D. Soskice (Eds.), *Varieties of capitalism: The institutional foundations of comparative advantage* (pp. 1–68). Oxford University Press.

Häusermann, S. (2018). The multidimensional politics of social investment in conservative welfare regimes: Family policy reform between social transfers and social investment. *Journal of European Public Policy, 25*(6), 862–877.

Hemerijck, A. (2015). The quiet paradigm revolution of social investment. *Social Politics, 22*(2), 242–256.

Hemerijck, A. (Ed.). (2017). *The uses of social investment*. Oxford University Press.

House of Commons. (2001). *Memorandum from the Trades Union Congress (TUC): The new deal—And inquiry by the House of Commons Employment Sub-Committee*. https://publications.parliament.uk/pa/cm200001/cmselect/cmeduemp/58/58ap24.htm

House of Commons. (2012). *Youth unemployment and the youth contract* [Second report by the Work and Pensions Committee]. https://publications.parliament.uk/pa/cm201213/cmselect/cmworpen/151/15102.htm

Hyman, R. (2001). *Understanding European trade unionism: Between market, class and society*. Sage.

Ibsen, C. L., & Thelen, K. (2017). Diverging solidarity: Labor strategies in the new knowledge economy. *World Politics, 69*(3), 1–39.

Jessoula, M., Graziano, P. R., & Madama, I. (2010). Selective flexicurity in segmented labour markets: The case of Italian "mid-siders." *Journal of Social Policy, 39*(4), 561–583.

Johnston, A., Kornelakis, A., & d'Acri, C. R. (2011). Social partners and the welfare state: Recalibration, privatization or collectivization of social risks? *European Journal of Industrial Relations, 17*(4), 349–364.

Kenworthy, L. (2017). Enabling social policy. In A. Hemerijck (Ed.), *The uses of social investment* (pp. 89–96). Oxford University Press.

Korpi, W. (1978). *The working class in welfare capitalism: Work, unions, and politics in Sweden*. Taylor & Francis.

Korpi, W. (1983). *The democratic class struggle*. Routledge.

Leonardi, S. (2008). Union organisation of employees in precarious and atypical work in Italy. *International Journal of Action Research, 4*(3), 203–224.

Madama, I., Natili, M., & Jessoula, M. (2013). *National report: Italy. Work package 5—The national arena for combating poverty*. Combating Poverty in Europe.

Martin, C. J., & Swank, D. (2012). *The political construction of business interests: Coordination, growth, and equality*. Cambridge University Press.

Morel, N., Palier, B., & Palme, J. (Eds.). (2012). *Towards a social investment welfare state?* Policy Press.

Mosimann, N., & Pontusson, J. (2017). Solidaristic unionism and support for redistribution in contemporary Europe. *World Politics, 69*(3), 448–492.

Neimanns, E., Busemeyer, M. R., & Garritzmann, J. L. (2018). How popular are social investment policies really? Evidence from a survey experiment in eight western European Countries. *European Sociological Review, 34*(3), 238–253.

Nelson, M., & Stephens, J. D. (2012). Do social investment policies produce more and better jobs. Towards a social investment welfare state. In N. Morel, B. Palier, & J. Palme (Eds.), *Towards a social investment welfare state?* (pp. 205–234). Policy Press.

Oliver, R. J. (2010). Powerful remnants? The politics of egalitarian bargaining institutions in Italy and Sweden. *Socio-Economic Review, 9*(3), 533–566.

Organisation for Economic Co-operation and Development. (2017). *Government at a glance 2017*. http://dx.doi.org/10.1787/gov_glance-2017-en

Rueda, D. (2005). Insider–outsider politics in industrialized democracies: The challenge to social democratic parties. *American Political Science Review, 99*(1), 61–74.

Rueda, D. (2006). Social democracy and active labour-market policies: Insiders, outsiders and the politics of employment promotion. *British Journal of Political Science, 36*(3), 385–406.

Sabel, C., Zeitlin, J., & Quack, S. (2017). Capacitating services and the bottom-up approach to social investment. In A. Hemerijck (Ed.), *The uses of social investment* (pp. 140–149). Oxford University Press.

Schmitter, P. C., & Streeck, W. (1999). *The organization of business interests: Studying the associative action of business in advanced industrial societies* [MPIfG discussion paper 99/1]. Max-Planck-Institut für Gesellschaftsforschung.

Seawright, J., & Gerring, J. (2008). Case selection techniques in case study research: A menu of qualitative and quantitative options. *Political Research Quarterly, 61*(2), 294–308.

Simoni, M. (2013). The left and organized labor in low-inflation times. *World Politics, 65*(2), 314–349.

Thelen, K. (2014). *Varieties of liberalization and the new politics of social solidarity*. Cambridge University Press.

Thelen, K., & Busemeyer, M. R. (2012). Institutional change in German vocational training: From collectivism towards segmentalism. In M. R. Busemeyer & C. Trampusch (Eds.), *The political economy of collective skill formation* (pp. 68–100). Oxford University Press.

Visser, J. (2019). ICTWSS Database. version 6.1. Amsterdam: Amsterdam Institute for Advanced Labour Studies (AIAS), University of Amsterdam.

Wintour, P., & Mulholland, H. (2011, November 25). Nick Clegg: £1bn youth jobs fund to prevent lost generation. *The Guardian*. https://www.theguardian.com/society/2011/nov/25/clegg-youth-jobs-generational-fairness

11

TRADE UNIONS, LABOR MARKET DUALIZATION, AND INVESTMENT IN EARLY CHILDHOOD EDUCATION AND CARE IN LATIN AMERICA

Melina Altamirano and Bárbara A. Zárate-Tenorio

11.1. INTRODUCTION

Early childhood education and care (ECEC) policies have experienced a substantial expansion in the last decades in Latin America, particularly after the 1990s. To date, virtually all countries have an ECEC program in place. However, the inclusiveness and quality of public childcare services vary widely across the region (Araujo et al., 2013). The political actors and coalitional dynamics underlying ECEC social policy reform also differ among countries. This variation is consequential as we expect actor configurations to influence social policies' distributive profiles (see Chapter 2 in this volume).

This chapter focuses on the role of trade unions in the recent expansions of ECEC services in Latin America. We identify and analyze whether unions have supported ECEC policy reforms and their role in the policymaking process. Membership composition and unions' relations with the government have analytical value for studying the link between organized labor and social investment in European and Latin American countries (see Chapter 10 in this volume for Europe). However, there are two specificities about the Latin American context that mark a sharp difference in outcomes. First, in most countries, the legacies of union–government relations during authoritarian regimes shape unions'

Melina Altamirano and Bárbara A. Zárate-Tenorio, *Trade Unions, Labor Market Dualization, and Investment in Early Childhood Education and Care in Latin America* In: *The World Politics of Social Investment (Volume I)*. Edited by: Julian L. Garritzmann, Silja Häusermann, and Bruno Palier, Oxford University Press. © Oxford University Press 2022. DOI: 10.1093/oso/9780197585245.003.0011 role in social policy reform processes in the post-transition period. Hence, the analysis of centralization and sectorial differences is less relevant than the focus on particular professions in the public sector (e.g., teachers' unions; see Chapter 6 in this volume) or the peak union organization. Therefore, unions are less "encompassing" than in some Western European countries. Second, many Latin American countries have large informal sectors of non-unionized labor market outsiders. While in Europe outsiders are generally characterized by relatively worse labor market conditions,[1] in Latin America they are usually excluded from the social security system.

We argue that the truncated nature of the welfare state in Latin America together with varying degrees of dualization of labor markets are crucial factors affecting trade unions' positions. In contexts of low dualization, social policy reforms are more likely to have direct consequences for the labor conditions of the formal workforce because welfare provision is less segmented. When organized labor's interests are affected, unions have more incentives to get involved in shaping social policies. Unions' involvement can either translate into defending reforms that benefit formal workers while expanding services or opposing measures that might affect their labor benefits. In contrast, social policy expansion is less likely to impact formal workers' labor conditions in highly dualized labor markets. Given the segmentation of welfare provision and the size of the informal sector, the cost of reforms that equalize the benefits between insiders and outsiders is higher, and financial constraints play a significant role. In these contexts, where formal labor conditions remain unaffected, it is unclear that organized labor will be a primary driver (or opponent) of policies aimed at extending benefits to labor market outsiders.

We focus on two crucial reforms that expanded ECEC public services to previously excluded segments of the population: Chile Grows up with you (*Chile Crece Contigo*) in Chile (2006) and the Daycare Program for Working Mothers (*Programa de Estancias Infantiles para Madres Trabajadoras*) in Mexico (2007).[2] In both cases, there was an emphasis on facilitating women's participation in the labor market (human capital mobilization). However, the centrality of the social investment component of human capital creation from an early age differed. In Chile, the objective of fostering cognitive and socioemotional skills in the early years was key, and there was a unified framework setting the standards to reach

1. See Emmenegger et al. (2012) for an analysis of the distinctive nature of dualization and its consequences in Europe.
2. The Daycare Program for Working Mothers (*Programa de Estancias Infantiles para Madres Trabajadoras*) ended in 2019. President López Obrador's administration (2018–2024) replaced it with a cash transfer to mothers with children aged 1–4 years. The analysis in this chapter covers the program's development up until 2018. Although the politics of the ECEC policy replacement are out of this chapter's scope, the coalitional dynamics underlying the design and implementation of the 2007–2019 program might provide important clues to understand the ensuing process.

these goals. In contrast, the Mexican reform focused on providing mothers with childcare while they worked, and the early childhood education component was secondary. Following the theoretical framework of this project, we classify the Mexican program as targeted in its distributive profile and identify mobilization of human capital as its primary function. *Chile Crece Contigo* sought to expand childcare services and consolidate a quasi-universal ECEC public system with a strong educational component. We classify this program as inclusive in its distributive profile and identify as its functions the creation and mobilization of human capital.

ECEC expansions in Chile and Mexico were introduced under presidencies from the left and center-right, respectively. In both cases, the federal governments were the main drivers or protagonists of the reforms. Neither in Chile nor in Mexico was organized labor a relevant actor in the agenda-setting stage. However, in contrast to unions in Mexico, which did not attempt to shape the policy at any stage of the process, unions in Chile have become highly involved in the post-reform period. Following Korpi's (2006) categorization, we find that Chilean unions have acted as consenters in the policymaking process after ECEC expansion.

11.2. LABOR MARKET DUALIZATION, TRADE UNIONS, AND THE POLITICS OF ECEC REFORM

According to International Labor Organization (ILO, 2018) estimates, more than half of Latin American workers lack formal labor benefits (44.6% had access to social security in 2015). There is also significant variation in the size of informality within the region. While some labor markets in Latin America are highly informal (e.g., Bolivia, Honduras, Guatemala), other economies show low levels of informalization (e.g., Uruguay, Costa Rica, Chile). Countries with large informal sectors have developed truncated welfare systems, where workers are eligible for social services depending on their (formal/informal) labor status. In contrast, in contexts where the informal sector is smaller, welfare services tend to be more encompassing of the workforce. Therefore, social policy reforms are more likely to include elements related to formal workers' labor conditions and benefits.[3]

We argue that the dualization of the labor markets and the fragmentation of the welfare systems have consequences for unions' positions regarding ECEC

---

3. Recent Latin American experiences of social policy expansion toward the universalization of certain social policies show that, in contexts of low-dualization, governments have been able to increase access in part through adjustments in payroll taxes and contributions. See Martínez-Franzoni and Sánchez-Ancochea (2014) for the case of Costa Rica and Pribble (2013) for the case of Uruguay.

policy reform. In highly dualized labor markets, welfare provision is likely to be truncated, with different systems for insiders and outsiders. Given varying benefits and financing sources across systems, the interests of both groups are neither aligned nor necessarily in conflict.[4] More importantly, new reforms aimed at extending benefits to outsiders might be unfeasible if they impose high costs on formal workers. Thus, governments will be more prone to introduce new policies for outsiders that do not rely on the organized workers' current benefits system. This partially explains the "layering" of policies in highly dualized labor markets (Haggard & Kaufman, 2008; Dion, 2009).[5] In this context, organized labor has fewer incentives to promote social policies that do not directly benefit their members. Therefore, it is improbable that trade unions will act as important drivers of policies that extend benefits to labor market outsiders. Yet as long as their interests are not hurt, they are unlikely to act as opponents of policy extensions.

In contrast, in contexts of low dualization, organized labor has more incentives to get involved in the process of social policy reform. In the case of formal workers, proposals for expanding services might impact their current system of benefits. Reforms may entail trade-offs between keeping current benefits and increasing access to an excluded group of informal workers (e.g., adapting services or reducing quality to finance the expansion). Therefore, when proposals coincide with the potential of cutbacks in their benefits scheme, unions' incentive to get involved in the policy process increases. Unions' strategies will depend on the specificities of the reforms. While organized labor has incentives to avoid proposals that come at the cost of current benefits, it also has an incentive to act on behalf of excluded workers by opposing lower-quality policies and mobilizing to secure policies that benefit unions.[6]

We claim that organized labor is more likely to mobilize and influence the policy process when proposals for the expansion of ECEC services directly affect the generosity or the quality of the services they receive. Similar to Durazzi

4. In contrast, see Rueda (2007) for the differences in preferences between labor insiders and outsiders in Europe.

5. The pattern of expansion of social assistance programs in Latin America since the 1990s reveals that governments in countries with more extensive social security coverage could increase access to services relying, at least partially, on social insurance institutions. In contrast, those with large informal sectors have resorted to noncontributory social programs layered on top of existing systems. See Haggard and Kaufman (2008) for an analysis of expansion in countries with widespread entitlements, such as Costa Rica and Uruguay. See Dion (2009) for a discussion of policy legacies and institutional layering in Mexico, where "new welfare institutions were created to meet the needs of new political constituents and a new economic development model, and as an alternative to reforms of ailing social insurance blocked by interest groups" (p. 66).

6. An alternative argument could be made based on ideology (see Chapter 13 in this volume). We acknowledge that a more leftist tradition of unions may play an important role in shaping the type of reform (i.e., in terms of quality and generosity/coverage). However, we argue that a crucial element that encourages unions to get involved in the policy process for ECEC expansion to outsiders in the first place is whether their interests and benefits are affected/threatened.

and Geyer (Chapter 10 in this volume), we expect unions to have a more prominent role when they perceive that welfare expansions might modify their contributions and benefits.[7] Moreover, we emphasize that this is more likely in contexts of smaller informal sectors and low fragmentation of welfare systems.

On the other hand, our argument also implies that informal sector workers face severe barriers to collective action that prevent them from playing a prominent role in shaping social investment policies from which they would benefit.[8] Recent work shows that, in contrast to labor market outsiders, the mobilization of insiders has been highly influential in increasing social security and welfare spending in Latin America (Zárate-Tenorio, 2014). Given the low mobilization capacity of outsiders and that noncontributory social investment may not primarily benefit the formal workforce, analyzing whether and under what conditions unions will engage in social policy reform and implementation becomes particularly relevant.

11.3. RESEARCH DESIGN AND CASE SELECTION

To explore the relationship between economic informality and the role of trade unions, we compare the processes of ECEC reform in Chile and Mexico, following a most similar design. The cases of Chile and Mexico are useful for our analysis for various reasons. First, in terms of potential explanatory variables, Chile and Mexico are comparable. They share economic characteristics such as the level of development, the persistence of inequalities, and a similar organization of production (Kurtz, 2002; Schneider, 2009). Chile and Mexico are also similar on various dimensions relevant to studying trade union roles regarding ECEC policies. For instance, the participation of women in the labor force has been consequential for the adoption of ECEC policies in advanced democracies and essential in shaping the positions of collective actors in this regard (Morgan, 2013). According to estimates from the Inter-American Development Bank, the two countries exhibit similar percentages of women (aged 15–64) in the labor force: 39.8% in 2006 and 44.7% in 2017 in Chile; 40.9% in 2006 and 41.2% in 2016 in Mexico (Inter-American Development Bank, 2016).

---

7. In certain policy areas and political contexts, the long-standing clientelistic relationships of public unions with governments might also prevent them from acting on behalf of the interests of their members or the ultimate beneficiaries of social investment policies. See Chapter 6 of this volume and Fernández (2012) for a discussion of the political role of the Mexican teachers' union (Sindicato Nacional de Trabajadores de la Educación, SNTE) that has resulted in rent extraction from the education budget.
8. Successful mobilization of informal workers is more likely when organizational capacity is provided by associations or churches and in electoral contexts where parties actively compete for the vote of outsiders (Agarwala, 2013; Garay, 2017).

In addition, the proportion of employed women affiliated with trade unions is low in both countries. In Mexico, the unionization rate for women was around 11.8% in 2005[9] compared to 9.6% in Chile in the same year (Dirección del Trabajo, 2015). Taking unionization as a whole, we also observe similarities. Labor representation is weak in both countries. In Mexico, the share of the economically active population affiliated with a trade union was 10.6% in 2007 (Bensusán and Middlebrook, 2013), while the rate was 12.9% in Chile in the same year (Dirección del Trabajo, 2015).[10]

Most importantly, both cases differ in terms of the key variable in our study: the magnitude of the informal sector. Mexico has a large informal sector as more than half of the population in the labor force works without social protection in unregistered jobs according to the estimates of the ILO (2018) (69.6% in 2005 and 68.4% in 2015). In contrast, only a third of the workers in Chile lack coverage from contributive social security (34.9% in 2005 and 32.2% in 2015).

Second, these two countries differ on the outcome of interest: the position of trade unions in the demand and politicization of ECEC social investment. As we show in the following sections, the role of organized labor in the politics of ECEC investment gradually diverged in both countries in the post-reform years. While Mexican unions continue to have a marginal role in ECEC policy design and implementation, Chilean unions have been more organized and effective in voicing their preferences and have chosen to participate in policymaking.

We also focus on Chile and Mexico because both countries carried out significant expansions of ECEC provision roughly within the same period (2006–2007). These parallel processes allow us to analyze the role of trade unions before and after two key innovations: the development of a comprehensive early childhood strategy in Chile and the introduction of noncontributory childcare services in Mexico. As noted, the expansion of ECEC services was implemented in Chile by the left/center-left *Concertación* administration of Michelle Bachelet (2006–2010), while the center-right government of Felipe Calderón (2006–2012) of the National Action Party (PAN, *Partido Acción Nacional*) initiated the Mexican reform. However, after the stage of ECEC reform in Chile, the next elected government was the center-right administration of Sebastián Piñera (2010–2014).[11] Therefore, although the design of ECEC policy expansion might have had different ideological underpinnings, the political context (in terms of the ideological leanings of parties in government) was not entirely dissimilar

9. Calculated as the share of the economically active population. Data from Bensusán and Middlebrook (2013) and Instituto Nacional de Estadística y Geografía (2006).

10. In Mexico, this estimate corresponds to salaried workers who are union members as a share of the economically active population (Bensusán & Middlebrook, 2013). In Chile, the rate is the population affiliated to a trade union as a share of the workforce with unionization potential, including salaried, self-employed, and domestic workers (Dirección del Trabajo, 2015).

11. In Mexico, the Institutional Revolutionary Party (PRI, *Partido Revolucionario Institucional*), the previously hegemonic party, regained power in 2012 with Enrique Peña Nieto (2012–2018).

afterward. Organized labor in both countries encountered proposed changes to ECEC services advanced by conservative governments in terms of their social policy preferences, but only in Chile did these proposals generate clear reactions from trade unions.

To explore the consequences of the dualization of labor markets in both countries for the role of trade unions in the expansion of ECEC services, we gathered information regarding the positions of organized labor as reported in each country's most relevant newspapers from 2005 to 2017. We relied on news articles from *El Mercurio* and *La Tercera* for Chile and from *Reforma*, *El Universal*, and *La Jornada* for Mexico.[12] We complemented this evidence with data from official sources. Building on this information, we traced the positions of organized labor and political actors in the processes of ECEC expansion in both countries.

11.4. COLLECTIVE LABOR REPRESENTATION

11.4.1. Chile

More than two decades after the transition to democracy in Chile, unions' political role continues to be limited. Almost nullified during the military dictatorship (1973–1990), organized labor entered the new democratic stage in a weak position. Indeed, several studies have found that even with the prominent role of the left in the *Concertación* governments after the return of democracy in the 1990s, labor unions have remained marginal actors (Etchemendy & Berins Collier, 2007; Leiva, 2012; Palacios-Valladares, 2010).[13] Until the labor reform of 2017, one of the legacies of the period of military rule was a series of regulations that restricted collective labor negotiations, which continued to reduce the ability of unions to leverage their position among workers (Cook, 2007). Unionization rates have remained consistently low in the last decades. Leiva (2012) estimates that the percentage of unionized workers was 15.1 in 1991, then declined to 11.1 in 2000 and was approximately 11.9 in 2008.[14]

According to the Direction of Labor, the Unitary Workers' Central (Central Unitaria de Trabajadores [CUT]), which emerged in 1988 as a union federation

---

12. We used a similar list of search terms adapted to each country (e.g., key political actors and policy programs) for each year in the period of analysis. In Chile we complemented the information with articles from *Sindical.cl*, a labor and union news website.

13. Scholars have also noted that post-transition governments sought to accommodate elite and business interests in the new democratic regime, which further limited the margin of action of organized labor (Haagh, 2002; Palacios-Valladares, 2010).

14. These estimates consider the total employed labor force. According to the author, the decline in the unionization rate is sharper when taking into account the waged labor force, from 21.2 in 1991 to 16.1 in 2008 (Leiva, 2012).

comprised of national multisectoral unions, is currently the largest labor organization.[15] However, given the low unionization rates, the percentage of workers represented by CUT is still limited (Antía, 2014; Arrieta, 2003).

Nonetheless, Chilean organized labor has followed new strategies in recent years. For instance, CUT has resorted to legal actions to challenge labor policies. Gutiérrez Crocco (2017) finds that, although the union federation has had limited success in mobilizing workers using calls for strikes, it has increasingly confronted authorities using legal mobilization (i.e., appealing in courts against labor reforms [p. 200]).[16] Organized labor has also gained relevance in the public discussion of childcare provision after the implementation of *Chile Crece Contigo*, especially when formal labor contributions have been part of the discussion of potential sources of financing for social policy expansion. In addition, low dualization has allowed unions to gradually frame their positions as relevant for most workers and with widely spread benefits.

11.4.2. Mexico

As in many Latin American countries, economic globalization has also weakened labor unions in Mexico. In contrast to Chile, however, one of the defining features of unionism in Mexico is the legacy of the one-party hegemonic regime under the rule of the PRI (1929–2000). During this period, the PRI firmly controlled the workers' movement. Control was exerted by granting particularistic concessions to union leaders in exchange for political support, which limited unions' autonomy, the nature of their demands, and the institutional opportunities to create independent labor movements (Bensusán, 2015; Bizberg, 2003). In the long run, this form of "rigid corporatism" resulted in a lack of representation of workers' interests by labor unions, which has worsened over time. Leaders switched their role to protect government's and employers' interests before those of workers (Bensusán, 2015). Political representation of labor experienced significant losses after the transition to democracy. For example, the number of representatives of the *Confederación de Trabajadores de México* (CTM; Confederation of Mexican Workers) in the Chamber of Deputies fell from 51 to four in the 1985–1988 and 2006–2009 legislatures, respectively (Bensusán & Middlebrook, 2012, p. 346).

The mobilization capacity of organized labor has also declined. While in 1978 the share of the economically active population that belonged to a union was 16.3%, in 2012 this figure dropped to 8.8% (Bensusán & Middlebrook, 2013). Regarding strike activity, Mexico has one of the lowest levels in the region, a legacy of the government's control over the labor movement. As a result, it is

---

15. CUT was formed after a similar organization, the Central Unica de Trabajadores, which was dissolved in the 1970s under the dictatorship.
16. Other firm-level unions, not necessarily affiliated to CUT, have also increasingly resorted to legal mobilization to challenge the government and denounce labor law violations (Gutiérrez Crocco, 2017, p. 201).

not surprising that union leaders often fail to advance workers' interests. In this context, organization and mobilization around issues related to social policy access have been minimal, and there have been few incentives to include informal workers in their collective efforts.

11.5. LABOR UNIONS AND THE POLITICS OF ECEC REFORM

11.5.1. Chile

Early childhood education was a prominent issue in Michelle Bachelet's first presidential campaign. The ECEC strategy, announced early in 2005, was an effort to universalize access to childcare services ("Michelle Bachelet Presenta sus Propuestas como Candidata Presidencial," 2005). According to media coverage of the election, gender issues were key in the race, and Bachelet made declarations pointing to discrimination against women and gender barriers to achieve economic and political power as fundamental problems in Chile (Marques-Pereira et al., 2015).[17] Women's groups, particularly the organization Comunidad Mujer, were quite active during this period, engaging in public dialogue and inviting presidential candidates to sign a pledge to implement work–family policies once in power ("El Factor Mujer," 2006).[18]

After the election, the Bachelet administration presented the ECEC reform as one of the national government's main priorities. It sought to advance the proposal without resorting to congressional approval. Although women's associations continued to press the issue and had strong preferences regarding concrete policies that they believed ought to be adopted, qualitative evidence suggests that the main forces steering the design and implementation strategy of the ECEC services were government officials within the administration. According to interviews carried out by Staab (2017), childcare provision became a central issue in the executive agenda following bureaucratic consensus around two goals: reducing poverty and increasing female labor participation. Government officials viewed this public policy intervention as a feasible reform that would generate mass social support.[19] In addition, these objectives reflected

17. According to Marques-Pereira et al. (2015), during her campaign, Bachelet made reference to gender in three ways: a) she framed it as a factor that made her more relatable to women and different from the political establishment, b) she emphasized gender issues in her government agenda, and c) she made a link between motherhood, strength, and a continuous effort to balance work and family objectives.

18. For instance, Comunidad Mujer, a civil society organization, carried out a public opinion study to identify preferences and needs among working women and developed a report with specific recommendations aimed at reconciling work and family life via labor reforms and public provision of childcare (El factor mujer, 2006).

19. This was the position from a former Budget Office official interviewed by Staab (2017).

the perspective of social investment, consistent with the overall goal of economic growth, human capital creation, and mothers' employability.[20] The initiative successfully generated a supporting coalition that brought together bureaucrats in different ministries (Staab, 2017).

In the first months of the administration, President Bachelet invited experts to form a commission, the Advisory Council for the Reform of Childhood Policy, to work on a proposal to guide the ECEC strategy. Among other recommendations, the Council suggested the possibility of delivering childcare services using a voucher system and of modifying the labor code to eliminate the requirement for employers with more than 20 female workers to provide childcare services (Consejo Asesor Presidencial para la Reforma de las Políticas de Infancia, 2006).[21] However, according to Staab (2017), the Bachelet administration opted to develop the new ECEC model following two strategies. First, it decided to modernize and expand childcare provision via the Junta Nacional de Jardines Infantiles (JUNJI; a public corporation) and Fundación Integra (a state-funded nonprofit foundation), favoring increased public provision over a voucher system. Second, the administration avoided proposing changes to the labor code, anticipating opposition in Congress and other social groups (p. 136). Indeed, although unions remained at the margins of the design and implementation of the ECEC reform during this stage, they publicly rejected proposals that shifted financing responsibility from employers to workers. Therefore, the administration refrained from implementing a tripartite model, favored by the Socialist Party of Chile (PS, *Partido Socialista de Chile*), with contributions from employers, workers, and the government (Staab, 2017).[22] Trade unions' priorities at the moment of the reform can help explain the limited role of organized labor in developing the ECEC strategy. Around 2006, CUT's agenda mostly centered on pension issues. President Bachelet appointed a commission, the Executive Advisory Council for the Pension System Reform, to analyze and prepare recommendations to reform the pension system. The commission elaborated the so-called Marcel Report, a document that presented a series of recommendations to modify the financing structure of the system. Unions strongly opposed the report's content, especially its proposal to increase the retirement age for women from 60 to 65 ("Rechazo a Informe Marcel," 2006). The

---

20. Indeed, Staab (2017) finds that policy objectives consistent with the social investment paradigm were already present during the second half of the Ricardo Lagos government (2000–2006) and that prominent actors in the Bachelet administration considered early education and female labor market participation as key factors in fostering economic development.

21. As discussed in the following sections, this issue continues to be contentious among unions, women's organizations, and the government. The main argument against this regulation is that it discourages employers from hiring more women.

22. The financing model, particularly the tripartite contribution alternative, emerged again as a key issue in the following years. As we discuss in the following sections, after the first stage of ECEC expansion, the Piñera and the second Bachelet administration put the topic on the agenda and again faced strong opposition from trade unions.

financing model, particularly the tripartite contribution alternative, emerged again as a critical issue in the following years. As we discuss in the following sections, after the first stage of ECEC expansion, the Piñera administration and the second Bachelet administration put the tripartite contribution on the agenda and once again faced strong opposition from trade unions.

In sum, ECEC expansion was probably not due to increased public demand or pressure from trade unions or women's organizations. Instead, the reform was mainly designed within the government to extend coverage, building on extant institutions and preventing modifications requiring legislative approval. The consensus among government officials around the relevance and urgency to transform childcare provision suggests a process of diffusion and adoption of social investment goals (Jenson, 2010) that permeated the policy agenda in Chile and elsewhere.

11.5.2. Mexico

In 2007, in the first year of his administration, President Felipe Calderón announced a new ECEC strategy: the Daycare Program for Working Mothers (*Programa de Estancias Infantiles para Madres Trabajadoras*). This program aimed to expand childcare services to the population in the informal sector, who lacks access to social security institutions (the Mexican Social Security Institute, IMSS, and the Institute for Social Security and Services for State Workers, ISSSTE). Formal workers' benefits include healthcare and other services such as IMSS and ISSSTE daycare networks.

The program departed significantly from the childcare provision model for formal workers. First, it was a social program administered by the Secretary for Social Development (Sedesol). The government sought to create a daycare center network independent from the contributory childcare provision system. Unlike the strategy in Chile, the ECEC reform in Mexico did not contemplate the expansion of childcare services that were already provided in public institutions. The design of the Daycare Program for Working Mothers created two groups of beneficiaries: working mothers with social security benefits, covered by IMSS and ISSSTE daycare centers, and mothers in the informal sector with access to the more recent daycare program.

The fragmentation of the ECEC model reflects the labor market dualization in Mexico, which has also impacted the role of trade unions in pressing for the expansion of these services. The Daycare Program for Working Mothers targeted the population in the informal sector, where organized labor has a minimal presence. Informal workers in Mexico continue to face various obstacles to organize and articulate policy demands effectively. Consequently, unions were not central actors in the design and implementation of the ECEC program. The policy was not the result of an increased social policy demand from organized informal workers or from women for public childcare provision.

Similar to the case of Chile, the program emerged within the administration. However, unlike *Chile Crece Contigo*, the Mexican government kept down spending when implementing this ECEC initiative (Altamirano, 2020). According to official figures, the combined budgets of the IMSS and ISSSTE daycare centers in 2009 amounted to three times the budget of the Daycare Program for Working Mothers. However, the latter had more children enrolled than the two contributory services together.[23]

Changes in the childcare provision model for the formal sector generated more reactions among unionized workers. Since 1997, the IMSS has expanded childcare provision by outsourcing services to private providers. The expansion of outsourced daycare centers was significant after 2000, during the PAN administrations of Vicente Fox and Felipe Calderón. From 2000 to 2009, the number of outsourced daycare centers almost doubled, and, in contrast, daycare centers at IMSS facilities stagnated ("Crece Subrogación de Guarderías IMSS," 2009a). The low level of institutionalization of this modality of childcare provision resulted, at least in the beginning, in less rigorous compliance with program and quality standards (Staab & Gerhard, 2010, 2011). Unionized IMSS workers favored the original institutionalized childcare model over the outsourced alternative. In their collective negotiations, they asked for more daycare centers at IMSS facilities ("Demanda SNTSS Más Dinero y Prestaciones," 2005). However, despite this pressure, the government gradually decreased spending in the traditional model and favored subsidies to privately owned centers.

11.6. POST-REFORM ECEC PROVISION AND LABOR UNIONS' PREFERENCES

11.6.1. Chile

The participation of labor unions, represented by CUT has been substantially more active after the reform implementation. A new proposal to extend ECEC services via funding from the workers' unemployment fund triggered unions' involvement. When organized labor perceived that its benefits could be affected, it decided to actively mobilize to support the existing model and oppose attempts to create a different ECEC model on top of the current system. In 2010, CUT participated in public discussions with the labor ministry to expand maternity leave from 3 to 6 months and extend these benefits to women in the informal sector (Frías Fernández, 2010, Vallejos, 2010). In general, unions have been vocal against modifications to the ECEC model they perceive to be detrimental to public financing and service quality.

23. Information given to the authors by IMSS, ISSSTE, and Sedesol via a request for access to public information.

The first administration of Sebastián Piñera (2010–2014), from the National Renewal Party (*Partido Renovación Nacional*), presented a bill before Congress to regulate childcare services under a new national daycare law. In 2013, shortly before the end of his term, President Piñera proposed to increase access to childcare services to women working in small firms and to finance this expansion using part of the employers' contributions to the workers' unemployment fund (Gobierno de Chile, 2013; Peña, 2013). The proposal included the possibility of providing female workers with vouchers to enroll their children in private daycare centers. The bill established that increased childcare access would be financed via the workers' unemployment funds without additional contributions from employers, aligning with employers' preferences and providing them with incentives for hiring women.[24]

In response, CUT publicly rejected the central aspects of the proposal, arguing that it intended to privatize ECEC provision, risking universal access to childcare services ("CUT Rechaza Aspectos del Proyecto de Ley Sobre Salas Cunas," 2013b). Bárbara Figueroa, the CUT leader, demanded that the expansion of childcare access be financed independently from the workers' unemployment fund ("CUT Pidió al Gobierno no Financiar Salas Cuna con Seguro de Cesantía," 2013). PS representatives in Congress backed the CUT's position during the beginning of the new administration of Michelle Bachelet (2014–2018), arguing that it intended to dismantle the workers' unemployment fund to pay for daycare centers (Toro, 2014). Figueroa and the CUT vice president for women's affairs declared that the bill could reduce the quality of childcare because it could incentivize private providers to expand their offer to more children without necessarily adhering to the Chilean early education program.[25] In turn, the union called for prioritizing public childcare provision and strengthening the role of JUNJI and Fundación Integra.[26]

In 2014, President Bachelet withdrew President Piñera's proposal from the legislative process in Congress. Her administration started drafting a new bill to finance the expansion of childcare services via a tripartite fund with additional contributions from the government and workers. Representatives from

---

24. The bill sought to modify the restriction in Article 203 of the Chilean labor law that requires employers to provide access for female workers to daycare centers only in the case of firms with more than 20 female employees. Civil society organizations, including Comunidad Mujer, have pointed out that this threshold has had a negative effect on female employment because employers have opted to keep the number of female employees below 20 (see Escobar, 2014; Sepúlveda et al., 2016).

25. In particular, the union leaders argued that the model proposed in the bill could have similar results to the expansion of after-school programs, which, they claimed, just offered extended childcare hours without teaching additional skills or following a curriculum.

26. The conflict with the government escalated by the end of 2013, and the CUT leader announced that President Piñera would be required to attend a meeting with the human rights commission at the Organization of American States to explain the lack of advancement in the negotiation mechanisms between the government and multi-firm unions ("CUT Lleva al Gobierno de Piñera Ante la Comisión de Derechos Humanos de la OEA," 2013).

opposition parties criticized Bachelet's decision to withdraw the bill. For instance, representative Claudia Nogueira from the Independent Democratic Union Party (*Unión Demócrata Independiente*) argued that working women who would have benefited from the bill proposed by President Piñera continued to be uncovered (Cámara de Diputados de Chile, 2014). By 2017, the labor minister, Alejandra Krauss, announced that the government would set aside the project of a new universal daycare law due to concerns about the financial viability of a tripartite fund and the limited time left to negotiate a deal in Congress under the Bachelet administration (Palacios, 2017). Sebastián Piñera won the presidential election for the second time in 2017 and sent a new ECEC reform proposal to Congress the following year. Again, the initiative sought to repeal Article 203 and to extend access to childcare for working mothers, regardless of the number of female employees in the workplace. In this proposal, the expansion would be financed by a new fund, with "an initial employers' contribution of 0.1% of the taxable income of each worker" (Sepúlveda et al., 2018, p. 9). The new proposal drew renewed criticism from union leaders, who argued that excluding informal workers and allowing parents' copayments in private daycare centers would deepen social inequalities and reduce state efforts in ECEC provision (Valdés, 2018).

We can draw two main conclusions from the process followed by the daycare bills proposed by the executive branch. First, labor unions had a more active role in discussing social investment reforms after the *Chile Crece Contigo* reform in 2006. Although unions were not central actors in expanding childcare services in the first Bachelet administration, they became more vocal in the following years. Gradually, they took strong positions in favor of public spending in childcare provision and against initiatives they perceived to be detrimental to the workers' labor benefits. CUT was a visible actor in the media in this period (although its actual political leverage remains limited). Second, given the relatively small size of the informal sector in the country, initiatives and regulations bearing on public childcare provision constitute issues that affect the workers broadly. As discussed, the *Chile Crece Contigo* model covers the bottom 60% of (lower-income) households on the income scale of the population. In addition, women in larger firms receive childcare benefits from their employers (given the current requirement in Article 203). And, as Sepúlveda et al. (2012) note, these benefits (*Chile Crece Contigo* and employer-provided childcare) are not exclusive. This relatively low level of fragmentation in the Chilean childcare provision model contrasts notably with the Mexican case. Consequently, the expansion of services that followed the 2006 reform generated policy feedbacks and incentivized labor unions to take a stronger position on the issue.

11.6.2. Mexico

In Mexico, the two childcare models (the contributory and noncontributory systems) have followed different paths. In 2009, the death of 49 children in an accidental fire in the ABC Daycare Center, a private facility in the northern city of

Hermosillo, Sonora, brought the quality of outsourced services of the contributory system to national attention. Investigations carried out by authorities at the IMSS found that the center did not comply with fire regulations and basic safety standards (IMSS, 2015).[27] Furthermore, reports on the irregularities in this and other outsourced facilities showed that some daycare center owners colluded to block efforts from unionized childcare workers to demand higher wages and improved work conditions. For instance, documents revealed that after an attempted strike of childcare providers at the ABC Daycare Center in 2004, the owners asked new employees to sign renewable 1-month contracts and a document renouncing their rights to organize collectively (Proceso, 2009).

In the following years, the IMSS's union, the Sindicato Nacional de Trabajadores del Seguro Social (SNTSS), opposed creating more outsourced centers. The union claimed that the outsourced facilities had inadequate labor protection for childcare providers and lacked the quality of the centers directly administered by the IMSS. In addition, workers demanded an increase in the budget allocated to daycare centers to improve the conditions of facilities and update educational material for children.[28] Government officials deemed these requests unfeasible. An IMSS official argued in 2010 that the union's increasing demands and the operation costs of daycare centers at IMSS facilities made it unsustainable for the institution to continue with the traditional model: "coverage per child in one of these [IMSS] daycare centers costs around 4,500 pesos, because of supplies, wages, benefits, and everything necessary for the center, but if I outsource the service . . . the cost is 2,483 pesos, so that is what the IMSS has done: outsource childcare provision" ("Prevén Más Subrogación en IMSS." 2010). Another issue concerns the work status of childcare providers at these outsourced centers. Employees at the centers are not government employees and do not have access to the same labor benefits as IMSS childcare center workers.

Collective organization of working parents in the informal sector who are beneficiaries of the Sedesol Daycare Program has been even less visible. Beneficiaries have been less effective in demanding changes or improvements

---

27. After the tragic incident at the ABC Daycare Center, nongovernmental organizations highlighted similar, if not greater, vulnerabilities in the Daycare Program for Working Mothers for the informal sector. For instance, the director of the Network for Children Rights in Mexico, Gerardo Sauri, expressed consternation at seeing an accident like this happening in an outsourced IMSS center with supposedly stricter quality standards compared to Sedesol centers: "we are worried . . . that there might be higher risks in Sedesol centers [that operate] with the logic that having a yard is enough to install a daycare facility." The former director of the National System for Family Development, Mario Luis Fuentes, echoed these concerns ("Urgen Revisar la Operación de Estancias," 2009).

28. In 2013, the national leader of the SNTSS declared that outsourced daycare centers were not staffed by unionized IMSS workers, "which entailed risks by not complying with the appropriate profile and skills required to take care of the workers' children" (SNTSS, 2013).

to the services provided. Childcare providers in these centers, who are not government employees, also faced obstacles to organizing. In this respect, President Calderón declared, "we cannot directly hire employees in the outsourced centers. The governor [in each state] must pay for teachers in elementary and secondary schools, . . . we know that constitutes a heavy load. Still, with the [outsourced] daycare centers, we are helping a previously uncovered sector. . . . These are excellent options that do not cost loads of money to the government" ("Espaldarazo de Calderón a Estancias Infantiles de Sedesol," 2009). The Sedesol daycare system thus became a social program in itself by providing self-employment opportunities. The model created a network of private providers who operated as contractors, running daycare centers in their adapted homes and hiring staff at low costs. These childcare providers received their income from the subsidy that the government provided for each enrolled child.

As with the outsourced IMSS model, the government favored this non-formal arrangement with providers. In 2012, President Calderón declared that an obstacle to providing preschool education in Sedesol daycare centers was that the teachers' union (SNTE) would become involved and hinder the development of the program: "Another key to the program's success is that we do not pay salaries to the owners of the daycare centers, so there is no employment relationship, and therefore, there is no union . . . the idea of incorporating preschool instruction is interesting, but the teachers' union, the SNTE, has to intervene to teach at this level, . . . and the program would be affected" (Ramos Pérez, 2012).[29]

In sum, the Mexican case illustrates how the labor market dualization resulted in a strong divide between informal and formal workers. In this context, unions do not have incentives to advance an inclusive ECEC agenda. Also, governments have so far prioritized low-cost options in part to avoid confrontation with unions. In Mexico, these conditions translate into a self-reinforcing equilibrium that leads to social policy fragmentation and inequality.

However, it is important to emphasize the value of this social investment initiative despite its limitations. Even considering the margin for improving the early childhood education component, the noncontributory daycare program allowed women in the informal sector to join the labor force, leaving their children in a structured environment providing educational activities and meals. Indeed, available impact evaluations of the Sedesol program show positive results in increased female labor participation, parents' satisfaction (Cejudo et al., 2012), and early childhood development indicators (Rizzoli-Córdoba et al., 2017).

29. In 2016, the secretary of education, Aurelio Nuño, signed an agreement with Sedesol to start offering preschool education at Sedesol daycare centers. The agreement was meant to be the first step in a process of coordination with the education secretaries of each Mexican state.

11.7. CONCLUSION

The analysis of the expansion in access to ECEC services in a comparative perspective provides crucial insights into the conditions under which unions are more likely to engage reforms of ECEC policies in Latin America. We argue that the fragmentation of welfare provision and the segmentation of the labor market partially explain union positions regarding ECEC policy expansion. In contexts of low dualization of the labor market, new social policy proposals are more likely to directly impact formal workers' current system of labor benefits and conditions. This, in turn, generates incentives for unions to become involved in the policymaking process of social policy expansion. In contrast, in contexts of high labor market dualization, new proposals are less likely to modify current conditions for formal workers due to the political costs this entails. In this scenario, it is less likely that organized labor will have incentives to speak for (or against) the expansions of policies to outsiders.

The analysis of the role played by labor unions during the reform processes in Chile and Mexico shows that labor unions have played a much more marginal role than theories on welfare state development in industrialized democracies would predict. Governments in both countries have been the *protagonists* in the coalition-formation and decision-making stages of the politics of ECEC social investment. In both cases, economic structural changes and legacies from the authoritarian period have contributed to the weakening of organized labor after the transition to democracy. However, relatively lower levels of dualization in Chile have resulted in unions defending ECEC public provision when there have been attempts to partially privatize these services or use workers' funds to finance the system. Therefore, we characterize Chilean unions as *consenters* in the period after the first reform. In contrast, labor unions in Mexico have been absent during the reform and post-reform periods. Higher levels of dualization in Mexico generate a more significant divide between the interests of labor insiders and outsiders.

Finally, our argument about the importance of dualization in ECEC provision has implications for inequality and poverty reduction objectives. Quality differences and fragmentation in service provision for insiders and outsiders reinforce inequalities and prevent broad coalitions from supporting and defending social investment policies.

ACKNOWLEDGMENTS

The authors' names appear in alphabetical order; both are equal collaborators on the chapter. The authors would like to thank Gabriela Francisco and Berta Díaz for their superb research assistance. Bárbara Zárate-Tenorio acknowledges the financial support provided by the Consejo Nacional de Ciencia y Tecnología (Council of Science and Technology), CONACyT.

REFERENCES

Agarwala, R. (2013). *Informal labor, formal politics, and dignified discontent in India*. Cambridge University Press.

Altamirano, M. (2020). Política social e igualdad de género en México, 2012–2018. *Foro Internacional, 60*(2), 755–789.

Antía, F. (2014). La dinámica política de la redistribución en Chile y Uruguay en los años 2000. [Unpublished doctoral dissertation]. Instituto de Estudos Sociais e Políticos, Universida de Estadual de Rio Janeiro.

Araujo, M. C., López Boo, F., & Puyana, J. M. (2013). *Overview of early childhood development services in Latin America and the Caribbean*. Inter-American Development Bank.

Arrieta, A. (2003). *Mercado de trabajo, organización y representación sindical y gremial*. International Labor Organization.

Bensusán, G. (2015). Organizing workers in Argentina, Brazil, Chile, and Mexico: The authoritarian-corporatist legacy and old institutional designs in a new context. *Theoretical Inquiries in Law, 16*, 131–161.

Bensusán, G., & Middlebrook, K. (2012). *Organized labor and politics in Mexico*. Oxford University Press.

Bensusán, G., & Middlebrook, K. (2013). *Sindicatos y política en México: Cambios, continuidades y contradicciones*. FLACSO-México.

Bizberg, I. (2003). El sindicalismo en el fin de régimen. *Foro Internacional, 43*(171), 215–248.

Cámara de Diputadas y Diputados de Chile. (2014, April 25). Diputada Nogueira Lamenta Decisión del gobierno de retirar proyecto de sala cuna universal." [Press release]. https://www.camara.cl/prensa/sala_de_prensa_detalle.aspx?prmid=97885

Cejudo, G. M., Michel, C. L., & Gerhard, R. (2012). *Metaevaluación del Programa de Estancias Infantiles (PEI)*. CIDE-CLEAR Regional Centers for Learning on Evaluation and Results.

Consejo Asesor Presidencial para la Reforma de las Políticas de Infancia. (2006). *Propuestas del Consejo Asesor Presidencial para la Reforma de las Políticas de Infancia*.

Cook, M. L. (2007). *Politics of labor reform in Latin America: Between flexibility and rights*. Penn State Press.

Crece subrogación de guarderías IMSS. (2009, July 9). *Reforma*.

CUT lleva al gobierno de Piñera ante la Comisión de Derechos Humanos de la OEA. (2013, October 24). *Sindical*. http://sindical.cl/cut-lleva-al-gobierno-de-pinera-ante-la-comision-de-derechos-humanos-de-la-oea/

CUT pidió al gobierno no financiar salas cuna con seguro de cesantía. (2013, December 22). *La Tercera*. https://www.latercera.com/diario-impreso/cut-pidio-al-gobierno-no-financiar-salas-cuna-con-seguro-de-cesantia/

CUT rechaza aspectos del proyecto de ley sobre salas cunas. (2013, October 14). *Sindical.* https://sindical.cl/cut-rechaza-aspectos-del-proyecto-de-ley-sobre-salas-cunas/

Dion, M. (2009). Globalization, democracy, and Mexican welfare, 1988–2006. *Comparative Politics, 42*(1), 63–82.

Dirección del Trabajo. (2015). *Más mujeres en los sindicatos. Sectores con alta sindicalización femenina.* https://www.dt.gob.cl/portal/1629/articles-106799_archivo_01.pdf

El factor mujer. (2006, January 12). *El Mercurio en Internet.* http://diario.elmercurio.com/detalle/index.asp?id={479a1890-0bc6-415a-b21d-c3d2d240b826}

Emmenegger, P., Hausermann, S., Palier, B., & Seeleib-Kaiser, M. (Eds.). (2012). *The age of dualization: The changing face of inequality in deindustrializing societies.* Oxford University Press.

Escobar, D. (2014). *Ley de salas cuna y sus efectos en la contratación de mujeres* [Unpublished master's thesis]. Pontificia Universidad Católica de Chile.

Espaldarazo de Calderón a estancias infantiles de Sedesol. (2009, June 11). *La Jornada.* https://www.jornada.com.mx/2009/06/11/politica/006n1pol

Etchemendy, S., & Berins Collier, R. (2007). Down but not out: Union resurgence and segmented neocorporatism in Argentina (2003–2007). *Politics & Society, 35*(3), 363–401.

Fernández, M. (2012). *From the streets to the classrooms: The politics of education spending in Mexico* [Unpublished doctoral dissertation]. Duke University.

Frías Fernández, P. (2010) Papel de los sindicatos y la negociación colectiva y su impacto en la eficiencia y la equidad del mercado de trabajo. United Nations Economic Commission for Latin America and the Caribbean.

Garay, C. (2017). *Social policy expansion in Latin America.* Cambridge University Press.

Gobierno de Chile. (2013). Proyecto de Ley de Salas Cuna. http://2010-2014.gob.cl/especiales/proyecto-de-ley-de-salas-cuna/

Gutiérrez Crocco, F. (2017). Coping with neoliberalism through legal mobilization: The Chilean labor movements new tactics and allies. In S. Donoso & M. von Bulow (Eds.), *Social movements in Chile: Organization, trajectories, and political consequences* (pp. 191–217). Palgrave Macmillan.

Haagh, L. (2002). The emperor's new clothes: Labor reform and social democratization in Chile. *Studies in Comparative International Development, 37*(1), 86–115.

Haggard, S., & Kaufman, R. R. (2008). *Development, democracy, and welfare states: Latin America, East Asia, and Eastern Europe.* Princeton University Press.

Instituto Mexicano del Seguro Social. (2015). *Capítulo VI. Seguro de guarderías y prestaciones sociales.* Informe al Ejecutivo y al Congreso de la Unión sobre la situación financiera y los riesgos del Instituto Mexicano del Seguro Social.

Instituto Nacional de Estadística y Geografía. (2006). *Mujeres y hombres en México* (10th ed.). Instituto Nacional de Estadística y Geografía e Instituto Nacional de las Mujeres.

Inter-American Development Bank. (2016). Sociómetro database. https://www.iadb.org/en/sociometro-bid/sociometro-bid

International Labour Organization. (2018). *Presente y futuro de la protección social en América Latina y el Caribe.*

Jenson, J. (2010). Diffusing ideas for after neoliberalism: The social investment perspective in Europe and Latin America. *Global Social Policy, 10*(1), 59–84.

Korpi, W. (2006). Power resources and employer-centered approaches in explanations of welfare states and varieties of capitalism: Protagonists, consenters, and antagonists. *World Politics, 58*(2), 167–206.

Kurtz, M. J. (2002). Understanding the third world welfare state after neoliberalism: The politics of social provision in Chile and Mexico. *Comparative Politics, 34*(3), 293–313.

Leiva, F. (2012). Flexible workers, gender, and contending strategies for confronting the crisis of labor in Chile. *Latin American Perspectives, 39*(4), 102–128.

Marques-Pereira, B., Paternotte, D., & Valenzuela, M. (2015). El género como recurso político: El uso estratégico del género por Michelle Bachelet (Chile) y Laurette Onkelinx (Bélgica). *Revista de la Academia, 20*, 155–182.

Martínez Franzoni, J., & Sánchez-Ancochea, D. (2014). Filling in the missing link between universalism and democracy: The case of Costa Rica. *Latin American Politics and Society, 56*(4), 98–118.

Michelle Bachelet presenta sus propuestas como candidata presidencial. (2005, March 19). *El Mercurio en Internet.* https://www.emol.com/noticias/nacional/2005/03/19/176500/michelle-bachelet-presenta-sus-propuestas-como-candidata-presidencial.html

Morgan, K. J. (2013). Path shifting of the welfare state: Electoral competition and the expansion of work–family policies in Western Europe. *World Politics, 65*(1), 73–115.

Palacios, J. P. (2017, February 2). Diputados activan ofensiva parar descongelar debate de derecho a sala cuna universal. *Pulso.*

Palacios-Valladares, I. (2010). From militancy to clientelism: Labor union strategies and membership trajectories in contemporary Chile. *Latin American Politics and Society, 52*(2), 73–102.

Peña, N. (2013, August 12). Proyecto de salas cuna incluirá financiamiento con seguro de cesantía. *La Tercera.*

Prevén más subrogación en IMSS. (2010, November 22). *Reforma.*

Pribble, J. (2013). *Welfare and party politics in Latin America.* Cambridge University Press.

Proceso. (2009). *ABC: Una historia de abusos y negligencia* (Special report).

Ramos Pérez, J. (2012, January 12). Sindicato arruinaría sistema de Estancias: FCH. *El Universal.*

Rechazo a informe Marcel. (2006, July 17). *El Mercurio en Internet.*

Rizzoli-Córdoba, A., Vargas-Carrillo, L. I., Vásquez-Ríos, R., Reyes-Morales, H., Villasís-Keever, M. A., O'Shea-Cuevas, G., Aceves-Villagrán, D., Muñoz-Hernández, O., & García-Aranda, J. A. (2017). Asociación entre el tiempo de permanencia en el Programa de Estancias Infantiles para niños en situación de pobreza y el nivel de desarrollo infantil. *Boletín Médico Del Hospital Infantil México, 74*(2), 98–106.

Rueda, D. (2007). *Social democracy inside out: Partisanship and labor market policy in industrialized democracies.* Oxford University Press.

Schneider, B. R. (2009). Hierarchical market economies and varieties of capitalism in Latin America. *Journal of Latin American Studies, 41*(3), 553–575.

Sepúlveda, A., Betancor, A., & Yachan, C. (2012). *Mujer y trabajo: Provisión de sala cuna, la esperada sustitución del artículo 203* (Serie Comunidad Mujer 16). Comunidad Mujer.

Sepúlveda, A., Poblete, P., & Yachan, C. (2016). *Mujer y trabajo: Sala cuna, un derecho para madres y padres trabajadores* (Serie Comunidad Mujer 35). Comunidad Mujer.

Sepúlveda, A., Poblete, P., Yachan, C., & Aros, N. (2018). *Sala cuna hoy. Una reforma laboral indispensable* (Serie Comunidad Mujer 44). Comunidad Mujer.

Sindicato Nacional de Trabajadores del Seguro Social. (2013). *Reprueba SNTSS nuevo esquema de subrogación de guarderías en el IMSS.*

Staab, S. (2017). The expansion of childcare services (2006–2010). In *Gender and the politics of gradual change: Social policy reform and innovation in Chile* (pp. 135–161). Springer.

Staab, S., & Gerhard, R. (2010). *Childcare service expansion in Chile and Mexico.* United Nations Research Institute for Social Development.

Staab, S., & Gerhard, R. (2011). Putting two and two together? Early childhood education, mothers' employment and care service expansion in Chile and Mexico. *Development and Change, 42*(4), 1079–1107.

Toro, P. (2014, April 24). Gobierno opta por nuevo proyecto de sala cuna con financiamiento tripartito y desecha el de Piñera. *La Tercera.*

Urgen revisar la operación de estancias. (2009, June 7). *Reforma.*

Valdés, F. (2018, November 22). Nueva ley de sala cuna universal, otro engaño a la clase trabajadora. *Sindical.cl.*

Vallejos, M. (2010, April 27). ¿Posnatal compartido o flexible? *La Nación.cl.* http://oge.cl/postnatal-icompartido-o-flexible/

Zárate-Tenorio, B. (2014). Social spending responses to organized labor and mass protests in Latin America, 1970–2007. *Comparative Political Studies, 47*(14), 1945–1972.

12

PUBLIC PREFERENCES TOWARD SOCIAL INVESTMENT

COMPARING PATTERNS OF SUPPORT ACROSS THREE CONTINENTS

Björn Bremer

12.1. INTRODUCTION

In the last few decades, social investment has become a popular concept among policymakers and academics. It is widely seen as a means to reform public services, generate growth, and address pressing social problems like inequality. Consequently, there has been a significant turn among governments toward social investment in the last few decades (Hemerijck, 2013; Morel et al., 2012). How is this supply of social investment policies reflected on the demand side? Following up on the preceding chapters on employer preferences (Chapter 9 in this volume) and trade unions (Chapters 10 and 11 in this volume), this chapter studies the third key dimension of the demand side: public opinion. A focus on public opinion is crucial because the changing occupational configuration of the post-industrial knowledge economy (see Chapter 8 in this volume) has transformed class structures across the advanced capitalist world. When studying social policy development in this context, a novel view on the policy demands of social classes is in order, not least in order to identify the underlying societal coalitions that may drive or impede the development of social investment.

In recent years, an increasing amount of research has shown that the popularity of social investment is broadly shared by citizens but that public preferences

Björn Bremer, *Public Preferences Toward Social Investment* In: *The World Politics of Social Investment (Volume I)*. Edited by: Julian L. Garritzmann, Silja Häusermann, and Bruno Palier, Oxford University Press. © Oxford University Press 2022. DOI: 10.1093/oso/9780197585245.003.0012 toward social investment are distinct from preferences toward more traditional consumption-oriented social policies (e.g., Busemeyer & Garritzmann, 2017; Fossati & Häusermann, 2014; Garritzmann et al., 2018; Häusermann et al., 2021; Neimanns et al., 2018): While the working class is the strongest and most consistent supporter of traditional transfer-oriented social policies (social consumption), parts of the expanded middle class seem to be the champions of social investment. Yet, the existing literature is limited by its empirical foundations: Due to a lack of survey data, it has mostly analyzed support for social investment in Western Europe. This ignores that the turn to social investment also occurred in other regions of the world (see Chapter 1 in this volume). Although the structural transformations that lead to new social demands have been particularly strong in the developed post-industrial economies, they have also changed the politics of welfare states in less developed countries. As a result, many countries in Central and Eastern Europe, Latin America, and North East Asia have adopted social investment policies, too.

Despite this popularity of social investment, we still lack an overview of how public support for social investment varies across countries and regions. This omission is a real gap in the literature because the changing configuration of public preferences interacts with the existing policy legacies, as Häusermann et al. emphasize in Chapter 2 of this volume. Countries have distinct forms and levels of social policies with feedback effects that structure the relative salience of different political conflicts (Beramendi et al., 2015; Gingrich & Ansell, 2012; Svallfors, 1997). Therefore, we know very little about whether and how public opinion drives social investment in different regions across the world. Which are the relevant societal groups that support social investment across different regions? And how do different political contexts and policy legacies influence the individual-level determinants of support for social investment?

This chapter addresses these questions by analyzing data from the Comparative Study of Electoral Systems (CSES) and the International Social Survey Programme (ISSP). Both surveys include data on attitudes toward different social policies in a large set of countries, which I use to measure attitudes toward different forms of social investment (education, public childcare, and paid parental leave) and traditional transfer-oriented policies (old-age pensions). I employ multivariate regression analysis and explore the determinants of attitudes on the individual level in two ways: First, I analyze preferences in a pooled sample, examining the broad pattern of support across three continents; second, I identify the regional specificities of preference configuration by estimating regression models for five broad regions separately.

The analysis shows that preferences toward the welfare state are multi-dimensional (e.g., Fossati & Häusermann, 2014; Häusermann et al., 2021; Neimanns et al., 2018): While the lower classes remain the core constituency for social consumption policies, the educated middle class has become the key constituency for social investment. However, there is also some intra-class heterogeneity: Women are more likely to support social investment than men, and young people are more likely to support it than older people. Moreover, the configuration of individual-level preferences is moderated by existing policies legacies. In regions with less developed welfare states, demand for social investment is on average higher and less divisive, and hence, it is more difficult to identify clear patterns of support than in regions with more mature welfare states.

To make these arguments, the chapter proceeds as follows. First, I briefly review the existing literature and develop a theoretical framework in Section 12.2. In Section 12.3, I elaborate on the data and methods that I use to test these hypotheses before I present my empirical findings in Section 12.4. Finally, I use the conclusion to summarize the main findings and caveats of my analysis, raising open questions that should be addressed by future research.

12.2. ATTITUDES TOWARD SOCIAL INVESTMENT: SOME EXPECTATIONS

In recent years, "social investment" has become a buzzword among policymakers and academics alike, which generated a new research agenda that attempted to understand the politics of social investment (Bonoli, 2005, 2013; Esping-Andersen, 2002; Hemerijck, 2013, 2017; Morel et al., 2012). Initially, the existing literature focused on causes and effects of these policies, but it hardly studied public opinion toward social investment. While scholars analyzed preferences toward specific policies like higher education (e.g., Ansell, 2010; Garritzmann, 2016), childcare (e.g., Goerres & Tepe, 2010, 2012), or active labor market policies (e.g., Rueda, 2005), there was little analysis of attitudes toward social investment policies more generally. This omission was partly due to a lack of data, but recently several contributions have emerged that attempted to fill this gap (e.g., Bremer & Bürgisser, 2022; Busemeyer & Garritzmann, 2017; Fossati & Häusermann, 2014; Garritzmann et al., 2018; Häusermann et al., 2021; Neimanns et al., 2018).

This collection of studies shows that social investment is, on average, very popular and that citizens hold coherent preferences on a range of social investment policies. Yet, preferences are distinct from attitudes toward more traditional consumption-oriented social policies: While the working class is the strongest and most consistent supporter of transfer-oriented social policies, parts of the expanded middle class are the champions of social investment. Specifically, Garritzmann et al. (2018) show that social investment policies are supported by people with a higher educational background and left-libertarian views. This remains true when citizens are confronted with cuts in other parts of the welfare state (Neimanns et al., 2018) or trade-offs with respect to higher taxes or government debt (Busemeyer & Garritzmann, 2017). The middle class thus attributes higher importance to social investment (Häusermann et al., 2021) and is the key actor in the politics of the welfare state and the main driver for social investment policies in Western Europe (Häusermann & Palier, 2017).

Mostly due to the lack of data, these existing studies have only focused on selected countries from Western Europe, and we know very little about how support for social investment varies across different regions and welfare state regimes. However, countries differ markedly in their provision of social policies, and these differences are important because existing welfare state policies have significant feedback effects (Beramendi et al., 2015; Gingrich & Ansell, 2012; Palier, 2010; Pierson, 1993; Svallfors, 2012). For example, Ansell (2010) argued that support for education spending is moderated by the existing institutions: High-income individuals are more likely to support spending on education if access to education is highly stratified (see also Busemeyer & Iversen, 2014; Garritzmann, 2015).

In order to account for the interaction of public opinion and policy legacies, as set out in Chapter 2 of this volume, we therefore need to broaden the scope of research on preferences for social investment. To this end, this chapter considers evidence from countries across three continents: Europe, Asia, and Latin America. To different degrees, social investment has become popular in countries across these continents, increasing the salience of such policies. In turn, this should also result in an increasing politicization of social investment, which begs the question of which societal groups are the core supporters of social investment.

Based on the assumption that individuals support policies from which they benefit, the supporters of social investment policies should have different characteristics than supporters of social consumption. The welfare state developed in response to the political mobilization of the working class (Esping-Andersen, 1985; Korpi, 1983; Stephens, 1979), but the distributive effects of new social policies like social investments are different than the traditional compensatory social policies. For example, in Western Europe, social investment is often stratified: It is formally available to everyone, but the middle and upper classes use it disproportionately. This results in a so-called Matthew effect: It benefits individuals who are already well-off (e.g., Bonoli & Liechti, 2018; Pavolini & van Lancker, 2018).[1] In contrast, in Latin America, social investment is often successfully targeted at lower-income classes (e.g., see Chapters 7 and 13 in this volume), and in Nordic countries social investment was—at least initially—inclusive (see Chapter 2 in Volume II [Garritzmann et al., 2022]).

There is also a value-based explanation for social investment support, though. As Beramendi et al. (2015) argue, there is a link between universalistic attitudes and preferences for investment. "Social investment" refers to policies whose future payoffs and distributive benefits are uncertain. These policies resonate

---

1. Examples of such policies include public spending on higher education (Garritzmann, 2016) and the provision of childcare (van Lancker & Ghysels, 2012).

closely with highly educated middle-class voters (Gingrich & Häusermann, 2015): They are more likely to have universalistic and egalitarian preferences, and their own advantageous position in the labor market is also the direct result of past investment policies. Valuing the well-being of future generations, they are likely to have a lower discount rate, which amplifies their support for social investment due to material self-interest. Consequently, socioeconomic class shapes preferences toward social investment differently than it shapes preferences toward social consumption: While the highly educated middle classes are the primary constituency for social investment, particularly in contexts where social investment is not targeted, the working class remains the primary constituency for social consumption (*hypothesis 1*).

The conflict between different socioeconomic classes is not the only relevant social conflict for the politics of social investment, though. As welfare states have become multi-dimensional, other lines of conflict are also salient, generating a significant amount of intra-class heterogeneity. To begin with, there is a generational conflict about social policies in the 21st century. Traditionally, the welfare state had a pro-elderly bias (Lynch, 2006). Assuming that age groups favor policies that benefit them, older citizens should have an interest in preserving this high level of social consumption and entitlements (Bonoli & Häusermann, 2009). At the same time, older people are less likely to benefit from social investment, the benefits of which mostly accrue in the future. Therefore, support for social investment is likely to decrease with age, while support for social consumption should increase with age (*hypothesis 2*).

Another divide that is salient for the politics of social investment is gender. In the past, women's movements have markedly influenced the development of welfare states (Huber & Stephens, 2000; Naumann, 2005; Sainsbury, 1996), which should also translate to the individual level for two reasons. Women are still the primary caregivers, but they have increasingly joined the labor force in the last few decades. They benefit from family policies which ease the conciliation of care and work, but they also benefit from other forms of social investment. At the same time, women also disproportionately gain from transfer-oriented policies because in many countries it is still difficult to combine paid employment with the provision of care for children or elderly. Therefore, women may be in general more supportive of both social investment and consumption than men (*hypothesis 3*).

Yet, the strength of these individual-level conflicts should depend on the policy legacies of different welfare state regimes. Public preferences interact with cross-country variations in economic systems and social policies, producing distinct patterns of public support for the welfare state for three reasons. First, preferences may vary with the absolute level that governments spend on compensatory social policies and social investment. While some regions have very well-developed welfare states (e.g., Western Europe), other regions devote fewer resources toward social policies (e.g., Latin America). In countries with less developed welfare states, public preferences for social investment might not be very different from preferences for consumption because the politics of social investment cannot be conceptualized in terms of trade-offs between the two different logics of welfare (see Chapter 13 in this volume); instead, demand for both types of social policy should be similarly high as there is a broad and diffuse coalition of interests that supports any expansion of the welfare state. Second, social investment also functions differently in different regions. In some countries, social investment is highly stratified, but it is more inclusive in others. In Latin America, for example, social investment is often targeted and combined with compensatory social policies in order to improve the social security for the lower classes. Finally, the salience of social investment greatly varies across regions. In regions like Eastern Europe and North East Asia, social investment is less politicized, especially compared to Western Europe and Latin America. For example, in North East Asia, social investment is primarily viewed as a valence issue to address the challenges associated with an aging society (see Chapter 11 in Volume II [Garritzmann et al., 2022]). In many Eastern European countries, on the other hand, public opinion generally favors a lean compensatory welfare state (see Chapter 7 in Volume II [Garritzmann et al., 2022]). This reduces the salience of social investment, which should also make it more difficult to make out clear supporting coalitions for social investment compared to Western Europe, where social investment has become much more politicized. Thus, the importance of individual-level determinants should vary across different countries and regions (*hypothesis 4*).

12.3. DATA AND METHODS

This chapter uses data from the fourth wave of the CSES and the 2012 wave of the ISSP to put these hypotheses to test. The fourth wave of the CSES included a large number of national election surveys that used a standardized set of questions. For this chapter, I use all available surveys from Asia, Europe, and Latin America which occurred between 2011 and 2016.[2] Also, the cross-national ISSP included a module in 2012 called "Family and Changing Gender Roles." From this module, I again use data from all countries in Asia, Europe, and Latin

2. These countries and elections include Argentina (2015), Austria (2013), Brazil (2014), Bulgaria (2014), the Czech Republic (2013), Finland (2015), France (2012), Germany (2013), Greece (2012), Hong Kong (2012), Iceland (2013), Ireland (2011), Japan (2013), Mexico (2012), Norway (2013), Peru (2016), the Philippines (2016), Poland (2011), Portugal (2015), Romania (2012), Serbia (2012), Slovakia (2016), Slovenia (2011), South Korea (2012), Sweden (2014), Switzerland (2011), Taiwan (2012), Thailand (2011), and the United Kingdom (2015). The election studies from Mexico (2015) and Montenegro (2012) are excluded because they do not include all variables necessary for the analysis.

America.[3] In total, I draw on data from 41 different countries and more than 75,000 individuals.[4]

From the two surveys, I use individual-level attitudes toward social investment and social consumption as the dependent variables. To get around the problem of data availability for attitudes toward social investment, I use policy-specific questions as proxies. These questions relate to education spending, public childcare, and paid parental leave. Additionally, I use attitudes toward spending on old-age pensions as a proxy for social consumption, which allows me to compare patterns of support for social investment with patterns of support for traditional social policies. Following existing research (e.g., Gingrich & Ansell, 2012; Neimanns et al., 2018; Rehm, 2011), I recode the dependent variable into a binary variable: 1 means support for the respective policy, while 0 means opposition. For example, for government spending on pensions and education, 1 means that individuals would like to spend more; 0 means that individuals support less or the same amount of spending. For parental leave, 1 means support for at least 3 months of paid parental leave; for childcare, 1 means support for public childcare as the most appropriate form of childcare.

The independent variables used in the analysis follow from the theoretical framework. To measure the importance of socioeconomic class, I use education, income, and occupation. Following the CSES, I categorize individuals into four different groups based on educational attainment and five country-specific income groups. I also use the class scheme from Oesch (2006a, 2006b) to categorize citizens into different classes based on their occupation. Specifically, I distinguish between occupational groups, as shown in Table 12.1. Note that occupational information is not available for all countries included in the CSES data set, and therefore, I include occupation in separate regression models. Finally, and in line with my hypotheses, I also include age and gender as well as other common control variables in the analysis.

To examine the patterns of support across different regions, I categorize countries into five different geographical groups: Western Europe, Southern Europe, Central and Eastern Europe, Latin America, and Central and East Asia. Due to a lack of cases for some regions, the categorization is not as detailed as the regions identified in the introductory chapters of this volume. Chapter 11 in this volume as well as Chapters 3 and 11 in Volume II (Garritzmann et al., 2022) pay more attention to regional differences in public opinion within Latin America, Europe, and Asia, respectively.

3. These countries include Argentina, Austria, Belgium, Bulgaria, Chile, Croatia, the Czech Republic, Denmark, Finland, France, Germany, Hungary, Iceland, India, Ireland, Japan, Latvia, Lithuania, Mexico, the Netherlands, Norway, the Philippines, Poland, Portugal, Slovenia, South Korea, Spain, Sweden, Switzerland, Taiwan, the United Kingdom, and Venezuela.
4. The ISSP has a module on the role of government that includes similar questions as the CSES. However, at the time of writing, the latest available data for the countries of interest was from 2006. Data from the 2016 module was not yet fully available.

Table 12.1 List of classes and occupational groups (based on Oesch [2006a])

Technical work logic	Organizational work logic	Interpersonal service work logic
Technical (semi-) professionals	Associate managers	Sociocultural (semi-) professionals
Production workers	Office clerks	Service workers

Note. The Oesch class scheme has eight different groups, distinguishing between four different horizontal work logics and two vertical levels. However, I can only construct six groups because the CSES does not include information on self-employment for every country.

I then analyze the data and test my hypotheses in two ways. First, I pool all countries and use multivariate logit regression analysis with country fixed effects to evaluate the determinants of individual-level support for social investment preferences. Second, I run the same logit regression models for each region separately in order to evaluate how the importance of different individual-level variables varies across regions. For each step, I also estimated other model specification to test the robustness of my results: I used hierarchical models with random effects where individuals are clustered in countries and countries are clustered in regions, I treated the dependent variables as ordered and estimated a multinomial analysis with fixed effects, and I also treated the dependent variables as continuous and estimated both ordinary least squares (OLS) regressions with fixed effects and OLS regressions with random effects. In general, these specifications did not substantially affect the results.

12.4. EMPIRICAL RESULTS

12.4.1. Determinants of individual preferences for social investment and consumption

The results indicate that in a pooled sample there is a distinct support coalition for social investment that differs from the support coalition for social consumption. Table 12.2 shows the results of regression analyses with education and income as key independent variables; Table 12.3 shows the results with occupational class as key variable. Note that the ISSP does not include a cross-national measure for income. Hence, income is not included in the analysis for public childcare and parental leave.

In line with hypothesis 1, the results indicate that socioeconomic class is an important predictor for both preferences toward social consumption and social investment, but it shapes these preferences differently: While lower socioeconomic classes are more in favor of social consumption than higher socioeconomic classes, the pattern is reversed for social investment. This result can best be illustrated graphically. Figure 12.1 plots the predicted probabilities of supporting

Table 12.2 Logistic regression—Support for different social policies by education and income

	Support for social policy			
	Pension	Education	Public childcare	Parental leave
	(1)	(2)	(3)	(4)
Education (ref. = primary)				
Secondary	−0.13***	0.06	0.14***	0.12***
	(0.04)	(0.04)	(0.05)	(0.04)
Post-secondary	−0.29***	0.01	0.25***	0.21***
	(0.06)	(0.06)	(0.06)	(0.06)
Tertiary	−0.58***	0.27***	0.38***	0.41***
	(0.05)	(0.05)	(0.05)	(0.05)
Income (ref. = 1st quintile)				
2nd quintile	−0.01	0.05		
	(0.04)	(0.04)		
3rd quintile	−0.07*	0.11**		
	(0.04)	(0.04)		
4th quintile	−0.18***	0.14***		
	(0.04)	(0.04)		
5th quintile	−0.32***	0.14***		
	(0.05)	(0.05)		
Age	0.01***	−0.002***	−0.001	−0.01***
	(0.001)	(0.001)	(0.001)	(0.001)
Female (1 = yes)	0.18***	0.10***	0.04	0.36***
	(0.03)	(0.03)	(0.02)	(0.03)
Married (1 = yes)	−0.10***	−0.04	0.11***	0.30***
	(0.03)	(0.03)	(0.03)	(0.03)
Unemployed (1 = yes)	0.09	0.001	0.13**	0.01
	(0.06)	(0.06)	(0.05)	(0.06)
Union member (1= yes)	0.08**	0.23***	0.27***	0.19***
	(0.04)	(0.04)	(0.03)	(0.04)
Constant	1.46***	2.06***	−3.56***	1.06***
	(0.10)	(0.12)	(0.19)	(0.09)
Observations	34,263	34,180	42,386	41,704
Log likelihood	−18,932.91	−18,245.63	−20,883.99	−18,379.80
Akaike information criterion	37,947.83	36,573.26	41,849.98	36,841.60

*p < 0.1, **p < 0.5, ***p < 0.01.

Table 12.3 Logistic regression—Support for different social policies by occupation

	Support for social policy			
	Pension	Education	Public childcare	Parental leave
	(1)	(2)	(3)	(4)
Occupation (ref. = managers)				
Office clerks	0.29***	0.06	−0.17***	0.05
	(0.05)	(0.05)	(0.06)	(0.06)
Production workers	0.57***	−0.09**	−0.17***	−0.12**
	(0.04)	(0.04)	(0.05)	(0.05)
Service workers	0.43***	0.01	−0.13***	−0.05
	(0.04)	(0.05)	(0.05)	(0.05)
Sociocultural professionals	0.09*	0.40***	0.10*	0.23***
	(0.05)	(0.05)	(0.05)	(0.06)
Technical professionals	0.10*	0.15**	0.01	0.09
	(0.06)	(0.06)	(0.07)	(0.08)
Age	0.01***	−0.003***	−0.001	−0.01***
	(0.001)	(0.001)	(0.001)	(0.001)
Female (1 = yes)	0.21***	0.05*	0.03	0.32***
	(0.03)	(0.03)	(0.03)	(0.04)
Married (1 = yes)	−0.14***	0.02	0.12***	0.33***
	(0.03)	(0.03)	(0.03)	(0.03)
Unemployed (1 = yes)	0.23***	0.05	0.10*	−0.01
	(0.07)	(0.07)	(0.06)	(0.07)
Union member (1 = yes)	0.02	0.23***	0.20***	0.17***
	(0.04)	(0.04)	(0.04)	(0.04)
Constant	0.55***	2.30***	−3.18***	1.43***
	(0.10)	(0.12)	(0.22)	(0.11)
Observations	30,937	30,891	29,172	28,699
Log likelihood	−17,203.99	−16,954.20	−14,891.77	−11,868.20
Akaike information criterion	34,485.98	33,986.39	29,869.54	23,822.39

$^{*}p < 0.1$, $^{**}p < 0.5$, $^{***}p < 0.01$.

the different social policies by an individual's level of education. Although there are differences in the level of support for the different social policies, the pattern is always the same: Support for social investment increases with education, while support for social consumption decreases with education. Education spending in the upper left panel is the only exception: In this case, only people with a tertiary education have a significantly higher probability of supporting it than others.

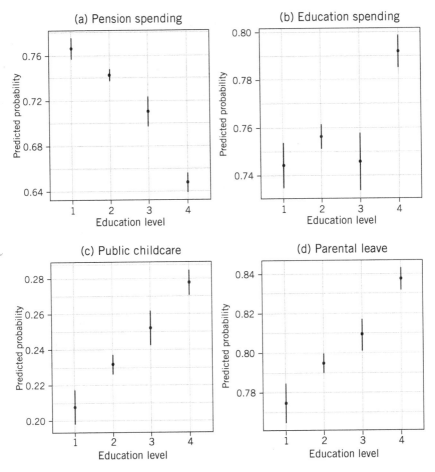

Figure 12.1 Predicted probability of supporting different social policies by education.
Note. The figure shows the predicted probabilities of supporting social investment by educational attainment. They are calculated from the respective models in Table 12.2. Education is coded in the following way: 1 = primary; 2 = secondary; 3 = post-secondary; 4 = tertiary.

Substituting occupational classes for education and income in the analysis indicates that class has a similar influence on preferences. The results are again illustrated by predicted probability plots in Figure 12.2. This figure shows that individuals from lower socioeconomic classes—including production workers, service workers, and office clerks—are the core supporters for additional pension spending, while higher socioeconomic classes are the core supporters for social investment. Especially sociocultural professionals are the true champions of social investment policies: They are most likely to support education spending, public childcare, and paid parental leave.[5] Depending on the issue, technical

5. Note that the dependent variables differ, which explains the very different levels of probability in Figure 12.1C as opposed to Figure 12.1A, B, and D: In the latter, respondents are asked

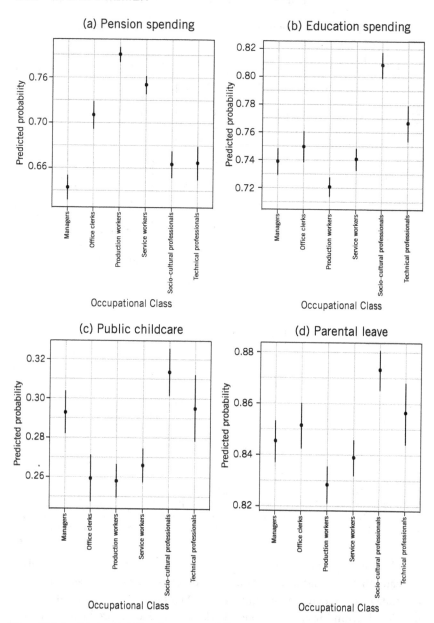

Figure 12.2 Predicted probability of supporting different social policies by occupation. *Note.* The figure shows the predicted probabilities of supporting social investment by occupation. They are calculated from the respective models in Table 12.3.

professionals and, to a lesser extent, managers are also supportive of social investment. Production and service workers as well as office clerks are relatively less enthusiastic about most forms of social investment.

about support for additional spending, while they are asked about the most appropriate form of childcare provision (public, family, private, other) in the former.

Taken together, these results clearly indicate that in terms of socioeconomic class the core supporters for social investment and social consumption are, indeed, very different (hypothesis 1): The educated middle classes are the champions of social investment; the working classes are the strongest supporters of transfer-oriented social policies. Although the effect sizes of education or occupational class on support for social investment are sometimes small, it is noteworthy that the pattern of support for social investment is the same across all three policies. Even when specific policies are very popular (e.g., education or paid parental leave), the expanded middle classes, and in particular social–cultural professionals, are significantly more supportive of social investment.

The results suggest that preferences toward social investment and social consumption are shaped not only by socioeconomic status, though. Several sociodemographic variables have significant effects on attitudes that are sometimes very large. First, age seems to influence preferences toward some social policies. As expected (hypothesis 2), age increases support for old-age pensions, but it decreases support for education spending and parental leave. It also has a negative effect on support for public childcare, but this effect is not statistically significant. In general, this effect of age may be explained by a life-cycle effect or a generational effect: Social policy preferences change either over the life cycle of individual respondents or over successive generations of cohorts.

Second, gender also influences preferences toward social policies as women are more likely to support both social investment and social consumption (hypothesis 3). They are strongly more supportive of additional spending on pensions and education as well as paid parental leave. For example, women have a 0.77 predicted probability of supporting education spending and a 0.74 predicted probability of supporting pension spending, whereas men have predicted probabilities of 0.75 and 0.70, respectively.[6] However, women are not more supportive of childcare being provided publicly than men, but this may again be due to the different nature of this variable as it asked not about policy generosity directly but about the best way of providing a service.

Finally, some control variables also have significant effects, including trade union membership and marital status. The former can be explained by narrow self-interest (as married people are more likely to benefit from family policies). Interestingly, trade union members are more likely to support both social investment and social consumption, but the effect of trade union membership on support for social investment is much larger than the effect on support for additional pension spending. This reflects the broad popularity of old-age pensions, but it also indicates that people with a left-wing ideology (as proxied by trade union membership) are much more likely to support state intervention in the economy by way of social investment than other individuals.

---

6. All calculations are based on Models 1 and 2 from Table 12.2, respectively.

12.4.2. Regional differences in the individual-level determinants for support for social investment and consumption

The problem with the pooled regression analysis is that it masks possible differences across regions. The samples from both the CSES and the ISSP include more countries from Western Europe than from other regions, and therefore, the results may be biased. Given the expectation that individual preferences interact with policy legacies, it is also important to analyze whether and how social policy preferences differ across contexts. To this end, I estimate all regression models separately for each region.

Tables 12.4–12.7 include results from multivariate regression models where support for the four different social policies analyzed here is used as the dependent variable. The models include the same explanatory variables used in Table 12.2, but regression models with occupational class as the key independent variables reveal similar patterns. In general, the results suggest that the determinants of preferences for social investment are comparable across regions. The findings from the pooled sample hold for most regions and policies, but there are some important differences, as expected (hypothesis 4).

To begin with, preferences for social investment appear more context-dependent than preferences for transfer-oriented social policies: The lower social classes are the core supporters of pension spending across all regions (see Table 12.4), but the support coalition for social investment is less clearly defined in some regions (see Tables 12.5–12.7). In Latin America, and to a lesser extent in Southern and Eastern Europe and Asia, it is difficult to make out any clear champions for social investment in the first place; and even where it is possible to discern individual-level differences in support for social investment, they are often smaller. For example, support for the public provision of childcare is clearly associated with a higher socioeconomic status in Western Europe but not in the other regions.

Similarly, the effect of other key independent variables on support for social investment also varies across regions (see Table 12.5–12.7). Age, gender, and trade union membership have a consistent effect in Western Europe, but they are less important for preferences in the other regions. Gender is a salient divide in Europe but not in Latin America and Asia (except for parental leave), while age has a significant effect on some policies, such as pension spending and parental leave, but not on others.

The results thus suggest that policy legacies interact with individual-level preference configurations. In particular, in regions where either welfare states are less developed (e.g., Latin America) or the salience of social investment is low (e.g., Eastern Europe), public opinion toward social investment is less clearly divided along class lines. This is especially true for Latin America, where education and income are hardly associated with preferences for higher education spending,

Table 12.4 Logistic regression—Support for additional pension spending by region

	Support for pension spending				
	Western Europe	Southern Europe	Eastern Europe	Asia	Latin America
	(1)	(2)	(3)	(4)	(5)
Education (ref. = primary)					
Secondary	−0.43***	−0.54***	−0.13	0.02	−0.12
	(0.10)	(0.18)	(0.10)	(0.10)	(0.08)
Post-secondary	−0.61***	−0.11	−0.45***	−0.33**	−0.17
	(0.12)	(0.30)	(0.14)	(0.13)	(0.15)
Tertiary	−0.96***	−0.79***	−0.67***	−0.37***	−0.30***
	(0.10)	(0.20)	(0.12)	(0.12)	(0.11)
Income (ref. = 1st quintile)					
2nd Quintile	−0.08	0.02	−0.03	−0.07	0.18**
	(0.07)	(0.15)	(0.10)	(0.10)	(0.09)
3rd Quintile	−0.20***	−0.35**	−0.01	−0.03	0.16*
	(0.07)	(0.15)	(0.10)	(0.11)	(0.09)
4th Quintile	−0.30***	−0.44***	−0.19*	−0.15	0.08
	(0.07)	(0.16)	(0.10)	(0.11)	(0.10)
5th Quintile	−0.56***	−0.58***	−0.30***	−0.13	−0.07
	(0.08)	(0.21)	(0.11)	(0.12)	(0.10)
Age	0.01***	0.01	0.02***	0.003	0.01***
	(0.001)	(0.004)	(0.002)	(0.002)	(0.002)
Female (1 = yes)	0.22***	0.34***	0.28***	0.08	0.01
	(0.04)	(0.09)	(0.06)	(0.06)	(0.06)
Married (1 = yes)	−0.05	−0.12	0.02	0.001	−0.15**
	(0.05)	(0.11)	(0.06)	(0.07)	(0.06)
Unemployed (1 = yes)	0.22*	0.16	−0.04	0.36*	−0.14
	(0.12)	(0.16)	(0.11)	(0.19)	(0.15)
Union member (1 = yes)	0.13***	0.10	0.04	0.02	−0.02
	(0.05)	(0.18)	(0.11)	(0.10)	(0.11)
Constant	0.54***	0.92***	1.75***	0.15	1.39***
	(0.16)	(0.31)	(0.22)	(0.21)	(0.15)
Observations	10,990	2445	8720	4880	7228
Log likelihood	−6749.43	−1456.80	−3715.47	−3113.53	−3793.54
Akaike information criterion	13,542.87	2941.60	7470.93	6259.05	7621.07

*$p < 0.1$, **$p < 0.5$, ***$p < 0.01$.

public childcare, or parental leave. Similarly, in Eastern Europe and Southern Europe, support for additional education spending and public childcare is more even across classes than in Western Europe. In all these instances, support for social investment is generally higher than in Western Europe. For example, in Latin America, the average predicted probability of supporting additional education spending (across all classes) is above 85%, but it is below 65% in Western Europe. This is also indicated by Figure A-12.1 in the Appendix, which shows that the support coalition for social investment is both broader and more diffuse in some regions with less mature welfare states than in Western Europe, like Latin America or, to a lesser extent, Southern and Eastern Europe. It may be evidence for a thermostatic model of public opinion (Soroka & Wlezien, 2010; also see Chapter 3 in Volume II [Garritzmann et al., 2022]): Support for social investment is higher in countries where such policies are less developed.

However, the differences across regions may also be explained by the different prevailing distributive profiles of social investment across regions. In Western Europe, social investment is often stratified: Although it is formally open to anyone, individuals who are already well prepared to take advantage of the knowledge economy benefit disproportionally. In combination with an existing high level of compensatory social policies, which often pits social investment against social consumption in the context of permanent austerity (Bremer & Bürgisser, 2022), this contributes to a clear division of public opinion along classes. In other regions, support for social investment cannot be conceptualized in terms of a trade-off between social investment and social consumption. For example, in Latin America, social investment policies combine elements of both logics because they are targeted at lower classes. Consequently, different classes may have different reasons to support social investment in these regions: While lower classes favor social investment for distributive reasons, the educated middle classes support it for reasons of universalism. This could explain why support for social investment is (even) higher in regions like Latin America than it is in Western Europe. Similarly, in North East Asia, a trade-off between social investment and social consumption is not apparent. Historically, these countries had relatively low levels of public social expenditure. Due to their aging societies, however, countries in the region have increased spending on both consumption and investment, which shows that there is not always a trade-off between these two logics. As social investment is, however, in general less targeted in Asia than it is in Latin America, there is still a division of public opinion toward education, parental leave, and, to a lesser extent, public childcare along classes, as shown by Model 4 in Tables 12.5–12.7.

Finally, the way that these patterns of support translate into an effective demand for social investment also depends on the size of the respective groups in the different regions. As argued, the expanded middle classes are the key actors in the politics of social investment. Yet, their size varies significantly across regions, partly as a result of welfare state legacies (see Oesch, 2015).

Table 12.5 Logistic regression—Support for additional education spending by region

	Support for education spending				
	Western Europe	Southern Europe	Eastern Europe	Asia	Latin America
	(1)	(2)	(3)	(4)	(5)
Education (ref. = primary)					
Secondary	0.04	0.02	−0.07	0.19*	0.16*
	(0.09)	(0.17)	(0.08)	(0.10)	(0.09)
Post-secondary	−0.08	−0.28	−0.07	0.29**	0.07
	(0.10)	(0.29)	(0.12)	(0.14)	(0.20)
Tertiary	0.32***	0.22	−0.01	0.42***	0.16
	(0.09)	(0.20)	(0.10)	(0.13)	(0.14)
Income (ref. = 1st quintile)					
2nd Quintile	0.09	0.12	−0.002	0.07	0.03
	(0.07)	(0.16)	(0.08)	(0.10)	(0.11)
3rd Quintile	0.03	0.0003	0.09	0.34***	0.13
	(0.07)	(0.16)	(0.08)	(0.11)	(0.11)
4th Quintile	0.12	0.01	0.11	0.20*	0.27**
	(0.07)	(0.18)	(0.09)	(0.12)	(0.12)
5th Quintile	0.07	−0.07	0.17*	0.31***	0.17
	(0.08)	(0.24)	(0.09)	(0.12)	(0.12)
Age	−0.003**	−0.004	−0.001	−0.002	0.0003
	(0.001)	(0.004)	(0.002)	(0.002)	(0.002)
Female (1 = yes)	0.08*	0.30***	0.16***	−0.03	0.05
	(0.04)	(0.10)	(0.05)	(0.06)	(0.07)
Married (1 = yes)	−0.05	−0.07	−0.02	0.08	−0.12
	(0.05)	(0.11)	(0.06)	(0.07)	(0.08)
Unemployed (1 = yes)	0.04	0.09	0.09	−0.28	−0.21
	(0.12)	(0.17)	(0.10)	(0.17)	(0.18)
Union member (1 = yes)	0.24***	0.72***	0.24**	0.26**	−0.02
	(0.05)	(0.24)	(0.11)	(0.11)	(0.15)
Constant	1.14***	1.12***	1.87***	0.05	1.97***
	(0.16)	(0.33)	(0.19)	(0.21)	(0.19)
Observations	11,019	2452	8627	4855	7227
Log likelihood	−6669.25	−1289.46	−4622.59	−2932.39	−2695.47
Akaike information criterion	13,382.50	2606.93	9285.18	5896.78	5424.93

*$p < 0.1$, **$p < 0.5$, ***$p < 0.01$.

Table 12.6 Logistic regression—Support for public childcare by region

	Support for public childcare				
	Western Europe	Southern Europe	Eastern Europe	Asia	Latin America
	(1)	(2)	(3)	(4)	(5)
Education *(ref. = primary)*					
Secondary	0.21**	0.25**	0.35**	−0.03	0.02
	(0.10)	(0.11)	(0.14)	(0.11)	(0.11)
Post-secondary	0.43***	0.16	0.42***	0.10	−0.06
	(0.10)	(0.15)	(0.15)	(0.19)	(0.17)
Tertiary	0.59***	0.18	0.46***	0.21*	0.15
	(0.10)	(0.13)	(0.15)	(0.13)	(0.15)
Age	0.0005	−0.001	−0.002	−0.0004	−0.004
	(0.001)	(0.003)	(0.001)	(0.003)	(0.003)
Female (1 = yes)	0.08**	0.12*	0.02	−0.09	−0.09
	(0.04)	(0.07)	(0.05)	(0.08)	(0.08)
Married (1 = yes)	0.16***	−0.05	0.02	0.29***	0.07
	(0.04)	(0.08)	(0.05)	(0.08)	(0.09)
Unemployed (1 = yes)	0.01	0.09	0.15*	0.40***	−0.06
	(0.10)	(0.11)	(0.09)	(0.15)	(0.19)
Union member (1 = yes)	0.32***	0.41***	−0.001	0.29***	0.28*
	(0.04)	(0.11)	(0.08)	(0.10)	(0.15)
Constant	−1.55***	−1.09***	−2.27***	−1.86***	−3.23***
	(0.14)	(0.20)	(0.19)	(0.17)	(0.25)
Observations	17,365	3492	9929	6874	4726
Log likelihood	−8889.04	−2154.29	−5585.62	−2310.17	−1902.81
Akaike information criterion	17,820.08	4328.58	11,205.23	4646.34	3829.62

$^*p < 0.1, {}^{**}p < 0.5, {}^{***}p < 0.01.$

For example, Figure 12.3 shows the size of the different occupational groups by region. This figure indicates that the group of sociocultural professionals, who are the strongest supporters of social investment, is considerably larger in Western Europe than in the other regions. Therefore, as Garritzmann et al. emphasize in Chapter 8 in this volume, we can also expect the politicization of social investment to vary across regions as a result of differences in the structural transformation of post-industrial societies (e.g., as a result of the occupational transformation). It influences how public opinion feeds into the political process and affects the size and composition of the support coalitions in different regions of the world.

Table 12.7 Logistic regression—Support for paid parental leave by region

	Support for parental leave				
	Western Europe	Southern Europe	Eastern Europe	Asia	Latin America
	(1)	(2)	(3)	(4)	(5)
Education *(ref. = primary)*					
Secondary	0.13	0.47***	0.33**	0.16*	−0.07
	(0.09)	(0.14)	(0.15)	(0.09)	(0.09)
Post-secondary	0.12	0.32*	0.52***	0.45***	0.11
	(0.10)	(0.19)	(0.17)	(0.14)	(0.14)
Tertiary	0.33***	0.48***	0.77***	0.63***	0.005
	(0.09)	(0.17)	(0.17)	(0.10)	(0.12)
Age	−0.02***	−0.01***	−0.003	−0.01***	0.0003
	(0.001)	(0.003)	(0.002)	(0.002)	(0.002)
Female (1 = yes)	0.43***	0.51***	0.43***	0.31***	0.03
	(0.04)	(0.10)	(0.07)	(0.06)	(0.07)
Married (1 = yes)	0.28***	0.39***	0.56***	0.32***	0.09
	(0.04)	(0.10)	(0.07)	(0.06)	(0.07)
Unemployed (1 = yes)	0.18*	−0.07	0.02	−0.15	−0.09
	(0.10)	(0.15)	(0.13)	(0.12)	(0.14)
Union member (1 = yes)	0.29***	0.02	0.06	−0.13	0.20
	(0.05)	(0.16)	(0.14)	(0.09)	(0.13)
Constant	2.52***	1.66***	0.86***	−1.32***	0.93***
	(0.16)	(0.25)	(0.21)	(0.14)	(0.16)
Observations	16,839	3507	9879	6838	4641
Log likelihood	−8011.03	−1452.22	−2912.89	−3387.46	−2517.53
Akaike information criterion	16,064.06	2924.45	5859.77	6800.93	5059.07

*$p < 0.1$, **$p < 0.5$, ***$p < 0.01$.

12.5. CONCLUSION

In conclusion, the analysis showed that social policy preferences are multi-dimensional: Attitudes toward social investment are distinct from attitudes toward social consumption across most regions of the world. Socioeconomic class is still an important source of preference formation, but it shapes preferences for social investment distinctively: While the lower classes remain the core constituency for traditional social policies, the expanded middle classes have become the key

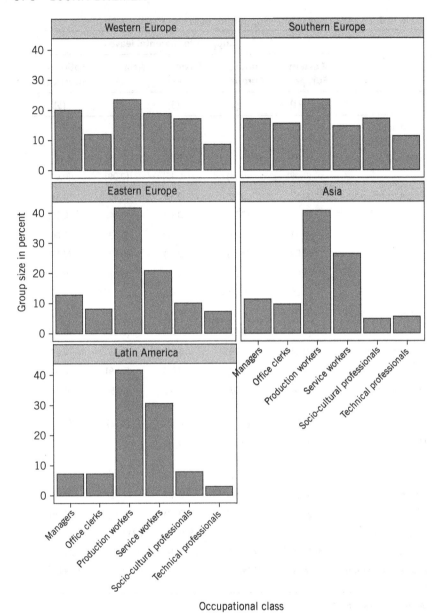

Figure 12.3 Relative occupation group sizes across regions.
Note. The figure shows the relative group size of different occupational groups by region, as reported in the ISSP survey (2012).

constituency for social investment policies. Yet, there is some intra-class heterogeneity in the demand for social investment: Older people are less willing to prioritize the needs of future generations, whereas women are generally more supportive of social investment than men.

Still, these individual-level effects also depend on the context in which people live. In mature welfare states, individual-level conflicts are clear-cut. Since the

expansion of social investment implies policy and fiscal trade-offs with traditional compensatory social policies, individuals support the policies from which
they benefit most. Influenced by the legacies of existing policies, the educated
middle classes are thus the key actors who support social investment. In contrast,
in regions with less developed welfare states, there are less distinct and countervailing class preferences. Particularly in Latin America, where social investment
policies are often targeted at the lower classes, individual-level conflicts are more
muted; rather, support for social investment is high across social classes, and
the potential support coalitions for social investment are thus broader and more
diffuse. Existing policies thus seem to have important feedback effects that influence the demand for social investment.

REFERENCES

Ansell, B. W. (2010). *From the ballot to the blackboard: The redistributive political economy of education.* Cambridge University Press.
Beramendi, P., Häusermann, S., Kitschelt, H., & Kriesi, H. (2015). *The politics of advanced capitalism.* Cambridge University Press.
Bonoli, G. (2005). The politics of the new social policies: Providing coverage against new social risks in mature welfare states. *Policy & Politics, 33*(3), 431–449.
Bonoli, G. (2013). *The origins of active social policy: Labour market and childcare polices in a comparative perspective.* Oxford University Press.
Bonoli, G., & Häusermann, S. (2009). Who wants what from the welfare state? *European Societies, 11*(2), 211–232.
Bonoli, G., & Liechti, F. (2018). Good intentions and Matthew effects: Access biases in participation in active labour market policies. *Journal of European Public Policy, 25*(6), 894–911.
Bremer, B., & Bürgisser, R. (2022). Public opinion on welfare state recalibration in times of austerity: Evidence from survey experiments. *Political Science Research and Methods.* Advance online publication.
Busemeyer, M. R., & Garritzmann, J. L. (2017). Public opinion on policy and budgetary trade-offs in European welfare states: Evidence from a new comparative survey. *Journal of European Public Policy, 24*(6), 871–889.
Busemeyer, M. R., & Iversen, T. (2014). The politics of opting out: Explaining educational financing and popular support for public spending. *Socio-Economic Review, 12*(2), 299–328.
Esping-Andersen, G. (1985). *Politics against markets: The social democratic road to power.* Princeton University Press.
Esping-Andersen, G. (2002). A child-centred social investment strategy. In G. Esping-Andersen, G. Duncan, A. Hemerijck, & J. Myles (Eds.), *Why we need a new welfare state* (pp. 26–65). Oxford University Press.
Fossati, F., & Häusermann, S. (2014). Social policy preferences and party choice in the 2011 Swiss elections. *Swiss Political Science Review, 20*(4), 590–611.

Garritzmann, J. L. (2015). Attitudes towards student support: How positive feedback-effects prevent change in the four worlds of student finance. *Journal of European Social Policy, 25*(2), 139–158.

Garritzmann, J. L. (2016). *The political economy of higher education finance: The politics of tuition fees and subsidies in OECD countries, 1945–2015.* Palgrave Macmillan.

Garritzmann, J. L., Busemeyer, M. R., & Neimanns, E. (2018). Public demand for social investment: New supporting coalitions for welfare state reform in western Europe? *Journal of European Public Policy, 25*(6), 844–861.

Garritzmann, J. L., Häusermann, S., & Palier, B. (Eds.). (2022). *The world politics of social investment: Vol. II. The politics of varying social investment strategies.* Oxford University Press.

Gingrich, J., & Ansell, B. (2012). Preferences in context: Micro preferences, macro contexts, and the demand for social policy. *Comparative Political Studies, 45*(12), 1624–1654.

Gingrich, J., & Häusermann, S. (2015). The decline of the working-class vote, the reconfiguration of the welfare support coalition and consequences for the welfare state. *Journal of European Social Policy, 25*(1), 50–75.

Goerres, A., & Tepe, M. (2010). Age-based self-interest, intergenerational solidarity and the welfare state: A comparative analysis of older people's attitudes towards public childcare in 12 OECD countries. *European Journal of Political Research, 49*(6), 818–851.

Goerres, A., & Tepe, M. (2012). Doing it for the kids? The determinants of attitudes towards public childcare in unified Germany. *Journal of Social Policy, 41*(2), 349–372.

Häusermann, S., & Palier, B. (2017). The politics of social investment: Policy legacies and class coalitions. In A. Hemerijck (Ed.), *The uses of social investment* (pp. 339–348). Oxford University Press.

Häusermann, S., Pinggera, M., Ares, M., & Enggist, M. (2021). Class and social policy in the knowledge economy. *European Journal of Political Research.* Advance online publication. https://doi.org/10.1111/1475-6765.12463

Hemerijck, A. (2013). *Changing welfare states.* Oxford University Press.

Hemerijck, A. (2017). *The uses of social investment.* Oxford University Press.

Huber, E., & Stephens, J. D. (2000). Partisan governance, women's employment, and the social democratic service state. *American Sociological Review, 65*(3), 323–342.

Korpi, W. (1983). *The democratic class struggle.* Routledge & Kegan Paul.

Lynch, J. (2006). *Age in the welfare state: The origins of social spending on pensioners, workers, and children.* Cambridge University Press.

Morel, N., Palier, B., & Palme, J. (2012). *Towards a social investment welfare state? Ideas, policies and challenges.* Policy Press.

Naumann, I. K. (2005). Child care and feminism in West Germany and Sweden in the 1960s and 1970s. *Journal of European Social Policy, 15*(1), 47–63.

Neimanns, E., Busemeyer, M. R., & Garritzmann, J. L. (2018). How popular are social investment policies really? Evidence from a survey experiment in eight western European countries. *European Sociological Review, 34*(3), 238–253.

Oesch, D. (2006a). *Redrawing the class map*. Palgrave Macmillan.

Oesch, D. (2006b). Coming to grips with a changing class structure: An analysis of employment stratification in Britain, Germany, Sweden and Switzerland. *International Sociology, 21*(2), 63–88.

Oesch, D. (2015). Welfare regimes and change in the employment structure: Britain, Denmark and Germany since 1990. *Journal of European Social Policy, 25*(1), 94–110.

Palier, B. (2010). *A long goodbye to Bismarck? The politics of welfare reform in continental Europe*. Amsterdam University Press.

Pavolini, E., & van Lancker, W. (2018). The Matthew effect in childcare use: A matter of policies or preferences? *Journal of European Public Policy, 25*(6), 878–893.

Pierson, P. (1993). When effect becomes cause: Policy feedback and political change. *World Politics, 45*(4), 595–628.

Rehm, P. (2011). Social policy by popular demand. *World Politics, 63*(2), 271–299.

Rueda, D. (2005). Insider–outsider politics in industrialized democracies: The challenge to social democratic parties. *The American Political Science Review, 99*(1), 61–74.

Sainsbury, D. (1996). *Gender, equality, and welfare states*. Cambridge University Press.

Soroka, S. N., & Wlezien, C. (2010). *Degrees of democracy: Politics, public opinion, and policy*. Cambridge University Press.

Stephens, J. D. (1979). *The transition from capitalism to socialism*. Macmillan.

Svallfors, S. (1997). Worlds of welfare and attitudes to redistribution: A comparison of eight Western nations. *European Sociological Review, 13*(3), 283–304.

Svallfors, S. (2012). *Contested welfare states: Welfare attitudes in Europe and beyond*. Stanford University Press.

van Lancker, W., & Ghysels, J. (2012). Who benefits? The social distribution of subsidized childcare in Sweden and Flanders. *Acta Sociologica, 55*(2), 125–142.

APPENDIX

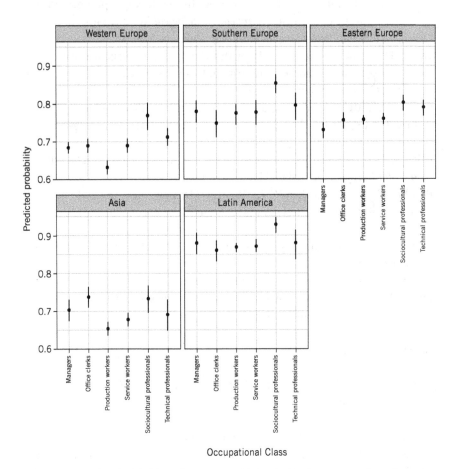

Occupational Class

Figure A-12.1 Predicted probability of supporting additional education spending by region.

PART IV

THE COMPARATIVE POLITICS OF SOCIAL INVESTMENT REFORMS

13

SOCIAL INVESTMENT AND NEOLIBERAL LEGACIES IN LATIN AMERICA

BREAKING THE MOLD?

Evelyne Huber, Claire Dunn, and John D. Stephens

13.1. A CONCEPTUAL TURN TO SOCIAL INVESTMENT?

If we start with the definition of the goals of social investment as aiming "to prepare, support, and equip individuals in a way that increases their chance to support themselves in the economy (notably through employment) and reduces their future risks of income loss and poverty," we can certainly find a range of policies that pursue these goals in Latin America. Nevertheless, we cannot really call the spread of social investment policies in Latin America a "turn to social investment" analogous to the European experience. The notion of a "turn" implies a turn away from something, in the European case from the passive or consumption-oriented welfare state to an active/activating or investment-oriented welfare state. In Latin America the passive welfare state was much less developed, covering in most cases not more than half the population. Coverage was obtained through formal sector employment, and by the 1990s roughly half of the population (ranging from about a quarter in Argentina and Chile to over three-quarters in Central American cases) worked in the informal sector. Even in the cases where coverage had been high during the peak of import substitution industrialization, it had been shrinking in the course of structural adjustment. To build on Ferrera's (2005) diagnosis of the weakness of the Southern European welfare state, Latin America was characterized by incomplete Fordism to an even

Evelyne Huber, Claire Dunn, and John D. Stephens, *Social Investment and Neoliberal Legacies in Latin America* In: *The World Politics of Social Investment (Volume I)*. Edited by: Julian L. Garritzmann, Silja Häusermann, and Bruno Palier, Oxford University Press. © Oxford University Press 2022. DOI: 10.1093/oso/9780197585245.003.0013 greater degree. Thus, the preoccupation in Latin America (as in most lower- and middle-income countries, see Chapter 5 in this volume) has been with expansion of coverage of welfare state programs—reaching those who had previously been excluded both from transfers and from services, specifically healthcare and education.[1]

In this chapter, we shall identify the types of social investment strategies pursued in Latin America as well as the main protagonists of these reforms. We shall further explore the institutional structures that shaped the reforms, particularly policy legacies and presidential partisan control over legislatures. We shall also take note of the power of antagonists of inclusive reforms.

To the extent that the concept of social investment has been adopted in Latin America, it has been with the aim of creating human capital and at the same time reducing inequality of opportunity. The emphasis has been on education, expanding secondary and tertiary enrollment and improving the quality of education, to close the gap between public and private education and within the public sector between schools with affluent and poor students. In some countries, most notably Brazil, these efforts began in the 1990s already. More recently, early childhood education and care (ECEC) has received more attention because of the great disadvantage with which poor children start school in Latin America. This disadvantage stems from both physical health problems like malnutrition and disease and relative cognitive deprivation. Accordingly, children's access to healthcare and adequate nutrition has assumed a prominent place in the pursuit of human capital improvements. At the same time, access to healthcare for all adults has become a policy goal.

In the context of high absolute poverty, that is, a large proportion of the population living under conditions that do not allow them to satisfy basic necessities, creating human capital cannot be divorced from alleviating poverty. Access to health services and schools is necessary but not sufficient for children to learn. Families must have the incentive to send children to school rather than involving them in hustling to contribute to the family economy. It is for this reason that the conditional cash transfer (CCT) programs have become so popular. They provide modest cash transfers mostly to families with children under the condition that these children regularly attend school and get health checkups. These programs illustrate the tight nexus between social investment and basic income strategies in Latin America extremely well.

In order to assess the significance of the reforms, or the extent to which they advance universalism in social policy, we need to look at expansion of coverage as well as the generosity of transfers and quality of services and at the degree of equality in generosity and quality of services for different income groups in

---

1. There were exceptions to this generalization. In Brazil and Uruguay, for instance, privileged public sector pensions weighed heavily on the budget; and thus, cutting this part of the consumption-oriented welfare state was a major preoccupation. However, other parts of the consumption-oriented welfare state were expanded, particularly the non-contributory pensions.

the society.[2] Expansion of coverage of poor-quality preschool education or expansion of health insurance without concomitant expansion of accessibility of quality services will not significantly improve the human capital and capabilities of a society, and therefore not fulfill the functions that define social investment. Advance toward universalism in social policy in turn is shaped by the partisan orientation of governments, by the parliamentary base of governments, and by policy legacies (Huber & Stephens, 2012). In addition, the strength of left parties even when in opposition and the strength of social movements engaged in the struggle for social investment contribute to advancement toward universalism via inclusive social investment (Anria & Niedzwiecki, 2016; see also Chapter 5 in this volume). The nexus between expansion of transfers to previously excluded groups and social investment policies in Latin America is a clear example of the importance of policy legacies for the social investment agenda (see Chapter 1 in this volume).

13.2. REASONS FOR THE SPREAD OF SOCIAL INVESTMENT POLICIES

There are multiple reasons why social investment policies along with social transfers spread in Latin America beginning in the 1990s and then accelerated after 2000. The most important is arguably the backlash against neoliberalism. This backlash was aimed at the social consequences of neoliberalism and the neoliberal reforms of social policy everywhere, whereas the backlash against economic policies like trade liberalization, privatization, and economic regulation varied greatly. It was negligible in countries like Chile and Uruguay but much stronger in countries like Bolivia and Ecuador. The backlash took the form of street protests that forced some incumbents from office and of anti-incumbent votes that forced politicians of all stripes to address the "social debt" incurred by Washington Consensus policies (Silva, 2009). Governments started investing more heavily in education and experimenting with pilot programs of CCTs in the 1990s. The second reason was the growing electoral strength of the left and the winning of the presidency by leftist candidates: Chavez in Venezuela in 1998, Lagos in Chile in 2000, Lula in Brazil in 2002, Kirchner in Argentina in 2003, Vazquez in Uruguay in 2004, Morales in Bolivia in 2005, Correa in Ecuador in 2006, Ortega in Nicaragua in 2006, Lugo in Paraguay in 2008, Funes in El Salvador in 2009, Humala in Peru in 2011, with all but Lugo and Humala

---

2. Martínez Franzoni and Sánchez-Ancochea, D. (2016) conceptualize universalism in social policy as composed of the three dimensions of coverage, generosity/quality, and equity. We shall adopt the concept with this meaning here. See their paper: More, Less or the Same Segmentation: The Case of Early Child Education and Care Services in Costa Rica and Uruguay, presented at the Meeting of Research Committee 19 of the International Sociological Association.

either re-elected or followed by another left president. These left governments became the protagonists of social investment, social protection, and minimum income strategies, based on their commitments to reducing inequality; and they were helped by the third reason—the commodities boom. The increase in demand for raw materials from Latin America, fueled in particular by the growth in China, greatly increased export revenue and tax revenue for Latin American governments.

We might add a fourth reason, particularly for late adopters of a particular type of social investment policies, the CCT programs—political learning. CCT programs became very popular, and in a 2007 article Hunter and Power credited the program with changing the electoral landscape in Brazil. Since then several studies have confirmed that indeed these programs strengthened political support for the governments administering them (e.g., De La O, 2013; Diaz-Cayeros et al., 2016). In fact, where these programs achieved wide coverage, as in Brazil, they became so popular that opposition candidates promised not only to preserve them but even to expand them (Pavão, 2016).

Some observers credit a change in thinking in the International Financial Institutions (IFIs), specifically the World Bank, the Inter-American Development Bank, and the Comisión Económica Para América Latina y el Caribe (CEPAL), with giving an impetus to social investment policies in Latin America. It is true that these institutions began to develop an official concern with poverty, inequality, and inclusion in the 1990s. However, it is not so much that they developed new ideas but rather that they allowed intellectuals with those ideas to influence their official reports. All through the 1990s there had been social scientists articulating an alternative to the residual social policy vision of the IFIs, visible, for instance, in the 1995 Copenhagen World Summit on Social Development; but for the most part they were not in positions of power in their home countries or in the IFIs, so their influence was limited. What changed to make their ideas more influential were political power relations. Moreover, after 2000, Latin American countries gained greater independence from the IFIs as they began to accumulate foreign exchange reserves. Thus, domestic politics became crucial.

Putting primary emphasis on domestic and international power relations is not to deny that particularly CEPAL made important contributions to the debate. CEPAL's annual publication *Social Panorama* offered outstanding research and stimulated important discussions. Arguably, based on its relations to the European Commission and particularly aid agencies from Germany, Spain, and Sweden, CEPAL contributed to steering the discourse in the direction of social rights (Mahon, 2015).

13.3. SPENDING PATTERNS

If we look at average spending patterns in the region from 1990 to 2015 (Table 13.1), we see an increase in spending on health, education, and social security

Table 13.1 Average spending as percentage of GDP, 1990–2015

Year	Education	Health	Social protection	Number of countries
1990	2.58	2.21	2.94	8
1991	2.65	2.18	2.92	8
1992	2.85	2.24	2.62	9
1993	3.24	2.36	2.72	9
1994	3.17	2.30	2.88	9
1995	3.23	2.28	3.29	11
1996	3.35	2.22	3.42	11
1997	3.42	2.25	3.64	11
1998	3.48	2.31	4.23	13
1999	3.60	2.43	4.28	15
2000	3.70	2.40	4.10	16
2001	3.99	2.59	4.18	16
2002	3.94	2.53	3.90	17
2003	3.97	2.59	3.80	17
2004	3.84	2.50	3.71	17
2005	3.83	2.50	3.68	17
2006	3.98	2.62	3.64	17
2007	4.06	2.59	3.80	18
2008	4.16	2.70	4.10	19
2009	4.57	3.08	4.73	20
2010	4.46	3.05	4.72	19
2011	4.37	3.11	4.66	19
2012	4.43	3.07	4.47	18
2013	4.52	3.10	4.55	18
2014	4.53	3.21	4.67	18
2015	4.73	3.48	5.24	16

Source. For all except Uruguay (all years) and Brazil (1995–1999): CEPALSTAT Bases de Datos y Publicaciones Estadisticas (2018). For Uruguay (all years) and Brazil (1995–1999): Evelyne Huber and John D. Stephens, Latin American Welfare Dataset, 1960–2014, University of North Carolina at Chapel Hill (2014).

and welfare; but the increase and level are highest in spending on social security and welfare.[3] This picture reflects the overall effort to expand the reach of the welfare state in all dimensions, transfers as well as services.

3. The data for this section comes from CEPALSTAT Base de Datos y Publicaciones Estadísticas https://statistics.cepal.org/portal/cepalstat/index.html?lang=es. Data for Uruguay come from our Latin American Social Policy Data Set (https://huberandstephens.web.unc.edu/) and are not updated as the latest CEPALSTAT data now exclude information from quasi-public pension funds and the social protection agency, which results in figures that are way too low for the Uruguayan case.

If we take a closer look at the economically most advanced countries (Argentina, Brazil, Chile, Mexico, and Uruguay) and Costa Rica (because of its long tradition of progressive social policy), over the period since 1990, we see a mixed picture[4]: Argentina and Mexico fit the general pattern, but spending on social security and welfare actually decreased in Uruguay and Chile.[5] In Brazil health spending and in Costa Rica health and education spending increased more steeply than social security and welfare spending (Table 13.2). Argentina, Brazil, and Uruguay all had made efforts to rein in expenditures on contributory pensions since the 1990s, but they all significantly expanded non-contributory social transfers, both in pensions and in transfers to the working-age population, most of the latter in the form of conditional transfers.

Tables 13.1 and 13.2 show that social spending in all categories increased on average in the 17–20 Latin American and Caribbean countries for which we have data. Countries where the welfare state was less developed expanded social security and welfare spending as much as or more than spending on health and education. This pattern clearly applies to Mexico. What is important to note here is that this category of spending includes the CCT programs, which can be seen as social investment programs. However, if the health and education infrastructure does not keep up with the demand generated by the required school enrollment and health checkups, the investment in CCTs will bring limited dividends. The main effect will be poverty alleviation, which is important but not sufficient to improve human capital.

Tables 13.3 and 13.4 show data on health and education spending since 2000; levels of spending at or above 3.5% and 5%, respectively, are in italics; years of left government are in bold. Health spending shows a strong commitment concentrated among the most advanced countries. Since 2000, they have consistently spent 3.5% or more of their gross domestic product (GDP) on health, with Argentina lagging behind until 2009. The increase is particularly steep in Uruguay after 2005, under the left *Frente Amplio* (FA) government, reflecting the important reform that introduced a single-payer system. In Chile, the steepest increase comes after 2005, with the implementation of *Acceso Universal con Garantías Explícitas* (AUGE), the signature reform of the *Concertación* under the Socialist Lagos. Left governments in Bolivia, Ecuador, El Salvador, and Nicaragua have shown a similar commitment to increasing spending on healthcare. The two countries that have higher than expected expenditures are Colombia and

---

4. These six countries together comprise more than 67% of the population of the area, so we get a picture of social investment as it affects some two-thirds of Latin Americans living in the region. As defined by *Social Panorama*, the Latin American region includes 18 countries (Argentina, Brazil, Bolivia, Chile, Colombia, Costa Rica, the Dominican Republic, Ecuador, El Salvador, Guatemala, Honduras, Mexico, Nicaragua, Panama, Paraguay, Peru, Uruguay, and Venezuela).

5. In Uruguay, the level of social security and welfare spending was the highest until 2008, when it was surpassed by Brazil. In Chile, remaining state obligations from before 1980, when the dictator Pinochet privatized the pension system, declined over time.

Table 13.2 Change in spending, 1998–2015

Country	Education 1998	Education 2015	Change in education 1998–2015	Health 1998	Health 2015	Change in Health 1998–2015	Social protection 1998	Social protection 2015	Change in social protection 1998–2015
Argentina	3.91	6.63	2.72	4.24	7.10	2.86	8.71	14.13	5.42
Brazil	5.53	5.06	–0.47	3.73	5.55	1.82	11.72	13.21	1.49
Chile	3.17	4.41	1.24	2.47	4.69	2.22	6.99	6.28	–0.71
Costa Rica	4.35	7.53	3.18	4.64	6.57	1.93	5.73	6.98	1.25
Mexico	3.46	3.70	0.24	2.05	2.75	0.70	1.70	3.83	2.13
Uruguay[a]	2.93	4.44	1.51	3.15	6.05	2.90	12.17	11.07	–1.10

[a] Uruguay data are from 2011 rather than 2015.

Source. For all except Uruguay and Brazil (1998): CEPALSTAT Bases de Datos y Publicaciones Estadisticas (2018).

For Uruguay and Brazil (1998): Evelyne Huber and John D. Stephens, Latin American Welfare Dataset, 1960–2014, University of North Carolina at Chapel Hill (2014).

384 EVELYNE HUBER ET AL.

Table 13.3 Government health spending as a percentage of GDP

	2000	2005	2006	2007	2008	2009	2010	2011	2012	2013	2014	2015
Argentina	1.2	2.7	2.9	3.1	3.1	3.7	3.7	3.6	4	4.3	4.5	4.9
Brazil	3.5	3.3	3.5	3.5	3.5	3.7	3.6	3.5	3.4	3.6	3.7	4.4
Chile	3.8	3.5	3.3	3.4	3.8	4.2	4	4	4.2	4.4	4.6	3.8
Costa Rica	4.3	4.3	4.7	4.7	5.2	5.7	5.9	6.2	6.1	6.3	6	4.1
Uruguay	4.2	4.5	4.8	4.2	5	5.1	5.2	5.3	5.9	6.3	6.4	3.2
Bolivia	2.4	2.8	2.7	2.8	2.8	3.2	3.1	3.1	3	3.3	3.7	4.1
Ecuador	1	1.7	1.8	2.2	2.3	2.7	3.2	3.7	4.2	4.4	4.5	2.5
Colombia	4.3	4	4.2	4	4.1	4.6	4.4	4.3	4.5	4.4	4.5	4.9
Mexico	2.5 [a]	2.5	2.4	2.5	2.6	2.9	2.9	3	3.1	3.2	2.9	2.9
Panama	5	4.1	4.5	4.3	4.3	4.2	4.2	3.7	3.5	4	4.2	4.4
Paraguay	2.4	1.9	2.2	2.2	2.2	3	2.9	3.3	4.1	3.5	4.1	4.3
Peru	2.3	2.5	2.3	2.2	2.1	2.5	2.5	2.4	2.6	2.8	3.1	4.2
Dominican Republic	0.9	1.5	1.5	1.7	2.1	2.3	2.5	2.7	2.8	2.8	2.6	
El Salvador	3.3	3.7	3.9	3.5	3.5	3.5	3.8	4.2	4	4.3	4.3	4.2
Guatemala	1.7	1.9	2	2	2.1	2.2	2	1.9	1.9	2.1	2.2	4.4
Honduras	3	2.9	3.1	3.2	3	3.7	3.4	3	3.4	3.2	2.9	1.8
Nicaragua	2.5	2.6	2.6	2.9	3.2	3.5	3	3.7	4	4	4.3	3.1

Note. Italics means 3.5% or more; bold means under left rule (beginning the year after the election).
[a] 2003.

Panama, both under right-wing governments. Both of them started out with a high level of health spending in 2000; Colombia stayed at roughly the same level, and Panama actually decreased its spending.

The comparable data on education spending are not as complete. Again, we see a concentration of high values among the most advanced countries and left governments. Costa Rica and Brazil saw particularly strong increases, closely followed by Argentina. The timing and politics of the increases are similar to those of health spending in Costa Rica, Argentina, and Uruguay; they all happened under left-leaning governments committed to reducing inequality in their societies.[6] Bolivia's effort under the leftist *Movimiento al Socialismo* rivals that of Costa Rica. Two more countries under left governments reached and surpassed the 5% threshold, Ecuador under Correa and Paraguay under Lugo. The only country that surpassed the threshold under right-wing governments in some years, but not consistently, is Mexico.

6. The *Partido Liberación Nacional* (PLN) in Costa Rica was historically a moderate left party. It did pursue neoliberal economic reforms in the wake of the debt crisis, and critics contend that it lost its commitments to left values then. What is clear is that the Citizens' Action Party emerged as a challenge from the left, but the PLN did retain a commitment to universalistic social policy.

Table 13.4 Government education spending as a percentage of GDP

	2000	2005	2006	2007	2008	2009	2010	2011	2012	2013	2014	2015	2016	2017
Argentina	4.6	**3.9**	**4.1**	**4.5**	**4.8**	**5.5**	5	**5.3**	**5.4**	**5.4**	**5.4**	**5.8**	5.6	
Brazil	3.9	**4.5**	**4.9**	5	**5.3**	**5.5**	**5.6**	**5.7**	**5.9**	**5.8**	**5.9**	**6.2**		
Chile	**3.8**	**3.3**	3	**3.2**	**3.8**	4.2	4.2	4		4.5	4.7	**4.9**	5.3	
Costa Rica	4.7		4.6	**4.7**	**4.9**	6	6.6	6.5	6.7	6.8	6.9	7.1	7.1	7.4
Uruguay	2.4	2.7	**2.9**	**4.2**				4.4	4.4	4.5	4.5	4.4		
Bolivia	5.5		**6.3**	7		8.1	7.6	6.9	6.4	6.3	7.3			
Ecuador						4.3	4.5	4.7	4.6	5	5.3	5		
Colombia	3.5	4	3.9	4.1	3.9	4.7	4.8	4.5	4.4	4.9	4.7	4.5	4.5	4.4
Mexico	4	4.8	4.7	4.7	4.8	5.2	5.2	5.1	5.1	4.7	5.3	5.2		
Panama	4.8				3.5			3.2						
Paraguay	4.6			3.5			3.8	5	5			4.5		
Peru	3.2	2.8	2.6	2.6	2.9	3.1	2.9	2.7	2.9	3.3	3.7	4	3.8	3.9
Dominican Republic	1.9			2										
El Salvador	2.8	3.2	3.5	3.6	4.5	4.7	4	**3.9**	**3.7**	**3.8**	**3.8**	**4**	3.9	
Guatemala		1.9	3	3	3.2		2.8	2.9	3	2.8	2.9	3	2.8	2.8
Honduras														
Nicaragua	3						4.5				4.1	4.1	4.1	4.3

Note. Italics means 5% or more; bold means under left rule (beginning the year after the election).

a 2003.

The pattern that emerges is of a strong commitment to social investment in the most advanced countries, which were also mostly governed by the left. A similar commitment in both health and education is visible in Bolivia and Ecuador under left governments, and the left governments in El Salvador and Nicaragua made a strong investment in health. Mexico under right-wing governments made a strong investment in education, and Colombia and Panama did so in health. So, we have seven countries whose governments since 2005 have been strongly and consistently committed to social investment: Argentina, Brazil, Costa Rica, Bolivia, and Ecuador, with Uruguay and Chile fully invested in health but lagging somewhat in education. We have five more countries where governments have invested strongly in either health or education: Colombia, Panama, Mexico, El Salvador, and Nicaragua. However, spending alone does not guarantee the desired improvement in human capital, which is why it is important to analyze the reforms of health and education policies undertaken by different governments.

13.4. TYPES OF SOCIAL POLICY REFORMS

As noted, the backlash against growing inequality and economic insecurity and declining quality of public services associated with Washington Consensus policies combined with the growing electoral strength of left parties forced governments of all political orientations to pay attention to the situation of the poor and the low-income population and to act as protagonists of social investment reforms. However, the manner in which left and right governments have designed and implemented such policies has differed markedly. Left governments have attempted to extend coverage to the entire population (either via targeted or inclusive reforms), to improve the quality of transfers and services (hence also serving the functions of human capital creation and preservation, not purely mobilization), and to reduce inequality in the generosity of benefits and quality of services available to different groups. Right governments have prioritized expansion of coverage (via targeted or stratified reforms) without much regard for quality and equity. Moreover, there have been significant differences between left parties in the areas they chose to reform and how they chose to reform, depending on their connections to organized social actors (Pribble, 2013) and the degree of control over the legislature. Policy legacies defined the nature of the problems and the options open to the reformers. In what follows, we shall demonstrate the importance of these political factors in a systematic comparison of social investment strategies under different governments.

13.4.1. CCT programs
One of the major social policy innovations in Latin America since the 1990s is the CCT program, versions of which have been implemented either as pilots or

Table 13.5 CCT programs

Country	Program name	Year implemented	Households covered (year)	% Population covered (year)	Cost (% of GDP)
Argentina	Asignación Universal Por Hijo	2009	2,027,740 (2016)	8.67 (2016)	0.59
Brazil	Bolsa Família	2003	13,569,567 (2016)	26.14 (2016)	0.45
Chile	Chile Solidario	2002	546,096 (2012)	13.37 (2012)	0.14
Costa Rica	Avancemos	2006	132,737 (2016)	3.48 (2016)	0.16
Mexico	Prospera	1997	6,073,764 (2016)	23.06 (2016)	0.43
Uruguay	Asignaciones Familiares	2008	145,506 (2016)	11.29 (2016)	0.36

Source. Non-contributory Social Protection Programmes Database, Social Development Division, ECLAC (2018).

full-scale programs in 18 countries in Latin America and the Caribbean (Table 13.5). These programs provide cash transfers to poor families on a number of conditions, most typically that their children attend school regularly and receive regular health checkups. CCTs have been implemented throughout the region with the two-pronged goal of alleviating poverty in the short term while also creating human capital to tackle the long-term goal of ending the cycle of poverty (Barrientos & Villa, 2016). CCTs have broad appeal, being widely supported by both left- and right-leaning governments. The appeal of the programs comes in part from their ability to produce results in the short term. CCT programs have reduced child labor as well as extreme poverty. An Inter-American Development Bank report found that, "Over time, CCT beneficiaries have become relatively less poor and more educated, tend to live in better quality dwellings, and are increasingly engaged in formal wage employment" (Stampini & Tornarolli, 2012). These results have been achieved by programs that, on average, cost only 0.3%–0.4% of GDP (Paes-Sousa et al., 2013). At such a low cost, CCTs are able to cover large populations in need through effective targeting mechanisms. In the largest program in the region, Brazil's *Bolsa Familia*, over 14 million families benefit (Robles et al., 2015). While *Bolsa Familia* is by far the largest program, other programs in the region, such as those in Mexico, Colombia, and Argentina, still cover well over a million families.

The big challenge in implementing these programs has been to keep them free from patronage (see also Chapter 15 in Volume II in Garritzmann et al., 2022). While success in doing so has varied, it has been higher than expected. Specifically, the two largest programs, those in Brazil and Mexico—countries with a strong tradition of patronage politics—managed to bypass subnational politicians and effectively target recipient families that met the criteria for eligibility. In contrast, Honduras is an example of heavy use of the CCT for clientelistic purposes by the right-wing central government (Richardson, 2017).

While the short-term achievements of CCTs are noteworthy, their impact on the long-term transmission of poverty through the creation of human capital has been less impressive, bringing into question the strength of CCTs as true social investment programs. The social investment portions of CCT programs, creating human capital through the education and health conditionalities, rely on having adequate and accessible health facilities and schools. As such, while CCTs are important programs because of their potential to facilitate increased use of health and education services, understanding their ability to serve as social investment programs depends on the public health and education systems, to which we will now turn.

13.4.2. Healthcare reforms by right and left governments

The cases of health sector reform in Mexico and Uruguay illustrate the differing goals and impacts of reform under right governments versus left governments. Essentially, the conservative *Partido Acción Nacional* (PAN) government in Mexico opted for expanding subsidized health insurance to the huge population without coverage, thus creating a parallel and inferior structure to coverage through the social security system, a stratified system of health provision. In contrast, the FA government in Uruguay unified the health insurance system by introducing a single-payer and per-person payment system, thus promoting inclusion and equality of service quality.

When Vicente Fox of the right-wing PAN won the presidency, ending the 71-year reign of the *Partido Revolucionario Institucional*, Mexico faced a healthcare system that failed to cover much of the population. Only around half of the population had health insurance. The formally employed received coverage through the Mexican Institute for Social Security (IMSS), and other groups such as the unemployed or informal sector workers received care that was not only often costly but also often of lower quality and limited availability at various Ministry of Health clinics and hospitals (Lakin, 2010).

The Mexican reform was a top-down process led by Secretary of Health Frenk. While the IMSS was initially consulted, it was quickly dropped from discussion and actively opposed the law (Ponce de León, 2018). Likewise, the Ministry of Finance opposed the law due to fiscal concerns, and the left-wing *Partido Revolucionario Democratico* (PRD) did not support the reform for both ideological and self-interested reasons because the implementation of the reform would overtake the health service the PRD had succeeded in implementing in Mexico City (Lakin, 2010).

In spite of this opposition, the *Ley General de Salud* passed both houses of the legislature easily (Gómez-Dantés et al., 2015). The reform known as *Seguro Popular* covers a specified number of services which, as of 2014, included 280 interventions and 59 high-cost interventions such as breast cancer treatment. Funding is provided by federal and state contributions as well as a sliding-scale payment by families, with the lowest two deciles of the income distribution not contributing at all.

Seguro Popular has had a major impact but has a number of serious shortcomings. As of 2013, just under 16% of the Mexican population had no health insurance, showing that the reforms have made drastic improvements in coverage levels but have fallen short of providing truly universal coverage (Gómez-Dantés et al., 2015). There have been a number of financing issues including delays in transferring funds from the federal to the state level as well as problems with states failing to meet their financial commitments to the system (Nigenda et al., 2015). This in turn means that services are underfunded and inadequate and that formal coverage does not guarantee access to care.

In contrast to Mexico's reform, the Uruguayan health reforms came under the first government of the left-wing FA coalition. Like Mexico, Uruguay had a fragmented health system prior to reform, with those employed in the formal sector contributing to and receiving care from *Institutos de Asistencia Médica Colectiva* (IAMCs) that were regulated by the state and required to be not-for-profit organizations. The poor, on the other hand, received care through the state *Administración de Servicios de Salud del Estado*. Since the size of the formal sector in Uruguay was comparatively large, a high percentage of the population enjoyed coverage.

The neoliberal reforms of the 1980s and 1990s had already reduced the size of the formal sector and thus the proportion of the population with coverage through the IAMCs, and with the financial crisis of 2001–2002 an even greater portion of the population became reliant on the public health system, which led to decreased quality of care and pressure for reform (Pribble, 2013). The FA held a majority in both houses of the legislature and lacked the close ties to the three key unions in the medical field that had held back the previous Colorado and Blanco governments from implementing reforms. The lack of close ties to these antagonistic organizations allowed the FA to move forward without concern for losing an important electoral coalition. In fact, the union with which the FA had close ties, the Inter-Union Plenary of Workers–National Convention of Workers, supported reform, having noted at its seventh congress in 2001 that its vision for the future of health in Uruguay should involve an active role for the state as a regulator (Fuentes, 2010).

The FA's proposal for health reform was approved while the party was still in opposition. The proposal included a constitutional reform to make health a fundamental right and to establish the responsibility of the state to help the population as well as a shift in focus from hospital care to primary care and prevention (Fuentes, 2010). In order to move forward with the reforms once in government, the FA pursued a negotiated reform process with the incorporation of social actors as opposed to the highly technocratic, top-down approach taken in the Mexican reform (Pribble, 2013).

The 2007 reforms resulted in increased coverage and improved quality of care provision in the public sector. The system was not fully integrated as both public and private providers continue to exist. However, the reform created the *Fondo Nacional de Salud* (FONASA) into which both private and public affiliates pay in a progressive manner. Contributors to FONASA have the option to affiliate with the public system or the private IAMCs, and then FONASA issues payment to the chosen provider. Since the aim of Uruguayan reforms was equity and the view dominated that healthcare is a right, there is no set list of interventions that are covered, as is the case in Mexico. While the Uruguayan reforms have not succeeded in covering the entire population without exception, the uncovered portion of the population is quite small. In addition, public hospitals and clinics have been constructed in previously underserved areas to increase access to health services (Pribble, 2013). Despite the continued existence of both public and private providers, quality of care across the system has been standardized.

The comparison between Mexico and Uruguay highlights the contrast in value commitments underpinning reform under a right-leaning government versus a left-leaning government. The PAN responded to the highly restricted access to healthcare with an insurance scheme that expands access but does not address differences in quality or continued reliance on out-of-pocket expenditures, thus perpetuating a stratified system. The FA was committed to extending access to equal quality healthcare to the entire population, regardless of ability to pay, as a matter of right. The spending figures presented in Table 13.3 underline this contrast; the Uruguayan reform was accompanied by a significant increase in public spending on healthcare, whereas spending in Mexico did not reflect an increased public commitment to healthcare.[7]

13.4.3. Healthcare reforms by left governments with different policy legacies and partisan control over legislatures

A comparison of Uruguay with Chile and Brazil highlights the impact of policy legacies and the power of antagonists on variation in reforms implemented by left-leaning governments with a commitment to equity in healthcare.

---

7. Since GDP per capita grew after 2003, real per capita health spending did increase somewhat; but the percentage of the GDP that was devoted to healthcare hardly increased at all.

Prior to reform, as in both Mexico and Uruguay, the Chilean system was fragmented with private health insurers, *Instituciones de Salud Previsional* (ISAPREs), and a public system, FONASA. People with formal sector jobs were able to choose the system to which they wanted their mandatory contributions to go, but in practice which system a person was a part of was determined largely by income, with the well-off contributing to ISAPREs, while lower-income groups were forced into the public system (Pribble, 2013). Unlike in Uruguay, the reforms implemented by the Pinochet dictatorship set up the ISAPREs as for-profit entities without regulation. Because those in the upper-income deciles chose to contribute to ISAPREs rather than FONASA and since ISAPREs could reject coverage to high-risk people, FONASA was forced to deal with the majority of the risk while also receiving a much smaller amount of the financial contributions.

The government of Ricardo Lagos from Chile's left-wing coalition, the *Concertación*, implemented the inclusive Chilean health reform AUGE. Right from the beginning of his term, Lagos noted the need for health reform using rights-based language and aiming at equalizing access to and quality of care.

The reform process in Chile began as a consultative process but ended up essentially being a technocratic decision-making process (Dannreuther & Giddeon, 2008). Lagos faced a set of policy legacies that placed more roadblocks in the way of his reforms than was the case in Uruguay. Crucially, the legacy of having unregulated and profit-driven ISAPREs made them a major antagonist of reform as it threatened their profit margins. Moreover, the ISAPREs received support from the larger and very powerful business community. In addition to resistance from the ISAPREs, the reform faced opposition from a strong presence of right parties in the legislature as, unlike the Uruguayan case, Lagos' coalition did not have a large enough majority in the Senate to pass the bill without some concessions to other parties. Right-wing parties succeeded in forcing the *Concertación* to abandon the proposed solidarity fund that was supposed to reduce the inequity in funding between the private and public sectors (Pribble, 2013).

The resulting AUGE reforms showed some similarities to the Mexican reforms in that they guaranteed coverage only for a set list of illnesses that would grow with the healthcare system's capacity to provide the services. However, AUGE created the healthcare *Superintendencia* to enforce the guarantees and help citizens hold the state and private insurers accountable (Pribble, 2013). Thus, in contrast to Mexico, the reform actually delivered what it promised; and this increased commitment was reflected in increased funding. By 2010, when the candidate of the right won the presidency, the reform had become so popular that he embraced it and promised an increase in the illnesses covered.

The Brazilian health reforms predated most other health reforms in the region and are unique in that a social movement pushed them forward more so than did a particular political party. The impetus for the reforms began in the 1970s with the emergence of the *sanitarista* movement. This was a social movement of medical professionals and academics pushing for health reform with greater public sector involvement and more equality. Under the military dictatorship healthcare services were largely only available for those employed in the formal sector who paid into the social security system. Health facilities were not easily available for the urban or the rural poor. Similarly, because the social security system contracted many services out to the private sector, fraud and waste followed as there were incentives to provide unnecessary treatments or to charge for services that were not actually provided (Weyland, 1995). The *sanitarista* movement took root among academics and medical professionals, who moved into government to push for bureaucratic reform, switching from a movement pushing for bottom-up reform to bureaucrats pushing for top-down reform. When the new constitution was written after the democratic transition, the *sanitaristas* were able to anchor the right to health care for all citizens in the constitution. However, the road to giving substance to this right remained difficult. The push for health reform faced opposition from President José Sarney of the conservative *Partido da Frente Liberal* along with other conservative politicians and the private medical industry, which opposed state regulation. Reforms found support, on the other hand, from state and municipal governments which stood to benefit from the decentralization proposed in the reform as well as from center-left and left parties (Weyland, 1995).

Despite increased coordination between the Ministry of Health and the health functions of the social security system, the health system remained stratified and fragmented between the public and private sectors. Those who are formally employed get social security or private insurance and use largely private providers, while the unemployed and those in the informal sector rely on the public sector. Likewise, the public system has ended up covering basic health and high-cost health services, while the private system provides the more profitable services (Elias & Cohn, 2003).

Under President Cardoso, significant progress was made from 1998 on as the federal government bypassed governors and worked directly with municipal governments through two new programs, the Health Community Agents Program and the Family Health Program, or PSF (Arretche, 2004). These programs greatly increased access to preventive and primary care in poor areas. They were particularly likely to get adopted by municipalities with left-of-center executives (Sugiyama, 2008). Presidents Lula and Dilma from the left-wing Workers' Party then further increased expenditures on health and promoted in particular the PSF. Nevertheless, the system as a whole remained stratified.

The Brazilian case, like the Chilean, highlights two obstacles to universalizing health reforms faced by left-wing governments committed to social investment in the form of equal access to quality healthcare for all. First, policy legacies in the form of private insurers and private providers generate powerful political opposition. Second, where party systems are highly fragmented and/or the executive does not have partisan majorities in the legislature, concessions are necessary that reduce the egalitarian thrust. In Uruguay, the private sector was regulated and not for profit, and the government controlled the legislature, which allowed for the introduction of a single-payer system with a strongly egalitarian effect, an inclusive system. In Chile, the for-profit private healthcare sector had powerful allies in the business community and right-wing parties, and the government lacked a partisan majority in the senate, which kept a single-payer option completely off the agenda and even forced the sacrifice of the equalization fund, preserving a stratified system. The Brazilian process was different as it was originally pushed forward by a social movement that managed to infiltrate the state, not by governments. When left-leaning presidents attempted to create the system that would realize the constitutional right to healthcare, they were in a comparatively weak political position as they also faced strong opposition from private providers and lacked partisan majorities in both houses in the context of an extremely fragmented party system. Accordingly, new services were added to the existing system, and the Brazilian system falls furthest among these three cases from the goal of an inclusive system guaranteeing access to equal-quality care for all.

13.4.4. Education reforms by left governments with different policy legacies and relations to civil society

The comparison between efforts in Uruguay and Chile to move toward equalizing access to quality education highlights again the importance of policy legacies and introduces an important additional variable, the relationship of left governments to civil society, specifically teachers' unions. Policy legacies have been much more favorable in Uruguay, but the close relationship between sectors of the FA and the teachers' union has essentially paralyzed reform efforts.

When the military government took power in 1973 in Uruguay it did not fundamentally change the education system, unlike in Chile, though it did cut funding to the system (Pribble, 2013). The funding cuts paired with increased enrollment led to a decrease in the quality of education and students moving out of the public system and into the private. With the return to democracy in 1984, the government increased public education funding, and enrollment in the public system grew with students from all income quintiles attending the public schools, in contrast to the highly segregated Chilean system (Pribble, 2013). However, Uruguay continued to experience a rather high dropout rate at the secondary level, particularly among lower-income groups, and pressures for reform mounted.

The first reform attempts came under the *Colorados*, one of the two traditional parties, in 1995 as it faced growing electoral pressure from the FA. The Sanguinetti administration's reforms included increased spending on public education, the implementation of universal and obligatory public preschool, full-day secondary education in high-risk areas, and improvements and standardization in the teacher training process (Pribble, 2013). The reforms faced opposition from the center-left FA, as well as from the teachers' unions, in particular the secondary school teachers' union, but were still put into effect.

When the FA first came to power, it ignored some of the Sanguinetti reforms while continuing others such as preschool education. The new government had this option since Sanguinetti's reforms were put in place without any legislative modifications (Pribble, 2013). The FA further increased spending on education, but the effect of the increased spending was largely limited to salary increases due to the FA's tight ties with the teachers' unions and the importance of these unions to the FA's electoral success (see also Chapter 6 in this volume on how clientelism degrades education spending). The 2008 general education law increased the number of decentralized education councils and provided for enhanced teacher representation on these councils and the central governing body.

The FA used a bottom-up approach to education reform in contrast to the top-down approach used by the *Colorados* before them and the *Concertación* in the Chilean case, but it has struggled to implement real change. In particular, the teachers' unions want higher salaries but refuse any salary increases tied to meeting certain educational goals and a no-strike pledge ("Uruguay Teachers Strike in Face of Sanctions", article published in the Buenos Aires Herald, August 27, 2015).

Education reform in Chile is in many ways a more complex process than in Uruguay due to the highly stratified system that was put in place during the Pinochet dictatorship. On the other hand, teachers' unions are not a force to be reckoned with. They were totally debilitated by Pinochet's decentralization of education. Moreover, the member parties of the *Concertación* did not maintain close relationships to any social movements.

Pinochet radically transformed Chilean education by decentralizing administration and implementing a tiered system. Students had the option to attend either a fully public school, a state-subsidized private school, or a fully private school. The central government paid a per-pupil subsidy to either a public or a private school depending on where parents chose to enroll their children. Private schools were able to set admissions criteria and charge fees beyond what the government subsidy covered. The resulting situation was a set of poorly funded, low-quality public schools; mid-range-quality, semi-private schools; and high-quality, all private schools, with enrollment in each type being largely based on income.

The Pinochet-era system created many entrenched interests that made future reforms very challenging. The left-wing *Concertación* governments made small steps toward improving public schools, but only the second government of Michelle Bachelet, under major pressure from student protests, began implementing larger structural changes. The first *Concertación* government led by Patricio Aylwin implemented targeted programs to improve education among the poorest-performing schools. The electoral incentives to move for change did not exist as public school enrollment had dropped below 50% of the total enrollment, making for a strong group of stakeholders in the private system (Pribble, 2013).

The next *Concertación* government under Frei implemented full-day school for all children. Previously private education was full-day, while public education was half-day, so this reform helped to level the field at least in terms of the number of hours of schooling students received. The Frei government also implemented a new system of teacher training and evaluation, which helped make the quality of teaching more similar across the three types of schools. Even though Frei's reforms had a wide-ranging group of beneficiaries, it took 2 years for the reforms to be passed by Congress as there were strong antagonists, including the right-wing parties, municipal governments, and some of the semi-private schools (Pribble, 2013).

The Penguin Revolution then brought education reform to the top of the agenda. This movement of secondary students formed in response to the great inequities in the quality of education and the consequent restricted chances of students from public schools to succeed in the entrance exam to gain access to the good public universities. Private universities and other tertiary education institutes had proliferated, many of them as for-profit institutions; but they were expensive. The student movement demanded an education reform that would have required a large injection of resources.

The reforms under Bachelet's first government imposed new regulations on private institutions including eliminating socioeconomic status or previous academic performance as allowable criteria for admission to semi-private elementary and middle schools and requiring that admissions criteria be made public (Pribble, 2013). In her second term, Bachelet passed the most significant reforms to the Pinochet-era system, but she continued to face student protests demanding even greater reforms. The reforms eliminated selective admissions as well as profits at state-subsidized schools. The proposal for free university education was temporarily held up in the Constitutional Court. The private sector and the right-wing parties argued that free university education is unaffordable and would require new taxes to cover the costs. Eventually, a targeted reform was implemented, offering free university education to students from poor families who pass the entrance exam. Thus, the highly stratified education system has been moved in a more inclusive direction but is far from having reached this goal.

13.4.5. Early childhood education under right and left governments

Early childhood education has been shown to yield important economic returns and to keep the gap between rich and poor from growing (Araujo et al., 2013). It is also an important policy tool to support women's labor force participation. As with health and general education, enrollment in ECEC programs has grown throughout Latin America, but coverage and quality vary widely. Most countries have wide coverage with some kind of preschool education for 4- to 6-year-olds but typically only for part of the day or part of the week. For the under-4 age group, coverage is much more restricted. In a comprehensive 2013 study, the Social Protection and Health Division of the Inter-American Development Bank found only six countries with more than 100,000 children enrolled in essentially full-day care: Argentina, Brazil, Chile, Ecuador, Jamaica, and Mexico (Araujo et al., 2013).

If part-time enrollment is taken into account, in both public and private institutions, coverage is considerably larger. By 2015, Brazil, Chile, Ecuador, and Uruguay enrolled 20% or more of the 0–3 age group; Uruguay was highest with 35% (Berlinski & Schady, 2015). In 2014 and 2015, Costa Rica and Uruguay adopted the goals of universalizing coverage (Martínez Franzoni & Sánchez-Ancochea, 2016). However, coverage remains very heterogeneous in institutional structure and quality, even in these two countries. Mexico and Chile offer wide coverage, but they also show very clear differences in goals and quality, reflecting the different value commitments of right and left governments.

Mexico has a variety of ECEC programs and has offered some services since 1973. Early services were limited to working mothers in the formal sector where a 1% payroll tax was used to fund guaranteed childcare provided by the IMSS. In 2011, the IMSS served 205,000 children (Araujo et al., 2013). In 2002, Mexico implemented mandatory preschool for children starting at age 3 and as of 2010 had 89% of children ages 3–5 enrolled in preschool. However, when looking at a breakdown of enrollment for each age group, it is clear that 3-year-olds are much less likely to be enrolled in preschool than are 4- and 5-year-olds (Organisation for Economic Co-operation and Development, 2014). Preschool teachers have completed teacher training usually with a focus on child development (Bennett & Tayler, 2006). In the programs available for children under the age of 3, however, quality is highly variable as teachers of early childhood education are not required to have teacher training.

In 2007, the administration of President Felipe Calderón of the right-wing PAN put in place the *Programa Estancias Infantiles* (*Estancias*). By 2011 it had grown to serve 266,000 children and thus was the largest child care program in the country (Araujo et al., 2013). *Estancias* aimed to increase access to childcare for low-income families that could not benefit from the IMSS programs and, by doing so, allow mothers to work, pursue education, or search for a job. Hence, it had merely activating purposes. The providers of childcare under this scheme are largely civil society organizations or individuals who run childcare centers from their homes or community centers with the assistance of a stipend from the government and a copayment from the families enrolling their children. Those who run such centers need not have formal training (Staab & Gerhard, 2011). Accordingly, the *Estancias* program does not reflect the goals of a social investment program; indeed, it has been criticized for providing low-quality services.

Even in rhetoric about the program, President Calderón did not discuss the program as an opportunity to create human capital but rather as an employment program mobilizing human capital by allowing poor mothers to enter the workforce (Staab & Gerhard, 2011). In line with the PAN's pro-business, pro-church, and pro-traditional gender roles positions, Calderón made it clear in his rhetoric that increasing women's employment was more of a necessity than a desired goal.

ECEC programs in Chile, in contrast, have come to reflect the principles of social investment much more clearly (see also Chapter 11 in this volume). Under the Lagos administration, ECEC programs actually followed mobilizing goals similar to those of the *Estancias* program, aiming primarily to increase female workforce participation. In 2004 the *Servicio Nacional de la Mujer* launched a pilot program of *comunicentros*, similar to *Estancias*, which provided home-based care financed by a government subsidy. This program did not last long, and under the Bachelet administration a turn toward social investment became clear. In the first year of the administration, the Bachelet government launched the *Chile Crece Contigo* program, with the goals of providing universal preschool education and initial education to all children under the age of 4 in the lowest two income quintiles.

Unlike in Mexico, Chilean initial education teachers are required to have a university degree in early childhood education, and support staff are required to hold a technical degree in early childhood education (Staab & Gerhard, 2011), reflecting goals of not only human capital mobilization but also creation. Additionally, as with the health reforms, the *Chile Crece Contigo* program goes beyond simply being a program that can come or go as the government pleases to being guaranteed by law as a right. This is not true for the Mexican case. In contrast to Calderón, Bachelet spoke of *Chile Crece Contigo* as a social investment program, noting, "I am convinced that initial education is fundamental, that all the effects of primary, secondary and later, of course, tertiary education won't be enough if we arrive late" (Staab, 2010).

13.5. CONCLUSIONS AND PROSPECTS

On the whole, progress in social investment has been decidedly mixed in Latin America. In comparison to Europe, much ground remains to be covered on both the passive and active sides of welfare state programs. The reach of social policies has expanded to previously excluded groups, both urban and rural. In particular, non-contributory social protection and minimum income programs like old-age pensions and child allowances have been expanded to people in the informal sector. School enrollments among the lowest income groups have expanded, and healthcare services have developed a larger reach. Governments of all stripes have introduced social programs, but governments of the left have been stronger protagonists of social investment devoted to creating human capital. The main antagonists of inclusive social investment policies have been private providers and insurers with a stake in the existing systems and their allies among business and right-wing parties. Most strategies have been targeted, improving but not transforming existing stratified systems. A clear exception is the *Frente's* healthcare reform in Uruguay.

CCTs are specifically designed to ensure that children do attend school and get medical checkups, and they have been introduced in some form in virtually every country. However, to realize their potential in creating human capital, these programs need to be linked to easily accessible high-quality education and healthcare services. It is in these areas that most Latin American countries still fall short as they have failed to transform their stratified systems. Moreover, CCTs are aimed at the school-age population, whereas ECEC remains woefully underdeveloped. Coverage in ECEC is expanding, at least part-time; but quality is a major issue in an institutionally highly heterogeneous context, which means that large numbers of children reach school age at a considerable disadvantage.

The trajectories of social investment in the countries with the most advanced economies and/or welfare states since the mid-1990s have been shaped by their policy legacies, economic conditions, and political commitments of incumbent governments. Costa Rica enjoyed the most favorable policy legacies with a unified inclusive healthcare system and a preponderantly public education system. The PLN government of Arias (2006–2010) built well on this foundation, strongly expanding expenditures in health and education, resulting in increased school enrollments at the secondary and tertiary levels and improvements in the public healthcare system. Mexico is at the other end of the spectrum, starting with a very low base of public social expenditures in all categories and heavily stratified healthcare and education systems with strong private participation. An effort to increase expenditures in the aftermath of the highly contested 1988 elections was cut short by the financial crisis of the mid-1990s and the conservative orientation of the post-2000 governments. Mexico reached a spending level of 5% of GDP in education only in 2009, and it has not even reached 3% in health expenditures.

Chile also entered the 1990s with highly unfavorable policy legacies. Not only had Pinochet drastically cut expenditures but he had also greatly stratified education and health services and cemented the role of private providers and insurers. The various *Concertación* governments steadily expanded social spending in both health and education; but Chile's spending effort remained only above Mexico's, and the health and education systems remained stratified. Public education at the primary and secondary levels is of clearly lower quality than publicly subsidized private and fully private education. At the tertiary level, many institutions are private and expensive, one of the key reasons for the ongoing student protest movement.

Brazil and Argentina both made very strong efforts in health and education expenditures. Brazil first significantly expanded efforts in education under Cardoso and then reached an even slightly higher level under Lula. In Argentina education spending greatly increased under the Kirchners. In health, we see similar spending increases under the left-leaning Lula and Kirchner governments. If we look at enrollment rates among students from the lowest income quintiles, Argentina maintained the leading position in enrollment at the secondary and tertiary levels (Figures 13.1–13.3). Brazil started from very low enrollment rates at every level and managed to catch up with the others at the primary level and even move ahead of Costa Rica and Uruguay at the secondary level.

Uruguay had one of the three highest averages in years of education in the adult population in 1990, along with Argentina and Chile. Education spending clearly increased under the FA, but the level remained similar to Chile's, below those of Costa Rica, Argentina, and Brazil. In contrast, the effort in health expenditures under the FA was much greater, and it was accompanied by the systemic transformation to a single-payer system. As a result of the comparative neglect of education, enrollment among the lowest quintile at the secondary and tertiary levels remained comparatively low, surpassing only Mexico's. On the positive side, the FA introduced compulsory preschool education and has made great efforts to expand quality ECEC, which will leave children better prepared to learn when they enter school.

Clearly, the end of the commodity boom is endangering social investment in Latin America everywhere because of a drop in available resources. Moreover, successful social investment requires careful long-range planning and follow-through. Accordingly, the effect of resource constraints will be felt particularly strongly in countries where political crises aggravate the problem. Brazil is at the

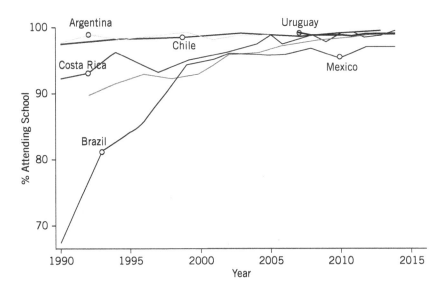

Figure 13.1 Share of 7- to 12-year-olds from the lowest income quintile who attend school, 1990–2014.

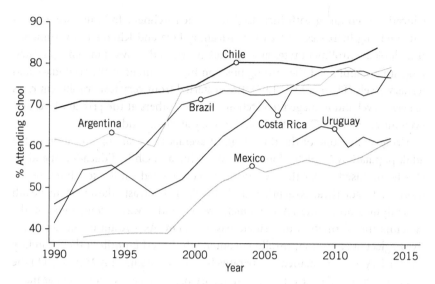

Figure 13.2 Share of 13- to 19-year-olds from the lowest income quintile who attend school, 1990–2014.

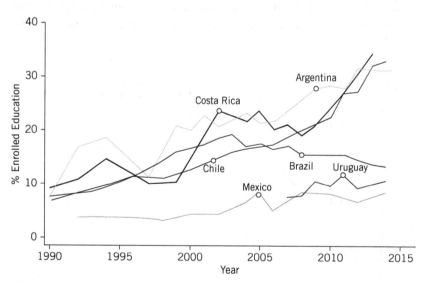

Figure 13.3 Share of 20- to 24-year-olds from the lowest income quintile enrolled in education, 1990–2014.
Source. CEPALSTAT Bases de Datos y Publicaciones Estadísticas, 2013.
This is the source for Figures 13.1–13.3.

top of the list of potential political paralysis. The corruption scandals and the political maneuvering around impeachment essentially destroyed policy consistency. The boldness of Macri's initiatives in Argentina and the historic mobilization capacity of the Peronists similarly indicate the potential for policy discontinuities. Mexico remains far behind in social investment efforts, and resource constraints are likely to keep it there. The three countries with better chances for continuing social investment efforts are Chile, Costa Rica, and Uruguay; but they face political difficulties as well. Costa Rica can build on favorable legacies and has strong public and political party support for investment in health and education, among the PLN and recent challengers on the left. However, the fractionalization of the party system has made the formation of legislative majorities increasingly difficult. Chile and Uruguay have made the most progress in ECEC, and they have significantly improved their healthcare systems. Where they need to work hard is on education reform—an area fraught with difficulty in Chile because of private sector interests and in Uruguay because of the important role of the teachers' union in the FA's support base. In addition, the victory of Piñera in Chile and tensions within the governing party in Uruguay make it all the harder to overcome these obstacles. In sum, even in the most advanced social policy contexts, Latin American political leaderships remain far from forging a consensus on the path toward a major public effort to improve social investment.

ACKNOWLEDGMENT

The authors would like to thank Diego Sánchez-Ancochea and the editors of this volume for helpful comments on an earlier draft.

REFERENCES

Anria, S., & Niedzwiecki, S. (2016). Social movements and social policy. *Studies in Comparative International Development, 51*(3), 308–327.

Araujo, M. C., López Bóo, F., & Puyana, J. M. (2013). *Overview of early childhood development services in Latin America and the Caribbean.* Inter-American Development Bank.

Arretche, M. (2004). Toward a unified and more equitable system: Health reform in Brazil. In R. R. Kaufman & J. M. Nelson (Eds.), *Crucial needs, weak incentives* (pp. 155–188). Woodrow Wilson Center.

Barrientos, A., & Villa, J. (2016). Economic and political inclusion in human development conditional income transfer programmes in Latin America. *Social Policy and Society, 15*(3), 421–433.

Berlinski, S., & Schady, N. (2015). *The early years: Child well-being and the role of public policy.* Inter-American Development Bank and Palgrave Macmillan.

Bennett, J., & Tayler, C. P. (2006). *Starting strong II: Early childhood education and care*. Organisation for Economic Co-operation and Development.

Dannreuther, C., & Gideon, J. (2008). Entitled to health? Social protection in Chile's Plan AUGE. *Development and Change, 39*(5), 845–864.

De La O, A. L. (2013). Do conditional cash transfers affect electoral behavior? Evidence from a randomized experiment in Mexico. *American Journal of Political Science, 57*(1), 1–14.

Diaz-Cayeros, A., Estevez, F., & Magaloni, B. (2016). *The political logic of poverty relief: Electoral strategies and social policy in Mexico*. Cambridge University Press.

Elias, P. E. M., & Cohn, A. (2003). Health reform in Brazil: Lessons to consider. *American Journal of Public Health, 93*(1), 44–48.

Ferrera, M. (2005). *Welfare state reform in southern Europe: Fighting poverty and social exclusion in Greece, Italy, Spain and Portugal*. Routledge.

Fuentes, G. (2010). El sistema de saludjo en la post dictadura: Análisis de la reforma del Frente Amplio y las condiciones que la hicieron posible. *Revista Uruguaya de Ciencia Política, 19*(1), 119–142.

Garritzmann, J. L., Häusermann, S., & Palier, B. (Eds.). (2022). *The world politics of social investment: Vol. II. The politics of varying social investment strategies*. Oxford University Press.

Gómez-Dantés, O., Reich, M. R., & Garrido-Latorre, F. (2015). Political economy of pursuing the expansion of social protection in health in Mexico. *Health Systems & Reform, 1*(3), 207–216.

Huber, E., & Stephens, J. D. (2012). *Democracy and the left: Social policy and inequality in Latin America*. University of Chicago Press.

Hunter, W. & Power, T. (2007). Rewarding Lula: Executive power, social policy, and the Brazilian elections of 2006. *Latin American Politics and Society 49*, (1), 1-30.

Lakin, J. M. (2010). The end of insurance? Mexico's Seguro Popular, 2001–2007. *Journal of Health Politics, Policy and Law, 35*(3), 313–352.

Mahon, R. (2015). Integrating the social into CEPAL's neo-structuralist discourse. *Global Social Policy, 15*(1), 3–22.

Martínez Franzoni, J., & Sánchez-Ancochea, D. (2016, August 25–27). More, less or the same segmentation: The case of early child education and care services in Costa Rica and Uruguay [Paper presentation]. Meeting of Research Committee 19 of the International Sociological Association, San José, Costa Rica.

Nigenda, G., Wirtz, V. J., González-Robledo, L. M., & Reich, M. R. (2015). Evaluating the implementation of Mexico's health reform: The case of *Seguro Popular. Health Systems & Reform, 1*(3), 217–228.

Organisation for Economic Co-operation and Development. (2014). *PF3.2: Enrolment in childcare and pre-schools*. OECD Family Database.

Paes-Sousa, R., Regalia, F., & Stampini, M. (2013). *Conditions for success in implementing CCT programs: Lessons for Asia from Latin America and the Caribbean.* Inter-American Development Bank.

Pavão, N. (2016). Conditional cash transfer programs and electoral accountability: Evidence from Latin America. *Latin American Politics and Society, 58*(2), 74–99.

Ponce de León, Z. (2018). *Political parties and policy reform: Expansion of health care in Latin America* [Unpublished doctoral dissertation]. University of North Carolina at Chapel Hill.

Pribble, J. (2013). *Welfare and party politics in Latin America.* Cambridge University Press.

Richardson, W. (2017). *The impact of conditional cash transfer design on program corruption rates: A case study of Mexico and Brazil* [Senior honors thesis]. University of North Carolina at Chapel Hill.

Robles, M., Rubio, M. G., & Stampini, M. (2015). *Have cash transfers succeeded in reaching the poor in Latin America and the Caribbean?* Inter-American Development Bank.

Silva, E. (2009). *Challenging neoliberalism in Latin America.* Cambridge University Press.

Staab, S. (2010). Social investment policies in Chile and Latin America: Towards equal opportunities for women and children? *Journal of Social Policy, 39*(4), 607–626.

Staab, S., & Gerhard, R. (2011). Putting two and two together? Early childhood education, mothers' employment and care service expansion in Chile and Mexico. *Development and Change, 42*(4), 1079–1107.

Stampini, M., & Tornarolli, L. (2012). *The growth of conditional cash transfers in Latin America and the Caribbean: Did they go too far?* Inter-American Development Bank.

Sugiyama, N. B. (2008). Ideology and networks: The politics of social policy diffusion in Brazil. *Latin American Research Review, 43*(3), 82–108.

Uruguay teachers strike in face of sanctions. (2015, August 27). *Buenos Aires Herald.*

Weyland, K. (1995). Social movements and the state: The politics of health reform in Brazil. *World Development, 23*(10), 1699–1712.

14

DIFFERENT PATHS TO SOCIAL INVESTMENT?

THE POLITICS OF SOCIAL INVESTMENT IN NORTH EAST ASIA AND SOUTHERN EUROPE

Margarita Estévez-Abe and Margarita León

14.1. INTRODUCTION

This chapter explores the degree to which Italy, Japan, South Korea, and Spain have or have not adopted the kind of childcare and paid parental leave programs recommended by the social investment (SI) perspective. In line with the conceptual approach adopted in this volume (see Chapters 1 and 2), we consider childcare to have the double function of "creation", that is, investment in human capital formation and "mobilization" of existing human capital for labor market participation. Short and well-paid parental leaves are also seen as crucial elements of human capital enhancement, especially for women. Hence, expansion of childcare provision and short, well-paid, and shared parental leaves will be considered as moving in an SI direction.

What can the comparison between our four countries offer? Italy, Japan, Korea, and Spain are four familialist welfare states. As Estévez-Abe et al. (2016, p. 302) argue, "although it is not a perfect fit, the concept of familialism—defined as an emphasis upon the family as the primary locus of welfare provision by way of intra- and inter-generational mutual aid and unpaid care work provided by mostly women—captures adequately the family resemblance of these four countries." As a result, the four countries have always performed rather poorly in promoting the employment of women and in reducing poverty. As

Margarita Estévez-Abe and Margarita León, *Different Paths to Social Investment?* In: *The World Politics of Social Investment (Volume I)*. Edited by: Julian L. Garritzmann, Silja Häusermann, and Bruno Palier, Oxford University Press.
© Oxford University Press 2022. DOI: 10.1093/oso/9780197585245.003.0014

demographers have noted, when we only look at Organisation for Economic Co-operation and Development (OECD) countries, fertility rates are higher in those countries where more women work. Our quartet is also a group of lowest-fertility countries. Combined with their good longevity records, these countries are all very rapidly aging as well.

Unsurprisingly, facing low fertility and demographic aging, our quartet of countries has been trying to move "beyond familialism" with varying degrees of success. Against the odds, the countries in this familialist quartet significantly expanded childcare provision at different junctures and did so in different ways with very different outcomes for women. None of them has become a new Sweden, but welfare state readjustments have been taking place in all four countries in the past decades. As a consequence, today, they all deviate from the pure familialist model in different ways. A number of scholars have written about how Spain expanded childcare more than Italy and/or how Korea expanded it more than Japan (An & Peng, 2016; Estévez-Abe & Kim, 2014; Estévez-Abe & Naldini, 2016; León & Pavolini, 2014; León et al., 2016, 2019). This chapter investigates these cross-national variations further. A country such as Spain which has expanded childcare services considerably since the first decade of the 2000s continues to have no paid parental leave. Why was the policy development in Spain so uneven? Why was Italy so progressive in the late 1960s and the early 1970s but became so dormant ever since? Why has Korea expanded its childcare services so dramatically, but its take-up rate of parental leave remains so low in comparison? What happened in Japan in 2014 to dramatically accelerate its policy change?

The choice of this group of familialist states is strategic for two reasons. The first is a practical reason. Unlike the Nordic economies, which are small in size and in population, the four countries studied in this chapter are very large economies. Italy and Spain are among the largest economies in the Eurozone, with populations 10 times bigger than those in small Nordic countries. The Korean economy is larger than that of Spain, and the Japanese economy is larger than the German. Whether these large economies can be reformed effectively has important economic implications beyond their borders. The second reason is an intellectual one. The quartet offers good test cases to assess if the SI model is applicable to countries beyond a handful of Northern Continental European and Nordic countries. Whether they can adopt the SI model or not also helps us understand the economic and political prerequisite for the politics of SI.

More specifically, the cross-national variations we observe do not readily lend themselves to the existing causal explanations for how work–family reconciliation policies expand, which, it is fair to say, are strongly influenced by Germany's "Swedish turn" (Morgan, 2013). Although there is a renewed and welcome attention on the role of party competition, the current literature still does not pay sufficient attention to the effects of electoral rules and the economic structure, which specify the context in which party competition takes place. By means of a four-country analysis, we highlight how specific electoral contexts affect government's capacity to adopt an SI turn—particularly in childcare—and how employers' interests intervene on any policy decisions that affect their human resources management practices.

The rest of the chapter proceeds in four sections. Section 14.2 provides a more in-depth account of the cross-national variations referred to in the introduction. It presents the current policy mix (parental leaves and childcare) in each of the four countries and identifies the key legislative decisions that led to the current policy mix. Section 14.3 evaluates the existing theories about family policy reforms and presents our causal argument. Section 14.4 traces the policy developments in our four countries. Section 14.5 briefly concludes.

14.2. POLICY MIXES AND THE KEY POLICY SHIFTS IN THE QUARTET

Our quartet of countries at times chose divergent paths and moved in the same direction at other times in their attempts to adjust to new socioeconomic challenges. As Saraceno (2016) points out, in her analysis of policy mixes in the four countries, Italy and Japan offer more income support to families with children in the form of more generous parental leaves, cash benefits, and tax deductions, in contrast to Korea and Spain, whose family-related spending is more skewed in favor of publicly subsidized childcare services. As Figure 14.1 shows, all four countries are below EU and OECD averages. Spain and Korea made greater efforts in providing childcare services but less so in cash transfers

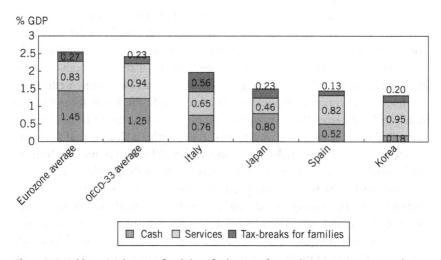

Figure 14.1 Public expenditure on family benefits by type of expenditure as a percentage of gross domestic product (GDP), 2013 and latest available.
Source. OECD (2017).

and tax breaks for families. Of the four, Italy is the most generous, but its generosity stands counter to the SI model as its overall family policy is biased toward tax breaks and cash benefits rather than SI policies.

With regard to childcare, Table 14.1 compares our four countries with other selected OECD countries for 2014 and 2017—the latest year for which OECD data are available. Italy and Spain have universal preschool education, and boast very high rates of enrollment on a full-time basis for preschool children even by international standards. The rates are slightly lower for Japan and Korea. However, in Korea, early childcare and education of preschool children became a universal right in 2013, and Japan made preschool for children aged 3–5 an almost universal right (the high-income groups still need to pay) in 2019. When we look at the enrollment rates for the youngest children (0–2), Korea has the highest rate in 2017, with the strongest increase since 2014, followed by Spain. Korea is the only country in the quartet that allows stay-home mothers to claim compensation for not using childcare centers: A home-care allowance is paid

Table 14.1 Proportion of children enrolled in formal childcare or preschool (2014–2017)

	Children aged 3–5, 2014	Children aged 3–5, 2017	Children aged 0–2, 2014	Children aged 0–2, 2017
Australia	67.4	84.0	32.0	39.6
Austria	83.3	89.3	19.2	21
Czech Republic	80.5	87.7	5.6	8.22
Denmark	95.5	97.5	65.2	55.4
Finland	73.8	79.5	27.9	31.2
France	100.3	100	51.9	56.3
Germany	97.0	94.6	32.3	37.2
Greece	47.0	65.3	13.8	23.4
Hungary	89.7	92.0	14.5	16.3
Italy	**95.1**	**93.9**	**24.2**	**29.7**
Japan	**91.0**	**91.4**	**30.6**	**35.1**
Korea	**92.2**	**94.6**	**35.7**	**56.3**
Netherlands	92.0	94.5	55.9	59.3
New Zealand	92.4	94.6	41.9	50.1
Norway	96.6	96.9	54.7	56.3
Spain	**96.7**	**97.1**	**38.1**	**36.4**
Sweden	94.3	94.1	46.9	46.6
Switzerland	48.1	49.5	38.0	—
United Kingdom	93.7	100	33.6	37.7

Source. OECD (2017), Japanese Ministry of Health, Labor and Welfare, annual updates on childcare and related facilities.

Table 14.2 Evolution of enrollment rates of under-3s in formal childcare (2001–2017)

Country	2004	2005	2006	2007	2008	2009	2010	2011	2012	2013	2014	2015	2016	2017
Germany	—	—	—	13.6	15.5	17.6	20.2	23.0	25.2	27.6	29.3	32.3	32.9	37.2
Italy	26.6	27.3	28.6	25.8	28.9	25.9	23.3	27.2	21.9	23.1	24.2	—	—	28.6
Japan	0.0	0.0	0.0	22.6	23.4	24.6	25.9	26.6	28.3	29.4	30.6	29.7	33.1	35.1
Korea	6.6	8.9	11.2	14.2	18.8	22.2	26.1	29.0	35.5	34.3	35.7	34.2	—	56.3
Spain	43.1	40.9	42.6	41.7	37.4	34.2	38.2	39.7	36.9	36.0	38.1	—	—	45.8

Source. OECD (2017), Japanese Ministry of Health, Labor and Welfare, annual updates on childcare and related facilities.

to families who look after their children at home. The rest of the countries do not link child allowance programs and public subsidies for childcare services as does Korea.

Table 14.2 looks at the evolution of enrollment rates of under-3s in formal childcare. As Estévez-Abe and Naldini (2016) argued, expansion of childcare services has been very rapid in Korea and Spain, while it was slow in Italy and Japan. However, there has been a big shift in Japan since 2014. In order to capture Japan's most recent changes, Table 14.2 includes information from Japanese government sources.

A simultaneous look at parental leave offers a better sense of the overall policy mix. As Table 14.3 shows, Japan has the most generous paid leaves for mothers. Japan offers almost 36 weeks of full-rate equivalent paid leave for mothers. Italy and Korea follow, with about 25 weeks each. Spain is one of the few advanced democracies without any paid extended leaves after the statutory 16 weeks of maternity leave (at 100% of earnings, see Table 14.3). However, after a number of parliamentary initiatives, paternity leave exclusively for fathers (or the second partner) has been improving continuously since 2017 to its current 12 weeks at full salary since January 1, 2020. Considering eligibility rules and take-up rates, the four countries differ substantially. The eligibility rules are more inclusive in Italy and Spain; both ask for a very short employment record for a new mother to qualify for the leave, and they grant paid maternity leave to self-employed women as well (Addabbo et al., 2016; Escobedo et al., 2016). This contrasts starkly with Japan and Korea, where only those who have been employed continuously for a year by the same employer qualify (Kim, 2016; Nakazato & Nishimura, 2016).

When we compare our four countries on their childcare and paid parental leave programs together, a pattern emerges. Korea and Spain both show higher rates of childcare enrollment and very low take-up rates of parental leaves (shown in Table 14.4) because of the low replacement rate in Korea and the absence of paid leave in the case of Spain.[1] Unlike in Italy and Japan, childcare services are

---

1. Some Spanish mothers resort to a creative solution by lumping together the statutory paid 1 hour a day "breastfeeding breaks" (1 hour a day until the child is 9 months old at 100% of salary).

Table 14.3 Comparative chart of paid leaves

	Spain	Korea	Italy	Japan
Maternity leave	16 weeks	12.9 weeks	21.7 weeks	14 weeks
Coverage (eligibility conditions)	100% of earnings up to a ceiling of €3642.00 in 2016.	100% ordinary wages for the first 60 days of maternity leave and maximum €1100 for the remaining 30 days.	80% of earnings with no ceiling for salaried workers. In the case of multiple or premature births, the length of leave increases by 12 weeks.	66.6% of the mother's average daily earnings for 6 months up to a ceiling of €3545 (minimum payment of €384/month and maximum of €2375). Remainder at 50%. Payment is tax-free, and the recipients are exempted from social insurance contributions.
	All employed women. Conditions: social security contributions (at least 180 days). Women <21, no conditions; women 21–26, only 90 days of social security contribution.	All female employees are eligible, whether on permanent or temporary contracts, must have been insured for 180 days prior.	All employees and self-employed women covered with social security contribution.	All female employees are eligible for maternity leave, but only those covered by the employees' health insurance systems are eligible for maternity benefit payment.
Right to time off work for breastfeeding	1 hour daily leave for the mother or the father until the child is 9 months old; 100% of salary. By consolidating breastfeeding leave, mothers can extend leave by 2 weeks or 4 weeks (for civil servants).		Until a child is 12 months old, the mother or the father is entitled to reduce hours (1 hour less per day if working 6 hours a day or less; 2 hours less per day if working longer) for breastfeeding, with full earnings compensation.	Unpaid breaks of at least 30 minutes twice a day for mothers with a child under 12 months.
Paternity leave	12 weeks (as of Jan. 2020) at 100% salary. Leave can be taken either full- or part-time, at a minimum rate of 50% of regular working time.	3–5 days; 100% salary paid for 3 days, unpaid for 2 days.	2 days; fathers can take 2 additional days if the mother agrees to transfer these days; 100% of earnings.	No statutory entitlement
Coverage (eligibility conditions)	All employees and self-employed (at least 180 days social security contributions)	All employees	All employees	

(continued)

Table 14.3 Continued

	Spain	Korea	Italy	Japan
Parental leave	4 weeks unpaid. Each parent is entitled to take leave until 3 years after childbirth.	52 weeks for parents with children under 6, paid 40% of ordinary wages (maximum €810 per month).	6 months per parent. 30% of earnings for a child under 6. Public sector employees 100% of earnings during first 30 days of leave.	Each parent can take leave, only entitled to 12 months after birth including maternity leave. 66% for the first 6 months, 50% the remaining time (the benefits are tax-exempt, hence the replacement ratios are much higher in real terms).
Coverage (eligibility conditions)	All employees. Unemployed and self-employed workers are not eligible.	Employees must have been insured for at least 180 days.	All employed parents, except domestic workers and home helps. Self-employed workers, 3 months.	Only applies to an employee employed on a fixed-term contract by the same employer for at least 1 year or likely to be kept employed.
Total paid leave available to mothers	16 full-rate equivalent weeks.	25 full-rate equivalent weeks.	25.2 full-rate equivalent weeks.	35.8 full-rate equivalent weeks.
Leave of absence to look after children	Maximum of 3 years unpaid. Social security contributions for old age and invalidity benefits are recognized during this leave.	Maximum 90 days unpaid for workers to look after their children, parents, or spouse on account of illness, accident, or old age.	Without limit for a child <3 years; 5 days a year per parent for a child aged 3–8 years. Unpaid. 2 years leave in the case of a serious need in their family: 100% earnings, up to €47,351 per year.	Up to 5 days per parent per year for a child <6 or up to 10 days per year if there are two or more children. Unpaid. When a family member requires constant care for a period of 2 weeks or more with a limit of 93 days, paid at 40% of earnings.
Reduction of working time	For workers with children under the age of 12 or older if disabled. Reduction can be for a maximum of 50% of working time with proportional salary reduction. Social security contributions remain 100% during first 2 years.	Working time reduction possible between 15 and 30 hours per week instead of using parental leave. All female workers who are within the first 12 weeks or beyond the 36th week of their pregnancies can reduce their working hours by 2 hours a day without reduction in pay. Payments are provided in proportion to the reduced working hours.	Employees who have parental responsibility for a child under 6 or a disabled child under 18 have a legal right to apply to their employers to work flexibly.	Until a child reaches the age of 3 years, parents have the right to reduce their normal working hours to 6 hours per day. There is no payment for working reduced hours. Employers may not require an employee with a child below compulsory school age to 1) work more than 24 hours per month or 150 hours per year of overtime or 2) work night shifts.

Sources: Authors' own elaboration from Escobedo et al. (2016); Nakazato and Nishimura (2016); Addabbo et al. (2016); Kim (2016); Salido and León (2016); Ministry of Health and Welfare, Korea (2015); and OECD (2017).

Table 14.4 Take-up rates or maternity, paternity, and parental leaves

	Spain	Korea	Italy	Japan
Take-up rate maternity leave	Benefit covered 64.7% of the 427,595 births in 2014. 85.6% of mothers (active in labor market) benefited from maternity leave in 2014. Mean number of days on leave has increased slightly to 134.4.	Number of employees taking maternity leave has increased on average by 12% per year, rising from 22,711 (4.6% of births) in 2002 to 95,259 (22% of births) in 2015.	Maternity leave is obligatory for employees. In 2012, 360,000 employees used maternity leave: 9% were temporary workers and 91% permanent workers.	Part of maternity leave is obligatory. Length of prenatal maternity leave 42.1 days, length of postnatal leave 54.5 days (2007 Basic Survey of Gender Equality in Employment Management).
Take-up rate parental leave	7.4% of births had parental leave in 2014. 10.4% women aged 25–59 who were working made use of parental leave. Women mostly took it just after maternity leave (64%) and most commonly for a maximum of 1 year (85%) and were working at that time report having used it (2012).	Number of employees taking parental leave 3763 (0.8% of the number of newborn children) in 2002; 87,339 (20% of newborn children) in 2015.	In 2012, parental leave was used by 285,000 employees (6.7% temporary contracts and 93.3% permanent contracts). 89% of employees using parental leave in 2012 were women, and 11% men (INPS).	86.6% of female workers who had given birth had started or applied for parental leave in 2014 (survey, 2014). The proportion increased by 3.6 percentage points from the previous year (2012). 33.8% took 10–12 months of leave; 22.4% took 12–18 months.
(Fathers' take-up rate in parentheses)	Paternity leave coverage was 55.4% (total number of births) in 2014. 74% of men who became fathers after the introduction of this leave and were working at that time report having used it (2012).	Proportion of male employees taking parental leave in 2015 was only 5.6% of total leaves.	(Introduced in January 2013, there is no information.)	46.8% of the workplaces surveyed provided their workers with non-statutory paternity leave. The proportion increased from the same survey in 2008 by 10.8. 52.9% of male workers at workplaces that provided this leave took it.

the only option available to working mothers in Korea and Spain. As a consequence, the inadequate parental leave boosts the demand for childcare services for infants below the age of 1. According to a 2012 survey in Spain, only 10.4% of women and 0.5% of men who were working when they became parents made use of unpaid parental leave (Meil et al., 2019). In Korea, for 20% of live births in 2015, one of the parents (mothers mainly) took parental leave. In Italy, the ratio of parents on parental leave in 2015 to the babies born in 2015 was 60%.[2] In Japan, the same ratio is 40% (authors' own calculations). Given the fact that only 2.3% of fathers took parental leave, this means that roughly 37% of new mothers took paid parental leave. It is worth mentioning that the recent improvement of paternity leave in Spain should be seen as an SI strategy aiming at a more equal sharing of caring time between partners. Constructing an indicator dividing the number of paternity benefits by the product of births and male employment rates (in the 22–54 age group), Flaquer and Escobedo (2020) observe that while the fathers' take-up rate was 63.9% in 2008, it had reached 86% in 2019.

Now let us move to a discussion of the timing of key legislative shifts behind the aforementioned cross-national patterns. In Italy, active legislative periods were from the 1970s until the late 1990s. Most of the key legislative decisions came by very early even by international standards. Italy universalized preschool education for ages 3–5 in 1968. Paid parental leave was introduced in 1971, and the program for private workers has remained more or less the same since, with 30% of salary replacement (public sector workers get 100%). The public responsibility for childcare provision (at the regional level) was legislated also in the 1970s. Nothing much happened after the active period of the 1970s until the late 1990s. The first decade of the 2000s saw a few legislative activities at the national level, but they all fell short of being considered as major legislation in terms of budgetary commitment or imposition of obligation on employers. In recent years, there have been again some national initiatives. The Fornero Reform in 2012 subsidized both formal and informal care instead of offering more generous paid parental leaves. Furthermore, some work–family reconciliation measures such as a tax credit for working mothers and an extension of paternity leaves were initially included in the Jobs Act package, but as explained in Chapter 5 in Volume II (Garritzmann et al., 2022), these initiatives were then dropped from the implementing decrees and did not materialize. As the authors of Chapter 5 argue, the post-crisis welfare expansion in Italy still favored the old social-protectionist path characterized by consumption-based programs over an investment-based SI strategy (see also Chapter 4 in Volume II [Garritzmann et al., 2022]).

---

2. A word of caution here is that this ratio overestimates the number of parents who take the leave. The Italian government statistics on the number of parents on parental leave lumps together parents of the newly born and those who are taking the leave care for older children. (The Italian parental leave allows parents to take paid time off until the child turns 12 years of age.)

In Japan, family policy issues emerged onto the national policy arena in the early 1990s and remained active throughout the first two decades of the 21st century. Unpaid parental leave was legislated in 1991. Although a meager paid benefit was added in 1995, significant improvements in the benefit did not happen until 2010 and then again in 2014. The 2014 reform raised the replacement wage close to 80% in real terms for the first 6 months of the parental leave and about 60% in real terms afterward. The government explained that it was advantageous for both the mother and the father to take 6 months off each. This was indeed a big policy shift, but the eligibility remained restrictive. As for publicly subsidized childcare, Japan introduced strictly means-tested public childcare services in the immediate postwar period. Despite the increase in female labor force participation, it was only in the 1990s that childcare provision emerged onto the national legislative agenda (Estévez-Abe, 2008). Policy efforts during the 1990s remained incremental. There was a renewed commitment to increase childcare provisions in the first decade of the 2000s (Estévez-Abe & Kim, 2014). However, it was in 2014 that the government announced a big policy shift (Estévez-Abe, 2019). In addition to the drastic improvement in paid parental leave, the government vowed to expand the supply of childcare services. Activation of female labor became the top national economic priority in 2014 for the first time. In 2017, the government decided to universalize free preschool education for ages 3–5 (implemented in 2019). Therefore, although Japan started with a strong familialist model, its recent investment in childcare and parental leave is a very significant departure from its initial welfare state design. However, Miura and Hamada point out in Chapter 12 of Volume II (Garritzmann et al., 2022) that Japan's social spending is still heavily biased in favor of "consumption-based" programs rather than SI-style "investment" programs. They also claim that even the latter programs are not sufficiently universalistic in Japan and conclude that Japan is moving to a partial or stratified SI. We agree with their analysis, but our four-country comparison demonstrates that this is not a problem unique to Japan; it is true of all four of our familialist cases to varying degrees.

In Korea, work–family reconciliation policy became highly active during the first decade of the 2000s and into the early 2010s. Korea introduced paid parental leave in 2001. However, the benefits were flat-rate and meager, and the policies that followed only marginally improved the rates. A big policy shift came in 2011, when an earnings-proportional paid leave was introduced (40% of wages). As for childcare, like postwar Japan, Korea only used to provide strictly means-tested childcare services. Middle-class families relied on unsubsidized private services. In 2004, Korea took a more universalistic turn on childcare policies and began subsidizing childcare for a greater share of the population, as described in Chapter 13 of Volume II (Garritzmann et al., 2022). From 2007 onward, the policy orientation in childcare shifted from a means-tested targeted one toward a more inclusive universalistic direction. The change from a progressive to a conservative government in 2008 did not alter the more universalistic policy orientation in line with the SI model. Public programs for childcare continued to be a salient electoral issue in the presidential elections as well as in the local elections in the Greater Seoul metropolitan area. While Korea appears to have embraced an SI approach, a word of caution is necessary. The aspect of activation of mothers' labor force remains weak as stay-home mothers can be paid benefits to look after their children at home and as the paid parental leave program only covers female full-time workers in Korea.

Spain shares with other Southern European countries a very strong consumption-oriented legacy (see Chapter 4 in Volume II [Garritzmann et al., 2022]). In this sense, Italy and Spain are like Japan. However, since the early 2000s, family policy expansionary trends have favored services against a much more limited use of tax breaks and transfers. Childcare for children 3 and older became universal in the early 1990s, two decades after Italy but sooner than many European countries thanks to its inclusion within the education system. Progress in childcare for children under the age of 3 has been more limited, although coverage rates have been increasing even during the 2008 economic crisis (León et al., 2019). The most recent political attempt to improve childcare services was in 2008 under the socialists. The Educa3 plan intended to support the creation of 300,000 new childcare places for children aged 0–2 in the 2008–2012 period. Compared to Italy, since the 1990s, Spain has kept spending less on a per-capita basis in covering the needs of families with small children. By contrast, its family policy expansion has gone decisively in the direction of universalizing childcare and increasing the share of caring time between mothers and fathers after childbirth. While parental leave continues to be unpaid, Spain provides 12 weeks of fully paid paternity leave just for fathers (or second partners) as of January 2019. This family policy model fits in with an inclusive SI approach, although insufficient transfers to low-income families explain Spain's very high levels of child poverty (León et al., 2019, p. 456).

14.3. WHAT EXPLAINS THE CROSS-NATIONAL VARIATIONS? THE LIMITS OF EXISTING EXPLANATIONS

How can we explain these variations among our quartet? Why is the family policy development in Spain geared toward childcare services much more than tax breaks, leaves, or transfers? Why was Italy so progressive in the late 1960s and the early 1970s but became so dormant ever since? Why has Korea expanded its childcare services so dramatically, but its take-up rate of parental leave remains so low in comparison? What happened in Japan in 2014 to dramatically accelerate its policy change?

The usual suspects do not seem to offer a ready explanation for the pattern of policy developments we observe in our quartet, as described in the previous section. Power resources theory has long been a very dominant explanation for welfare state development. More recently, there is a growing awareness about the limitations of the power resources model (Bonoli, 2005; Bonoli & Reber, 2010; Ferragina & Seeleib-Kaiser, 2015; Morgan, 2013; Chapter 15 in this volume). Today, an increasing number of studies offer reasons why the power resources model has lost its explanatory capacity. Such reasons include the following: 1) complex political spaces in Western democracies are not so easily pinned down to traditional left–right divisions (Häusermann & Kübler, 2010); 2) the changes in the party systems make the crafting of electoral coalitions more complex, with alignments and strategies almost impossible to predict (Beramendi et al., 2015; see also Chapter 2 in this volume); 3) compared with old social risks, new social risks affect more heterogeneous groups whose interests are harder to identify, and thus, these groups have less capacity to mobilize collectively at the level of either politics or industrial relations (Bonoli, 2005); and 4) policy legacies and magnitudes of problems (Häusermann & Kübler, 2010; Palier & Martin, 2007; Chapter 2 in this volume).

Our quartet helps us go beyond some of the problems embedded in the Eurocentric explanations. European literature generally assumes similar electoral systems—proportional representation systems—and similar economic structures—where relatively large companies dominate. Most studies on recent work–family reconciliation policies have been inspired by the experiences of Northern Continental European countries such as Germany and the Netherlands. These are countries that adopt proportional representation and where there are established parties that are aligned with well-organized unions and employer associations. In contrast, the four countries under study here have very different economic structures when compared to Northern Continental European economies and include different electoral systems.

Like Estévez-Abe and Naldini (2016), we argue that the institutional context of party competition is critical in understanding why work–family reconciliation policies appear on the national legislative agenda and get legislated. The most important point we make is that party competition over votes does not always concern nationwide vote allocation: Under winner-take-all electoral systems, voter preferences in competitive districts carry oversized importance. This means that even policy preferences of a relatively small segment of the voting population can propel political parties to change their policy menus to cater to their needs. We argue that big policy shifts began to occur in Korea precisely because of the specific characteristics of the Korean electoral context. Of course, for electoral pledges to become credible promises, "pledge makers" have to be able to control the legislative agenda. Estévez-Abe and Naldini (2016) argue that party leaders in Korea and Spain possessed such abilities as decisive electoral winners formed the governments—until the situation changed in Spain in very recent years—while in Italy and Japan, frequent turnovers of prime ministers unrelated to electoral cycles weakened the tie between electoral pledges and policy outcomes (also see Estévez-Abe & Kim, 2014). In Japan, however, as a direct consequence of the electoral and other political reforms in the 1990s, the prime minister's tenure began to lengthen in the early 2000s, providing the prime minister with greater powers over the legislative process (Estévez-Abe, 2008).

We also highlight the importance of economic structure, which conditions the configuration of employers' policy preferences. Overall, employers are important actors in explaining the development of SI policies (see Chapter 9 in this volume). But employers' preferences matter little in legislation concerning public subsidization of childcare services—unless the government explicitly forces employers to share the costs. However, the consent of employers is critical for any meaningful paid childcare leave to be legislated, and there are three structural "necessary conditions" for this consent to materialize: 1) dominance of large corporations as employers in the economy, 2) the preexistence of a corporate leave program and a statutory option that will subsidize their corporate programs, and/or 3) the presence of a severe labor shortage that makes employers need to hold onto female employees even after they become mothers (Estévez-Abe, 2019). Lambert (2008) very aptly noted that the generosity of paid parental leaves seems to correlate with corporatism. We argue that it is not corporatism per se but the predominance of large-scale employers that matters for paid parental leave that actually gets implemented. Smaller employers are always wary of statutory leaves regardless of the skill components of the workers they employ. For small employers, the cost of managing the temporary loss of an employee is too great. For large employers, the situation is different as they have more resources and capacity to adjust.

14.4. HISTORICAL EVIDENCE—POLITICAL TRAJECTORIES

Historically speaking, our quartet breaks up into two respective pairs: Italy and Japan, on the one hand, and Korea and Spain, on the other. Italy and Japan both were democratized after World War II and experienced rapid economic growth, which continued into the 1970s. Until their party systems collapsed—more spectacularly in Italy—after the Cold War, the two countries were prototypical "one party–dominant" democracies (Pempel, 1990), where a catch-all conservative party ruled (the Christian Democrats [CD] in Italy and the Liberal Democratic Party [LDP] in Japan). The CD and the LDP shared many similarities, partly because of functional similarities in the respective electoral systems in the two countries (Estévez-Abe, 2008). In the two countries, the ruling parties were mere coalitions of political bosses, who engaged in the clientelistic exchange of favors and votes. Their welfare states reflect the long periods of such clientelistic politics (Estévez-Abe, 2008; Ferrera, 1996; Lynch, 2006).

In Italy and Japan, socioeconomic changes began to weaken the conservative grip on political power in the 1960s and led to the rise of progressive forces within society. Progressive candidates began to seize control of wealthy urban municipal governments in Japan. In Italy, left-wing parties seized control of Northern cities. In both countries, the conservatives fought back with a mixture of carrots and sticks. Carrots often came in the form of social policies and their functional equivalents (see Ferrera [1996] for Italy, Estévez-Abe [2008] for Japan, and Lynch [2006]). At the national level, the ruling LDP government preemptively adopted the popular policies of progressive municipal governments and announced its commitment to build a new welfare state. It was during this period that Japan introduced the only two universalistic programs that the country had ever introduced: free elderly medical care and the children's allowance (Estévez-Abe, 2008). The LDP in Japan preemptively introduced "left-wing" policies and succeeded in avoiding the situation where it had to form a center-left coalition government. In Italy, the CD, unable to form a stable government on its own, formed a center-left coalition government under Aldo Moro in 1968. In Japan, by the late 1960s, large corporations had succeeded in their fight against ideological unions; more pragmatic enterprise unions had become the dominant unions within the private sector, opening possibilities to negotiate and engage in mutually beneficial economic arrangements with their employers (Garon & Mochizuki, 1993; Gordon, 1993). The only ideological unions in Japan hence were public sector unions. Italian large corporations did not fight back as hard as the Japanese large corporations did. Although both countries had very large shares of workers employed in small enterprises, the nature of large corporations differed markedly. Japan's economy was mostly privately owned, while a much larger share of Italy's economy was publicly owned. In the 1970s, more than 20% of publicly traded corporations in the Italian stock market were controlled by the government (Aganin & Volpin, 2005).

In Italy, the kind of employer-initiated "private" profit-sharing pact that characterized Japanese industrial relations never emerged; instead, the political arena was where the class struggle took place. The persistence of more ideological unions led Italy onto a different path. The youth mobilization in the 1960s combined forces with ideological unions and led to the growing presence of left-wing parties in the national parliament. Under Prime Minister Moro's center-left coalition government, Italy introduced universal access to preschools and paid parental leave as well as a law that stipulated the public responsibility to offer childcare services in 1971 (Ballestrero, 1979). The progressive legislation, however, had its limitations. The wage replacement rate for the new parental leave was very low (30%). While the benefit level was raised for public sector workers, it remained low for the private sector. This signals that even the historic compromise only resulted in an unrealistic program design. Unless the benefit level is higher, the take-up rate will remain low, which probably made it palatable to the employers.

The kind of center-left coalition government that was formed in Italy in 1968 did not happen in Japan until the early 1990s. This means that the amount of compromise the LDP had to make to socialists remained minimal until the early 1990s. No universalization of preschools as a state-provided education program took place in Japan because, with no socialist coalition partners to force them, the LDP had no reason to invest in the expansion of the public sector, which would increase membership of ideologically oriented public sector unions. However, in the early 1990s, the LDP lost control of the House of Councilors (the Upper House). Forced into a minority position, the LDP government had to accept some policy concessions to the left. The legislation of unpaid parental leave in 1991 was one of those concessions. In 1993, Japan formed its first non-LDP center-left co-alition government since the US occupation when a group of LDP politicians left the party and orchestrated a vote of non-confidence against the LDP government, and this government put childcare policies at the top of the national agenda. This non-LDP center-left coalition government was succeeded by another center-left coalition (LDP-Socialist) in 1994. This second center-left government introduced the first paid parental leave; however, the benefit levels remained very low (at 25% of wage replacement), just like the Italian paid parental leave.

Interestingly, the party systems in Italy and Japan both went through transformations after the end of the Cold War. Both countries introduced elec-toral reforms and adopted similar mixed systems—a combination of propor-tional representation (PR) and single-member district (SMD) tiers—around the same time. To make a long story short, a new electoral context gave rise to a different kind of party competition—between two camps, center-left and center-right—in the two countries. In Japan, where the mixed system had a very dominant SMD logic, a quasi-two-party system began to develop (Estévez-Abe, 2008). In Italy, two broad camps of party alliance began to form, giving rise to pe-riodic shifts in power from center-left to center-right and back to center-left until the recent emergence of anti-system parties changed the new status quo (Picot, 2012). In Japan, the first turnover of power did not occur until 2009 and then again in 2012. While the party competition was intensifying in the two coun-tries, for reasons that we cannot go into here due to space limits, political power was far from being concentrated, and most prime ministers did not last very long. Both countries experienced a series of weak governments and high turn-over of prime ministers (see Estévez-Abe & Naldini, 2016). The inability of party leaders to hold onto power to actually legislate what they promised meant that the increased party competition was not producing legislative outcomes. As we shall see, the situation dramatically changed in Japan more recently.

In contrast, both Korea and Spain are late developers. Spain democratized in the mid-1970s—but had had a democratic period before it ended in a civil war that led to the rise of a fascist regime. Korea only became a democracy in the late 1980s without ever having had any democracy earlier because the au-thoritarian regime was preceded by a long duration of Japanese colonial rule.

Building of modern welfare states did not begin in earnest until after they became democracies—although democratic Spain had inherited the social security system from General Franco's regime (Rodríguez Cabrero, 2011). Interestingly, it was the two late-comers that behaved more like "normal democracies." Unlike Italy and Japan, Korea and Spain experienced periodic and very clear alternations of power (Estévez-Abe & Naldini, 2016). In Spain, several years after the democratic transition, the *Partido Socialista Obrero Español* (PSOE) seized power in 1982. In Korea, the progressive Kim Dae-jung unexpectedly became the president in 1998. In Spain, the PSOE and the conservative *Partido Popular* (PP) would alternate power and ruled as a majoritarian government—even when the ruling party was in the minority; because of Spain's peculiar political party system, it still ruled as the de facto majoritarian party (see Field, 2016). Although Spain has a closed-list PR, its electoral system works very differently from other European PR systems. Its small district size favors large political parties and thus produces strong majoritarian tendencies (Hopkin, 2005). Importantly, their political systems gave Korean and Spanish voters a very clear choice of government—either conservative or progressive. Korean presidents and Spanish prime ministers possessed more legislative power than their counterparts in Italy and Japan, who had a hard time harnessing their grip on power. Between 1995 and 2015, Korea had five presidents, Spain had four prime ministers, while Italy and Japan would go through rapid successions of prime ministers for one reason or another. The critical point here is that the choice of the government and elections were not clearly linked in Italy and Japan as they were in the two new democracies.

The clearer link between elections and governments in Korea and Spain meant that political parties competed more on policies (see Estévez-Abe & Naldini, 2016). The reaction of young voters against the recent authoritarian past meant that progressive policies concerning gender equality were not necessarily viewed as "women's policies" but rather as policies to democratize their societies further. This meant that when the socialist government in Spain universalized preschool education in 1990, the National Organic Law of Education, the issue was not female activation or catering to female voters but a matter of social equality. The political intention was to give children of working-class families an opportunity for early education in order to level the playing field so that these children would have a better chance to succeed. Main efforts were placed in universalizing access to preschool for children aged 3–5, leaving childcare for younger children largely unresolved (Ibáñez & León, 2014, p. 278). The expansion of access to tertiary education that had taken place under the socialist government meant that more highly educated women were joining the labor force. Hence, the universalization of preschool education, whatever the immediate political intention might have been, helped highly educated women who wanted to work. Given the fact that economically better-off women supported the conservative PP, the PP did not roll back PSOE-legislated initiatives. In fact, the presence of highly educated women among the voting base of the Spanish right is substantially higher than that of the main center-right party in Italy (León et al., 2019). This reflects a deeper transformation from the social demand side (higher access of women to employment and further education and more progressive views on motherhood). The difference marked a steady convergence between the two main parties in Spain regarding their main lines of action on family policy.

Similarly, the election of a progressive president in Korea brought new policy issues on to the agenda. Kim Dae-jun, the first progressive to win the office, did not have strong organized support and hence courted groups that had been active in the democratic movement. Feminists were invited into this administration as the new president had created the Ministry of Gender Equality (Estévez-Abe & Kim, 2014). With the backup of the president, new programs such as paid parental leave were introduced (Peng & Wong, 2008; Song, 2012). When another progressive, Roh Moo Hyun, won and succeeded Kim Dae-jun, he began to introduce a more universalistic approach to childcare. His tilt in favor of universalistic childcare provision was partly a way of countering the threat from a progressive independent candidate, Chung Mong-Joon, during the electoral campaign (Lee, 2016). The Korean electoral landscape used to be dominated by highly personalistic regionalism: In the early days of Korean democracy, people would vote for the party whose leader was from their region. While such electoral regionalism persisted, urbanization and internal migration into the area surrounding Seoul increased the number of competitive districts in parliamentary elections (Jong, 2016; Yoon, 2017). The electoral necessity to cater to more progressive urban voters—who were also younger—increased. This need was greater for Roh, whose region of origin did not match the region that traditionally supported his party (Lee, 2016). Roh's government prepared a major childcare program (the Saessak Plan), which gradually loosened the qualifying household income levels to include ever-growing numbers of families with access to subsidized childcare services (Song, 2012; see also Chapter 13 in Volume II [Garritzmann et al., 2022]).

The actual complete universalization of childcare and preschool came in steps overlapping two conservative governments. Conservative President Lee Myung-bak and his party decisively became pro-subsidization of childcare costs after conservatives suffered significant losses in local elections in 2010 in the Greater Seoul area. Progressive candidates had won in formerly conservative areas including the mayoral position of Seoul by promising more public subsidies for the cost of childrearing. Since the Greater Seoul area includes competitive districts, catering to the wishes of urban voters became an important electoral strategy for both progressives and conservatives (Jong, 2016; Lim, 2018). It was in this context that President Lee, his successor Park Geun-hye (also conservative), and their party supported the universalization of childcare.[3] President Lee introduced an earnings-related paid parental leave in 2011 and introduced partial universal

---

3. Korea imposes a strict 5-year, one-term limit on its presidents.

childcare for 0–2, 5-year-olds. Korea then completely universalized childcare for children 0–5 years old in 2013—making Korea the only country among our quartet to grant universal free childcare to all preschool children. This is not to say that the progressives and conservatives advocated the same policies. President Lee opted for a voucher system and granted those families that did not use childcare services an option to receive a "home care allowance," hence significantly weakening the activation and educational aspects of the childcare policy (Lee, 2016; Song, 2012).

Most recently, there have been very interesting developments in Italy and Japan. As noted, even when party competition increased after the introduction of electoral systems that encouraged more bimodal partisan competition, for reasons identified elsewhere, party competition failed to produce bold shifts in policies in the two countries (see Estévez-Abe & Naldini, 2016). When the LDP returned to power in 2012, it implemented the final changes to complete the process of concentration of power in the hands of the prime minister—a chain of reforms that had started in the late 1990s. Prime Minister Abe not only preemptively adopted the popular work–family reconciliation policies of the rival party, Democratic Party of Japan, but placed work–family reconciliation policy as his government's top policy goal (one of the three arrows of the so-called *Abenomics*, known as *Womenomics*). Once Prime Minister Abe had seized complete control over his party's legislative agenda, he ran a campaign on these issues in the 2014 elections. After a landslide victory, he found creative ways to increase funding for childcare facilities as well as for paid parental leaves (for more details on the Japanese case, see Estévez-Abe [2019] and Chapter 12 in Volume II [Garritzmann et al., 2022]). As we saw in section 2 in this chapter, the enrollment rate of small children in formal care began to expand rapidly. Although less dramatic than in Japan, Italy saw some renewed activities. In the 2013 general elections, the populist anti-establishment Five Star Movement did extremely well, emerging as the third largest party in its first election. It had successfully attracted the support of many disgruntled youth who suffered underemployment and constituted a disproportionate share of precarious employment. The party secretary of the Democratic Party (center-left), Matteo Renzi, strategized to counter Five Star's challenge by reorienting his party much more toward the concerns of labor market outsiders: His vision was to introduce policies oriented toward younger generations, which materialized as the Jobs Act. Renzi, in an intra-party coup, displaced Prime Minister Letta to install himself as his successor. The Jobs Act redesigned leave policies to make them more flexible and easier for workers with precarious contracts to use. For workers who had the right to paid parental leave but found it difficult to take advantage of it, the Renzi government introduced a "babysitter voucher" as an alternative option. The Renzi government seemed as if it were set to make real changes finally, but the resignation of the prime minister after his failed constitutional reform bid brought back business as usual (see Chapter 5 in Volume 2 [Garritzmann et al., 2022]).

Although we do not have the space to fully elaborate, we need to say a few more words about the politics of parental leave. As we have seen, governments sometimes introduced paid parental leave because of increased party competition. However, generally speaking, even when such leaves were introduced, they remained very meager among our quartet. This is because of their economic structure. The four countries under study here have had very different employment structures, whereby the majority of workers work in very small enterprises or are self-employed. As Chapter 9 in this volume explains, small enterprises are likely to resist the introduction of leaves. Even if the leaves were fully subsidized by the government, small enterprises do not have the capacity to manage the leaves of the few employees they have. Japan, however, is the only country that deviates from the rest. Although the Japanese employment structure resembled that of Italy for most of the postwar period, the larger enterprises began to hire more workers relative to the smaller ones. Today, Japan's employment structure looks markedly different (OECD, 2015). The recent expansions in paid parental leaves in Japan occurred as the younger cohorts of workers began to shrink in size just as the baby boomers began to retire from the largest corporations upon reaching the corporate retirement age. It is the combination of the dominance of larger firms and the acute labor shortage that have changed the calculations of what used to be highly male-chauvinistic Japanese corporations. In the absence of large waves of skilled or unskilled migration, female labor is highly in demand for both skilled and unskilled work. The expansion of paid parental leave in Japan also took place by ensuring that the redistributive component was minimal: Most parents who are eligible are labor market insiders.

14.5. CONCLUSION

This chapter has looked at cross-national variations in the politics of childcare and parental leave in four familialist welfare states: Italy, Japan, Korea, and Spain. Faced with rapidly aging populations, our four countries have been trying to make a SI turn with different degrees of success. Ruling out the usual explanations, we have demonstrated how the institutional context of party competition is crucial in understanding why and when childcare policies and parental leave programs appear on the national legislative agenda. In the cases of Korea and Spain, governments possess more legislative power than their counterparts in Italy and Japan, and thus electoral promises can more easily enter the policy agenda. Clearer links between national elections and governments mean that political parties compete more on policies. But electoral politics alone is not sufficient to understand the trajectories of our four countries in parental leave. We have argued that the economic structure, to the extent that it shapes employers' preferences and labor shortages, is part of the explanation.

REFERENCES

Addabbo, T., Cardinali, V., Giovannini, D., & Mazzucchelli, S. (2016). Italy country note. In A. Koslowski, S. Blum, & P. Moss (Eds.). *International review of leave policies and research* (pp. 190–202). International Network on Leave Policies and Research.

Aganin, A., & Volpin, P. (2005). The history of corporate ownership in Italy. In R. K. Morck (Ed.), *A history of corporate governance around the world: Family business groups to professional managers* (pp. 325–366). University of Chicago Press.

An, M. Y., & Peng, I. (2016). Diverging paths? A comparative look at childcare policies in Japan, South Korea and Taiwan. *Social Policy & Administration, 50*(5), 540–558.

Ballestrero, M. V. (1979). *Dalla tutele alla parità*. Il Mulino.

Beramendi, P., Häusermann, S., Kitschelt, H., & Kriesi, H. (2015). *The politics of advanced capitalism*. Cambridge University Press.

Bonoli, G. (2005). The politics of the new social policy providing coverage against new social risks in mature welfare states. *Policy and Politics, 33*(3), 431–449.

Bonoli, G., & Reber, F. (2010). The political economy of childcare in OECD countries: Explaining cross-national variations in spending and coverage rates. *European Journal of Political Research, 49*, 97–118.

Escobedo, A., Meil, G., & Lapuerta, I. (2016). Spain country note. In A. Koslowski, S. Blum, & P. Moss (Eds.). *International review of leave policies and research* (pp. 325–339). International Network on Leave Policies and Research.

Estévez-Abe, M. (2008). *Welfare capitalism in postwar Japan*. Cambridge University Press.

Estévez-Abe, M. (2019, June 22). *The varieties of politics of work–family reconciliation: Parties, employers and demography* [Paper presentation]. Annual Conference of the Council of European Studies, Madrid, Spain.

Estévez-Abe, M., & Kim, Y. S. (2014). Presidents, prime ministers and politics of care—Why Korea expanded childcare much more than Japan. *Social Policy & Administration, 48*(6), 666–685.

Estévez-Abe, M., & Naldini, M. (2016). Politics of defamilialization: A comparison of Italy, Japan, Korea and Spain. *Journal of European Social Policy, 26*(4), 327–343.

Estévez-Abe, M., Yang, J. J., & Choi, Y. J. (2016). Beyond familialism: Recalibrating family, state and market in Southern Europe and East Asia. *Journal of European Social Policy, 26*(4), 301–313.

Ferragina, E., & Seeleib-Kaiser, M. (2015). Determinants of a silent (r)evolution: Understanding the expansion of family policy in rich OECD countries. *Social Politics, 22*(1), 1–37.

Ferrera, M. (1996). The "southern model" of welfare in social Europe. *Journal of European Social Policy, 6*(1), 17–37.

Field, B. (2016). *Why minority governments work: Multilevel territorial politics in Spain*. Palgrave.

Flaquer, L., & Escobedo, A. (2020). Las licencias parentales y la política social a la paternidad en España. In L. Flaquer, T. Cano, & M. Barbeta-Viña (Eds.), *La paternidad en España: La implicación paterna en el cuidado de los hijos* (Politeya: Estudios de Política y Sociedad 37 (pp. 161–190). Consejo Superior de Investigaciones Científicas.

Garon, S., & Mochizuki, M. (1993). Negotiating social contracts. In A. Gordon (Ed.), *Postwar Japan as history* (pp. 145–166). University of California Press.

Garritzmann, J. L., Häusermann, S., & Palier, B. (Eds.). (2022). *The world politics of social investment: Vol. II. The politics of varying social investment strategies*. Oxford University Press.

Gordon, A. (1993). Contests for the workplace. In A. Gordon (Ed.), *Postwar Japan as history* (pp. 373–394). University of California Press.

Häusermann, S., & Kübler, D. (2010). Policy frames and coalition dynamics in the recent reforms of Swiss family policy. *German Policy Studies, 6*(3), 163–195.

Hopkin, J. (2005). Spain: Proportional representation with majoritarian outcomes. In M. Gallagher & P. Mitchell (Eds.), *The politics of electoral systems* (pp. 375–394). Oxford University Press.

Ibáñez, Z., & León, M. (2014). Early childhood education and care provision in Spain. In M. León (Ed.), *The transformation of care in European societies* (pp. 276–300). Palgrave Macmillan.

Jong, J. (2016). Regionalism and candidate nomination system in the 2014 Korean general local elections. *Jichi Soken, 448*, 91–114.

Kim, H. (2016). Korea country note. In A. Koslowski, S. Blum, & P. Moss (Eds.). *International review of leave policies and research* (pp. 211–216). International Network on Leave Policies and Research.

Lambert, P. (2008). The comparative political economy of parental leave and child care: Evidence from twenty OECD countries. *Social Politics: International Studies in Gender, State and Society, 15*(3), 315–344.

Lee, S. C. (2016). Democratization, political parties and Korean welfare politics: Korean family policy reforms in comparative perspective. *Government and Opposition, 44*, 1–24.

León, M., Choi, Y. J., & Ahn, J. S. (2016). When flexibility meets familialism: Two tales of gendered labour markets in Spain and South Korea. *Journal of European Social Policy, 26*(4), 344–357.

León, M., & Pavolini, E. (2014). Social investment or back to familism: The impact of the economic crisis on care policies in Italy and Spain. *South European Society & Politics, 19*(3), 353–369.

León, M., Pavolini, E., Miró, J., & Sorrenti, A. (2019). Policy change and partisan politics: Understanding family policy differentiation in two similar countries. *Social Politics, 28*(2), 451–476.

Lim, S. (2018). Perceptions of unfairness and a weak universal welfare state in South Korea. *Japanese Journal of Political Science, 19*(30), 376–396.

Lynch, J. (2006). *Age in the welfare state: The origins of social spending on pensioners, workers, and children.* Cambridge University Press.

Meil, G., Lapuerta, I., & Escobedo, A. (2019). Spain country note. In A. Koslowski, S. Blum, I. Dobrotić, A. Macht, & P. Moss (Eds.), *International review of leave policies and research 2019* (pp. 445–458). International Network on Leave Policies and Research. http://www.leavenetwork.org/lp_and_r_reports/

Morgan, K. J. (2013). Path shifting of the welfare state electoral competition and the expansion of work–family policies in Western Europe. *World Politics, 65*(1), 73–115.

Nakazato, H., & Nishimura, J. (2016). Japan country note. In A. Koslowski, S. Blum, & P. Moss (Eds.). *International review of leave policies and research* (pp. 203–210). International Network on Leave Policies and Research.

Organisation for Economic Co-operation and Development. (2011). *Doing better for families.*

Organisation for Economic Co-operation and Development. (2015). *Entrepreneurship at a glance.*

Organisation for Economic Co-operation and Development. (2017). *OECD family database.* www.oecd.org/social/family/database

Palier, B., & Martin, C. (2007). Editorial introduction. From "a frozen landscape" to structural reforms: The sequential transformation of Bismarckian welfare systems. *Social Policy & Administration, 41*(6), 535–554.

Pempel, T. J. (1990). *Uncommon democracies: The one-party dominant regimes.* Cornell University Press.

Peng, I., & Wong, J. (2008). Institutions and institutional purpose: Continuity and change in East Asian social policy. *Politics & Society, 36*(1), 61–88.

Picot, G. (2012). *Politics of segmentation: Party competition and social protection in Europe.* Routledge.

Rodríguez Cabrero, G. (2011). The consolidation of the Spanish welfare state (1975–2010). In A. M. Guillén & M. León (Eds.), *The Spanish welfare state in European context* (pp. 59–74). Ashgate.

Saraceno, C. (2016). Varieties of familialism: Comparing four southern European and East Asian welfare states. *Journal of European Social Policy, 26*(4), 314–326.

Song, J. (2012). The politics of family policies in Korea. *Korea Observer, 43*(2), 209–231.

Yoon, J. (2017). Cross-pressure and the change of regional voting: Evidence from the 14th to the 18th Korean presidential election. *Korean Party Studies Review, 16*(3), 5–45.

15

SOCIAL INVESTMENT OR CHILDCARE ON THE CHEAP?

QUALITY, WORKFORCE, AND ACCESS CONSIDERATIONS IN THE EXPANSION OF EARLY CHILDHOOD EDUCATION AND CARE

Kimberly J. Morgan

15.1. INTRODUCTION

In recent years, governments in many advanced industrialized countries have expanded the supply of early childhood education and care (ECEC), informed at least in part by social investment rationales. Yet, the logics of these interventions have varied, depending on the breadth of access to the services and their potential effects on human capital. An inclusive approach makes services broadly, if not universally, available, while more stratified and targeted policies produce more limited access (see Chapters 1 and 2 in this volume). And while ECEC programs mobilize human capital by supporting workforce participation, they also can help create human capital if they are of high quality and provided by well-trained staff. Understanding the implications of ECEC expansions for social investment thus requires analysis of *how* program development occurs, with attention to job quality, program quality, and inclusion. This raises a further question: Why do governments pursue ECEC policies that follow different social investment logics?

This chapter investigates this question by focusing on six countries that have significantly expanded the availability of ECEC in recent years but vary in how

Kimberly J. Morgan, *Social Investment or Childcare on the Cheap?* In: *The World Politics of Social Investment (Volume I)*. Edited by: Julian L. Garritzmann, Silja Häusermann, and Bruno Palier, Oxford University Press. © Oxford University Press 2022. DOI: 10.1093/oso/9780197585245.003.0015 this expansion has occurred: France, Germany, Ireland, New Zealand, Norway, and Slovenia. Many of these countries have couched their reforms in the language of social investment yet adopted variable policy architectures. Norway, New Zealand, and Slovenia have fostered inclusive human capital creation and mobilization. Ireland is furthest from this approach, with its more targeted ECEC initiatives, class-stratified access, and programs of dubious quality. France and Germany are more mixed models, with elements of universalism and stratification and varied access to programs that are high-quality and support employment.

Two factors explain these different logics. One is whether ECEC programs are administered by educational or social welfare administrations, which shapes protagonists involved in program expansion. When services are lodged within educational ministries, they gain powerful bureaucratic allies in domestic politics that often work in tandem with unionized public sector workers. Linking ECEC with primary education, both bureaucratically and in labor relations, helps assure better working conditions and pay for staff, which in turn has positive ramifications for program quality. It also increases attentiveness to curriculum. Three of the countries with high-quality ECEC programs, New Zealand, Norway, and Slovenia, moved all of their early childhood programs under education ministries in recent decades.

A second factor concerns the influence of another set of protagonists: left parties. Both conservative and left parties have, in recent years, promoted expansions of ECEC programs, at times using social investment rationales. Yet, left parties are more likely to develop programs that not only mobilize human capital but also create it through quality care and broad-based access. Left parties evince greater support for publicly provided or heavily subsidized services, both assuring greater access (by making them affordable to parents) and supporting better jobs for workers in them. Conservative parties have, at times, expanded ECEC programs somewhat grudgingly while still harboring a preference for the male-breadwinner family. And market-oriented liberal parties often prioritize budget balance, are less attentive to public sector workers, and believe that markets deliver a superior product at less cost to government—particularly for their upper-income voters who are best able to find and pay for childcare in the marketplace. Thus, to the extent that center-right politicians embrace social investment, they tend to put forward an economistic and neoliberal vision of it as a set of inputs designed to maximize economic productivity. By contrast, left parties are more likely to develop policies that emphasize the "social" dimension of social investment.

15.2. SOCIAL INVESTMENT LOGICS IN ECEC

ECEC exemplifies many of the goals of social investment—to invest in human development, improve the efficient use of human capital, and promote social inclusion (Morel et al., 2012). ECEC can contribute to these goals by offering developmentally stimulating programs to young children that also enable parents to be in paid employment, thereby both creating and mobilizing human capital. High-quality ECEC can shape cognitive and social development during the crucial first 5 years of a child's life, with potentially lasting effects on capacities for lifelong learning (Organisation for Economic Co-operation and Development [OECD], 2017, p. 31). ECEC also can provide employment, often for less skilled and/or lower-income women. In short, ECEC programs can support multiple social investment goals.

However, many of these aims will not be met if programs are mediocre and access to quality care is stratified by socioeconomic status. The greatest developmental gains for children come from high-quality services, whereas poor-quality programs can negate these benefits (Gambaro et al., 2014, pp. 3–6; Melhuish, 2015, p. 10). Moreover, the benefits of ECEC are most significant for children experiencing some form of disadvantage, owing to low family income, migrant status, and/or disability (Gambaro et al., 2014, p. 6). Yet, many political scientists and sociologists studying ECEC have focused on the quantitative expansions in services and neglected quality and inclusiveness (e.g., Blome, 2017; Bonoli & Reber, 2010; Ferragina & Seeleib-Kaiser, 2015; Fleckenstein & Lee, 2014; Morgan, 2013). Much of this scholarship has identified the electoral dynamics that have driven reform owing to changing social values, intensified partisan sparring over the welfare state, and/or the rising influence of women in political parties and government. Among countries engaging in expansion, however, there are considerable differences in how they go about doing it. What explains these differences?

This chapter focuses on six countries that have made significant changes in quantitative provision but vary in how this expansion has occurred. The countries also represent different welfare regimes: conservative (with a Christian democratic version in Germany and a statist version in France), liberal (Ireland and New Zealand), social democratic (Norway), and former communist (Slovenia). Figures 15.1 and 15.2 show trends in ECEC provision for under-3s and 3- to 5-year-olds in five of the six countries, showing how they have expanded ECEC provision for under-3s from 2005 to 2019. As these figures are from household survey data in Europe, comparable figures for New Zealand are not available; but enrollment in licensed early childhood education expanded by more than 60% for children aged 2 and under and 13% for children aged 3–5 between 2000 and 2019.[1] OECD data shows that 47.6% of children in New Zealand aged 0–2 were enrolled in services in 2018, while 94.6 children aged 3–5 were in ECEC services in 2017.[2]

What comparative measures capture quality and access? Child development specialists evaluate program quality according to structural and process measures

---

1. Author's calculation based on data from the New Zealand Ministry of Education. Note that in 2014 the system for calculating enrollment rates changed, and thus the estimate of the expansion of services should be treated as approximate.
2. OECD family policy database.

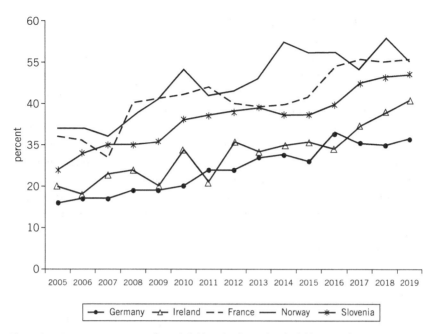

Figure 15.1 Participation rates in formal childcare and preschool, children aged 0–2.
Note. Author's calculations from EU-SILC data of children in ECEC for more than 0 hours/week.

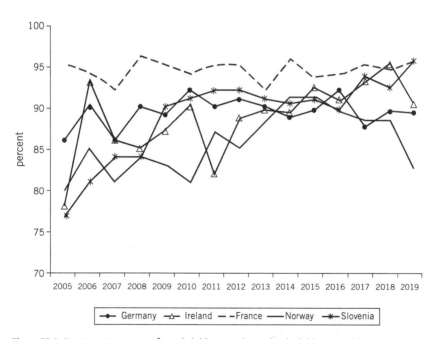

Figure 15.2 Participation rates in formal childcare and preschool, children aged 3–5.
Note. Author's calculations from EU-SILC data of children in ECEC for more than 0 hours/week.
The scale in this figure differs from that of Figure 15.1 to facilitate viewing the country trends.

(Ishimine & Tayler, 2014, p. 273; Slot, 2018). The former concept is often conveyed by child–staff ratios, maximum group size requirements, health and safety regulations, and requirements concerning staff qualifications and continuing professional development (CPD). Process quality aims to capture the nature of interactions between staff and children yet is difficult to measure cross-nationally. There is some relationship between structural and process quality: Interactions between staff and children appear better when class sizes are smaller, the ratio of children to staff is lower, and workers have higher educational qualifications and opportunities for CPD (Eurofound, 2015, pp. 18–26). Moreover, these indicators convey something about the quality of the jobs created in the ECEC sector: Lack of training, low qualification levels, and high-stress environments produce higher turnover rates and undermine the ECEC sector as a source of decent-quality jobs. These structural measures thus help capture quality levels that have ramifications for both children and staff (see Table A-15.1 in the appendix).

To compare the accessibility of services to disadvantaged populations, there are some instructive measures of outcomes, such as the gap in ECEC attendance rates according to parents' income or education level. Such measures may imperfectly capture access barriers as some families of lower socioeconomic status or from minority communities may prefer not to send their children to early education programs. However, when services are free or their cost declines, use of these services goes up, revealing the importance of price as a motivating factor for many (Ellingsæter, 2014, pp. 60–61). When services are expensive, access becomes stratified by income. Subsidies for low-income parents may broaden access, but if services remain expensive, middle-income families may struggle to afford them. In analyzing the particular cases, I will bring in information about the cost of services.

Finally, the most easily comparable indicator is spending per child: Countries that spend more on ECEC likely pay their staff better, assure wider access, and support higher-quality services. Although this does not say enough about what they spend money on, this measure nonetheless provides useful information about the commitment of public resources. Inadequately subsidized private markets of care generate poor-quality programs that are expensive for parents, putting them out of reach for lower-income people (Lloyd & Penn, 2010). As personnel costs are the dominant expense in childcare services, poorly subsidized private markets can only exist if employees receive very low wages (Morgan, 2005). For these reasons, spending per child offers evidence about the quality of services and the jobs within them.

15.3. ECEC QUALITY AND ACCESS IN EXPANSION COUNTRIES

Examining how ECEC development has occurred reveals different social investment logics. In some countries, expansion occurred alongside a commitment to quality services, decent jobs in the profession, and broad access to services. In other countries, these goals are far from being met. Before developing an explanation for these patterns, it is necessary to examine the varying social investment logics.

15.3.1. Inclusive creation and mobilization of human capital: Norway, New Zealand, and Slovenia

Norway, New Zealand, and Slovenia all have expanded their ECEC systems in ways that both mobilize and create human capital. During the first decade of the 2000s, both New Zealand and Norway achieved expanded access through either public programs or public–private partnerships that prioritized nonprofit organizations, while Slovenia's services are almost entirely public. In all three countries, a high level of provision has generally not come at the expense of the quality of the workforce and the services delivered. Moreover, in Norway and Slovenia, children from lower–socioeconomic status families have been participating in these programs in percentages comparable to those of families from higher up the socioeconomic ladder, although access in Norway has a steeper class gradient.

Norway had been a relative laggard among Nordic countries in ECEC provision. That changed during the first decade of the 2000s when governments began a massive increase in state funding for ECEC programs that promote both child development and parental employment. Between 2000 and 2013, government funds for investment and operating costs rose from 0.5% of gross domestic product to 1.4% (Engel et al., 2015, p. 30). At the same time, governments took steps to shore up the quality of the programs. In 2006, the government moved responsibility for all ECEC from the Ministry of Children and Equality to the Ministry of Education and Research and adopted a new national curriculum (Engel et al., 2015). Greater focus was put on pedagogic considerations, with an eye to cognitive development and making sure disadvantaged populations—especially immigrant and low-income families—had access to the programs (Ellingsæter, 2014, p. 55).

To foster inclusion, municipalities were required to ensure that all children have a preschool place by 2009, a ceiling was placed on parental fees, and government spending increased to cover 85% of operating costs, enabling a significant decline in the cost of services and improving access (Ellingsæter, 2014; Engel et al., 2015, p. 30). Although access to early childhood education is less stratified by socioeconomic status than in some countries (Figure 15.3), there are gaps linked to income, ethnic origin, and education. For instance, the gap in participation rates between minority-language children and the majority population is high for young children: a 30 percentage point gap for 1-year-olds, 18 percentage points for 2-year-olds, and 9 points for 3-year-olds (Engel et al., 2015, p. 40).[3] One reason for enduring stratification may lie in the fact that fees, though capped, are 15% of the cost of services, higher than in neighboring countries

---

3. The gap is still present but smaller for 4- and 5-year-old children.

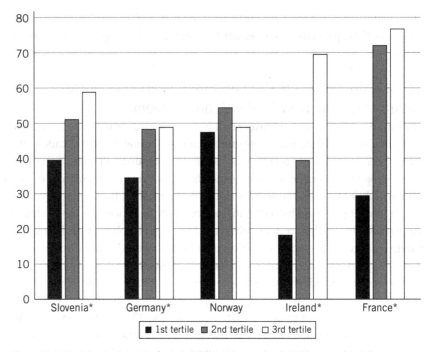

Figure 15.3 Participation rates in formal childcare or preschool, children aged 0–2, by equivalized disposable income tertile, 2019 or latest available.
Note. Unavailable for New Zealand. For countries marked with * the differences across income groups are statistically significant (*p* < 0.05). The figures are based on center-based care, organized family day care, and paid childminders, whether registered or not. The first tertile is the lowest and the third tertile, the highest.
Source. OECD Family Policy Database.

(e.g., they are 7% in Sweden), and lower-income parents generally pay a higher proportion of their income for childcare than do those with higher incomes (Engel et al., 2015, p. 40).

Although the ECEC expansion largely occurred through privately run services, which make up 50% of programs, private and public centers must follow the same requirements for staff education and teacher–child ratios and use the national curriculum (Haug, 2014, p. 374). For-profit centers, which make up a small percentage of privately owned programs, have to demonstrate that they do not compromise staff education and working conditions or educational goals (Haug, 2014, p. 375). In 2010, 96% of head teachers and 83% of pedagogues had the education required for their position, and a 2008 survey showed that the rapid expansion of programs did not erode structural quality measures (Ellingsæter, 2014, pp. 67, 69).

The expansion of childcare services in New Zealand since the start of the 2000s also occurred with a focus on improving quality, assuring decent pay and working conditions for staff, and reaching disadvantaged groups. ECEC expert

Peter Moss has lauded New Zealand for developing programs with "a broad and holistic concept of 'education-in-its-broadest-sense' in which learning and care really are inseparable and connected to many other purposes besides" (quoted in May, 2014, p. 147). Since 1986, the Department of Education oversees all ECEC services, and it follows an internationally renowned ECEC curriculum, *Te Whāriki* ("a mat for all to stand on" in Māori). In addition, New Zealand's centers have low child–staff ratios: In 2014, the average full-time equivalent number of children to staff was 3.9 for children under age 3 and 6.6 for children 3 and older, compared to the OECD averages of 8.5 and 13.8, respectively (Ministry of Education, 2016, p. 9). In center-based services, national standards require that at least 50% of staff have a recognized teaching qualification—a bachelor's degree in early education or equivalent credential. Although some governments have aspired to having 100% of staff in teacher-led ECEC services with such a credential, as of 2017 just under 69% had ECE qualifications (Ministry of Education, 2017). Programs are somewhat less adapted to parental work schedules, however: For instance, children under 3 generally are in programs, on average, 20 hours/week. The ECEC system is therefore more oriented toward creating human capital than mobilizing it.

New Zealand has taken steps to draw in children from disadvantaged backgrounds. An equity funding measure since 2002 delivers higher subsidies to programs serving low-income families, and in 2007, the government instituted 20 hours of free care for all 3- and 4-year-old children, producing a 32% drop in the cost of services in 2007 (May, 2014, p. 157). There remain some disparities, although they are less stark than in the past. A 2017 national survey of childcare use found that for children whose parents' annual income was $30,000 or less, 55% were in some kind of formal care arrangement[4] compared to 59% for those earning $70,000–$10,000 and 79% of those earning $100,001–$150,000. There also are gaps by ethnic origin: 70% of European-origin children were in some type of formal childcare compared to 66% of Māori children, 53% of Pacific peoples, and 54% of Asian-origin children.[5]

Slovenia also expanded ECEC in an inclusive, human capital–creating way. Slovenia built upon its existing system—inherited from the communist era—of both public funding and provision in a unified model of education and care (Kaga et al., 2010). The programs are under the ambit of the education ministry, and all children are entitled to a full-time place by the age of 11 months, although not all municipalities have succeeded in providing this (Schreyer & Oberhuemer, 2018b, p. 1067). Enrollment has rapidly expanded in recent years,

---

4. Formal ECE refers to childcare centers, public kindergartens, play centers, *Kōhanga reo* ("language nests," which aim to promote the Māori language), play groups, and organized home-based care.

5. A 2009–2010 national survey of childcare use found that for families earning $20,000 or less, 39.6% of children aged 0–6 were in formal childcare compared to 68.6% of those whose parents earned over $70,000 a year (Statistics New Zealand, 2010, p. 4).

and extensive subsidies keep the programs affordable: All approved public and private providers can receive subsidies worth around 80% of costs per child (Formánková & Dobrotić, 2011, p. 417; Stropnik & Šircelj, 2008, p. 1044). The average cost for a kindergarten place is €140/month, but municipalities determine fees based on income (Formánková & Dobrotić, 2011, p. 417; Vidmar, 2015, p. 315): Parents in the lowest income group pay nothing, while the maximum ranges from €450 to €500 for 3- to 6-year-olds and from €350 to €450 for under-3s (Schreyer & Oberhuemer, 2018b, p. 1069). Given the general accessibility of services, Slovenia has a relatively small gap in ECEC participation according to income gradient (Figure 15.3).

Although private actors have, since the 1990s, been allowed to operate programs and receive public funding, and some nonprofit associations have stepped in to run such services, 96% of children are enrolled in public services (OECD, 2016a, p. 7; Stropnik, 2001). Staff are highly qualified: Preschool teachers have a college degree and often are assisted by someone with an upper secondary–level education in early childhood education, and CPD is required (Vidmar, 2015, p. 314). Most positions are full-time and permanent contracts, with salaries close to the average salary (Humer & Hrzenjak, 2016). Moreover, the average child–staff ratio is one of the lowest in the OECD (OECD, 2016a, p. 7). An overarching curriculum applies to the entire age group. These various features ensure that ECE centers are "homogeneously of high quality—at least in terms of structural quality," while measures of process quality are high yet more variable (Vidmar, 2015, p. 315).

15.3.2. France and Germany: Mixed models in quality and stratification

France is often held up as an ECEC pioneer and role model because of its universally available, publicly funded (and largely publicly provided) preschool education that starts at the age of 3.[6] The system has deep historical roots and is well entrenched as a foundation of the education system, being staffed by teachers who receive training and pay identical to that of teachers in primary schools (Morgan, 2006).[7] A national curriculum guides the activities and orientations of the preschools.[8] These programs do not match the workday, but combined with after-school care (which is widely available), they can help foster parental employment. They cost relatively little to parents (who pay for after-school care and lunchroom costs), and as nearly 100% of children aged 3–5 attend them,

---

6. A small number of children aged 2 to 2 and a half also attend preschools.
7. The highly trained staff has long been given as a rationale for the high child–teacher ratios in preschools. However, some have questioned the quality of these programs given that high ratio.
8. Some criticize the curriculum for being excessively focused on formal school preparation and the lack of teacher training geared toward the specific needs of this age group. See Agacinski and Collombet (2018).

disparities of access are small. In 2019, the mandatory school age was lowered from 6 to 3.

However, services for children under the age of 3—*crèches* (childcare centers), *assistantes maternelles* (family day care), and the like—have taken a different trajectory. Although *crèches* are not educational institutions, since 2000 they have been required to develop educational and social plans and report on how they intend to meet these objectives (Fagnani, 2014, p. 89). Historically, the *crèches* were created to address concerns about infant mortality and were staffed by trained personnel. However, as demand for these programs grew with rising rates of mothers' workforce participation, governments have repeatedly sought to promote cheaper forms of care—most notably through licensed and subsidized home-based care (*assistantes maternelles*). Moreover, many low-income parents also rely on a low, flat-rate benefit available for those caring for their own children under the age of 3. These benefits for parents (largely mothers) to care for children at home have been justified in the name of providing parents "free choice" in matters of child care, but given the low benefit and lack of available childcare, these policies instead reinforce income and gender inequalities by drawing low-income women out of the workforce (Jenson & Sineau, 2003).

The expansion of ECEC places since the first decade of the 2000s has been largely through home-based care, with implications for the quality, quality of employment, and access for lower–socioeconomic status groups (Figure 15.4). Moreover, while previously many 2-year-old children attended the *école maternelle*, this dropped from 35% in 2002 to 11.5% in 2015, while the supply of other center-based forms of care grew at a slow pace (Collombet et al., 2017, p. 3). Home-based caregivers generally lack educational qualifications and are not required to have any, beyond 120 hours of training before beginning in this role—training that is said to be generally "inadequate and ad hoc" (Vandenbroeck & Bauters, 2017, p. 183). In 2005, 49% were found to not have "any qualification," while 35% had "very low qualifications" (Fagnani, 2014, p. 89). Government policies to improve remuneration expanded the number of children allowed in home-care arrangements from three to four (Fagnani, 2014, p. 94), thus potentially further undermining quality.

Current policy also does not assure broad access, thereby augmenting stratification in access. Even with subsidies, home care fees are much higher than those for the public centers that are in short supply and distributed unequally across the territory (Observatoire de la petite enfance, 2019, pp. 23, 34). Income-based stratification in access to ECEC services is therefore very large (Figure 15.3). The gap reflects the low availability of public *crèches* and the fact that home care programs are more expensive than the *crèches* and thus often out of reach for lower-income families.[9]

---

9. There also is a tax subsidy for parents who hire individuals to care for children in their own home. This subsidy is received by only a small percentage of generally wealthy families.

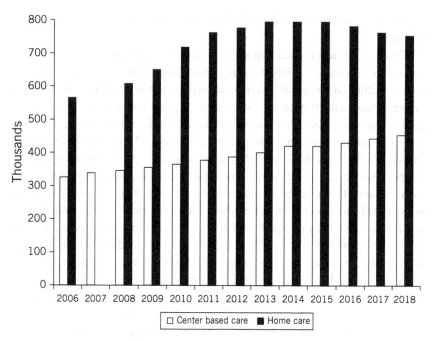

Figure 15.4 Places in French center-based and home-based care (thousands) for under-3s, 2006–2018.

Note. The data covers metropolitan France and overseas departments. Comparable data for individual care in 2007 is not available.

Source. Observatoire de la petite enfance, various years.

Germany also significantly expanded its ECEC system starting in the 1990s and accelerating after 2000—a reversal from its past policy orientation of encouraging parental (mostly maternal) care of young children and part-day programs for preschoolers. Among the policy rationales driving the expansion since 2005 were promoting work–family reconciliation, bolstering the fertility rate, and responding to the "Pisa shock"—the revelation by the OECD's Programme for International Student Assessment that German youth had comparatively poor educational outcomes, especially for those of migrant origins (Oberhuemer, 2014, pp. 121–122). Federal government funding thus sought to stimulate growth in ECEC places, and provision rapidly expanded, mostly under public or private nonprofit auspices (Leu & Schelle, 2009, p. 6; Oberhuemer, 2014, p. 127).[10] In contrast to France, most of the expansion has been in centers rather than home-based care. Significant regional variation in program policies reflects historical factors—for instance, the eastern regions built upon the well-developed ECEC programs they inherited from the communist era—and significant authority given to the *Länder* in this area.

10. Only 1.7% of providers are non-corporate, for-profit entities.

Table 15.1 Percentage of children in early childhood centers and publicly subsidized family day care, 2012

Percentages	Under 3			3 to under 6		
	Total	With migration background	Without migration background	Total	With migration background	Without migration background
Germany	28	16	33	93	87	96
Western Länder	22	15	26	93	89	95
Eastern Länder	49	26	53	96	74	100

Note. "Migration background" = at least one parent of foreign origin.
Source. Oberhuemer (2014).

Germany is one of the few OECD countries that mandates access to ECEC provision at an early age (OECD, 2016b, p. 3): A 2009 childcare law required that all 1- and 2-year-old children whose parents request it have access to a place by 2013. In 2017, just over 30% of children under the age of 3 were in ECEC services, as were 87% of 3- to 5-year-olds. There remain some gaps in access based on socioeconomic status: A national study from 2012 found large disparities in access to programs based on one's migration origins (Table 15.1). However, the income gradient is much lower than in France (Figure 15.3). As in France, Germany also offers a subsidy for parents to "choose" caring for their own children at home. As in France, the lack of fully available services for under-3s and the possibility of receiving this low payment tend to augment class inequalities in women's workforce participation.

All services for children below school age (5 or 6, depending on the *Länder*) are under the ambit of the Federal Ministry of Family Affairs, Senior Citizens, Women and Youth. However, unlike many other countries that mandate a particular curriculum, some of the *Länder* have only non-binding guidelines for these programs (OECD, 2016b, p. 6). Moreover, according to Rauschenbach and Riedel (2015, pp. 1–2), Germany has been "one of the few countries in Europe where ECEC professionals are not trained at universities," and thus staff "have remained out of touch with the processes of increasing scientification and the upgrading of qualifications undergone by other professions since the 1960s and were unaffected by the wave of academization that swept numerous professions in the social and educational sectors at that time." As a result, some specialists have raised concern about the quality of these programs. A national study on childcare quality in 2009 found that 80% of centers it evaluated were mediocre, and less than 10% were ranked as being of good quality, with centers in the East of lower quality than those in Western *Länder* (Oberhuemer, 2014, p. 139). A 2018 law aims to improve the situation by making up to €5.5 billion available to the *Länder* between 2019 and 2022, with the states choosing from a toolkit of quality-enhancing measures in return for federal funds.[11] Qualifications for core staff also have been upgraded from a non-tertiary to a university-level degree.

15.3.3. Targeted social investment falling short on quality: Ireland

Among the countries examined here, Ireland has invested the least in service expansion and ranks lowest on many measures of quality and inclusion. After having minimal policy with regard to early childhood programs, change began in the late 1990s, justified in part by social investment objectives (Wolfe et al., 2013, p. 192). Between 2000 and 2006, Irish governments tapped the European Regional Development Fund to provide capital grants for childcare, leading the supply of places to nearly double.[12] An additional, yet still inadequate, staffing grant sought to subsidize personnel costs in these centers, and the National Childcare Investment Fund took over for the EU program between 2006 and 2010 (Devitt, 2016, p. 231). To help parents with the cost, the government increased the child benefit in the early 2000s and added an Early Childcare Supplement (ECS) in 2006—a universal benefit that allowed the government to avoid choosing between support for parental and non-parental care (Wolfe et al., 2013, p. 198).[13] In 2009, the supplement was replaced with a year of free preschool (3 hours/day for 38 weeks)—a measure equal to only 35% of the cost of the ECS, thereby saving the government money during the financial crisis; and a new National Childcare Investment Program replaced the older staffing grant with a subsidy for childcare providers to cover the costs of parents on welfare who are using the services (Wolfe et al., 2013, p. 197). In September 2016, a new measure came into effect that expands the entitlement to 3 hours/day of free care, and starting in October 2019, an Affordable Childcare Scheme offers demand-side subsidies for families earning up to €60,000 a year. Providers of ECEC services are private, with 70% being for-profit and the rest nonprofit organizations (Schreyer & Oberhuemer, 2018a, p. 578).

Despite the increased investment in ECEC, there remain problems of quality, quality of jobs, and access. Until 2010, there were no educational requirements for personnel working with younger children, and even those responsible for running ECEC programs faced no educational requirements and were not required to have professional experience in ECEC or training to do it (Eurydice & Eurostat, 2014, pp. 100–101, 111, 113). That started to change in 2010, when governments began

---

11. The *Gesetz zur Weiterentwicklung der Qualität und zur Teilhabe in der Kindertagesbertreuung*, or Gute-KiTa-Gesetz.

12. In 1999–2000, there were 56,803 children aged 0–12 in childcare, including 37,619 3- to 6-year-olds (23.6% of the age group) and 12,515 1- to 3-year-olds (12.8%), and 2337 under 1 (4.8%) (ADM, 2000, p. 41).

13. The total benefit per child under 6 was therefore €2800/year, 5 times what it had been in 1999 (Wolfe et al., 2013, p. 198).

requiring progressively higher standards for room leaders and assistant staff.[14] As of 2017, all room leaders must have at least vocational qualifications that do not require bachelor's degree–level work. A higher capitation payment is available to services in which the room leader has a bachelor's degree (usually following 3 years' education) and assistants have a vocational qualification (Pobal, 2016, p. 78). However, pay in this sector is low: A 2016 study found hourly pay rates to range from €10.27 to €13.28, compared to the average industrial wage of €21.46 (Duignan, 2018, p. 571).

Studies of ECEC quality have found many services deficient (Devitt, 2016, p. 232). The system is largely market-driven, with limited attempts to plan provision (Wolfe et al., 2013, p. 194). Only parents from some disadvantaged families benefit from public funding (beyond the 1 year of free 3 hours/day free care for 3- and 4-year-olds), and costs of ECEC are some of the highest in Europe (Wolfe et al., 2013, p. 194). Implications for access according to income level can be seen in Figure 15.3. A 2013 study also highlighted the social class stratification of access to services, with the proportion of children in center-based childcare highest for children of professional/managerial households (34%) and lower for other groups (26% in non-manual households, 16% in skilled manual/ semi- or unskilled, and 24% in households that never worked or are unclassified) (Murray et al., 2016, p. 118). This class stratification extends to women's employment as the negative impact of childcare cost on employment is greater for lower–socioeconomic status women, whose households pay more on childcare relative to income than do those higher up in the income distribution (Russell et al., 2018).

15.4. EXPLAINING THE DIFFERENT SOCIAL INVESTMENT LOGICS OF ECEC PROVISION

Why do these expansionary ECEC policies vary in their social investment logics? Institutional and partisan factors have shaped the kinds of protagonists involved in these reforms. Where education ministries oversee ECEC services, they and their unionized allies are important advocates for inclusion and quality services. Left political parties also push for programs that both mobilize and create human capital. Together, these two factors have shaped whether or not the expansion of ECEC has occurred while also promoting quality programs, quality of the work environment, and broad-based access.

15.4.1. Institutions: Bureaucratic auspices

One of the most significant determinants of ECEC programs being oriented toward the related goals of promoting quality services and quality of the work

---

14. About half of the staff are room leaders (Pobal, 2016, p. 74).

environment for staff is whether programs are overseen by education ministries. Research generally shows that lodging all services for young children in one bureaucratic home improves access, quality, and the status/conditions of employment (OECD, 2017, pp. 64–65). Moreover, it is important to have these programs under education ministries that prioritize their educational content, often by requiring that they adhere to a coherent curriculum. In addition, education ministries can be potent actors in domestic politics—they are responsible for one of the largest spending items in the budget, one that ultimately touches on every member of society. Related to this, teachers' unions are influential actors in industrial relations, particularly given the decline of blue-collar unions. Thus, having ECEC programs located in educational ministries and their staff covered by teachers' unions helps protect these programs from cuts and puts powerful protagonists behind them who can push for higher pay for staff and improved working conditions.

The six cases examined in this chapter offer support for these arguments. In New Zealand, Norway, and Slovenia, all programs are the responsibility of education ministries. New Zealand brought its programs under the education ministry in 1986, Slovenia did so in 1993, and Norway made a similar shift in 2006. This meant that educational objectives pushed from within these ministries influenced the ECEC expansion. It also helped ensure either that staff would have comparable pay and working conditions to teachers in the primary education system (as in Slovenia) or that the failure to align these professions would become a source of political debate and pressure (as in New Zealand). As Humer and Hrzenjak (2016) remark about ECEC staff in Slovenia, "Although public childcare is an exceedingly feminized field of work, employees have secondary or tertiary degrees, most have full-time and permanent contracts, and their salary is close to the average salary in Slovenia. Teachers in public kindergartens are unionized and have a strong public voice." By contrast, Irish and German programs are entirely under welfare ministries, and France's ECEC system is divided between education (for 3- to 6-year-olds) and family/social welfare (for children under 3).

In fact, France illustrates the differing political dynamics in the two sectors. Since the 1980s, economic slowdown and high unemployment resulted in austerity policies that have either cut welfare state programs or stalled their expansion. The public *crèches* have fallen victim to these forces: Because of high staff qualifications and other regulations designed to promote high-quality programs, successive governments have found them too expensive to develop into a universally available service (Jenson & Sineau, 2003). The staff and their union allies have been unable to prevail against these pressures, and thus while the quality of these programs has been maintained, much of the ECEC expansion since the 1980s has been in home childcare or other types of centers (such as *micro-crèches* and *crèches familiales*), where regulatory requirements are lower.

By contrast, the *écoles maternelles* have stronger political allies. The Education Ministry is a strong force in domestic politics, with education being the single largest item in the public budget.[15] Moreover, although unionization rates have dropped among teachers, they remain higher than those of other workers (Dobbins, 2017). That said, budgetary austerity has also hit the educational sector in recent years, with one consequence being a declining willingness of preschools to accept children under the age of 3. In so doing, the costs of caring for these younger children have shifted to the family insurance funds and contributed to the growing reliance on the less skilled *assistantes maternelles* (Périvier, 2015, p. 125). The shift of under-3s away from the system also reflects a gradual move since the 1970s to draw the preschools closer into the education system and further from being a mode of care (Garnier, 2011). However, budgetary means have not fully kept up, spurring critiques about the high child–teacher ratio in these programs and the need for increased spending (Agacinski & Collombet, 2018).

In New Zealand, not only are ECEC programs under the Department of Education but teachers' unions also have incorporated ECEC staff. Prior to the 1980s, early childhood education had been viewed as distinct from the education system, but union organizing of childcare workers during the 1980s and 1990s helped bridge the gap between this workforce and kindergarten teachers (May, 2007, p. 136). In 1994, the childcare workers' union merged with the main teachers' union, creating the New Zealand Educational Institute—*Te Riu Roa*—one of the largest unions in the country and the main union for pre-primary, primary, and secondary school workers. The union worked to align the salaries of primary school teachers with those of secondary school teachers and then to do the same for kindergarten teachers. In 2004, it negotiated a pay parity deal for teachers in early childhood education settings.

By contrast, the fact that ECEC services largely are under social welfare departments in Ireland and Germany helps explain why the ECEC expansion in those countries has not been done in a way that is as supportive of high-quality social investment. Ireland's ECEC system for children below age 4 is under the Department of Children and Youth Affairs, while the Department of Education and Skills is responsible for primary education, which is classified as starting at age 4 (Eurydice & Eurostat, 2014, p. 191). Germany has a long tradition of subsidiarity in the social welfare sector, whereby local governments contract with nonprofit associations in order to deliver services in the youth and welfare sectors. The expansion of ECEC in the first decade of the 2000s largely came through similar arrangements, rather than challenging them. And while there has been much discussion in Germany of

15. This does not include the social security funds.

the need to improve educational requirements for those working in ECEC services, subsidiarity and federalism may help explain the failure to upgrade qualifications as these are left largely for *Land* governments to determine (Haasler & Gottschall, 2015, p. 84).

15.4.2. Actors: Left parties

The case studies also generally reveal that having left parties in power has shaped how ECEC expansions took place. Left parties are not solely responsible for promoting expansions of ECEC: In the 21st century, conservative and centrist parties also have been willing to direct resources toward these programs (Morgan, 2013). Yet they operate with a particular set of motivations or political constraints. Some of these parties have religious roots and continue to have social conservatives as an important voting bloc, leading them to favor policies supportive of mothers caring for children at home. Even as they may attempt to reach out to new constituencies—younger people, working parents, and the like—they often face countervailing pressures from their traditional support base. They are therefore more inclined toward compromise measures, such as more generous care leave benefits, that divert resources away from greater investments in ECEC and thereby reinforce class and gender inequalities. Other center-right parties hold a liberal market orientation, and thus prefer to deploy public resources in a way that maximizes private, and especially for-profit, services. Yet this likely works against the objectives of shoring up quality, particularly as for-profit childcare providers often skimp on staff pay and qualifications to maximize profits. More generally, liberal market–oriented political forces tend to espouse an economistic version of the social investment model that focuses on the hoped-for "output" of higher productivity and economic growth through targeted spending.

Left parties view ECEC from another perspective. Today, these parties most commonly have within their voting constituencies working women, educated strata, young people, public sector workers, and unionized workers more generally (Morgan, 2013). As a result, these parties tend to favor direct public spending on ECEC services or else funding that goes toward well-subsidized nonprofit organizations. Their union backers push for decent wages and working conditions. And their traditional concern for the well-being of disadvantaged populations makes them mindful of accessibility to a wider swath of the electorate rather than to the wealthier voting blocs who likely vote for the center-right. In other words, it is left parties that put the "social" in social investment.

We can see these different left–right orientations playing out in the country cases. In Slovenia, for instance, during the transition away from communism in the 1990s, there were strong political debates over the future of family policy. Some advocated a familialist system that would enable mothers to care for young children at home, while others called for maintaining the existing parental leave system—which had been modeled after the Swedish one (Korintus & Stropnik, 2009, pp. 150–151)—as well as the established infrastructure of ECEC services (Formánková & Dobrotić, 2011). Conservative parties favored the former direction, with some proposing a 3-year paid leave. Yet, ultimately, pushback by center-left parties, as well as various organized groups such as employers, prevented this development (Formánková & Dobrotić, 2011, p. 417). Then, throughout the first decade of the 2000s, the period when ECEC services expanded, Slovenia was governed by either center-left governments or mixed center-right/center-left governments.

In New Zealand, even as left and right parties came to agree on the need for ECEC development, they have differed in *how* this should be done, with the National Party often favoring demand-side subsidies and for-profit programs, while the Labour Party has pushed for supply-side subsidies that promote non-profit services and been more attentive to workforce, pay, and training issues. Many of the most significant moves with regard to quality, access, and the quality of employment have been made under Labour governments. In 1986, a Labour government brought early childhood education programs under the Education Ministry, while another Labour government that came to power in 1999 sought to improve availability and affordability of services while also ramping up staff qualifications (Mitchell, 2015, p. 293). The government set a goal of having all staff in teacher-led services meet requirements for educational qualifications by 2012 and instituted a system of subsidies whereby centers with higher proportions of qualified staff would receive more funding.

When a conservative government returned to power in 2008, however, it dropped the word "free" from the promised 20 hours of free care and sought to target spending toward the most disadvantaged families (May, 2014; Mitchell, 2015, p. 294). The government also reduced targets for staffing qualifications (the goal now being that 80% of staff working with children over age 2 and 50% of those working with children below the age of 2 have a teacher qualification), eliminated funding for professional development, and lowered government subsidies for centers with higher proportions of qualified staff (May, 2014, pp. 156–157; Mitchell, 2015, p. 294). Maximum sizes for centers also were doubled (Mitchell, 2015, p. 294). The overall structure of the ECEC system was preserved yet with less emphasis on universalism and quality.

Norway also has long had a left–right divide on ECEC. Conservative parties resisted policies to encourage paid work by mothers of young children, and a center-right government created a cash-for-care benefit in 1998 to support parents caring for children under the age of 3 (Leira, 1998). However, in 2003 the opposition (which included the Labour Party) was key to the development of a compromise among all the parties on childcare (Ellingsæter et al., 2017, p. 154), leading ultimately to passage of the Kindergarten Act in 2005. In 2006, a left-leaning government returned to power, which augmented funding for ECEC in an effort to achieve "full coverage" (Ellingsæter et al., 2017, p. 154). Greater focus was put on pedagogy, with an eye to both children's cognitive development and making sure that disadvantaged populations—especially immigrant and low-income families—had access to these programs (Ellingsæter, 2014, p. 55).

In line with the latter goals, in 2012, a red–green government abolished the cash-for-care leave for children aged 2, in part because of concerns that low-income and minority children were not entering preschool due to this policy (Ellingsæter, 2014, p. 58). Instead, the government placed a mandate on municipalities to assure that all children have a place in preschool by 2009 and instituted reforms to cap parental fees and increase government spending on these programs (Ellingsæter, 2014). In short, although left and right parties broadly have agreed on the need to expand the ECEC system, center-left governments have played an essential role in promoting high-quality social investment during a time of rapid growth.

Where conservative parties have held the reins of government during ECEC expansions, they have been less committed to supply-side policies that would assure higher-quality and more broadly accessible services. In France, both socialist and conservative governments have encouraged the development of family day care over the public *crèches*, but many of the policies most supportive of this sector have come under conservative governments. The latter also have been most favorable to subsidizing parents who stay at home to care for their children during the first 3 years. These policies divert resources away from public services while also undermining the labor force attachment of the women who accept these subsidies. Many are lower-income mothers whose connection to the labor market may already be marginal. Similar policies to encourage lower-income mothers to become home day care operators do not provide a pathway toward stable, high-quality employment but instead one of marginal wages and limited future opportunities.

In Germany, the expansion of ECEC services in the first decade of the 2000s largely took place under Christian democratic or grand coalition governments, yet the Christian Democratic Union/Christian Social Union has been subject to cross-pressures from socially conservative constituents and party members (see also Chapter 3 in Volume II [Garritzmann et al., 2022]). One result was the decision to allow single-earner families to receive a monthly benefit for 14 months, no matter their level of income. A second move came, after 2009 elections led to the Social Democratic Party's (SPD) exit from the government, with the adoption of a flat-rate monthly benefit for parents of 1- and 2-year-olds who "choose" to care for their children at home rather than use the childcare space to which they are entitled (Morgan, 2013, pp. 98–99).[16] With

16. After a federal court quashed the latter subsidy as something that should be left to state governments, some such as Bavaria began offering the benefit.

the SPD back in the coalition and in control of labor, social affairs, and family ministries, it has been able to shape laws such as the aforementioned "Good Day Care Act" that directs more money toward ECEC quality improvements (David & Stark, 2018, p. 105).

Further evidence of the continued influence of socially conservative forces can be found at the subnational level. Even though the federal government has prioritized expanding ECEC services, *Land*-level governments play a major role in determining how public resources are spent (Busemeyer & Seitzl, 2018). Thus, as several studies have shown, subnational differences in ECEC systems are related to the partisan composition of *Land* governments, with left party participation predictive of higher spending (Busemeyer & Seitzl, 2018) and enrollment rates (Andronescu & Carnes, 2015).

In Ireland, center-right governments were behind much of the ECEC expansion during the first decade of the 2000s yet tended to do so haltingly, through the promotion of private services, and with minimal public investment. Irish childcare policy was slow to take off at all—a reflection of the influence of both Catholic social conservatism and economic liberalism that had produced minimal family support policies as a whole (Devitt, 2016, p. 219). This began to change in the late 1990s and early 2000s, largely owing to labor shortages and growing awareness that educated women in paid work helped sustain the economic boom (Weishaupt, 2009). By the late 1990s, a center-right government sought to encourage the development of childcare services without riling up its social conservative supporters. As a result, their initial policies targeted childcare support to the disadvantaged while pouring public resources into an expanded universal child benefit that did nothing to help develop the supply of services (Weishaupt, 2009). Faced with pressure by a large array of organized interests, including both labor unions and employer groups, a center-right government then instituted a more significant reform in the 2006 national Child Care Investment Program. Yet by the end of the government's term, the economic crisis had set in, producing austerity measures and some retrenchment in these policies. Only with the shift to a center-left government in 2011 would there be a renewed commitment to ECEC, including some of the staff quality-promoting measures noted in this chapter. Even so, the Irish system still has a long way to travel to promote inclusive and high-quality social investment.

15.5. CONCLUSION

This chapter aimed to move beyond the tendency of welfare state scholars to study cross-national trends in ECEC policy largely in terms of levels of provision and adaptability to the needs of working parents. Social investment can follow distinct logics, depending on whether policy interventions not only mobilize (women's) human capital but also shape the development of human capital through quality programs. Good-quality ECEC services also depend on a staff that has strong educational qualifications, decent pay, prospects for professional training and development, and reasonable working conditions. Not all countries aim at promoting broad access to services as some instead target interventions toward the poor, while others produce access that is stratified by income. All of these elements of ECEC systems are complicated to study cross-nationally, which likely explains why comparative scholars often neglect them.

Explaining different logics of social investment in ECEC requires analysis of both institutional context and the key protagonists involved in pushing policy change. Where ECEC programs are bureaucratically located influences how reforms have unfolded. In countries with unified systems under education ministries, all programs tend to have a strong educational orientation. The institutional home also shapes protagonists: Education ministries tend to have a good bit of power in politics, as do the unionized teachers who work in this sector. These actors often work to protect the pay and working conditions of ECEC staff. Another vitally important set of actors are social democratic or labor parties, which are more inclined than conservative or liberal parties to pursue ECEC expansions promoting high-quality, inclusive social investment. Even as conservative parties have abandoned a lot of their earlier reticence or opposition to mothers' employment and become supporters of ECEC, they often resist expanding these programs in ways that not only promote mothers' employment but also foster a quality working environment for staff and broadly accessible, high-quality services for children.

REFERENCES

ADM. (2000). *National Childcare Census Report Baseline Data 1999–2000*. Dublin: Area Development Management Ltd.

Agacinski, D., & Collombet, C. (2018). *Un nouvel âge pour l'école maternelle?* (Note d'analyse 66). France stratégie.

Andronescu, C. G., & Carnes, M. E. (2015). Value coalitions and policy change: The impact of gendered patterns of work, religion and partisanship on childcare policy across German states. *Journal of European Social Policy*, *25*(2), 159–174.

Blome, A. (2017). *The politics of work–family policy reforms in Germany and Italy*. Routledge.

Bonoli, G., & Reber, F. (2010). The political economy of childcare in OECD countries: Explaining cross-national variation in spending and coverage rates. *European Journal of Political Research*, *49*(1), 97–118.

Busemeyer, M. R., & Seitzl, L. (2018). The partisan politics of early childhood education in the German *Länder*. *Journal of Public Policy*, 38(2), 243–274. https://doi.org/10.1017/S0143814X16000313

Collombet, C., Maigne, G., & Palier, B. (2017). *Places en crèche: Pourquoi l'Allemagne fait-elle mieux que la France depuis dix ans?* (Note d'analyse 56). France stratégie.

David, D., & Stark, H. (2018). Cinquante ans après mai 68: Ou en sont les gauches en France et an Allemagne? *Allemagne d'aujourd'hui*, 226, 100–110.

Devitt, C. (2016). Mothers or migrants? Labor supply policies in Ireland 1997–2007. *Social Politics*, 23(2), 214–238.

Dobbins, M. (2017). Teacher unionism in France: Making fundamental reforms an impossible quest? In T. M. Moe & S. Wiborg (Eds.), *The comparative politics of education: Teachers unions and education systems around the world* (pp. 87–113). Cambridge University Press.

Duignan, M. (2018). Ireland—ECEC workforce profile. In P. Oberhuemer & I. Schreyer (Eds.), *Early childhood workforce profiles in 30 countries with key contextual data* (pp. 555–575). Systems of Early Education and Professionalisation-Revised (SEEPRO-R). www.seepro.eu/ISBN-publication.pdf

Ellingsæter, A. L. (2014). Towards universal quality early childhood education and care: The Norwegian model. In L. Gambaro, K. Stewart, & J. Waldfogel (Eds.), *An equal start? Providing quality early education and care for disadvantaged children* (pp. 53–76). Policy Press.

Ellingsæter, A. L., Kitterød, R. H., & Lyngstad, J. (2017). Universalizing childcare, changing mothers' attitudes: Policy feedback in Norway. *Journal of Social Policy*, 46(1), 149–173.

Engel, A., Barnett, W. S., Anders, Y., & Taguma, M. (2015). *Early childhood education and care policy review: Norway*. Organisation for Economic Co-operation and Development.

Eurofound. (2015). *Early childhood care: Accessibility and quality of services*. Publications Office of the European Union.

Eurydice & Eurostat. (2014). *Key data on early childhood education and care in Europe: 2014 edition* (Eurydice and Eurostat Report). https://ec.europa.eu/eurostat/documents/3217494/5785249/EC-01-14-484-EN.PDF/cbdf1804-a139-43a9-b8f1-ca5223eea2a1

Fagnani, J. (2014). Equal access to quality care: Lessons from France on providing high-quality and affordable early childhood education and care. In L. Gambaro, K. Stewart, & J.e Waldfogel (Eds.), *An equal start? Providing quality early education and care for disadvantaged children* (pp. 77–99). Policy Press.

Ferragina, E., & Seeleib-Kaiser, M. (2015). Determinants of a silent (r)evolution: Understanding the expansion of family policy in rich OECD countries. *Social Politics*, 22(1), 1–37.

Fleckenstein, T., & Lee, C. S. (2014). The politics of postindustrial social policy: Family policy reforms in Britain, Germany, South Korea, and Sweden. *Comparative Political Studies, 47*(4), 601–630.

Formánková, L., & Dobrotić, I. (2011). Mothers or institutions? How women work and care in Slovenia and the Czech Republic. *Journal of Contemporary European Studies, 19*(3), 409–427.

Gambaro, L., Stewart, K., & Waldfogel, J. (Eds.). (2014). Introduction. In L. Gambaro, K. Stewart, & J.e Waldfogel (Eds.), *An equal start? Providing quality early education and care for disadvantaged children* (pp. 1–28). Policy Press.

Garnier, P. (2011). The scholarization of the French *école maternelle*: Institutional transformations since the 1970s. *European Early Childhood Education Research Journal, 19*(4), 553–563.

Garritzmann, J. L., Häusermann, S., & Palier, B. (Eds.). (2022). *The world politics of social investment: Vol. II. The politics of varying social investment strategies.* Oxford University Press.

Haasler, S. R., & Gottschall, K. (2015). Still a perfect model? The gender impact of vocational training in Germany. *Journal of Vocational Education & Training, 67*(1), 78–92.

Haug, P. (2014). The public–private partnerships in ECEC provision in Norway. *European Early Childhood Education Research Journal, 22*(3), 366–378.

Humer, Z., & Hrzenjak, M. (2016). Socialization of childcare in Slovenia and its impact on informal care markets. *Laboratorium, 8*(3), 52–67.

Ishimine, K., & Tayler, C. (2014). Assessing quality in early childhood education and care. *European Journal of Education Research, Development and Policy, 49*(2), 272–290.

Jenson, J., & Sineau, M. (2003). Reconciling republican equality with "freedom of choice." In J. Jenson & M. Sineau (Eds.), *Who cares? Women's work, childcare, and welfare state redesign* (pp. 88–117). University of Toronto Press.

Kaga, Y., Bennett, J., & Moss, P. (2010). *Caring and learning together: A cross-national study of integration of early childhood care and education within education.* UNESCO.

Korintus, M., & Stropnik, N. (2009). Hungary and Slovenia: Long leave or short? In S. B. Kamerman & P. Moss (Eds.), *The politics of parental leave policies* (pp. 135–157). Policy Press.

Leira, A. (1998). Caring as social right: Cash for child care and daddy leave. *Social Politics, 5*(3), 362–378.

Leu, H. R., & Schelle, R. (2009). Between education and care? Critical reflections on early childhood policies in Germany. *Early Years, 29*(1), 5–18.

Lloyd, E., & Penn, H. (2010). Why do childcare markets fail? Comparing England and the Netherlands. *Public Policy Research, 17*(1), 42–48.

May, H. (2007). "Minding," "working," "teaching": Childcare in Aotearoa/ New Zealand, 1940s–2000s. *Contemporary Issues in Early Childhood*, 8(2), 133–143.

May, H. (2014). New Zealand: A narrative of shifting policy directions for early childhood education and care. In L. Gambaro, K. Stewart, & J. Waldfogel (Eds.), *An equal start? Providing quality early education and care for disadvantaged children* (pp. 147–170). Policy Press.

Melhuish, E. (2015). *Provision of quality early childcare services* [Discussion paper]. Early Childcare Services, Czech Republic. https://ec.europa.eu/social/BlobServlet?docId=14879&langId=en

Ministry of Education. (2016). *How does New Zealand's education system compare? OECD's education at a glance 2016*. https://www.educationcounts.govt.nz/__data/assets/pdf_file/0011/176528/Education-at-a-Glance-2016-New-Zealand-Summary-Report.pdf

Ministry of Education. (2017). *The national picture: What does the ECE census 2017 tell us about ECE teaching staff?* https://www.educationcounts.govt.nz/__data/assets/pdf_file/0003/184557/ECE-Summary-page-Teaching-staff.pdf

Mitchell, L. (2015). Shifting directions in ECEC policy in New Zealand: From a child rights to an interventionist approach. *International Journal of Early Years Education*, 23(3), 288–302.

Morel, N., Palier, B., & Palme, J. (2012). Beyond the welfare state as we knew it? In N. Morel, B. Palier, & Jo. Palme (Eds.), *Towards a social investment welfare state? Ideas, policies and challenges* (pp. 1–30). Policy Press.

Morgan, K. J. (2005). The "production" of child care: How labor markets shape social policy and vice versa. *Social Politics*, 12(2), 243–263.

Morgan, K. J. (2006). *Working mothers and the welfare state: Religion and the politics of work–family policies in western Europe and the United States*. Stanford University Press.

Morgan, K. J. (2013). Path shifting of the welfare state: Electoral competition and the expansion of work–family policies in western Europe. *World Politics*, 65(1), 73–115.

Murray, A., McGinnity, F., & Russell, H. (2016). Inequalities in access to early care and education in Ireland. In J. Williams, E. Nixon, E. Smyth, & D.y Watson (Eds.), *Cherishing all the children equally? Ireland 100 years on from the Easter rising* (pp. 107–131). Oak Tree Press.

Oberhuemer, P. (2014). The case of Germany. In L. Gambaro, K. Stewart, & J. Waldfogel (Eds.), *An equal start? Providing quality early education and care for disadvantaged children* (pp. 121–146). Policy Press.

Observatoire de la petite enfance. (2019). *L'accueil du jeune enfant en 2017*. Caisse Nationale des Allocations Familiales.

Organisation for Economic Co-operation and Development. (2016a). *Education policy outlook for Slovenia.*

Organisation for Economic Co-operation and Development. (2016b). *Starting Strong IV country note: Germany.*

Organisation for Economic Co-operation and Development. (2017). *Starting Strong 2017: Key OECD indicators on early childhood education and care.*

Périvier, H. (2015). Accueil des jeunes enfants: Enjeux et perspectives. *Regards, 2*(48), 119–129.

Pobal. (2016). *Early years sector profile 2015-2016.* https://www.pobal.ie/app/uploads/2018/06/Early-Years-Sector-Profile-Report-2015-2016.pdf

Rauschenbach, T., & Riedel, B. (2015). Germany's ECEC workforce: A difficult path to professionalization. *Early Child Development and Care, 186*(1), 61–77.

Russell, H., McGinnity, F., Fageh, É., & Kenny, O. (2018). *Maternal employment and the cost of childcare in Ireland* [Working Paper 73]. Economic & Social Research Institute.

Schreyer, I., & Oberhuemer, P. (2018a). Ireland—Key contextual data. In P. Oberhuemer & I. Schreyer (Eds.), *Early childhood work-force profiles in 30 countries with key contextual data* (pp. 576-589). Systems of Early Education and Professionalisation–Revised (SEEPRO-R). www.seepro.eu/ISBN-publication.pdf

Schreyer, I., & Oberhuemer, P. (2018b). Slovenia—Key contextual data. In P. Oberhuemer & I. Schreyer (Eds.), *Early childhood workforce profiles in 30 countries with key contextual data* (pp. 1065-1078). Systems of Early Education and Professionalisation–Revised (SEEPRO-R). www.seepro.eu/ISBN-publication.pdf

Slot, P. (2018). *Structural characteristics and process quality in early childhood education and care: A literature review* [Working Paper 176]. Organisation for Economic Co-operation and Development–Education.

Statistics New Zealand. (2010). *New Zealand childcare survey 2009.*

Stropnik, N. (2001). Childcare in Slovenia: An example of a successful transition. *Child: Care, Health and Development, 27*(3), 263–278.

Stropnik, N., & Šircelj, M. (2008). Slovenia: Generous family policy without evidence of any fertility impact. *Demographic Research, 19*, 1019–1058.

Vandenbroeck, M., & Bauters, V. (2017). Family day care: The trilemma of professionalisation, sustainability, and fairness in Flanders, France and Germany. In E. J. White & C. Dalli (Eds.), *Under-three year olds in policy and practice* (pp. 177–189). Springer.

Vidmar, M. (2015). Contextualizing ECEC research: The case of Slovenia. *International Journal of Early Years Education, 23*(3), 313–328.

Weishaupt, J. (2009). Money, votes or "good" ideas? Partisan politics and the effectiveness of the European Employment Strategy in Austria and Ireland. *European Integration online Papers (EIoP)*, *13*(1), Article 14.

Wolfe, T., O'Donoghue-Hynes, B., & Hayes, N. (2013). Rapid change without transformation: The dominance of a national policy paradigm over international influences on ECEC development in Ireland 1995–2012. *International Journal of Early Childhood*, 45, 191–205.

APPENDIX

Table A-15.1 ECEC quality indicators

Country/structure of ECEC system	Public spending on ECEC, %GDP and USD PPP/child	Staff education requirements	Staff–child ratios and group size regulations	Continuing professional development
Norway Unified under education ministry	1.3% GDP $11,400 (0–5) $11,800 (0–2) $11,100 (3–5)	Core practitioner (ages 0–5) Bachelor's level Assistants No requirements Home care No requirements	Ratios 1:3 (ages 1–2) 1:6 (ages 3–5) Group size No requirements Home care 1:4	n/a
New Zealand Unified under education ministry	0.9% GDP $4400 (0–5) $800 (0–2) $8500 (3–5)	Teacher-led center staff: bachelor's degree or equivalent as recognized by Education Council	Ratios 1:5 (ages 0–2) Aged 2 and over: 1 teacher for 1–6 kids; 2 for 7–20; 3 for 31–30; 4 for 41–50, etc. Home care 1:2 (age 0–2) 1:4 (age 2+)	n/a
Slovenia Unified under education ministry	0.5% GDP $2400 (0–5)	Core practitioner (ages 0–5) Bachelor's level Assistants Upper secondary (4 years) Home care Upper secondary education required	Ratios 1:6 for 0–2-year-olds 1:9 for 3-year-olds 1:11 for 4–5-year-olds Group size 12 for 0–2 17 for 3-year-olds 22 for 4–5-year-olds Home care 1:6	Mandatory for core practitioners and assistants

Country / Ministry	Spending	Core practitioner qualifications	Ratios / Group size / Home care	In-service requirement
France — Divided between education and welfare ministries	1.3% GDP $7400 (0–5) $7200 (0–2) $7600 (3–5)	Core practitioner center care: Bachelor's level Core practitioner education: Master's level Assistants: Upper secondary; 1 year (under-3s), 2 years (3–5-year-olds) Home care: No education requirement; mandatory 120-hour course	Ratios (care): 1:5 (ages 0–2), 1:8 (age 3) Ratios (education): No requirements Group size: No requirements Home care: 1:4	Optional for childcare center staff Mandatory for teachers and assistants in preschools
Germany — Unified under welfare ministry	0.6% GDP $5600 (0–5) $3600 (0–2) $7700 (3–5)	Core practitioner (ages 0–5): Bachelor's level Assistants: Post-secondary non-tertiary Home care: No education requirement; mandatory training, courses vary by Land	Ratios: 1:4–8 (ages 0–2), 1:9–20 (ages 3–5) Group size: 8–15 (ages 0–2), 15–28 (ages 3–5) Home care: 1:5	Mandatory in only two Länder: Mecklenburg-Western Pomerania and Thuringia
Ireland — Divided between education and welfare ministries	0.3% GDP $2500 (0–5)	Core practitioner (ages 0–5): Below bachelor's No assistants Home care: Post-secondary non-tertiary education	Ratios: 1:3 (ages 0–1), 1:5 (age 1), 1:5 (age 2), 1:8 (ages 3–5) Group size: No regulations (under 3) 22 (ages 3–5) Home care: 1:5	n/a

Note. Spending from 2015 or latest available, for formal day-care/pre-primary programs. *Core practitioner* refers to "an individual who leads the practice for a group of children at the class- or playroom-level and works directly with children and their families. Core practitioners may also be called pedagogues, educators, childcare practitioners, pedagogical staff, pre-school, kindergarten or early childhood teachers" (Eurydice, 2019). Home care child–staff ratios are for children under age 3. ECEC = early childhood education and care; GDP = gross domestic product; n/a = not available; PPP = purchasing power parity. *Sources.* OECD family policy database. Staff education requirements are from Eurydice, *Key Data on Early Childhood Education and Care in Europe* (2019). New Zealand adult–child ratios from http://www.legislation.govt.nz/regulation/public/2008/0204/latest/DLM142637.html

16

THE POLITICS OF SOCIAL INVESTMENT IN THE KNOWLEDGE ECONOMY

ANALYTICAL INSIGHTS FROM A GLOBAL COMPARISON

Julian L. Garritzmann, Silja Häusermann, and Bruno Palier

16.1. INTRODUCTION

Welfare states around the globe are challenged by the transformation of industrial societies into post-industrial knowledge economies. While several welfare
reform strategies are theoretically possible (see Chapters 1 and 2 in this volume),
social investments with their focus on human skills and capabilities seem to
be an obvious and appropriate welfare reform strategy to support individuals,
families, and countries in this "great transformation". A look at different countries around the globe shows, however, that countries differ enormously in the
welfare reform strategies they pursue in terms of the degree to which they have
introduced and expanded social investments as well as regarding the type of established social investment policies. Some have even chosen not to follow a social investment reform strategy at all (for an overview, see Chapter 17 in Volume
II [Garritzmann et al., 2022]).

The overall objectives of the World Politics of Social Investment (WOPSI) project and the two volumes that are its key outputs are, first, to provide an analytical
approach that allows us to characterize, systematize, and describe the different
reform strategies; second, to provide a systematic comparative and descriptive
overview of the different welfare reform strategies, especially the different types

Julian L. Garritzmann, Silja Häusermann, and Bruno Palier, *The Politics of Social Investment in the Knowledge Economy*
In: *The World Politics of Social Investment (Volume I)*. Edited by: Julian L. Garritzmann, Silja Häusermann, and Bruno Palier,
Oxford University Press. © Oxford University Press 2022. DOI: 10.1093/oso/9780197585245.003.0016

of social investment reforms, in democracies around the globe; and, third, to explain this variation.

We collectively argue that politics is at the heart of these differences. As Palier et al. (Chapter 1 in this volume) and Häusermann et al. (Chapter 2 in this volume) explain, we theorize that in order to understand and explain the empirical variety of social investment policies, we need to analyze how collective political actors and (new) social political demands interact with policy legacies and institutions, resulting in different processes of politicization and of coalition-building between protagonists and consenters of social investment (or antagonists that oppose social investment). In presenting the theoretical framework underpinning our research (see Chapter 2 in this volume]), we argued that the interaction of legacies, socioeconomic factors, and social demand for social investment is likely to shape the politicization of social investment, while the corresponding reform coalitions are especially crucial in shaping the actual reforms.

The empirical contributions show that in this regard differentiating the functions and distributive profiles of social investment is important because it appears that the factors shaping politicization are more influential in affecting which *functions* of social investment are politicized, while the reform coalitions are crucial in order to understand the resulting *distributive profiles*. Figure 16.1 offers a graphical recap of the argument, originally illustrated in Figure 2.1 but now "empirically enriched" in the sense that it highlights those factors that our research found to be important in the politics of social investment.

More specifically, we posed seven analytical research questions in the introduction to this volume (see Chapter 1):

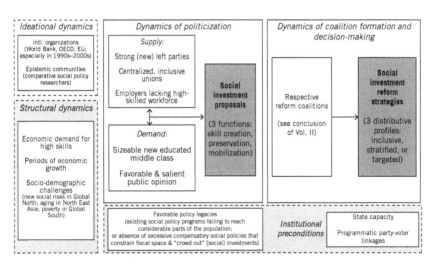

Figure 16.1 The politics of social investment: A graphical summary of our theoretical framework enriched by empirical findings.

1) *Classifying social investment proposals and reforms*: How can we conceptually distinguish, characterize, systematize, and describe different social investment policies? Do all social investment policies follow the same political logic, or are there systematic differences?

2) *Social demand*: What are the public/social demands for social investment? Which social groups have a stake in social investment policies? Who are the politically relevant social groups? What do they want? And under what conditions do they get what they want?

3) *Collective actors*: Who are the protagonists, antagonists, and consenters of social investment proposals or reforms? In particular, we focus in this chapter on the following questions: What do collective actors want? And under what conditions are collective actors protagonists, antagonists, or consenters of (different types of) social investment?

4) *Socioeconomic and institutional scope conditions*: What role do structural dynamics play in the politics of social investment? What are the scope conditions for (successful) social investment reforms? How do political institutions shape the politics of social investment?

5) *Salience*: How politically salient are social investment proposals, programs, and reforms (overall and relative to other welfare reform strategies), and how does this affect the politics of social investment?

6) *Policy legacies*: Are welfare state legacies influential? If so, how? Do they facilitate, slow, or block reforms?

7) *Coalition formation dynamics*: Which political coalitions are relevant for the adoption of social investment reforms? Which types of coalitions lead to which types of social investment reforms?

Drawing on all the findings presented in both volumes, this chapter aims to provide systematic answers to the first four questions. The conclusion of Volume II (Chapter 17 [Garritzmann et al., 2022]) will answer the remaining research questions by providing a descriptive overview of reform strategies around the globe and will summarize what we have learned about the role of politicization and salience, about policy legacies, and about how different reform coalitions lead to different policy outputs.

While both volumes examine the politics of social investment around the globe, the present volume is more oriented around the "independent variables" (i.e., collective actors, social demands, and political and socioeconomic scope conditions), whereas the second volume takes the perspective from the "dependent variables" (i.e., investigating the different welfare reform strategies region by region). Thus, the present volume predominantly asks, what is the role of factor X? (e.g., state capacity, democracy, or trade unions), whereas Volume II asks, what were the politics of welfare reforms in region Y? Of course, both volumes speak to all of our research questions. However, since they emphasize different perspectives and focal points, we split answering the questions *systematically* between the two conclusions.

In order to avoid excessive length, we refrain from summarizing each chapter individually and jump straight to a comparative analytical discussion of what we have learned from the global perspective about the politics of welfare states in the knowledge economy. We start by discussing our typology of nine types of social investment in detail, before moving to social demands and collective actors. Before concluding with thoughts about the prospects for social investment, we discuss how socioeconomic and institutional scope conditions affect our arguments and findings, which are particularly relevant in a broad global comparison such as ours.

16.2. ANALYTICAL INSIGHTS: WHAT HAVE WE LEARNED?

16.2.1. Classifying social investments

Our WOPSI project conceptualizes social investment as policies that aim to "create, preserve, and mobilize human skills and capabilities" (see Chapters 1 and 2 in this volume). This definition—explicitly and intentionally—covers a potentially wide range of policies, from early-life interventions (e.g., early childhood education and care policies or parental leaves) to education policies, some family policies, work–life balance policies, conditional cash transfers, active labor market policies, and lifelong learning, to name but some of the best-known programs.

How can we conceptually systematize and distinguish different social investment policies? The existing literature on social investment usually has treated social investments as a single concept or "paradigm." Sometimes two "variants" are distinguished, a "Nordic version" and an "Anglo-Saxon third way version," with the former seeing social investment and social compensation as complementary and the latter regarding them as substitutes (Hemerijck, 2017; Morel et al., 2012). Yet this distinction is more about how social investment policies interact with other social policies and less about variation within the set of social investment policies. This is especially visible in the many normative discussions about social investments, such as the discussions about "Matthew effects," where the assumption is that all kinds of social investment policies are normatively questionable because they apparently benefit the already better-off (Cantillon, 2011; Nolan, 2013).

By contrast, our research results demonstrate empirically that, while social investment should indeed be regarded as one welfare reform strategy and one welfare paradigm on the basis of the mechanisms it relies on, we need to distinguish different types of social investment policies in order to be able to recognize and acknowledge the empirical variety of approaches and their respective political logics. More specifically, we have learned from cross-regional and cross-national comparison that it is helpful to distinguish *nine different types* of social investment policies as they pursue distinctive immediate goals and result in different outcomes. We propose to differentiate social investments along two dimensions: their *functions* (skill creation, skill mobilization, or skill preservation) and their *distributive profiles* (inclusive, stratified, or targeted), resulting in nine types of social investments, as shown in Table 16.1 and originally introduced in Chapter 1 in this volume.

Combining both dimensions leads to nine types of social investments, which—as the global comparison shows—is helpful because each type follows a different political logic and results in different outcomes. For one, this differentiation helps to take descriptive stock of social investment efforts around the globe. The broad comparison teaches us that while many countries around the world have established social investments, these are of very different types. For example, simplifying greatly we could say that while countries in the Global South have concentrated more on skill creation policies (often in a targeted form), countries in the Global North have combined skill creation (especially with early-years interventions), skill mobilization, and skill preservation policies; but with very different distributive profiles (more inclusive in Nordic Europe, largely stratified in Continental and Central and Eastern Europe as well as in North East Asia, and targeted in most of North America).

At the same time, the differentiation is important because it reflects the varied impact of socioeconomic and political factors on the politics of these policies. For example, while parties of different leanings have established social investment policies, the types of social investment policies they have chosen to support vary quite systematically, with left-wing and social liberal parties often pushing for inclusive social investment policies, whereas Christian democratic parties (and conservative parties to some extent) foster social investments in a stratified form. To mention another example, while women are found to be generally more supportive of social investment, they are particularly supportive of skill

Table 16.1 Nine types of social investment strategies

Function \ Distributive profile	Inclusive social investment	Stratified social investment	Targeted social investment
Creation of skills and capabilities			
Mobilization of skills and capabilities			
Preservation of skills and capabilities			

mobilization and skill preservation policies (Garritzmann & Schwander, 2021; see also Footnote 2 below).

We argued in the theoretical framework of this volume (see Chapter 2) that the interaction of legacies, socioeconomic factors, and social demand for social investment is likely to shape the politicization of social investment, while especially the respective reform coalitions are crucial in shaping the respective reforms. The empirical contributions show that in this regard differentiating the functions and distributive profiles of social investment is important because it appears the factors shaping the politicization are more influential in affecting which *functions* of social investment are politicized, while the reform coalitions are crucial in order to understand the resulting *distributive profiles*.

The differentiation of nine types of social investment implies that, more often than not, it will be misleading to make general statements about social investments (such as "social investments create Matthew effects" or "women support social investments" or "unions support social investments") because whether or not these statements are true depends on the respective types of social investments. The distinction is also crucial when trying to understand the role of specific political or socioeconomic factors in the politics of social investment (as this volume does) as well as when analyzing the politics of social investment in particular regions (as volume II does).

16.2.2. The role of social demands and public opinion in the politics of social investment

What are people's attitudes toward social investment? Which social groups demand and support social investment reforms, and who are the main opponents? Do people in different country contexts have similar preferences, or do attitudes vary systematically across world regions? Under what conditions does public opinion matter for the politicization of social investment and for policymakers to be responsive? Several chapters in both volumes of the WOPSI project address these questions, most explicitly the comparative analysis of Bremer (Chapter 12 in this volume) as well as Busemeyer and Garritzmann (Chapter 3 in Volume II [Garritzmann et al., 2022]) for Western Europe and Hong et al. (Chapter 11 in Volume II [Garritzmann et al., 2022]) for North East Asia. Together, these chapters provide a consistent and systematic overview on (the role of) public opinion in the politics of social investment. Here, we highlight five core findings.

First of all, and most fundamentally, people do hold (rather) consistent preferences toward social investment. Furthermore, attitudes toward social investment are distinct from attitudes toward other welfare strategies such as social compensation or workfare. Indeed, people hold multidimensional welfare preferences. This finding appears in Busemeyer and Garritzmann's (Chapter 3 in Volume II [Garritzmann et al., 2022]) detailed analysis of Western Europe using principal component analysis (see also Fossati & Häusermann, 2014;

Garritzmann et al., 2018), as well as in Bremer's (Chapter 12 in this volume) comparison of several policy areas in Western, Central, and Eastern Europe, Latin America, and North- and Southeastern Asia. That people's views on social investment differ from their views on other welfare reform strategies is important because it shows that social investment policies follow a distinct political logic. Therefore, the finding substantiates the theorization of current welfare politics as multidimensional and open to varying coalitional dynamics.

Second, Bremer (Chapter 12 in this volume), Busemeyer and Garritzmann (Chapter 3 in Volume II [Garritzmann et al., 2022]), and Hong et al. (Chapter 11 in Volume II [Garritzmann et al., 2022]) analyze the lines of conflict over social investment in order to understand which social groups are supportive of or opposed to social investments. They conclude that we can clearly identify groups supportive of social investment, as well as groups that are more or less explicitly critical of social investments. Social investment support is particularly strong among the new educated middle class and individuals identifying with the political left (economically and/or socially)[1] and tends to be stronger among younger people, women,[2] and trade union members. While this pattern emerges most strongly in Western Europe, it also appears in Central and Eastern Europe, Latin America, and North and Southeastern Asia, with some important qualifications (discussed in the following paragraphs).

The lowest support for social investment, in contrast, is found among the traditional working class ("production workers") and among people who identify as both economically right wing and socially right wing (i.e., traditionalist, authoritarian, nationalistic), who electorally often vote for radical right populists. This is one reason why radical right populist parties are the most vocal opponents of social investment policies in many countries (see Chapters 2 and 8 in Volume II [Garritzmann et al., 2022]).

A third important insight is that these generalized findings require some qualification. While similar patterns can be identified across countries, important variations in both the lines of conflict over and the degree of support for social investment are noteworthy across contexts (Chapter 12 in this volume). The social cleavages over social investment are clearest and most pronounced in Western Europe (particularly Nordic and Continental Europe), arguably because these countries have among the strongest policy legacies in social compensation; as such, the policy and fiscal trade-offs of social investment expansion might be

---

1. This is true on both the economic and the social dimensions (see also Garritzmann et al., 2018), as well as for both mainstream and radical left voters (see Häusermann et al., 2020).
2. But see the nuanced discussion in Garritzmann and Schwander (2021), who show that women are particularly supportive of skill mobilization and skill preservation policies and less so of additional skill creation policies, arguably because—especially in younger generations—women tend to be more highly skilled than men but still have more difficulties as they de facto carry the dual burden of work and family life. Accordingly, they benefit less from additional skill creation policies but more from skill mobilization and preservation policies.

most visible and articulated, leading to clearer lines of conflict. In regions with less established compensatory legacies, such a trade-off between social investment and social compensation is less pressing, as discussed in Chapter 13 in this volume. While similar patterns appear in all world regions we studied, Bremer's (Chapter 12 in this volume) comparative analysis concludes that

> preferences for social investment appear more context-dependent than preferences for transfer-oriented social policies: The lower social classes are the core supporters of pension spending across all regions . . . but the support coalition for social investment is less clearly defined in some regions. . . . In Latin America, and to a lesser extent in Southern and Eastern Europe and Asia, it is difficult to make out any clear champions for social investment in the first place.

Along these lines, Hong et al.'s (Chapter 11 in Volume II [Garritzmann et al., 2022]) detailed study shows that, while there is increasing support for social investment policies in North East Asia, it is difficult to identify clear-cut advocates and opposition groups in public opinion, especially in Korea and Japan (but distinct groups are visible in Taiwan).

Fourth, social investment reforms are generally popular and often achieve higher public support levels than does the expansion of other welfare reform strategies (social compensation or workfare). This is particularly true for education policy (which receives very high support levels in many countries) but also for other social investment areas. Moreover, as Hong et al.'s longitudinal analysis shows, public opinion has become more supportive of social investment expansion, even among males in North East Asia, who arguably constitute an unlikely support group in several respects.

Again, this finding on the high popularity of social investment comes with provisos. The first is that the degree of public support for social investment differs across regions. One reason for this is policy legacies and the respective types of capitalism. Another, related reason is that the relative size of the different social groups differs. Since the new educated middle class is simply (much) larger in Northern and Continental Europe than in Southern, Central, and Eastern Europe, North East Asia, and Latin America, it is not surprising that the level of support for social investment measured at the country or regional level would be higher (see Chapter 12 in this volume; Beramendi et al., 2015). The second proviso stems from the fact that this high popularity mainly holds for unconditional survey questions; as soon as policy or fiscal trade-offs are acknowledged (e.g., "an expansion of social investment would come at the expense of higher taxation or cutbacks of social compensation"), public support drops to lower levels (see Chapter 3 in Volume II [Garritzmann et al., 2022]; see also Busemeyer & Garritzmann, 2017; Häusermann et al., 2020). This means that the degree to which and the way social investment reforms are politicized and framed in the public debate affect what role public opinion plays in the politics of social investment. For example, while there appears to be high and widespread support for social investment policies in Southern Europe, this support weakens significantly when respondents are reminded of the costs of such policies. Along these lines, Ronchi and Vesan (Chapter 5 in Volume II [Garritzmann et al., 2022]) and Bürgisser (Chapter 4 in Volume II [Garritzmann et al., 2022]) show how social investment reform efforts were aborted in many instances when fiscal constraints became tighter. Moreover, as we discuss next, how public opinion affects reforms will depend on the saliency of the issue and respondents' welfare priorities.

The fifth core finding relates to the question, under what conditions do people's preferences matter for the politicization and the policymaking process of social investments? Busemeyer and Garritzmann (Chapter 3 in Volume II [Garritzmann et al., 2022]) argue that the influence of public opinion vis-à-vis other political forces depends on two factors: 1) the political salience of an issue and 2) the degree of consensus among the public on that issue. Public opinion matters the most when an issue is salient among the general public, and a large majority of people agrees on the direction of the reforms, what Busemeyer et al. (2020) term "loud politics." The influence of public opinion is smallest under "quiet politics," that is, when an issue is not salient (Culpepper, 2010), in which case organized interests are much more influential (see also Chapters 9–11 in this volume). In a third scenario of "loud but noisy politics," public opinion is loud enough to propel an issue onto the political agenda; but if people do not agree on the direction of policy reforms, the signal becomes noisy and the direction of reforms will depend on the partisan makeup of government. Hong et al. (Chapter 11 in Volume II [Garritzmann et al., 2022]) demonstrate that this reasoning helps explain variation in the politics of social investment in North East Asia as the influence of public opinion has varied depending on salience, the strength of the supporting coalitions, and policy legacies. Moreover, in addition to this "direct" influence, public opinion can indirectly affect the politics of social investment, as Estévez-Abe and León (Chapter 14 in this volume) and Hong et al. (Chapter 11 in Volume II [Garritzmann et al., 2022]) show. They argue that public opinion mattered because the electoral institutions created incentives for policymakers to be responsive to (parts of) public opinion, leading to intensified partisan competition over social investment, which ultimately triggered social investment expansions.

16.2.3. The role of collective actors in the politics of social investment

What is the role of collective actors such as political parties, trade unions, employer organizations, and international organizations in the politics of social investment? Who are the protagonists, antagonists, and consenters of social investment proposals and reforms? We answer these questions both in the next paragraphs and in the conclusion of Volume II (Chapter 17 [Garritzmann et al., 2022]). Here, we focus on the following questions: What do collective actors want? Under what conditions do their preferences matter for reform outputs? In the conclusion of Volume II, we provide additional insights by reporting on who the actual protagonists, consenters, and antagonists were in specific reforms in specific regions.

Before delving into the account of distinctive actor types, we start with four general observations. First, the project's worldwide analysis reveals that—unlike what simpler theories assume—the preferences, strategies, and influence of collective actors are not fixed and stable across time and space but are rather contingent on specific contexts, particularly policy legacies and political institutions, as well as on characteristics of the respective policy issue such as its political salience. This is yet another reason why legacies feature so prominently in our theoretical framework and analysis. Therefore, rather than asking what does actor X want?, we prefer the more nuanced question, under what conditions is actor X a social investment protagonist, antagonist, or consenter?

A second general observation is that all collective actors have different, partly contradictory motives, leading to trade-offs both for themselves and in their interaction with other actors. For example, as has been shown for a long time in political science, political parties aim to simultaneously maximize their policy impact, vote share, and to seek office, which can lead to "hard choices" for parties when several of these goals collide (Müller & Strøm, 1999). Similarly, organized interest groups such as employer associations and labor unions are torn between different logics (e.g., a logic of membership and a logic of influence) (Schmitter & Streeck, 1999). Understanding these trade-offs helps us to understand the—sometimes counterintuitive—positioning, strategic negotiation, and influence of collective actors. It is this range of motivations that underlies the significance our theoretical account places on political decision and agency.

A third insight is that no collective actor in any democratic country analyzed here has fully achieved its preferred policy. While this might sound trivial, it reminds us that all political actors have to make concessions because they are rarely in the position of holding the majority and are involved in constant negotiations and power struggles with other collective actors and legacies. This inevitably leads to "less pure" policy packages (as discussed in Chapter 17 in Volume II [Garritzmann et al., 2022]). As mentioned by Esping-Andersen (1990) for compensatory social policies, class politics of the welfare state are most often politics of class coalitions (see also Häusermann, 2010; Manow et al., 2018). This is no different for the politics of social investment.

Fourth, the analysis shows that actors seek to exercise influence at several points during the policy cycle: They aim to influence a) the politicization of social investments (the degree as well as the framing of the discussion, as analyzed in Chapter 17 in Volume II [Garritzmann et al., 2022]), b) the reform process and the design of the resulting policies, and c) the policies' implementation process.

For example, as Pavolini and Seeleib-Kaiser (Chapter 9 in this volume) describe, employers in Germany helped to politicize and lobby for inclusive dual-earner, dual-care family policies as social investment protagonists during the politicization and reform stage; employers in the United Kingdom aimed to influence the reform process and watered down some social investment policies during the policy implementation period; and employers in Italy paid lip service to the expansion of social investment during the politicization process and acted as (partial) social investment consenters during the reform and implementation phases. While our research systematically examines the first two elements (politicization and reform coalitions), we shed less systematic light on the implementation period, which, accordingly, might be a rewarding field for future research.

Next, we look in more detail at the role of a selection of actors, starting with international organizations and then moving to political parties, unions, and producer groups.

16.2.3.1. International organizations

What role have international organizations played in developing and disseminating social investment ideas? How and when have international organizations contributed to the politicization of social investment? In this volume, Jenson and Mahon (Chapter 3) and de la Porte and Palier (Chapter 4) answer these questions by tracing the ideational dynamics of social investment and studying how the social investment paradigm has emerged in three powerful international organizations. Jenson and Mahon analyze the Organisation for Economic Co-operation and Development (OECD) as particularly influential for the Global North and the World Bank for the Global South, and de la Porte and Palier focus on the European Union, particularly the European Commission.

Both chapters focus on these powerful international organizations for several reasons. In line with a sizable literature, they argue that the OECD, the World Bank, and the European Union are influential actors despite the fact that they (especially the OECD and the World Bank) usually cannot directly affect countries' policymaking processes. They are nonetheless crucial actors because they develop and transfer knowledge and expertise between countries, are highly visible and vocal actors giving policy recommendations, and (especially the World Bank and the European Union) provide resources to countries to follow through with their agenda. These international organizations thus are crucial in the development and dissemination of policy ideas, such as those on social investment. Moreover, they (can) support domestic social investment protagonists by providing expertise, resources, and additional legitimacy. Besides ideational influence, the international organizations can in some circumstances also directly affect policymaking, for example, by providing resources or by tying conditions to those resources. Indeed, as several chapters in these volumes show, international organizations have indeed been important for the development of social investments, especially in Central and Eastern Europe and Latin America.[3]

A first major takeaway that both chapters highlight is that ideas have not "just emerged" from nowhere. Rather, ideas and the specific understandings and conceptualizations of social investment are the result of tough and continuous intellectual and political battles between different groups with different interests within these international organizations. In short, the ideational dynamics of social investment are full of politics, and the development and dissemination of social investment are highly political processes. In line with our theoretical framework (see Chapter 2 in this volume), the policy ideas that the OECD, the World Bank, and the European Union have developed, proposed, and disseminated are the results of interactions between protagonists, antagonists, and consenters of social investment within these organizations and across their member nation states.

Indeed, neither the OECD nor the World Bank nor the European Union should be treated as a coherent, monolithic, unitary actor with a single policy goal and an unambiguous and consistent understanding of social investment. Rather, there are strong and diverse subgroups within each organization that push for different policy goals, different policy instruments, and different framings of social investment. Within the OECD, for example, the Economics Department; the Directorate of Employment, Labor, and Social Affairs; and the Education Directorate lobbied for very different versions of social policy in general and social investments in particular; and we can only understand the resulting policy proposals by delving into these intra-organizational discussions (see Chapter 3 in this volume). Thus, talking about the ideas and the roles of "the" OECD, "the" World Bank, or "the" European Union can be misleading as these international organizations are not coherent unitary actors, and their positions, proposed policies, and policy framings have changed over time as a result of intra-institutional dynamics.

Furthermore, context, in particular the macroeconomic environment, has significantly affected the positions of all three international organizations because changing contexts have shifted the balance of power of different groups and the respective dominant ideas within these international organizations. To name but two important examples, the 1997 financial crisis in Asia and Latin America put into question the neoliberal views of the international organizations recommending reforms in the Global South and led to a progressive turn toward the social investment perspective; later, the financial crisis that began in 2007–2008 and the subsequent Great Recession have partly shifted the focus and

---

3. See Chapters 7–9 in Volume II (Garritzmann et al., 2022) on Central and Eastern Europe and Chapter 13 in this volume and Chapters 14–16 in Volume II (Garritzmann et al., 2022) on Latin America.

relative salience that these organizations placed on social investments toward a broader agenda of inclusive growth, which nevertheless continues to include some of the social investment perspective (see Chapter 3 in this volume).

A second major takeaway regarding the role of international organizations is that from the start and until the present day, social investment has been framed and used by these organizations mainly in order to achieve economic goals, particularly economic growth. The mandates of the OECD and the World Bank, and to a considerable degree the European Union, follow an economic imperative. While social goals have also become more prominent in all three organizations, they often have been secondary to economic goals. More concretely, as Jenson and Mahon (see Chapter 3 in this volume) show, social investment as a policy paradigm only gained traction in the OECD and the World Bank once other policy approaches had failed to deliver on economic growth; these organizations as well as national policymakers thus started looking for new policy ideas to foster growth. The ambiguity of the notion of "investment" was the key to winning over economically oriented actors within these institutions. The same is also true in the European Union, where the European Union could endorse important social policy action only when it was presented as a "productive factor" (see Chapter 4 in this volume). All three organizations have thus framed social investments particularly with reference to economic goals.

A closer look at the specific types of social investment policies that the three organizations have proposed reveals a third crucial takeaway: All three have taken strong and clear positions on the different *functions* of social investment but largely left discussion on the *distributive profiles* to national policymakers. That is, the OECD, the World Bank, and the European Union have emphasized skill creation, skill mobilization, and skill preservation policies to different extents and at different times and designed policy packages that highlight these functions. Yet, they have not engaged much with the distributive profiles that the policies implemented in the different member states have taken (i.e., whether these are inclusive, stratified, or targeted).[4] More concretely, the World Bank has focused on skill creation policies, the OECD on skill mobilization and some skill creation policies, and the European Union on skill creation and skill mobilization policies. That is, the international discourse has been dominated by a focus on skill creation in the Global South, whereas in the Global North emphasis was placed on skill creation and skill mobilization, especially on integrating women to a higher degree in the labor market. Skill preservation in either region is hardly on the agenda of these international organizations.

A fourth insight is that the timing of the emergence and development of social investment ideas is highly similar across all three organizations. Initial ideas had

---

4. A partial exception was the World Bank's emphasis on targeted social (investment) policies to combat poverty, which over time, however, have become more inclusive as part of their "inclusive growth" agenda.

emerged in the OECD, the World Bank, and the European Union already in the (late) 1980s; but they became more prominent during the 1990s, partly as a result of the declining belief in the "Washington Consensus" (see Chapter 3 in this volume) and partly—in the EU—because of a shift from center-right to center-left governments in several EU member states (see Chapter 4 in this volume). During the first decade of the 21st century, social investment ideas gained momentum in all three organizations, backed by powerful protagonists both on the international level and within pivotal member states. With the onset of the global financial crisis and Great Recession, however, the relative salience of social investment declined again as countries and international organizations have concentrated on macroeconomic policies, social protection, and fiscal consolidation, with social investment hardly being considered as a potential policy solution to these socioeconomic problems. In the late 2010s, as Jenson and Mahon (see Chapter 3 in this volume) show, social investment ideas have been merged into another, partly broader policy paradigm around the idea of "inclusive growth." While the core ideas of the social investment paradigm remain very present in the "inclusive growth initiative," the focus has shifted more toward inequality as an inhibitor of economic growth; and the range of policy tools to achieve these goals has widened, moving beyond policies that aim at creating, preserving, and mobilizing human skills and capabilities.

That is, the definition and understanding of social investment, as well as the relative salience of social investment vis-à-vis other policy paradigms (e.g., "liberalization and privatization," "fiscal consolidation," "social protectionism"), have changed repeatedly over time. De la Porte and Palier (Chapter 4 in this volume) tellingly characterize this process of constant redefinition within the European Union as an "incremental metamorphosis" because the understanding of social investment has gradually become broader, more encompassing, and more salient (with a decline, however, since the global financial crisis).

16.2.3.2. Political Parties

Which political parties are protagonists, antagonists, and consenters of social investment and under what conditions? And what kinds of social investment policies, if any, do they support? Our research addresses these questions by studying the preferences, strategies, and behavior of political parties in various parts of the globe. Drawing on this empirical material, a general pattern emerges.

In countries of both the Global North and the Global South and in both democracies and non-democracies, the political left—especially new left parties (i.e., left parties that place particular focus on left-libertarian social progressive values, including green and ecological as well as gender issues [see Kitschelt, 1988])—can generally be regarded as the most vocal and most consistent protagonist of social investment policies, particularly of inclusive social investments and of a more encompassing social investment approach that introduces skill creation, skill mobilization, and skill preservation policies. The large-N macro-comparative quantitative chapters by Barrientos (Chapter 5 in this volume), Chen and Kitschelt (Chapter 6 in this volume), and Huber et al. (Chapter 13 in this volume) show that the presence of (strong) left parties in government ceteris paribus increases the likelihood of social investment reforms being enacted. The same finding emerges in the detailed qualitative process-tracing comparative case studies in both volumes, especially Horn and van Kersbergen (Chapter 2 in Volume II [Garritzmann et al., 2022]), Bürgisser (Chapter 4 in Volume II [Garritzmann et al., 2022]), Rossel et al. (Chapter 16 in Volume II [Garritzmann et al., 2022]), de la Porte and Palier (Chapter 4 in this volume), Huber et al. (Chapter 13 in this volume), and Morgan (Chapter 15 in this volume). These chapters also show that, whereas all left parties in general are social investment protagonists, the degree to which they prioritize social investment vis-à-vis social compensation differs (in situations where these trade-offs occur), with new left parties favoring social investments and radical and traditional left parties favoring social compensation, arguably due to their different electorates.

That said, a few qualifications are also in order as the partisan politics are more complex than a simple left–right perspective would suggest. To start with, the global comparison teaches us that the partisan politics of social investment differ to some degree across contexts and regions, mostly because of predominant policy legacies and institutional factors. In some contexts, especially in North East Asia, in Latin America, and in Central and Eastern Europe, such partisan differences are hard to discern at first glance. For instance, Huber et al.'s (Chapter 13 in this volume) finding that both left and right parties in Latin America have introduced and expanded social investment policies, especially conditional cash transfers, seems to indicate that there are few partisan differences. The same is true for North East Asia: On the surface, Shim's (Chapter 10 in Volume II [Garritzmann et al., 2022]) analyses of the parliamentary and media agenda might give the impression that social investment is a "problem-driven valence issue" adopted by policymakers of the left and the right. Relatedly, it also appears surprising initially that, like their right-wing counterparts, many left-wing parties in Central and Eastern Europe have been relatively skeptical about social investments, especially public early childhood education and care. A historical perspective can explain this, though: Because of the Soviet legacy of extensive state dominance, several social investment policies, particularly public childcare, are perceived as "forced commodification" or "forced defamilialization" by both elites and the general public.

However, a closer look at these regions and around the world reveals that despite seemingly similar attention to and a similar degree of politicization of social investments, different political parties have promoted very different types of social investment (another reason that distinguishing social investment types is crucial). Indeed, political parties have mattered for social investment policies in all world regions. But how they have mattered varies in at least four noteworthy respects.

First, as several chapters report, even if governments of different ideological leanings introduce similar numbers of bills, the distributive profile of social investment policies differs under different party coalitions. Social investments under left-wing governments tend to be more inclusive in their distributive profile, while social investments under right-wing governments tend to take a targeted or stratified form.[5] The same pattern is found in the strictness of requirements attached to conditional cash transfers (Chapter 16 in Volume II [Garritzmann et al., 2022]), which have become the cornerstone of many Latin American countries' welfare reform strategies.

Second, as Morgan's chapter on the quality of childcare (Chapter 15 in this volume) demonstrates most clearly, left and right parties differ in the degree to which their social investment strategies are comprehensive and emphasize quality. Right-wing governments tend to concentrate only on the skill mobilization function of childcare policies, whereas left-wing governments appear to pay more attention to a combination of skill mobilization and skill creation through more emphasis on the quality of childcare (see also Chapter 14 in Volume II [Garritzmann et al., 2022], for Latin America). Similarly, Altamirano and Zárate-Tenorio (Chapter 11 in this volume) explain that right-wing Latin American governments' provision of early childhood education and care has remained highly stratified and, for poorer social strata, of low quality (i.e., not capacitating).

Third, left parties tend to place much more emphasis on the social dimension of social investments, whereas right parties focus on their economic dimension. This is especially evident in the framing of and justification for the policies but also in the actual reforms (see Chapter 10 in Volume II [Garritzmann et al., 2022]).

Fourth, left-leaning political parties typically follow through with the social investment agenda not only by proposing and enacting social investment proposals and bills but also by providing the necessary services to make social investments effective. In Hemerijck's (2018) terms, left parties make sure to provide the necessary "institutional complementarities" for the "social investment life-course multiplier" to work. Huber et al. (Chapter 13 in this volume) trace this pattern clearly for the case of conditional cash transfers in Latin America and the complementary public services needed to implement these conditions.

Moving beyond the simple left–right dichotomies, distinctive patterns also emerge when looking at the roles and strategies of established party families. For example, several chapters show that *socialists*, *social democrats*, and *social*

5. See, for example, the chapters on Western Europe (Chapters 2–4 in Volume II [Garritzmann et al., 2022]), on Latin America (Chapter 13 in this volume and Chapters 14–16 in Volume II [Garritzmann et al., 2022]), and on North East Asia (Chapter 14 in this volume and Chapters 10–13 in Volume II [Garritzmann et al., 2022]).

liberals—especially new left parties (placing particular focus on left-libertarian social progressive values, including green and ecological as well as gender issues [see Kitschelt, 1988]) with electorates among or reaching out to voters of the new middle class—have been core protagonists of countries' social investment efforts, partly for ideological reasons as well as because of social demand from their electoral base.[6] The pattern is most visible in Nordic Europe, where these parties have been dominant in government (see Chapter 2 in Volume II [Garritzmann et al., 2022]), but also appears in entirely different contexts, for example, in Korea (see Chapter 13 in Volume II [Garritzmann et al., 2022]) and in the Baltics (see Chapter 7 in Volume II [Garritzmann et al., 2022]). Moreover, this relationship is visible not only at the national level but also at the regional level (e.g., as Prentice & White, Chapter 6 in Volume II [Garritzmann et al., 2022], show on the Canadian subnational level; see also Kleider et al. [2017] and Garritzmann et al. (2021) for a comparative regional analysis), as well as on the supranational EU level (see Chapter 4 in this volume). This finding is also mirrored in Busemeyer et al.'s (2013) analysis of party manifestos, which indicates that especially socialist, social democratic, and social liberal parties have placed particular emphasis on social investments in their manifestos, leading to a greater degree of politicization over time.

Christian democrats, in contrast, have continued to place more emphasis on compensatory social policies (and partly retrenchment and fiscal austerity) and have—for a long time—paid less attention to social investment, particularly to its dual-employment, dual-career model, which was perceived to be at odds with Christian democrats' preferred male-breadwinner ideal. This was the case until the first or even the second decade of the 21st century, for example, in Germany, Ireland, Chile, the Netherlands, Switzerland, Spain, and Austria, to name but a few prominent examples (see Chapters 3 and 5 in Volume II [Garritzmann et al., 2022] and Chapter 15 in this volume). More recently, however, several prominent Christian democratic parties (such as the German Christian Democratic Union [CDU]/Christian Social Union [CSU]) have undergone a modernization process, often for electoral reasons, aiming to appeal more to female voters (see, e.g., Morgan, 2013; Schwander, 2020) and became consenters or even protagonists of social investment. When the party was in office, the resulting policies frequently took a stratified form, benefiting particularly middle-class

---

6. This appears both in the macro-quantitative large-*N* comparative chapters by Barrientos (Chapter 5 in this volume), Chen and Kitschelt (Chapter 6 in this volume), and Huber et al. (Chapter 13 in this volume) as well as in the quantitative text-based analyses of parliamentary and media agendas in North East Asia (see Chapter 10 in Volume II [Garritzmann et al., 2022]), Latin America (Chapter 14 in Volume II [Garritzmann et al., 2022]), and (Southern) Europe (Chapter 4 in Volume II [Garritzmann et al., 2022]). Moreover, several of the comparative case study chapters vividly underpin this finding, diving more deeply into the underlying reasons for these partisan strategies (see also Häusermann, 2018). This assessment holds similarly for Green parties (see Bremer & Schwander, 2019; Röth & Schwander, 2021).

voters. Still, this repositioning has not taken place in all Christian democratic parties.

Fiscal conservative, social conservative, and *economic liberal parties'* first-order preference has continued to be a lean (welfare) state (i.e., a welfare reform strategy of marketization). This is most visible in Japan under the dominating Liberal Democratic Party (LDP), which has long been reluctant to expand public early childhood education and care, widen access to (public) higher education, or introduce and expand skill mobilization and reconciliation policies to facilitate women's labor market entry (this has changed since the mid-2010s though, for electoral reasons). Another example is the Republican Party in the United States, which has favored privatized investment in skills, hindered the expansion of several family policies, and even retrenched or inflated some preexisting public social investments that had been installed under Democratic control (see Chapter 6 in Volume II [Garritzmann et al., 2022] and Garritzmann [2016] on higher education). A similar story unfolds in Korea, where the conservatives introduced home-care cash allowances, which undermined the expansion of public early childhood education and care policies (see Chapter 14 in this volume). As a final example, consider how EU policy has shifted from an explicit emphasis on social investment toward mere activation, balanced budgets, and fiscal austerity when majorities shifted from the center-left (in the late 1990s) toward conservative forces and a conservative-led Commission (after the middle of the first decade of the 2000s) (see Chapter 4 in this volume). If conservatives introduced social investments at all, the programs mostly took a stratified form, while economic liberals were more inclined toward a targeted form.

Radical right populist parties, finally, appear to be the most outspoken and forceful antagonists of social investment. Such parties' core electorates tend to be production workers and the petty bourgeoisie, as well as more generally people identifying with traditionalist, authoritarian, and nationalist values who show only weak support for social investment (see Enggist & Pinggera, 2020; Häusermann et al., 2020; Pinggera, 2020). Thus, in line with the preferences of their electorate and at least partly due to ideology, radical right populist parties have—when in office—followed a welfare reform strategy of social protectionism and more or less explicitly acted as antagonists to social investment. The clearest examples are to be found in the Visegrád countries (see Chapter 8 in Volume II [Garritzmann et al., 2022]), where radical right populist parties have moved from an implicit to an explicit antagonism toward social investment. The only social investments that they used were active labor market policies as these were predominantly financed by the European Union and could—at least partly—be exploited for (clientelistic) political reasons.

Again, though, these general patterns need to be qualified, in this case taking into account how intra-party dynamics affect the partisan politics of social investment. Shim (Chapter 10 in Volume II [Garritzmann et al., 2022]), for example, shows that some members of parliament (MPs) are more likely to introduce social investment bills in the legislature than others are. In particular, women (see Morgan, 2013), newly elected MPs, and party-tier legislators (in contrast to directly elected MPs) tend to be more active in promoting or supporting social investment. This is an important addition since it points at the micro-level dynamics behind partisan effects.

Together the macro-quantitative and qualitative comparative case study chapters in both volumes paint a complex but encompassing picture. Generally speaking, political parties have impacted social investment in all regions, yet *how* they have mattered has varied between regions and depending on their political leanings and party family. For example, in some regions, though it appears at first glance as if both left- and right-wing parties have politicized social investments to a similar degree, a closer look reveals that the relative emphasis on and commitment to actual social investment reforms have differed, as have the resulting policies, especially regarding their distributive profiles.

Looking around the world more generally, left-wing parties—especially new left parties—can be regarded as the most vocal and most persistent social investment protagonists, particularly of inclusive social investments and pushing for an encompassing approach combining skill creation, mobilization, and preservation. Right parties have been found to be more reluctant or even openly opposed to social investment, but some notable differences between Christian democratic, conservative, economic liberal, and radical populist right parties appear. The analyses also point out, however, important shifts that have happened among several right-wing parties, especially among Christian democrats but also among conservatives, in several places. These changes can be traced back to vote-seeking motivations as parties have sought to reach out to new voting groups (e.g., the CDU/CSU in Germany; cf. Morgan [2013] and Chapter 3 in Volume II [Garritzmann et al., 2022]) or reacted to reinforced political opposition from the left, competing particularly for (younger and more female) urban voters (e.g., in North East Asia; see Chapter 14 in this volume). That is, the degree and kind of party competition can also affect the party politics of social investment. The resulting social investment policies under right-wing predominance have often focused only on skill mobilization, been of lower quality, and often took a targeted or stratified form.

16.2.3.3. Trade unions and employer associations

What role do organized interests, particularly the social partners (employers and trade unions), play in the politics of social investment? Several chapters in both volumes add new insights into the preferences, strategies, and impact of social partners, most explicitly Chapters 9–11 and 14 in this volume. The main finding that emerges is that, in contrast to the assumption of simplistic views and theories, the preferences and impact of employer associations and labor unions are not stable and fixed in the realm of social investment but highly context-dependent. Depending on many contextual factors including especially policy legacies and institutional settings, both employers and unions can be protagonists, antagonists, or consenters of social investments. Therefore, as for political parties, the more relevant question becomes, *under what conditions* are the social partners social investment protagonists, antagonists, or consenters? The chapters identify a range of factors that influence whether the social partners are supportive of, opposed to, or indifferent to social investment reforms. More specifically, we need to take into account factors at three levels: the micro-level of individual firms and individual unions; the meso-level of the collective actors (i.e., organizational characteristics); and the macro-level of the interaction of employer associations, unions, and governments.

Pavolini and Seeleib-Kaiser (Chapter 9 in this volume) describe how *employers' and employer associations'* positions on social investment differ both between and within countries, depending on their risk structure (their skill needs, the risks their employees face, the gender balance of their workforce, sector differences, skill shortages) and on institutional features, particularly the type of labor market coordination (corporatist, sector coordination, or pluralist). Their comparative case studies on two social investment policy areas in Germany, Italy, and the United Kingdom exemplify this point as they find that employers in the three countries took very different positions on and had different impacts on reforms as policy legacies created different environments: While German employers were particularly supportive of social investment reforms and became protagonists ("the good"), British employers mostly opposed social investment expansions ("the bad"), while Italian employers were "selective consenters" ("the ugly"). Estévez-Abe and León (Chapter 14 in this volume) show that the importance of context applies equally to other world regions. Their cross-regional comparison of four familialist welfare states (Italy, Spain, Japan, and Korea) reveals that employers' positions and influence on social investment depend in particular on the type of economic structure.

When looking systematically at *trade unions*, Durazzi and Geyer (Chapter 10 in this volume) find that whether unions are social investment protagonists, antagonists, or consenters depends on the characteristics of their members (their skill level, gender, age, and employment sector), as well as on organizational and institutional factors, particularly the degree of union density and union centralization which shape unions' degree of inclusiveness. Empirically, focusing on the economically most advanced countries, the authors identify four country groups with regard to institutional factors and illustrate the varying union positions and influence in a set of diverse comparative case studies. For example, an Austria–Germany comparison reveals that because Austrian unions were more centralized, had higher union density, and were institutionally more involved in the policymaking process, the resulting social investment reforms (especially in vocational education and training) were more inclusive than under Germany's moderately centralized, medium-high density, and medium-high union involvement, which contributed to more stratified reforms. As a second example, consider the British unions, which, because of their low degree of centralization, low density, and low institutional involvement, were simply sidelined in the policymaking process. A similar constellation appears in most of Central and Eastern Europe, where trade unions were considerably weakened after the breakup of the Soviet Union because they were associated with the authoritarian past, when trade union membership was obligatory for many workers (see Chapters 7–9 in Volume II [Garritzmann et al., 2022]).

Altamirano and Zárate-Tenorio (Chapter 11 in this volume) continue along these lines, studying unions in Latin America. They make the case that, just like in Europe, policy legacies and institutional settings strongly affect union preferences and their influence. More specifically, "the truncated nature of the welfare state in Latin America with varying degrees of dualization of labor markets is a crucial factor that shapes trade unions' positions." Focusing on the case of early childhood education and care policies, the authors demonstrate that, because of authoritarian legacies that had weakened unions, unions played no role in the politicization of social investments in Chile and Mexico. However, in the policy design and policy implementation stages, their role depended on the degree of the country's labor market dualization: When dualization was lower, unions became somewhat more relevant but only as consenters, not as protagonists.

Finally, several chapters focus on the role of *teachers' unions*, which are arguably the most directly involved in and affected by skill-creating social investment policies. Again, the finding that emerges from the comparison is that their positions and influence on social investment policies are highly context-dependent. In Latin America, teachers' unions have complicated, vetoed, or diluted (inclusive) social investment reforms in many countries because the reform proposals threatened their preexisting privileges and standing (see Chapters 6 and 13 in this volume). By contrast, in looking at early childhood education and care policies in several OECD countries, Morgan (Chapter 15 in this volume) reveals that, in the absence of clientelistic linkages, the active involvement and support of teachers' unions were indispensable in raising the quality of both the type of education and the teachers' working conditions.

Thus, having looked at many types of collective actors including international organizations, political parties, and social partners, our global comparison teaches us that their positions on social investment are not fixed and stable across countries and time but are highly dependent on a range of micro-, meso-, and macro-level factors. Put differently, it is insufficient and misleading to assume— as simpler theories do—that collective actors hold specific given positions irrespective of context. While such generalizations are tempting, they unfortunately produce inaccurate or incorrect conclusions. We rather need to look more closely and acknowledge the empirical complexity around the globe. When we do, we can find protagonists, consenters, and antagonists among all collective actor groups, varying according to the context in which they act. This is far from saying that their positions are random or accidental; they are highly systematic but in a more complex way than simpler theories assume. Importantly, this is another reason why the party politics and coalition formation processes around social investment are so crucial because—depending on legacies, preferences, and institutional settings—different coalitions of collective actors can form, leading to very different types of social investment reforms (see Chapter 17 in Volume II [Garritzmann et al., 2022]).

16.2.4. Socioeconomic and institutional scope conditions of social investment reforms

In presenting the theoretical framework underpinning our research (see Chapter 2 in this volume), we argued that both the politicization of social investment and the actual reform process happen against the background of socioeconomic factors and are influenced and moderated by political institutions. Especially in a broad worldwide comparison of very different contexts such as ours, it is therefore essential to explore to what degree these arguments are dependent on specific socioeconomic and institutional contexts, particularly given our finding that the positions, strategies, and influence of political actors are contingent on contexts. Therefore, we need to explore the socioeconomic and institutional scope conditions of our arguments and findings more explicitly. In other words, how externally valid are our arguments and findings?

In the following we address a range of questions to explore the scope conditions. What are the socioeconomic and institutional scope conditions of (successful and sustainable) social investment reforms? Do reforms only happen at certain levels or within certain kinds of economic development? How do changes in the type of capitalism, especially an increasing development toward post-industrial knowledge economies, affect social investment reforms? What role do political institutions (democracy, electoral systems, types of political linkages) play? Does state capacity matter? In particular, the four chapters in Part II of this volume (Chapters 5–8) address these and related questions most explicitly by studying the political and economic conditions surrounding social investment reforms in a large number of countries (96, 66, 16, and 110, respectively) on all continents. In what follows, we systematize their findings, focusing first on socioeconomic developments and then on political institutions.

16.2.4.1. The role of economic growth and development

Since Wagner (1890), the notion has been prominent in welfare state research that countries' welfare effort is affected, if not determined, by their level of economic development. Richer economies (e.g., in terms of gross domestic product per capita) on average tend to spend more on welfare and tend to have more generous welfare policies. Does this also apply to social investment? How does economic development affect social investment reforms? What role does economic growth play for social investment policies? While several chapters cover this relationship, two chapters (see Chapters 5 and 6 in this volume) address these questions explicitly. Their macro-quantitative analyses of many developing or low- and middle-income countries support the notion that economic development is positively associated with countries' social investment effort: Wealthier nations tend to spend more on social investments. This finding also appears in Huber et al. (Chapter 13 in this volume), in which the authors conclude that the early 21st-century commodities boom in Latin America had created favorable economic conditions for expansion of social investments, while the boom's end has presented challenges for the (future of) social investments. Additional evidence comes from the analysis of Southern Europe, particularly Spain, which had started developing social investments during an economic upswing in the late 1990s and early 2000s but stopped and reversed many of these reforms once the financial crisis and Great Recession set in. This underpins once more that when resources are scarce or when the political discourse is framed as if they were (Blyth, 2013), policy and fiscal trade-offs become more pressing.

Yet, the relationship between economic development and social investment effort is far from deterministic as outliers do exist, such as Venezuela, the United States, Costa Rica, or Brazil: some rich countries "underinvest" (from a functionalistic perspective) in the sense that they spend less than Wagner's law would predict whereas some poorer countries "overinvest", spending considerable amounts despite being economically less advanced (see Chapters 5 and 6 in this volume). A second caveat is that even if higher economic development is associated with more social investment effort, this does not tell us anything about the *type* of social investment policies enacted. For example, a wealthy country could spend heavily on social investments but design them in a targeted or stratified way so that only certain social strata benefit. Third, we need to keep in mind that the relationship can be bidirectional: As economic development affects social investment reforms, higher social investment efforts can also contribute to economic growth. In fact, in many countries social investments are adopted for that very reason and have been promoted by the World Bank, the OECD, the European Union, and policy entrepreneurs with the main motivation to foster economic growth (see Chapters 3 and 4 in this volume; Hemerijck, 2017).

Additional insights on this complex relationship come from Garritzmann et al. (Chapter 8 in this volume), who examine the emergence of the knowledge economy and how it affects both labor markets and the politics of social investment. More specifically, they analyze how two of the most important structural changes in today's capitalism, namely educational expansion and labor market occupational change, affect the politics of social investment. The goal is to understand how these two "megatrends" have created different socioeconomic environments in different countries, offering policymakers different incentives to politicize and enact different kinds of social investment policies. Using data for 110 countries over 140 years, enriched by insights from qualitative case studies, the authors trace how fundamental structural change affects the politics of social investment.

The main argument is that the two megatrends of educational expansion and labor market change create different environments for policymakers. The authors show that the respective level of *demand* for skills and *supply* of skills creates incentives for policymakers to focus on and politicize different *types* of social investments, particularly regarding their functions: Skill *creation* policies are much more likely to be politicized when the supply of skills is low and especially when demand for skills outstrips supply; skill *mobilization* is more likely to be politicized when a considerable supply of skills exists but still they are not matched well with labor market demand; and skill *preservation* policies are more likely to be politicized when the supply of skills exceeds demand in order to protect workers from skill redundancy and skill decay.

16.2.4.2. Democracy and social investment

A prominent argument in welfare state research is that democratization has fostered welfare state expansion (see, e.g., Flora [1986], Korpi [1983], and somewhat more recently the comparative analysis in Haggard & Kaufman [2008] or Segura-Ubiergo [2007] for Latin America). Does the same hold for social investment policies? Is a certain degree of democracy necessary for social investment reforms? As our research has shown, democracy in itself is *not* a necessary condition for social investment reforms. In their large-N analyses, neither Barrientos (Chapter 5 in this volume) nor Chen and Kitschelt (Chapter 6 in this volume) detect signs of democracies being more likely to establish social investments than non-democracies. On the one hand, several democracies have not established social investments at all or introduced them late or only partially. On the other hand, several autocratic regimes have made use of social investments to foster their countries' economic development or in order to pacify the electorate or relevant elites in a Bismarckian-inspired logic.

Does this mean that democracy does not matter? Chen and Kitschelt (Chapter 6 in this volume) offer a more nuanced answer, arguing that we need to take a closer look as the *quality* of democracy plays an important role. Differentiating between two types of political linkages between people and elites (programmatic and clientelistic), they demonstrate in a multi-method setup that *programmatic* linkages are a necessary condition for social investment reforms. When *clientelistic* practices prevail, in contrast, reforms that prima facie look like social investments (e.g., increased education spending) de facto turn into consumption rather than investment because they are used for political vote-buying purposes and fail to deliver on the promises of the social investment paradigm. While democracy in itself thus seems to not be a necessary condition for adopting social investment reforms, the quality of democracy matters. In this sense our theoretical framework treats democracy as a scope condition for social investment reforms because all the mechanisms the framework entails (e.g., party politics or the influence of public opinion) rely on programmatic democratic partisan linkages and do not apply to either clientelistic or autocratic policymaking (see Chapter 2 in this volume).

16.2.4.3. State capacity and social investment

What role does state capacity play? Is a certain level of state capacity (i.e., a state's ability to make and effectively implement policy decisions) necessary for social investment reforms? These questions are addressed in several of the chapters in Part II of this volume, most explicitly by Bogliaccini and Madariaga (Chapter 7) but also by Chen and Kitschelt (Chapter 6) as well as by Jenson and Nagels (Chapter 15 in Volume II [Garritzmann et al., 2022]). Bogliaccini and Madariaga show that state capacity is a necessary but in itself not sufficient condition for successful and sustainable social investment reforms. They argue that state capacity matters at three crucial moments: first, during the policymaking process; second, during the policy implementation stage; and third, in the long run because it affects policy legacies. Their comparative analysis of 16 Latin American countries demonstrates clearly that a certain level of state capacity is necessary for social investment reforms: Countries lacking capacity have failed to either adopt reforms or implement them even despite having promising political coalitions in favor of social investment. Thus, state capacity is necessary.

But state capacity alone is not sufficient for social investment reforms to be successful since some countries with high state capacity have failed to establish reforms because they lack the essential pro-social investment coalitions. Bogliaccini and Madariaga demonstrate this with a case study from Uruguay, but we can equally add examples from Europe and North America, where countries certainly have high state capacity but still differ considerably in the degree and kind of social investment adopted (see contributions in Volume II for details [Garritzmann et al., 2022]). Thus, two crucial scope conditions for successful and sustainable social investment reforms have been identified: state capacity and reform coalitions of social investment protagonists favorable to reforms (discussed more systematically in Chapter 17 in Volume II [Garritzmann et al., 2022]).

A related finding is that a certain aspect of state capacity, namely the functioning of bureaucracies and the role of policy experts, matters a great deal to the politics of social investment, particularly in the Global South. Technocrats and experts have—under certain macroeconomic conditions—pushed for the introduction and expansion of social investments and diffused social investment ideas, particularly in Latin America but also to some degree in Europe and North East Asia (see particularly Chapter 3 in this volume and Chapter 15 in Volume II [Garritzmann et al., 2022]).

16.2.4.4. Political institutions

How do political institutions affect the politics of social investment? The detailed empirical chapters in both volumes indicate that several institutions have had an effect on the politics of social investment, especially electoral institutions, corporatism, and the geographical distribution of power.

Several chapters, most explicitly those by Estévez-Abe and León (Chapter 14 in this volume) as well as Shim (Chapter 10 in Volume II [Garritzmann et al., 2022]), point to the role of electoral institutions as an explanation of variation in the politicization of social investment and resulting reforms. Estévez-Abe and León argue that social investments are more likely to be politicized under winner-take-all majoritarian electoral systems that set incentives for parties to focus on competitive districts (rather than their nationwide vote share). This effect helps explain why social investment has become more politicized in Korea and Spain and why these countries have established more encompassing social investment policies than Japan and Italy have, despite similar legacies. Shim shows that electoral institutions matter as he detects that MPs in North East Asia who have been elected on a party-tier ticket (rather than being directly elected) are more likely to introduce social investment bills.

Besides electoral systems, the type of macroeconomic organizational institutions matters for the politics of social investment, particularly the degree and kind of corporatism. This is most visible in the interaction of social partners and governments, as touched upon in Section 16.2.3.3. and 16.2.3.4. in this chapter. As the chapters in Part III of this volume argue (Chapters 9–11), the roles social partners play differ across institutional contexts. Jointly, the chapters identify a somewhat asynchronous relationship. While employers appear to always be involved (as protagonists, antagonists, or consenters) in the politics of social investment that are connected to the labor market (i.e., parental leaves and vocational education and training), what the unions do depends much more on institutional contexts as they can be—and de facto are—entirely sidelined in the political process in several countries. Whether or not policymakers can ignore their interests or have to take them into account (if they do not want to) is determined by political institutions, particularly corporatism. When institutionally involved, unions are much more powerful actors in the politics of social investment.

An additional relevant institution is federalism and decentralization, or more generally the distribution of power within multilevel governance systems. This is most visible in the big federal countries, especially Canada, Germany, and the United States. As Busemeyer and Garritzmann (Chapter 3 in Volume II [Garritzmann et al., 2022]) and Prentice and White (Chapter 6 in Volume II [Garritzmann et al., 2022]) show, there is considerable within-country variation across subnational entities regarding social investment policies (e.g., between Québec and the rest of Canada or between the more conservative-led and the more progressive-led Bundesländer in Germany). As other work has shown, however, this is more generally the case in decentralized political systems and not only under federalism (Kleider et al., 2017; Garritzmann et al., 2021).

Finally, Morgan (Chapter 15 in this volume) points to an important quasi-institutional factor that is relevant for the politics of social investment, namely whether social investment is organized under and administered by ministries of education (MoEs) or other ministries. Morgan argues that when administered by MoEs, more attention is paid to the quality of social investments and more generally on their skill creation aspects. When organized under ministries of labor or social affairs, by contrast, social investments often are more oriented toward skill mobilization.

In sum, our research identifies a range of socioeconomic and institutional factors that affect the politics of welfare state reform and help explain the variation in social investment strategies around the globe. Yet, as theorized in Häusermann et al. (Chapter 2 in this volume), whether the socioeconomic and institutional factors actually lead to reforms and what form these changes take depend on the interaction of political actors and the type of political coalitions that exist.

16.3. CONCLUSION AND OUTLOOK: THE PROSPECTS FOR SOCIAL INVESTMENT

Politics is at the heart of welfare state reforms as countries around the world are challenged to compete in increasingly post-industrial, globalized knowledge economies. Why do some countries focus more on social investments as a welfare reform strategy and others less so or not at all? What explains the different types of social investment policies that result?

Drawing from all the chapters in both volumes and thus the results of our WOPSI research project, this concluding chapter has provided comparative analytical insights on four aspects of the politics of social investment. First, we discussed how we can conceptually systematize and characterize social investment policies, distinguishing nine types of social investments along two dimensions, namely the functions of social investments and their distributive profiles. Second, we drew conclusions on the population's demands for social investments, identifying the relevant social groups, their preferences and group sizes, and conditions under which their preferences matter. Third, we turned toward collective actors to examine under what conditions different political actors are protagonists, antagonists, or consenters of social investments and what types of social investment they prefer. Fourth, we reviewed socioeconomic and institutional factors, summarizing what we have learned about the role of economic growth and other socioeconomic aspects as well as about the role of democracy, state capacity, programmatic linkages, and specific political institutions in the politics of social investment. The remaining research questions raised by our research project will be addressed more systematically in the conclusion of Volume II (Garritzmann et al., 2022), which provides a descriptive overview of reforms around the globe and examines the role of political salience, legacies, and reform coalitions.

As we have shown, despite the broad focus of our research in terms of country coverage, time periods, and policy areas, we *are* able to systematize, describe, and explain the (great) variety of social investment strategies in countries around the globe with a (relatively) concise and parsimonious theoretical framework. While global comparisons remain notoriously difficult because of the wide range of explanatory factors, the variety of concrete policies, and simply the amount of knowledge that is necessary to understand and fully acknowledge this variation, such assessments are extremely valuable and productive and provide new insights. Yet, these are only possible as we as a group of more than 50 policy experts can draw on each other's expertise.

16.3.1. The prospects for social investment

Based on the insights we gained from this research, it seems possible to conclude with a general assessment of the likelihood of future social investment reforms in democratic countries around the globe. What are "most likely" and what are "least likely" scenarios for (successful and sustainable) social investment reforms? Which actors, factors, and contexts make it more likely that social investment becomes politicized and which make reforms more or less likely? Put differently, which countries are likely to adopt (which kinds of) social investments soon and which are unlikely? As we try to answer these questions, it is important to emphasize that the following discussion should be understood as *probabilistic* (and not deterministic) and *configurational*; that is, it is not one factor alone that drives results.

To begin, we identified several factors that indeed make it more likely that social investment becomes *politicized*. A first crucial factor is strong left parties (especially strong new left parties), often connected to strong public demand for social investment, particularly when a sizable new middle class electorally and publicly voices demands to expand social investment. Clearly then, electoral alignment has important consequences for the politics of social investment. Yet, we also found another path to the politicization of social investment, namely, when strong left opposition parties and a favorable public opinion force non-left governing parties to compete on the issue. Social investment is also more likely to become politicized when the notion and its promoters receive (ideational and financial) support from international organizations (as was the case most clearly in the 1990s and early 2000s). In addition, the presence of centralized and inclusive unions contributes to the politicization of social investment. Another favorable factor is strong economic demand for social investment, that is, when a country's economy is based on skill-intensive workers who (at least partly) lack these skills. This often results in employers becoming social investment protagonists or at least consenters, supporting social investment policies. Socioeconomic factors also matter as the politicization of social investment is more likely in periods of economic growth and with the emergence and politicization of new social risks (in the Global North) or the need to find new and more effective policy tools to address poverty, informal work, and inequalities (in the Global South). Finally, some political institutions matter, especially electoral institutions that set incentives for elected politicians to respond to demands for social investment, even if this is only voiced by a subgroup of society.

Going further, our findings allow us to point to a range of factors and actors that make it more likely that certain *types* of social investment will become politicized. Under what conditions are skill *creation*, skill *mobilization*, and/ or skill *preservation* policies more likely to become politicized? Figure 16.2 summarizes our results in a simple arrow graph.

In the first place, our comparative review shows that skill *creation* policies are politicized by (a combination of) several international organizations (the World Bank, the OECD, and the European Union), some political parties (especially [new] left parties), centralized and inclusive unions (particularly teachers' unions), and MoEs and in economic conditions of high persistent poverty or in contexts of low supply but high economic demand for skills. Skill *mobilization* policies are politicized by some international organizations (the OECD, the European Union), several political parties ([new] left parties but also center-right parties), several trade unions, employer associations (especially in contexts where a large human capital stock exists but is not well connected to the labor market), and ministries of labor or social affairs and demanded by (high-skilled) female voters. Skill *preservation*, finally, is politicized by some international organizations (the OECD, the European Union), some parties (especially old and new left parties but partly also center-right parties), and (high-skilled) female workers and in contexts where skill supply exceeds economic demand for skills.

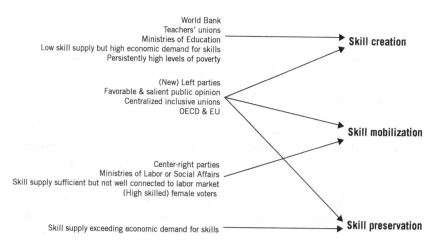

Figure 16.2 Main actors and factors contributing to the politicization of different types of social investment.

Figure 16.2 additionally shows that while some factors make it more likely that only a specific type of social investment becomes politicized (e.g., the World Bank has pushed mainly for skill creation policies), other factors make it more likely that several social investments are jointly more likely to become politicized in a more holistic approach (e.g., [new] left parties aiming for a combination of skill creation, mobilization, and preservation). So, which factors contribute to the politicization of a single, specific type of social investment (creation or mobilization or preservation) and which lead to a combination of several types? Figure 16.2 provides an answer when we look at the different number of arrows (1, 2, or 3) from each factor. We find that (new) left parties, a favorable and salient public opinion, centralized and inclusive unions, and the OECD and European Union help to politicize all three types of social investments together. A core argument here, forcefully proposed for example in Hemerijck's (2018) concept of a "life-course multiplier," is that each of these policies is most effective when surrounded and supported by other kinds of social investment policies, leading to institutional complementarities. Yet, as illustrated in Figure 16.2, several factors and actors contribute to the politicization of a narrower social investment approach, politicizing only one or two types of social investment (e.g., the World Bank or most center-right parties).

Beyond politicization, we identified a range of factors that make it more likely that social investment *reforms* are successfully adopted and sustained. By and large, the actors and factors making reform more likely are similar to those that we identified for the politicization of social investment, but we also note important differences. First, starting with the similarities, we find that—as with politicization—strong (new) left parties strongly increase the likelihood of actually enacting social investment reforms but also detect an alternative mechanism (i.e., when strong left opposition parties and a favorable public opinion force non-left governing parties to enact reforms). Second and again as in the case of politicization, strong social political demand for social investment matters (i.e., when a sizable new middle class electorally and publicly demands expansion of social investment). Third, while we found that public demand is important to politicize social investment, we can concretize the role of public opinion further for the likelihood of reforms: Reforms are more likely when public opinion is in favor of the expansion of social investment, more specifically when social investments are salient on the political agenda and the general public holds rather coherent positive views on the issue (rather than being polarized).

Fourth, centralized and inclusive unions make reforms more likely, especially teachers' unions. The exception are teachers' unions in contexts of clientelism, which can undermine social investment reform efforts. Fifth, employers can make reforms more likely but only when requiring yet lacking high-skilled workers; otherwise, they often become important antagonists, preferring lower taxation over additional public investments. Sixth, (ideational and financial) support from international organizations increases the reform likelihood. Seventh, two economic factors are relevant: Social investment reforms are more likely when there is strong economic demand for social investment (i.e., when a country's economy is based on skill-intensive workers) as well as in periods of economic growth, facilitating reform effort (which was less relevant for the politicization of social investment).

Finally, our contributions point to two institutional preconditions for success, namely, a high level of state capacity and the presence of political party-voter linkages (i.e., the absence of clientelistic linkages). Several political and socioeconomic factors make it more likely that social investment reforms are adopted.

Of course, there is also the possibility that no reform takes place at all, that social investment policies are not implemented or sustained, or that welfare reforms take a different direction that does not include social investment. Such developments are more likely in certain contexts, that is, under low state capacity, when clientelistic (rather than programmatic) political linkages prevail, and when strong and costly social compensatory policy legacies exist, crowding out social investments (see Chapter 17 in Volume II [Garritzmann et al., 2022]). Moreover, several political factors make social investment reforms less likely: radical right populist parties in particular but also dominant fiscal or social conservative parties (unless they are challenged by strong political opponents); low social political demand for social investment (i.e., when a sizable old working class of production workers and/or office clerks and managers electorally and publicly voices demands for either welfare protectionism or market liberalism); public opinion that is either hostile to social investment or very polarized on the issue; low issue salience among the general public (even if public opinion is favorable); when unions are weak, decentralized, or segmented; when employers find an already sufficiently skilled workforce and/or favor low taxation and low costs over investments; when there is no support from—or even opposition of—international organizations (which empirically was the case before the 1990s or for certain countries highly indebted after the financial crisis); or when teachers' unions are involved in contexts of clientelism. Finally, economic contexts matter as social investment reforms are less likely when there is low economic demand for social investment, that is, when a country's economy is not based on skill-intensive workers or already has abundant skilled workers (because of either domestic or migrant workers), and in periods of zero or negative economic growth.

Our research also found that the resulting *type* of social investment policy is particularly shaped by the type of reform coalition (i.e., the interaction of social investment protagonists, antagonists, and consenters). We discuss this more systematically in the conclusion of Volume II.

16.3.2. Both overly pessimistic and overly optimistic predictions are unjustified

Taken together, all this implies that social investment reforms are least likely to happen in those contexts where they could be most influential in helping individuals, families, companies, and countries with the transformation from agrarian or industrial into post-industrial knowledge economies. That is, in contexts where countries could benefit economically and socially from an increased focus on high-skill production, up-skilled labor markets, and high ed-ucational enrollment levels, the expansion of social investment is less likely to happen. Very often, these countries exhibit a set of factors that have been shown to be detrimental to the development of social investment. Conversely, social investment expansion (or maintenance) is most likely and politically easiest in those contexts that have already established (some) social investments success-fully. In that sense there is a "country-level Matthew effect" or, in Horn and van Kersbergen's (Chapter 2 in Volume II [Garritzmann et al., 2022]) terms, a "po-litical flywheel": The countries that have implemented social investment policies in the past are more likely to continue to develop them. One could call this the "tragic irony" of welfare reform.

Nonetheless, in our view both overly optimistic and overly pessimistic predic-tive outlooks are unjustified: Neither will all countries around the globe success-fully reform their welfare states in a one-size-fits-all fashion (as many optimists assume or hope for) nor will it be only the Nordic European countries that manage a high and sustainable social investment effort (as many pessimists as-sume). Simply put, our analysis shows that this is not an all-or-nothing story, in which countries either establish inclusive, encompassing, high-quality "Nordic European" social investment or do not have any social investment at all. Rather, there are many different types of social investment and many different polit-ical pathways to achieve social investments ("equifinality"). Our analysis has demonstrated that we have detected traces of social investment in (almost) all countries around the globe, which in itself is already a remarkable finding.

While the comparison across many countries and regions shows that it is difficult to implement, establish, and sustain social investments, in particular *inclusive, encompassing, high-quality* social investments, nothing says that it is impossible. There is indeed room for political agency and for successful reforms. Four counterintuitive examples from different world regions underpin this point.

First, Japan can—for several reasons—be regarded as a most unlikely case of social investment reforms. Its welfare state is highly focused on male indus-trial workers; its public debt level is enormous, arguably leaving little space for new and costly policy programs; its politics continue to be dominated by a "tri-angle" of predominant conservative parties, powerful employer associations, and a strong hierarchical and conservative bureaucracy; public opinion tends to be skeptical of progressive proposals such as the integration of women in the labor market; and unions as well as (new) left parties are weak. In fact, throughout the 20th century social investments were meager at best. Since 2014, however, Japan has—first silently but increasingly explicitly—expanded social investment policies, although none of the above-mentioned factors that usually impede the introduction and expansion of social investments had disappeared. Why, then, has this happened? As Miura and Hamada (Chapter 12 in Volume II [Garritzmann et al., 2022]) and Estévez-Abe and León (Chapter 14 in this volume) explain in detail, this change can be traced back to shifts in the electoral arena as incentives have emerged for conservative LDP politicians to start emphasizing and competing electorally on social investment agendas.

Second, Germany—long depicted by scholars and journalists as the "sick man of Europe" with an anachronistic but unreformable welfare state—has equally and unexpectedly undergone substantial welfare reform in the early 21st century. While certainly not all of these reforms follow a social investment strategy (also showing some market liberalism and social protectionism), a social investment orientation is nowadays clearly evident in many policy areas. How did this change come about? Some of the core reasons lie in a feminization and movement toward the left within the Christian democratic parties (Morgan, 2013), intertwined with an increasingly social investment–friendly public opinion (see Chapter 3 in Volume II [Garritzmann et al., 2022]). These factors have combined with the forceful support of German employers, who switched from being social investment antagonists to protagonists (or at least consenters) in order to improve Germany's economic competitiveness (Seeleib-Kaiser, 2017). Again, transformative change toward social investment came about unexpectedly but strongly.

Third, several Latin American countries that had been argued to be caught in a "low-skill trap" (Schneider, 2013) enacted substantive welfare reforms in the early 21st century. Led especially by left-wing governments (e.g., in Brazil) several countries have to a considerable extent managed to break away from the legacy of truncated social protection welfare states, labor market dualization and informality, and clientelism by implementing investment-oriented conditional cash transfer programs. These programs were not only accompanied by an expansion of the necessary services but also specifically designed to defy the threat of clientelistic capture.

Fourth, we would highlight that even the Nordic countries, which are often regarded as the world's "social investment champions" because of their inclusive, encompassing, and generous social investment approach, have not just somehow "miraculously received" social investment policies from nowhere. Here—just like everywhere else—the introduction, expansion, and maintenance of social investment policies have been and continue to be a tough political battle as argued by Horn and van Kersbergen (see Chapter 2 in Volume II [Garritzmann et al., 2022]). While from a 21st-century perspective it might appear obvious and straightforward that they have inclusive social investments, it was not clear at all in the early 20th century that they would move in this direction. Rather, political battles at that time and throughout the mid-20th century were fought not only about the type of social investment but more fundamentally about the type of welfare reform strategy.

In sum, while several factors make it more (or less) likely that (a certain type of) social investment becomes politicized and is enacted in reforms, the development or non-development of social investment policies is far from predetermined, and there always remains space for political agency. It is in this respect that we believe both overly optimistic and overly pessimistic predictions are unjustified and point at politics at the core of these dynamics.

REFERENCES

Beramendi, P., Häusermann, S., Kitschelt, H., & Kriesi, H. (2015). Introduction: The politics of advanced capitalism. In P. Beramendi, S. Häusermann, H. Kitschelt, & H. Kriesi (Eds.), *The politics of advanced capitalism* (pp. 1–64). Cambridge University Press.

Blyth, M. (2013). *Austerity: The history of a dangerous idea.* Oxford University Press.

Bremer, B., & Schwander, H. (2019, June 20–22). *The distributive preferences of green voters in times of electoral realignment* [Paper presentation]. 26th Conference of Europeanists, Madrid, Spain.

Busemeyer, M. R., Franzmann, S. T., & Garritzmann, J. L. (2013). Who owns education? Cleavage structures in the partisan competition over educational expansion. *West European Politics, 36*(3), 521–546.

Busemeyer, M. R., & Garritzmann, J. L. (2017). Public opinion on policy and budgetary trade-offs in European welfare states: Evidence from a new comparative survey. *Journal of European Public Policy, 24*(6), 871–889.

Busemeyer, M. R., Garritzmann, J. L., & Neimanns, E. (2020). *A loud, but noisy signal? Public opinion and the politics of education reform in western Europe.* Cambridge University Press.

Cantillon, B. (2011). The paradox of the social investment state: Growth, employment and poverty in the Lisbon era. *Journal of European Social Policy, 21*(5), 432–449.

Culpepper, P. (2010). *Quiet politics and business power: Corporate control in Europe and Japan.* Cambridge University Press.

Enggist, M., & Pinggera, M. (2020). *Radical right parties and their welfare state stances—Not so blurry after all?* [Working paper].

Esping-Andersen, G. (1990). *The three worlds of welfare capitalism.* Polity Press.

Flora, P. (1986). *Growth to limits: The Western European welfare states since World War II.* Walter de Gruyter.

Fossati, F., & Häusermann, S. (2014). Swiss policy preferences and party choice in the 2011 Swiss election. *Swiss Political Science Review, 20*(4), 590–611.

Garritzmann, J. L. (2016). *The political economy of higher education finance. The politics of tuition fees and subsidies in OECD countries, 1945–2015.* Palgrave Macmillan.

Garritzmann, J. L., Busemeyer, M. R., & Neimanns, E. (2018). Public demand for social investment: New supporting coalitions for welfare state reform in western Europe? *Journal of European Public Policy, 25*(6), 844–861.

Garritzmann, J. L., Häusermann, S., & Palier, B. (Eds.). (2022). *The world politics of social investment: Vol. II. The politics of varying social investment strategies.* Oxford University Press.

Garritzmann, J. L., Röth, L., & Kleider, H. (2021). Policy-making in multi-level systems: Ideology, authority, and education. *Comparative Political Studies, 54*(2), 2155–2190.

Garritzmann, J. L., & Schwander, H. (2021). Gender and attitudes towards welfare state reform: Are women really social investment promoters? *Journal of European Social Policy, 31*(3), 253–266.

Haggard, S., & Kaufman, R. R. (2008). *Development, democracy, and welfare states.* Princeton University Press.

Häusermann, S. (2010). *The politics of welfare state reform in continental Europe: Modernization in hard times.* Cambridge University Press.

Häusermann, S. (2018). Social democracy and the welfare state in context: The conditioning effect of institutional and party competition. In P. Manow, B. Palier, & H. Schwander (Eds.), *Welfare democracies and party politics: Explaining electoral dynamics in times of changing welfare capitalism* (pp. 150–170). Oxford University Press.

Häusermann, S., Pinggera, M., Ares, M., & Enggist, M. (2020). *The limits of solidarity. Changing welfare coalitions in a transforming European party system* [Working Paper]. University of Zurich.

Hemerijck, A. (2017). *The uses of social investment.* Oxford University Press.

Hemerijck, A. (2018). Social investment as a policy paradigm. *Journal of European Public Policy, 25*(6), 810–827.

Kitschelt, H. P. (1988). Left-libertarian parties: Explaining innovation in competitive party systems. *World Politics, 40*(2), 194–234.

Kleider, H., Röth, L., & Garritzmann, J. L. (2017). Ideological alignment and the distribution of public expenditures. *West European Politics, 41*(3), 779–802.

Korpi, W. (1983). *The democratic class struggle.* Routledge & Kegan Paul.

Manow, P., Palier, B., & Schwander, H. (2018). *Welfare democracies and party politics: Explaining electoral dynamics in times of changing welfare capitalism.* Oxford University Press.

Morel, N., Palier, B., & Palme, J. (2012). *Towards a social investment state? Ideas, policies and challenges.* Policy Press.

Morgan, K. J. (2013). Path shifting of the welfare state: Electoral competition and the expansion of work–family policies in western Europe. *World Politics, 65*(1), 73–115.

Müller, W. C., & Strøm, K. (1999). *Policy, office, or votes? How political parties in western Europe make hard decisions.* Cambridge University Press.

Nolan, B. (2013). What use is "social investment"? *Journal of European Social Policy, 23,* 459–468.

Pinggera, M. (2020) Congruent with whom? Parties' issue emphases and voter preferences in welfare politics. *Journal of European Public Policy, 28*(12), 1973–1992.

Röth, L., & Schwander, H. (2021). Greens in government: The distributive policies of a culturally progressive force. *West European Politics, 44*(3), 661–689.

Schmitter, P. C., & Streeck, W. (1999). *The organization of business interests: Studying the associative action of business in advanced industrial societies* [Discussion paper]. Max Planck Institute for the Study of Societies.

Schneider, B. R. (2013). *Hierarchical capitalism in Latin America. Business, labor, and the challenges of equitable development.* Cambridge University Press.

Schwander, H. (2020). Electoral demand, party competition, and family policy: The politics of a new policy field. In P. Manow, B. Palier, & H. Schwander (Eds.), *Welfare democracies and party politics: Explaining electoral dynamics in times of changing welfare capitalism* (pp. 197–224). Oxford University Press.

Seeleib-Kaiser, M. (2017). The truncated German social investment turn. In A. Hemerijck (Ed.), *The uses of social investment* (pp. 227–234). Oxford: Oxford University Press.

Segura-Ubiergo, A. (2007). *The political economy of the welfare state in Latin America: Globalization, democracy, and development.* Cambridge University Press.

Wagner, A. (1890). *Grundlegung der politischen Ökonomie. Teil I: Grundlagen der Volkswirtschaft.* C.F. Winter'sche Verlagshandlung.

INDEX

Tables and figures are indicated by *t* and *f* following the page number

welfare state(s) (*cont.*)
  liberal, 12
  maturity, and politicization of social
    investment, 81–82, 94
  neoliberal, 4
  "new politics of," 65
  policies, feedback effects, 354
  public preferences toward, 352–353
  public support for, 355–356
  reforms (*see* welfare reform)
  restructuring, contemporary era, 64n2
  Schumpeterian, 4
  social investment as new paradigm for, 3–4
  and social investment policy, 96, 126
  universal basic service, 61n1
welfare state literature, 287
welfare system(s)
  in Europe and English-speaking
    countries, 11–14
  in Latin America, 332–334
  and new social risks, 7
  in North East Asia, 14–15
  as social investment systems, 5
  socioeconomic context, 5
  traditional, 5
well-being, 127
Western economies
  educational attainment in, 257–259, 258f
  educational expansion in, 255–259
  enrollment in primary, secondary, and
    tertiary education, 254–258, 254f
Western Europe. *See also* Western economies
  distributive effects of social investment in, 17
  economy, changing composition, 263, 264f
  individual-level support for social policies in,
    364–368, 365t, 366, 367t–369t
  occupational group sizes in, 370f
  political demand and supply in, 74
  salience of social investment in, 356
  social investment policies in, 11, 354
  social investment support in, 352–354, 460
  support for education spending in, predicted,
    by occupational class, 374f
Why We Need a New Welfare State, 151
women, 7–8
  changing roles, 64
  employment
    in familialist welfare states, 404–422
    and fertility rates, 405
  in labor force, 112
    and ECEC reform, 334
  labor market participation by, familialism
    and, 404
  and social investment support, 352, 355,
    458–460, 460n2

  and social policy, in Spain, 419–420
  in society, 6
  support for social consumption, 355
  in unions, in Latin America, 335
Womenomics, 421
work conditions, in LMICs, 178
workers
  with high general skills, in Europe, 290, 291t
  with low general skills, in Europe, 290, 291t
  with specific skills, in Europe, 290, 291t
work–family balance, 114
work–family life course, 126
  OECD's social investment approach and,
    111–115
work–family reconciliation policy(ies)
  corporatism and, 416
  electoral systems and, 405–406, 415–416
  employers and, 416
  in familialist welfare states, 405–422
  historical political trajectories and, 416–422
  party competition and, 415–416
workforce mobilization, EU focus on, 133
working-age population, educational
    attainment, 257–259, 258f
working class, 74–75
  and social investment support, 460
  social policy preferences, 352–353
  and support for social consumption, 355
  and support for social policies, 363
  traditional industrial (male), and social
    investment, 29
working conditions, EU social investment
    and, 160
work–life balance, 6–7
  European Commission and, 160
work schedule(s), flexible, 113
World Bank, 31, 109–110
  development agenda, 115–118
  development paradigm, 111
  economic goals of, 466
  education indicators, 208
  emphasis on skill creation, 466
  emphasis on targeted social investment
    policies, 466n4
  investment in children, 115–118
  and politics of social investment, 464–467
  poverty-reduction objective, 111, 115–118
  and prospects for social investment, 482–483
  and shared prosperity, 123–126
  and social assistance in LMICs, 185
  social development agenda, 115–118
  social investment ideas, timing of emergence
    and development, 467
  social investment perspective, 110, 127
    new challenges to, 119–120, 123–126